Women Criminals

WOMEN CRIMINALS

AN ENCYCLOPEDIA OF PEOPLE AND ISSUES

Volume 2
Women and Crime: Biographical Profiles, A–Z

Vickie Jensen, Editor

 ABC-CLIO

Santa Barbara, California • Denver, Colorado • Oxford, England

Library of Congress Cataloging-in-Publication Data

Women criminals : an encyclopedia of people and issues / Vickie Jensen, editor.
    v. cm.
  Includes index.
  ISBN 978-0-313-33713-0 (hardcopy : alk. paper) — ISBN 978-0-313-06826-3
(ebook) 1. Female offenders—Encyclopedias. 2. Female offenders—
Biography—Encyclopedias. I. Jensen, Vickie, 1967–
  HV6046.W654 2011
  364.3'740922—dc22   2011009906

ISBN: 978-0-313-33713-0
EISBN: 978-0-313-06826-3

15 14 13 12 11   1 2 3 4 5

This book is also available on the World Wide Web as an eBook.
Visit www.abc-clio.com for details.

ABC-CLIO, LLC
130 Cremona Drive, P.O. Box 1911
Santa Barbara, California 93116-1911

This book is printed on acid-free paper ∞

Manufactured in the United States of America

CONTENTS

Preface   xi

Acknowledgments   xv

VOLUME ONE
ISSUES RELATED TO WOMEN AND CRIME

Introduction: Women Criminals and the Crimes They Commit   3
Vickie Jensen and Kristyan M. Kouri

Women and Criminal Offending: Societal-Level Perspectives   25
Jennifer Schwartz and Arina Gertseva

Women and Criminal Offending: Individual-Level Perspectives   53
Vickie Jensen, Lizette Barrientos, and Annie Neimand

Women and Sexual Offending   81
Rebecca Trammell and Sharon S. Oselin

Age and Women's Offending   99
Carolyn Rebecca Block and Nicole T. Carr

Diversity and Women's Criminal Offending   121
Vickie Jensen, Yasmin Serrato, Nayla Huq, and Crystal Kelly

Victimization and Women's Offending   139
Vickie Jensen and Venessa Garcia

Political Women and Criminalization   163
Karren Baird-Olson and Carlos Moran

Issues in Women's Crime around the World   177
Rosemary Barberet

Women and Policing   187
Jennifer C. Gibbs

Women, Law, and the Legal System   209
Celesta A. Albonetti

Criminal Justice System and Women: Corrections and
Correctional Issues   241
Barbara A. Koons-Witt and Gillian M. Pinchevsky

VOLUME TWO
WOMEN AND CRIME: BIOGRAPHICAL PROFILES, A–Z

A

Ah Toy	277
Allen, Wanda Jean	279
Allitt, Beverly	282
Anthony, Casey	284
Aquash, Anna	289
Atkins, Susan	291

B

Baker, Josephine	297
Barfield, Velma	299
Barker, Ma	302
Barrows, Sydney	303
Bàthory, Elizabeth	306
Beets, Betty	308
Bell, Mary	310
Bevan, Catherine	312
Bishop, Amy	314
Bobbitt, Lorena	318
Bombeek, Cecile	321
Bonny, Anne	323
Borden, Lizzie	325
Borgia, Lucrezia	328
Boyd, Belle	330

Brinvilliers, Marquise de	333
Broderick, Betty	335
Brown, Debra	337
Brown, Joyce Ann	341
Buck, Marilyn	343

C

Cheng Chui Ping	347
Cheng I Sao	349
Clark, Judith	352
Cleghorn, Mildred	355
Cook, Ann	357
Cora, Belle	360
Corday, Charlotte	362
Cotton, Mary	364

D

d'Aquino, Iva (Tokyo Rose)	367
Dann, Laurie	370
Davis, Angela	372
Devi, Phoolan	374
Devlin, Bernadette	377
Dhanu	379
Doss, Nannie	382

Drexler, Melissa 384
Dumont, Eleanor 387
Dyer, Amelia 389

E

Ebadi, Shirin 393
Edmonds, Sarah 395
Ellis, Ruth 398
Everleigh, Ada 400
Everleigh, Minna 403

F

Fair, Laura 407
Falling, Christine 408
Fallmer, Clara 410
Fisher, Amy 412
Fleiss, Heidi 415
Fonda, Jane 416
Frank, Antoinette 419
Fugate, Caril 422

G

Garcia, Guin 427
Gillars, Mildred Elizabeth
    Sisk (Axis Sally) 429
Gindorf, Debbie 431
Goldman, Emma 434
González Valenzuela, Delfina;
    María de Jesús González;
    and Eva González 437
Good, Sandra 439
Gottfried, Gessina 441
Greenhow, Rose 443
Gunness, Belle 446

H

Harris, Clara 449
Harris, Jean 451
Hayashi, Masumi 453

Hearst, Patty 457
Helmsley, Leona 460
Hindley, Myra 462
Hollander, Xaviera 464
Homolka, Karla 468
Howard, Katherine 470
Huckaby, Melissa 473
Huerta, Dolores 476
Hughes, Francine 479
Hutchinson, Anne 482

J

Jegado, Hélène 485
Jones, Genene 487

K

Kasabian, Linda 491
Kelly, Gladys Cannon 494
Khaled, Leila 498
Krenwinkel, Patricia 501

L

La Voisin, Catherine 507
Lafave, Debra 508
Lebron, Lolita 511
Letourneau, Mary Kay 513
Lewis, Teresa 515
Little, Joan 521

M

Mandela, Winnie 525
Mandelbaum, Mother 528
Mapp, Dollree 530
Marie Antoinette 534
McKnight, Regina 536
Metyard, Sarah; and Sarah
    Morgan Metyard 540
Montespan, Marquise de 542

N

Newton, Frances — 545

O

Osborn, Sarah — 549

P

Pagan, Dylcia — 553
Parker, Bonnie — 554
Parks, Rosa — 557

R

Rachals, Terri — 561
Riefenstahl, Leni — 563
Riggs, Christina — 566
Rosenberg, Ethel — 568

S

Sanger, Margaret — 573
Scholl, Sophie — 576
Shakur, Assata — 578
Shigenobu, Fusako — 581
Smith, Susan — 584
Snyder, Ruth — 586
Soliah, Kathleen — 589
Spooner, Bathsheba — 591
Steinem, Gloria — 593
Stewart, Martha — 596

Stone, Lucy — 599
Surratt, Mary — 602
Suu Kyi, Aung San — 605

T

Taketa, Gwen — 611
Tinning, Marybeth — 613
Tubman, Harriet — 615
Tucker, Karla Faye — 618

V

Van Houten, Leslie — 623
Van Lew, Elizabeth — 627

W

Wall, Rachel — 631
Wanrow, Yvonne — 633
West, Rosemary — 635
Whitney, Charlotte Anita — 637
Wuornos, Aileen — 641

Y

Yaklich, Donna — 645
Yates, Andrea — 646
Young, Lila — 649

Z

Zwanziger, Anna — 653

APPENDICES: STATISTICS AND REPORTS ON WOMEN AND CRIME

A. *Arrests*   656

B. *Offenders According to Victimization Data*   677

C. *Gender, Prisoners, and the Death Penalty*   680

D. *Death Penalty for Female Offenders,* by Victor Streib   690

Selected Bibliography   713

Index   719

About the Editor and Contributors   741

Women and Crime: Biographical Profiles, A–Z

Volume two provides brief biographical descriptions of women who primarily have been convicted of crimes. Included among them, however, are women who have been arrested for crimes against unjust laws, such as Rosa Parks, or who have advocated against what they have considered unjust laws, such as Gloria Steinem. Below, in alphabetic order is the list of women profiled, and below that, the list of women profiled, listed in chronologic order by their birth, when known. The group spans from the 15th century through today.

Alphabetic List

Ah Toy
Allen, Wanda Jean
Allitt, Beverly
Anthony, Casey
Aquash, Anna
Atkins, Susan
Axis Sally. *See* Gillars, Mildred Elizabeth Sisk
Baker, Josephine
Barfield, Velma
Barker, Ma
Barrows, Sydney
Bàthory, Elizabeth
Beets, Betty
Bell, Mary
Bevan, Catherine
Bishop, Amy

Bobbitt, Lorena
Bombeek, Cecile
Bonny, Anne
Borden, Lizzie
Borgia, Lucrezia
Boyd, Belle
Brinvilliers, Marquise de
Broderick, Betty
Brown, Debra
Brown, Joyce Ann
Buck, Marilyn
Cheng Chui Ping
Cheng I Sao
Clark, Judith
Cleghorn, Mildred
Cook, Ann
Cora, Belle
Corday, Charlotte

Cotton, Mary
d'Aquino, Iva (Tokyo Rose)
Dann, Laurie
Davis, Angela
Devi, Phoolan
Devlin, Bernadette
Dhanu
Doss, Nannie
Drexler, Melissa
Dumont, Eleanor
Dyer, Amelia
Ebadi, Shirin
Edmonds, Sarah
Ellis, Ruth
Everleigh, Ada
Everleigh, Minna
Fair, Laura
Falling, Christine
Fallmer, Clara
Fisher, Amy
Fleiss, Heidi
Fonda, Jane
Frank, Antoinette
Fugate, Caril
Garcia, Guin
Gillars, Mildred Elizabeth Sisk (Axis
    Sally)
Gindorf, Debbie
Goldman, Emma
González Valenzuela, Delfina;
    María de Jesús González; and Eva
    González
Good, Sandra
Gottfried, Gessina
Greenhow, Rose
Gunness, Belle
Harris, Clara
Harris, Jean
Hayashi, Masumi
Hearst, Patty
Helmsley, Leona

Hindley, Myra
Hollander, Xaviera
Homolka, Karla
Howard, Katherine
Huckaby, Melissa
Huerta, Dolores
Hughes, Francine
Hutchinson, Anne
Jegado, Hélène
Jones, Genene
Kasabian, Linda
Kelly, Gladys Cannon
Khaled, Leila
Krenwinkel, Patricia
La Voisin, Catherine
Lafave, Debra
Lebron, Lolita
Letourneau, Mary Kay
Lewis, Teresa
Little, Joan
Mandela, Winnie
Mandelbaum, Mother
Mapp, Dollree
Marie Antoinette
Marquise de Montespan. *See*
    Montespan, Marquise de
McKnight, Regina
Metyard, Sarah; and Sarah Morgan
    Metyard
Montespan, Marquise de
Newton, Frances
Osborn, Sarah
Pagan, Dylcia
Parker, Bonnie
Parks, Rosa
Rachals, Terri
Riefenstahl, Leni
Riggs, Christina
Rosenburg, Ethel
Sanger, Margaret
Scholl, Sophie

Shakur, Assata
Shigenobu, Fusako
Smith, Susan
Snyder, Ruth
Soliah, Kathleen
Spooner, Bathsheba
Steinem, Gloria
Stewart, Martha
Stone, Lucy
Surratt, Mary
Suu Kyi, Aung San
Taketa, Gwen
Tinning, Marybeth
Tokyo Rose. *See* d'Aquino, Iva
Tubman, Harriet
Tucker, Karla Faye
Van Houten, Leslie
Van Lew, Elizabeth
Wall, Rachel
Wanrow, Yvonne
West, Rosemary
Whitney, Charlotte Anita
Wuornos, Aileen
Yaklich, Donna
Yates, Andrea
Young, Lila
Zwanziger, Anna

Chronological List
(by Woman's Birth Date)

Borgia, Lucrezia, 1480–1519
Howard, Katherine, 1521?–1542
Bàthory, Elizabeth, 1560–1614
Hutchinson, Anne, 1591–1643
Brinvilliers, Marquise de, 1630–1676
Osborn, Sarah, 1640–1692
La Voisin, Catherine, 1640–1680
Montespan, Marquise de, 1640–1707
Bevan, Catherine, 1680–1731
Bonny, Anne, 1697–1720?

Spooner, Bathsheba, 1746–1778
Marie Antoinette, 1755–1793
Wall, Rachel, 1760–1789
Zwanziger, Anna, 1760–1811
Metyard, Sarah; and Sarah Morgan
    Metyard, ?–1762
Corday, Charlotte, 1768–1793
Cheng I Sao, 1775–1844
Cook, Ann, 1786–1826
Gottfried, Gessina, 1798–1828
Jegado, Hélène, 1803–1851
Greenhow, Rose, 1814–1864
Mandelbaum, Mother, 1818?–1894
Stone, Lucy, 1818–1893
Van Lew, Elizabeth, 1818–1900
Tubman, Harriett, 1820–1913
Surratt, Mary, 1823–1865
Cora, Belle, 1827?–1862
Ah Toy, 1828–1928
Dumont, Eleanor, 1829–1879
Cotton, Mary, 1832–1873
Dyer, Amelia, 1839–1896
Edmonds, Sarah, 1841–1898
Boyd, Belle, 1844–1900
Gunness, Belle, 1859–?
Borden, Lizzie, 1860–1927
Whitney, Charlotte Anita,
    1867–1955
Goldman, Emma, 1869–1940
Fair, Laura, 1850–?
Barker, Ma, 1871–1935
Everleigh, Ada, 1875–1960
Everleigh, Minna, 1878–1948
Sanger, Margaret, 1879–1966
Fallmer, Clara, 1892–?
Snyder, Ruth, 1895–1928
Gillars, Mildred Elizabeth Sisk (Axis
    Sally) (1900–1987)
Young, Lila, 1902–1967
Riefenstahl, Leni, 1902–2003
Doss, Nannie, 1905–1965

Baker, Josephine, 1906–1975
Parker, Bonnie, 1910–1934
Cleghorn, Mildred, 1910–1997
González Valenzuela, Delfina (ca.
 1911–?); María de Jesús González
 (ca. 1924–?); Eva González (n.d.)
Parks, Rosa, 1913–2005
Rosenburg, Ethel, 1915–1953
d'Aquino, Iva (Tokyo Rose),
 1916–2006
Lebron, Lolita, 1919–2010
Helmsley, Leona, 1920–2007
Scholl, Sophie, 1921–1943
Harris, Jean, 1923–
Ellis, Ruth, 1926–1955
Huerta, Dolores, 1930–
Barfield, Velma, 1932–1984
Bombeek, Cecile, 1933–
Steinem, Gloria, 1934–
Mandela, Winnie, 1936–
Brown, Joyce Ann, 1936?–
Fonda, Jane, 1937–
Mapp, Dollree, 1937–
Beets, Betty, 1937–2000
Stewart, Martha, 1941–
Tinning, Marybeth, 1942–
Kelly, Gladys Cannon, 1942–1987
Hindley, Myra, 1942–2002
Fugate, Caril, 1943–
Hollander, Xaviera, 1943–
Wanrow, Yvonne, 1943–
Davis, Angela, 1944–
Good, Sandra, 1944–?
Shigenobu, Fusako, 1945–
Suu Kyi, Aung San, 1945–
Aquash, Anna, 1945–1975
Pagan, Dylcia, 1946–
Ebadi, Shirin, 1947–
Hughes, Francine, 1947–
Krenwinkel, Patricia, 1947–
Shakur, Assata, 1947–

Soliah, Kathleen, 1947–
Taketa, Gwen, 1947–
Broderick, Betty, 1947–
Devlin, Bernadette, 1947–
Buck, Marilyn, 1947–2010
Khaled, Leila, 1948–
Atkins, Susan, 1948–2009
Clark, Judith, 1949–
Kasabian, Linda, 1949–
Van Houten, Leslie, 1949–
Cheng Chui Ping, 1949–
Jones, Genene, 1950–
Barrows, Sydney, 1952–
Garcia, Guin, 1953–
West, Rosemary, 1953–
Hearst, Patty, 1954–
Little, Joan, 1954–
Yaklich, Donna, 1956?–
Wuornos, Aileen, 1956–2002
Bell, Mary, 1957–
Devi, Phoolan, 1957–2001
Dann, Laurie, 1958–1988
Allen, Wanda Jean, 1959–1989
Tucker, Karla Faye, 1959–1998
Harris, Clara, 1960–
Hayashi, Masumi, 1961–
Letourneau, Mary Kay, 1962–
Rachals, Terri, 1962–
Brown, Debra, 1962–
Falling, Christine, 1963–
Gindorf, Debbie, 1964–
Yates, Andrea, 1964–
Bishop, Amy, 1965–
Fleiss, Heidi, 1965–
Newton, Frances, 1965–2005
Allitt, Beverly, 1968–
Lewis, Teresa, 1969–2010
Bobbitt, Lorena, 1970–
Homolka, Karla, 1970–
Frank, Antoinette, 1971–
Smith, Susan, 1971–

Riggs, Christina, 1971–2000
Fisher, Amy, 1974–
Dhanu, 1974–1991
McKnight, Regina, 1977–

Drexler, Melissa, 1978–
Lafave, Debra, 1980–
Huckaby, Melissa, 1981–
Anthony, Casey, 1986–

A

Ah Toy (1828–1928)

Ah Toy gained fame in the California Gold Rush as an independent prostitute, peepshow entertainer, brothel madam, and pursuer of legal justice. Always an independent businesswoman, she shared no earnings with a pimp. Toy stood out among Chinese men and women for having engaged the American judicial system as both a plaintiff and defendant on numerous occasions, as well as for her beauty. She participated as an American, unlike most other Chinese living in the United States at this time, who preferred to withdraw from the mainstream society, living as foreigners in a foreign land. Very little is known about her early life, and sparse and conflicting information exist about her life in San Francisco, but she still has gained some historical relevance in California history.

Male Chinese workers began arriving in California in 1848 and had been leaving their home in China to work abroad. High taxes from the Opium Wars, as well as floods and droughts, exacerbated the economic depression peasant farmers were already facing. Upon hearing of Gold Mountain, they came to California. Here they worked the mines abandoned by white miners. Toy left China at the age of 20 for the same reason: to take advantage of opportunities in America. While she was the second Chinese woman to arrive in California, remaining one of two women for many years, Chinese men numbered in the hundreds. Such little female companionship hiked the value of her services, allowing accumulation of significant wealth.

Toy was a very well-known prostitute in her time, so much that she was referenced in San Francisco travel books. She was considered attractive because of her height and her "lily-bound aristocratic feet" (Pryor, 2003). Most Chinese women were viewed as short with big "peasant" feet (Pryor, 2003). Toy exploited myths for her own gain. Scholars do not explicitly state what these myths are, but they imply that she turned a profit from the exotic stereotypes of Asian women.

Sex work was her livelihood, but she was never under the supervision of an employer. She had the freedom to offer services as she saw fit, but it may have misled patrons into believing that they could take advantage of her. Most Chinese people living in San Francisco managed disputes amongst members of their ethnic community. Toy, on the other hand, pursued justice through the American judiciary system. On numerous occasions, she had been both a plaintiff and defendant. In her best-known court case, Toy charged certain miners with defrauding her by paying for services with brass fillings covered in gold. She accepted payment from patrons in gold, which she weighed herself with her own scale. As evidence, she brought the brass-filled gold pieces to the courthouse, but the judge dismissed the case as her accusations against those specific miners had no evidentiary basis.

In 1850, Ah Toy moved out of her Chinatown alley into a larger house more representative of her wealth and status, and she became a madam. Gentry (1964) references then contemporary, anti-Chinese historian F. Soule, who accused Toy of sending enticing letters to young Chinese women to immigrate to the United States, purportedly encouraging prostitutes to arrive in the hundreds. Many of them, voluntarily or involuntarily, became prostitutes at her brothel. Those who felt coerced either committed suicide or sought sanctuary in Christian missions.

In August 1852, community members showed that they were threatened by Toy's experience with the American judicial system. Toy accused the notorious Chinese leader Yee Ah Tye of extortion. He demanded that her prostitutes pay him a tax so she threatened to take him to court, and he pursued the extortion no further. The police caused deep fright amongst most Chinese, and Yee Ah Tye feared Toy's close connections with the police, believing they would protect her interests against his, despite the illegality of both operations.

In spite of her purported ties to the police, in 1854, Toy was discriminated against as a Chinese woman when she was arrested, convicted, and fined for keeping a disorderly house. Over the next few years, she saw charges of this type, whereas white madams and prostitutes did not. Such treatment was increasing over the years, causing Toy to sell her house and belongings in 1857 to return to China. However, it seems that her departure from San Francisco was brief as she was arrested again in 1859 for disorderly housekeeping.

In the 1850s, anti-Chinese feeling was growing. In 1851, a law was passed to charge a special tax on foreign miners, particularly the Chinese. In 1854, California extended its law against African Americans and Native Americans, forbidding testimony in court for the Chinese, making it impossible for violent crimes against the Chinese to be prosecuted in court. They were viewed as a comical, insular community that only socialized amongst themselves, and the few women present were criticized as "the filthiest and most abandoned of their sex," accused of spreading syphilis (Gentry, 1964: 55). Toy specifically became a subject in a pseudoscientific study comparing internal biological differences between white and Chinese women. Even in this climate, Toy was able to continue her trade despite the discrimination she faced that caused her to leave the country temporarily.

In addition to litigating against swindlers in court, Toy defended her house and livelihood against the Vigilante Committee who, in 1851, investigated brothels.

They were commissioned to have Toy deported. When head vigilante John Clark, in his efforts to shut down her operations, discovered his father at her brothel, he stopped his investigation. Soon after, John Clark became Toy's lover.

Ah Toy stood out among the Chinese in San Francisco. She was singular in gender, height, beauty, courage, social connection with Chinese and non-Chinese, wealth, and health. The average Chinese prostitute died young, having been forced to service even the most obviously diseased clients. Toy, on the other hand, as reported in the February 2, 1928, issue of the San Francisco *Examiner*, died in San Jose days after her 100th birthday, outliving most first arrivals from China.

Resources

Corr, William. 1996. "How Chinese Women Came of Age in San Francisco." *Daily Yomiuri*. September 15, p. 15.

Gentry, Curt. 1964. *The Madams of San Francisco.* Garden City, NY: Doubleday & Company.

Public Broadcasting System. 2006. "American Experience: The Gold Rush | People & Events | Chinese Immigrants and the Gold Rush." Retrieved April 6, 2010. http://www.pbs.org/wgbh/amex/goldrush/peopleevents/p_chinese.html.

Pryor, Alton. 2003. *Fascinating Women in California History.* Roseville, CA: Stagecoach Publishing.

Stephens, Autumn. 1992. *Wild Women: Crusaders, Curmudgeons and Completely Corsetless Ladies in the Otherwise Virtuous Victorian Era.* Berkeley, CA: Conari Press.

Nayla Huq

Wanda Jean Allen (1959–1989)

Wanda Jean Allen was the sixth woman put to death since the reinstatement of the death penalty in the United States in 1976. She was executed as a result of her 1989 conviction for killing her intimate partner, 29-year-old Gloria Leathers. Allen's execution was carried out by the state of Oklahoma on January 11, 2001, in the Oklahoma State Penitentiary in McAlester. Oklahoma had not executed a woman since 1903, when Dora Wright was executed for murder of a child. Both Wright and Allen were African Americans. Allen's execution was the first of a black woman in the United States since 1954. There is some evidence that her sexuality, mental abilities, and legal representation led to controversy about her death sentence.

Allen was born in 1959 to Mary and Bill Allen. She was the oldest of eight children. Allen's father remained in the home only until the youngest sibling was born, leaving Allen's mother to continue to raise the children single-handedly. Allen aided her mother in caring for the younger children but also spent some of her youth in foster homes and facilities for juvenile delinquents. During her youth, Allen suffered from two head injuries. In two IQ tests conducted later, Allen tested at 69 when she was 15 years old and at 80 while she was on death row in the mid-1990s; these IQ scores are indications that she was mentally deficient. These conflicting scores would raise further dispute in her subsequent capital punishment case.

As indicated, Allen had previous interactions with the criminal justice system. These included infractions that occurred during adulthood

Wanda Jean Allen pleads with the Oklahoma Clemency Board to spare her life during a clemency hearing in Oklahoma, in 2000. Allen was executed by lethal injection in Oklahoma. Allen's execution was the first of a black woman in the United States since 1954. (AP/Wide World Photos)

as well as her first murder charge. Allen admitted to fatally shooting her childhood friend Detra Pettus on June 29, 1981. Allen reported that the shooting was the result of an argument between herself and Pettus. There was no trial for this incident as Allen pled guilty to first-degree manslaughter. She served approximately two years in prison of the four year sentence—the result of a plea bargain.

Allen met Gloria Leathers while serving the prison sentence on the first homicide charge. The two women began an intimate relationship soon after Leathers was released in 1986, and they eventually resided together. Allen reported that her relationship with Leathers was mutually verbally and physically abusive, with Leathers often moving out of their shared home after some of their altercations. As a result of what would be their final dispute, Leathers went to file a complaint against Allen based on a disagreement over the ownership of some of the property in the home. Immediately after filing the complaint at a police station in a suburb of Oklahoma City, Oklahoma, on December 1, 1988, Allen shot Leathers in the abdomen at close range. They were outside the police station. Leathers died four days later.

Allen maintained that she shot Leathers in self-defense because Leathers struck Allen in the face earlier that day, and Allen believed Leathers was going to attack her outside the police station. Allen had visible marks to her face when photographed upon her arrest after Leathers succumbed to her injuries. Leathers' mother and the police involved in the case asserted that Allen did not shoot Leathers in self-defense.

In her trial, Allen was represented by a private attorney who had never before tried a capital punishment case and was working with especially limited monetary resources (only $800) that would have allowed him to hire investigators and expert witnesses. The attorney agreed to be retained by Allen and her family prior to the prosecutor's decision to try Allen as a capital case. Though the attorney asked that the trial judge remove him from the case or that he be assisted by a public defender, the judge denied the motion. The capital trial took place and was concluded in less than five months after Leathers' death and Allen's arrest.

The issues considered in the finding of guilt, the sentencing, and the ultimate execution of Allen centered on the intersectional identity of Allen as a poor black lesbian woman with questionable mental and developmental capacity. In her capital trial, the prosecution continually referred to Allen's sexual orientation and that she was the "man" in the relationship with Leathers, thus placing traditional heterosexual standards on lesbian relationships. Also, though both Leathers and Allen were African American women, the often-shared stereotype of lesbians and black women as that of masculine and emasculating women may have affected the legal processing and media interpretation of Allen and her capital punishment trial.

Allen's sexual orientation was also a factor frequently highlighted in community advocacy and media coverage of her case. Though Allen identified as a lesbian prior to her conviction and through much of her incarceration, she stated that through her religious transformation in prison to Christianity, she no longer identified as a lesbian because it is viewed as a sin (Cohen, 2001). Interviews with religious leaders in the black community of Allen's hometown revealed skepticism regarding Allen's sexual conversion to heterosexuality and believed her declaration to be a ploy to secure support from the black community that would hopefully lead to a gubernatorial commutation of her sentence.

Only a short time prior to Allen's scheduled execution, Allen was denied a stay of execution by Oklahoma governor Frank Keating. This denunciation followed a lengthy series of failed pleas on Allen's behalf to have her conviction overturned or her death sentence commuted to a lesser sentence. Arguments referring to Allen's limited intelligence and mental capacity were refuted by Governor Keating and the prosecution who argued that Allen knew her homicidal actions were wrong and that she knew the consequences of such actions.

Allen's case received increased national attention and was highlighted by death penalty opponents on the eve of her execution. On the execution gurney, Allen proclaimed, "Father forgive them. They know not what they do" (Hines, 2001). She was executed by lethal injection minutes later. Allen was 41 years old at the time of her death.

Resources

Cohen, Aaron Buckley. 2001, March 13. "Who was Wanda Jean?—Black woman executed in the United States." *Advocate*.

Hines, Rochelle. 2001, January 12. "Wanda Jean Allen becomes first black woman executed in United States since 1954." *Associated Press*.

Hillary Potter

Beverly Allitt (1968–)

Beverly Allitt, a female serial murderer, is a classic "Angel of Death" type of serial killer who is typically a doctor, nurse, or other health worker. She operated out of the United Kingdom, killing children who attended the Grantham and Kesteven Hospital. She is thought to have suffered initially from Munchausen syndrome, a condition in which a person secretly causes his or her own illnesses or injuries in order to get sympathy and attention, and then later Munchausen syndrome by proxy, a condition in which a person, usually a parent, or in this case, a caregiver, secretly causes illnesses or injuries to another person, usually a child, in order to gain attention and sympathy.

Allitt had pronounced personality problems identified as early as age 13. By her late teens she had a history of medical appearances for injuries that where either self-inflicted or appeared to be invented. Doctors commented that many of her illnesses appeared to be psychosomatic. It was eventually concluded that she suffered from Munchausen syndrome. While training for her nurse's certificate, she missed 130 days of class and had difficulty finding placement. She eventually settled in Grantham and Kesteven Hospital in Grantham, England. Although she had just qualified to work, she expressed the desire to work as a special care nurse. She was told she would have to get experience working with seriously ill children before she would qualify. Days later, children started to mysteriously collapse on her watch.

Her first victim, seven-week-old Liam Taylor, died while receiving treatment for a common cold. The second victim, 11-year-old Tim Hardwick, came in suffering from severe bouts of epileptic shock and passed away under Allitt's care. It was assumed a prolonged attack was the cause. Three-month-old Becky Philips suddenly stopped breathing and died while being treated at the hospital. Becky was a twin, and therefore her sister was brought in for testing. She was found to be perfectly healthy and normal but then suddenly experienced bouts of being unable to breathe while Beverley was watching her. The last bout arrested her heart, and, although doctors were able to bring her back to life, she suffered irreparable brain damage.

Allitt's last victim was 15-month-old Clare Peck, an asthmatic who stopped breathing April 22, 1991, two hours after being placed under Allitt's care. Clare Peck's death was blamed on asthma. Her blood analysis revealed high levels of potassium. All the children's deaths had one thing in common: Allitt's presence on the ward. It was found that the 26 children who had died or become ill had been injected with either insulin or potassium. Allitt was charged with 4 counts of murder, 11 counts of attempted murder, and 11 counts of causing grievous bodily harm. The defense argued that the children had died from natural causes. The prosecution was able to establish that Allitt had committed these acts in order to receive attention and appreciation from staff, as she pretended to care for the children.

Allitt went to live with Tracey Jobson, of Peterborough, while awaiting trial. Although they were considered to be friends, Tracy's son Jonathan began suffering dizzy spells shortly after her arrival. These spells were accompanied with cravings for chocolate. Allitt offered the teenager a drink, and at the bottom of the glass Jonathan found a chalky substance. He later collapsed, stating that he was unable to see and that he had pains in his stomach and head. Ms. Jobson recalled that Allitt did nothing to help. He survived the attack. It was discovered later that Jonathan's blood sugar was very low, and he had received diabetic tablets intended for his grandmother. Beverly Allitt was charged with attempted murder of Jonathan, for which she was eventually cleared. The trial was also delayed because Allitt was said to be suffering from severe anorexia; the legal proceedings eventually continued while she was in hospital. Allitt stated she did not wish to testify and maintained her innocence.

Before her trial, when being interviewed by police, she stated, "My nursing means more to me than living" (Jenkins, 1993a). When further asked about her competence given the accusations she replied, "I am not competent, far from it. I know I am not competent. I am one of the bloody crappiest nurses out. I am the lowest of the low." (Jenkins, 1993a) She then stayed quiet, including for the remainder of the trial process. By October 1993, while beginning to serve 13 life sentences, Allitt admitted to committing nine of the murders (Jenkins, 1993c). She also admitted to smothering some infants when the injection did not produce desired results.

Allitt displayed classic symptoms of Munchausen syndrome in her younger years before her murderous career. In essence, she had graduated from faking her own symptoms to injuring others and subsequently attempting to save her victims, her "heroism" getting the attention she desperately needed. She could also get attention while offering comfort to bereaved family members. In the condition of Munchausen syndrome by proxy, the offenders stop mimicking symptoms of severe illness in their own bodies and begin to create symptoms in others to gain personal attention. In 2007, a high court confirmed that Allitt would have to continue to serve a minimum of 30 years in prison, the original sentence given in 1993.

Resources

Jenkins, Lin. 1993a, May 18. "Killings Fed a Craving for Attention." Retrieved July 15, 2011, from ProQuest Newsstand.

Jenkins, Lin. 1993b, May 29. "Judge Gives Allitt 13 Life Terms for Crimes Against Children." *Times* (London).

Jenkins, Lin. 1993c, October 15. "Serial Killer Allitt Admits None of the Crimes she Denied." *Times* (London), A3

Kelleher, M. D., & Kelleher, C. L. 1998. *Murder Most Rare.* New York: Dell.

Hannah Scott

Casey Anthony (1986–)

Casey Anthony was one of the most media-scrutinized women criminals of the 21st century. What began as a search for her missing two-year-old daughter, Caylee, in 2008 swelled into a sensationalized case of the disappearance and homicide of a child whose mother partied rather than grieved while her daughter was allegedly missing for 31 days. The notoriety of this case and its connection to societal ideas about motherhood make it notable. Legally, this case also raises questions about the delicate balance between a fair trial and the right of the public to access key court materials.

Casey Anthony was born on March 19, 1986, the second child of George and Cindy Anthony. They lived in Niles, Ohio, where George was a sheriff's deputy and Cindy was nurse and stay-at-home mom. Shortly after Casey's birth, George resigned as a deputy and went to work with his father to earn more money for the family. Shortly thereafter, George left employment with his father, took a second mortgage on the home, and started a used car lot. That business failed, the couple declared bankruptcy, and they lost their home.

Cindy Anthony's parents had just moved to Florida, and in 1989 the family left Ohio to seek a chance to start over in Orlando, Florida. Casey was three at the time. They purchased the home they would live in through her childhood, adolescence, and early adulthood. It was also the home that would become famous later as the home of Casey's missing daughter and the site of the police investigation.

Early in her school years, Casey Anthony was an average to good student and did not get into any noticeable trouble. Cindy had taken a job as a nurse, and George worked several different jobs but was rendered disabled at least twice and had financial trouble related to gambling and bad investments. In her senior year of high school, Casey started missing a large number of classes and eventually stopped attending school, resulting in her failure to graduate from high school. She successfully hid this from her parents who prepared for a graduation up until the school notified them a few days before.

Casey Anthony took a job with Kodak at Universal Studios after leaving high school. In early 2005, she met Jesse Grund, and they had been dating seriously by June when she revealed to Jesse that she was pregnant and that it was his child. They became engaged even though Jesse was not sure it was his. Her family, on the other hand, appeared to ignore or try to hide the pregnancy. Her mother, Cindy, "didn't have a clue" (Fanning, 2009: 82), and when Casey appeared at a relative's wedding obviously pregnant, her parents insisted that she was bloated and had female problems. Cindy insisted that Casey couldn't be pregnant because she would have had sex to get pregnant, and Casey said she hadn't. Casey finally told her parents the truth less than two months before giving birth.

Despite the shock, George and Cindy Anthony anxiously prepared for the arrival of their granddaughter and were present at the birth. Cindy Anthony was the first to hold little Caylee Marie, born August 9, 2005. Casey reportedly became upset with her mother about this and began what would be a conflict and rivalry-filled relationship between them over Caylee. Casey would often complain that her parents, particularly her mother, were overbearing and controlling, and she expressed great resentment against them. At the same time, Casey and Caylee both lived in Casey's parents' home.

Caylee's arrival was initially greeted with happiness as Casey appeared to enjoy being a mother. As time passed, while she was loving and patient when she was with Caylee, Casey appeared more discontent with motherhood and more willing to leave Caylee with family and friends while she pursued her social life. Casey also began engaging in more notable lies to elicit support and money, and she was caught stealing from family members. After Caylee was born, she simply quit going to work at her job and was eventually dismissed for "job abandonment" (Fanning, 2009: 90).

In June 2006, Casey Anthony broke off her relationship with Jesse Grund. From that point, Casey lied about a job at Universal Studios as an event planner—a job she clearly did not have the education for. She also continued her party life, even suffering from suspected alcohol poisoning in November 2007. Her complaints about motherhood to friends increased, and when she did not leave Caylee with a friend or her parents, she sometimes took Caylee with her to drinking parties overnight at men's houses.

On March 17 and 21, 2008, disturbing searches attributed to Casey Anthony were done on the family computer. According to prosecutors, the searches involved the terms "chloroform," "alcohol," "neck breaking," as well as other death-related searches, although it was later found that the prosecutors misreported the number of times "chloroform" was searched; it was apparently searched only once (Alvarez, 2011). It was in late spring that Casey met Tony Lazarro and began smoking marijuana. She reportedly had sex with Tony while two of Tony's friends, strangers to Caylee, were with the little girl in the living room. On Father's Day, Caylee went to visit her great-grandfather with her grandmother Cindy. The visit allegedly ended with a loud argument between Cindy and Casey, and, in one version, Cindy allegedly put her hands around Casey's neck. The next day, Casey told her father that she would be working late, and she and Caylee would be staying with the nanny. That was the last time George Anthony saw his granddaughter.

That night, Casey Anthony was recorded on surveillance camera with Tony Lazarro at a movie rental store, and as Lazarro's testimony at trial would confirm, she spent the night and most of the next day with him. Caylee was not with them and not seen again. For the next 31 days, Casey appeared to go about her daily business shopping, spending time with friends, and partying at her favorite club. Not one of her friends saw Caylee, but none of them saw Casey upset or distraught. When asked by her friends and family, Casey had a variety of explanation including vacations, being with Zanny the nanny, and so forth. She would not allow her mother, Cindy, to talk to Caylee on the phone. On June 27, her Pontiac was found abandoned and towed. Around July 2, Casey stole money and checks from her friend Amy Huizenga—a crime for which she was later arrested, charged, and pleaded guilty to. On July 2, Casey Anthony received a tattoo with the Italian phrase "*Bella Vita*" (meaning "beautiful life"). That night, she posted on MySpace the following: "On the worst of days, Remember the words spoken. Trust no one, only yourself. With great power, comes great consequences. What is given, can be taken away. Everyone lies. Everyone Dies. Life will never be easy" (Fanning, 2009: 149).

On July 15, George Anthony retrieved Casey's towed car from the tow yard, and he noticed a foul smell. Cindy Anthony, trying to remove the smell, found Amy Huizenga's number on the front seat. She found Amy, who led her to Tony Lazarro. Casey Anthony came home on the July 16, at the insistence of her parents, to a confrontation about the whereabouts of Caylee. Cindy Anthony called 911 and uttered the now famous words: "There's something wrong. I found my daughter's car today and it smells like there's been a dead body in the damn car" (Hewitt, 2008: 48). Casey then told her parents and, later, investigators, that Caylee was taken by the nanny whom she identified as Zenaida Gonzalez. When asked about the length of time before she reported her missing, Casey replied that she was looking for her herself. She was arrested at that point, charged with child neglect, providing false statements to police, and obstruction of justice, and held on $500,000 bond. Casey provided several key falsehoods to the police including her alleged job at Universal, allegedly speaking with two nonexistent coworkers about looking for Caylee, leaving Caylee with Zanny the nanny, and allegedly leaving Caylee at the Sawgrass Apartments to stay with Zanny. Ultimately she was released only to be arrested again in the theft from Amy Huizenga and released again for that trial, resolved in 2010 with a guilty plea. Investigators continued to look into Caylee's disappearance, and on October 2, 2008, Casey Anthony was named the prime suspect in the disappearance of her daughter.

On October 14, 2008, prosecutors presented their case against Casey Anthony to a grand jury. They returned with an indictment for capital murder, aggravated manslaughter of a child, aggravated child abuse, and four counts of providing false information to a law enforcement officer. On October 28, 2008, Anthony entered her plea of not guilty. The trial was set for early 2009, though it would actually not begin until more than two years later. Without the body of Caylee, the search continued for her, while Casey denied any knowledge of her whereabouts. On December 11, 2008, a meter reader found the skeletal remains of Caylee Anthony in plastic garbage bags in a wooded area less than a mile from the Anthony house. As trial testimony would gruesomely detail, the remains had been there for several months, long enough for roots to grow through the skeleton and animals to gnaw at her bones. Duct tape with a heart sticker attached was found on the skull, still attached to small amounts of hair. A tattered Winnie the Pooh blanket identical to the one Caylee had was found with the remains as were other items of hers. As the medical examiner stated on December 19, death was ruled as a homicide by unknown means. Preparation for trial in an already publicized case took on a new intensity.

There were two legally interesting aspects to this case. The first involved the massive quantity of investigation documents available to the public prior to the trial. Thousands of pages of statements, photos, reports, and other evidence were released in the discovery phase after the prosecution and defense attorneys had had ample time to study them. This release resulted in media access to every intricacy of the investigation through Florida's unique statute that allows such access. The abundance of information available to the public prior the trial had a potential impact on the jury pool, which ultimately was selected from a nearby county through several days of questioning about knowledge about the trial. Ultimately, a jury was seated and sequestered, but there were many who were excused due to having prior knowledge of the case and forming opinions about it.

The second interesting legal aspect to this case was the role of the scientific, expert testimony. Experts were called in to testify not only to the standard forensic characteristics of the scene—status of the body, insect and plant evidence—but also to analysis of the odor coming from the trunk of Casey Anthony's car. This was the first time such evidence about odor had been admitted into a capital murder trial. It was added to an already circumstantial case.

The trial began on May 24, 2011. The defense's opening arguments were surprising and unexpected. Jose Baez, lead defense attorney, argued in opening statements that Caylee had actually died of a drowning accident in the family's pool and that George Anthony discovered her and helped cover it up. Casey was a loving mother who lied because she was sexually abused by her father and brother, and this family was good at keeping secrets. Sexual abuse was, however, not substantiated at trial. The defense's case relied heavily upon challenging the foundation of the scientific evidence and raising reasonable doubt about both the cause of death and key players, including Casey's father.

The prosecution contended that Anthony killed Caylee because she sought freedom from her responsibilities of motherhood. She was the only one who benefited from Caylee's death. They argued that Casey had drugged the child with chloroform, put duct tape over her mouth, and transported the body in her car until she could dump the remains in the woods. Expert testimony would identify the odor of human decomposition and presence of chloroform in the car. The prosecution provided evidence as well about Casey's lies and odd behavior, actions that seemed unlikely for a distraught mother searching for her child. Thirty prosecution witnesses alone were called to testify, including Casey Anthony's mother, father, brother, and friends.

Taking just 10 hours over two days to decide, the jury returned its verdict on July 5: Casey Anthony was acquitted on the most serious charges of premeditated murder, manslaughter, and aggravated child abuse. They returned guilty verdicts on the four lesser charges of providing false information to law enforcement. The judge gave her the maximum possible sentence for the crimes she was convicted of: four one-year terms to be served consecutively. Casey Anthony was returned to jail while her time served for the theft charge (she pled guilty in 2010) and time already served under this case was calculated. Casey Anthony was ultimately released on July 17, 2011, in the very early hours in the morning and whisked away from public sight. Anthony is facing several civil suits connected to the case as well as repaying the cost of the investigation.

The Anthony case seems to demonstrate the way society addresses women homicide offenders as either sick or evil. If they cannot be identified as sick somehow, then they are viewed as evil. This is even truer when the female is seen as violating an essential woman's nature as mother. The jury acquitted on the basis of reasonable doubt around the cause of death, despite strong feelings about her culpability. Despite this acquittal, the case still draws protest from those who refuse to accept the verdict and who call for justice for Caylee. Threats have been hurled at Anthony, her defense team, and even the jurors. It is clear that Anthony, while acquitted by the court, was convicted in the proverbial court of public opinion, which could not forgive or believe a mother who did not report her child missing for 31 days.

Resources

Alvarez, Lisette. 2011, July 18. "Software Designer Reports Error in Anthony Trial." *New York Times*. http://www.nytimes.com/2011/07/19/us/19casey.html?_r=1&ref=caseyanthony.

Burke, Cathy. 2011, June 11. "Thrown to Wolves: Tot Bones Gnawed." *New York Post*, 15.

Colarossi, Anthony. 2011, June 2. "Attorneys Question Lead Investigator in Casey Anthony Case as Trial Continues." *Orlando Sentinel*, B8.

Colarossi, Anthony. 2011, May 25. "Casey's Defense: Caylee Drowned." *Orlando Sentinel*, A1.

Fanning, Diane. 2009. *Mommy's Little Girl: Casey Anthony and Her Daughter Caylee's Tragic Fate*. New York: St. Martin's Press.

Hayes, Ashley. 2011. "After Nearly 3 Years, Casey Anthony to Stand Trial in Daughter's Death." May 23, 2011. www.cnn.com/2011/CRIME/05/23/florida.casey.anthony.trial/index.html?iref=allsea

Hewitt, Bill. 2008, August 11. "Little Girl Lost." *People* 70: 48–53.

Pafundi, Brian. 2010. "Note: Public Access to Criminal Discovery Records: A Look Behind the Curtain of the Criminal Justice System." 21. *University of Florida Journal of Law and Public Policy*. 227.

Richey, Warren. 2011, June 5. "Casey Anthony Case Resembles Real-Life CSI Crime Drama." *Christian Science Monitor.*

Richey, Warren. 2011, May 24. "Casey Anthony Trial: Defense Says Toddler Caylee Drowned by Accident." *Christian Science Monitor.*

Vickie Jensen

Anna Aquash (1945–1975)

In the fight for American Indian rights, Anna Mae Pictou Aquash emerged as a memorable figure, an activist whose death exposed the bitter relationship of the people she dedicated her life to and the U.S. government. Even now, decades after her frozen corpse was found on a remote ranch outside the Pine Ridge Reservation in South Dakota, the slaying of Anna Mae remains shrouded in controversy.

Anna Aquash was an activist involved with the American Indian Movement. Aquash was murdered shortly after a shootout on the Pine Ridge Reservation in 1975. (Courtesy: Robert A. Pictou-Branscombe)

Born March 27, 1945, in a small Mi'kmaq Indian village in Nova Scotia, Canada, Anna Mae Aquash was raised by a single mother who had to leave school at an early age. Aquash's childhood was marked with struggle and poverty. Her mother, Mary Ellen Pictou, raised Anna Mae and two other daughters on her own before marrying again. The family moved to a nearby Mi'kmaq reservation where Aquash grew up in a home without heat, water, or electricity. The family survived on food they grew themselves. Adding to her hardships, Aquash struggled with racism when she attended school outside the reservation.

Aquash eventually found her calling in Boston. She had moved there with a boyfriend who eventually became the father of her two daughters. She worked in factories to help support her family, attending some college. Eventually, she worked at a day care center in an African American neighborhood where she garnered praise for her dedication to the community. The work inspired her to join the growing Indian rights movement where she met Nogeeshik Aquash. A young Anna Mae and her new boyfriend Nogeeshik Aquash traveled together to a protest march in Washington DC in 1972 in which hundreds gathered to express grievances American Indians had with the government.

The needs of the Indians led Anna to the Sioux tribe's Pine Ridge Reservation in South Dakota where Anna and Nogeeshik eventually married.

Even now, the Pine Ridge Reservation remains to many in the Sioux community a symbol of broken promises by the U.S. government. Poverty, joblessness, crime, and lack of social services persist. The disconnect between federal agents and the Sioux people who live there contributed to a deeper distrust of the U.S. government, fueling bloody clashes. Tensions between American Indian Movement (AIM) activists, federal authorities, and government factions on the reservation resulted in dozens of deaths.

These were the conditions Anna Mae Aquash saw when she arrived in Pine Ridge in the early 1970s, just as the AIM was gaining momentum; AIM called on the U.S. government to acknowledge its broken treaties. Though the civil rights movement had called for equality for all during the 1960s, American Indians remained largely isolated from the national dialogue. Nonetheless, members of AIM had been encouraged by the results.

In 1973, members of AIM barricaded themselves in the village of Wounded Knee in South Dakota, the site of an infamous, blood massacre of a century before. A 71-day standoff followed. At the time, Anna Mae Aquash's role was unique, because the AIM was largely a patriarchal one, but she established herself as a guard and a supply courier. She also caught the attention of agents from the FBI. The FBI considered AIM an extremist organization. To this day, some American Indians believe the FBI was so concerned about AIM that they planted spies within the group to track their moves.

After the stand-off, Anna Aquash's work continued with AIM, and her activism to garner support for AIM took her to various cities, including Los Angeles. However, a shadow of doubt had been cast upon her from those back at Pine Ridge. Some thought Anna Mae Aquash was a snitch because she seemed to always be around when arrests occurred.

In June 1975, two FBI agents were searching for a robbery suspect at Pine Ridge. The agents were killed in a gunfight with AIM members. Later that year, police stopped a motor home carrying the alleged shooter, activist Leonard Peltier. Peltier eventually was convicted of the deaths. Aquash was among those riding in the motor home when it was pulled over, and rumors circulated that she had tipped off authorities. She was arrested, but after being released on her own recognizance, she sought refuge at an AIM safe house in Denver.

One month later, a small group of AIM members kidnapped Aquash from the Denver home. She was taken to South Dakota then driven to a remote ridge on the reservation and killed. Her frozen body was later found by a rancher. She had no identification on her, only a bracelet that many said Aquash always wore.

Her friends back at Pine Ridge began to believe that Aquash had been murdered by the FBI. Aquash's hands had been cut off by FBI investigators proof, AIM members said, that the agency was trying to cover up her death so that her body could not be identified. The doctor who conducted the first autopsy, W. O. Brown, ruled she had died of exposure. She was buried in an unmarked grave until her friends demanded that her body be exhumed and a second autopsy conducted. The second autopsy showed she had been shot execution-style in the back of the head with a .38-caliber gun. Later, Brown stated that he had unintentionally overlooked the bullet wound.

But the investigation into who killed Aquash languished for years. Her friends and some AIM members continued to blame the FBI for Aquash's death, saying that the agency had begun false rumors that she was an informant. Federal authorities have always denied wrongdoing.

Nearly 30 years later, a dogged investigation by a Denver police detective led to two former AIM members as Aquash's killers: John Graham and Arlo Looking Cloud. Graham, the gunman, was convicted of murder but not first-degree murder, which requires premeditation. He is currently serving a mandatory life sentence in prison. Suspect Thelma Rios continues to await trial in Rapid City, South Dakota, for Aquash's murder. Arlo Looking Cloud, an accused conspirator, was captured on March 27, 2004, Aquash's birthday. He was found guilty and is currently serving a life sentence for murder. Another suspect, Richard "Dickie" Marshall, was found not guilty in Aquash's murder in an April 2010 trial in Rapid City.

Resources

Arrillaga, Pauline. January 11, 2004. "Victim's spirit invoked to solve case." *Los Angeles Times,* A1

Henricks, Steve. 2007. *The Unquiet Grave: The FBI and the Struggle for the Soul of Indian Country.* New York: Da Capo Press.

Sonneborn, Liz. 1998. *A to Z of Native American Women.* New York: Facts on File.

Susan Abram

Susan Atkins (1948–2009)

Susan Atkins is best known as a Manson family member who was convicted of murdering Gary Hinman and Sharon Tate along with six other people in August 1969. Susan claimed for many years that she did not have a big part in the killings and that did not actually kill anyone. However, her own statements revealed that she stabbed Voytek Frykowski in the legs and restrained Sharon Tate while Charles "Tex" Watson stabbed her. Atkins served much of her life sentence at the California Institution for Women at Chino, along with Patricia Krenwinkel and Leslie Van Houten, other Manson followers and convicted murderers who are also housed there. In 2008,

Atkins was diagnosed with brain cancer and moved to the California Central Women's Facility in Chowchilla where she remained until she died on September 24, 2009.

Born Susan Denise Atkins in San Gabriel, California, on May 7, 1948, Atkins moved to Santa Clara when she was just 6 months old. Atkins' youth was marred with parental favoritism of her brothers, Michal and Steven; sibling incest (by Michael); and sexual molestation by Michael's friends, her father's friends, and random family friends. Both of

Susan Atkins is shown as she is about to leave the Los Angeles County Mens' Jail after meeting with Charles Manson, in 1971. Manson, acting as his own attorney, had asked to question Ms. Atkins, who was a principal witness before the grand jury that indicted the hippie "family" in the slayings of actress Sharon Tate and six others. (AP/Wide World Photos)

her parents were alcoholics. Until the age of 15, Atkins lived with her family in the middle-class Cambrian Park area of San Jose, California. A self-conscious, quiet girl, Atkins joined the glee club and choir where she was able to express herself in ways that otherwise she could not. In 1962, Atkins' mother died of cancer. After her death, relatives looked after Atkins and her brothers, but they could no longer pay for her mother's hospital bills. Atkins' relationship with her father went sour after he began drinking more heavily. He eventually sold the house in San Jose and moved to Los Banos, California. By this time, Michael had moved out and joined the Navy. Her father eventually left Atkins with her younger brother Steven.

Depressed and wanting to be on her own, at age 18, Atkins eventually left high school to support herself. She eventually moved to San Francisco where she took a variety of jobs, including as a secretary and a topless dancer. Depressed and lonely, she got involved with the drug and hippie crowd in Haight-Ashbury; she especially liked marijuana and LSD, and after hanging out with some sailors one evening, her Crazy Sadie identity was born. It was in 1967, at the age of 19, that Atkins met Charles Manson, who visited the house she shared with friends and played guitar. A few weeks later, police raided the house, leaving Atkins homeless. She joined Manson and others who planned a summer road trip to Los Angeles. While creating a fake ID for Atkins, Manson and another man gave her the nickname Sadie Mae Glutz.

Manson and his family eventually settled at Spahn Movie Ranch, which was located in the San Fernando Valley in Southern California. Atkins had learned about men at a young age but not about love. She felt that she learned and received that from Manson. "Getting hit by the man you love is no different than making love to him . . . Charlie gives me what I need" (Watkins, 1979: 73). On October 7, 1968, Atkins gave birth to a son whom Manson named Zezozece Zadfrack Glutz. The boy's father was Bruce White, whom Atkins met while the family was traveling through New Mexico in 1967. White came along and lived with them for about a month in the Topanga Canyon area but left just before the family eventually settled at Spahn Ranch. Once convicted, Atkins' parental rights were immediately terminated. None of her family took in the child. He was adopted later on by a family who renamed him "Paul." Atkins had no contact with her son after her incarceration in 1969.

In the summer of 1969, the Manson family came under the suspicion of law enforcement for auto thefts and harboring runaways. Manson encouraged drug dealing in order to make money; in fact, many of the women were used as "entertainment" for the dealers who frequented the ranch. During this time, Manson talked about "Helter Skelter," the inevitability of a race war which he described as an apocalyptic battle in which blacks would rise up against their white oppressors and kill them. Influenced by the Beatles' *White Album*, which he played endlessly, Manson claimed that during the war, the family would be safe. At the end of this war, family members would be made into gods and eventually rule the Earth when blacks realized that they could not do it by themselves. Though the plans undoubtedly sounded insane to outsiders, everyone in the family believed anything that came out of Manson's mouth.

At that time, someone suggested to Manson that he contact Gary Hinman who had just received a large monetary inheritance. Manson wanted Hinman to join the family and share his newfound wealth. On July 25, 1969, Manson sent Atkins, Bobby Beausoleil, and Mary Brunner to meet with Hinman. When Hinman confirmed that he did not inherit any money (which turned out to be true), Beausoleil beat him severely. Manson later showed up, infuriated that Hinman still claimed he had no money. In a rage, he sliced Hinman's face with a sword and cut his ear. Then, Manson ordered Atkins and Brunner to remain with Hinman and help him. According to Mary Brunner's testimony, two days later, Beausoleil returned to Hinman's residence and killed him while Brunner and Atkins watched from the kitchen. Atkins claimed to have put a pillow over Hinman's face, but Brunner denied witnessing that. After Hinman's death, Beausoleil left a bloody handprint and other revolutionary words on the walls to deflect attention away from Manson and onto the Panthers.

The Hinman killing did not seem enough for Manson so he contemplated other murders. On August 9, 1969, Atkins accompanied Charles "Tex" Watson, Linda Kasabian, and Patricia Krenwinkel to the Tate residence where Manson had indicated something ominous was going to happen. During the grand jury testimony, Atkins insisted that while she remained in the car, Watson told everyone there that they were to get the money from the people inside and then kill them. Atkins assisted with tying up the victims. She struggled with Voytek Frykowski and stabbed him repeatedly in the legs. While waiting for Watson, Atkins also restrained Sharon Tate. Later, with Tate's blood, she scrawled "Pig" on the front door. But Watson testified that he alone stabbed and killed Tate. Atkins claims that her role in the murders was mostly passive. However, many people argue that it was much more serious that she would admit.

The next night, August 10, Manson told his crew that the murders of the previous night were too messy and that he needed to show them how to do it correctly. So, Manson gathered up Atkins, Patricia Krenwinkel, Watson, Linda Kasabian, Leslie Van Houten, and Steve Grogan, who all eventually found themselves at the home of wealthy grocers Leno and Rosemary LaBianca in the Los Feliz area of Los Angeles. Manson and Watson went inside the home and tied up the couple. He then sent in Krenwinkel and Van Houten, demanding that followed Tex's orders. Manson told them to write on the walls with the victims' blood and then to make it back to Spahn Ranch. Manson took Atkins, Kasabian, and Steve Grogan to Venice Beach to murder an acquaintance, actor Salidin Nader, whom Kasabian had met previously while hitchhiking. While dropping them off, Manson instructed them to kill Nader and then come back to the ranch. Nader was not killed because Kasabian went to the wrong apartment.

Eventually, Manson and his followers left Spahn Ranch and relocated to Baker Ranch in Death Valley. However, in October 1969, police raided this ranch and family members were arrested for arson and auto theft. The charges were dropped, and everyone except Atkins could go. While in prison, a former family member, Kathryn Lutesinger, had suggested that Atkins was a part of the Hinman murder. Atkins went to another prison, where she bragged to her cell mates, Ronnie Howard and Virginia Graham, about the family's involvement in the Tate–LaBianca murders. Atkins shared with these women that she killed Sharon Tate, but later, she asserted that she said it only to show how tough and bad she was. Eventually, police arrested Manson, Watson, and Krenwinkel, based on the information they received. They issued a warrant for Kasabian, but she could not be located at the time.

Hoping to avert the death penalty, Atkins testified before the Los Angeles grand jury that Manson ordered them to go to the house in "creepy-crawly outfits" and to kill everyone there. Atkins told the grand jury how she restrained Sharon Tate while she begged for her and her baby's life. When asked if she killed Tate, Atkins denied it. She claimed she watched Watson stab her to death. However, Atkins claimed that she stabbed Frykowski in the legs. In exchange for this testimony, the Los Angeles DA's office proclaimed that Atkins' statements had been very helpful to police. Yet, right before the trial, Atkins recanted that testimony, claiming it was not true. However, years later, she maintained that it was a truthful accounting of what had occurred in the Tate residence that night.

There was a global reaction to the Manson murders and subsequent trial. From the very beginning, the media exposure reached unprecedented levels. Atkins was later tried with Manson, Krenwinkel, and Van Houten on charges of first-degree murder. The three girls shaved their heads, carved an "X" in their foreheads, and continually disrupted the courtroom with giggling in order to show solidarity and loyalty to Manson. In March 1971, the group was convicted and given the death penalty. Following this trial, Atkins was tried for the Hinman killing. Sharing the truth about that crime, Atkins also received another death sentence. However, in 1972, the California Supreme Court, in *People v. Anderson*, ruled the death penalty unconstitutional, leaving Atkins with a life sentence in prison.

Susan Atkins, Patricia Krenwinkel, and Leslie Van Houten were housed at the California Institution for Women at Frontera. Atkins did not maintain close contact with either woman, both of whom had ignored Atkins for many years immediately following the trial. Nonetheless, during her time in prison, Atkins involved herself in nearly every type of programming the prison offered. Her goal centered on self-transformation, for she always worked toward successful re-entry into society once on parole. She became a born-again Christian in 1974, involved herself in 12-step programs, and over her last four decades made significant contributions to community programs. Atkins helped save the lives of inmates and was awarded two commendations for these efforts. Atkins married twice while in prison. She first wed Donald Lee Laisure in 1981. From 1987 until her death, she was married to James Whitehouse, a Harvard-trained lawyer who represented Atkins at her parole hearings in 2000 and 2005.

Atkins had some difficult times during her incarceration, especially with psychiatrists. Despite several negative reports, she was considered a model prisoner by many supporters including reformed inmates whom she helped; prison teachers who enjoyed her as a student; and prison clergy and counselors impressed by her abilities to be a role model for others. Diagnosed with brain cancer in 2008, Atkins was eventually transferred to the California Central Women's Facility in Chowchilla. Despite her progress, Atkins had been continually denied parole, including at one hearing on September 2, 2009, where she had been wheeled into the hearing room on a hospital gurney. Susan Atkins was near death from her cancer at this point, finally dying on September 24, 2009.

See also Good, Sandra; Kasabian, Linda; Krenwinkel, Patricia; Van Houten, Leslie

Resources

Atkins, Susan, with Bob Slosser. 1978. *Child of Satan, Child of God.* New York: Bantam Books.

Bugliosi, Vincent, and Curt Gentry. 1974. *Helter Skelter: The True Story of the Manson Murders.* New York: W.W. Norton & Company.

CNN.com/Crime. 2009, September 25. "Ex-Manson follower Susan Atkins dies." http://www.cnn.com/2009/CRIME/09/25/california.manson.atkins/index.html, accessed July 2, 2010.

Sanders, Ed. 1989. *The Family: The Manson Group and Its Aftermath.* New York: New American Library/Signet.

Schiller, Lawrence. 1970. *The Killing of Sharon Tate: The Exclusive Story of Susan Atkins.* New York: Signet.

Watkins, Paul, and Guillermo Soledad. 1979. *My Life with Charles Manson.* New York: Bantam Books.

Woo, Elaine. 2009, September 26. "Charles Manson follower Susan Atkins dies at 61." *Los Angeles Times,* http://articles.latimes.com/2009/sep/26/local/me-susan-atkins26, accessed July 2, 2010.

Sue Cote Escobar

Axis Sally. *See* Gillars, Mildred Elizabeth Sisk

B

Josephine Baker (1906–1975)

Josephine Baker (1906–1975) was a legendary multiracial American-born dancer, singer, actor, entertainer, and civil rights activist. She served as an undercover agent for the French Resistance during World War II. In the 1950s, the FBI kept extensive files on her alleged un-American activities.

Baker was born on June 3, 1906, as Freda Josephine McDonald in St. Louis, Missouri. According to her personal and official autobiography, her childhood was characterized by poverty and racism. She received little formal education and had to work as a cleaner to support her family. She became a street performer at a young age, and her professional career began as she toured with the Jones Family Band and the Dixie Steppers.

In New York, Baker quickly earned fame and fortune at the Plantation Club. She traveled to Europe in 1925 and became an instant sensation. Her popularity soared in Paris for her exotic and erotic act. Her French audiences were awed by her sexuality, stage presence, and elaborate productions. Baker later settled in France and was declared a French citizen in 1937.

During World War II, Baker was active in the French Resistance. She performed extensively for French troops in various locations, and she even served in the French Auxiliary Air Force as a sublieutenant. In addition, Baker worked undercover for the intelligence branch of the French Resistance and smuggled secret messages coded in her sheet music from Portugal. Baker received the Croix de Guerre and the Legion d'Honneur for her service during the war.

The FBI compiled a 359-page file on Josephine Baker in her lifetime, though she was never proven to have engaged in any criminal activities, and she was never charged or convicted for any wrongdoings. The files contain various pieces of information, memos, letters from the public, newspaper and magazine articles, and other items that contain information on Baker's political activities.

The intersection of racial and Cold War politics in the 1950s United States triggered the FBI to keep an extensive file on Baker. Her active involvement in the Civil

Rights Movement and her international fame and exposure were argued to be the prime cause for the FBI's scrutiny.

Baker first came under the FBI's attention in the early 1950s when she was initially refused service at the Stork Club in New York City. She subsequently received very slow service, and she left the club angrily. She believed that the incident was racially motivated. She decided to initiate a boycott of the club, and she received support from the National Association for the Advancement of Colored People (NAACP).

To generate public support, the NAACP appealed to Walter Winchell, a newspaper columnist who was regarded as an ally of the NAACP and the African American community. Instead, Winchell attacked

Josephine Baker, a young dancer from New York City's Harlem neighborhood, was the star attraction in the 1920s at the Folies Bergères in Paris. (Library of Congress)

Baker and labeled her as a fascist and a communist sympathizer, and he further commented on her act as being morally indecent. Baker filed a libel law suit against Winchell and the Hearst newspaper corporation in return. The case became a sensation, and the FBI began to collect information on Baker.

According to Regester (2000), the FBI files contain detailed documentation of her professional as well as personal activities to discredit her involvement in the Civil Rights Movement and her international popularity. According to one of the files, she had a Russian maid, and the FBI used the maid's racial background to claim that Baker secretly wanted to deny her racial identity. In other files, Baker was also labeled as anti-American when she gave lectures in various countries on racial segregation and racism in America.

Baker's international fame and support, along with her staunch position on the Civil Rights Movement and Cold War politics, have been suggested as the primary causes of the intense investigation by the FBI. Baker's leadership role in the formation of the World League Against Racial Discrimination further fueled the FBI's claims that she was involved in un-American activities and was a threat to national security. The organization was to establish branches in Cuba, Guatemala, and El Salvador, and these nations were regarded as the top enemies of the United States. The FBI also used her visit to Cuba and her meeting with Fidel Castro as confirmation of her anti-American stands.

Ultimately, the FBI was effective and successful in portraying Baker as communist sympathizer and a significant threat to the national security of the United

States. The State Department also kept records of her travels and activities overseas. The mainstream press appeared to be significantly influenced by the FBI's effort. However, no charges were ever filed against Baker, and her alleged anti-American activities were never substantiated by any solid evidence nor formally charged in the courts.

Resources

Baker, Jean-Claude, and Chris Chase. 1993. *Josephine: The Hungry Heart*. New York: Random House.

Baker, Josephine, and Joseph Bouillon I. 1976. *Josephine*. New York: Harper & Row.

Dudziak, Mary L. 1994. Josephine Baker, Racial Protest, and the Cold War. *Journal of American History,* 81: 543–570.

Regester, Charlene. 2000. The Construction of an Image and the Deconstruction of a Star—Josephine Baker Racialized, Sexualized, and Politicized in the African-American Press, the Mainstream Press, and FBI Files. *Popular Music and Society* 24: 31–84.

Wood, Ean. 2000. *The Josephine Baker Story*. London: Sanctuary.

Kay Kei-ho Pih

Velma Barfield (1932–1984)

Velma Barfield is 1 of only 50 women executed in the United States between 1900 and 2006. She was put to death for the poisoning murder of her husband, and she confessed to killing three other people. Margie Velma Bullard, born in North Carolina on October 29, 1932, was the second of nine children born to Lillie and Murphy Bullard. Velma, as her parents always called her, had a troublesome childhood. Her father was abusive towards her and very violent towards her mother and older brother, Olive. According to Barfield, her father raped her when she was 13 years old. She also felt rejected and unloved by her mother.

In December 1949 when she was only 17, Velma married Thomas Burke, whom she began to date the year before at age 16. Their son Ronald Thomas was born on December 15, 1951, and their daughter Kim was born on September 3, 1953.

Condemned murderer Velma Barfield is shown during the taping of an interview in October 1984. (AP/Wide World Photos)

Around the age of 30 when Velma began to have trouble with anxiety, Thomas began to drink heavily. In 1966, Thomas's father died suddenly from a heart attack at the age of 60, and Thomas turned to more alcohol to cope. Velma was fearful of Thomas when he drank. In 1967 when Thomas was arrested for drunk driving, Velma had him committed to Dorothea Dix State Hospital in Raleigh, North Carolina. After he signed himself out, he continued to drink. In 1967, Velma suffered a nervous breakdown, was taken to a hospital, and was given vitamin shots and sedatives. She was released after a week with a prescription for tranquilizers. This was the beginning of her addiction to prescription medications including tranquilizers, painkillers, Valium, and sleeping pills. Velma went to various doctors who all prescribed her medications without knowing she was getting prescriptions elsewhere. As Thomas's drinking problem escalated, Velma threatened to divorce him.

In April 1969, Thomas came home drunk, started smoking, ignited a fire, and died of smoke inhalation. After his death, Velma increased her abuse of prescription medications.

Velma married Jennings Barfield, the widower of one of her co-workers, in August 1970. She continued to take pills and overdosed several times. Jennings, who was sick with emphysema and diabetes, refused to follow doctor's orders. Approximately six months after they were married, Velma poisoned him. She tried to convince herself that he died because of pre-existing medical conditions. After the death of two husbands, Velma experienced another great loss when her father died at the age of 61 from lung cancer. Despite the lack of a good relationship with her father, she was devastated by his death. Soon after, she moved in with her mother and began to take out loans to pay for medications using her mother's home as collateral. Drugs controlled Velma's life. In 1974, Velma poisoned her mother. The autopsy did not reveal poison; the cause of death was ruled a heart attack. Once again Velma denied that the death was a result of the poison. After her mother's death, Velma moved in with her daughter and son-in-law. As her money dwindled, she began to write checks on a closed account and was arrested and served four months in jail for check fraud.

In 1976, Velma Barfield accepted a job caring for Montgomery Edwards, a 94-year-old blind and bedridden man. His 84-year-old wife Dollie paid Barfield $75 a week and gave her room and board. In September 1976, Barfield met their nephew, Stuart Taylor, whom she started dating despite him being married. Over time, Dollie Edwards became critical of Barfield. In January 1977 when Montgomery Edwards died at the age of 95, Barfield stayed with Dollie although their relationship was quite tense. Four weeks after Montgomery's death, Velma Barfield poisoned Dollie Edwards who died in the intensive care unit of the hospital in February. Dollie Edwards was Velma's third victim.

One week after Dollie's funeral, a young woman asked Barfield to care for her mother, 76-year-old Record Lee, and her father, 80-year-old John Henry Lee. To cope with the bickering between John Henry and Record, Barfield was taking numerous drugs a day. After only a few weeks working for the Lees, Barfield used one of their checks to pay for a prescription for herself. John Henry contacted police about the forged check, but no one suspected Barfield. Velma Barfield began to poison John Henry Lee in April 1977, and he died June 4, 1977. Since the medical report said he died of a heart attack, Barfield convinced herself that he was old and had problems; it wasn't the poison that killed him. Barfield continued to care for Record for a few months before quitting.

At that time she again started to date Stuart Taylor, whose wife had since died from kidney disease. After the two became engaged, Barfield stole one of his blank checks and forged his name. When Stuart found out, he forgave her. Stuart Taylor died on January 31, 1978, at the age of 56. Velma Barfield agreed to an autopsy because she didn't think any poison would be discovered, and she already convinced herself that though the poison that she had given him made him sick, he really died from the flu. Taylor's autopsy revealed arsenic poisoning, and Velma Barfield was suspected. Barfield's son Ronnie convinced her to confess in March 1978. She confessed to also poisoning Lillie Bullard, Dollie Edwards, and John Henry Lee. Jennings's body was exhumed and traces of poison were found, but Velma never confessed to poisoning him. She was charged only with the first-degree murder of Stuart Taylor and pled not guilty by reason of insanity. Velma Barfield took the stand in her defense, testifying that she never meant to kill people—she just wanted to make them sick. She was found guilty and sentenced to death in 1978. Velma's son and daughter blamed drugs for their mother's actions, and both supported her during the trial proceedings and while she was on death row.

In prison Barfield became religious and was convinced she never would have killed anyone if not for the pills. While in prison, she stopped taking prescription medications and is said to have helped many other inmates.

In the six years Velma Barfield was on death row, her sentence was unsuccessfully appealed numerous times and she received several stays of execution. She was executed by lethal injection on November 2, 1984. She was the first woman to be executed in the United States since 1976.

Resources

Barfield, Velma. 1985. *Women on Death Row*. Nashville, TN: Oliver-Nelson Books.

Bledsoe, Jerry. 1998. *Death Sentence: The True Story of Velma Barfield's Life, Crimes and Execution*. New York: Dutton.

Kelleher, Michael D., and C.L. Kelleher. 1998. *Murder Most Rare: The Female Serial Killer*. Westport, CT: Praeger.

Shana Maier

Ma Barker (1871–1935)

In a time when women still were expected to be docile and caretakers, remaining in the home, Ma Barker rose to notoriety as the mastermind behind the Barker-Karpis Gang and was named a female public enemy by the FBI.

Arizona "Ma" Barker was born near Ash Grove, Missouri, on October 8, 1871. She later moved to Tulsa, Oklahoma, when her mother, Emma Reynolds, remarried Reuben Reynolds (aka James Reynolds) who was a watchman and worked at an oil exposition there. Barker grew up with her four sisters, one half-sister, and one half-brother.

Barker had several aliases, including "Effie Gordon," "Ma," "Mother," "Arrie," and commonly "Kate." Under the name "Arrie Clark," she married George E. Barker, a filling station operator, on September 15, 1892. They had four sons: Herman, Lloyd, Arthur ("Doc"), and Fred. The Barkers were relatively poor, relying on George's low salary, and Ma left George in 1928 amid speculation of her infidelity. Ma Barker later was associated with Arthur Dunlop (also known as George Anderson) whom the FBI speculated was murdered by Ma's son Fred and Alvin Karpis for allegedly tipping off the police.

There is no indication that George was involved in the criminal activity of his family, although he profited from it. The FBI reported that George was fearful for his life, that he was afraid of Ma Barker and the boys.

Ma Barker's sons were involved in quite a bit of delinquency as juveniles, quickly escalating to bank robbery, burglary, and homicide. Between 1915 and 1935 throughout Arkansas, Missouri, and Oklahoma, the Barker boys were involved in numerous crimes. One of the earlier crimes recorded was a highway robbery arrest of Herman on March 5, 1915, in Joplin, Missouri. While there is some dispute about the extent of Ma's participation in the criminal activity of her sons, there is no doubt that she knew what they were doing, and she clearly benefited from the "proceeds" of their crime.

While in prison on a burglary charge, Fred (the youngest and reportedly Ma's favorite son) met Alvin Karpis, who came home with Fred upon release, and together they formed the Barker-Karpis Gang including the other Barker brothers (when they were not incarcerated) and other associates they met in the penitentiary or while on the run. Ma moved with the gang throughout Oklahoma, Missouri, Minnesota, Kansas, and finally to Florida.

Ma Barker. (UPI/Bettmann/Corbis)

The FBI referred to Ma Barker as the mastermind of the gang, planning their crimes of bank robberies and kidnappings. However, in his biography, Karpis disagreed, claiming Ma was merely a caretaker, never involved with the crimes; Karpis said that, in fact the gang sent Ma to the movies when they engaged in criminal activity. Given that Ma downplayed the importance of education to her sons, the FBI speculated that she was the most intelligent of the gang—and the only one capable of plotting their crimes.

One of the final crimes committed by the gang was the kidnapping of a bank president, Edward George Bremer, on January 17, 1934, for which they received $200,000 ransom. Ma did not accompany the boys in this criminal endeavor; instead, she and the other women of the gang stayed behind in their apartments. She and a couple members of the gang did, however, move the ransom money from the kidnapping from its hiding place to Fred's Ohio apartment.

Despite her involvement with the Barker-Karpis Gang, Ma Barker was never tried or convicted. On January 16, 1935, when the FBI tried to execute a warrant on Ma and her son Fred in their cottage near Oklawaha, Florida, Ma and Fred began a gun fight which resulted in their deaths. The FBI reports finding a machine gun next to Ma Barker's left hand. The other Barker brothers were either killed or imprisoned.

In a time when women were fighting for the right to vote and were expected to remain in the home, Ma Barker violated gender stereotypes by leading a criminal gang. She was labeled by the FBI as a "female public enemy" in a press release for *Every Week Magazine*, making Ma Barker a household name.

Resources

deFord, Miriam Allen. 1970. *The Real Ma Barker: Mastermind of a Whole Family of Killers*. New York: Ace.

Federal Bureau of Investigation. 1936. "Barker-Karpis Gang (summary)." FBI Records: The Vault. Washington, DC: U.S. Department of Justice, Federal Bureau of Investigation. http://vault.fbi.gov/Barker-Karpis%20Gang%20Summaryy

Hornberger, Francine. 2002. *Mistresses of Mayhem: The Book of Women Criminals*. Indianapolis, IN: Alpha.

Jennifer C. Gibbs

Sydney Barrows (1952–)

The story of Sydney Biddle Barrows, otherwise known as the "Mayflower Madame," demonstrates that people from all walks of life can and do break laws. A descendent of William Brewster, an English separatist who sailed to America on the Mayflower, Barrows was formally charged with the crime of promoting prostitution on October 16, 1984. Her legal transgressions also call attention to the relationship between gender roles and women's crimes. In a society that places an inordinately high premium on a young woman's ability to present oneself in a sexual and desirable manner, her sexuality became a valuable commodity—something that could be bought and sold within the context of a lucrative but illegal sex market.

Though Barrows was born into a family whose names were listed on the pages of the social registry, she was far from rich. At the time of her high school graduation, she learned that the money set aside for her college tuition had been used to pay her boarding school expenses. Undeterred, she enrolled in a fashion buying and merchandising program at the New York City Fashion Institute of Technology, paying her tuition with the use of student loans and the money she earned through part-time employment. Finishing at the top of her class, she readily landed a number of retail positions. But after losing one such job, and in desperate need of money, she found work as a part-time receptionist at a local escort service.

As she answered phones, and saw that the poorly run service was owned and operated by an individual who habitually defrauded his female employees, she began to envision a well-run escort service that was not only profitable but treated its workers fairly. Partnering with Gina, a friend and fellow receptionist, she instituted Cachet, an exclusive and upscale escort service.

Providing an alternative to the typical shady escort operations found in and around New York City, Barrows took pride in the way she treated her "girls." She paid them 60 percent of their fees, allowed them to keep all of their tips, and supplied them with health care. Male patrons were carefully screened, and her young female employees could refuse to spend time with any man they were uncomfortable with.

Landing a job with Barrows was not easy. Unattractive young women lacking in poise and diction were turned away, making this humane alternative to the typical escort service open only to a select few. The "young ladies," as they were referred to, were expected to acquire a sophisticated wardrobe, practice careful grooming, and maintain an appropriate weight. She did, however, hire as many as 172 young escorts over the course of the four-and-a-half years she was in business.

Why did such bright and competent women, who were often drawn from the ranks of college students and business professionals, moonlight as professional escorts? Money! "Manhattan is an appallingly expensive place to live," Barrows wrote in her 1986 autobiography *Mayflower Madame: The Secret Life of Sydney Biddle Barrows*, "and even a girl making $25,000 in an executive training program would have a difficult time paying her bills without a second income. [And] hour for hour, our girls were among the highest-paid professional women in the country" (168).

Barrows became sole owner of Cachet after her partner opted out of the business. Barrows came to the attention of the New York City vice squad after the disgruntled owner of the townhome that served as her business headquarters tipped off the police. Vice officers, posing as "johns" attempting to render services, arrested four of her employees, and these arrests led to the eventual raid of Cachet's townhome headquarters. Learning of the arrest warrant issued for her the very next day, she acted upon the advice of her attorney and surrendered to district attorney officials several days later.

The half day Barrows spent in police custody on October 16, 1984, stands in sharp contrast to the upper middle class lifestyle was accustomed to. Fingerprinted and handcuffed upon surrender, she was transferred to a grimy holding pen for a total of five hours before being forced to join a line of 12 women handcuffed to a long chain. The entire group was eventually loaded into the small windowless back compartment of a police van. They were forced to sit on each other's laps or on the floor prior to being driven to the courthouse in cramped unventilated darkness. Once in court with her legal team, Barrows was formally charged with promoting prostitution. Pleading "not guilty" to the crime, she was released on $7,500 bail.

Although the prosecution's case against her was weak—running an escort service is not a crime in that clients paid for a young woman's time rather than for any particular sexual act—she reluctantly accepted a plea bargain for taking the case to trial would not only add to her already exorbitant legal fees but also introduce the slight possibility of jail time. What's more, a trial would force her former clients and employees to break their anonymity when ordered to testify against her in court. So on July 19, 1985, Barrows pled guilty to the crime of prostitution in the third degree and was ordered to pay a $5,000 fine—a penalty her attorney Risa Dickstein described as a "kiss on the wrist" (Barrows, 1986: 358).

In the weeks and months following her arrest and subsequent plea, Barrows' story was covered by both the tabloids and news organizations alike, making her an instant celebrity, and her best-selling autobiography *Mayflower Madame* (1986) was later turned into a television movie.

Barrows' her newfound celebrity status was not without drawbacks. The stigma of her arrest made it difficult to find work, and the money earned from her autobiography went to pay her legal fees. A second book, *Etiquette for Consenting Adults* (1990), did not sell well at all. As a result, she could not make ends meet.

She was not down for long. She married legal scholar and TV producer Darnay Hoffman in 1994, and her third book, *Just Between Us Girls* (1996) served as a springboard for a successful lecture series for wives intent on keeping their husbands from seeking sexual solace with the use of high-class prostitutes.

How does Barrows make sense of her foray into the illegal world of prostitution? She steadfastly contends that U.S. prostitution laws are in desperate need of reform. As she wrote in her 1986 biography, the illegal nature of prostitution provides an "attractive operating ground for gambling, drugs, violence, and even organized crime" (366). Likening sex work to one of the many service industry jobs she asserts, "Like their counterparts in the other helping professions our girls brought tenderness and comfort into our clients' lives" (365). It therefore comes as no surprise to learn that Barrows does not believe she did anything wrong.

Resources

Adler, J., and Johnson, P. 1984. The Mayflower Madame. *Newsweek*. October 29.

Barrows, S. B. 1986. *Mayflower Madam: The Secret Life of Sydney Biddle Barrows*. New York: Arbor House.

Biography. 1995. *Mayflower Madame: The Sydney Biddle Barrows Story*. A&E. DVD.

Goldman, David. 1996. Love for Sale: The Sydney Biddle Barrows Case. *Biography* 1(9): 14.

Stanley, A. 1984. The Classy Madame. *Time*. October 29.

Kristyan M. Kouri

Elizabeth Bàthory (ca. 1560–1614)

Countess Erzsebet (Elizabeth) Bàthory was a legendary female serial murder who either murdered her victims or directed other women in her employ to kill on her behalf. Even though she operated around the turn of the 17th century, she remains one of the most significant and prolific murderers of all time. She is also, as of this writing, the earliest documented case of a female serial murderer. Although she was tried for killing over 80 people, several claims put her victim count from 300 to 600 or more individuals.

According to Seagrave (1992), Bàthory was born to Gyorgy, a soldier, and Anna the sister of the king of Poland, in 1560. She was promised to Count Ferencz Nadasdy at age 11. Many of the Bàthory family were described as drunks; Satan worshippers, and incestuous, murderous sadists who tortured servants. Penrose (1970) documents quite eloquently that the family was notorious for their torture activities. There is substantial evidence that the environment in which Erzsebet Bàthory grew up in may have played a role in her choice of entertainment. The countess was also prone to "fits." She often complained of stabbing pains both in her head and behind her eyes. It has been suggested by Seagrave (1992) that these fits may have been bouts of epilepsy, something the family was also known to suffer from. She married Count Nadasdy on May 8, 1575, at the age of 15, retaining her maiden name of Bàthory, thus signifying her family's higher status. They moved into the Castle of Csejthe in northern Hungary.

Before her husband's death in 1604, she was known to have tortured many of the female servants of the castle. She eventually incorporated a variety of barbaric implements and built torture chambers wherever she moved to. In her collection were a number of long pins, a pair of flesh-tearing silver pincers, and a torture manual her husband had acquired while fighting the Turks. She would pierce, cut, sear, and burn all parts of the body including breast and vaginal areas, or she would have her trusted servants do it for her while she watched, screaming expletives and insults at her victims until she passed out. She also enjoyed flagellation, something taught to her by her aunt.

Women victims were taken from the lower classes, so as to not attract attention from the existing authorities. If these women went missing, the disappearance was rarely investigated especially if a member of the aristocracy was implicated. Some young women were convinced to come willingly with the enticement of employment as maids. Still others were simply drugged, or physically overpowered, and taken to the castle. Those who were brought to Bàthory were said never to leave the castle. The dead were buried, left to rot, or sometimes thrown over the castle walls to be eaten by wild animals. Eventually, she sought women from non-peasant classes.

At some time directly after the turn of the century, her husband died. By this point, it was believed that Erzsebet Bàthory was quite mad. It is unclear whether she was as active torturing young women before his death, but it was remarked that after he died, her activities were at a feverish level. As her need to torture grew, so did her need for victims. She moved to torturing strangers when her supply of local servants ran out. Before she was caught, she would direct a number of trusted servants to bring victims to the castle. With pressure from his public, King Matthias of Poland, whose father attended the Bàthory wedding, was forced to order an investigation. Count Thurzo, Bàthory's closest neighbor conducted a raid on the castle on December 29, 1610. She and her dedicated servants were caught in the midst of a torture session.

Countess Elisabeth Bàthory was put on trial January 2, 1611. She was accused and convicted of killing 80 young women, a number related to the number of individual remains found at the scene by the raiders. It is estimated that she killed many more over the years that she was operating. Although three of her assistants were put to death, Countess Bàthory, protected by birthright, was allowed to live. Parliament decided that she be confined to a room in her own castle. She died there three-and-a-half years later on or around August 21, 1614.

Despite the many accounts of her crimes and her significant victim pool, she was not recognized as being in the serial killer class of offenders until the early 1990s. She is a prime example of how gendered stereotypes can interact with social class. Before this time she was most often not included in many popular encyclopedias on this subject. Where her actions were documented, she remained unclassified as a serial murderer or labeled erroneously as a "Black Widow," even though she did not murder her husbands or lovers.

The activities of Countess Bàthory have been recounted in several books. Some of these documents include a grotesque legend of the countess and her activities that had built up over the centuries. The legend was that Erzsebet Bàthory initially got the blood of a young servant girl on her skin and supposedly became convinced that her skin, under the blood, looked younger. It was stated that, aided by her servant Doretta Szentes, or Dorka, and two others, Countess Bàthory began bathing at four every morning in the blood of virgins. She was said to either drink the blood directly out of the body or to drain it into her bathing tub. This version of events, as with many legends, is almost wholly false. The legend, however, is revealing in that it suggests that she killed to protect beauty and youth, not to gain power or experience pleasure through violence. The former reflects traditionally feminine sources of power, while the latter being masculine. Trial documents do state that some exsanguination of victims was performed, but this was due to Bàthory's practice of alchemy and rituals of "black magic" as opposed to warding off old age.

Resources

Penrose, V. (1970). *The Bloody Countess*. London: Creation Books.

Seagrave, K. (1992). *Woman Serial and Mass Murderers: A Worldwide Reference, 1580 through 1990*. London: McFarland & Company.

Hannah Scott

Betty Beets (1937–2000)

Betty Lou Dunevant, born March 12, 1937, in North Carolina, was the second of four children born to James and Louise Dunevant. Louise Dunevant had severe mental health issues, and Betty's father James drank heavily and was physically abusive towards Betty Lou.

At the age of 15, Betty Lou met Robert Franklin Branson. She married him in 1952, right after completing ninth grade, and they had their first child Faye one year later. Betty Lou and Robert had marital problems, and Betty Lou even attempted suicide. However, they continued to have children together. After the birth of their second daughter, Connie, Betty Lou and Robert moved to Texas. Their third daughter, Shirley, was born in 1959, followed by the birth of Phyllis in 1962, Robert Franklin II in 1964, and Bobby in 1966. In 1969, after 17 years of marriage and six children, Betty Lou and Robert divorced. Betty Lou received custody of the children.

One year later, in 1970, Betty Lou married Billy York Lane. Billy York Lane abused Betty Lou, and the two divorced within one year. After the divorce, Billy saw Betty Lou at a bar dancing with another man and became jealous. Betty Lou told police that Billy followed her home that evening and threatened to kill her so she shot him twice. She claimed it was self-defense. However, both shots were in Billy's back. Billy, who survived the shooting, at first told police a story very different from Betty's account of the night. Billy claimed that Betty Lou called him at his daughter's house and asked him to come over. He later recanted his story and told police that he had threatened Betty Lou. As a result of the incident, Betty Lou received only a fine, and Betty Lou and Billy York Lane married for a second time. They divorced again after one month.

In 1978, Betty Lou married Ronnie Threlkeld (her third husband and fourth marriage), and they moved to Arkansas. At that time, Betty Lou's youngest son Bobby, who was still living with her, started to notice his mother's mental instability. Ronnie Threlkeld soon left Betty Lou, and she filed for divorce. Betty Lou soon met Doyle Wayne Barker at a gas station, and the two married in October 1979. She divorced him in January 1980, but he returned to Betty Lou, and the two married for a second time in 1981. According to Betty Lou, Barker was abusive so she shot him in 1981, stuffed him in a sleeping bag, and stuffed him in the closet. She then called her daughter, Shirley, and confessed the murder. Shirley helped her mother bury Doyle Wayne Barker in the backyard, and Betty Lou told friends, family, and neighbors that Barker simply disappeared.

While working in a club, Betty Lou met James Donald Beets. The couple married in Texas in August 1982, and although Jimmy Don's son Jamie did not like Betty Lou, Betty Lou's children were fond of Jimmy Don and claimed that he was never abusive towards their mother. Betty Lou soon began to take out life insurance policies on Jimmy Don listing herself as the beneficiary. She told her son Robby that she planned to kill Jimmy Don to collect the life insurance money. Betty Lou shot Jimmy Don Beets with a .38 Colt revolver while he was asleep in their home on August 6, 1983. She confessed to her son Robby and daughter Shirley, and Robby helped Betty Lou bury Jimmy Don in the yard. Betty Lou called the police to report Jimmy Don missing. The next day, she and Robby put Jimmy Don's empty fishing boat in a nearby lake, spilling Jimmy Don's heart medication in the boat; they wanted to make it look like Jimmy Don had a heart attack and fell overboard, although Jimmy Don's son Jamie never believed that story. The police found the empty boat on August 12, 1983.

After having too much to drink, Betty Lou told Gerald Albright, a man with whom she was having an affair, that one of her husbands was buried in her yard. Albright reported this to the police who obtained a search warrant for her yard. They found the bodies of Jimmy Don Beets and Doyle Wayne Barker and arrested Betty Lou Beets on June 8, 1985. Bail was set at $1 million. Betty Lou's daughter Shirley was also arrested in connection with the murders. Both Shirley and Robby confessed their involvement in the murders; Shirley reported to the police that while she was incarcerated in a cell next to her mother, Betty Lou confessed to killing Jimmy Don Beets.

Betty Lou Beets pled not guilty to the murder of Jimmy Don Beets but was indicted for murder on June 11, 1985. Robby and Shirley testified against their mother.

Despite the efforts on Betty Lou's defense attorney, E. Ray Andrews, Betty Lou Beets was found guilty and sentenced to death for the murder of Jimmy Don Beets in a Texas court in October 1985. Although she was charged with the murder of Doyle Wayne Barker, she never went to trial for Barker's death because of the death sentence that was imposed on her for the murder of Beets.

Betty Lou Beets, who claimed her father and all five husbands abused her, appealed the court's ruling, claiming the jury should have been allowed to consider her history of abuse. Battered women's advocates agreed that her history of abuse should have been entered as mitigating evidence. She also claimed her counsel, E. Ray Andrews, was ineffective. Despite her appeals and a few stays of execution, Betty Lou Beets was executed by lethal injection in Texas on February 24, 2000. She was 62 at the time of the execution, and she was the fourth woman to be executed in the United States since 1976.

Resources

Fox, James A., and James Levin. 2005. *Extreme Killing: Understanding Serial and Mass Murder.* Thousand Oaks, CA: Sage Publications.

Pence, Irene. 2001. *Buried Memories: The Chilling True Story of Betty Lou Beets, the Texas Black Widow.* New York: Pinnacle Books.

Shana Maier

Mary Bell (1957–)

Mary Flora Bell was a child convicted of manslaughter in the cases of two other children. Her actions caused a sensation in 1968 when she was convicted, at 11 years of age, for the murders of two boys in Newcastle-upon-Tyne, England. Mary Bell murdered four-year-old Martin Brown by strangulation on the day before her 11th birthday, May 25, 1968. It is believed she was alone during this incident. The second murder, on July 31, 1968, also involved the strangulation of a young boy—three-year-old Brian Howe. Though it is believed both Mary and her friend Norma Bell (no familial relation) were present during the murder, only Mary was convicted for Howe's death.

Mary Flora Bell was born on May 26, 1957, in Newcastle-Upon-Tyne, England, to 16-year-old Betty Bell. Mary's father is unknown. It is believed that Betty Bell attempted to kill her daughter several times, usually by drug overdose, within the first several years of her life. Additionally, relentless abuse was the norm within the home in which Mary was raised. Betty Bell engaged in prostitution and often used Mary as a sexual prop during these encounters. Many believe that the brutality of her mother, the unknown genetics of her father, and the damage caused by the numerous drug overdoses Mary suffered may have been catalysts to her violent actions.

Although Mary was convicted of manslaughter in the deaths of Martin Brown and Brian Howe, her friend Norma Bell was acquitted of both deaths. On the day four-year-old Brown was found dead in an abandoned house (May 25, 1968), it was Mary and Norma who informed his aunt of the horrible tragedy. When Martin was taken to the hospital and pronounced dead, the pathologist conducting his autopsy could not determine a cause of death. There were no external injuries, except for a small bruise on his knee. The doctor believed the boy's death might have occurred from poisoning, but this was ruled out once test analyses showed no signs of chemicals or drugs within the boy's system.

Following Martin's death, several incidents served to illuminate Mary's interest in violence and her involvement in Martin's deaths. First, Mary and Norma approached Martin's family members to ask morbid questions, including whether Martin was missed. Then the girls asked if they could see the little boy's body in the casket.

Additionally, on the day following Martin's death (Mary's 11th birthday), Mary was found strangling Norma's younger sister. Norma's father intervened. Then, on the morning of May 27, 1968, it was discovered that the local day nursery (day care center) had been broken into, and messages related to Martin's murder had been left behind. A security alarm was promptly installed in the building. On Friday of that same week, Mary and Norma set off the building alarm and were caught by the police. They denied ever having broken in before and were sent home with their parents to await an appearance date in juvenile court.

A final incriminating incident focused on Mary's visit to Brian Howe's home a few days prior to his death. During that visit, she told the Howe family that Norma had strangled Martin Brown, and she even demonstrated how Norma had done it. Only days later, Mary strangled Brian Howe exactly as she had described the strangulation of Martin Brown's. Unlike Martin, however, Brian had puncture wounds in his thighs, his genitals were partially skinned (a pair of scissors was found near the scene), and a razor had been used to scratch "M" into his stomach. The physical wounds found on Brian's body, compared to the lack of violence on Martin's body, illuminate the fact that Mary, similar to many individuals who murder multiple times, had become more violent during her murders.

The nine-day trial against Mary Bell and Norma Bell began on December 5, 1968. The prosecutor suggested that whoever had killed Martin Brown had also killed Brian Howe. He furthered his case by describing the suspicious behaviors of both Mary and Norma.

Norma first took the stand during the trial. She told the court that Mary had shown her how to kill a little boy or girl and that Mary had also told her about the "accident" of Martin Brown. When Mary was called to the stand, her odd and violent behavior following Martin's death was immediately questioned. In addition, handwriting experts analyzed the notes left behind at the day nursery; their analysis indicated that both girls had participated in writing those notes.

As the trial proceeded, Mary and Norma continually told opposing stories. Though both girls denied having a role in the death of Martin Brown, each admitted that they had been together with Brian Howe at the time of his death. However, their testimonies conflicted regarding how Brian was killed. Mary claimed that Norma killed him, while Norma accused Mary of Brian's murder.

The jury took under four hours to return a verdict. Norma was judged "not guilty" of manslaughter in both cases; Mary was found guilty of manslaughter in both Martin's and Brian's deaths.

At the time of judgment, British authorities were unsure where Mary should serve her sentence. She eventually was remanded to an "all boys" facility, the Red Bank Special Unit, from February 1969 until November 1973. Later, in 1977, she was moved to a less secure facility, from which she escaped, though she was recaptured after only a few days. Shortly before her parole in 1980, Mary was moved to a hostel where she met, and became pregnant by, a married man. She was officially released on May 14, 1980, at age 23.

At the time of her initial incarceration, Mary Flora Bell was judged to be a severe risk to other children. Though diagnosed with a psychopathic disorder, Britain had no treatment or hospital suitable to provide appropriate care for Mary. Consequently, she was imprisoned without treatment.

After rendering a decision, Mary Bell's trial judge commented that he hoped the matters they had all had to deal with would be put behind them and forgotten. The judge's comments, coupled with the lack of adequate treatment resources and age- or gender-appropriate incarceration facilities, might have reflected a larger societal problem in the denial that young female children were capable of such aggression and violence.

Resources

Scott, Shirley Lynn. *Mary Bell*. Court TV, Crime Library, Retrieved August 10, 2007. http://www.crimelibrary.com/about/authors/scott/

Sereny, Gitta. 1995. *The Case of Mary Flora Bell: A Portrait of a Child Who Murdered.* London: Pimlico.

Sereny, Gitta. 1998. *Cries Unheard*. London: Macmillan.

Devon Thacker Thomas

Catherine Bevan (1680–1731)

Catherine Bevan was accused of killing her husband, Henry Bevan, with the help of their servant Peter Murphy. She was burned for her crime, a punishment typically reserved for black slaves (though she was white), whereas her alleged partner in crime, a white indentured servant, was hanged (Williams 1999, 22). The legal reason for the separate sentences is that a woman killing her husband was considered "petit treason" (Loyd 1908, 36). Catherine Bevan's execution is a significant event in American history as it illustrates the differential societal expectations of men and women in early America. Her case exemplifies that, among other formal and informal social mechanisms, white male power was maintained through the disparate treatment of men and women in the criminal justice system. While little has been written on her life, her ostensibly heinous demise caused some scholarly inquiry and speculation regarding her guilt. Her account of the event was not documented. The treatment of her execution by the news media of that day, and earlier historians, exemplifies the patriarchal approach to crime.

During separate interrogations, Peter Murphy accused Catherine Bevan of the murder, claiming that she had sent him off to buy vitriol, which she then mixed into her husband's wine (Jones 1996, 37). According to Peter Murphy, when Henry Bevan did not immediately die after drinking the poisoned wine, Catherine Bevan ordered him to beat Henry Bevan to death. He claimed to have refused and was dispatched to find the neighbors on the false pretense that her husband had taken ill (37). Peter Murphy asserted that, during his absence, Catherine strangled Henry Bevan to death. Peter Murphy maintained this story, until the day of the trial, when he confessed that he lied about the aforementioned, saying only that Catherine Bevan had not disapproved of the murder (37).

No real detail exists on the circumstances of Catherine Bevan's relationship with Peter Murphy nor the nature of the relationship with her husband. Some evidence suggests that the community did not feel as much malice towards her as, for example, sentiments printed in the *Pennsylvania Gazette*. There was a clear suspicion that Peter Murphy was as responsible as Catherine Bevan was, but little record of this possibility exists other than his retraction on the day of the trial. By some accounts, Henry Bevan had allegedly told neighbors that he was being abused by both Catherine Bevan and Peter Murphy (Jones 1996, 36). Perhaps due to these rumors, a magistrate had ordered an exhumation, and upon opening the coffin, it was discovered that Henry Bevan was covered in bruises (Jones 1996, 36). It has largely been assumed that she was having an affair and, together with her lover, she murdered her husband. Catherine Bevan's historical treatment is testament to the timelessness of stories involving love affairs and murder. Another motive has not been considered.

Sentenced by the Court of New Castle County in Delaware, Catherine Bevan's fate was to be burned in New Castle on September 10, 1781. The *Pennsylvania Gazette* reported that she was unrepentant as opposed to her accomplice who expressed remorse (September 23, 1971). Indeed, she was said to deny any part in the crime up until the very end. It seems that Peter Murphy might have confessed to the murder (Loyd 1908), though little else is known about the trial. What is known is that her execution was unique. Apparently her demise was to be quickened by the noose that had been tied around her neck (Fiske 1902, 381). Unfortunately for Catherine, the rope either broke or was tampered with because she fell into the fire. She managed to slip out of her hand and foot constraints but, upon attempting to jump out of the fire, she was thrust back in by the sheriff who had to hold her there until she died (Browning 1912, 170). The nature of her demise, whether fairly sentenced or not, was severe enough to cause a reevaluation of the efficacy of public burnings, at least pertaining to white men *and* women.

Peter Murphy was hanged and Catherine was burned, meaning she was treated more punitively because burning is not only more excruciating, but also a desecration of the body (Banner 2003, 71). Her account of the events is not available suggesting that, when it comes to the murder of a husband where the circumstances appear unambiguous, the testimony of the wife was not considered important. Nevertheless, her suffering appeared to change early American society because hers was the last public burning on record (Walker 1998).

Resources

Banner, Stuart. 2003. *The Death Penalty.* Harvard University Press.

Browning, Charles. H. 1912. *Welsh Settlement of Pennsylvania.* Press of Devine Co.

Fiske, John. 1902. *The Historical Writings of John Fiske.* Houghton, Mifflin and Company.

Jones, Ann. 1996. *Women who Kill: With Previously Unpublished Material on the "Battered Women's Syndrom*e. Beacon Press.

Loyd, William H. Jr. 1908. "The Courts of Pennsylvania in the Eighteenth Century prior to the Revolution." *University of Pennsylvania Law Review and American Law Register.* University of Pennsylvania Dept. of Law, University of Pennsylvania Law School.

Walker, Samuel. 1998. *Popular Justice: A History of American Criminal Justice.* Oxford University Press.

Williams, William H. 1999. *Slavery and Freedom in Delaware, 1639–1865.* Rowman & Littlefield.

Corina Schulze

Amy Bishop (1965–)

Amy Bishop came to widespread attention in the United States in February 2010 as the perpetrator of a series of deadly workplace shootings at the University of Alabama, Huntsville (UAH). Bishop, a mother of four and a researcher with a PhD from Harvard University, was accused of murdering three of her colleagues and wounding three others during a routine faculty meeting. The killings were allegedly motivated by Bishop's failure to receive tenure and the likely termination of her job as a professor. Homicides committed by women are relatively rare, and mass homicide with firearms, such as the one allegedly perpetrated by Bishop, is nearly unheard of, especially in a school or college setting. While the rarity of this event is enough to proclaim Bishop an important woman criminal, Bishop also provides an example of the importance of intersections of race, class, and gender in the criminal justice treatment of previous incidents including her involvement in the shotgun death of her brother, violent confrontations in public, and an alleged bombing plot. Bishop's middle-class status as a white woman clearly had an influence on how those cases were handled.

Bishop was born on April 24, 1965, in Braintree, Massachusetts, into an upper-middle-class background. She is the daughter of Samuel and Judith Bishop. Not much is specifically known about her childhood except that she was raised in a highly educated home with the general expectation that she would go to college and become part of the community of educated citizens.

Bishop had her first brush with the law in 1986, at age 20, when she fatally shot her 18-year-old brother Seth with a shotgun in their family home in Braintree. Bishop was briefly detained and questioned in connection with the shooting, but police at the time ruled it an accident and released Bishop into the custody of her mother. No charges of any sort were filed against Bishop at the time with regard to the death or the discharge of the weapon.

The investigation into the 1986 shooting was reopened in the wake of the UAH killings. Braintree officials first claimed that the original police report had been lost, but it was later rediscovered. According to the original report and other law enforcement documents, shots had been fired in several different rooms of the Bishop's home. Following the shooting, Bishop tried to steal a car at gunpoint from a local car dealer, claiming her husband was trying to kill her. Investigators also found a news clipping in Bishop's room about a woman who killed a family member with a shotgun and then stole a car to make her getaway.

After the UAH shootings, officials in Braintree revisited the case of Seth Bishop's shooting death. On June 16, 2010, after review of the evidence, Bishop was indicted in Norfolk County, Massachusetts, for the murder of her brother. The incident created a statewide scandal in Massachusetts with accusations that Bishop's initial release, the subsequent loss of police records, and her later indictment were all politically motivated. Bishop's status as a woman may have also contributed as she did not fit the profile of a "dangerous" killer. This lack of concern about Bishop's dangerousness is underscored by the fact it took police 11 days to interview her after the shooting.

Despite her role in the shooting death of her brother, Amy Bishop went on to receive her bachelor's degree in biology in 1988 from Northeastern University in Boston. In 1989, Bishop married James Anderson, whom she had met at a science fiction convention while they were undergraduates at Northeastern. She earned a PhD in genetics from Harvard University in 1993 and continued to teach and do research at Harvard until 2003, notably as an instructor at the Harvard Medical School. In 2003, Bishop was hired into a tenure-track position as an assistant professor of biology at UAH. Bishop's career in biology has included several achievements, including at least one patent associated with her research. She and her husband, James Anderson, also worked together to develop a "portable cell incubator" intended as an alternative to growing cell cultures in Petri dishes. Anderson raised $1.25 million from his employer, Prodigy Biosystems, to fund the research. Bishop had also written several unpublished novels, had found a literary agent, and was reportedly very serious about getting her novels published. Some described Bishop and her husband as Star Trek lovers ("trekkies") and "nerdy." As of February 2010, they were the parents of four children, including a son who was a sophomore biology major at UAH.

Beneath the seemingly idyllic surface, Bishop was suspected of or directly involved with several encounters that would be discussed, in retrospect, as potential red flags of trouble ahead. In 1993, Bishop and her husband, James Anderson, were investigated in a failed mail-bomb attack on Dr. Paul Rosenberg, Bishop's former boss at Children's Hospital Boston. According to documents at the Bureau of Alcohol, Tobacco and Firearms (ATF), Rosenberg had forced Bishop to resign her job in the neurobiology lab for not meeting the job's requirements. According to the same documents, Bishop was extremely upset over the loss of her job, and Anderson told witnesses of his desire to do physical harm to Dr. Rosenberg. Search warrants were issued against Bishop and Anderson, and both of them were questioned repeatedly by ATF investigators, but no one was ever charged in the incident. The case was reopened for further investigation after the UAH shootings but, again, resulted in no charges.

In 2002, Bishop became enraged at another mother in a Massachusetts International House of Pancakes restaurant who had taken the last child booster seat available. Bishop punched the woman, was charged with assault, and was sentenced to probation and mandatory anger management classes. Accounts that emerged after the UAH shootings painted a picture of a woman who screamed at people who crossed her and called police to report individuals who bothered her, including children who rode bicycles too close to her homes in both Massachusetts and Alabama. Colleagues and others, after the fact, claimed that she couldn't get past slights against her and that she was filled with a rage that boiled just below the surface.

In March 2009, Bishop was denied tenure at UAH, a decision that would result in the loss of her job. She appealed the decision in November of that year, spending many hours writing letters and talking to colleagues, but her appeal was rejected. Her colleagues at UAH cited poor teaching, frequent complaints from students, and insufficient research and publication as the reason for the denial. According to family members, Bishop saw the loss of tenure as the "end of the world."

On February 12, 2010, Bishop is alleged to have shot several of her colleagues during a routine meeting of the biology faculty. What follows is a description of the alleged events that has not been legally substantiated in the court system. Bishop is described as removing a 9 mm handgun from her purse and methodically shooting her fellow professors. She was described as being cold and unemotional as she shot them one by one. One colleague of Bishop's, Debra Moriarty, crawled under the table when the shooting started. During a pause in the shooting, she grabbed Bishop's leg and begged her to stop. Instead, Bishop turned the gun on her and chased her from the meeting room into the hallway. She pointed the gun at Moriarty's face and pulled the trigger, but it had either run out of ammunition or malfunctioned and did not fire. Moriarty then ran back into the meeting room and locked the door. By this time, survivors in the room had already called the Huntsville police. Bishop left the gun in a nearby bathroom and surrendered herself to police minutes later outside the building. When it was over, three colleagues were killed, and two colleagues and a staff assistant were wounded. Killed in the shootings were professors Gopi Podila, Maria Ragland Davis, and Adriel D. Johnson, Sr. Professors Luis Rogelio Cruz-Vera and Joseph G. Leahy and staff assistant Stephanie Monticciolo were also shot but survived the attack.

As of September 2011, Bishop was still in the Huntsville jail awaiting trial for capital murder for the UAH killings, as well as facing a Massachusetts murder charge for the shooting death of her brother in 1987. The trial date for Bishop in Alabama has been set for March 2012 when the state will pursue the death penalty. Bishop's defense team filed court papers indicating their pursuit of a not guilty by reason of insanity plea, requiring the demonstration of both mental illness or defect and the inability to appreciate the wrongfulness of her actions. As of June 2011, psychological examination and testing was underway with respect to Bishop's legal sanity. Authorities decided not to press further with the case of the alleged bombing plot.

Amy Bishop provides one picture of how race and class privilege interact with gender. The fact that Bishop is a woman from a middle/upper-class background and is white appears to have made it more difficult for authorities to see her as fitting the model of a dangerous criminal, and she was given consideration that men and nonwhite women of working and lower classes may not have been given in the same circumstances. This case is still progressing, and more influence of race/class/gender will undoubtedly be noticeable as the judicial process moves forward. This case has also raised questions related to the structure and stress of the tenure system in many U.S. universities, a system that challenges many women and men in academia. While there can be gender overtones to the system of tenure, Bishop's alleged violent response to being denied tenure stands as the only known case of violent retaliation committed by a woman in this setting.

Resources

Amy Bishop Faculty Web Page. http://www.web.archive.org/web/20070820140857/www.uah.edu/colleges/science/biology/amy/amy.htm. Retrieved October 8, 2010.

Associate Press. 2010a. "Accused UAH Shooter Amy Bishop Won't Be Charged in 1993 ArtBombing."http://blog.al.com/wire/2010/09/accused_uah_shooter_amy_bishop.html. September, 30, 2010. Retrieved October 8, 2010.

Associated Press. 2010b. "1986 Shooting by Professor Reexamined." *New York Times*. June 6, 2010. A22.

Associated Press. 2010c. "Professor's Killing of Brother Will Be Focus of an Inquest." *New York Times*. February 26, 2010. A 16.

Dewan, Shaila, Stephanie Saul, and Katie Zezima. 2010. "For Professor, Fury Just Beneath the Surface." *New York Times*. A1.

Harlow, John. 2010. "Professor in Campus Killing Spree had Been Rejected for Job." *Sunday Times* (London England). February 14, 2010. 33.

"I'm Mad as Hell and I'm Not Going to Take This Anymore!" 2010. *Women in Higher Education* 19(3): 28.

Jonsson, Patrik. 2010. "Amy Bishop Case: Why No Red Flags Were Waved Before Shooting Spree." *Christian Science Monitor*. February 17, 2010.

Meadows, Bob. 2010. "Murder on Campus A Professor's Rage." *People Weekly*. March 8, 2010. 123.

Jonsson, Patrik. 2010. "Beat-Up Cars and Neuron Computers: Broken 'Dream' of Amy Bishop?" *Christian Science Monitor*. February 18, 2010.

Kolata, Gina. 2010a. "A Case for Tenure that Some See as Falling Short." *New York Times*. February 21, 2010. A18.

Kolata, Gina. 2010b. "A Murder Suspect's Worth to Science." *New York Times*. February 23, 2010. D4.

Roop, Lee. 2010. "Amy Bishop to Face Capital Murder Charge in Huntsville's First." http://blog.al.um/breaking/2010/06/army_bishop_to_face_murder_char.html. June 16, 2010. Retrieved October 8, 2010.

"Science and Violence: The Career of Amy Bishop." 2010. *Chronicle of Higher Education* 56: 25.

Tanenhaus, Sam. 2010. "Violence that Art Didn't See Coming." *New York Times*. February 28, 2010. AR1.

Wadman, Meredith. 2010. "Life After Death." *Nature* 465: 151–155.

Zezima, Katie. 2010. "Police are Criticized in 1986 Shooting." *New York Times*. February 23, 2010. A15.

Christopher Volak

Lorena Bobbitt (1970–)

Lorena Bobbitt was involved in one of the more sensational televised court cases of the 1990s. Her singular attack against an abusive husband, and its aftermath,

Lorena Bobbitt meets reporters in Virginia after her acquittal, in 1994. (AP/Wide World Photos)

revealed a disconnect between men and women and their respective attitudes towards marital violence and gender-based revenge. Born Lorena Leonor Gallo in 1970, she was raised in a working-class family in Caracas, Venezuela. In 1986, she and her family decided to immigrate to the United States. While her family eventually went back to Caracas, Lorena decided to stay. She made plans to attend school, eventually ending up employed at a friend's nail salon. During an outing with friends, she met a handsome marine, John Wayne Bobbitt. They were married on June 18, 1989, and set up house in Manassas, Virginia.

In a 1993 *Vanity Fair* interview, she described the marriage as troubled from the start. Over the next few years, there were conflicts over John's drinking and heavy spending (not helped by his fitful employment after departing the Marines), his infidelity, and his violent attacks beginning in the first month of their marriage. At one point, Lorena became pregnant, but she reports that John pressured her into having an abortion. Over the ensuing years, police, neighbors, and friends would be asked to intervene in the couple's violent arguments.

On the early morning of June 23, 1993, Lorena reported that a drunken John woke her out of a sound sleep and raped her. According to her own account, she went to the kitchen in a daze, got a knife, returned to the bedroom, and cut off a sizable chunk of her husband's penis. She subsequently threw the "body part" out of a car window while fleeing the scene. She wound up at the home of her best friend, where the police were notified. The police retrieved the organ and took it to a local hospital where John Wayne Bobbitt was waiting. He underwent 9.5 hours of surgery to have it reattached.

Lorena Bobbitt was charged with malicious wounding, with conviction creating the potential of a 20-year prison sentence. John Wayne was also charged with committing marital sexual assault, which carried the same penalty. Interestingly, the prosecutor tried both cases with jury trials.

John Wayne's trial, which ended occurred first, ended in an acquittal. Lorena's trial, which was videotaped, occurred later, in January 1994. Her defense attorney argued that she was rendered temporarily insane as a result of the rape, combined with years of marital abuse, and thus was unable to restrain the "irresistible impulse" (Margolick, 1994, para 18) to injure her husband. The term "irresistible impulse" refers to a crucial element in Virginia's insanity defense. The prosecution introduced into evidence statements Lorena made to police at the time of the event, when she said, "He always have orgasm and he doesn't wait for me to have orgasm. He's selfish, I don't think it's fair, so I pulled back the sheets and I did it" (Margolick, 1994, para 22). Also brought up were information on her past thefts from an employer and a department store. The defense countered with experts on battered woman's syndrome, as well as evidence of John's past physical abuse of Lorena. This last point was conceded by the prosecutors who argued that it did not justify her attack.

On January 21, after brief deliberations, the jury acquitted Lorena Bobbitt of all charges, finding her temporarily insane in the attack on her husband. She was ordered to submit to court-imposed psychiatric evaluation and was placed in a mental facility for a few weeks, after which she was released.

There was tremendous societal response to Lorena's act and to her trial. Everything about the case was analyzed from various angles, in both public and private settings. Overall, the incident was viewed as a dramatic expression of the so-called battle between the sexes. Accordingly, media accounts tended to contrast sympathetic female responses with horrified male ones.

Battered women's advocates regarded both Bobbitt trials as indicators of American attitudes towards violence against wives (marital rape in particular), as well as on the acceptability of female revenge. In other quarters, questions were raised about the use of the battered women's syndrome to explain Lorena's actions. Allen Dershowitz (1994) viewed her defense as exemplifying the so-called abuse excuse, decrying it as an unacceptable method of avoiding criminal responsibility.

Lorena Bobbit's trial also reinforced a shift toward more prodigious media coverage of certain types of court cases, in particular on television. Another effect was the mainstreaming of explicit discussions of the male anatomy, previously a forbidden topic in mass media.

A key component of reaction to the case involved humor. From famous comedians to people on the street, jokes, limericks, one-liners, and so forth about the Bobbitt incident were traded with abandon. Linda Pershing describes how these jokes reflected complex societal responses, along dimensions of gender, class, and ethnicity, to the event and its participants.

Feminist reaction to the incident was conflicted. Some thought Lorena Bobbitt should not be lionized for committing violence. Others were unhappy about the use of insanity defense, as it made her appear weak and lacking agency, thus reinforcing traditional female stereotypes. Still others deemed her a "symbol of innovative resistance against gender oppression," as quoted in one *New York Times* letter to the editor (Morris, 1994, para 3). Many feminists viewed the negative responses to Lorena Bobbitt as reflecting class and ethnic bias.

The years subsequent to the incident were a mixed bag for both John Wayne and Lorena. He parlayed his misfortune into a minor degree of fame, appearing on the

Howard Stern show and later becoming a porn actor. In 2003, he was convicted of domestic assault on Joanna Farrell, his third wife.

Lorena Bobbitt maintained a lower profile. Thrust into sudden celebrity, she was named one of *People Magazine*'s most intriguing people of 1993. A candidate for the presidency of Ecuador (the land of her birth) famously took her to lunch. After the couple's divorce in 1995, she reclaimed her maiden name. However, in 1997, she was arrested for hitting her mother but was acquitted of the charge shortly afterwards. Since then, she has stayed out of the public eye. Nevertheless, Lorena Bobbitt's particular response to marital abuse ensures she will not soon be forgotten.

Resources

Court TV. 1997. *Trial of Lorena Bobbitt.* Winstar. Videocassette.

Dershowitz, Alan. M. 1994. *The Abuse Excuse And Other Cop-Outs, Sob Stories, and Evasions of Responsibility.* Boston: Little, Brown, and Company.

Filetti, Jean S. 2001. From Lizzie Borden to Lorena Bobbitt: Violent women and gendered justice. *Journal of American Studies* 35: 471–484.

Margolick, David. (1994, January 22). Lorena Bobbitt acquitted in mutilation of husband. *New York Times*, 1, 7.

Masters, Kim. 1993. Sex, lies, and an 8-inch carving knife. *Vanity Fair* 56: 168–172.

Morris, Stephanie. (1994, January 19). Mrs. Bobbitt is a symbol of feminist resistance [Letter to the Editor]. *New York Times.* A20.

Pershing, Linda. 1996. His wife seized his prize and cut it to size: Folk and popular commentary on Lorena Bobbitt. *NWSA Journal* 8: 1–35.

Angela Taylor

Cecile Bombeek (1933–)

Cecile Bombeek was an atypical serial murderer who targeted elderly people in a geriatric wing of CPAS Wetteren Hospital in Belgium. Bombeek, who sought out victims who were in her care, is an angel of death type of serial murder. This serial killing form is a play on words taken from the phrase "angels of mercy," a euphemism for nurses, who often provide comfort while someone is suffering. Although Bombeek appeared to be nursing her targets back to health, she was actually killing them. Eventually, it was revealed that she was a morphine addict who stole from her clients and who admitted to killing three elderly patients in her care with insulin overdoses, but she is suspected of several more.

Cecile Bombeek, also known as Sister Godfrida of the Apostolic Congregation of St. Joseph, had a marked behavior change after surgery to remove a brain tumor in 1975. After the surgery Bombeek developed consistent and severe headaches for which she was given pain medication and to which she became addicted. In 1977, while Bombeek was employed at the hospital, the 38-bed ward experienced higher than normal death rates. The nurses on the ward decided to keep a diary and, through their entries, realized that all the deceased had died while under Sister Godfrida's care. They also documented that Bombeek would administer "tortures" like roughly ripping out patients' catheter tubes.

The hospital suspected the nun of misdeeds and attributed them to her drug addiction, which was a criminal offense in 1977 in Belgium. By August 1977, they had sent Sister Godfrida for drug rehabilitation, for a third time, which proved unsuccessful. After being released from rehabilitation, she expressed interest in coming back to the hospital and to her nursing career. Fearing more deaths, the hospital confronted her with the crimes to which she partially confessed. Sister Godfrida had been charged with theft initially, stealing almost $30,000 from her elderly clients to support her addiction to morphine. Community members also noted that she shared a rather lavish lifestyle with her roommate, a nun who taught school in the same town. Townspeople suspected that Cecile Bombeek had affairs, including one with her roommate and another with a retired priest. She later confessed to killing three of her clients because they were "too difficult at night" (A Nun's Story, 1978). A judge ordered the three bodies exhumed, along with two others. Governing board member Dr. Jean-Paul De Corte commented, "It could just as well be 30 people as three" (A Nun's Story, 1978). In the year she worked at the facility, 21 of 38 elderly people died while she was on shift. In March 1978, Cecile Bombeek was sent for psychiatric evaluation. She was found not fit to stand trial and, subsequently, interred in a psychiatric facility.

This case is interesting as the hospital tried to deal with this threat internally by sending Bombeek to addiction counseling. Had this worked, the case probably would never have become public. It was Bombeek's lack of rehabilitation that forced the hospital to seek charges against her, thus bringing negative attention to the hospital. Although a somewhat marginalized case of serial murder committed by a female, it is one of the few recorded cases in Belgium.

Resources

Dodende susters bij ons [Killer nurses among us] (2010, Mar. 28). *Nieuwsblad.be*. Retrieved June 24, 2010, from http://www.nieuwsblad.be/article/detail.aspx?articleid=O32O54H8.

The Nun's Story (1978, March 13). *TIME Magazine* [Electronic version]. Retrieved July 15, 2011, from http://www.time.com/time/magazine/article/0,9171,919411,00.html.

Yorker, B.C., Kizer, K.W. Lampe, P., Forrest, A.R.W., Lannon, J.M., and Russlee, D.A. (2006). Serial murder by healthcare professionals. *Journal of Forensic Science* 51(6): 1362–1371.

Hannah Scott

Anne Bonny (ca. 1697–1720?)

Anne Bonny was thought to be a headstrong, independent woman who was ahead of her time. Her actions, breaking conventional wisdom of what a woman could do during the 1800s, are evidence of this. Women of this time were expected to behave in a sedate, subservient manner, but Anne Bonny rebelled against society and its male-dominated world. She became a pirate, a plunderer, and a sailor.

The exact details of Anne Bonny's birth is unknown, but she is believed to have been born around 1697 to 1700 in Country Cork, Ireland. She was the daughter of a prominent lawyer, William Cormac, and his wife's maid, Mary Brennen. When the scandal of William Cormac having an affair with his wife's maid became public, all three of them left Ireland for America. In the New World, they established themselves as successful plantation owners in South Carolina.

When Anne was 16 years old, she married a man named James Bonny, who was an opportunist and small-time pirate. He thought by marrying Anne that he would eventually own the family plantation. Anne's father disowned her before James Bonny could get to fulfill his plans for the family plantation. James and Anne left for New Providence, known as "a den of iniquity" and "a pirate's paradise" (*Anne Bonny*, 2011).

Marriage for Anne was not a pleasant life experience. At first, she was a dutiful wife waiting for her husband to return from sea. Even after he gave up pirating and became an informer for Governor Woodes Rogers, Anne was discontented. Most of Anne's friends on the islands were pirates and earned their livelihoods from piracy. When Anne Bonny saw that her friends were being arrested for the rewards offered to informers, she was even further disenchanted with the new life chosen by her husband.

Anne Bonny and Mary Read were convicted on the island of Jamaica in 1720 for acts of piracy. Both were found to be pregnant while awaiting execution and were spared hanging, though Read died in prison. (Library of Congress)

Captain Jack Rackham (known as Calico Jack) offered Anne Bonny a chance to get away from her husband. She escaped her marriage with him and disguised herself as a man on Calico's ship. During the journey, Anne stayed in disguise for a long time, mainly because sailors of the time thought that a woman on a ship was bad luck. It is said that she was so vicious and fought so well with both pistol and cutlass that no one questioned her. The one fellow pirate who did challenge her lost his life with the tip of her cutlass. However, when she became pregnant, her gender was revealed. Jack and Anne agreed that the pirate's life and a ship was no place to give birth to a baby. They sailed to Cuba, where Anne stayed with friends until she had the child.

Unfortunately, the baby was born two months premature and died one hour after birth. This loss crushed Anne. Her former husband, who still lived on the island, discovered that Anne and her new pirate husband Calico Jack were in the vicinity in the town of New Providence. He sent troops to arrest them both for piracy. They were dragged before the governor in the middle of the night. He was angry and refused to be merciful or allow others to show mercy to the couple. He wanted the two pirates to be hanged.

Governor Woodes Rogers commanded that Anne be whipped and returned to her rightful husband. He also allowed Calico Jack to be set free. The next evening Anne and Jack escaped and returned to piracy. This time Anne Bonny was not the only woman on board Jack's ship as Mary Read joined the crew.

In October 1720 Anne Bonny's life of piracy came to an end. Governor Lawes of Jamaica heard of their presence in his jurisdiction and sent troops to commandeer their ship and bring them to trial. The crew was unprepared for the assault. Lawes's troops did not strike until the day after Jack had captured a commercial vessel, and he and all the men aboard ship were in a postcelebration drunken state. Their incapacitation left only Anne and Mary to fend off the troops. The two women became so disgusted with the men for not fighting back that they periodically turned their guns on their own crew before they were all captured. The whole crew was condemned to hang, but Anne and Mary received a stay of execution because they were both pregnant. Mary died in prison along with her unborn child.

Anne, however, survived, and when Jack received permission to speak to her before his hanging, she said to him "I'm sorry, Jack, but if you had fought like a man you would not now be about to die like a dog. Do straighten yourself up" (Carlova 1964, 194). Anne Bonny never was executed, but there is some disagreement about what happened to her. The most common story is that her father intervened through his powerful connections. Yet another version was that she escaped with an unknown lover. What actually happened to Anne Bonny will probably never be known, but given her life and actions, she was a woman who embraced an alternative life, one of adventure and piracy, both unusual qualities for a woman of that day and time.

Resources

Anne Bonny: Fearless Female Pirate. http://www.essortment.com/anne-bonny-fearless-female-pirate-21541.html.

Carlova, John. (1964). *Mistress of the Seas.* New York: Citadel Press.

Defiant Women: Pirates. *Anne Bonny.* members.tripod.com/cathreese/DefiantWomen/ pirates/abonny_mread.html.

Gooch, Steve. (1978). *The Women Pirates, Ann Bonny and Mary Read.* London: Pluto Press.

Jones, Deanna J. *Ahoy, Matey! That Pirate Has Breasts! Pirates, Fact and Legend.* www.piratesinfo.com/biography/biography.php?article_id=26.

James David Ballard and Nune Sogomonyan

Lizzie Borden (1860–1927)

Lizzie Borden took an axe
And gave her mother forty whacks.
And when she saw what she had done,
She gave her father forty-one.

—Victorian playground verse

Lizzie Borden was tried for and acquitted of the brutal murders of her father and stepmother in 1892. The case signified the power of wealth in the court of law as well as the court of public opinion, and it was the first to gain national media coverage in the United States. Also significant to the Borden murders was the fact that the accused was a well-respected woman during an era when women of Lizzie's background were viewed as morally superior.

Lizzie Borden, defendant accused (and acquitted) of murdering her parents. (Chaiba Media)

Lizbeth Andrew Borden, also known as Lizzie Borden, was born in Fall River, Massachusetts, on July 19, 1860. Sarah Borden, wife of Andrew Borden, gave birth to two girls, Lizzie and Emma, but died of complications from uterine congestion in 1863. Soon after, Andrew married his second wife, Abby Durfee Gray, to whom he was devoted. While Lizzie and Emma lived most of their lives with their stepmother, Lizzie was not particularly fond of her stepmother and was known to call her "Mrs. Borden."

The Borden family was one of the wealthiest in Fall River. Andrew Borden was an undertaker whose successful investments made him a rich man. Nevertheless, the family of four lived in a small four-bedroom house in a run-down neighborhood. The household consisted of Andrew, Abby, Lizzie, Emma, and the maid Bridget. The day before the murders, Abby's brother, John V. Morse, came for a brief visit.

While Abby and Emma Borden were reported to be shy women, Lizzie was very active in the community. She taught Sunday school, was Secretary to the Fruit and Flower Mission, and worked with the Women's Christian Temperance Union. Lizzie had also toured Europe in 1890, as was the fashion of young American women at the time. Historians claim that Lizzie had disputes with her father for want of a more lavish house and life. Additionally, it is reported that Lizzie and Emma resented their stepmother for standing in the way of getting their rightful inheritance. Emma was not as outgoing as Lizzie in her activities and was reported to be a quieter person. However, it was this reported conflict between Lizzie and her parents that was used as the motive for the charges of murder. There was also contradictory testimony from John V. Morse that Andrew Borden was going to write a new will leaving his half-million dollar estate to his wife but only $25,000 each to Lizzie and Emma. Upon later testimony, Morse stated that Andrew Borden did not tell him of the will.

Just after 11:00 AM on August 4, 1892, the bodies of Andrew Jackson Borden and Abby Durfee Gray Borden were found hacked to death with an axe in their own home at 92 Second Street, Fall River, Massachusetts. Andrew Borden was found lying neatly on a couch with his head crushed from 18 blows, 13 of which crushed his skull. Abby Borden was later found lying on the floor of an upstairs bedroom. She sustained 13 blows, 11 to the head and 4 of them crushing her skull. Reportedly, one blow to the neck nearly severed her head. It was Lizzie Borden who found her father's body and summoned for the maid, Bridget Sullivan, to fetch Dr. Bowen. Lizzie Borden was charged and tried for the murders of her father and stepmother.

The case against Lizzie Borden, from the onset, was riddled with problems and eventually resulted in her acquittal. While justice officials were convinced of Lizzie's guilt, premised on the belief that she killed her father and stepmother for the inheritance, they could not link any evidence to Lizzie. Even the closest person to a witness, Bridget Sullivan, did not provide testimony that could incriminate or exonerate Lizzie. However, during the investigation of the case, there were four events reported to have occurred on August 3, 1892, that would point to the guilt of Lizzie. First, at 7:00 AM that morning, Abby Borden visited Dr. Bowen to report that she and Andrew were violently sick complaining of stomach pains and vomiting. She claimed that they were being poisoned, but the doctor sent her home informing her that she had mild food poisoning. Lizzie and Bridget reported also being sick; however, the fact that Lizzie went out that day did not convince authorities of her condition.

Second, Eli Bence, the chemist of Smith's Drug Store, claimed that Lizzie tried to buy Prussic acid. Bence reported that Lizzie told him that she needed it to clean her sealskin cape. Bence refused to sell her the Prussic acid without a prescription because it was too strong. Two of Bence's assistants testified that Lizzie was in the store, but she denied she was near the store. During the trial, however, the three justices (as was the law at the time) ruled that because the autopsies failed to reveal evidence of poison, Bence's testimony was irrelevant and inadmissible. Third, Lizzie's step-uncle, John V. Morse, had visited on August 3, 1892, but he and Lizzie did not see each other until after the murders. Fourth, Lizzie visited her friend Alice Russell and, in an agitated state, claimed that someone was trying to kill her family. These last two events were used to show that Lizzie had premeditated the acts and could not account for her whereabouts.

After the murders, Alice Russell testified during the inquest that she saw Lizzie burning a dress. (For a review of the inquest transcripts and photographs see http://www.frpd.org/lizzie/index.htm.) Lizzie told her friend that the dress had been stained with paint. It was this testimony that lead to Lizzie being charged for murder. However, just as Bence's testimony was ruled inadmissible, so was the inquest transcript. The judges ruled that Lizzie's testimony was made by a person not formally charged and could not be used.

The trial against Lizzie Borden lasted 14 days (June 5, 1983–June 20, 1893). Lizzie was charged with three murders: one charge for the murder of Andrew Borden, one for Abby Borden, and one for both. The defense presented witnesses that would argue that there was a mysterious man near the home and that Lizzie did not have motive. But in the end, many claimed that Lizzie bought her freedom by employing highly influential lawyers and paying more than any lawyer would make in a year. Justice Dewey gave the jury its charge. It has been claimed that his charge was a second summation of the defense's case. It should also be pointed out that Justice Dewey was appointed to his position by one of Lizzie's attorneys, Robinson, when he was governor. After slightly over one hour of deliberation, Lizzie was found not guilty of all three murders.

There are many theories that propose how Lizzie Borden killed her father and stepmother and more that claim that she did not do the crime. There were many factors that made it popular to accuse Lizzie. Two popular arguments used to publicly convict Lizzie were that she was a greedy rich woman who could not live the lavish life she wanted to live and that she was a spinster who did not have a future. However, it seemed that other more powerful factors exonerated her of the crimes. Lizzie was wealthy, came from a prominent family, an ardent church-goer, active in the community, and a woman. During this era, it was not acceptable to think of a woman of such stature as a murderer.

The killing of Andrew and Abby Borden was the first murder case to gain national media coverage in the United States. The town of Fall River maintained support for this church-going woman from a respected family. In the lead to support Lizzie were the suffragettes and the Women's Christian Temperance Union. The media, however, focused on the dress-burning testimony of Alice Russell and tried to speculate as to whether Lizzie was the murderer.

Five weeks after the trial, Lizzie and Emma bought a lavish 13-room Victorian mansion in a prominent section of Fall River. They named the estate Maplecroft. Lizzie, who changed her name to Lizabeth A. Borden, continued her lavish lifestyle of travel and theater going. In 1897, Lizzie was arrested and charged with stealing two inexpensive paintings from Tilden-Thurber Company, a store in Fall River. While the case was settled out of court, there was a brief revival of the 1891 theft of some of Andrew Borden's property, including some money and jewelry taken from their 92 Second Street home. Seven years later, Lizzie met and developed a strong relationship with an actress named Nance O'Neil. It was this two-year relationship and a very large party that Lizzie threw for the actress and her theater company that led to an estranged relationship between Lizzie and Emma. Emma moved out and the sisters remained estranged for the last 20 years of their lives. Lizabeth A. Borden died on June 1, 1927, from complications of a gall bladder operation. Though she was acquitted of the charges, she continues to be viewed as the woman who gave her mother 40 whacks with an axe.

Resources

Engstrom, Elizabeth. 1997. *Lizzie Borden*. New York: Forge.

Fall River Police Department. 1893. *Inquest Testimony of Lizzie Borden*. http://www.law. umkc.edu/faculty/projects/ftrials/LizzieBorden/bordeninquest.html

Filetti, Jean S. 2001. From Lizzie Borden to Lorena Bobbitt: Violent women and gendered justice. *Journal of American Studies* 35: 471–484.

Kent, David. 1992. *Forty Whacks: New Evidence in the Life and Legend of Lizzie Borden*. Emmaus, PA: Yankee Books.

Klein, Shelley. 2003. *The Most Evil Women in History*. New York: Barnes & Nobles Books.

Pearson, Edmund. 1937. *Trial of Lizzie Borden*. New York: Doubleday, Doran & Company.

Porter, Edwin H. 1893. *The Fall River Tragedy: A History of the Borden Murders*. Fall River, MA: Press of J.D. Munroe.

Venessa Garcia

Lucrezia Borgia (1480–1519)

Lucrezia Borgia was a powerful noblewoman of the Italian Renaissance who was accused of several misdeeds, including having attempted to murder her first husband (allegedly committed in complicity with her family) and following merciless political strategies and sexual depravity. The illegitimate daughter of Rodrigo Borgia, a dissolute and ambitious man, who later became Pope Alexander VI, and his

Portrait painted by Bartolomeo Veneto and generally believed to be Lucrezia Borgia. Borgia was a noblewoman and patron of the arts during the Italian Renaissance. (Veneto, Bartolomeo. *Portrait of a Woman* (n.d.), Städelsches Kunstinstitut, Frankfurt)

mistress Vannozza Cattanei, she was born in Subiaco on April 18, 1480. Among her three brothers, Cesare Borgia, in particular, was actively involved in the bloody plots and ruthless crimes that have historically sullied Lucrezia Borgia's reputation. Portrayed by the painter Bartolomeo Veneziano in his famous "Portrait of a Woman," she was blessed with fine beauty, an ivory complexion, and golden hair.

In 1493, when she was only 13 years old, her father agreed to give her in marriage to Giovanni Sforza, Lord of Pesaro, with an extravagant and opulent celebration, aimed at establishing a political alliance with his powerful family. Soon thereafter, however, the unscrupulous Pope Alexander VI was determined to acquire more advantageous political allies and eliminate his daughter's husband. To that extent, he and his son Cesare Borgia were believed to have plotted Giovanni Sforza's execution. It is unclear whether Lucrezia Borgia herself was involved in the criminal plan against her husband or if she became aware of it through her brother and, instead, helped Giovanni Sforza to flee safely to Rome.

In any event, after the failure of the original plan, Pope Alexander VI and Cesare Borgia attempted to persuade Giovanni Sforza to grant Lucrezia a divorce. He steadily refused and even accused his wife of paternal and fraternal incest. In response, Pope Alexander VI initiated a marriage annulment procedure on the grounds that the marriage had not been consummated because of Giovanni Sforza's impotence. Although he was offered all of Lucrezia's dowry by Pope Alexander VI in return for his agreement, Giovanni Sforza initially resisted to verify such an accusation, claiming that his previous wife, Maddalena Gonzaga, had actually died giving birth. He also refused to prove his virility before the papal legate. Lucrezia, on the other hand, was scrupulously examined and declared still a virgin. Therefore, the marriage was annulled by Pope Alexander VI, and Giovanni Sforza was resigned to signing a declaration of impotence due to the Borgias's threats.

Newly freed from marriage, in 1498, Lucrezia Borgia entered a second marital union with Alfonso d'Aragona, Duke of Bisceglie, with whom she was deeply in love and had her first child, Rodrigo d'Aragona. However, the newlyweds' happiness did not last and was soon sacrificed for the reasons of state. Cesare Borgia had recently entered a political alliance with Louis XII, King of France, who was claiming the territory of the Duchy of Naples, which belonged at that time to the Aragona's family. On July 15, 1500, Alfonso d'Aragona was attacked by unknown assailants in Rome but managed to survive thanks to the loving and faithful care of his wife. Cesare Borgia was suspected of having been the secret instigator of the attack, which was confirmed one month later by the fatal assault committed against Alfonso d'Aragona by his executioner. The murder of her beloved spouse commissioned by her own brother cast Lucrezia into a state of despair. She retired to the fortress of Nepi grieving for Alfonso, while her father was already contemplating a third illustrious marriage for her with Alfonso d'Este, a legitimate heir to the Duchy of Ferrara.

The infamy of the Borgias and, in particular, the many rumors regarding the direct involvement of Lucrezia Borgia in the intrigues and misdeeds committed by her family as well as her alleged incestuous relationships with her father and brother concerned the bridegroom. However, pressured by Pope Alexander VI and Cesare Borgia, and other realpolitik considerations, Alfonso d'Este agreed to marry Lucrezia in 1501. Soon thereafter, she moved permanently to the court of Ferrara where she became a generous patroness of the arts and distinguished herself for her moderate life, finally atoning for her questionable past. She died in Ferrara on June 24, 1519, after having given birth to her eighth child and was buried in the convent of Corpus Domini.

Several authors have been inspired by Lucrezia Borgia's virtues and offenses throughout the ages. In 1816, Lord Byron visited the Biblioteca Ambrosiana in Milan and remained so fascinated by what he called "the prettiest letters in the world" exchanged between the poet Pietro Bembo and Lucrezia Borgia that he stole a preserved lock of her golden hair. In 1833, Victor Hugo wrote the drama *Lucrèce Borgia* loosely based on her life that also inspired Gaetano Donizetti's opera *Lucrezia Borgia*, which was performed in 1833 at La Scala in Milan.

Resources

Bradford, Sarah. 2004. *Lucrezia Borgia: Life, Love and Death in Renaissance Italy*. London: Viking, Penguin Group.

Erlanger, Rachel. 1978. *Lucrezia Borgia: A Biography*. New York: Hawthorn Books.

Benedetta Faedi Duramy

Belle Boyd (1844–1900)

Belle Boyd was famous in the Southern state where she was born and infamous in the Northern states during the Civil War, first because of her loyalty and nursing support for the Confederate troops and later due to her spying against the Union

Maria Isabella "Belle" Boyd, a Confederate spy, provided critical information about Union troop movements during the Civil War, most notably during the Shenandoah Valley Campaign in 1862. (Library of Congress)

Army. She epitomizes the role of women in protecting their homes and families in time of war, especially in the South where resources were limited. Their men were gone from home, and women, by necessity, turned from their traditional roles to include aiding and supporting the Confederacy in time of peril.

Maria Isabelle Boyd was born in Bunker Hill, West Virginia, May 9, 1844, to parents from well-respected and prosperous backgrounds. When Boyd was 10, her family moved near the town of Martinsburg, West Virginia, where her father ran a store and worked at farming. Belle was the oldest of eight children and from the beginning showed a strong determination to go her own way and to challenge propriety. Her best known biographer, Louis Sigaud, reports that when she was 11 she rode her horse into the family dining area after being excluded from an adult dinner party, saying: "my horse is old enough, isn't he"? (1944, 1) When she was 12, her parents sent her to be educated in Baltimore, Maryland, at the Mount Washington Female College, where she was introduced to Washington, D.C., society. Her family hoped she would become a proper Southern woman, eventually marry well, and settle in Martinsburg, now a part of the state of Virginia. Boyd spent four years at the college studying music, classical literature, and French, all the while holding a secret desire to be an actress. Any attempts to try the stage were postponed, however, when upon graduation she returned to Martinsburg to be near her mother. Her father, at age 44, had enlisted to serve with General Stonewall Jackson's Confederate troops.

Boyd recounted how, shortly after she arrived home, Union soldiers from units occupying nearby Martinsburg broke into her family home and roughly insisted that a Union flag be flown from the roof. Her mother adamantly refused and one soldier became threatening whereupon Boyd drew a pistol that she carried for protection and shot him to death (Boyd, 1865, 14). Instead of enraging the Union's commanding officers, Boyd won sympathy and attention from them as well as adoration from her Southern neighbors. The commanding officer sent frequent patrols to check on the Boyd family's safety and well-being after the incident. It appeared that at 17, her comely looks and intelligence worked in her favor to gain sympathy, even when she killed a Union soldier.

Boyd began to observe Union troop movements and to gather information from them to forward to Confederate leaders, often using servants as couriers. She was an excellent horsewoman and frequently rode through the Shenandoah Valley herself to deliver messages and supplies. She was apprehended by Union forces several times but they did little more than warn her to stop her aid to their enemy while continuing to let her visit freely among them. As a result, she escalated her covert work and was rewarded when the Confederacy officially appointed her a courier for generals Stonewall Jackson and Pierre Beauregard. In addition, General Jackson made her a captain and honorary aide-de-camp on his staff.

In early 1862, Boyd was arrested by the Union and sent to Baltimore to be interrogated but was held scarcely a week and then sent home. Once more, she had charmed her way out of a situation that could have ruined the rest of her life. Some said she was let off easily because Union officers did not know what to do with her since they were reluctant to imprison an 18-year-old girl. Still others said it was because she was a brilliant talker and had the best legs in the South (Belle Boyd, 1).

By the spring of 1862, Boyd had moved to Front Royal, Virginia, to live with an aunt. She continued to support the Confederacy from this location by delivering important information to the Confederate army about how Union forces planned to destroy bridges as they moved across the countryside. She often wore disguises and, at one point, went on foot between the two armies risking Union gunfire to deliver a message when no courier would volunteer. For this effort, she received a letter of appreciation from General Jackson but also brought unwanted attention to herself from Union officers who put her under close surveillance. The next time she ventured out, she was captured and taken to Washington to the Old Capitol Prison, which was reportedly not a pleasant experience. After a month, she was once again freed to return to Virginia with a warning not to resume her role as a spy and courier.

Boyd's freedom was short-lived this time, however, since the federal government arrested her again in a few months even though she only had been visiting relatives and friends, basking in her reputation as a heroine. The federal government had grown increasingly uneasy about her potential danger to the Union. Taking no chances that she might revert to her old ways, they once again sentenced her to the Old Capitol facility for several months, where she suffered a severe case of typhoid fever. Upon being released, she went back home to regain her strength.

Shortly after her return and just before her 20th birthday, the Confederacy called upon her again. This time Boyd was asked to sail to England with messages pleading for help from the British. Her ship barely cleared the harbor when it was captured by a Union vessel being used to blockade ports. Before she was forcibly removed, she and her maid managed to destroy the secret documents. This time Belle was sent to prison in Boston for a short time before being released on the condition that she go to Canada, never to return. However, fate intervened again.

The Union naval officer, Samuel Wylde Hardinge, Jr., commander of the vessel that captured Boyd, fell in love with her and because his attention was diverted to her, the captain of the blockaded vessel escaped. As a result of his actions, Hardinge was removed from the Navy. He followed Boyd to Canada and, from there, arranged passage to England for both of them from Quebec. On August 25, 1864, they were married in London. He tried to return to the United States but was captured and imprisoned for nearly a year. He and Belle had a daughter in 1865, while he was in prison, and the health problems he developed while prison left him in such poor physical condition that he died just a year later, leaving Belle with a baby and no money. In 1865, Belle Boyd Hardinge wrote a book, *Belle Boyd in Camp and Prison*, in 1865 hoping to realize enough profit to support herself. Initially, it was not initially well received, and because the proceeds were insufficient, at the age of 22, she took up a long-desired acting career on the stages of Great Britain. She had modest success, and after the war, she returned to the United States to try her acting skills both in New York and with stock companies on tour. She passed the next four years on tour until one of her admirers persuaded her to marry him and retire from the stage. Her new husband, John Swainston Hammond, was a well-to-do business man and former Union Army officer. They were married for 14 years, had four children, but were divorced in 1884.

Within a few weeks after her divorce at age 40, Belle married a debonair actor, 16 years younger than she. Because her new husband, Nathaniel Rue High, Jr., could not support her and her children, she returned to the stage as a lecturer to entertain audiences with stories of her war adventures. Her act was so successful that she was in demand for the next 15 years until her death from a heart attack at the age of 56, in June, 1900. At her funeral, her pallbearers were four Union veterans of the Civil War, and she had had three husbands who were Northerners. She was forced by circumstances to use her ingenuity and to combine the best of her Southern charm with her will to survive.

Resources

"Belle Boyd." *Civil War Home*. http://www.civilwarhome.com/belleboyd.htm.

Boyd, B. 1865. *Belle Boyd in Camp and Prison*. New York: Blelock & Co.

Faust, Drew G., and Kennedy-Nolle, Sharon. 1998. *Belle Boyd In Camp and Prison*, Louisiana State University Press.

Sigaud, Louis. 1945. *Belle Boyd: Confederate Spy*. Richmond, VA: Dietz Press.

Marcia Lasswell

Brinvilliers, Marquise de (1630–1676)

Marie Madeleine Marguerite d'Aubray (Marquise de Brinvilliers) was a French famous serial poisoner, whose trial rocked the royal court of Louis XIV and engaged the public imagination. The highly born Marie Madeleine Marguerite d'Aubray was the eldest of five children of Antoine Dreux d'Aubray, a civil lieutenant of the city of Paris. In 1651, Marie Madeleine Marguerite d'Aubray married Antoine Gobelin, Marquis de Brinvilliers and Baron de Nourar, thus entering, at the age of only 17, the dissolute French aristocratic society. Within only a few years of her marriage, she became accustomed to libertine practices as well, especially since her husband was not much concerned about her but rather indulged in his own debauchery.

In fact, she became the mistress of Gaudin de Sainte-Croix, an attractive young army officer of ill repute that Brinvilliers had met in 1659 when they were serving in the same regiment and with whom he had become a bosom friend. The affair between the two was initially tolerated by her husband until it collided with his financial interests. In fact, when, following Gaudin de Sainte-Croix's advice, Brinvilliers began to consider initiating legal action to separate her fortune from that of her husband who was lavishly dissipating their joint patrimony, a public scandal unfolded. Concerned about the negative consequences for the entire d'Aubray family, Antoine Dreux d'Aubray and two of his sons urged Marie to break off her relationship with Gaudin de Sainte-Croix. Her resistance led her father to extreme action in requesting the king to issue an order of arrest, or *lettre de cachet,* against Gaudin de Sainte-Croix.

In 1663, the chevalier Gaudin de Sainte-Croix was publicly arrested in the name of the king and immediately transported to the fortress-prison of the Bastille in Paris. Such a public insult could not be forgiven by either the marquise or her paramour. During his three months of custody, Gaudin de Sainte-Croix made the acquaintance of the Italian poisoner Exili who had joined several royal households, been accused of many crimes, and, thus, was feared by every European court at that time. Initiated into the practice of poisoning by his comrade, Gaudin de Sainte-Croix made practical use of his skill upon his release from prison. Indeed, under his guidance, Brinvilliers began experimenting with lethal poisons, testing them on her own servants and hospital patients. Still enraged with her own family and aspiring to appropriate the entire fortune, she finally poisoned her father in 1666 and her two brothers in 1670. The crimes were not detected; the autopsies stated that Antoine Dreux d'Aubray had died of natural causes, and both his sons of "malignant humour."

However, in 1672, upon the mysterious death of Gaudin de Sainte-Croix, which probably occurred during one if his lethal experiments, a casket containing incriminating letters and conclusive evidence against Brinvilliers was discovered by the police. She promptly fled to London and later to Holland. Finally, in 1675, she was arrested in a convent at Liége and transported back to France. During the trial, Brinvilliers was denied the aid of a legal counsel and, hence, stood alone in her own defense. The marquise stubbornly refused to admit that she had poisoned her father and her two brothers, even when the court beseeched her: "You are now perhaps at the end of your life. I beg of you to reflect seriously over your wicked conduct, which has brought upon you not only the reproaches of your family, but even of those who participated in your evil life" (Stokes 1912, 226). In her defense speech, she proclaimed her innocence and accused her former lover Gaudin de Sainte-Croix of having deceived her "because, under a wise and good outward appearance, there was hidden one of the blackest and most detestable souls in the whole world" (229). Her defiant attitude upset the judges who eventually found her guilty. When she was subjected to painful torture, she finally confessed to having poisoned her father and her two brothers as well as having attempted to poison her sister-in-law and her husband several times.

Brinvilliers was beheaded publicly and burned on a pile of wood in 1676. Considered as a dissolute criminal until the day of her execution, she then became a martyr for the populace. Her murder case revealed that poisoning was the obscure cause of many mysterious deaths that had occurred in the elite French society. In fact, just before her execution, she exclaimed: "Out of so many guilty people must I be the only one to be put to death?. . . . [and yet,] half the people in town are involved in this sort of thing, and I could ruin them if I were to talk" (Somerset 2003, 40). In the end, Brinvilliers did not betray them. However, those to whom she alluded were later implicated in a larger scandal referred to as the Affair of the Poisons, which affected the royal court of Louis XIV and involved some of his closest courtiers.

See also La Voisin, Catherine; Montespan, Marquise de

Resources

Somerset, Anne. 2003. *The Affair of the Poisons: Murder, Infanticide and Satanism at the Court of Louis XIV.* London: Weidenfeld & Nicolson.

Stokes, Hugh. 1912. *Madame de Brinvilliers and Her Times 1630–1676.* London: Thomas Nelson and Sons.

Benedetta Faedi Duramy

Betty Broderick (1947–)

On November 5, 1989, Betty Broderick, a socialite and mother of four, killed her ex-husband, Dan and his new wife, Linda, while they were sleeping. All she ever wanted in life was to be a supermom, but a bitter divorce caused her to be consumed with hatred and thoughts of revenge which led to the killing. Betty Broderick is currently serving two consecutive 15-to-life sentences for the double murder. She was eligible for but ultimately denied parole in January 2010. She may apply for another parole hearing in 2013.

Betty Broderick was born Elisabeth Anne Bisceglia in 1947 and grew up as one of six children in Eastchester, New York. Growing up in a large, Catholic, working-class family and attending Catholic girls' schools, Betty was trained to be a loving wife of one man and the mother of his children.

When she was 17, Betty's parents allowed her to travel to Notre Dame with friends. At a football game there, she met Dan Broderick, a handsome pre-med student. It was love at first sight for Betty. They dated during the next three years and were married in a glamorous wedding on April 12, 1969.

Weeks into the marriage, both Betty and Dan felt as if they had made a mistake, but they had big dreams for the future and worked hard to build a good life. Dan continued his medical studies while Betty worked multiple jobs and raised the children they soon had. The Brodericks were living the American dream. Betty was a model mother and wife, which was an asset to Dan's developing career. She worked diligently to create and maintain the perfect family life for her husband and children.

Betty helped to support the family while Dan attended Cornell Medical School and later, Harvard Law School. After law school, Dan led the stereotypical life of a young male lawyer climbing the social and financial ladder as his wife took care of their four children and the home. Betty was leading the life of a socialite. As Dan began to make millions of dollars annually, their marriage began to crumble. Dan was not attentive to Betty, and they had arguments about how to spend their money. Success drove them further apart, even as they were active in San Diego's social scene.

By 1983, Dan was having an affair with 21-year-old Linda Kolkena, whom he had met at a party. Betty continuously confronted Dan who denied any romantic involvement. The repeated denials fueled Betty's anger and desperation as more evidence mounted against Dan. According to Betty, Dan told her she was crazy and imagining things as well as being fat, old, boring, ugly, and stupid.

As Dan publicly flaunted his relationship with Linda, Betty felt deserted, humiliated, and angry. She spun out of control. When Dan filed for divorce two years later, Betty desperately clung to her imagined fairy tale life. Instead of accepting the end of the marriage, she started on a path of revenge that lasted for years. Betty became obsessed with retaliating against Dan and, ultimately, against Linda.

During the Christmas holidays in 1985, Dan and Linda took the children on vacation. Betty felt unloved, useless, lonely, and discarded. She broke into Dan's home and vandalized it. She was obsessed with a man who no longer wanted her.

The next several years were riddled with complex legal maneuverings by Dan and his professional colleagues. The San Diego legal community cooperated with Dan in his campaign to deprive Betty of the couple's shared assets even though Betty had supported Dan while he built his career. In addition, Dan obtained temporary custody of their children, and Betty was denied visitation until she received psychological counseling. Dan knew the legal ropes and used them to manipulate his legal team until he successfully beat down Betty. Frustrated by the legal manipulations, Betty lashed out. Dan ensured that she was punished legally, including having her jailed for contempt of court.

The couple's divorce was finalized in January 1989. Betty received a $28,000 lump sum and a sizeable alimony award despite her role in amassing the couple's multimillion dollar wealth. Betty was livid. On November 4, 1989, Betty received a letter from Dan threatening to take her to court, throw her in jail, and keep her from ever speaking with her sons, who were in his full custody. The next day, Betty went to Dan's home and shot and killed Dan and Linda while they were sleeping.

Betty's first trial ended with a hung jury, but she was later convicted of two counts of second-degree murder on December 11, 1991. Betty has never shown remorse or regret. She continues to claim she acted in self-defense on the basis that the emotional and psychological abuse by Dan caused her to kill him and Linda. Betty Broderick resides at the Central California Women's Facility at Chowchilla.

Resources

Stumbo, B. (1994). *Until the Twelfth of Never.* New York: Pocket Books/Simon & Schuster.

Taubman, B. (2004). *Hell Hath No Fury: A True Story of Wealth and Passion, Love and Envy, and a Woman Driven to the Ultimate Revenge.* New York: St. Martin's True Crime Books.

A Woman Scorned: The Betty Broderick Story. (1992). Made-for-television movie. Patchett Kaufman Entertainment.

Jo-Ann Della Giustina

Debra Brown (1962–)

Debra Denise Brown is one of relatively few women sentenced to death in the United States. However, like many women involved in crime, Brown may never have committed any crimes had it not been for the influence of her male accomplice. Over the course of approximately one month in the summer of 1984, 21-year-old Debra Denise Brown took part in a five-state crime spree with her 28-year-old boyfriend Alton Coleman. By the end of the spree, the couple had committed at least 13 armed robberies, 2 kidnappings, 7 rapes, and 7 murders. Brown was convicted of murders in both Indiana and Ohio. She was sentenced to die in both states for her crimes, though her death sentence in Ohio was commuted to a life sentence in 1991.

Debra Denise Brown was born on November 11, 1962, in Waukegan, Illinois. Brown was 1 of 11 children in what by many accounts was a respected family. According to Brown's mother, however, the family may have had problems that were unknown to those outside the family. Lottie Mae Brown, Debra's mother, told the FBI that Brown's father had severe mental problems. She reported that he often

Alton Coleman and Debra Brown express little emotion as they are arraigned on a series of charges, including two counts of aggravated murder, as an unidentified sheriff's deputy stands guard, 1985. (Bettmann/Corbis)

drank to excess and physically abused his children and other family members. According to psychologists who testified at trial on Brown's behalf, she was often physically and sexually abused as a child, and she suffered from strong feelings of rejection and abandonment. Records indicated that she did poorly in school where she was often truant and tested low on standard IQ tests.

Brown had no criminal record at the age of 21 years when she met Alton Coleman. Coleman, however, had a criminal record for rape and assault when the couple met, and Brown's life changed dramatically after they met. Brown broke off an engagement with another man and moved in with Coleman soon after the two met. According to Brown's mother, Debra changed drastically after meeting Coleman. Like many abused women, Brown stopped talking to her family as the relationship developed. Mrs. Brown believed that Coleman completely controlled her daughter. She also believed that Coleman beat Debra and may have prostituted her.

There is little doubt that Debra Brown committed the crimes for which she was convicted and sentenced. Moreover, she likely committed several other crimes for which she was never charged. On June 18, 1984, Coleman and Brown abducted seven-year-old Tamika Turks and her nine-year old-aunt, Annie Turks, as they walked home. Coleman reportedly raped Tamika while Debra held her down. Then, the couple strangled and beat her to death. Coleman and Brown also attacked Annie. They forced her to perform oral sex on both of them before Coleman raped her and they both beat her. Amazingly, Annie Turks survived and later identified Brown and Coleman as the couple who had attacked her and killed her niece.

Before Annie Turk identified Coleman and Brown, however, the couple continued on a five-state crime spree. Twenty-five-year old Donna Williams was the next to fall prey to Coleman and Brown. Williams was reported missing in Michigan on June 19, and witnesses identified Brown and Coleman as the last to be seen with her. On July 11, Donna's body was discovered in Detroit. She had been raped and strangled to death. Very few details of how her life ended are known because prosecutors decided not to prosecute the case in Michigan since it is a non-death penalty state.

On June 24, Coleman and Brown abducted a woman in Michigan and demanded she drive them to Ohio. She purposely crashed her car and fled. Coleman and Brown were not deterred. On June 28, they invaded Palmer and Maggie Jones' home in Dearborn Heights, Michigan. They beat the couple with a club and then took $86 and the couple's car. Then, on July 2, Coleman and Brown beat a Detroit couple and stole their car. The Detroit couple's car was soon found in Toledo, Ohio, where Coleman and Brown had assaulted another couple and stolen their car.

On July 7, Coleman and Brown began killing again. After spending the night with Virginia Temple and her 10-year-old daughter Rachelle in Toledo, Ohio, Coleman and Brown are believed to have strangled both of them to death after Coleman raped Rachelle. The next to die was 15-year-old Tonnie Storey. Brown and Coleman abducted her as she walked to a computer class in Ohio. The couple raped and strangled Tonnie to death in Ohio.

Just days after Tonnie Storey's death, Marlene and Harry Walters invited Coleman and Brown into their house on the pretense of talking about a trailer the couple was selling. Coleman and Brown attacked the couple. Harry Walters survived, despite severe injuries. Marlene, however, was bludgeoned to death. Interestingly, Coleman and Brown have each claimed that Brown murdered Marlene while Coleman and Mr. Walters were in the basement. Nevertheless, both were found guilty for the murder, and Coleman received a death sentence for Mrs. Walters's murder.

Despite a massive hunt by the FBI, Alton Coleman and Debra Brown continued to evade police. On July 16, they abducted Oline Carmichal and drove him to Dayton, Ohio, where they left him locked in trunk of his car unhurt. Then on July 17, Coleman and Brown attacked an elderly minister and his wife before stealing their car. On July 18, Eugene Scott and his car were reported missing in Dayton. Mr. Scott was found hours later in a ditch. He had been stabbed repeatedly and shot four times in the head. Though they have not been charged with this crime either, this is believed to be Coleman and Brown's final crime before they were apprehended in Evanston, Illinois, on July 20, 1984. The couple went quietly when five officers surrounded them. Coleman is reported to have been armed with a knife while Brown had an unloaded .38 Special in her purse.

Prosecutors in the five states where Brown and Coleman committed their crimes met to decide how to proceed with the trials. The strongest cases in death penalty states were prosecuted first. Prosecutors had much evidence against both Brown and Coleman including fingerprints at the scenes, eyewitness testimony, and confessions. Brown's defense counsel did not claim Brown was innocent, but instead attempted to convince the jury that she should not be sentenced to death because their was mitigating evidence to suggest that Alton Coleman dominated and controlled her before and throughout the crime spree.

Psychologists who evaluated Debra Brown for trial reported that she tested as mildly retarded on the Wechsler IQ test. Two psychologists believed that Brown had a dependent personality disorder. They also agreed that she was dominated and controlled by Alton Coleman when she took part in the five-state criminal spree with him. Finally, Dr. Suran testified that, independent of her relationship with Alton Coleman, he did not believe that she would have committed any of the offenses for which she was charged. More than one jury, however, disagreed, finding Brown guilty of murder and sentencing her to death.

Despite the defense's arguments and the psychological testimony, in May 1985, Brown was found guilty of murder for the deaths of Tonnie Storey and Marlene Walters in Ohio. She was sentenced to death for Storey's murder and to life in prison for Walters's murder. On May 7, 1986, Brown was convicted again; this time for the murder of seven-year-old Tamika Turks in Gary, Indiana. Brown was again sentenced to death. However, she also received a 40-year sentence in Indiana for child molestation in an assault and attempted murder of nine-year-old Annie Turks. The four remaining murders of Eugene Scott, Virginia Temple, Rachelle Temple, and Donna Williams are not likely to be prosecuted. With more than one death sentence Brown, additional prosecutions are not likely to be seen as cost-effective.

At the time this entry was written, Debra Denise Brown was still under the sentence of death in Indiana. Yet she remains incarcerated in Ohio, where her Ohio death sentence was commuted to life imprisonment in January 1991 by Ohio governor Richard Celeste. Governor Celeste commuted the death sentences of all four women on Ohio's death row before he left office in 1991. Celeste is believed to have selected death row cases such as Brown's that suggested the offender was mentally impaired. Celeste, however, may have also considered the evidence suggesting that Brown had been in a battering relationship when she committed her crimes. In addition to commuting Brown's sentence, before he left office, Celeste granted clemency to 25 women convicted of killing or assaulting intimate partners who had physically abused them.

Alton Coleman was also prosecuted (separately from Brown) for the murders and rapes for which Brown was convicted. He was also found guilty for the murders of Tamika Turks, Tonnie Storey, and Maureen Walters as well as Verita Wheat, who he killed in Wisconsin before he and Brown began their spree. Coleman received the death penalty for each of the four murders. Coleman was executed on April 26, 2002, in Ohio for the murder of Maureen Walters.

Resources

Debra V. Brown v. State of Indiana. 1998, July 17. Supreme Court of Indiana, 697 N.E.2d 1132; 1998 Ind. LEXIS 2437.

Gribben, Mark. 2006. "Alton Coleman & Debra Brown: Odyssey of Mayhem Deadly Duo." *Court TV Crime Library.* www.crimelibrary.com

Jones, Meg. 2002. "18 Years Later, Circle of Death Will Close with Killer's Execution." *Milwaukee Journal Sentinel*, April 16, 2002.

Kim Davies

Joyce Ann Brown (1936?–)

After 9 years, 5 months, and 24 days in prison, Joyce Ann Brown was declared innocent. She had been wrongfully convicted for murder due to eyewitness error. On May 9, 1980, in Dallas, Texas, Brown's mother called to inform her that the local newspaper was reporting that the police were looking for Joyce for the murder and robbery of a local fur shop owner. On Tuesday, May 6, at about 1:00 PM, two black women had shot and killed the owner of Fine Furs By Rubin and had escaped with stolen furs in a 1980 brown Datsun rented by a Joyce Ann Brown.

Because Brown, 44 years old, had been at work on the day of the crimes, she decided to go to the police to correct the error. Upon entering the police station, she was promptly arrested.

Numerous inconsistencies immediately arose concerning Brown's case. The police quickly discovered that the Joyce Ann Brown, who had rented the brown Datsun, was not the same Joyce Ann Brown in custody. In fact, the authorities located the Joyce Ann Brown who had rented the car, discovering that she was from Denver, Colorado. The Colorado native also claimed to have been at work at the time of the murder and robbery and that she too had witnesses to confirm her story. She further stated that she had allowed a friend (Rene Taylor) to borrow the rental car.

Police briefly focused on Taylor (knowing she had a criminal record and specialized in fur store robberies). They even found Taylor's fingerprints in the getaway car. However, police never actually located Rene Taylor for questioning or to clear Brown's name. Therefore, they searched the home of the woman they had in custody: Joyce Ann Brown from Dallas, Texas. Although the search produced nothing linking her to the crime, police, nevertheless, began building a case against her.

For example, police uncovered previous arrest records against Brown for prostitution. Brown told authorities the charges had been brought during a time when she had to help support her family, but police viewed the past arrests as a sign of her criminality.

On Tuesday, September 20, 1980, the case of *The State of Texas vs. Joyce Ann Brown* was called in the Dallas County Court. During her trial, evidence repeatedly indicated that Joyce Ann Brown was not at the scene of the crime, and stress might have caused the witnesses to be mistaken in identifying her. Brown further testified that she did not have a car that day, making it impossible for her to drive to the store and commit the crimes. Additionally, several of her co-workers swore that she was at work on the day of the crimes. Though it seemed that the defense might, in fact, be able to prove Brown's innocence, the prosecution produced a surprise witness: Martha Jean Bruce.

Bruce, who had shared a jail cell with Brown while she was awaiting trial, testified that Brown bragged about committing the crime. However, the prosecution omitted the fact that Bruce had a prior conviction for lying to a police officer. In fact, it was the omission of this information that ultimately freed Joyce Ann Brown.

On October 23, 1980, the all-white jury in Brown's case found her guilty of aggravated robbery. One month later, she was sentenced to life in prison.

At one point during her imprisonment, there was a glimmer of hope. Rene Taylor, the woman actually implicated by evidence in the case, was apprehended in Michigan. Though she confessed to the robbery and murder of the man for whom Brown was imprisoned, Taylor refused to disclose the identity of her accomplice in the crime. Thus, Joyce Ann Brown remained in prison as the assumed accomplice.

After several years in prison, Brown again found hope when, at the end of 1983, the case of a man named Lenell Geter was revisited by the Texas court system. The court found that he was, in fact, innocent of crimes for which he had been convicted. By January 1984, Geter left prison a free man. Upon Geter's release, Joyce's attorney filed a writ in her behalf, and, on January 20, 1984, Joyce Ann Brown again appeared in court. The judge was charged with determining whether Joyce had received a fair trial. Upon arriving at court, however, Brown learned that her hearing had been postponed for six months.

When the hearing finally went forward, numerous witnesses testified on behalf of Brown, including Rene Taylor. Taylor not only testified that she did not know Brown before the crime but that she did not know Brown at the time of the crime, or even after the crime. Taylor also had taken a polygraph test, and the administrator of the test informed the court that Taylor's results paralleled her testimony. Though Brown was confident that Taylor's testimony would prove her innocence, the judge noted his intention to consider all evidence and announce a decision at a later time.

In September 1984, Joyce Brown learned that her case had been sent to the Texas Criminal Court of Appeals to be reviewed for a new trial. A few months later, Joyce received a letter from her attorney notifying her that the higher courts had ruled against her. There would be no new trial. Her attorney also informed her that he was filing a writ for a discretionary review. On February 22, 1985, Joyce Brown was notified that the Texas Criminal Court of Appeals had denied her request for a discretionary review.

Brown spent three years writing letters to ask different individuals and organizations for help. Finally, in 1988, Jim McCloskey, founder and director of Centurion Ministries, a group that fights for the freedom of innocent prisoners, became interested in Brown's case. It was recognized that McCloskey's group was extremely discriminating as to whom they chose to help. As a small group with minimal financial resources, Centurion Ministries only accepted compelling cases in which the group was confident that the accused "criminals" were actually innocent beyond doubt and by evidential fact. Therefore, when Joyce Ann Brown's case was accepted by the McCloskey's group, her potential to regain her freedom increased exponentially.

New evidence proved that Bruce (the prisoner who had testified in Joyce's original trial) had lied under oath when asked about her criminal background. Additionally, the media initiated new and increased coverage of Brown's case. Ultimately, on November 1, 1989, a Dallas court reversed her conviction on the grounds that the prosecution had failed to tell the jury about Martha Jean Bruce's prior conviction. After more than nine years in prison, on November 3, 1989, Joyce Ann Brown was free.

Joyce Ann Brown's story is significant in a number of ways. First, Brown authored a book, *Justice Denied*, in which she discussed her beliefs regarding the effect on her case of having an all-white jury. She felt the jury and authorities wanted to find her guilty, regardless of testimony or evidence. She believed that race relations in the United States at that time allowed for, and often led to, a peremptory assumption of guilt and imprisonment of black individuals. Brown's case also publicly demonstrated the profound impact a grassroots activist group of individuals is capable of exerting to catalyze change. Finally, following the example of Centurion Ministries, Joyce Ann Brown launched Mothers (Fathers) for the Advancement of Social Systems (MASS). Her initial goal was to support the wrongfully convicted; however, she soon expanded the organization's mission to include helping ex-offenders and their families to become self-sufficient, law-abiding citizens.

Resources

Brown, Joyce Ann. 1990. *Joyce Ann Brown: Justice Denied*. Chicago: The Noble Press.

MASS, Inc. *The Joyce Brown Story*. Retrieved August 10, 2007. http://www.massjab.org/content-brown.asp

Devon Thacker Thomas

Marilyn Buck (1947–2010)

Marilyn Buck described herself as an anti-imperialist and antiracist activist whose use of extreme measures to support her various causes was the source of her many run-ins with the United States government. Born in 1947 and raised in Jasper, Texas, Buck grew up in a family that strongly supported the Civil Rights Movement.

Throughout the 1960s, Buck participated heavily in protests against racism and against the Vietnam War. As a teenager, Buck became interested in the causes of Native American, Palestinian, Iranian, and Vietnamese sovereignty, and in 1967, she joined the iconic Students for a Democratic Society, an activist group of the radical New Left. As a student at the University of Texas, Buck was politically active and moved to California in 1968 to work with San Francisco Newsreel, a radical filmmaking collective. She later went on to become the only white member of the Black Liberation Army.

In 1963, Marilyn Buck was convicted of purchasing two boxes of handgun ammunition for the Black Liberation Army. Three years into her 10-year sentence for that crime, Buck was given a furlough from prison. Rather than return to prison, however, Buck escaped and went underground. She managed to stay

An FBI photo of Marilyn Buck in 1982. (AP/Wide World Photos)

underground until 1981, when she provided a safe house and weapons to the perpetrators of the 1981 Brinks robbery. The Brinks robbery was an armed robbery in which Kathy Boudin and other members of the Weather Underground and the Black Liberation Army stole over $1 million from a Brinks armored car at the Nanuet Mall in Nanuet, New York. Later that day, the robbers were stopped by police and were engaged in a shoot-out. Two police officers and a Brinks guard were killed in the ensuing gunfire. The license plates of the getaway vehicles were traced to a New Jersey apartment rented by Marilyn Buck. When they searched the apartment, police found bomb-making materials, weapons, and detailed blueprints of six Manhattan police precincts. Police also found papers linking Marilyn Buck to another apartment, located in Mt. Vernon, New York, which was only 20 minutes away from the site of the robbery. Inside this second apartment, police found clothing belonging to Marilyn Buck, who had accidentally shot herself in the leg when attempting to draw her weapon during the shoot-out. They also found ammunition, guns, and ski masks.

In 1983, Marilyn was recaptured and charged in the successful removal of Assata Shakur from a United States federal prison. In 1985, Buck and six others were convicted in the Resistance Conspiracy Case: the bombing of the United States Capitol building to protest United States policy toward Grenada and Latin America. This bombing occurred on November 7, 1983, and was directed toward the Senate. The bomb was planted in the capitol's north wing and was hidden under a bench. The explosion blew the door off Democratic leader Robert C. Byrd's office door and caused quite a bit of physical damage to the building. Immediately preceding the blast, a caller claiming to be a member of the Armed Resistance Unit warned the capitol switchboard that a bomb had been placed near the chamber to retaliate against United States activity in Lebanon and Grenada.

When Marilyn Buck was captured, she received four separate court trials. Buck was charged with conspiracy to support and free political prisoners and for support of the New African Independence struggle through robbery. In 1988, Marilyn was indicted for conspiracy to protest and alter government policies through use of violence against government and military buildings. For this, she received an additional 10 years because of her involvement in the conspiracy to bomb the capitol. Buck received a total sentence of 80 years, of which she served 33 years at the Federal Corrections Institute at Dublin in California. She was, then, transferred to the Federal Medical Center (FMC) Carswell in Fort Worth, Texas, because of terminal cancer. She was released on July 25, 2010, from the Carswell Center, but she died less than two weeks later in Brooklyn. Two of her co-conspirators in the bombing of the capitol have been released from prison, one was never captured, and two others remain in prison for their crimes.

Marilyn Buck remained an activist and prolific writer throughout her incarceration. She won the poetry prize from the PEN Prison Writing Program, contributed poetry and essays to a variety of collections and other publications, and authored a book of poetry titled *Rescue the Word* in 2001. Post-9/11, according to an article in the *Harvard BlackLetter Law Journal*, Buck and other political prisoners were isolated from other prisoners and denied access to their attorneys. Buck gave regular interviews on this subject and on other aspects of prison life throughout her years of incarceration. She also participated in other forms of artistic expression, namely sculpting. Marilyn continued to be outspoken in her continued support of her causes and attempted to bring awareness to the plight of women prisoners, political prisoners, and minority prisoners. Through her publications and her artwork, Marilyn Buck gained many supporters over the Internet, and although she was considered by the United States government to be a domestic terrorist, Marilyn Buck was an ideological martyr to others.

Resources

Buck, Marilyn. 2000. Prisons, Social Control, and Political Prisoners. *Social Justice* 27: 25.

Buck, Marilyn. 2001. *Rescue the Word*. Oakland, CA: Friends of Marilyn Buck—AK Press

Buck, Marilyn, David Gilbert, and Laura Whitehorn. 2001. *Enemies of the State*. Montreal: Abraham Guillen Press.

Day, Susie. 2001. Cruel But Not Unusual: The Punishment of Women in U.S. Prisons, an Interview with Marilyn Buck and Laura Whitehorn. *Monthly Review* 53: 3.

Elijah, J. Soffiyah. 2002. The Reality of Political Prisoners in the United States: What September 11 Taught Us About Defending Them. *Harvard BlackLetter Law Journal* 18: 129–137.

Fox, Margalit. 2010, August 5. Marilyn Buck, Imprisoned for Brinks' Holdup, Dies at 62. [Obituary] *New York Time*s.

Willmott, Donna. 2003. Introduction to Marilyn Buck's Incommunicado: Dispatches from a Political Prisoner. *Social Justice* 30: 102–103.

Ariel E. Allison

C

Cheng Chui Ping (1949–)

Chinese snakeheads (i.e., human smugglers) are among the most audacious and organized in transnational illegal human migration. Few smugglers, male or female, have ever ascended to the height and notoriety as that enjoyed by Cheng Chui Ping (aka Zheng Cui Ping; the Snakehead Queen). To U.S. law enforcement agencies, she was considered the "Mother of all Snakeheads" and a cut-throat underground banker. But she was well-respected and affectionately called Yi-Ping-Jie (or Big Sister Ping) in social circles in New York's Chinatown and her home village in China.

The exact circumstance of how Sister Ping entered the United States has remained a mystery. A *Time* magazine report claimed that she first entered Hong Kong from mainland China and then came to the United States in 1981 and, somehow, obtained naturalization papers (Barnes 2000). Among the first few people who knew how to organize smuggling operations, Sister Ping began smuggling Chinese immigrants in the early 1980s. Her early clients were mostly relatives and villagers from her hometown in Shengmei in coastal Fujian Province.

During the early days, she would personally travel back to her hometown, recruiting and coordinating smuggling operations. She typically transported her clients first to Canada by using fraudulent documents and then across the border into the United States. Hong Kong was often used as a transit point. With the help of corrupt officials in China, she was able to obtain the necessary travel documents for her clients. Her smuggling routes later expanded to Mexico, Belize, and other Central American states.

Stories of her successful operations quickly spread in her hometown and adjacent townships. Villagers came looking for her in droves. At the height of her operations, Sister Ping owned restaurants, a clothing store, and real estate in Chinatown, as well as apartments in Hong Kong and a farm in South Africa (Federal Bureau of Investigation [FBI] 2006). Estimates varied as to how big her operation had become at the pinnacle of her smuggling career. Some claimed that she was transporting hundreds in each operation by boats. The U.S. government estimated that, for more than a decade, Sister Ping smuggled as many as 3,000 illegal immigrants from her native China into the United States, amassing more than $40 million from her smuggling business (FBI 2006).

Sister Ping was also involved in money laundering. Although often overshadowed by her reputation as the "Mother of all Snakeheads," people close to her claimed that she was far more successful at underground banking than she was any of her other business ventures. Her entry into the underground banking business, though fortuitous, was perfect in timing. After illegal immigrants settle down, their immediate need is to send money home. The remittance is used to repay the smuggling debt and to support family members back home. This is no easy task when illegal immigrants cannot use mainstream banking institutions. Even for legal immigrants, conventional banks are slow, and transactions are expensive for the small amounts of money they send home. In the late 1980s, the demand for underground banking services exploded when waves of illegal immigrants arrived, found jobs, and wanted to send money home to pay smuggling debts and to sponsor other family members for the same journey.

Sister Ping's reliable and timely money transferring operation quickly won her more clients. Prospective migrants in China would borrow money from her, while smugglers would count on her for payment assurance. She in turn collected smuggling fees from clients and their families. In an environment where business transactions are neither legally recognized nor protected, her banking business served a vital role in facilitating these transactions. Much of the transmitting was done in so-called mirror transfers, in which she took in the money in the United States and placed a call to instruct her partners in China to deliver the money either in U.S. dollars or Chinese yuan to her clients' families. When individuals and even legitimate businesses wanted to send money to the United States, the process was reversed. No money was physically transmitted. This practice continues today in many overseas Chinese communities.

People who used her service had nothing but praise for her. As her reputation grew, she needed no advertisement. Both smugglers and illegal immigrants used her banking service to send money home or to finance smuggling operations. Her fees and exchange terms were always superior to those offered by legitimate banks. Unlike the Bank of China, the only official bank from China with overseas branches, that forced customers to convert their U.S. dollars into Chinese currency at unfavorable official rates, Sister Ping's clients had a choice of either receiving their remittances in dollars or Chinese yuan with much more favorable black market rates.

The U.S. government claimed that Sister Ping continued to smuggle Chinese immigrants while she was supposedly cooperating with the FBI (Mata Press Service 2006). She was believed to have been involved in the ill-fated smuggling operation the *Golden Venture* incident, in which a freighter was deliberately beached in the Rockaways off Queens in June 1993, after the transfer boat failed to show up to ferry the illegal immigrants ashore. Gangsters onboard urged some 300 illegal immigrants to jump the ship and swim to "freedom." Many did. Ten of them drowned.

Facing indictments following the *Golden Venture* incident, Sister Ping evaded authorities for years by hiding in her native Shengmei village. While in hiding, her son and husband continued to live in the United States and traveled to China on occasion. In April 2000, Sister Ping ventured to see her son, returning to the United States, off at Hong Kong's Chek Lap Kok airport. She did not know that her son was being watched. With the help of Hong Kong police, Sister Ping was detained at the airport. At the time of her arrest, she was holding three different passports: one from Hong Kong, one from the United States, and one from Belize. Authorities later claimed that Sister Ping had managed to make several visits back to the United States under different identities. She fought extradition for three years, hoping her wealth and official connections could somehow save her. In the end, none panned out. In July 2003, she was handed over to the U.S. authorities for trial.

For more than a decade, Sister Ping's many exploits became almost legendary. Her reputation loomed so big in the Chinese smuggling community that many snakeheads in the United States and China claimed to be her associates. Many of them simply were trying to boost their otherwise obscure status to attract clients or to charge higher fees. Sister Ping's saga finally came to an end on March 16, 2006, when she was sentenced in a federal court in New York to 35 years on charges of conspiring to commit alien smuggling, hostage taking, money laundering, and laundering ransom money (U.S. Immigration and Customs Enforcement 2006).

Resources

Barnes, Edward. 2000. "Two-faced Woman." *Time*, July 31: 48–50.

Federal Bureau of Investigation. 2006. "The Case of the Snakehead Queen: Chinese Human Smuggler Gets 35 Years." *News Release*, March 17. http://www.fbi.gov/page2/march06/sisterping031706.htm.

Mata Press Service. 2006. "Mother of All 'Snakeheads' Gets 35 Years in Jail." *Asian Pacific Post,* March 27. http://www.asianpacificpost.com.

U.S. Immigration and Customs Enforcement. 2006. "Sister Ping Sentenced to 35 Years in Prison for Alien Smuggling, Hostage Taking, Money Laundering and Ransom Proceeds Conspiracy." *News Release*, March 16. http://www.ice.gov/graphics/news/newsreleases/.

Sheldon X. Zhang

Cheng I Sao (1775–1844)

Cheng I Sao, known by many names, including Ch'ing Yih Szaou, Lady Ching, and Mrs. Ching, was the most powerful and notorious pirate in the Sea of China. Not only did she gain tremendous wealth, but she had a dangerous reputation and ran a well-organized marauding operation, while maintaining good relations with her subordinate pirates and the poor on land. Accounts of her history are conflicting, but historians agree that she was a very powerful and financially successful pirate among males and females. Her story begins with her marriage to another very successful pirate, Lord Ching.

Most accounts of her early life place her as a prostitute that Lord Ching married. Others state that she was born and raised on a pirate ship, as Chinese pirates lived as families on their junks.

The Sea of China was home to numerous women pirates, but Lady Ching was a legendary success. She inherited her husband's fleet of 500 ships and 70,000 people, becoming more wealthy and powerful than any male pirate had been.

In the 19th century, people were driven to piracy due to an increasing birth rate and food shortage while the royals lived in luxury, and the mandarins, imperial bureaucrats, grew wealthy by extortion. The excesses of the wealthy caused disaffection among the people. Piracy was of great concern to the Chinese emperor who tried to curb Lord Ching's marauding by appointing him Master of the Royal Stables with the title Golden Dragon of the Imperial Staff. However, this royal bribe was to no avail as Lord Ching was soon back to plundering at sea at the helm of his fleet arranged into six squadrons, each with its own colored flag.

The emperor battled the Chings three times. During the third time, in 1808, the imperial fighters seemed to be gaining a victory on the pirates but were surprised when the pirates, including Lady Ching, boarded the royal ships with sabers in both hands, leaving the imperial fleet in ruins. When attacking the coast of present-day Vietnam, a typhoon disrupted their operations. Some scholars say that Lord Ching died there, while others recount him being taken to land, tortured, and killed. There are also conflicting reports as to Lady Ching's reaction. According to some sources, she retreated, while others claim that she dared the pirates to prove themselves under a female commander. Prove themselves they did, and from then on, Lady Ching became the pirate queen.

Some historians portray Lady Ching as politically maneuvering into her position as commander. Another historian portrays her as having inherited her powerful position, claiming that it was common for captain's wives to have been made first lieutenant, then succeed them as captain upon his death. Lady Ching is unique in the level of her success as the most powerful pirate who has terrorized Chinese waters.

Any ship that crossed her path was raided. Captives unable to purchase their freedom could choose between an excruciating death or conversion to piracy. Captured women and children were sold into slavery. Lady Ching also collected protection money from people along the coasts. The goods taken from farmers were compensated for. Some histories portray her as an extortionist who also raided farms, while others paint her as being on good terms with those people with whom she did business.

Lady Ching was a careful business woman, keeping exact records of plunder and expenses. She ran her operations like a legitimate business; she called "plundering" a 'transferring shipment of goods" (Klausmann, 1997: 40). She maintained discipline herself and amongst her pirates by issuing rules of conduct, including those applied to keeping the common loot communal. She made sure that her ships were always equipped with weapons and provisions, and she had good relationship with her crew. Strict punishments were levied against violators of the codes of conduct, which prevented the pirates from using violence against women, especially the female captives. Furthermore, she did away with the cruel practice of hanging captured women and children by their hair on the ships. Instead, female captives of high standing not sold into slavery could be purchased by the pirates to be their wives, and the women were to be treated as people of high standing. Klausmann suggests that these reforms were not rooted in a feminist ideal; rather, treating captured women well was practical, because women jumping overboard caused a financial loss.

Politically, she organized her fleet as a constitutional monarchy in which she was the absolute monarch. Lord Ching had already divided the fleet into six squadrons with their own color flag. To this she added a council with a prime minister, all of whom were chosen by her.

Some accounts also speak of a P'aou or Pao, a child captive she had made into her adoptive son, or Lord Ching's right-hand man, because of some special quality he possessed. Some historians claim that she married Pao; however, most histories cast him as the leader of the red squadron and prime minister of the fleet. With Pao's assistance, Lady Ching maintained a strong intelligence network allowing her to keep up on who to pursue, and who considered pursuing her.

There is also conflicting information as to the end of her seafaring career. A rivalry ensued between Pao and the black or yellow squadron leader inciting a battle that left Pao defeated, and 160 ships under the rival's squadron abandoned Lady Ching. This mutineer sought amnesty from either the Chinese government or the governor of Macau, trading in his ships and possibly some plunder for life on land. Having been weakened from this loss of ships, Lady Ching also negotiated with this formal political body for a life on land. She was able to secure provisions and money for her thousands of crewmembers, and she lived as a wealthy woman until her death in 1844. Some accounts say that she ran a brothel and a smuggling ring, while others says she married the governor of Macau; still others say she lived as an honorable first lady who engaged in smuggling.

Resources

Beagle Bay. 2009. Publisher's book publication webpage—Book entitled *Women Pirates*. Retrieved on March 28, 2010, from http://www.beaglebay.com/women_pirates.html.

Gosse, Philip. 1932. *The History of Piracy*. New York: Tudor Publishing Company.

Klausmann, Ulrike. 1997. *Women Pirates and the Politics of the Jolly Roger.* Montreal, Canada: Black Rose Books.

Koerth, Maggie. 2006. "Most Successful Pirate Was Beautiful and Tough." *CNN.* Retrieved March 28, 2010, from http://www.cnn.com/2007/LIVING/worklife/08/27/woman.pirate/index.html.

Ossian, Robert. "Rob Ossian's Pirate's Cove—Biographies—Cheng I Sao." Retrieved on April 8, 2010, from http://www.thepirateking.com/bios/sao_cheng_i.htm.

Stapleton, David. 2001. *Chen I Soa.* "Pirates Hold—Pirate History and Beyond—Pirate Roster." Retrieved March 28, 2010, from http://piratehold.buccaneersoft.com/roster/cheng_i_soa.html.

Stephens, Autumn. 1992. *Wild Women: Crusaders, Curmudgeons and Completely Corsetless Ladies in the Otherwise Virtuous Victorian Era.* Berkeley, CA: Conari Press.

Nayla Huq

Judith Clark (1949–)

Arrested for her participation in an armed robbery that ended in three murders, Judith Clark's actions drew societal attention to the use of violence in radical activism. Clark was born November 23, 1949, in Brooklyn, New York to a politically active Jewish family. As an infant, her family moved to the Soviet Union. After experiencing several disappointments with the Communist Party, they returned to the United States when Clark reached age three. Her parents eventually decided to discontinue their political involvement with the Communist Party. Despite the loss of political commitment by her parents, she decided to rekindle the family's involvement by pursuing her own political agendas.

As the years passed, Clark became increasingly involved in radical social movement organizations. In the 1970s, Clark participated in the Weathermen, and by 1981, she was active in the May 19 Communist Organization. Participation in these groups reinforced her political agenda through collective cohesion in the form of group conformity. She eventually became mentally and emotionally dependent on group acceptance. The strict moral codes within these organizations distanced her from her family and close friends, making it difficult for her to sustain personal relationships outside the radical organizations she was involved in.

After giving birth to her daughter in 1980, Clark was briefly removed from her activist lifestyle. Although the birth drew Clark closer to her family, she still felt a strong obligation to the May 19 Communist Organization. Participation in grassroots organizations gave her a sense of collective identity and emotional fulfillment. Unfortunately, political activism and a drive for social justice subsequently lead to her incarceration.

On October 20, 1981, Clark participated in a politically motivated crime that took the lives of three people. Members of the May 19 Communist Organization and Black Liberation Army, including Clark, attempted to rob a Brinks truck in Nyack, New York. During the robbery, the extremists shot and killed Brinks truck security guard Peter Paige while attempting to escape with $1.6 million. The shooters then changed cars and entered another get away vehicle that was driven by Clark. As she was driving away from the scene, they were stopped by a police barricade. After several shoots were fired, the radicals killed police officers Waverly Brown and Edward O'Grandy. Although Clark was not one of the shooters, she was one of the three participants arrested on the scene.

During the pretrial period, Clark and three other participants were transported between several jails and correction facilities. The trial lasted from August 8, 1983, to the end of September of that year. Throughout the proceedings, Clark decided not to have a legal counsel and represented herself. She also voluntarily removed herself from the court proceedings. Clark was housed in the basement holding cells of the courthouse and appeared in court twice during the trial. On October 6, 1983, she was charged with three counts of felony murder and was sentenced to three consecutive sentences of 25 to life.

Immediately following the trial, she was taken to a special housing unit (SHU) at the Bedford Hills Correctional Facility for Women in New York State. She was held in the SHU for several weeks and was eventually released into the general population with assistance from the prison-appointed attorney. She was then placed back into SHU for two years after being charged with conspiracy to escape in September of 1985.

Judith Clark experienced serious depression that arose from social isolation and the lack of intellectual stimulation. Through a series of interviews by Dr. Gilda Zwerman, a professor of sociology, Clark began changing her attitudes and perspectives. She also started taking college courses through the mail and received a bachelor's degree from Mercy College Bedford in 1990 and a master's degree in 1993 from the Vermont College of Norwich University. She has also used her experience to create scholarly writings and promote social change. Her writings have been published in the *New Yorker*, the *Prison Journal*, *Doing Time*, *Fortune News*, and other literary journals. In addition to her scholarly writings, she has worked for Bedford Hills Children's Center and co-founded the AIDS Counseling and Education during her incarceration.

Clark's actions brought societal awareness to politically motivated violence in the form of radical activism. When violence is present in social movements, there is a possibly of individuals becoming physically injured or killed. Although her supporters contend that she is a political prisoner, she believes that the attachment to anti-imperialism led to her rebellious behavior. Clark and another defendant,

David J. Gilbert, were once involved in the radical Weathermen organization. The Weathermen were labeled as a domestic terrorist organization by the FBI for their rioting and attacks against banks, police departments, and government offices. Kuwasi Balagoon is another defendant that was involved in the Black Partner Party and held black separatist political views. A fourth defendant Kathy Boudin, along with the other defendants, was involved or affiliated with the Black Liberation Army and was seeking to establish governance of the Republic of New Afrika. Therefore, the defendants argued that they were being treated as prisoners of war, and there cases should have been adjudicated by nations. Since the trial, Clark has also become active in antiviolence programs that use discussion as an alternative to violent behavior.

After receiving support from her family and legal counsel, Clark began taking steps towards an appeal. In 2002, attorneys Leon Friedman, Lawrence Lederman, and Michael L. Hirschfeld filled an appeal on her behalf. They argued that her placement in the holding cells caused her to be removed from the hearings, and she was denied the right to counsel because she chose to represent herself. On September 21, 2006, nearly four years after the appeal, the district court judge ruled in her favor, and she was granted the right to a new trial. On February 26, 2007, her legal counsel addressed the Federal Court of Appeals, but in 2008, the court reversed the opinion of the district court and denied her request for a new trial.

Today, Clark contends that she has a great deal of remorse for her involvement in the killings. She has since removed herself from extreme activism and committed herself to helping others. Clark has since written a letter to her supporters about the impact she believes her actions have had on the victims' children. On August 23, 2001, the victims' families spent several months opposing the parole of another defendant Kathy Boudin, whose parole was denied and later granted in 2003. Chief Van Cura, South Nyack and Grand View police chief, and the victims' families have expressed the impact the killings have had on the lives of their families.

Resources

Burrell, Jocelyn, and Suheir Hammad. (2004). *Word: On Being A (Woman) Writer.* New York: The Feminist Press.

Clark v. Perez. (2006a). 05 Civ. 698. U.S. Dist. 450 F. Supp. 2d 396.

Clark v. Perez. (2006b). U.S. Dist.

Clark v. Perez. (2008). 510 F. U.S. App. 3d 382.

Farber, M. A. (1982, February 16). Behind the Brink's Case: Return of the Radical Left. *New York Times,* A1.

Feron, James. (1982, September 23). State Acts of Brink's Defendant. *New York Times,* B1.

Foderaro, Lisa W. (2006, October 1). New Trial for Woman in 1981 Brink's Case Is Reopening Old Wounds. *New York Times.*

Friends of Judith Clark. http://www.judithclark.org. Retrieved September 20, 2007.

Hanley, Robert. (1983, August 23). Fannie Mae Tests Transit Program. *New York Times,* B2.

Hudson, Edward. (1983, August 9). Protest Marks Opening of Brink's Murder Trail. *New York Times,* B1.

Mahoney, Joe. (2003, August 23). Death Penalty Upheld for N.O. Ex-Cop. *Daily New (New York),* 10.

Margolick, David. (1982, October 1). In Brink's Holdup Case, Tactics Used by Lawyers Differ Widely. *New York Times,* B1.

Suddath, C. (2008). A Brief History Of The Weathermen. *Time International (Canada Edition), 172*(16), 12.

Worth, Robert. (2001, August 23). Parole Denied for Radical in Fatal 1981 Robbery. *New York Times,* B1.

LaSheila S. Yates

Mildred Cleghorn (1910–1997)

Mildred Imoch Cleghorn was the first chairperson of the Fort Sill Apache Tribe. Known also by her Apache names Eh-Ohn and Lay-a-Bet, Cleghorn ascended through historical accident from intense marginalization to renowned stateswoman. She began her life as a human remnant of the last vestige of Native American independence and as a reminder of the historical mistreatment of Native Americans by the U.S. government. Though not a criminal by most meanings of the term, she was labeled as beyond the law before was she born, and she grew to challenge, change, and utilize the law for the benefit of all Native Americans.

Historically, Apaches migrated from Athabaskan heritage to the southwestern United States and northern Mexico. Those who settled in southwestern New Mexico, southeastern Arizona, northern Sonora, and northern Chihuahua came to be known as the Chiricahua Apaches. They constituted at least four culturally and geographic distinct bands: the Bedonkohe, Chihenne, Chokonen, and Nednai. Although they originally came from distinct groups, they became loosely affiliated as a tribe, first as settlers described them and later as a function of their own defenses against settlers' incursions.

Gradually restricted to the Fort Apache and San Carlos reservations, the Chiricahua were the last Native American group to resist federal incursion, led by a series of seminal names in Native American history, including Cochise and Goyaałé (aka Geronimo). A series of incidents in which Chiricahua leaders were ambushed, murdered, and mutilated led to more than two decades of wars during which the Chiricahua were relentlessly pursued by both federal troops (led by generals George Cook and Nelson Miles) and Mexican soldiers. Most were killed, captured, or surrendered. The final 34, including Geronimo and Cochise's son Naiche, surrendered on September 5, 1886. The U.S. federal government then forcibly relocated 394 Chiricahua Apaches in railroad boxcars to Army facilities in Florida, then Alabama, and ultimately, in 1894, to the Fort Sill reservation in Oklahoma.

The Chiricahua remained at Fort Sill as "prisoners of war" until a 1912 act of Congress freed them and permitted them to settle in the surrounding area. However, although each family was promised 160 acres, a house, a well, and a year's rations, two families received 158 acres and most received 80 or less. "The families weren't allowed to live together," Cleghorn told the Associated Press in a 1996 interview. "So they scattered us all over. If we wanted to go visit someone, it would be an all-day trip. I guess they were afraid of another uprising." Worse, resistance from non-Indian locals regenerated tensions from earlier history. The Chiricahua were thus offered land by the Mescalero Apaches near Ruidoso, New Mexico. In 1913, about two-thirds (some 183) relocated to the Mescalero reservation, while the rest (accounts give a range from 78 to 84) remained at Fort Sill, intent that the United States would fulfill its promise of local lands. After struggling through decades of drought and the depression, the Fort Sill Chiricahua were aided somewhat by the Oklahoma Indian Welfare Act of 1936, and after four more decades of effort, they finally organized as a federally recognized tribe in 1976.

On December 11, 1910, Cleghorn was among the last Chiricahua Apaches to be born under "prisoner of war" status. Her grandfather had fought with Geronimo, and her parents and grandparents had been among those imprisoned and triply relocated. When she was three years old, her family left Fort Sill in a wagon to settle a 40-acre plot (a fourth of what had been promised) near Apache, Oklahoma. She thus began life beyond the margins, a poor and culturally distant female with no tribe and no home.

Cleghorn attended school in Apache, as well as the Haskell Institute in Kansas, then earned a degree in home economics from Oklahoma State University in 1941, and completed a human relations fellowship at Fisk University in 1955. She served as a home extension agent for several years in Kansas, Oklahoma, and New Mexico; as a home economics teacher for 16 years on reservations in Oklahoma; and later as a kindergarten teacher. She married William G. Cleghorn, whom she met while teaching in Kansas, and gave birth to their daughter, Peggy. Throughout this time, she perfected the art of crafting traditional dolls, creating a series clothed to represent the 40 tribes she encountered as a teacher; this series of dolls has been exhibited at the Smithsonian Institution in Washington, D.C.

In 1976, when the Chiricahua tribe became formally recognized, she became its first tribal chairperson. She held that position until 1995, devoting significant efforts to preserving and sustaining the tribe's history and culture. She was recognized with a string of accolades, including the Ellis Island Award in 1987 and the Indian of the Year Award in 1989, and also served as secretary of the Southwest Oklahoma Intertribal Association as well as treasurer of the American Indian

Council of the Reformed Church of America. In 1996, Cleghorn was a lead plaintiff in an unsuccessful class action lawsuit filed on behalf of over 300,000 Native Americans against the federal government alleging destruction of important documents and mismanagement of hundreds of millions of dollars in Indian monies held in trust fund accounts with the Bureau of Indian Affairs. On April 15, 1997, she was killed in an automobile accident near Apache.

Resources

Abner, Julie L. 2000. "Mildred Imoch Cleghorn." In *Native American Women: A Biographical Dictionary*, eds. Gretchen M. Bataille and Laurie Lisa. New York: Routledge.

Stockel, H. Henrietta. 1991. *Women of the Apache Nation: Voices of Truth.* Reno: University of Nevada Press.

Stockel, H. Henrietta. 2000. *Chiricahua Apache Women and Children: Safekeepers of the Heritage.* College Station: Texas A&M University Press.

Thrapp, Dan L. 1988. *The Conquest of Apacheri.* Norman & London: University of Oklahoma Press.

Ellis Godard

Ann Cook (1786–1826)

Ann Cook, a Southern belle in her youth, was seduced by a powerful politician, Colonel Solomon P. Sharp, and in turn she seduced Jereboam Beauchamp. She was questioned but never tried for conspiracy to murder Sharp. As was commonly the case in the Regency Era, Cook's behavior as a seducer of Jereboam and as an aggressive woman was pitted against the crime of Sharp's seduction of Cook and the romantic pact between Beauchamp and Cook to avenge her honor. This case, known to many as the Kentucky Tragedy (also known as the Sharp-Beauchamp Tragedy), is a perfect example of betrayal and seduction. Ann Cook, who had stepped out of her gender role expectation, was viewed as a monster by some. In the end, however, romanticism won, and Ann Cook was defined as a victim.

Not much is known about Ann Cook. Born in 1786, Ann Cook came from a wealthy, well-known, and well-educated family who frequently traveled to Frankfurt, Kentucky, especially during legislative sessions. Ann and her sister Mary were prominent belles who traveled elegantly in four-horse drawn carriages. This particular story begins around 1818, when Ann Cook claimed to be seduced by Solomon Sharp, a prominent lawyer and politician one year her minor. (It should be noted that various accounts of this story identify different dates. For example, Ann Cook's pregnancy has been noted as occurring in 1818, 1819, and 1820. We chose the more frequent year of 1818 [Johnson, 1993].)

Cook became pregnant, and she claimed that Sharp was the father; however, the baby was stillborn which caused her heartache. Her relationship with Sharp and her resulting pregnancy put a dent in her reputation, and she fell from society. Adding to her tragedy, Sharp denied that the baby was his, even claiming that the baby was mulatto. As a result, Cook was forced to remain unwed and live with her family at their farm.

In 1824, Ann Cook met another young lawyer by the name of Jereboam Beauchamp. One shocking piece of this story, to those living in this era, was that Beauchamp was 16 years younger than Cook. Some claim that upon learning of her seduction, Beauchamp sought her out and proposed marriage. Upon Beauchamp's proposal, Cook made it clear that the only way that she would marry him was if he helped kill her ex-lover Solomon Sharp who had denied paternity to her stillborn child. After a hostile confrontation between Sharp and Beauchamp, in which Sharp continued his denials, Cook and Jereboam married and worked closely to devise a plan to murder Sharp.

Sharp made further accusations that Cook had sexual affairs with other men, which further angered Beauchamp. On November 6, 1825, Beauchamp stabbed Sharp to death after persuading Sharp to open the door to his home. Beauchamp went so far as to cover his face with a black mask in order to hide his identity while traveling at night on the streets. His intention was to make passersby think that he was African American. He also wore socks made out of a very heavy material so that his footprints could not be identified. Fueled by her anger, Ann Cook had laced the tip of the knife with poison hoping that when it went into Sharp's chest, it would kill him instantly. When Sharp answered the door, Beauchamp pulled his knife from beneath his shirt and ripped off his mask in order to let Sharp know who killed him.

After the murder, the couple hoped that the crime would go unsolved and that they could go on with their lives. They planned to move to Missouri to ensure that they would not be caught. Suspicion quickly fell onto Beauchamp, however, and he was arrested for the murder of Solomon Sharp. Ann Cook was questioned and later released because she was not in the area where the murder was committed.

On May 19, 1826, after a trial was conducted, Beauchamp was sentenced to death by hanging. He was to be executed on June 7, 1826. Cook begged the warden that she be allowed to stay in the jail cell with her husband before he was executed. Having entered into a suicide pact, Cook smuggled poison and a knife into the jail. When the poison did not work, they proceeded to stab themselves. Cook stabbed herself twice and died. However, Beauchamp's self-inflicted injury did not kill him. He was revived, cleaned up, and watched very closely until he was hanged a few hours later. Literary writers point out the irony that all three victims died of stab wounds to the same area of the chest. Cook and Beauchamp were buried in the same casket in a lover's embrace.

This case inspired literary and historical works. For example, the renowned author Edgar Allen Poe constructed a drama by the name of *Politian* (1835) that is believed to be inspired by the real-life story of this tragedy of betrayal and lies. William Gilmore Simms, as well as Thomas Holley Chivers and Robert Penn Warren, wrote novels based on the Kentucky Tragedy. It has been stated that Poe's work closely resembles the true story of Ann Cook. Warren's work *World Enough and Time* (1950) is said to be the most realistic account of the Kentucky Tragedy, although his character portrayal of the main female character is the least like Ann Cook. Unlike his literary counterparts, Warren minimized the romantic aspects of the story and was most true to the facts. This case has also been the subject of many published theses and dissertations within literature.

Of importance to the social fabric at the time was the romanticism of Beauchamp's drive to avenge Cook's honor. Various news and literary accounts of the Sharp-Beauchamp Tragedy indicate that Beauchamp acted within the code of the era. When a woman of worth is seduced and then denied status, justice is warranted. This can be seen in seductions laws in early 20th-century America. In cases of seduction, a woman had legal recourse. However, she was only provided recourse if she did not violate the patriarchal bargain by stepping out of her gender role. In Cook's case, her family's good reputation, her wealth, and her marriage to a prominent male saved her reputation as a good woman deserving of justice. And, although Ann Cook took her own life, her memory was not persecuted by society.

Resources

Beauchamp, Ann Cook and W.R—n. 1826. *Letters of Ann Cook, Late Mrs. Beauchamp, to her friend in Maryland: Containing a Short History of the Life of that Remarkable Woman.* Washington, D.C.

Beauchamp, Jereboam O., and Beauchamp Ann. (1826). The confession of Jereboam O. Beauchamp: who was hanged at Frankfort, Ky., on the 7th day of July, 1826, for the murder of Col. Solomon P. Sharp. *Filson Historical Society.* Retrieved March 19, 2008, from http://memory.loc.gov/cgi-bin/query/r?ammem/fawbib:@field(DOCID+@lit(bbf0086)).

Coleman, Winston J. 1950. *The Beauchamp-Sharp Tragedy: An Episode of Kentucky History During the Middle 1820s.* Frankfort, KY: Roberts Print.

Johnson, Fred M. 1993. New Light on Beauchamp's *Confession. Journal of the Kentucky-Tennessee American Studies Association,* 9. Retrieved March 19, 2008, from http://spider.georgetowncollege.edu/HTALLANT/border/bs9/fr-johns.htm.

Gates, W. B. 1960. William Gilmore Simms and the Kentucky Tragedy. *American Literature* 32, 158–66.

Justus, James S. 1962. Warren's *World Enough and Time* and Beauchamp's *Confession. American Literature* 33, 500–511.

Kimball, William J. 1971. Poe's Politian and the Beauchamp-Sharp tragedy. *Poe Studies* 4, 24–27.

Norman, Michael, and Beth Scott. 2002. *Haunted Heritage: A Definitive Collection of American Ghost Stories.* New York: Forge Books.

Erin Elizabeth Gourley and Venessa Garcia

Belle Cora (1827?–1862)

Belle Cora was an important madam in San Francisco during the gold rush days. She was romantically involved with Charles Cora who killed U.S. Marshal William H. Richardson. Richardson's murder prompted a new rise in the Committee of Vigilance, a citizen group that formed to try to rid San Francisco of crimes related to the corruption in city officials.

Two versions of Belle Cora's early life are known. She was born either Arabella Ryan or Clara Belle Ryan. One version has her as the daughter of a minister from Baltimore. She supposedly became pregnant, was denounced by her parents, and ended up in New Orleans in 1849, where her baby was born and died (Levy, 1941: 149). It was here she met Charles Cora. Another version is that she was the daughter of Irish-Catholic parents in Baltimore. Belle and her sister Anna quit school to work in a dressmaking shop, which happened to be next to the Lutz, a house of questionable means. The girls decided it was more profitable to wear the dresses instead of making them and so became involved with the Lutz. It is said that Belle eventually quit and drifted to Charleston where she became mistress to a man who was later killed. From there she went to New Orleans in 1849, where she met Charles Cora, a gambler (Gentry, 1964: 77). Of the two versions, the second seems to be the one most believed.

After Belle Ryan left New Orleans with Charles Cora, they eventually booked a passage on a side-wheeler bound for San Francisco. Upon arrival, on December 28, 1849, they immediately left for Sacramento, where some say that Belle provided financial support for Charles's high-stakes gambling. After Sacramento, Belle left for Sonora where, under the name of Arabelle Ryan, she became the madam of a house of ill repute at the age of 23 (Levy, 1941: 150–154). She later returned to San Francisco sometime in 1852 and set up her own house at Dupont Street, complete with white picket fence and flower garden. Her place was directly across from Ah Toy, another madam. In an eight-block radius, there existed over 100 of these houses. It was said that Belle's place was the most lavish and her girls the prettiest. Belle Cora regularly held dinner parties where the most noted of the city came, including the mayor, aldermen, judges, and members of the legislature (Gentry, 1964: 83). It was said that Belle and Charles spent a good deal of time in high society together.

The event that led to the eventual shooting of U.S. Marshall Richardson happened Thursday, November 15, 1855, when Belle and Charles attended a play at the theater. This play was also attended by Richardson and his wife, who were sitting directly in front of Belle and Charles. When Richardson's wife found out who was sitting behind them, she asked her husband to get them expelled. The proprietor refused, and the Richardsons left instead. Richardson went looking for Charles Cora. They confronted each other on the street on November 17, and Charles Cora shot Richardson. Cora was soon arrested. The newspapers sensationalized the event, calling it murder. The public was split on whether Belle Cora or Mrs. Richardson was actually responsible (Gentry, 1964: 86–88).

Belle hired Colonel E. D. Baker to represent Charles. She advanced Baker $15,000 (in gold) of the $30,000 he had asked for a retainer. Belle also tried to pressure Mrs. Maria Knight, a witness, into adjusting her remembrance of what she saw to help out Charles Cora. The first trial in January 1856, ended in a dead-locked jury (Gentry, 1964: 88–92). Charles Cora remained in jail for his next trial.

Meanwhile, an event put Charles Cora's life in danger. James Patrick Casey, who was a member of the San Francisco County Board of Supervisors, had a running dispute with James King over an anonymous letter published in the newspaper which accused King of attacking the U.S. Marshall who had taken Richardson's place (Senkewicz, 1985: 7). Casey was arrested after shooting King on May 14, 1856. The Committee of Vigilance decided that they would make an example of both Casey and Charles Cora. They were taken to the committee's headquarters, where two vigilantes were provided for Charles Cora's counsel and where they were tried by the vigilante executive committee. Found guilty, they were both sentenced to hang.

After Belle gained permission to stay with Charles on the day of the hanging, May 22, 1856, Father Michael Accolti, a Catholic priest, united Belle and Cora in marriage (Senkewicz, 1985: 172). Belle Cora became an immediate widow and had an elaborate funeral for Charles Cora. When she found she could not be buried next to him because of space, she had his body transferred from the Mission Dolores Cemetery to the Calvary Cemetery (Levy, 1941: 222).

The aim of most respectable women at the time in San Francisco was to change the social atmosphere from one of sexual immorality to one more civilized, but they were not organized and so there was only surface reform. An unspoken tolerance for vice was maintained as long as the offenders were discreet (Jeffrey, 1979: 138–141). Many women in San Francisco believed that Belle Cora should be made to leave town. A request was sent to the newspaper asking the Committee of Vigilance to compel Belle Cora to leave. A woman named Gertrude responded to the women's request by arguing "that women ought not to persecute their own sex," going so far as to call the women's own virtue into question. She went on to say that all "true women" would agree with her (Jolly, 2003: 7). The request was ignored.

Belle continued to run her establishment until February 1862, when she caught pneumonia and died at the age of 35. She was buried in the Calvary Cemetery next to Charles Cora. Their bodies were later moved to the Mission Dolores Cemetery (Levy, 1941: 222).

Resources

Gentry, Curt. 1964. *The Madams of San Francisco: An Irreverent History of the City by the Golden Gate*. Garden City, NY: Doubleday.

Jeffrey, Julie Roy. 1979. *Frontier Women: The Trans-Mississippi West 1840–1880*. New York: Hill and Wang.

Jolly, Michelle. 2003. Sex, Vigilantism, and San Francisco in 1856. *Common-Place: The Interactive Journal of Early American Life* 3–4: 1–10.

Levy, Jo Ann. 1941. *They Saw the Elephant: Women in the California Gold Rush*. Norman: University of Oklahoma Press.

Senkewicz, S. J. 1985. *Vigilantes in Gold Rush San Francisco*. Stanford: Stanford University Press.

Cora Marie Bradley

Charlotte Corday (1768–1793)

Marie-Anne Charlotte de Corday d'Amont, descendent of a poor but aristocratic Normandy clan, was born in the French village of Les Champeaux, on July 27, 1768. Corday grew up at the Manor of Cauvigny and at the Ferme du Bois, both not far from her birthplace. She was the fourth daughter of Charlotte-Marie Gautier des Authieux and Jacques-François de Corday. At the age of eight, Corday went to live with her uncle, Abbot de Corday, a parish priest on Vicques, who began her education. After her mother's death, when Corday was 12, she was admitted to a convent in the city of Caen. Corday stayed there until it closed, when she moved away to live with another relative, Mme. de Bretteville-Gouville. Interested in affairs of state, Corday involved herself in French political questions, especially in the causes of the Girondists—a moderate political French group led by Jacques-Pierre Brissot.

Charlotte Corday in jail following her assassination of Jean-Paul Marat on July 13, 1793. She was executed for her crime four days later. (Library of Congress)

Corday left for Paris to join the fight against the Jacobins, a reactionary group headed by

Robespierre who was causing large-scale violence throughout France. Jean-Paul Marat was a spokesman and one of the strongest defenders of the terrorist politics of the Jacobins. Corday thought Marat's opinions, expressed in public or in his newspaper (the *L'Ami du Peuple*, or "Friend of people"), incited violence. Further, she held him responsible for the September's Massacres—an episode of extreme cruelty during the French Revolution, which resulted the death of half of the incarcerated population of Paris. She also feared the imminent possibility of a civil war. She believed Marat's death would end all of the violence.

Impelled by those thoughts and already involved in the Girondist ideology, she traveled to Paris, arriving there on Thursday, July 11. She lodged in the Hotel de la Providence on Vieux Augustins Street. In the night of July 12, Corday wrote the *Adresse aux Français amis des lois et de la paix* ("Speech to the French who are friends of law and peace"), in which she gave the motives of her futures acts; this speech was found after the murder.

On the morning of July 13, Corday bought a large kitchen knife. Hiding the knife under her scarf, she headed to Marat's residence on Cordeliers Street. At first, citing illness, he declined to receive her. An hour later, Corday tried again, and once more her presence was refused, this time by Marat's partner, Simone Evrard. Dissatisfied, Corday wrote a note to Marat, passing herself by an informant who knew about a Girondist conspiracy plan in the city of Caen. At night, she came back to Marat's place, and, finally, Marat accept her presence, curious about details of that message she sent him before.

Jean-Paul Marat had a skin disease which caused severe itching over his body, obligating him to stay immersed in long baths; therefore, Marat received his guests in the bathroom. And so, it was in the bathroom that Corday met Marat. Corday began the meeting by telling him about the conspiracy she mentioned in her the letter. Marat attentively took note of the Girondist's names provided by Corday, and, by the end of her speech, he guaranteed her that the offenders would be guillotined. In this moment, after those words, Corday pulled the knife out of her scarf and stuck it into Marat's chest, who exclaimed *"Aidez, ma chère amie!"* ("Help me, my dear friend!"). People in the residence discovered the crime immediately, and Charlotte Corday was arrested and imprisoned in the Conciergerie. On July 17, only four days after her arrival in Paris, Corday was beheaded by the guillotine.

After her death, the Jacobins guided a detailed necropsy in Corday's body, with the purpose of determining whether she was a virgin. They hoped to locate a lover who might have helped her plan the murder. No one ever knew if Corday's head was buried with her body. Years after Marat's murder, the Italian Cesare Lombroso (1835–1909)—pioneer of the Italian positivist school that related crimes to biological characteristics—analyzed a skull that was claimed to belong to Corday. He distinguished elements that indicated that the "angel of crime" was, in fact, an innate criminal; afterward, it was found out that skull never belonged to Corday (Darmon 1991, 13–16).

The political panorama in France did not alter after Marat's death, and the violence of the Jacobin era continued; however, Corday achieved a heroine status among the people she fought for.

Resources

Corday, Michel, and Elsie Finnimore Buckley. 1931. *Charlotte Corday*. New York: E.P. Dutton.

Darmon, Pierre. 1991. *Médecins et assassins à la Belle Epoque*. Translated to Portuguese by Regina Grisse de Agostino. São Paulo: Paz e Terra.

Goldsmith, Margaret L. 1976. *Seven Women Against the World*. Westport, CT: Hyperion Press.

Robert, Henry. 1959. *Les Grands Procès de L'Historie*. II Serie. Translated to Portuguese by Juvenal Jacinto. São Paulo: Globo.

Scherr, Marie. 1970. *Charlotte Corday and Certain Men of the Revolutionary Torment*. New York: AMS Press.

Shecaira, Sérgio Salomão. 2008. *Criminologia*. São Paulo: RT.

Camila Kühl Pintarelli

Mary Cotton (1832–1873)

Mary Ann Cotton is a female serial murderer, typically classified as a "black widow" in that she targeted her husbands, lovers, most of her own children, and several extended family members. It is known that she killed 15 people, although it is estimated that she may have killed as may as 21. She is one of Britain's most notorious killers of the 19th century.

Born Mary Ann Robson, in 1832, she was brought up a strict Methodist in the village of Low Moorsley, England, to young teenage parents, Michael and Mary Robson. When Mary Ann was 14, her father, a coal miner, died in an accident. Before the age of 20, she married William Mowbray. They moved to Devon and had five children, three of which died. The second to die, a daughter also named Mary Ann, age four, was diagnosed as having gastric fever. They returned to the northeast of England, where Mary Ann had three more children. She insured members of her family with the British and Prudential Insurance Company; all of her family members whom she had insured, save Isabella Mowbray, died. Isabella was placed with her maternal grandmother, Ms. Stott.

In 1865, Mary Ann married a second time to George Ward, of Sunderland. She met him at the Sunderland Infirmary, where he was a patient. Sources conflict as to how long she was married to George, but the marriage was ended when he also succumbed to gastric fever. She then went to work as a housekeeper for John Robinson, a widower with five children. They were soon married. In 1867, Mr. Robinson lost three children inside a two-week period. Mary Ann became pregnant and, after the deaths, visited her mother. She too soon succumbed to gastric fever, although Mary Ann did not collect any insurance monies. Isabella came home with Mary Ann but soon died, like all the rest. Isabella's life was insured. Robinson eventually realized his wife was putting him in considerable debt and asked for separation. She left and took their child with her. This baby was later returned to Robinson on New Years Day, 1870, after being abandoned in 1869 at Mary Ann's sister's home.

She was then introduced to Frederick Cotton by his sister Margaret Cotton. Shortly after Mary Ann met Frederick, Margaret Cotton died mysteriously under Mary Ann's care. In 1871, Mary Ann married Frederick even though she was still married to John Robinson. They lived in West Auckland, County Durham. At age 39, on September, 19, 1871, Frederick died of gastric fever. Her newly born son, Robert, died a short time later. Joseph Nattrass, a lover, moved in to her home but died in March 1872, followed the following month by Cotton's 10-year-old son, and three months later by his brother, Charles, age 7. Before the death of this last child, she was reported to have commented that this child would go like the rest of the Cotton family, and she would not be bothered for long.

It was this last string of deaths that aroused suspicion. The doctor, having seen too many deaths in one family, refused to sign a death certificate for the death of Cotton's second son. The authorities were brought in, and the child was examined. Arsenic was found in his stomach. His brother and Nattrass were exhumed. Arsenic was found in both.

While awaiting trial, Mary Ann gave birth to yet another child in January 1873. This one was adopted out to another family. The defense tried to argue that Mr. Cotton's seven-year-old boy may have licked the arsenic off the wallpaper in her home. The prosecution brought forth evidence that Mary Ann had purchased arsenic and soft soap, supposedly for killing bedbugs, shortly before the child's death. She was found guilty of murder and sentenced to death. She was hanged on March 24, 1873. The execution was botched, and it took her three minutes to die.

The Cotton case illustrates the power of gender to blind local authorities and laypeople as to the nature of her murderous activities. Although there were higher rates of infant and child mortality in this era, Cotton was able to kill her husbands and lovers, all of her own children, and many of the children that she came in close proximity to when she married into existing families, without being suspected of causing their deaths. Her gender and her perceived maternal instincts blinded most who stood by as Cotton experienced tragedy after tragedy. If Cotton had been a male, most certainly people would have become suspicious earlier in her killing career. Even when Mary Ann Cotton was able to foreshadow, and eventually predict with accuracy, the deaths of family members, the authorities were not notified. It was not until a family doctor insisted on an autopsy that her deeds were unraveled.

This case is significant as it is one of the first cases where a female serial murderer was assumed to be motivated, at least in part, by financial gain. During the Victorian era, despite the fact that a queen held the monarchy, women could not own property, had similar legal rights to that of children, were unable to vote, and could not initiate legal actions. Employment prospects were minimal. Most women could find work only as either teacher or housekeepers, and they were not allowed to have their own banking accounts. The so-called ideal woman was clean and pure, tending house and her own children. What is clear is that Cotton played into the ideology of ideal femininity and used it to hide a sinister deeds. Her children, stepchildren, husbands, and lovers became a source of income for Mary Ann Cotton, as many were insured, with herself as the sole beneficiary.

Resource

Appleton, A. (1973). *Mary Ann Cotton: Her story and trial*. London: Michael Joseph.

Hannah Scott

D

Iva d'Aquino (Tokyo Rose) (1916–2006)

The notorious name "Tokyo Rose" may have already been forgotten by many American people, and perhaps young Americans have never even heard the name of Tokyo Rose. The life story of Tokyo Rose is a true story about Iva Ikuko Toguri d'Aquino, a second-generation Japanese American woman, who was tried and convicted of treason in the United States in 1949. After serving 6 years of incarceration, out of the original sentence of 10 years (with a $10,000 fine), she was paroled in 1956 (Duss, 1979). Since her parole, the name of Tokyo Rose (or Iva) has disappeared from the public. Her name briefly reappeared when she regained her U.S. citizenship back in 1977 (Duss, 1990: 334), and when she passed away on September 26, 2006 (August, Barovick, McDonnough, and Salemme, 2006: 21).

Even though Iva d'Aquino's trial ended over half of the century ago, the question about who Tokyo Rose was (or whether she even existed) remains unanswered. Perhaps the more important question is how and why Iva d'Aquino was tried and convicted of treason when there was no convincing evidence against her. It is ironic that, despite the fact that Iva d'Aquino was loyal to the United States throughout her ordeal and did not consider adopting Japanese nationality while staying in Japan, she received neither a fair trial nor equal protection under U.S. law. Unfair treatment of Iva d'Aquino might have stemmed from the rampant American anti-Japanese prejudice that came out of the Pearl Harbor bombing and World War II; it may be that she was made the scapegoat for a hatred for Japanese people and the Japanese government. In fact, Iva d'Aquino was guilty in American people's minds before her trial began. Because of such harsh treatment, some people equate Iva's trial with a "witch hunt" (Duss, 1990: 150).

Iva d'Aquino was born on July 4, 1916, in Los Angeles, California, as Jun and Fumi Toguri's second-oldest child (Duss, 1979). After d'Aquino graduated from UCLA with a degree in zoology in 1940, she had the opportunity to visit her maternal aunt in Japan. Although she did not have any interest in Japan, she was asked to visit her aunt, who was ill, on behalf of her mother, who could not go because of her own illness. Her original plan was to stay in Japan for a short time and to return home in the spring of 1942. However, when the war between Japan and the United States broke out on December 7, 1941, Iva d'Aquino lost the opportunity to return to the United States, despite her efforts to go back home. Around the same time, the U.S. government ordered Japanese Americans, including d'Aquino's family, to move to relocation camps in various parts of the United States with short notice.

After d'Aquino lost the opportunity to leave Japan, she started working at the Monitoring Division of the Domei News Agency, where she listened to the news about the movements of Allied armies, and also at Radio Tokyo as a typist (Duss, 1990). At Radio Tokyo, d'Aquino was eventually selected as a female voice for the Japanese propaganda show, *Zero Hour*, which intended to make radio listeners (i.e., GIs) feel homesick, that is, "feeling like zero" (Howe, 1990: 234). This program was produced by a prisoner of war (POW)

Mrs. Iva "Tokyo Rose" Toguri d'Aquino is released from a federal women's reformatory in 1956. (Library of Congress)

Charles Cousens (an Australian) and managed by Cousens with two additional POWs, Wallace Ince (an American) and Norman Reyes (a Filipino) (Duss, 1990: 76–83). Her job for *Zero Hour* was to read a script written by Cousens. Later, Iva d'Aquino took the radio name of Orphan Ann at Cousens's suggestion (Duss, 1990: 81–82). Radio listeners initially gave the name Tokyo Rose to any English-speaking Japanese women on *Zero Hour*, and when soldiers were asked at Iva d'Aquino's trial if Tokyo Rose and Orphan Ann were the same people, they could not make the distinction between Tokyo Rose rumors and the Orphan Ann broadcasts (Duss, 1990: 183). Regardless of the origin of Tokyo Rose, soldiers' (mis) identification was one of the reasons that Iva d'Aquino ended up being involved in the Tokyo Rose story.

There were many key players who were implicated in the case of Tokyo Rose. Two reporters, Clark Lee at *International News Service* and Harry Brundidge at *Cosmopolitan*, played powerful roles in finding Tokyo Rose in Japan and identifying Iva d'Aquino as Tokyo Rose (Duss, 1990). They tricked Iva d'Aquino and her husband, Filipe d'Aquino, into signing the agreement that "Iva Ikuko Toguri is the one and original 'Tokyo Rose' who broadcasted from Radio Tokyo" (Duss, 1979: 22). However, the truth was that she was one of the five to six announcers working at Radio Tokyo at the time, and she had never identified herself as Tokyo Rose on the air. However, because the story was publicized in the media, the U.S. government was compelled to investigate the story of Tokyo Rose. Subsequently, Iva d'Aquino was arrested for treason without a warrant for her arrest and imprisoned in Japan for one year.

Although Iva d'Aquino was allowed to leave Japan on September 25, 1948, within one year of her arrival in San Francisco, she was indicted for treason by a grand jury. Her trial started on July 5, 1949 (Duss, 1979). Thomas DeWolfe, who was one of the prosecutors assigned to the Tokyo Rose case, played an important role in convicting d'Aquino. Throughout the trial, DeWolfe suppressed evidence brought by the defense team and ignored the perjury committed by George Naka-moto Mitsushio and Kenkichi Oki, who were Iva d'Aquino's supervisors at Radio Tokyo (Duss, 1979). These two men were Japanese Americans like Iva d'Aquino, but during the war, they denounced their American nationalities and adopted Japa-nese nationalities.

Iva d'Aquino was charged with eight counts of treason but was found guilty of only the sixth count by the jury (Duss, 1990). This sixth count was based on statements made by both Mitsushio and Oki before the grand jury: "On the day during October, 1944, the exact date being to the Grand Jury unknown, said de-fendant, at Tokyo, Japan, in a broadcasting studio of the Broadcasting Corporation of Japan, did speak into a microphone concerning the loss of ship" (Duss, 1979: 134). Originally, the jury had a split vote with three jurors who voted against her conviction. However, when the jury foreman, John Mann, asked Judge Michael Roche to clarify the instruction for the sixth count, Judge Roche was unwilling to clarify, and instead demanded a speedy verdict. Judge Roche's eagerness to end the case quickly influenced the jurors' decisions to vote for a guilty verdict (Kut-ler, 1978: 107).

Iva d'Aquino was convicted of treason because a number of key players orches-trated efforts to convict her regardless of the evidence so that the U.S. government could find someone guilty and demonstrate the symbol of (in)justice to American people. Because of this symbolic gesture, Iva d'Aquino had to endure the label of traitor to her beloved country and was incarcerated for six years. After her six years of imprisonment in U.S. federal prison, d'Aquino was released on January 28, 1956. She then moved to Chicago, where her family owned a store and where she lived until her death in 2006. President Gerald Ford pardoned d'Aquino on January 19, 1977.

Resources

August, Melissa, Harriet Barovick, Kaili McDonnough, and Elisabeth Salemme. 2006. "Died. Iva Toguri D'Aquino, 90." *Time*. October 9, 168: 21.

Duss, Masayo. 1979. *Tokyo Rose*. New York: Kodansha International.

Duss, Masayo. 1990. *Tokyo Rose* (new edition). Tokyo: Bungei Shunjyu.

Federal Bureau of Investigation. "Iva Toguri d'Aquino and "Tokyo Rose." Famous Cases and Criminals. http://www.fbi.gov/about-us/history/famous-cases/tokyo-rose.

Howe, Russell W. 1990. *The Hunt for "Tokyo Rose."* Lanham, NY: Madison Books.

Kutler, Stanley, I. 1978. The "Tokyo Rose" Case and Bureaucratic Administration of Justice ("Tokyo Rose" to Kanryotekishiho). *Jurist* 674: 101–107.

Yoko Baba, George Kikuchi, and Yumiko Watanuki

Laurie Dann (ca. 1958–1988)

In 1988 Laurie Dann walked into a school and opened fire in a classroom in a suburb of Chicago, Illinois. She killed one eight-year-old child and wounded five other children and an adult male. She committed suicide before she could be apprehended. In 1990, three reporters chronicled this story in a book *Murder of Innocence*, which later became the basis of a movie by the same name in 1993. She remains one of the few examples of female mass murderers in the United States and around the world.

Born to an accountant and his wife, Norman and Edith Wasserman, around 1958, Laurie Wasserman grew up in Glencoe, an affluent suburb of Chicago. She was described as a shy and withdrawn person by many. Laurie was married to Russell Dann, an insurance broker, on September 11, 1982. In 1985, Laurie Dann became known to Illinois police after a series of disputes with her husband. Their relationship ultimately ended in separation in 1986. Later, Russell survived being stabbed in the chest with an ice pick while he slept, missing his heart by an inch. There was not enough evidence to prosecute Laurie. She accumulated two charges: a misdemeanor offense after harassing her in-laws by phone and a shoplifting charge.

Laurie had a history of exhibiting odd behavior, such as spending hours riding the elevator in her high rise. She lived on various college campuses, passing herself off as a student, but never actually enrolled in any classes. In the years preceding the shootings, Dann had purchased three guns. In May, 1986, Dann purchased a high-powered Smith and Wesson .357 Magnum. In November, 1987, she purchased a second .32 caliber gun from the same maker. On

Laurie Dann, shown in this 1988 photo, shot six children at a Winnetka, Illinois, elementary school and then killed herself. The school shooting spree left one child dead and five youngsters wounded. (AP/Wide World Photos)

December 29, 1987, she bought a .22 caliber, semi-automatic Beretta. Just prior to the shootings, the family she had been baby-sitting for had informed Dann that they would be moving to New York. She had also started to threaten an ex-boyfriend with death threats which were being investigated by the FBI.

On the morning of the shootings, Laurie attempted to burn down a daycare center but was unsuccessful. She presented poisonous orange drinks to six family homes where she had been employed. Days previous, she made and delivered crispy rice treats to two Northwestern University fraternity houses and to workers in a graduate school building. She had also mailed as many as 24 packages of food products to various recipients in three states, including her ex-husband and her former psychiatrist; these packages were received days after her death.

At approximately 10:30 AM on May 20, 1988, Dann walked into Hubbard Woods Elementary School in Winnetka. She shot a boy of six in the chest, then proceeded to a second-grade classroom and shot five other children, ages 7–9, one of whom, Nicholas Corwin, age 8, died. She then fled the school, but when her car hit a boulder, she left her car and entered the residence of Phil Andrew, also in Winnetka. At first she claimed to have been raped but then she eventually shot Phil Andrew, a 20-year-old college student, and then committed suicide.

After her death it was uncovered that she had stopped seeing her psychiatrist almost two months prior and was taking both lithium carbonate and an experimental drug, Anafranil. Her psychiatrist admitted that after she had stopped coming to appointments, he had begun commitment proceedings, but there was insufficient evidence at the time to support his petition. After the shootings, he disclosed that no one had told him about the guns she had purchased until after her rampage.

Much of the media attention that followed the shootings was focused on her parents' protective behavior of their daughter. Critics argued that they should have been more forthcoming about their daughter's behavior to authorities. Her father acknowledged that he had tried to get her to voluntarily commit herself. Several lawsuits were launch against them, claiming the parents were negligent. These suits are significant in that they raised the question of accountability of parents of adult children who engage in criminal activity.

Most mass murders of this kind are typically committed by males, often acting alone. Dann does share in common many of the features of these lone gunmen, including that she had a perceived catastrophic loss (the family she was caring for was leaving thereby leaving her out of a job and without a support network), she was a loner, and she suffered through bouts of depression for which she was supposed to be taking medication. These conditions resulted in a "breaking point" in which she took her aggressions out on the students of a nearby elementary school and in a university, after which she took her own life. Why she chose these targets as an outlet for her aggression is unclear, as she left no suicide note to explain her actions. What is clear is that she clearly had interest in being at post-secondary educational institutions, as evidenced by her choices of places to live, but she had been unable to be an integral part of this culture as she did not enroll.

Additionally, these shootings re-opened several debates in Illinois including one on gun control and another on institutionalizing the mentally ill against their will. Many agreed that Laurie Dann "fell through the cracks" of the system given her gun purchases and her odd and threatening behavior. Laurie Dann's is one of the few examples of a female mass murderer who used a handgun to kill her victims.

Resources

Black, Lisa, and Bonnie Miller Rubin. 2008. "Old hurts, new lives emerge two decades after Dann shootings." May 20. *Chicago Tribune*. Accessed August 15, 2010, from http://articles.chicagotribune.com/2008–05–20/news/0805190613_1_hubbard-woods-school-laurie-dann-amy-moses.

Kaplan, J., G. Papjohn, and E. Zorn. 1990. *Murder of Innocence: The Tragic Life and Final Rampage of Laurie Dann, "The Schoolhouse Killer."* New York: Warner Books.

Hannah Scott

Angela Davis (1944–)

Angela Yvonne Davis is an internationally known African American feminist educator, activist, organizer, and philosopher. For 40 years, she has been a leading advocate for civil rights and an active organizer against all forms of oppression in the United States and globally. Davis gained notoriety in 1970, when she was the third woman to be placed on the FBI's Most Wanted list after being charged with conspiracy, kidnapping, and murder in a Marin County, California, courthouse incident. After being acquitted of all charges, she remained an anti-prison activist and is currently a professor at the University of California at Santa Cruz.

Davis was born into a Birmingham, Alabama, middle-class family on January 26, 1944. Both her parents were college educated. Her mother was a teacher; her father owned and operated a service station. Living in the Jim Crow South, Davis experienced segregation in all areas of her life. When she was four years old, her family moved from a government housing project to what had previously been an all-white neighborhood that was experiencing white flight and terrorist bombings against its black residents.

Davis attended segregated schools until she was selected for an American Friends Service Committee program that sent her to a New York City high school when she was 14 years old. The Little Red Schoolhouse in Greenwich Village was a small, private, integrated school that had a progressive educational program. Being exposed to the ideas of socialism and communism, Davis became

Civil rights activist and communist Angela Davis addresses the press at the University of California, Berkeley, where she received a standing ovation following her first class, in 1969. University regents had banned her employment, but she had support from the school's chancellor and faculty. (AP Photo/David F. Smith)

involved in a Communist Party youth organization, Advance, which was active in the civil rights movement.

In 1961, Davis received a full scholarship to Brandeis University. After her first year, she attended the World Festival of Youth and Students in Helsinki, Finland, where she met revolutionary youth from around the world, including Cuba. That experience changed her life. She decided to major in French and spent her junior year studying in France. In 1965 she graduated magna cum laude as a member of Phi Beta Kappa and then attended the University of Frankfurt to study philosophy.

During her time in Germany, Davis felt isolated from the growing Black Power movement in the United States. To be more connected, she transferred to the University of California at San Diego in 1967, where she became involved with the black movement. While in graduate school, Davis briefly belonged to the Student Non-Violent Coordinating Committee and the Black Panther Party, but she left both organizations because of her Marxist views. In 1968, she joined the Communist Party and the Che-Lumumba Club, a black collective within the Communist Party.

In 1969, Davis began teaching in the philosophy department at the University of California at Los Angeles, but she was not reappointed to a second year because of her membership in the Communist Party and her radical political activities. In 1970, she became active in the Soledad Brothers Defense Committee, which supported three black inmates, including George Jackson, who were charged with killing a prison guard in Soledad Prison. In an effort to free the Soledad Brothers, Davis spoke to community organizations, attended court hearings, demonstrated against the California Department of Corrections, and raised money for their defense.

On August 7, 1970, George Jackson's brother, Jonathan, used a shotgun that was legally registered to Davis in an attempt to free three San Quentin prisoners who were on trial in the Marin County courthouse. The courtroom takeover also intended to publicize the plight of all political prisoners in the United States. During the failed escape attempt, the trial judge and three people, including Jonathan Jackson, were killed. Davis was charged with conspiracy, murder, and kidnapping, and was placed on the FBI's Ten Most Wanted List. She fled to New York City, where she was arrested two months later and extradited back to California. The National

United Committee to Free Angela Davis organized a worldwide "Free Angela" movement to raise money for her defense. Davis was released on bail in February 1972, and on June 4, 1972, an all-white jury acquitted her of all the charges.

Shortly after her trial, Davis harnessed the momentum of her defense committee and cofounded the National Alliance Against Racism and Political Repression. She also began teaching at San Francisco State University (1979–1991).

During the 1980s, Davis was a member of the National Committee of the Communist Party. She ran for United States vice president on the Communist Party ticket in 1980 and 1984. Although Davis is no longer a member of the Communist Party, she still considers herself a communist.

Davis is currently on the advisory board of the Committees for Correspondence for Democracy and Socialism, which was formed by former Communist Party members in the early 1990s. She also serves on the board of directors for both the National Alliance Against Racist and Political Repression, which she cochaired from 1973 to 1993, and the National Black Women's Health Project. As a member of the advisory board of the Prison Activist Resource Center and Critical Resistance, an international movement to end the prison industrial complex, Davis continues to actively work for prison rights and the freedom of political prisoners, including Mumia Abu-Jamal; Puerto Rican political prisoners such as Dylcia Pagan; and Leonard Peltier.

Davis has been teaching in the history of consciousness department at the University of California at Santa Cruz since 1992 and lectures worldwide on Marxist theory, racism and sexism in the criminal justice system, the prison industrial complex, and the abolition of all prisons. She is the author of several books including *Blues Legacies and Black Feminism*; *Women, Culture, and Politics*; *Women, Race, and Class*; *Abolition Democracy: Prisons, Democracy, and Empire*; and *Are Prisons Obsolete?*

Resources

Davis, A. (1988). *Angela Davis: An Autobiography.* New York: International Publishers.

Davis, A. (2003). *Are Prisons Obsolete?* New York: Seven Stories Press.

James, J., ed. (1999). *The Angela Y. Davis Reader.* Oxford and Cambridge, MA: Blackwell.

Jo-Ann Della Giustina

Phoolan Devi (1957–2001)

Named after a flower and later called a goddess, Phoolan Devi was labeled the Bandit Queen of India at age 24 when she was charged with 48 major criminal offenses including kidnapping-for-ransom and raiding of villages. In particular, she was

Bandit Queen Phoolan Devi displays her old photograph to media persons at her residence in New Delhi, 1997. Phoolan had gone underground for a while after a court ordered her arrest for her alleged role in the Behmai Massacre case where she allegedly gunned down 20 upper-caste men to avenge her rape. (AP/Wide World Photos)

charged with murdering 22 high-caste Hindu men (the upper class in Hindu society) in Behmai just south of New Delhi, the capital of India. This is the true foundation of Phoolan Devi's significance. In the history of Indian banditry, a low-caste woman had never been accused of killing so many high-caste men. Her crimes created social and even political reactions when the family members and the supporters of her victims held protests near governmental places calling for justice. She was on the run from the police officials of three different states for a year. At many occasions she eluded capture while many were killed in their pursuit of her and her gang of seven men.

Born in a small village named Gorha Ka Purwa, in Uttar Pradesh, and raised in a mud house that had a roof made of straw, Phoolan spent her childhood wondering why her family never had enough to eat. She was the second of four children, three girls and a boy. Her father had spent his life savings on fighting a case to regain his inheritance, which had been stolen by his brother. According to her autobiography, Phoolan was strong; she could run faster and carry heavier things than the other girls; and she believed she got her strength from her anger. Married at age 11 to a widower, she was mistreated and raped by her husband, who was three times her age.

In the late 1970s, Phoolan was abducted by a gang of outlaws. The gang leader had abducted her, wanting to rape her, but the deputy leader of the gang, Vikram, was from the same caste as Phoolan and protected her. In the end, Vikram was forced to kill the leader and take over control of the gang. Under his control, they raided the village where Phoolan's abusive husband lived, and after stabbing him, she dragged him and displayed his suffering to the other villagers. Once this was done, the gang left him to die with a note warning against older men marrying young girls.

As time passed, Vikram and Phoolan were attacked due to growing tensions within the gang. Vikram was killed, and Phoolan was abducted by another group of men from Behmai village, where she was raped multiple times by Thakurs, high-caste men. She eventually escaped, and on February 14, 1981, she and her gang, dressed as police officers, returned to the village and shot all of the Thakur men in the village after her gang failed to produce all of her kidnappers and assaulters.

After the massacre, the government of India decided to make Phoolan an offer for her surrender in 1983. She agreed to surrender only if the government officials met her conditions. Her conditions included that she surrender her arms only before Mahatma Gandhi and Goddess Durga and not before the police. (In Hinduism, Durga is a warrior goddess who embodies feminine energy and fights demons.)

She also made the government agree to not sentence her to death and to give her brother a job in the Indian government. Additionally, she asked for a plot of land for her father and that her entire family should be escorted to the event of her surrender. Lastly, she had negotiated for all of her charges to be dropped. While she succeeded in her demands, the charges were eventually revived against her in Uttar Pradesh in 1997 despite being assured that all cases against her would be dropped at her surrender. Phoolan Devi was jailed for 11 years and released on parole in 1994.

After being released, she started Eklavya Sena, a group that taught self-defense to lower caste people. During this time, she also married Umaid Singh, a New Delhi business contractor. In 1996, Phoolan Devi ran for a seat in the parliament as a Samajwadi Party candidate and was successfully elected as a member of parliament. On July 25, 2001, Phoolan Devi was shot and killed as she was getting out of her car in front of her home in New Delhi. Her attackers escaped. The murderers have since been identified as Sher Singh Rana, Dheeraj Rana, and Rajbir. Sher Singh Rana later surrendered and confessed to the murder, which he claimed was revenge for the deaths of 22 Thakurs at Behmai.

There have been various works on the representation of Phoolan Devi's life, as she herself was illiterate. The biographical works on Phoolan Devi that have been published portray the phenomenal interest that the "bandit queen" generated in Western imagination. The first was written by Richard Shears and Isobelle Giddy: *Devi: The Bandit Queen* (1984). Several years later another attempt was made to document the life of Phoolan in Mala Sen's *The Bandit Queen: The True Story of Phoolan Devi* (1991). Another genre in which Phoolan Devi's story was captured was a film called *Bandit Queen*, directed by Shekhar Kapoor (1994), based on Mala Sen's book. Some have criticized the film for its sensational and oversexualized depiction of Phoolan's story. For instance, Madhu Kishwar (1994) criticizes the director of the film for "making it a formula-ridden Rape-Revenge story thus robbing [Phoolan's] life of all its richness and complexity" (35). In fact, Phoolan Devi herself also made an attempt to prevent the film from being released due to its violation of sexual privacy. The latest addition to the list of tributes to the legend is the autobiographical recounting *I Phoolan Devi, The Autobiography of India's Bandit Queen*, compiled by Marie-Therese Cuny and Paul Rambali, based on recordings of Phoolan's own recounting of her story (the recordings were later transcribed). Feminists have discussed the authenticity of representations of Phoolan Devi's life in terms of power relations that play out when there are attempts made to illustrate an illiterate person's life experiences.

Resources

Devi, Phoolan, Cuny, Marie-Therese, and Rambali, Paul. 1997. *I, Phoolan Devi*. London: Warner.

Fernandes, Leela. 1999. Reading "India's Bandit Queen": A Trans/national Feminist Perspective on the Discrepancies of Representation. *Signs* 25 (1): 123–152.

India's Bandit Queen. 1995. A film directed by Shekhar Kapoor.

Kishwar, Madhu. 1994. Film Review. "The Bandit Queen." *Manushi*. 84: 34–37.

Ravi, Srilata. 1999. Marketing Devi: Indian Women in French Imagination. *Journal of Comparative Poetics* (19) 131–150.

Sen, Mala. 1991. *India's Bandit Queen: The True Story of Phoolan Devi*. London: Harvill.

Preeta Saxena

Bernadette Devlin (1947–)

Bernadette Devlin McAliskey became a Northern Irish civil rights activist during the tumultuous 1960s and 1970s. She was born on April 23, 1947, to a Catholic nationalist family in Northern Ireland. While a psychology major at Queen's University, she participated and was arrested in the first Northern Ireland Civil Rights Association marches in 1968 and 1969. Radicalized by the police attacks against demonstrators, she became a leading figure in the student civil rights movement, which challenged discrimination against Catholics and undemocratic voting rules. Devlin helped to establish the radical People's Democracy group, a student organization that lobbied for fair elections, freedom of speech and assembly, fair allocation of houses and jobs, and repeal of the Special Powers Act, which authorized the internment of Northern Irish freedom fighters.

In 1969, at the age of 21, Devlin was the youngest woman to ever be elected to the British Parliament. While she had sympathies to the Irish Republican Army, she remained nonpartisan in her pursuit of unity among the Irish people. Her radical leftist anti-imperialist program argued for a socialist workers' republic that would end all repressive laws against the poor, workers, and small farmers.

In August 1969, Devlin participated in a demonstration by Catholic youth protesting the British occupation of Northern Ireland. The incident had been sparked by the police spraying the Catholic neighborhood in Derry with riot gas. Activists responded by setting up barricades and using petrol bombs to beat them back. Devlin was in the frontline of the resistance, which marked the beginning of 30 years of armed resistance to the British occupation of Northern Ireland. She was arrested and charged with inciting a riot. She served four months of a six-month jail term in Armagh Gaol; her arrest sparked street rioting in two Northern Ireland cities.

In 1971, Devlin announced that she was pregnant and unmarried, and she was determined to have her baby despite her decision being controversial in her conservative Catholic district. Although she later married the baby's father, Michael McAliskey, she never regained her status in the community.

Devlin was addressing protesters in Derry on January 31, 1972, when the British army's paratroop regiment opened fire, killing 13 civilians. After this Bloody Sunday and an ensuing demonstration, she punched the Tory Home Secretary Reginald Maudling in the House of Commons and accused him of being responsible for the death of the civil rights marchers.

Photo of former member of parliament Bernadette McAliskey (née Devlin) when she was 21 years old, in 1969. (AP/Wide World Photos)

The British assumed direct rule over Northern Ireland in March 1972, and Devlin became a passionate opponent of the British occupation of Northern Ireland.

After Devlin lost her bid for reelection in 1974, she co-founded the Irish Republican Socialist Party (IRSP), whose founding members were primarily former members of Sein Féin, the political wing of the Irish Republican Army. Their philosophy followed that of James Connolly, an Irish Marxist who was executed for his role in the Easter Rising of 1916. He had maintained that the struggle for national liberation is inseparable from the fight for socialism in Ireland. Devlin split from the IRSP in 1975 because of the militarism of its paramilitary wing, the Irish National Liberation Army.

Nevertheless, Devlin continued to support Irish republican causes, including the plight of political prisoners in Ireland. During the 1980–1981 Irish Hunger Strike, she was a member of the National Executive Committee of the National Armagh/H-Block Committee. In January 1981, she and her husband survived an assassination attempt when Loyalist paramilitary gunmen burst into their farmhouse near Belfast and shot them.

Devlin remains active in the struggle for civil liberties and freedom in Northern Ireland and for human rights issues worldwide. She is a leading critic of the Good Friday Agreement (also known as the Belfast Agreement), which is a peace document signed in 1998 by the British and Irish governments. The accord calls for the creation of an elected assembly and an executive committee comprised of both nationalists and unionists. The agreement was ratified by 94 percent of voters in Ireland and 71 percent in Northern Ireland.

In 2003, Devlin was seized at Chicago's O'Hare airport, where she was en route from Dublin to New York for a short vacation. Despite her attempts to convince the U.S. Immigration and Naturalization Service that she was not a terrorist, she was deported to Northern Ireland.

Resources

Coogan, P. (2002). *The IRA*. New York: Palgrave Books.

Devlin McAliskey, B. (1969). *The Price of My Soul*. New York: Random House.

Irish Republican Socialist Party. "Irish Republican Socialist Movement: 20 Years of Struggle." http://irsp.ie/Background/history/irsm20yrs.html

Jo-Ann Della Giustina

Dhanu (1974–1991)

Dhanu (Thenmuli Rajaratnam) was a beautiful young Sir Lankan woman who was also the first suicide bomber to use a suicide belt during a terrorist attack. She had many aliases including Anbu, Kalaivani, and her most famous alter ego, Dhanu. She assassinated India's Prime Minister Rajiv Gandhi, the highest-ranking political leader ever killed by a suicide bomber.

Rajaratnam was from a small town called Jaffna in Sri Lanka. During her youth, she was gang raped by the Indian Peace keeping Force (IPKF), and her four brothers were reportedly killed by the Indian military during a raid of her village (Cragin and Daly, 2009). Contrary to the stereotype of a suicide bomber, she did not come from an impoverished family nor was she highly impulsive or mentally unstable. In addition, she was not brought up with a rigorous religious fundamentalist education that typically serves religion as an underlying motivation for suicide terrorism.

Women who have experienced unfortunate social circumstances are more likely candidates for recruitment by terrorist insurgents as an option for justification. Most Sri Lankan women play maternal and supportive roles within their families. Within the Tamil community, unmarried young women normally live under the supervision of the father and/or brother(s) until they are married (Jayasena, 2009). Young women's lives are restricted to the private sphere, and they have limited freedom to pursue their personal goals in a hegemonic society (Balasingham, 1993). Nonetheless, according to the Hindu faith, being a victim of rape makes a woman an outcast and, therefore, tarnishes her social status in the Tamil community. "The main belief of the Tamil women fighters is that their participation in armed struggle will bring them advantages in the future, in a society at peace" (Schalk, 1994: 163).

Tamil women were recruited by indoctrinating them with the ideology that they have a chance to create a new society that would allow women to live their lives with equal human rights, self-respect, and honor (Balasingham, 1993). For instance, "[the] LTTE woman combatant is transformed into a public figure engaged in 'masculine' activities and repudiating patriarchal norms of womanhood" (Del Mel, 2001: 206). They were told that they will be liberated from the structures of oppression embedded in their society. Since many of these women were not satisfied with the social status quo, Rajaratnam may have been easily persuaded to join the national conflict based on gender-related motivations. According to Herath, "ethnic sentiments of the violation of female honour take precedence in public discourse, within which women are reconstructed as craving vengeance for the disgrace they suffered" (2006: 3). In this specific case, although the exact motive behind the crime is unclear, Rajaratnam's motivations for the attack may have been a combination of factors such as to proclaim equal social status, regain purity, and reclaim the honor for herself as well as for her family.

Her outward appearance showed a typical young woman but the only thing that separated her from the average girl was her affiliation as a female suicide bomber in the terrorist group Liberation Tigers of Tamil Eelam (LTTE) (also known as the Tamil Tigers). She was reported to have nerves of steel and a soldier-like mentality. She was a member of the LTTE since the mid-1980s and had gone through the selection and training as a suicide bomber since the late 1980s in the female suicide bomber division, which is also known as the Black Tigresses or Suthanthirap Paravaikal (The Freedom Birds).

She killed herself and 16 others when she attacked Rajiv Gandhi, India's chief political figure in 1991. With a strap of grenades hidden underneath her gown, she presented a flower garland to Gandhi at a political campaign in Tamil Nadu, India. According to accomplices, she was the designated assassin who was sent to Madras, the largest city in the southern Tamil Nadu region of India, where Rajiv Gandhi was scheduled to address crowds at a major political campaign.

Her trip to Madras was the first time that she had ever travelled beyond the jungles of Jaffna, Sri Lanka. She was provided with money and support from the LTTE to achieve her mission. Three weeks before the actual attack, she, with the help of handlers, prepared and rehearsed the mission. Her support group consisted of a squad of three other individuals that was sent by the LTTE. Besides this preparation, she took an advantage of her short stay in Madras by enjoying life like a tourist. In the last 20 days of her life, she went to the market, the beach, and local restaurants; she even went to see six movies at a local cinema. She bought herself jewelry, new dresses, cosmetics, and her first pair of glasses.

On May 21, 1991, she was dressed in a beautiful long dress for her presentation of the garland to the target. Beneath the dress was a belt which was three inches wide, made from denim and leather, with a Velcro closure. Inside were grenades that had been inserted to lie diagonally along the backbone. In addition to the explosives in her lower back area, there was a power pack and a manual switch for detonation. The explosives were composed of 10,000 steel balls, approximately 2 mm in diameter known as RDX or Research Department Explosive, which are widely used in the military. As she waited for Gandhi, she was smiling with a garland in her hands. The moment before garlanding Gandhi, she "accidently" dropped the garland at his feet, touched his feet, bent over, and manually pulled the switch to detonate the bomb at the exact moment when Gandhi and she would receive the full force of the explosion.

According to the investigators, two members of the LTTE were at the attack site with her. They were present to guarantee that she reached her target. The third squad member served as the cameraman who was recoding live footage of the attack as the bomb exploded. The cameraman man was too close the explosion and was killed. The tapes were later discovered by Indian police investigators, and this evidence was later used to clarify the assassination plot.

For Rajaratnam, the assassination of Rajiv Gandhi may have been considered a personal victory. The motivation for the crime came from the damage that was done to her and her loved ones by the Indian troops. It is widely believed that Dhanu's possible motivation was vengeance or revenge for the rape and killings of family troops that were sent to Sri Lanka by Gandhi. Having been raped at the hands of the Indian soldiers had attacked stigma to her (and destroyed her prospect of marriage). Terrorism may have been the only way to remove that stigma.

Even though Dhanu was not alive for the sentencing, seven years after the attack, an Indian court convicted 26 individuals for the conspiracy to assassinate Gandhi. To this day she is viewed as a hero to the Tamil women of Sri Lanka and an example for other Freedom Birds of LTTE.

Dhanu did not commit this act unknowingly. She was aware of the penalty of her actions, and she still conducted her mission to its bloody end. According to Ana Cutter, the former editor of Columbia University's *Journal of International Affairs*, "Acting as a human bomb, is an understood and accepted offering for a woman who will never be a mother" (in Pape 2005, 230). Dhanu's life story is still been used among the Tamils in the jungles of Jaffna to recruit new members. She is also remembered in the larger social context—she is honored at the national hero's day ceremony of the LTTE martyrs.

Resources

Balasingham, Adele. 1993. *Women Fighters of Liberation Tigers*. Jaffna, SL: LTTE Publications.

Cragin, Kim, and Sara A. Daly. 2009. *Women as Terrorists: Mothers, Recruiters, and Martyrs*. Santa Barbara, CA: Praeger Publications.

De Mel, Neloufer. 2001. *Women and the Nation's Narrative: Gender and Nationalism in the Twentieth Century.* Lanham, MD: Rowman and Littlefield.

Herath, Tamara. 2006. *Women's Global Connection Conference Proceedings, 2006.* London School of Economics and Political Science. 1–6 http://wgc.womensglobalconnection.org/conf06proceedings/Herath, T%20In%20My%20Honor.pdf

Jayasena, Karunya. 2009. *Motivations of Female Suicide Bombers from a Sociological Perpsective.* Unpublished Master's thesis. Department of Sociology, California State University, Northridge.

The Ministry of Defense Sri Lanka. 2006. *The Untold Story of Rajiv Gandhi's Assassination.* Colombo, Sri Lanka: National Public Security Law and Order.

The Office of Law Enforcement and Federal Air Marshal Service (FAMS) Special Report. 2011. "Female Suicide Bombers." *Transportation Security Administration* (TSA), 1–91. http://info.publicintelligence.net/TSA-FemaleSuicideBombers.pdf.

Pape, Robert. 2005. *Dying to Win.* New York: Random House.

Rao, Rama. 2006. LTTE admits killing Rajiv Gandhi, apologizes to India. *Asian Tribune,* June, 1–2.

Schalk, P. 1994. "Women Fighters of the Liberation Tigers in Tamil Ilam: The Martial Feminism of Atel Palacinkam." *South Asia,* 14: 163–195.

Karunya Jayasena

Nannie Doss (1905–1965)

Nannie Doss is a female serial murder who confessed to killing four husbands and is suspected of killing five other family members using arsenic placed in prunes and, in some cases, asphyxiation. It is also suspected that she killed her second and third child by her first husband as well as asphyxiating several other family members. Nannie suffered from headaches all of her life, which she blamed on a head injury received as a child while on a train after it suddenly stopped.

Nancy Hazel was born on November 4, 1905, into the poor farming family of Loulisa ("Lou") and James Hazel in Blue Mountain, Alabama. She was the oldest of four sisters and one brother, although there is some evidence to suggest that Nancy was born before Lou and James married. Early on, she developed both her nickname, Nannie, and a penchant for romance magazines. James was rumored to be strict and physically abusive, and he worked all the children in the fields, often taking them out of school. In 1921, at the age of 16, she met and married Charley Braggs. Her new mother-in-law would prove to be as dominating as the family she left. She had four daughters in four years, starting in 1923. Both Nannie and Charley engaged in extramarital affairs. In 1927, the Braggs family lost two middle children within weeks of each other. Charley took the oldest, Melvina, and left, returning a year later with a new girlfriend and another child. Nannie took back Melvina, and Nannie, along with Melvina and the youngest, Florine, left Blue Mountain, to move in with Nannie's parents in Anniston, Alabama where Nannie worked in cotton mill.

She married Frank Harrelson in 1929. Although handsome, and initially romantic, Frank was an alcoholic. He became abusive, but she stayed married to him for 16 years. Early in 1945, Melvina became pregnant with her second child, asking Nannie to care for her. Although Melvina's daughter was born, it survived one hour. Melvina recalls having a dream of seeing her mother press a hat pin, which others commented she had been playing with previously, into the baby's head. Melvina's other son died six months later while under Nannie's care, on July 7, 1945, diagnosed with "asphyxia" from unknown causes. Nannie had insured the child for $500. A short time after September 16, 1945, when after a night of drinking Frank insisted on having sex, Nannie spiked his liquor bottle with arsenic, and he died at age 38, over the course of that evening.

Two years later, she moved to Lexington, Kentucky, to meet and marry Arlie Lanning after a long letter writing courtship. He too drank and had affairs. Her response was to leave for days on end, but then they would reconcile. The town sympathized with her martyr status, given Arlie's actions. Arlie died after two days in pain in February 1950. On April 21, 1950, after realizing that Arlie had left the entire estate to his sister, she was seen leaving the house with her television shortly before the house exploded and burned to the ground. The insurance check was made out to the estate, the executor of which was Nannie.

In 1952, she married Richard L. Morton, whom she met through another "Lonely Hearts" column. They moved to Okmulgee, Kansas. All was good, until Nannie's mother came to visit in January 1953. She fell ill with stomach pains and died within days of her arrival. Richard died in May of similar symptoms. On July 13 of that same year, she married Samuel Doss, age 58, in Tulsa, Oklahoma. He was a miser, did not like noise or magazines, often turning off the television and not allowing Nannie's favorite reading material in the house. He died October 6, 1953, after signing all his assets over to his wife. The doctor who was treating Samuel became suspicious, having released him a few days earlier with a clean bill of health. He ordered an autopsy which would indicate lethal levels of arsenic in his system. In November 1954, Nannie Doss was interrogated by police, eventually confessing to killing four of her husbands but not to killing any other family members. The court trial was centered on the murder of her husband Samuel. She was convicted and sentenced to life in prison, dying there of cancer in 1965.

The motivation for these crimes is somewhat unclear. Doss states that she was always looking for the perfect husband. She simply did not find the right one: two were drunks, two were physically abusive, three were adulterers, and the last was too restrictive. Nannie would also leave on prolonged trips, and it is suggested that she was also adulterous. Doss also operated in a time when divorce was difficult, thereby permitting few options to women in unhappy marriages. Further, Nannie Doss may have also been partially motivated by finances, although it is suspected that she did not profit enough to make a living off her crimes. Doss did insure many of her victims or had assets signed over to her before they died.

The Doss case impacted police practice and legislation. Her nurturing persona and "motherly" nature allowed many of her murderous actions to go unnoticed. There were at least nine suspicious deaths before a doctor took notice and began to investigate. After her conviction, the case inspired work toward laws that mandated autopsies for all suspicious deaths. It was acknowledged that had this case been forced into investigation earlier in the process, lives could have been saved. It has also been suggested that she was spared the death penalty in Oklahoma because of her gender, as she was allowed to plea bargain on Samuel's murder. Finally, although this woman clearly had killed several innocent victims, she was not acknowledged in writings about serial murders until the early 1990s. Before this time, she was merely labeled as a so-called Black Widow killer, a term given to women who killed husbands, lovers, and often other family members. Her case, and others like it, illustrate the power of gender in the criminalizing of female deviance. In the past, women like Doss were rarely labeled serial killers. It wasn't until a few authors and academicians began pointing to the body counts of killers like Doss that that changed.

Resource

Manners, Terry. 1995. "Nannie Doss." In Terry Manners (ed.), *Deadlier Than a Male: Stories of Female Serial Killers*, 68–103. London: Pan.

Geringer, Joseph. "Nannie Doss: Lonely Hearts Lady Loved Her Man to Death." Notorious Murders: Women Who Kill." TruTV Crime Library. http://www.trutv.com/library/crime/notorious_murders/women/doss/1.html.

Hannah Scott

Melissa Drexler (1978–)

On June 6, 1997, in Lacey Township, New Jersey, Melissa Drexler committed a shocking crime. At age 18, she strangled or suffocated her healthy baby boy and placed him into the bathroom trash receptacle at the restaurant where she was attending her high school prom. This crime against the baby, posthumously named Christopher, earned her the title Prom Mom. Her crime is remarkable because it contradicts deep societal beliefs about a mother's instinct.

Neonaticide is the murder of an infant in the first 24 hours of birth and is commonly committed by teenagers and women in their early twenties. Research

Melissa Drexler, center, departs Monmouth County Courthouse with defense co-counsel Donald Venezia and her mother, Marie Drexler, after arraignment in 1997, in New Jersey. Melissa Drexler was charged with the murder of her newborn son during her high school prom. (AP/Wide World Photos)

indicates that adolescent girls who become pregnant often have immature cognitive development because they sometimes take risks without considering the outcomes. Many of these girls possess low self-esteem and have sex after succumbing to peer pressure. They also may lack the ability for more mature responses to an unwanted pregnancy. To exacerbate the problem still further, American society promotes a double standard of sexuality where only women experience stigma for premarital sex, and women more often bear the burden of an accidental pregnancy physically and financially.

Melissa Drexler came from a close-knit, middle-class Catholic family. An only child, she was the pride and joy of her parents. Though Melissa Drexler was not popular, she had a boyfriend for a couple of years and a few female friends. Her friends called her sweet, the kind of person who would do anything for them. Melissa Drexler had plans for a career in the fashion industry and was taking classes at a vocational school with plans to continue her education at a community college. The unique circumstances surrounding Melissa Drexler's accidental pregnancy interrupted her plans.

Women who commit neonaticide rarely have histories of substance abuse and mental illness, and Melissa Drexler was no exception. Premeditation and denial of an unwanted pregnancy are common, however. Drexler was assisted in her denial by the fact that she was thin and did not look pregnant. Drexler told no one about her pregnancy, did not seek prenatal care, and went to the prom even after her water broke that morning. Short labor and deliveries with minimal pain are common in cases of neonaticide; Melissa Drexler remained in the bathroom stall about a half hour while insisting to her concerned girlfriend that she was fine.

Dissociative states also frequently accompany neonaticide, consisting of an out-of-body experience, where the perpetrator does not realize she is committing a crime. Having dealt with the reality of a baby in a dissociative state, Melissa Drexler cleaned up but left blood spattered in the bathroom. She returned to the prom, ate a salad, laughed, and danced with her boyfriend. After authorities asked about the blood left in the bathroom, Melissa continued to state that she was fine; admitting to the reality of giving birth only after the baby was found.

Because family members have kept to themselves and provided no information to the media, the exact reasons for Melissa Drexler's denial and isolation are not clear, and court transcripts have not been made public record, either. However, psychological reports reveal that Drexler thought being pregnant out of wedlock was a serious and shameful problem that she wanted to hide. One can speculate further that because Catholic doctrine prohibits premarital sex and abortion, Drexler did not want to disappoint her parents, and the pregnancy would interfere with her career plans.

No statute in the United States exists for neonaticide per se, and charges in such cases have ranged from a misdemeanor for unlawful disposal of a body to first-degree murder. Sentences can vary from probation and therapy to life in prison, depending on the charge. Light sentences are sometimes given when forensic evidence fails to verify that the baby was born alive. The oxygen found in Christopher was either due to his taking a breath or attempts at his revival, but authorities proved strangulation or suffocation. Drexler originally pleaded not guilty while her lawyer spoke of her dissociative disorder and denial in an attempt to get a lighter sentence. However, neither "neonaticide syndrome" nor "neonaticide dissociative disorder" is widely accepted in the psychiatric community, and therefore sentencing does not necessarily take into account the exceptional circumstances surrounding neonaticide.

Drexler's plea bargaining avoided a possible minimum sentence of 30 years for murder and child endangerment. The judge in the case said her crime was not excusable, even though it was explainable. He believed the court had to send a message to prevent other women from killing their newborns, convicting Drexler of aggravated manslaughter and gave her the maximum prison sentence of 15 years for the crime. She was paroled after serving 37 months as a model prisoner.

Because of the special psychological state of women who commit neonaticide, and because few women are repeat offenders, some claim that deterrence is not accomplished by prison sentences, which have no purpose but to punish. These women would benefit the most by therapy, but it is seldom part of sentencing and, when given, is inadequate. Some experts believe that solutions aimed at producing confident young women with the resources to make mature decisions ought to occur in the family, at school, and in the community. Many experts also see value in sex education and pregnancy prevention programs aimed at the adolescent population. In addition to reshaping the socialization processes that contribute to neonaticide, more emphasis might be placed on responses that are more therapeutic. Many states in the United States now have "safe haven" laws that allow mothers and sometimes fathers to anonymously and without fear of criminal charges leave a newborn baby at designated hospitals and clinics.

Resources

Resnick, P. 1970. Murder of the newborn: A psychiatric review of neonaticide. *American Journal of Psychiatry 126*(3), 73–82.

Schwartz, Lita Linzer, and Natalie K. Isser. 2007. *Child Homicide: Parents Who Kill*. Boca Raton, FL: CRC Press.

Spinelli, Margaret G. (ed.) 2003. *Infanticide: Psychosocial and Legal Perspectives on Mothers Who Kill*. Washington, D.C.: American Psychiatric Publishing.

Loretta I. Winters

Eleanor Dumont (1829–1879)

Eleanor Dumont, born Simone Jules, was the first known professional blackjack player in history. Nicknamed "Madame Moustache" later in life, she was known as a highly regarded card dealer in the mining camps and gambling houses of the Pacific coast. She specialized in the game of vingt-et-un (French for 21), which we now call blackjack. Dumont has been described as one of the greatest professional woman gamblers and one of the most colorful. She was rumored to have spoken several languages and was obviously French, but beyond that she was a mystery. Little is known about her early life. She may have run honest betting tables, simply beating her customers as a result of the so-called house edge, but she won more often than she lost. As a result, some believe that Eleanor Dumont may have been a card cheat. It was not unusual for traveling card gamblers of that time to use various methods to cheat their patrons.

Historical accounts of Eleanor Dumont begin in Nevada City, California, in 1854. Early accounts describe that she arrived "one day on the stagecoach, a pretty, fresh-faced, dark-eyed woman, apparently about twenty years of age, and her stylish appearance created much commotion among the rough inhabitants of the town" (Piatt, 2007). French women held a certain fascination to the men of the West, and Eleanor Dumont capitalized on this fascination; however, it is unclear if Dumont was actually born in France or if she was the daughter of Creole parents from New Orleans (Rutter, 2005).

Shortly after arriving in Nevada, she opened up her own gambling establishment. It has been said that this establishment had carpets and crystal chandeliers, and served free champagne. Dumont did not allow any rowdy behavior, cussing, arguments, chewing, or smoking in her establishment. Patrons were instructed to wear jackets, ties, and some sort of hat if they wished to enter and play at Madame Dumont's tables. Historical accounts during this time suggest that she enticed male patrons in the womanless gold-rush camps with her virtue and flaunted chastity.

Dumont's Nevada City prosperity continued until 1855, when eventually the gold ran dry in the mining town. When the Nevada city boom went bust, Madame Dumont followed the gold and silver rushes of the period from one mining camp to another. Some suggest that her mania for gambling and the love of excitement were insatiable and that is why for the next five years she wandered from camp to camp. Others who report her as card cheat suggest that she moved towns each time her trickery and deception were discovered. She moved to Columbia in 1857, to Virginia City in 1859, and then to Pioche in 1861. While in Pioche, Dumont was reported to have fallen in love with Jack McKnight and married him. At this point she gave up her gambling, and they settled down in a ranch in Nevada. McKnight deserted Dumont shortly after they were married, and he disappeared with all of her money.

The extensive traveling, long night hours, liquor, men, and passing years took their toll on Madame Dumont's figure and complexion. It became more difficult for Madame Dumont to attract patrons to her tables. Dumont's looks were fading and the hair above her lip had grown into a prominent mustache, earning her the nickname "Madame Moustache." Under the circumstances, it became more and more difficult to keep her male patrons at arm's length. Dumont began practicing prostitution in order to supplement her dwindling income. It has been reported that Madam Dumont opened a parlor house in San Francisco between the 1860s and mid 1870s.

Dumont's last stop was the boom mining camp of Bodie in Northern California in May 1878. In Bodie, she decided to set up shop once again with an added attraction of prostitution. She opened up two-story combination gambling saloons and parlor houses with prostitutes upstairs. It has been suggested that it was Madame Dumont who led Martha Jane Canary, aka Calamity Jane, into the flesh trade. Dumont struggled to survive in Bodie. On September 8, 1879, Eleanor Dumont's body was found several miles from Bodie alongside the road. She had allegedly committed suicide, evidenced by an empty bottle that smelled of morphine discovered lying next to her body. Some also say she left a note declaring, "I am tired of life."

Eleanor Dumont was never charged with a crime related to card cheating or prostitution; in fact, she was never charged with any crime. Although no real known motive exists for her alleged behavior, many believe that it is never enough for chronic card players to win big just once; there is always the temptation to double their earnings. This is believed to have been the case for Madame Dumont. Although she was an honest card dealer in her early career, it was not long before the joys and benefits of winning may have led her to use dishonest tactics to prevail in her games. Although Dumont was known by some for being a card cheat and stealing naïve gambler's money, she has also given something back to society. Vingt-et-un, the game she made so popular, is today the well-known and famous game of blackjack. In 2006, she was nominated to the Blackjack Hall of Fame in recognition of her success in the game. Although on that occasion she was not selected, her contribution to the history of blackjack still remains notable today.

Resources

Enss, Chris. 2006. *Pistol Packin' Madams*. Guilford, CT: Globe Pequot Press.

Green, Emma. 2003. Biography of Eleanor Dumont. *Lucky Blackjack*. http://www.lucky blackjack.com/eleanore-dumont.html.

Lackmann, Ronald. 1997. *Women of the Western Frontier in Fact, Fiction, and Film*. Jefferson, NC: McFarland Press.

Piatt, Michael H. 2007. The Death of Madame Mustache: Bodie's Most Celebrate Inhabitant. *Bodie History*. http://www.bodiehistory.com/madame.htm.

Rutter, Michael. 2005. *Upstairs Girls: Prostitution in the American West*. Helena, MT: Farcountry Press.

Sexton, Timothy. 2009. Madame Moustache: Hair Today, Gone Tomorrow. *Women Gamblers of the Wild West, Part 2*. http://www.associatedcontent.com.

St. Eleanor Dumont: Evangelist of Blackjack. 2009. *Ladies Betting*. http://www.ladiesbet ting.com/st-eleanor-dumont-evangelist-blackjack.html.

Kathryn A. Branch and Rebecca Csikos

Amelia Dyer (1839–1896)

Amelia Elizabeth Dyer was a female serial murderer, also known as the "Reading Baby Farmer," who killed anywhere from 7 to as many as 50 infants in the United Kingdom over an estimated 20-year period. Dyer took advantage of weak protections for infants born to unwed mothers during the Victorian era. Not much is known about this killer's life before her actions started to come under suspicion when she moved to Reading, England, from Bristol in 1895 with her daughter, son-in-law, and a female associate. What is known is that while in Bristol, she was committed to psychiatric hospitals for insanity twice, thereby suggesting that she had a history of mental illness while she operated the service she has now become so well known for.

Baby farms became useful to women who found themselves pregnant with a child, usually out of wedlock. Often women would offer services to "women in trouble" by offering to care for the child, as would an orphanage, or to offer to find the child a home with parents seeking children. Often the proprietors of such institutions would require a modest fee and baby clothing for the adoption service; the fee was higher if the child would have to have an extended stay. The baby farming industry, however, was unmonitored, and periodically children and infants would not find their way to either care situation. Because the children born to these women were a source of embarrassment and were often the result of sexual relations outside of marriage, social protections for these young clients were minimal. Once these children were given away, they were rarely, if ever, checked upon by the birth mother. The English government, partly due to the laws governing births out of wedlock, refused to monitor such services.

Amelia Dyer took advantage of the lack of regulation regarding unwanted infants and opened her own baby farm, but with much more sinister purposes. She would attract clients to her services by advertising in local papers posing as a childless family looking to adopt or nurse children for a fee and adequate clothing for the child. After receiving payment, Amelia would strangle the infants with white tape, wrap them in brown paper, sometimes place the bodies in a carpet bag, and then throw them in the Thames River. The clothes would be pawned, when possible.

Eventually, a barge man found an infant floating in the river. Examination of the paper revealed a very faint name and address, which would eventually be linked back to Amelia Dyer. Police decided to send a women in, posing as a prospective client in need of adoption services, to gather evidence about the business she was running. Dyer was eventually charged with the death of the infant found in the river, and her son-in-law, Arthur Palmer, was charged as an accomplice. The Thames River was eventually dragged uncovering the bodies of six other infants, all bound in the same way. Examination of her home revealed many baby clothes, pawn tickets, and numerous letters to clients, suggesting that many women had given her their children, although no children were found in the home.

She was tried in May 1896. She pleaded guilty to seven murders. Dyer exonerated her son-in-law and his wife in a written confession in a statement made before she was executed. Although the defense argued that Amelia was insane, citing her previous psychiatric commitments, she was found fit to stand trial. The prosecution effectively argued that the commitments were simply a ploy to give the appearance of insanity. She was hanged on June 10, 1896, at Newgate Prison.

The case of Amelia Dyer, and of other women who acted as so-called baby farmers during the Victoria era, highlighted the inadequacies of the English government in protecting children. Eventually the Infant Life Protection Act (1897) and the Children's Act (1908) were drafted to increase protections afforded to children who were fostered or adopted. These acts also required that authorities be notified about any child, age seven or younger, who had died or changed custody within 48 hours after the event.

The murders of Amelia Dyer highlight the strong effect that gender, coupled with a clientele who was desperate to part with their unwanted children, and a high infant mortality rate, had in Victorian England. Suspicion had grown around Amelia Dyer for years prior to her apprehension, but no one was either interested or concerned enough for the clientele to investigate the allegations surrounding her. Most accepted the explanation of adoption or death by natural causes as reasonable as the alternative would have been to acknowledge that these little clients had no government protection.

Resources

"Baby Farming. A Tragedy of Victorian Times." Capital Punishment in the U.K. http://www.capitalpunishmentuk.org/babyfarm.html

Rattle, Allison, and Allison Vale. *Amelia Dyer, Angel Maker: The Woman who Murdered Babies for Money.* London: Andre Deutsch.

Hannah Scott

Shirin Ebadi (1947–)

Shirin Ebadi, an Iranian lawyer and human rights activist, was accused of conspiracy against the Islamic government officials of Iran. In June 2000, Ebadi was banned from practicing law and was jailed in solitary confinement at Evin. In weeks to follow, Ebadi's imprisonment received tremendous international attention, shedding light on human rights issues in Iran.

Shirin Ebadi was born in an upper middle-class, academic, and Muslim-practicing family in Hamadan, Iran. Ebadi's father was a professor and writer in commercial law while her mother dedicated her time to the upbringing of her four children. Ebadi's family moved to Tehran when she was one year old, and she has lived in Tehran ever since. Ebadi's father was a longtime supporter of Mossadegh, the Iranian prime minister whom, in 1951, was democratically elected to the parliament. In 1953, Mossadegh was forced out of his office through a military coup planned by the CIA and British government. After the overthrow of Mossadegh, Ebadi's father was demoted to a lower-ranking position and never promoted back to his senior level. Thus, political oppression was directly experienced by Ebadi family. However, as Ebadi stated, "The legacy of my father's sidelining was that our house became an irredeemably politics-free zone" (Ebadi and Moaveni, 2007: 13).

Ebadi obtained her doctorate in law from Teheran University at age 24 and held a variety of positions in the Justice Department. In 1975, during the Shah's regime, Ebadi became the chairperson of the Tehran Court and was the first woman in the history of Iranian justice to serve as a judge. Although the Shah's secular government was ruling Iran at that time, Ebadi remarked that Iran was culturally governed by patriarchy.

Following the victory of the Islamic revolution in February 1979, Ebadi and other female judges were dismissed from their posts and were offered clerical duties. According to the fundamentalists' interpretation, Islam forbids that women serve as judges. Ebadi and other female judges protested and soon were given a small promotion to a new position at the Justice Department, titled as "law expert." Ebadi, who could not tolerate the situation any longer, requested for an early retirement and applied for her license to work as a defense attorney. While her early retirement was accepted, her licensing application was turned down because Iran's Bar Association was closed during the government's state of transition.

Consequently, Ebadi became housebound, yet she used her time to write several books about children, women, and refugee rights. Her first book, *The Rights of the Child*, won the first prize at Al-zahra University and was translated to English by UNICEF. During this period, Ebadi also took on an advocacy role, campaigning for changes in law, particularly for women and children; she founded the Association for Support of Children's Rights. She published a number of articles in Iranian journals and became a lecturer at Tehran University. In 1992, Ebadi succeeded in obtaining her license to practice law. Ever since then, Shirin Ebadi has defended many cases, often free of charge. Ebadi's fight on behalf of abused children and women led to reformulation of Islamic law, granting mothers the right for children's custody. However, most

Shirin Ebadi is an Iranian human rights activist and winner of the 2003 Nobel Peace Prize. Ebadi is a Muslim lawyer and judge who campaigns for peaceful and democratic solutions to Iran's social problems. (Nobel Foundation)

of Ebadi's cases are highly controversial political cases. Ebadi represented Dariush Forouhar, an intellectual who was stabbed to death together with his wife at their home in 1998. Along with the attack on the Forouhar family, many other nonconformists were murdered, creating an environment of terror among Iranian dissidents. The responsibility for these murders fell on official hardliners, who were determined to end the more liberal climate that was adopted by Iran's new president, Khatami.

While Ebadi was documenting evidence for Forouhars' murder case, she videotaped Amir Farshad Ebrahimi, one of the perpetrators of violence against several reformers. In this video, Ebrahimi stated that he was following the order of a well-known fundamentalist to attack the reformers. After this confession, Ebrahimi was detained by the judiciary, and while in custody, he recanted his statements claiming that the video was a "forced confession."

In days to follow, Ebadi was attacked by print media that has been in control of the fundamentalists ever since the victory of Islamic revolution. Ebadi along with few other human rights lawyers were accused for blemishing the revolution. On June 28, 2000, Ebadi was brought to Evin, where she was interrogated on a daily basis. Each session began with the judge's sonorous recitation of Koranic verses, followed by hours of circular and repetitive questions.

During her stay at Evin, Ebadi had two preliminary trials. The plaintiffs consisted of members from the extremist right, paramilitaries, and the hard-line press.

During the second preliminary trial, Ebrahimi was put on the stand, and to everyone's surprise, he stayed loyal to his original story that Ebadi had videotaped. At this point, Ebadi's case was covered daily by major international news media, which were putting pressure Islamic fundamentalists to justify Ebadi's arrest. Nonetheless, 25 days after Ebadi passed through the iron gates of Evin, she received a call from her judge that her case was dismissed and she could be released. Ebadi's case not only shed light on the violation of human rights in Iran, it also strengthened the voice of reformists in Iran.

In December 2003, Ebadi was awarded the Nobel Peace Prize for her efforts for human rights and democracy. The Norwegian committee also recognized Ebadi for being a courageous person who has never heeded the threats to her own safety while standing up as a sound professional. Ebadi as an activist is known for using a peaceful approach that promotes democratic solutions. She argues for a new interpretation of Islam that unites the laws of the faith with vital human rights. On many occasions, Ebadi has called herself a feminist who is against patriarchy not Islam.

Now in her sixties, Ebadi has no plans to retire and continues to present politically charged cases that focus on the issue of human rights in Iran. Ebadi lectures at Tehran University regularly and lives with her husband, an electrical engineer. She and her husband have been married for 32 years and have two daughters.

Resources

Astele, C. B. 2007. "Nobel Women Serve As Role Models." *Progressive Christian* 181: 9.

Ebadi, Shirin, and Azadeh Moaveni. 2007. *Iran Awakening: A Memoir of Revolution and Hope.* New York: Random House.

Frangsmyr, Tore. 2004. *Les Prix Nobel.* http://nobelprize.org/nobel_prizes/peace/laureates/2003/index.html.

Hubbard-Brown, Janet. 2007. *Shirin Ebadi: Champion for Human Rights in Iran.* New York: Chelsea House Publication.

Moghadam, Valentine M. 2002. "Islamic Feminism and Its Discontents: Toward a Resolution of the Debate." *Sign* 27: 1135–1171.

Sedghi, Hamideh. 2007. *Women and Politics in Iran: Veiling Unveiling and Prevailing.* New York: Cambridge University Press.

Stiehm, Judith Hicks. 2006. *Champions for Peace: Women Winners of the Nobel Peace Prize*, 6th edition. Lanham, MD: Rowman and Littlefield.

Ladan Dejam

Sarah Edmonds (1841–1898)

Sarah Emma Edmonds served as a nurse, a spy, and a general's aide after enlisting in the Union Army during the Civil War. To avoid being limited by roles typically assigned to women, she masqueraded as a man. All of her young life, she preferred associating with boy companions, including her one brother, who was a disappointment to their father due to his frail build and poor physical health. As the fifth daughter of six children, she was always aware of her father's disappointment that she was not the son he longed for. To try to compensate for being female, Sarah Emma showed interest in fishing, hunting, and horsemanship, all activities that she believed her father wanted from a son.

Emma, as she was called by her family, was born in New Brunswick, Canada, into a family of immigrants from Scotland and Ireland in the early 19th century. Her father, Isaac Edmonds, was from Scotland and her mother, Elizabeth Leeper, from Ireland. The family was Anglican, and Emma remained deeply religious all of her life. She spoke of her faith as the source of her strength, both in yielding to her disapproving father and later during the hardships she endured in military service. She was wiry and hard muscled from farm work, and although small in stature, she handled a horse as well as any of the boys of her acquaintance. Growing up, she often rebelled angrily against restrictions placed on girls. When she reached adolescence, she took a job as a millinery assistant to earn enough money to escape from her father, who had grown abusive to her, and from her mother, who lacked the strength to stand up for her. When she was 16, she disappeared from New Brunswick without a trace, leaving her family and friends to wonder for over a decade what had become of her.

It was when she left home that Emma Edmonds began to pass herself off as a young man. She reasoned that a boy traveling alone would be safer and more readily employable than a girl. She adopted the name of Franklin Thompson and sold Bibles to support herself, first in rural New Brunswick and then in Nova Scotia. Her winning personality made her successful at her enterprise, and after several months, she moved on to Flint, Michigan, where she sold Bibles door-to-door.

When the Civil War broke out, "Franklin Thompson" joined the Flint Union Greys, a volunteer company, and later, became part of Company F, Second Michigan Regiment of Volunteer Infantry. The Regular Army of the United States numbered less than 20,000 soldiers at the time, and volunteers were urgently needed. As a result, no physical examination was required, and Frank Thompson was robust, healthy, and held his own at training camps. Emma was convinced that no one suspected her true gender.

By June 1861, Emma Edmonds was on the front line in Virginia, where her company fought at Blackburn's Ford, the first Bull Run and Peninsular campaigns. She was assigned to deliver mail and tend the wounded, and then she was hired as an aide to a company colonel during the Battle of Fredericksburg. She lived daily with fear that her real identity would be discovered and that she would be court-martialed or put in prison, but no one seemed to suspect that she was a male.

Emma Edmonds's life in the military included serving as a spy behind Confederate lines. These experiences only increased her need to take extra precautions to conceal the fact that she was a woman in order to avoid the jeopardy of what the enemy might do, if they came to realize that she fooled them in more ways than one. On one occasion, she made herself up with black face and a curly black wig to resemble a slave boy. At least one other time, she was "disguised" as a young woman. She wrote later of her dangerous roles: "I am naturally fond of adventure, a little ambitious, and a good deal romantic, and this together with my devotion to the Federal cause and determination to assist to the extent of my ability in crushing the rebellion, made me forget the unpleasant items, and not only endure, but really enjoy, the privations connected with my perilous position" (Dannett, 1960, 125).

In the spring of 1863, Emma Edmonds's regiment was moved to Kentucky, where she became so ill with fever and weakness that she needed medical care. Afraid that hospitalization would unmask her identity, she deserted her company and made her way to Ohio. Now, she had added Army deserter to her list of ways that she could be arrested. Once in Ohio, she resumed her own identity as Emma Edmonds to seek needed medical treatment. It took several weeks for her illness to abate, but as soon as she was able, she began work on a fictionalized version of her army experiences in which she depicted herself as a nurse instead of a soldier. The novel was published when the war ended and eventually sold 175,000 copies. Sarah Emma Edmonds was one of perhaps four hundred women to enlist as men in the Union Army; however, she was the most well-known because of the popularity of her novel (Edmonds, 1865).

Emma Edmonds returned to nursing in 1864 and went to hospitals in battle areas from Harper's Ferry to West Virginia. It was in Harper's Ferry that she met a widower, Linus H. Seelye from New Brunswick, and they began a courtship that ended in marriage when the war was over. They returned to Canada for a few months, but both had a wanderlust that led them back to Ohio, then to Michigan, Illinois, Texas, Louisiana, and Kansas. They lost three young children to illness, finally adopting and raising two boys from an orphanage that Emma ran for a time in Louisiana.

In 1882, Emma Seelye applied for a veteran's pension after soliciting endorsements from men with whom she had served. Letters of recommendation from those who had known the soldier, Frank Thompson, swore on oath that they never questioned her identity as a man or doubted her loyalty and bravery. Their affidavits were presented to Congress, and in 1884, she was placed on the pension roll under the name of Sarah E. E. Seelye, alias Franklin Thompson. Her pension of $12 a month was paid for 14 years until her death. While she was still alive and could enjoy the gesture, she was allowed to join a chapter of the Grand Army of the Republic, the only woman so honored. When she died in 1898, she was buried in La Porte, Texas, but on Memorial Day, 1901, her grave was moved to the Grand Army of the Republic portion of the Washington Cemetery in Houston, Texas.

In 1937, in Fort Scott, Kansas, where the Seelyes lived for 12 years, the townspeople belatedly publicized Emma's war adventures with articles in the local newspapers, complete with pictures of Franklin Thompson. Not only her military exploits with the Union Army hiding her identity as a woman were recounted, but the articles also extolled her lifetime of helping those less fortunate than she by reporting that she was a legend due to her bravery, nobleness, and true character.

Resources

Dannett, Sylvia. 1960. *She Rode With the Generals: But Her Regiment Thought She Was a Man*, Thomas Nelson and Sons, New York.

Edmonds, Sarah Emma. 2006. *Soldier, Nurse and Spy In the Union Army: The Adventures and Experiences of a Woman in Hospitals, Camps, and Battlefields*, W. S. Williams, 1865. Reprinted by Diggory Press, Cornwall, England.

Fort Scott Tribune Monitor. January 17, 1884–January 27, 1884.

Marcia Lasswell

Ruth Ellis (1926–1955)

In July 1955, Ruth Ellis became the last woman to be hanged in England and Wales. Her execution was controversial, and huge crowds gathered to protest outside the jail the night before she was due to be killed. Over 100,000 people had signed a petition requesting that her conviction for murder be reduced to manslaughter, which would have saved her from the gallows, and numerous other petitions demanding a reprieve were gathered. However, the protests were to no avail, and Ellis was the 15th and final woman to be hanged before the death penalty was abolished in England and Wales in 1965. She was 28 years old and the mother of two children.

Ruth Ellis shot her partner, David Blakely, in the back as he was leaving a pub on Easter Monday, 1955. They lived together, although Blakely was engaged to be married to another woman. He also had a number of other relationships while he was with Ellis, which had made her intensely jealous. He was a heavy drinker and was physically violent

Ruth Ellis, sentenced to death for the shooting death of racing driver David Blakely in 1955. (AP/Wide World Photos)

toward her. She had on occasion been hospitalized after being beaten by him. Ten days before she shot him, Blakely punched Ellis in the stomach and caused her to miscarry their child. On the night of the shooting, Ellis was accompanied by her friend, Desmond Cussen, with whom she had been involved in a sexual relationship. He helped her to procure the gun with which she killed Blakely.

Ruth Ellis had her first child when she was 17 and unmarried. At the age of 18, she became a nude model and then a club hostess. She met her husband, George Ellis, in 1950 through her work in the club. Their marriage fell apart, and they separated prior to the birth of her second child, a daughter, in 1953. During their divorce proceedings, Ruth did not oppose George's request for custody of their daughter, who went to live with him. David Blakely, an upper middle-class man who was five years younger than Ruth, moved in with her before her divorce had been finalized.

During her trial, the prosecution stressed that Ruth had been engaged in sexual relationships with men to whom she was not married and described Desmond Cussen as her "alternative lover." During her testimony, she referred to an illegal abortion (abortion became legal in England and Wales in 1967) she had had earlier on in her relationship with David Blakely, and she explained that she had refused his proposal of marriage at this time because she was not in love with him and deemed marriage unnecessary.

By the standards of the 1950s, when marriage and motherhood were regarded as the ideal situation for women, Ruth Ellis appeared to be a deviant and overly sexual woman. She did not live according to the conventions of the era, and her job as a club hostess was widely regarded as a type of prostitution. She had peroxide blonde hair and wore tailored suits and stiletto shoes. This made her appear glamorous, but also confident and unbowed. She was unrepentant about shooting David Blakely because she felt that he deserved it and she admitted that she had fully intended to kill him.

Ellis's defense counsel was ineffectual and called only two witnesses—Ellis and a psychologist. Her lawyer argued that she was not guilty of murder but rather of manslaughter due to provocation. However, he cross-examined only 2 of the 16 prosecution witnesses and did little establish why David Blakely's mistreatment of, and violence towards, Ruth should be considered important to the case. The judge ruled that manslaughter due to provocation could not be accepted as a valid defense, leaving the jury little option but to find her guilty of murder, which it did after 14 minutes' deliberation.

In 1955, murder automatically carried the death penalty, although the home secretary could choose to commute the sentence to imprisonment. This happened in nearly all cases of women convicted of murder, and the failure to reprieve Ruth Ellis was widely interpreted at the time and since to reflect disapproval of her "immoral" lifestyle and lack of respectability. The uproar that surrounded her execution was perceived to have contributed to the 1957 introduction of the law that made the defense of manslaughter due to diminished responsibility, which made it possible to use "instability of mind," not just insanity, a viable defense to murder.

The fate of Ruth Ellis remained controversial long after her death. There have been questions surrounding the involvement of Desmond Cussen in the murder and whether he should have been tried along with her. In 2003, the Criminal Cases Review Commission examined her case and ruled that her conviction for murder was sound according to the state of the law at the time.

Resources

Ballinger, A. (1996). "The Guilt of the Innocent and the Innocence of the Guilty: The Cases of Marie Fahmy and Ruth Ellis." In A. Myers and S. Wight (eds.), *No Angels: Women Who Commit Violence*. London: Pandora.

Ballinger, A. (2000). *Dead Woman Walking*. Aldershot, UK: Ashgate.

D'Cruze, S., S. Walklate, and S. Pegg. (2006). *Murder: Social and Historical Approaches to Understanding Murder and Murderers*. Cullompton, UK: Willan.

Farran, D. (1990), *The Trial of Ruth Ellis*. Manchester, UK: University of Manchester.

Marks, L., and T. Van Den Bergh. (1977). *Ruth Ellis: A Case of Diminished Responsibility?* London: Penguin.

Lizzie Seal

Ada Everleigh (1875–1960)

The first-born daughter of well-to-do parents in a small village in Kentucky was the last person imaginable to become one of the most prominent madams in United States' history. Born Ada Lester, her privileged young life provided her with the graces to become a typical Southern belle who in her teen years had her choice of suitors. She was genteel, strikingly attractive, and reportedly an ideal daughter. She was quiet and cautious, reluctantly allowing her only sister, Minna, two years younger and more aggressive, to lead her in social activities and relationships with males.

Minna was the more popular of the two and found a husband when she was 19. Ada, then 21, followed within a few weeks by accepting the proposal of the brother of her sister's new husband. Each daughter was given a lavish wedding attended by elite friends of their lawyer father and socialite mother. Soon, however, both discovered that they had married abusive men, and Minna began to plan for them to run away. The sisters had always wanted to be on the stage and decided to join a traveling troupe of actors as a way of escaping their disappointing husbands and also of seeing the country. Ada waited for her sister to leave her husband to travel to Washington, D.C., to find employment for them. When a touring repertory company offered them places, Ada joined her sister, and without looking back they began a tour of Midwest cities. Eventually in 1898, the acting group settled in Omaha, Nebraska, where the Trans-Mississippi Exposition was being held. The touring company attracted visitors from all over the West to their performances. Ada, who was proving to be an astute business woman, soon became aware that men who traveled to Omaha without their families were ready to pay for entertainment that their acting troupe provided and also for other types of female company and amusement as well.

An unexpected and sizable inheritance came to the sisters during their Omaha acting tour. While the source of the gift was never clearly identified, their grandmother died at about this time, and it was rumored that she left a sizeable inheritance to the young women. Looking for ways to invest their money, the sisters decided to open a "home away from home" for male visitors to the exposition to enjoy. Their aim was to provide good food, abundant alcohol, and beautiful women in a luxurious club atmosphere. It was clearly designed to be a bordello, even though neither sister would engage in prostitution personally. The ever-cautious Ada proposed that they change their last name so they could not to be traced to the Lester family in their small Kentucky hometown. Their grandmother, from whom the inheritance probably originated, always signed her letters "Everly yours," and Ada suggested they honor her with a slight variation to become the Everleigh sisters.

With Ada as business manager and Minna acting as hostess, the club was an instant success. After two years, the exposition closed, and even though they had doubled their money, their clientele, the visitors, left town. Locals were reluctant to be seen in their establishment or else were too frugal to part with the fees charged. Since their business was no longer welcome in Omaha, they determined that they would do well to settle in a large city where there would be a steady supply of men away from home. Buoyed by their previous two successful years, they decided to open an establishment in Chicago, Illinois, which they did on February 1, 1900. It was an establishment such as Chicago had never seen. When they opened its doors, the men came based on word of mouth only. There were no printed announcements, no illuminated signs, and a temperature of below zero on opening night. By 8:00 PM, customers began to find their way to the Dearborn Street address, and the sisters were encouraged with their successful beginning, which netted them a $100 profit after expenses for their first night in business (Washburn, 1936, 26).

As the business manager, Ada Everleigh paid salaries and hired the staff. Her young ladies were required to have good faces and figures and were carefully warned to treat customers with the greatest respect. She engaged musicians and bought a $15,000 gold-leaf piano, established an art gallery, and built a well-stocked library for use of guests. Due to the prominence of their patrons, Ada chose not to give regular payoffs to police or other city officials believing her prominent clientele was protection enough. However, she did arrange to provide "Everleigh girls" for First Ward Democratic events.

As a result of Ada's careful management and the popularity of the club, the nightly receipts soon grew to $2,500, equivalent to approximately $50,000, according to 2010 Consumer Price Index (Measuring Worth.com). The club telephone (Calumet 412) was listed in the Chicago directory as a residence under the name: Ada Everleigh. The number was used regularly when customers such as newspaper men and physicians were needed for after-hours emergencies.

For 11 years, Ada managed the establishment with such financial efficiency that a fortune in cash, jewels, art work, books, and other bordello furnishings was amassed. When religious crusaders began to demand the closing of all such houses in 1911, the sisters decided to take a vacation for six months, leaving the mansion shuttered and letting their employees go. Their last night in operation, October 24–25, 1911, was celebrated with friends and clients who drank champagne and predicted that the club would reopen at a later date. Great crowds gathered in the streets to watch men in tuxedos, wearing tall, silk hats leave in their carriages at the end of the evening while the police watched until the lights went out and everyone but the two sisters had departed. Within a week, Ada and Minna left for a six-month European vacation, hoping to reopen the club upon their return. However, the climate was even more hostile when they came back to Chicago, and reluctantly, Ada put most of the furnishings up for sale and planned to move with her sister to New York City.

Ada Everleigh had never considered marriage after her first unhappy effort but as she was planning to leave for New York City, a wealthy heir to a Chicago fortune begged her to marry him. She reported that she was tempted since she had grown fond of him but when he proved reluctant to pay to have her gold-leaf piano accompany her, she turned him down. The prized piano, along with many of the furnishings and art work from the Dearborn Street house, made the move to New York City, where they remained with her until her death (Washburn, 1936, 154).

The next years passed quietly in an elegant New York apartment on the east side. Ada had roses in every room and pictures of her favorite "girls" from the club. In her sitting room, some of the same easy chairs in which her customers once sat were used by friends from the old days who came to call. She attended the theater regularly, had several social groups to which she belonged, and renewed ties with her family to whom she sent checks. Ada Everleigh, who resumed the name of Lester, left life in Chicago as she entered it in the first place, easily and with no regrets. She outlived her sister Minna by 12 years, dying at age 84, and was buried beside Minna in a Virginia cemetery just outside the nation's capital.

Resources

Chicago Sun-Times, files of Chicago newspapers, 1910–1911.

Measuring Worth. www.Measuringworth.com/uscompare/SevenWays (used to compute the relative value of a U.S. dollar amount, 1774 to Present).

Wallace, Irving, *The Sunday Gentleman*, Simon & Schuster, New York, 1965.

Washburn, Charles, *Come Into My Parlor*, Knickerbocker Publishing Company, New York, 1936.

Marcia Lasswell

Minna Everleigh (1878–1948)

Born near Louisville, Kentucky, Minna Lester was the daughter of a prosperous attorney and his wife who were parents of three boys and one other daughter. She and her sister Ada went on to become the famed owners of the most prominent and luxurious bordello in Chicago. From her earliest days, Minna was the center of any event where she was present. Her reddish hair and dominant personality made her stand out in a crowd, and her intelligence and wit drew males and females alike to enjoy her company. Even though she and her older sister Ada were educated similarly in private schools and tutored to be Southern ladies, they could not have been more different. Minna was the assertive leader, and her sweet, round-faced sister, Ada, who was two-and-a-half years older, let Minna set the pace. One may have suspected that Minna would break rules and continue to surprise her parents and contemporaries; however, few would have suspected that she would lead herself and her lady-like sister into fame as bordello owners.

At 19, Minna married a local, young man in an extravagant early afternoon ceremony, in which she ordered that breakfast be served. She was known for late rising and took advantage of a new trend for mid-day ceremonies (Washburn, 1936, 14). As expected, it was but a short time until her sister, Ada, now 21, married the brother of Minna's new husband. It took but a few weeks, however, for both to regret their unions and confide to each other that the brothers were abusive. Together, they plotted to disappear without warning as a way to avoid a scandal directly. Since each had always dreamed of being an actress, joining a traveling road company seemed their best avenue of escape. It was decided that Minna, with her natural charm and her ability to meet and befriend strangers, would go to Washington, D.C., to find suitable positions for both of them. Ada, less adventurous and more practical, would follow when Minna had located willing employers. A struggling repertory company agreed to take the attractive sisters with them on a tour of Midwest cities. Ada joined Minna, touring large and small towns over several months, before arriving in Omaha, Nebraska, just as a large trade show opened a two-year run in that growing city.

After several weeks in Omaha, an unexpected windfall of $35,000 came their way from the will of a family member. Calculated in current terms, this would have amounted to approximately a quarter of a million dollars (Measuring Worth.com). Searching for investment ideas, Minna hit upon the idea of opening an exclusive club to entertain men who were visiting the exhibition. To hide their identities, they changed their last name to Everleigh, and the new establishment was named the Everleigh Club. For two years, until the exhibition closed and the visitors left town, the club did such a thriving business that their inheritance more than doubled. However, once the exhibition left town, so did the majority of their clientele. Minna urged a move to a more hospitable city, and after inquiries, Chicago, Illinois, was chosen because an established madam in that wide-open city was looking for a buyer for her imposing building and practice on South Dearborn Street. The mansion had been open for pleasure since the World's Fair in 1893, and the proprietor was ready to retire. The deal was set and the Everleigh sisters began weeks of extensive remodeling and refurnishing.

On Thursday, February 1, 1900, the grand opening of the Everleigh Club, the most luxurious in the city, inaugurated a period in which the sisters would become infamous in Chicago history. Minna, only 22 years old, presided as the hostess for elaborate dinners served to guests in a room ornately decorated in mahogany wood with gold-leaf trimmings. Midnight repasts of caviar, lobster, and good wine were offered for under $50. The fee for admission was $10, and to go upstairs, there was a minimum charge of $25. Minna saw to it that those who did not spend at least $50 were seldom admitted to the club a second time ($50 in 1900, was equivalent to approximately $1,000 in 2006 [Measuring Worth.com]).

Minna was astute enough to spot trends in the making that served as publicity for the club. The fad of drinking champagne from a lady's slipper was born at the Everleigh Club as she watched, amused, when one of the ladies, dancing barefoot on a table, knocked over a bottle of champagne, spilling it into her shoe. One of the regular customers lifted the shoe and drank from it saying: "boot liquor . . . the darling mustn't get her feet wet" (Washburn, 1936, 79). As if on cue, each man in the room took a slipper and followed the pattern. When word spread, the practice soon became a custom across society circles in other parts of the country.

After 11 years of entertaining politicians, important business men, and royalty, the Everleigh Club was targeted by reformers of the Progressive Era, who described it as "the most famous and luxurious house of prostitution in the country" (Chicago Vice Commission, 1911). During the weeks leading up to orders to close, Minna's humor never left her, as she demonstrated when an evangelist led thousands to pray in front of the club. Her response was: "I am so sorry to see so many nice young men coming down here for the first time" (Washburn, 1936, 108). Upon advice from her business-minded sister and politician friends, she agreed to a lengthy European junket until matters cooled off.

Upon their return to Chicago six months later, nothing had changed. Lacking any encouragement from officials to open for business again, the sisters became convinced it was time to retire. Minna, now 34 years old, was still attractive with her graceful, boyish body and auburn curls. She had ample funds to start a new life as a patron of the arts and theater, and she yearned for a chance to read the hundreds of leather-bound volumes she had collected.

New York City provided Minna with the anonymity she desired as she quietly settled into a life of a middle-aged dowager, joining women's clubs and playing hostess to poetry readings. She destroyed all of the records of her former life and became known once again as Minna Lester. She considered the Everleigh sisters dead and allowed that all she needed to be happy was "a roof and one quart of champagne a week" (Washburn, 1936, 247). She preceded her sister, Ada, in death by 12 years and was buried at age 70 in a small cemetery outside Washington, D.C.

Resources

Chicago Vice-Commission Report, June 1, 1911.

Measuring Worth. www.Measuringworth.com/uscompare/SevenWays (used to compute the relative value of a U.S. dollar amount, 1774 to Present).

Wallace, Irving, *The Sunday Gentleman*, Simon & Schuster, New York, 1965.

Washburn, Charles, *Come Into My Parlor*, Knickerbocker Publishing Company, New York, 1936.

Marcia Lasswell

F

Laura Fair (1850–?)

On November 3, 1870, Laura D. Fair boarded an Oakland to San Francisco ferry and shot her lover of seven years, Alexander P. Crittenden, in the heart. She took a seat on the ferry, and when she was arrested by the Harbor Police, stated calmly, "I don't deny it, and I meant to kill him. He ruined both myself and my child" (Lamott, 1963: 5). Fair's trial was widely reported and became a national sensation. Crittenden was a respected attorney and family man, shot in front of his wife and children. Fair had been widowed twice and divorced once, and she had a daughter from one of her previous marriages. The contrast between respectable, middle-class Crittenden and Fair, a woman who ran a boarding house and had experience a life-time of financial precariousness, made the case extremely newsworthy. Mark Twain's first novel (coauthored with Charles Dudley Warner), *The Gilded Age*, published in 1873, contains a character closely based on Laura Fair.

The defense at Fair's trial, held in April 1871, was temporary insanity caused by "scanty and retarded menstruation" (French, 1964: 303), a tipped womb, and Crittenden's failure to fulfill his promise to divorce his wife and marry her. She gained the support of local feminists, who attended her trial daily in order to demonstrate their opposition to the immorality of men who deceived and "ruined" women. The prosecutor was Crittenden's partner in law. He disdained Fair's insanity defense and asserted that she was a "free lover," as were the women who attended court to support her. The prosecution called character witnesses to testify to her lack of chastity. She was found guilty of murder in the first degree and sentenced to hang. While she was awaiting execution, leading 19th-century feminist Susan B. Anthony visited San Francisco. She visited Fair in jail, and at the close of a suffrage speech delivered that evening, stated that if all men treated women as chivalrously as they maintained, Laura Fair would not be in prison.

Fair's execution was stayed by the Supreme Court, and a new trial was ordered to take place in New York on the grounds that the defense should not have closed the arguments in her first trial, and evidence of her bad character for chastity should not have been allowed. At her second trial in September 1872, Fair was acquitted on the grounds of temporary insanity. Fair proposed a lecture tour on the topic of American morals. She drafted a speech that she planned to give at a hotel in San Francisco exhorting American to avenge their outraged names, in order to "strike a terror to the hearts of sensualists and libertines" (Jones, 2009: 204). Such a large crowd gathered in protest against her lecturing on this topic that it was deemed unsafe for her to appear in public and Fair published her speech as a pamphlet entitled *Wolves in the Fold*.

The case of Laura D. Fair is perhaps emblematic of the "cult of true womanhood" that existed in late 19th-century America, where women were idealized as placid, domestic creatures who experienced no sexual desires, but were unfortunately prone to illness, insanity, and hysteria. Limited conceptions of femininity meant that Fair was seen as either a wanton, overtly sexual "bad" woman, or as an irrational "mad" woman at the mercy of her own faulty biology. To an extent, she managed to evade both of these representations through her willingness to defend her actions in the language of 19th-century feminism.

Resources

Babcock, B. A. (2001), "Women Defenders in the West," *University of Nevada Law Journal*, Spring, 1–18.

French, B. M. (1964), "Mark Twain, Laura D. Fair and the New York Criminal Courts," *American Quarterly*, 16(4): 545–561.

Jones, A. (2009), *Women Who Kill*, New York: Feminist Press.

Lamott, K. C. (1963), *Who Killed Mr. Crittenden?*, New York: David McKay.

Twain, M., and C. D. Warner. (2001), *The Gilded Age*, New York: Penguin Books.

Lizzie Seal

Christine Falling (1963–)

Christine Laverne Slaughter Falling is a modern-day child serial murderer operating in the early 1980s. The pattern of her murders showed signs of what some consider the typical disorganized serial murderer; she also demonstrated some symptoms of someone who has Munchhausen Syndrome, but she was not identified as a serial murderer until the late 1990s when included in many serial murder anthologies as such. Over her criminal career, she had a sealed juvenile record and six charges of check fraud, in addition to the eventual murder charges levied against her.

Falling was born on March 12, 1963, to a very young mother (age 16) and a significantly older spouse (age 65). Falling was considered mentally challenged and diagnosed epileptic. It is known that at age 9 she and her sister, Carol, were removed from the home as a result of domestic violence. By then, she had started to exhibit

Christine Falling, led into Florida county court by Officer Lasseter, 1982. Ms. Falling changed her plea to guilty and was immediately sentenced to two concurrent life sentences for the murder of two local infants she was babysitting. (AP/Wide World Photos)

disturbing behavior such as strangling cats to see if they really had nine lives. She later dropped out of junior high school. In 1977, at age 14, she entered into a six-week marriage with a 20-year-old man, which ended in spousal violence. In 1979, she was found "delinquent" and at risk of running away.

Few job opportunities were open to young Falling given her personal appearance, lack of education, and her "dull wittedness." She began to take jobs as a babysitter. Shortly after her marriage, she also began to exhibit signs of Munchhausen Syndrome, showing up at hospitals with symptoms of conditions that were eventually found to be nonexistent.

The first recorded incident of harming a child came on February 25, 1980, when Cassidy Marie Johnson, age two, was brought into the local hospital in Blountstown, Florida, with a blunt force trauma to her head. Falling said the child had fallen out her crib as the result of losing consciousness. She died three days later as a result of her injuries. One doctor wrote a note to police indicating his suspicions about the babysitter, but the lead was not followed. Later, another child in her care, Kyle Summerlin, age three, was brought into hospital and died with a diagnosis of "meningitis."

Falling moved on to Lakeland, Florida, and continued to care for children. Shortly after her arrival, Jeffrey Davis, age 4, suddenly "stopped breathing" under her care. Autopsy revealed that the child had a mild inflammation of the heart, but it was not though enough to kill a child. At Jeffrey's funeral, Jeffrey's 2-year-old cousin Joseph Spring, also being taken care of by Falling, was found to have died in his sleep while taking a nap. Doctors concluded that Joseph had the same viral infection that was attributed to Jeffrey's death. Shortly after Spring's death, two other children in her care became critically ill and were hospitalized, but they recovered.

In July 1981, she moved to Perry, near Blountstown, Florida, and began work caring for an elderly man, William Swindle, age 77. He died the very first day she began working, apparently due to natural causes. That same month she was left in charge of her stepsister's infant, eight-month-old Jennifer Daniels, who stopped breathing. Then, on July 2, 1982, Travis Coleman, a 10-week-old infant, died in Falling's care. Autopsy revealed that the baby had been smothered. Falling was arrested and charged with this murder. She confessed to killing three children (Johnson, Daniels, and Coleman) by smothering them as she had seen on television, using a blanket to cover their faces. She said that she was following orders from voices telling her to kill the baby.

Facing six potential death sentences, Falling plead guilty in December 1982, in exchange for the state not prosecuting her for the death of Swindle or for the death of the two cousins in Lakeland. Falling later stated that she did not know why she had killed these children. Other statements suggest that Falling killed children when they became too noisy. In her confession she stated her method of killing was simple, smothering her victims with a blanket so no one could here them scream. In another confession specifically directed at the death of Johnson she stated:

> She got kinda rowdy or something. Anyway, I choked her until she quit breathing and she had turned purple. . . . Her heart had stopped beating and her pulse had stopped and she wasn't breathing. So I tried to get her back to breathing and I couldn't. So then I went and called the sheriff [*sic*] department. (Florida Baby Sitter Pleads Guilty, 1982, 8)

This case is interesting for several reasons. First, although Falling clearly had mental health issues as a child and as a teen, these problems were not addressed. Even after her arrest, there are reports that she received "psychiatric assessment" in Tallahassee but was later allowed to enter into a plea bargain with the state, suggesting she was of sound mind, when clearly there was evidence of both Munchhausen Syndrome and possible schizophrenia. There was also evidence of depression in her background and possible suicide attempts. She was eventually sentenced to life in prison in Homestead, Florida.

Resource

Florida Baby Sitter Pleads Guilty to Murdering Three in Her Care. 1982. *New York Times*, December 4: 8.

Hannah Scott

Clara Fallmer (1892–?)

At the age of 15 or 16 (her official age is unclear), Clara Fallmer made the headlines in Alameda County, California. She was charged with shooting and killing Charles La Due in public view. Miss Fallmer alleged that Mr. La Due had promised her marriage, but instead he abandoned her. Fallmer was pregnant. The defense and prosecuting attorneys both tried to plan what the character of the case should be in terms of what people wanted to believe. Miss Fallmer's lawyers argued in defense of her injured womanhood. The prosecutors constructed her as a lying harlot. "Neither side could afford the simple truth—that Fallmer was neither waif nor wench, but essentially a woman, with ordinary feelings and passions" (Friedman, 1994).

The headline of the first article on page 9 in the *San Francisco Call* newspaper on Tuesday, August 3, 1897, read: "Discarded, She Had Revenge: Charles V. La Due Seriously Wounded by Clara Fallmer. Then She Shot Herself. The Two Had Been Keeping Company for Some Time. He Is Well Known In Alameda. She Has Been in Trouble Before. Both Are in a Precarious Condition." According to the article, La Due's mother was not happy with his relationship with Fallmer. In addition, Fallmer's brother, K.R. Fallmer, was described as being not pleased with the relationship. In the article, it was reported that K.R. Fallmer approached La Due and asked him to stop keeping company with Clara Fallmer and to instead allow her to go to school. La Due promised to do so. The article suggested that La Due had planned on "dropping her acquaintance" but did not do so because Clara Fallmer intimidated him with what at the time seemed to be an idle threat.

Historical accounts speculated about the history of the relationship between Charles La Due and Clara Fallmer. The truth would finally be revealed on December 22, 1897, when Fallmer took the stand at her trial. Fallmer recounted for the court that La Due presented her with a ring, that he had asked her to marry him shortly after Christmas, and that she had consented to his request. Fallmer also described how she later ended the love affair after believing that the marriage proposal was false and that La Due never really had any intention of marrying her, but then they reconciled and the engagement was back on. On a trip to San Francisco, she plead with La Due to fulfill his contract of holy matrimony but instead he retrieved his hat and began to leave. While attempting to keep La Due in the restaurant to hear her, Fallmer was struck by La Due leaving her unconscious on the floor.

Young, pregnant, and unwed, Clara Fallmer went to the train station on the evening of August 2, 1897, armed with a revolver and what many would describe as a broken heart. Witnesses say they saw Fallmer call La Due over to her once he departed the train car. They appeared to have a conversation. Then the passengers departing the train at Park Street Station were greeted by two shots from a revolver. Within a few seconds, two bodies laid motionless in front of Kneinal Pharmacy. La Due's body dropped to the ground first, and Fallmer's followed shortly thereafter. Fallmer had shot La Due in the shoulder with the revolver and then turned the gun on herself. There was never any question about who committed such a heinous act because the smoking gun was still in the hand of the murderess, but everyone wondered why she had done it.

Historical accounts suggest that Clara Fallmer was not a stranger to the law. On February 11, 1895, Fallmer and two other girls were arrested for vagrancy. Her father, Rudolph K. Fallmer, a well-known newspaper agent on the broad-gauge local train, would come to her defense saying his daughter was wrongfully charged and that he was going to bring charges against the woman who accused his daughter for defamation of character. A little over a year later, Clara Fallmer would find herself back in the *San Francisco Call* but this time she would actually be the victim. Andrew Frank, the owner of a saloon, had either sold or given Clara Fallmer liquor even though she was legally underage. Her brother went to the Board of Trustees in hopes that they would annul Frank's liquor license.

Historical accounts also suggest that the Fallmer family tree comprised several members that may have had suffered from mental illness. According to the *San Francisco Call* newspaper, Fallmer told the matron while she was incarcerated that her older sister as well as her grandparents had taken their own lives. Fallmer also discussed an incident four years prior to the La Due murder in which she had shot her younger sister in the hand.

Her attorney, A.A. Moore, Jr., would argue that she had shot Charles La Due, her lover, during a state of emotional insanity. Her attorney made sure that she was perceived as an innocent young lady whose womanhood was wounded by her lover. Historical accounts describe that Moore had Fallmer carry a bouquet of violets and dress in a thick navy-blue veil, gloved hands, and a knee-length dress. She was painted as a picture of wounded innocence. After hearing about how Charles La Due had seduced and abandoned Fallmer, the jury appeared to have felt sympathetic towards her. Clara Fallmer was quickly and easily acquitted.

Resources

"Alameda's City Hall, The Fallmer Girl's Father Indignant That She Should Be Arrested for Vagrancy." *San Francisco Call*, February 11, 1896: 13.

Fisher, George. "Historian in the Cellar." Law, Society And History: Essays on Themes in the Work of Lawrence M. Friedman, Robert W. Gordon and Morton J. Horwitz, eds., 2006; Stanford Public Law Working Paper No. 117.

Friedman, L. (1994). *Crime and Punishment in American History*, reprint. New York: Basic Books.

Michelson, Miriam. (1898, January 5). "The Sins of Children Shall Be Visited Upon The Parents." *San Francisco Call*, 6.

Kathryn A. Branch and Anise Loney

Amy Fisher (1974–)

Amy Fisher, "the Long Island Lolita," was only a teenager when she was sent to prison for shooting the wife of her older married lover, Joey Buttafuoco. She was demonized by some in the media as an evil temptress; by others she was considered a victim of a sick and greedy man almost twice her age.

Amy Fisher was born and raised in communities on Long Island, New York. She moved from Wantagh to Merrick (both in Long Island) when she was 13 years old.

Amy Fisher leaves the Albion Correctional Facility in Albion, New York, 1999. Fisher, who spawned tabloid headlines and television movies as the teenager who shot her lover's wife in the head, walked out of the upstate prison after being paroled. (AP/Wide World Photos)

Both parents worked full-time making her a latch-key kid. According to Amy, this was a bad age to move and also a bad age to be left unsupervised. Merrick was more upscale than Wantagh, and her parents spoiled her with a sports car, expensive clothes, and forth. She hung out with what she termed the "B crowd" and early on ditched the B crowd to start hanging out with older girls who had already graduated from high school. This change in friends apparently initiated her change in behavior. Instead of being home by 11:30 PM, she was suddenly not going out until 11:30 PM. The signs of a troubled teen were there: slipping grades, new older friends, and staying out late.

Amy's parents unfortunately did not catch on to the signs that something was wrong with their teenage daughter. Amy describes her mother as good-natured and kind. Her father, on the other hand, had a trigger temper and physically abused her. The abuse occurred often when she was younger and when her mother was not home, but once when she was 16 years old, he physically assaulted her and she ran away for a few days. Her parents filed a police report, and her father told police that Amy was an awful, incorrigible child. Around this time, Joey Buttafuoco came into Amy's life.

Joey Buttafuoco, a married body shop repairman in his mid-thirties, started dating the 16-year-old Amy Fisher in July 1991. According to Amy, throughout their time together, he repeatedly mentioned that he wanted to kill his wife. He also repeatedly mentioned that it would be better if Amy did it because she was only a kid and would not go to jail. Mr. Buttafuoco, of course, denied the claims he ever said anything to Amy about killing his wife.

On May 19, 1992, Amy and an acquaintance, Peter (who had acquired the gun for her), drove to Massapequa to shoot Mary Jo Buttafuoco. Amy went alone to the doorstep and told Mary Jo that Amy's sister was having an affair with Joey. Mary Jo then turned around to call Joey. Amy, embarrassed by the thought that Mary Jo would call Joey, started hitting her repeatedly with the gun. Amy then walked away not knowing that the gun had gone off. Peter made her return to the house for the gun and that is when she found out the gun had malfunctioned and had shot Mary Jo while Amy had been hitting her with it.

Amy went about her life for the next two days and then was arrested a block from her home. She was interrogated without her parents there for many hours until she confessed to the crime. The media frenzy then began. Amy purports the reason that her case was so celebrated was because she was considered a rich, white, spoiled brat that had committed attempted murder. This was not the typical attempted murder case.

The media laid the Amy/Joey love affair on thick, all the while Joey continued to deny that he had this affair. Joey exploited Amy by giving exclusives to certain media outlets. It is reported by Amy that her lawyer Eric Naiburg tricked her into meeting with author Sheila Weller to write "her story." Amy in her own book many years later denies that much of her own story is actually in that first book. Further, the movies that were made were also mostly sensationalist.

During all the media frenzy, Amy, at the behest of her lawyer, pleaded to reckless assault with depraved indifference, receiving a prison sentence of 5 to 15 years. She never actually thought that she would be spending the seven years that she did in prison. Naiburg, her lawyer, had promised her and her mother that the most she would spend would be three years. Amy maintains that if she had known how long her sentence would end up being she would have gone to trial. However, an upstate New York prison is where she spent the majority of the next seven years.

During her stay in prison, she was harassed and sexually abused by the guards. They were not impressed with the publicity that Amy brought in with her, and she was viewed as a spoiled, rich kid. Fighting against the abuse only got her into more trouble within the prison. The guards would throw her into solitary confinement and continue with the ridicule.

Amy Fisher's life continues to take odd twists and turns. While she is currently a wife and mother, she reportedly was rumored to have left her husband for a brief reunion with Buttafuoco. The reunion was meant to spawn a reality show, which to date has not happened. Amy eventually made peace with Mary Jo (who is now divorced from Joey), and Fisher worked at a newspaper, the *Long Island Press*. It has been reported that she no longer works there, has made a sex tape, and plans to star in adult films. Fisher's story is one of a victimized girl, and her life continues to be riddled with drama.

Resources

"Amy Fisher." *A&E Biography*. http://www.biography.com/articles/Amy-Fisher-235415.

Amy Fisher: My Story (TV film). (1992). Jaffe/Brownstein Films/NBC.

The Amy Fisher Story (TV film). (1993). ABC Productions/American Broadcasting Company.

Casualties of Love: The Long Island Lolita Story (TV film). (1993). The Sokolow Company/CBS.

Fisher, Amy, and Robbie Woliver. (2004). *If I Knew Then . . .*: Lincoln, NE: I Universe.

Rebecca Hayes-Smith

Heidi Fleiss (1965–)

Heidi Fleiss, "the Hollywood Madame," rocked show business upon her arrest in 1993. Many producers, business moguls, and stars were afraid of the release of Heidi's client list. Heidi Fleiss to this day has never released that list, but the rapid success and notoriety that was achieved during and immediately after her reign as the Hollywood Madame has remained with her and continues to interest the news media.

Heidi Fleiss was born to a teacher, Elissa Fleiss, and a pediatrician, Dr. Paul Fleiss, in 1965. She had five siblings and a relatively happy and conventional upbringing. As a teenager, her innate business-savvy was exemplified through her babysitting business. She started out as a babysitter and gained a status as the neighborhood's best. She then became so busy that she started hiring out her friends and keeping a portion of their earnings. It was clear that she had a knack for business and managing money.

Despite her knack for business, her teenage years were still awkward. Heidi had trouble fitting in and did poorly in school. She eventually dropped out of school in the 10th grade. Over the next few years, she held different jobs, including waitressing, but it was when she met millionaire Bernie Cornfeld that her life and career changed. Their relationship led to her becoming accustomed to a lavish lifestyle, and upon their breakup she began to seek this life out.

Convicted Hollywood madam Heidi Fleiss, shown in this 1995 file photo, faced a maximum sentence of five years for money laundering and tax evasion in directing a prostitution ring for the rich and famous. (AP/Wide World Photos)

Ivan Nagy, a filmmaker, was the next influential person in Fleiss's life, and he introduced her to Elizabeth Adams, aka "Madam Alex." Madam Alex ran the most prosperous call girl service in Hollywood, and Heidi quickly rose up the ladder from prostitute employee to an assistant to Madam Alex. The relationship between Heidi and Madam Alex soon became rocky, and Heidi decided to go into business for herself.

Heidi's success quickly skyrocketed. She threw lavish parties at her mansion, where drugs and rock stars like Mick Jagger were welcome. Heidi Fleiss sent call girls all over the world and made millions within months. This lifestyle came crashing down in June 1993 when she was arrested and charged with five counts of pandering (soliciting customers for prostitutes) and possession of illegal narcotics. On December 2, 1994, the jury found her guilty on three counts of pandering. She was sentenced to three years in prison and fined. The verdict, however, was later overturned due to jury misconduct. The criminal charges did not stop there.

During the state trial, a federal grand jury indicted her on 14 counts of conspiracy, money laundering, and income tax evasion. In the midst of the media frenzy and court appearances, Fleiss tested positive for methamphetamines and was ordered to drug treatment. It seemed her reign as the Hollywood Madam was coming to an end.

In August 1995, Fleiss was convicted in federal court of conspiracy, money laundering, and income tax evasion. She was sentenced to 37 months in a minimum-security prison. She also entered a plea bargain with the state of California for pandering, and she was sentenced to 18 months in prison to run concurrent with the 37 months that was already sentenced. Two other pandering charges were dropped by Los Angeles prosecutors.

Heidi spent over two years in a prison in Dublin, California, where she was harassed by other inmates. She was released to a halfway house in November 1998 to finish out her time. She requested to be returned to prison (it is speculated for safety reasons), and this request was granted. Finally in September 1999, after three years in prison, she was released.

After her release from prison, it appeared that things were looking up for Fleiss. She wrote a book called *Pandering*, she and longtime friend Victoria Sellers came out with a DVD titled *Sex Tips*, and she was dating actor Tom Sizemore. Tom Sizemore abused her throughout the relationship, and in 2003, she filed charges against him for domestic abuse. In August 2003, Sizemore was convicted on six charges which included physical abuse, harassment, and vandalism.

Heidi Fleiss has not shrunk from attention, and she still appears on television, including appearances on a celebrity drug and alcohol rehabilitation program in 2009 called *Celebrity Rehab with Dr. Drew*. Fleiss's tumultuous past still follows her, but she continues to embrace it and goes on.

Resources

Bell, Rachel. *Courtroom Television Network*. http://www.crimelibrary.com/notorious_murders/celebrity/heidi_fleiss/index.html. Accessed March 1, 2007.

Fleiss, Heidi. (2002). *Pandering*. Los Angeles, CA: 1 Hour Entertainment.

"Times Topics: Heidi Fleiss." *New York Times*. http://topics.nytimes.com/top/reference/timestopics/people/f/heidi_fleiss/index.html?scp=1-spot&sq=heidi%20fleiss&st=cse. Accessed August 22, 2010.

Rebecca Hayes-Smith

Jane Fonda (1937–)

During a time of rapid social change and a push toward gender and racial equality, Jane Fonda emerged as an outspoken figure. Famous for her many movies, Fonda's public image changed from a sex symbol (for her roles in movies such as *Barbarella* [1968]) to political activist. Some viewed this change of persona as negative. Because of her support of controversial groups, she was monitored for some time by the FBI and arrested several times while protesting the Vietnam War. Fonda remains known today as a part of 1960s and 1970s history, and she continues work as both activist and actress.

Jane Fonda was born on December 21, 1937, to actor Henry Fonda and his second wife, Frances Seymour Brokaw. She had an older stepsister, Frances; a younger brother, Peter; and a younger sister, Amy, who was adopted during her father's third marriage to Susan Blanchard. Jane Fonda spent much of her childhood isolated from Hollywood, living on a nine-acre ranch in Brentwood, California, until her mother moved the family closer to Jane's father, who was acting on Broadway. They rented a house in Greenwich, where they lived with Jane's maternal grandmother. Suffering from mental illness, Fonda's mother committed suicide in 1950 when Jane was 12 years old. Following her death, Jane and Peter lived in New York with their father and his wife. She characterized her father in her 2005 biography as emotionally uninvolved.

Jane's first acting experience was participating in high school plays, but at that time she did not consider acting as a profession. After attending Vassar College, she briefly studied painting in Paris. Back in New York, she began modeling and acting. In 1965, she married director Roger Vadim, with whom she had a daughter three years later. They divorced; and she was later married to Tom Hayden, with

American actress and anti–Vietnam War activist Jane Fonda seated at a North Vietnamese antiaircraft gun during a visit to Hanoi in July 1972. Propaganda broadcasts of Fonda's trip were a coup for the North Vietnamese and an affront to many Americans. Years later, Fonda apologized for her actions. (AP/Wide World Photos)

whom she had a son and adopted a daughter. Her third marriage was with media mogul Ted Turner; they separated in 2001.

Fonda has an extensive acting resume but also is well-known for her popular exercise videos. While she retired from acting in 1992, recently Fonda has continued her acting career in films such as *Monster-In-Law* (2005) and *Georgia Rule* (2007), and has revitalized her antiwar protesting. Fonda, who has been described as a feminist, is also involved in organizations encouraging the prevention of teenage pregnancy and other causes supportive of equality.

Aside from her famous family and her own celebrity for her acting career and starring in exercise videos, Jane Fonda was known for her political activism. Perhaps inspired by her father's activism and his time spent in the Navy, she was an outspoken critic of the Vietnam War and negatively dubbed "Hanoi Jane" for her 1972 visit to North Vietnam in which she campaigned for the communist regime and denounced U.S. military involvement in the war. She was criticized in particular for the many photographs of her aboard an anti-aircraft gun. Some report that at least one senator argued that she should be arrested for treason. Fonda's intentions were to support the war-resisters inside the military and, broadly, to support equality for all; however, in retrospect, she realizes and apologizes for the unintended consequences of hurting U.S. soldiers.

Fonda's so-called criminal career—or lack thereof—stemmed from her political activism. Her involvement with the criminal justice system began in 1970 when she was arrested in Seattle, Washington, for her participation in protests against the U.S. government procurement of Native American lands for use as military bases and training grounds for soldiers for the Vietnam War. She was issued a letter of expulsion from Fort Lawton for her involvement in a protest there on March 8, 1970, and she was arrested for entering a tactical area of Fort Lewis, another military base south of Fort Lawton. Fonda was arrested again by military police in May of that year for distributing pamphlets at a protest at Fort Hood, Texas.

Later that year, Fonda was campaigning for the Vietnam Veterans Against War (VVAW) and the Winter Soldier Investigation, which were war crimes hearings. On November 3, she flew into Cleveland, Ohio, to begin a fundraising tour of colleges and universities. At the airport, U.S. Customs searched Fonda's luggage, finding pills, and refused her request to use the bathroom. When she tried to push the agents aside, Fonda was charged with drug smuggling and assaulting the police and spent 10 hours in jail. The pills were actually vitamins and prescribed medication, and the charges against Fonda were eventually dropped.

For some time in the late 1960s and early 1970s, the FBI had Jane Fonda under surveillance, as she supported the Black Panther Party, a sometimes violent political group that supported civil rights. The FBI was not the only organization to monitor Fonda; in fact, Mary Hershberger, who organized a collection of Fonda's speeches, found transcripts of Fonda's speeches only through the CIA (Fonda had not documented them). Other agencies, including the U.S. Secret Service (USSS) and the National Security Agency (NSA), also spied on her.

Jane Fonda was active in a time of dramatic social change, and she played an important role in history. The 1960s and 1970s were characterized by much social unrest, stemming from an unpopular war in Vietnam and public perceptions of a government unfair to racial and ethnic minorities and women. Today, many still perceive Fonda only as "Hanoi Jane", as evidenced by a recent incident in which a Vietnam veteran spat on her. In the 2004 presidential race, the Republican Party attempted to discredit Democrat John Kerry, a Vietnam veteran who had protested the Vietnam War, by associating him with Jane Fonda and the VVAW. Photos of John Kerry attending the same rallies as Jane Fonda circulated extensively. While George W. Bush won the election, it cannot be said that the Fonda connection had a serious impact on the public's opinion in either direction. Despite such controversy, her activism continues today, with a focus on issues such as education for girls and women across the world and reproductive rights.

Resources

Fonda, Jane. 2005. *My life so far.* New York: Random House.

Hershberger, Mary. 2004. Peace work, war myths: Jane Fonda and the antiwar movement. *Peace & Change*, 29: 549–579.

Hershberger, Mary, ed. 2006. *Jane Fonda's words of politics and passion.* New York: New Press.

Kinney, Katherine. 2003. Hanoi Jane and other treasons: Women and the editing of the 1960s. *Women's Studies*, 32: 371–392.

Jennifer C. Gibbs

Antoinette Frank (1971–)

Convicted of three murders and armed robbery while serving as a member of the New Orleans Police Department (NOPD), Antoinette Frank is one of two women offenders serving on death row in the state of Louisiana. These murders symbolize the prevalence of corruption and crime that has existed in the NOPD.

A native of Opelousas, Louisiana, Frank's ambitions of a career in law enforcement began at an early age. As a young adult, she was actively involved with the Opelousas Junior Police and the New Orleans Explorers. Frank further pursued her career ambitions at age 20 by applying to the NOPD. During the review process, her application encountered several problems regarding her employment history and psychological stability. Despite low scores on the psychological examination and inconsistencies on the application, she was able to obtain employment in the department.

At age 24, Frank became acquainted with 18-year-old Rogers LaCaze. They met while he was hospitalized from a shooting that she was investigating in November 1994. Aware of his criminal lifestyle, she continued her involvement with him after he was discharged from the hospital. She soon became involved in his small-time crimes, providing him with transportation and security. She often allowed him to ride with her on calls, having him pose as an officer in training. As the relationship continued, she became increasingly engaged in misconduct. The last crime she committed was a robbery of the restaurant she worked as a part-time security officer. It was during this robbery three people were killed.

New Orleans Police Department ID photo of former police officer Antoinette Frank, who was convicted of killing her law enforcement partner and two other people during a robbery attempt at a restaurant, 1995. (AP/Wide World Photos)

The murders of Cuong Vu, 18 years old, his sister Ha Vu, 24, and officer Ronald Williams, 25, took place on March 4, 1995, at Kim Anh Vietnamese Restaurant. Frank and LaCaze entered the establishment after casing it out with two previous visits. During the robbery, LaCaze shot officer Williams three times with a 9 mm pistol as Frank began looking for money. When she finally found the cash, she then used same 9 mm pistol to shoot Cuong and Ha Vu, leaving both victims dead on the scene. Unaware that there were witnesses, Frank and LaCaze fled the scene.

After dropping LaCaze off at an apartment, she borrowed a marked police car from the NOPD 7th District station to respond to the shootings and returned to the scene. She was unaware that the siblings of Cuong and Ha Vu, who also worked at the restaurant, had witnessed some of the events. Quoc Vu, the victims' brother, made the emergency call after witnessing the tragic events, and Chau Vu, their sister, told the other investigating officers that Frank and an accomplice were responsible for all three murders. Frank then contested this, stating that she heard shots fired in the dining room while she was in the kitchen area and began immediately moving the staff to the rear exit. Afterwards, Frank stated that she then proceeded to the police department to report the emergency. Uneasy about Frank's statement, the investigating officers then took her to the police station for further questioning. She later admitted to committing the violent crimes and killing two of the victims.

In July 1995, LaCaze was the first to go on trial; he was later convicted of murder and given the death sentence. The trial of Antoinette Frank took place September 5, 1995, at the Criminal District Court for the Parish of Orleans in the courtroom of Judge Frank J. Marullo. Frank's defense attorney argued that she was innocent and was merely an accomplice in the murders. On September 12, 1995, after 40 minutes of deliberation, the jury found her guilty. She was charged with three counts of first-degree murder and was recommended for the death penalty. On October 1995, a judge sentenced her to death by lethal injection. An appeal was later was a made based on the fairness of the court and on May 22, 2007, the Louisiana Supreme Court upheld the decision, ruling that Frank had been properly sentenced. Frank's death was scheduled for July 15, 2008, however; she was given a 90-day stay of execution on May 16, 2008, to file her an appeal. A second death warrant was signed on September 11, 2008, the second warrant signed by Judge Marullo. Frank's execution date was rescheduled for December 8, 2008. On November 24, 2008, the Louisiana Supreme Court recalled the warrant, and the case is currently pending post conviction appeals. On January 4, 2010, it was decided that the case would remain in Judge Marullo's courtroom at the Orleans Parish Criminal District Court. As of August 2011, she remains on death row.

This case brought nation attention to police misconduct and departmental shortcomings in the NOPD. It brought public awareness to the inadequate employment system, the low pay of police officers, and the internal corruption within the department. Prior to her employment, the department restructured the hiring system to insure the recruitment of qualified candidates, yet, Frank still managed to be employed.

The murders also drew societal attention to other corruption that took place between police officers and drug dealers. A year prior to the murders, an FBI operation led to the conviction of 10 police officers involved in guarding a warehouse stocked with cocaine. Both Frank and the convicted officers' crimes were connected to off-duty jobs. Many officers of the NOPD were underpaid and took additional work to sustain a living. The low pay scales of police officers made it difficult to hire and sustain qualified candidates. In addition to underpaying officers, residential restrictions was another deficiency with the department. The employment pool was limited to Orleans Parish residents. These restrictions also limited the department's efforts in recruiting qualified employees.

Today, Frank is currently an inmate at the Louisiana Correctional Institute for Women in St. Gabriel, Louisiana. She recently revealed that she experienced physical abuse and violence at the hands of her father. In November 1995, a skeleton with a bullet hole in the skull was recovered from underneath the house of her father. She had apparently reported her father missing over a year prior to the killings. The identity of the human bones remains undetermined.

Resources

Bones found under home of policewoman who killed 3. (1995, November 8). *Washington Post,* A13.

Filosa, Gwen. (2007, May 23). Death penalty upheld for N.O. ex-cop. *Times-Picayune.* http://blog.nola.com/topnews/2007/05/death_penalty_upheld_for_no_ex.html

Filosa, Gwen. (2008, February 27). Convicted killer Antoinette Frank appears in court. *Times-Picayune.* http://www.nola.com/news/index.ssf/2008/02/convicted_killer_antoi nette_fr.html

Filosa, Gwen. (2008, November 26). Louisiana Supreme Court cancels execution for Antoinette Frank. *Times-Picayune.* http://www.nola.com/news/index.ssf/2008/11/the_ louisiana_supreme_court_ha.html

Filosa, Gwen. (2010, January 4). Antoinette Frank case to stay in Marullo's courtroom. *Times-Picayune.* http://www.nola.com/crime/index.ssf/2010/01/antoinette_frank.html

Gwynne, S. (1995). Cops and robbers. *Time* 145(11), 45.

Herbert, Bob. (1995, September 15). In America; Killer cops. *New York Times,* A35.

Hustmyre, Chuck. (2003). Blue on blue: Murder, madness and betrayal in the NOPD. *New Orleans Magazine*, February, 44–47.

Nabonne, Rhonda. (2008, May 16). Stay of execution granted in cop killer case. *Times-Picayune.* http://blog.nola.com/twoyearslater/2008/05/stay_of_execution_granted_in_ c.html

New Orleans officer is convicted of 3 killings in robbery attempt. (1995, September 12). *New York Times,* A20.

Policewoman guilty of slaying 3. (1995, September 12). *Washington Post,* A02.

Sanz, Cynthia, and Joseph Harmes.(1995). A killer in blue. *People*, September, 131–113.

Sarma, Bidish J., Robert J. Smith, and G. B. Cohen. (2009, Fall). Struck by lightning: *Walker v. Georgia* and Louisiana's proportionality review of death sentences. 37. *Southern University Law Review* 65.

State of Louisiana v. Antoinette Frank. (2001). 99-KA-0553 Supreme Court of Louisiana 99–0553.

State of Louisiana v. Antoinette Frank. (2007). 1999-KA-0553 Supreme Court of Louisiana 1999–0553.

LaSheila S. Yates

Caril Fugate (1943–)

Murder by women and girls is rare. Multiple murders by women and girls are even rarer, and female spree killers, those who kill several victims at different locations within a short period of time with no "cooling off" period, are the rarest of them all. Caril Fugate is one of a very small group of women who has been defined as a *spree killer.* Fourteen-year-old Caril Fugate and her 19-year-old boyfriend Charles

Charles Starkweather, 19, and his girl-friend, Caril Fugate, 15, were the objects of a sensational manhunt in connection with six slayings in Nebraska, 1958. (AP/Wide World Photos)

Starkweather made history in 1958 with a crime spree that resulted in the murders of 11 people which shocked their bucolic community of Lincoln, Nebraska, and the entire nation. Although it is not clear whether Fugate took part in the murders, she was sentenced to life in prison for the murder of one of the victims killed, and she was believed by many to have helped her boyfriend with some of the other murders. If Fugate did murder anyone, however, it is highly unlikely, by all accounts, that she would have taken part in such violent crimes without the influence of her older boyfriend.

There is little known about Caril Ann Fugate's background. Born July 31, 1943, she was just 13 years old when she met Charles Starkweather through her older sister's boyfriend. Fugate was a native of Nebraska who had never left the state until the murderous spree with Starkweather. Although Starkweather found Fugate amazingly intelligent, she had been held back a year in elementary school and had been labeled a slow learner by her teachers. Caril Fugate's mother and father divorced in 1951. Fugate lived with her mother, her stepfather, and her baby stepsister. While her stepfather, Marion Bartlett, was strict, records do not indicate that Caril was abused. By many accounts, she was a typical lower-class teenage girl with a mild rebellious streak who found the older rebellious Charles Starkweather, a James Dean look-a-like, attractive.

It is not clear what led them on their killing spree or whether Caril Fugate committed any of the murders herself. Some surmise that Fugate's stepfather did not approve of her relationship with Starkweather, and this upset Starkweather. Before the murder spree began, Starkweather killed a gas station attendant, Robert Colvert, in December 1957. However, it wasn't until the following month that Starkweather got Fugate involved.

Sometime in late January 1958, Starkweather brought his .22 rifle to Fugate's home. While the exact details of the murders remain unknown, Caril Fugate's stepfather, Marion Bartlett, her mother, Velda Bartlett, and her two-and-a-half-year-old half sister, Betty Jean, did not survive Starkweather's visit to the family's home in Lincoln, Nebraska. Evidence found at the time of the murders, however, suggested that Starkweather and Fugate had lived in the house for six days with the bodies of Fugate's family, who are believed to be killed on January 21, 1958. When friends or family members came to the house, Fugate reportedly told them that her family was sick with the flu. The young couple, however, became worried when receiving more visits from family members, and they packed up and left the house.

Fugate's extended family soon discovered the bodies of Fugate's family, and the police began looking for Starkweather and Fugate. The couple had driven to Bennet, Nebraska, on January 27, where Starkweather may have thought he could get help from a family friend named Augusta Myer. Apparently, Starkweather and Meyer argued, and Starkweather shot Meyer to death. Later that same evening (January 27, 1958) when their car got stuck in the snow, teenagers Robert Jensen and Carol King offered Starkweather and Fugate a ride. Apparently, Starkweather demanded they drive him and Caril back to the Meyer farm. They stopped at an old storm cellar, where Starkweather shot Robert Jensen and may have attempted to rape Carol King before shooting her as well. It has been reported that Caril Fugate was jealous of Starkweather's attention toward King and that she demanded Starkweather stab King as well. Caril Fugate denies that she played any role in the killing.

After killing King and Jensen, Starkweather and Fugate continued on their way. They took the teens' car and drove back to Lincoln where Fugate allegedly chose a house where the couple would spend the night on January 28. The house was owned by Lauer and Clara Ward, who were then murdered along with their maid Lillian Fencl. Starkweather and Fugate took the Wards' car and continued their journey on January 29. Radio announcers warned listeners of the couple's activities as police set up roadblocks throughout Lincoln. Nebraska governor Victor Anderson called out the Nebraska National Guard to help capture the fugitives.

Starkweather and Fugate, however, had already fled to Wyoming where they tried to change vehicles again. Starkweather shot Merle Collison and attempted to steal his car, but Starkweather was unable to disengage the parking brake. Joe Sprinkle, believing there had been an accident, stopped to help when he noticed Collison was slumped over and Starkweather had a rifle. Sprinkle and Starkweather struggled over the rifle as deputy sheriff William Romer drove by and noticed the two men fighting. When Romer approached, Fugate momentarily distracted the deputy by yelling that she needed help which allowed Starkweather to drive off, but he was apprehended quickly, and the murderous spree ended on January 29, 1958, with a total of 10 dead.

Fugate and Starkweather were each found guilty in separate trials. Starkweather was sentenced to death on May 23, 1959 and executed on July 25, 1959. At the time of her trial, Fugate was the youngest women ever charged with murder in the United States. In her trial, which began on October 27, 1958, Fugate was also found guilty of murder. Fugate's attorneys argued that she was an unwilling captive of Starkweather and that she did not take part in the murders of her family or others. They maintained that Fugate only stayed with Starkweather out of fear for her life and to protect her family who she believed were still alive. However, law enforcement officers reported that she failed to make these claims when she was apprehended, and Starkweather also testified against her. The jury failed to believe that Fugate acted out of fear, and they found her guilty of the murder of Robert Jensen on November 21, 1958, for which she received a life sentence. Fugate's attorneys attempted to gain a new trial, but the judge overturned the motion for a new trial on December 20, 1958, and held that her sentence of life in prison would stand. Again on January 21, 1959, Fugate's attorneys attempted to get her a new trial. This time they requested a suspended sentence and a new trial with the State Supreme Court of Nebraska. On February 6, 1959, the Nebraska Supreme Court refused Fugate both a new trial and a suspended sentence.

On October 31, 1973, Fugate's sentence was commuted to a term of 30 to 50 years by the Nebraska State Pardon Board. All reports indicate that Fugate was a model prisoner, which may have played a role in the Nebraska Board of Parole's decision to parole her the first time she came up for parole after her sentence was commuted. On June 21, 1976, after serving 18 years of her sentence, Caril Fugate was paroled and relocated to Michigan where a job was waiting for her. A couple who had seen a documentary film on Caril and believed her to be innocent had arranged for her to move to Michigan after her parole.

Fugate was forbidden to do interviews about the murders as a condition of her parole. After her parole was up in 1981, she appeared on a 1983 television program called *Lie Detector* where she passed a lie detection test and maintained that she was not a willing accomplice to Charles Starkweather. Since this 1983 television appearance and interviews she granted at the time of the program, she has mostly stayed out of the public eye and led a quiet life working at a hospital. Still, Fugate remains a topic of conversation on various true crime Internet sites on which individuals comment about her innocence or guilt. Some bloggers have reported that she has married.

The killing spree of 1958 was horrendous and terrifying to a nation that had seen very few murderous rampages. Since that time, the couple's murderous spree has served as inspiration for both films and music. *Badlands* and *Natural Born Killers* are two of the most acclaimed films based on the multiple murders by Starkweather and Fugate. Bruce Springsteen's 1982 song "Nebraska" was also inspired by the 1958 killing spree. More recently, in 2005, Liza Ward, a granddaughter of two of the victims of the Starkweather/Fugate killings, published *Leaving Valentine*, which is a fictional account of the murders told from three viewpoints; including Fugate's point of view.

Resources

Davies, Kim. 2007. *The Murder Book.* Upper Saddle River, NJ: Prentice Hall.

Dzwonkowski, Ron. 1983. "Killer's Companion Takes Lie Detector Test." *Spokane Chronicle,* February 16: 90.

Levin, Jack, and James Alan Fox. 1985. *Mass Murder: American's Growing Menace.* New York: Plenum Press.

Lincoln City Library. "The Starkweather Timeline." Accessed on June 26, 2010, at http://www.lincolnlibraries.org/reference/StarkweatherTimeline.pdf.

Newton, Michael. 1998. *Waste Land.* New York: Pocket Books.

Weiser, Charles. 1976. "Carol Fugate Leaves Prison for Michigan." *St. Petersburg Times,* June 21: 5.

Kim Davies

G

Guin Garcia (1959–)

On January 16, 1996, Guinevere "Guin" Garcia was the first woman to be scheduled to be executed in Illinois in almost 60 years when Illinois governor Jim Edgar commuted her sentence to natural life in prison. She had been convicted of killing her husband four months after being released from prison for killing her baby daughter.

Garcia was born in 1959 to an alcoholic mother and an absent father. When she was 18 months old, her mother died after failing from an apartment window. Garcia's maternal grandmother gained custody of her, but failed to protect her from the repeated sexual abuse by one of her uncles. The molestation began when Garcia was six years old and continued through her adolescence. One time, her grandmother came into the room while her uncle was forcing intercourse on her, but her grandmother merely walked out of the room, closing the door.

By the age of 11, Garcia was drinking alcohol heavily. At age 14, she was gang-raped by five boys at a birthday party. The perpetrators were arrested but were not convicted. In addition to enduring emotional and psychological traumas throughout her life, Garcia experienced at least three head injuries, one requiring hospitalization. Due to interpersonal difficulties and intense conflicts with her grandparents, Garcia dropped out of high school and soon began working as a stripper/call girl in a local bar.

When Garcia was 16, Garcia's grandfather gave written consent, in exchange for $1,500, for her to marry a 28-year-old Iranian student who was seeking permanent residency in the United States. Shortly after Garcia gave birth to their daughter, Sara, they divorced. Garcia was living the life of an addict and a prostitute so her grandmother cared for Sara. Because the uncle who had molested Garcia was living in her grandmother's home, Garcia was afraid that he would also molest Sara. As a result, 18-year-old Garcia suffocated her baby daughter with a plastic bag.

The infant's death was ruled an accident, but her death tormented Garcia who set fires on the anniversaries of Sara's birth and death because she was upset and remorseful about her baby's death. Eventually she confessed to killing her daughter. She was convicted and sentenced to 20 years in prison.

While in prison, Guin married George Garcia, an older man who had been one of her clients when she was a prostitute. She was released on parole after 10 years' incarceration and lived with her husband for only a few weeks. Then she moved in with her grandparents and began a relationship with another man. A few months later Guin, armed with a .357 Magnum, went to her husband's home. The couple quarreled, and after a struggle for the gun, Guin shot him at point-blank range.

The prosecution argued, and the jury agreed, that Garcia had killed her husband in an effort to obtain money from him. In contrast, Garcia claims that he had tormented her mentally and physically for 15 years and that she killed him in the heat of passion. There were several accounts that George Garcia inflicted severe physical and sexual abuse on Guin throughout their relationship. On one occasion, supported by medical records, he had placed glass inside Guin's vagina, causing a two-inch laceration of her vaginal and rectal wall.

Guin Garcia was convicted of first-degree murder. At her sentencing hearing, Dr. Lyle Harold Rossiter, Jr., a forensic psychiatrist, testified that she suffered from a very serious mental disorder and was under the influence of an extreme emotional or mental disturbance at the time of the murder. Still, Guin Garcia was sentenced to death.

After losing her initial appeals, Garcia stopped all her appeals. Nevertheless, several death penalty opponents, including Amnesty International and Bianca Jagger, fought to save her life against her wishes. In televised interviews with journalist Carol Marin, Garcia stated that she was responsible for the murders and was taking responsibility, and described herself as an alcoholic who would kill again if she were abused. The only thing she felt would help her was to go back to her childhood. She wanted one day to be a child and not be afraid. Just prior to her commutation, which she did not seek, she stated that she asked for no sympathy and wanted to die with dignity and self-respect. She equated further appeals with a lack of dignity and begging the legal system, which she refused to do.

On January 16, 1996, Illinois Governor Jim Edgar stopped Garcia's execution, and he commuted her death sentence to life in prison without the possibility of parole. She is currently residing at Dwight Correctional Center in Illinois.

Resources

People v. Garcia, 165 Ill. 2d 409, 651 N.E.2d 100 (1995).

Rapaport, E. Equality of the Damned: The Execution of Women on the Cusp of the 21st Century. *Ohio North University Law Review* 26 (2000): 581.

Schmall, L. Forgiving Guin Garcia: Women, the Death Penalty and Commutation. (1996). 11 *Wisconsin Women's Law Journal*. 283.

Jo-Ann Della Giustina

Mildred Elizabeth Sisk Gillars (Axis Sally) (1900–1987)

Mildred Elizabeth Sisk Gillars was an American who was convicted of treason for broadcasting Nazi propaganda radio programs for Radio Berlin during World War II. Nicknamed "Axis Sally" by American soldiers, she used her sultry and sexy voice to demoralize American soldiers and talk about the futility of war against Germany during her daily radio program titled *Home Sweet Home*. Gillars was one of the first women to be convicted of treason in the United States (Fugate 1998, 38).

Mildred Elizabeth Sisk was born on November 29, 1900, in Portland, Maine, to Vincent and Mae Hewitson Sisk. After her parents divorced in 1907, her mother re-married and Mildred adopted her stepfather's last name. During her early years, Mildred's family moved around a lot. She graduated from high school in Conneaut, Ohio, in 1917 and attended Ohio Wesleyan University in Delaware, Ohio,

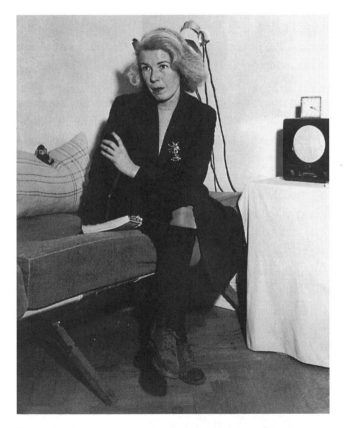

Mildred Gillars, aka Axis Sally, in a prison cell in Germany on January 25, 1947. Axis Sally was a commentator on Radio Berlin who broadcast German propaganda to Allied troops during World War II. She was eventually returned to the United States and convicted of treason. (National Archives)

and Hunter College in New York City with the hopes of pursuing a drama career. Gillars spent much of her time as a young adult struggling to be an actress. In 1929, she went to Paris with her mother for six months to study music. She returned to Europe in 1933 and worked various jobs before beginning her career in German radio. In 1940, Gillars was hired by her former Hunter College professor and lover, Max Otto Koischewitz, to work with the German Radio Broadcasting Company in Berlin. She eventually became one of the most highly paid radio personalities, earning an income of 3,000 deutsche marks a month.

In 1943, Gillars launched the radio program *Home Sweet Home*. While she introduced herself as "Midge at the mike," she became known as Axis Sally by American GIs (Thomas 1999, 328). Gillars was known for beginning her shows by saying "Hello gang. Throw down those little old guns and toddle off home. There's no getting the Germans down." (Associated Press 1988). During her radio programs, Gillars played popular music interspersed with political commentary, humorous skits, and so forth, all the while playing on the loneliness, fear, and homesickness of American soldiers (Fugate 1998, 53–54). Gillars frequently referred to herself as a "one hundred percent American girl" (Fugate 1998, 54). Her radio broadcasts were beamed to American forces in North Africa and Italy. While Gillars admittedly played an active role in promoting Nazi propaganda during the war, she maintained the view of herself as a patriot stating, "I love America, but I do not love Roosevelt and all his kike boyfriends" (Thomas 1999, 327). On May 11, 1944, Gillars participated in the doomsday drama, written by Koischewitz, entitled *Vision of Invasion*. In the drama, which was broadcast to soldiers preparing for doomsday, Gillars played the role of a GI's mother, crying out to American soldiers, "Everybody says the invasion is suicide. The simplest person knows that. Between seventy and ninety per cent of the boys will be killed, or crippled for the rest of their lives!" (Bergmeier and Lotz 1997, 58).

Gillars continued broadcasting her propaganda programs until the fall of Nazism. After the war, she went into hiding and was discovered hiding in the cellar of a bombed-out building in Berlin. Gillars was brought back to the United States in 1946 where she was held in jail until her trial in 1949. Upon return, she was viewed as a traitor and was charged with giving aid and comfort to the enemy from December 11, 1941, through May 6, 1945. The 10-count indictment accused Gillars of violating her allegiance to the United States and said she "knowingly, intentionally, willfully, unlawfully, feloniously and treasonably did adhere to the enemies of the United States (*New York Times* 1948, 11). Her trial in 1949 captured public attention due to the soap-operatic quality of Miss Gillars and her crime.

News accounts of Gillars's capture and criminal trial provide evidence of the complexity of motives behind Gillars activities. According to reports by the *New York Times*, after being captured, Gillars stated that she had become Axis Sally because of the "outlet for dramatic expression" (*New York Times* 1946, 20) and the salary she earned from her work with the German radio. At trial, she tearfully insisted that she never meant to harm the United States. She appeared to contradict herself, stating that she acted of her own free will and yet blaming her involvement on her love for Koischewitz and fear of reprisals from the Nazis.

Gillars was convicted of one count of treason for her involvement with the *Vision of Invasion* broadcast. She was sentenced to 10 to 30 years in prison for her acts of treason and was fined $10,000. She appealed her conviction unsuccessfully and was paroled after serving 12 years in the federal prison in Alderson, West Virginia.

Mildred Gillars died on June 25, 1988. Obituaries documenting the death of the infamous propagandist and traitor Mildred Gillars, aka Axis Sally, were published in various newspapers including the *Washington Post*, the *New York Times*, the *Chicago Tribune*, and the *London Times*. While Mildred Gillars was only one of the Americans who were tried for treason for their activities during World War II, her case stood out due to the continuing debates about whether her radio broadcasts amounted to treason against the United States. After her trial, there was a general disagreement in society about whether Mildred Gillars deserved the death penalty. Did her actions equate to treason? The Axis Sally case illustrates the complexities inherent in the Constitutional definition of treason and the difficulties in determining exactly what types of activities constitute treason. Many of the same issues that arose in the case of Axis Sally are being raised in relation to cases of treason by American citizens in the on-going war against terrorism.

Resources

Associated Press. 1988. "Nazi Propagandist Dead at 87." July 1. Retrieved online from the Lexus-Nexus Academic database.

Bergmeier, Horst J.P., and Rainer E. Lotz. 1997. *Hitler's Airwaves: The Inside Story of Nazi Radio Broadcasting and Propaganda Swing*. New Haven: Yale University Press.

Fugate, Tally Dawn. 1998. *"The Berlin Bitch": An American Voice of Nazi Propaganda*. Master's Thesis. Edmond: University of Central Oklahoma.

New York Times. 1946. "'Axis Sally' Tells Why She Broadcast." December 26, 20.

New York Times. 1948. "Indictment Calls Axis Sally a Traitor." September 11, 11.

Thomas, Theodore N. 1999. "Gillars, Mildred Elizabeth Sisk ('Axis Sally')." In Kenneth T. Jackson (Ed.), *The Scribner Encyclopedia of American Lives. Volume Two: 1986–1990*. Biography and Genealogy Master Index (326–327). Farmington Hills, MI: Thomas Gale.

Note: Various articles on this case appear in the *New York Times* for the years 1949, 1950, and 1988.

Rashi K. Shukla

Debbie Gindorf (1964–)

Debra Lynn Gindorf was convicted of first-degree murder after being found guilty for killing her two children in March 1985. Gindorf, who suffered from postpartum depression and psychosis, is currently serving a mandatory minimum sentence of natural life in prison for her crimes. At the time of Ms. Gindorf's offense, post-partum depression was not recognized as an illness, nor was it available as legal defense.

Debra Lynn Rutkowski was born to Donna and Walter Rutkowski on April 19, 1964, in Waukegan, Illinois. After her parents' divorce at the age of 10, she spent her time shifting between her parents' homes. Debra dropped out of high school during her junior year at Zion-Benton High School in Zion, Illinois.

In 1982, 18 years old and pregnant with her first child, Debra married Randy Gindorf. The marriage between Debra and Randy Gindorf was unstable and turbulent. Randy abused Debra both mentally and physically. Debra had a miscarriage after a beating by Randy. In 1984, while pregnant with her son Jason, Debra was granted a divorce on the grounds of physical cruelty. However, the problems that plagued the marriage persisted. Debra was an unemployed single mother who relied primarily on governmental support to care for her children.

Debra Gindorf experienced severe depression after the births of both of her children. She sought assistance for her depression and was diagnosed with chemical depression while pregnant with Jason. Due in part to her unstable life circumstances, she did not receive appropriate therapy and medication. Although she was experiencing severe depression after the birth of Jason, Gindorf was described by neighbors as a responsible and conscientious mother.

According to court documents, it is unclear whether Gindorf decided to kill her children the night of the offense or sometime before. On the basis of the suicide notes she wrote to her children, it appears that her original intent was suicide.

In March 1985, after deciding to commit suicide, Gindorf asked a friend to take her to the store to purchase sleeping pills. On March 28, 1985, suicidal, extremely depressed, and drinking, Debra crushed the sleeping pills, placing them into three piles. She then mixed the pills into her children's drinks, feeding the mixture to 23-month-old Christina and 3-month-old Joshua. Debra put the children to bed and cared for them as they became sick. She then consumed the last pile of crushed sleeping pills. The next morning, Debra Gindorf awoke to discover that she had vomited up the pills. Her children, however, were dead. She spent the next several hours trying to commit suicide by inhaling fumes from her gas oven, attempting to suffocate herself with a pillow, and by slashing her wrists with a kitchen knife. Unsuccessful in her suicide attempts, she walked to the police station and reported her crimes.

The key question in this case revolves around *why* Debra Gindorf committed her crimes. At trial, two expert witnesses testified that Ms. Gindorf's psychotic episode and "departure from reality" were likely the result of Gindorf's severe mental illnesses and posttraumatic stress disorder (Butterfield, 2006: 4). This argument was rejected, however, on the basis of testimony from the state's expert witness and lay witnesses who provided evidence supporting the notion that although Gindorf suffered from a mental illness, she was "able to tell right from wrong" (4) and was "capable of conforming her conduct to the requirements of law" (4), thus defeating Illinois' two-pronged test for insanity.

Gindorf's suicide notes to her children provide insight into her motives for suicide. In her letter to Christina she wrote, "Mommy had too many problems in her head, that she couldn't deal with, no matter what decision she made. Mommy was *very* depressed and unhappy woman . . . Mommy wanted you and loved you very much (emphasis in original)" (Petition for Executive Clemency, 2003: 7). In her letter to Joshua, she added, "Even tho I'm not around *I still love you very very much* . . . (emphasis in original)" (Petition for Executive Clemency, 2003: 7). She later commented on her motives on March 25, 1985, stating, "there was really no concern that what I was doing was wrong or anything like that. It was just all about us leaving" (Skalski, 2004: 1). In a later interview, Debra described how she views her offense in retrospect, telling a reporter, "I don't ever say 'when I killed my kids' . . . Even though it happened with my own hands, it wasn't me who killed them, it was the illness" (Zorn, 2009: 1).

Although Debra Gindorf was deemed mentally ill by the court, she was found guilty of two counts of murder following a bench trial. She received a mandatory sentence of natural life imprisonment. Attorneys for Gindorf filed clemency petitions in 1989, 2000, and 2003, but the petitions were unsuccessful. In May 2009, Governor Pat Quinn finally gave her a commuted sentence for time served.

Today there is a greater awareness of postpartum depression and its consequences within psychiatry, the criminal justice system, and society. However, little was known about the severity of such mental illnesses at the time of Gindorf's crimes. Postpartum depression or psychosis was not even included in the American Psychiatric Association's Diagnostic and Statistical manual until 1994, years after Gindorf's trial and initial appeal. In recent years there have been a number of high-profile cases similar to Gindorf's in which mothers have been absolved of criminal responsibility or received more lenient sentences. The Committee to Free Debra Gindorf continues to work to free Gindorf and raise awareness for postpartum depression. In a letter to her supporters, Gindorf commented on the significance of her case, stating, "Regardless of whether I get released or not, just knowing that, because of my case, some of you have spread awareness of postpartum illness to others is awesome, gratifying and satisfying to me!" (Gindorf, n.d.).

Resources

Butterfield, Jessica. 2006. Comment: Blue mourning—postpartum psychosis and the criminal insanity defense, waking to the reality of women who kill their children. *John Marshall Law Review* 39: 515. Retrieved February 4, 2008, from the Lexis-Nexus academic database.

Gindorf, Debra Lynn. n.d. A Message of Thanks from Debra Gindorf. Retrieved December 13, 2007, from www.freedebra.org.

The People of the State of Illinois, Plaintiff-Appellee, v. Debra Lynn Gindorf, Defendant-Appellant. No. 2–86–0147. Appellate Court of Illinois, Second District. 159 Ill. App. 3d 647; 512 N.E. 2d 770; 1987 Ill. App. LEXIS 3008; 111 Ill. Dec. 381. Filed August 10, 1987. Retrieved February 4, 2008 from Lexis Nexus Academic, Federal and State Cases database.

Petition for Executive Clemency. 2003. Pardon Docket No. 24126, Before the Illinois Prisoner Review Board, Advising the Honorable Rod R. Blagojevich, Governor, In the Matter of Debra Lynn Gindorf, Register No. N-67063, P.O. Box 5001, Dwight, Illinois 60420, Retrieved December 13, 2007, from www.freedebra.org.

Skalski, Ginny. 2004. Citing postpartum illness, woman who killed children seeks clemency. April 29. Associated Press State & Local Wire.

Zorn, Eric. 2009. Quinn brave where Blago was cowardly—announces he will release Debra Gindorf. May 1. *Chicago Tribune.*

Rashi K. Shukla

Emma Goldman (1869–1940)

Emma Goldman burst onto the American cultural scene during a tumultuous period in history characterized by a wide and ever growing disparity between the haves and the have-nots. As a powerful public speaker and social activist, she was arrested for public order crimes such as "inciting a riot" and the dissemination of illegal materials. Goldman looked upon her time in prison in a positive light, viewing it as an opportunity to bring public attention to her many causes, which, over the course of her lifetime, included freedom of speech, workers rights, legal access to birth control, and opposition to forced conscription into the army.

She was born on June 27, 1869, to a Jewish family living in a region of Eastern Europe now known as Lithuania. In search of greater economic opportunities, her family eventually moved to Saint Petersburg, Russia, the heart of economically oppressive and anti-Semitic Czarist Russia. As a result of the harsh living conditions, she chose to immigrate to the United States at the age of 16, joining family members

1901 mugshot of Emma Goldman taken after her arrest in President McKinley's assassination case. (Library of Congress.)

who had settled in Rochester, New York, some years earlier. Having worked as a seamstress in Russia, she quickly found similar employment in the United States. But she soon found the long hours and regimented factory atmosphere far more repressive than what she had experienced in her homeland, noting that the Russian factory working conditions, which permitted the women to sing, allowed for the development of a strong sense of camaraderie. Moving to New York City after a brief and unhappy marriage to a fellow Russian immigrant, she immediately became involved with the anarchist cause (one of many popular social movements, including socialism and "radical" labor, aimed at alleviating economic oppression and massive income disparities).

Anarchism stands in opposition to any kind of organized governmental entity in the belief that the state serves to stand in the way of individual liberty and any kind of real social progress. Anarchists believe that if the constraints of organized government could be completely removed, people would naturally move toward collectivistic living situations that fostered cooperation rather than competition.

Joining forces with notable anarchists such as Johann Most and Alexander Berkman, Goldman gradually began speaking on behalf of the cause, and she became a powerful public orator, lecturing to crowds of more than 8,000 people at the height of her popularity. Developing a passionate belief in individual freedom, she ignored many social conventions of the day, taking on as many as 20 lovers over the course of her lifetime

Charged with inciting a riot in 1893, her first arrest occurred as a result of her participation in a demonstration involving scores of unemployed women and girls in New York's Union Square who were demanding work. As she marched alongside the downtrodden workers, she carried a red banner with a quote that stated "demonstrate before the palaces of the rich; demand work. If they do not give you work, demand bread. If they deny you both, take bread, it is your sacred right" (Falk, 1984: 26).

After being convicted of inciting a riot, she was sentenced to a year in Blackwell Prison, where she was trained in nursing. This training subsequently led to her long career in midwifery. Goldman's second arrest came in 1901 after police officials made the assumption that one of her fiery speeches induced audience participant Leon Czolgosz to shoot and kill President William McKinley. Suspected of planning the crime, she was arrested and held in a Chicago jail for several weeks, but she was ultimately set free after convincing law enforcement officials that she hardly knew Czolgosz and was in no way connected with the assassination.

Continuing with her progressive activities, she founded *Mother Earth* magazine in 1906—a periodical dedicated to disseminating information in support of the anarchist cause. Soon thereafter, she was arrested while attending an anarchist meeting in New York City and charged with violating the dictates of the newly instituted Anarchist Exclusion Act, but after being bailed out of jail by her anarchist comrades, the charges against her were dropped. A similar arrest took place in San Francisco two years later for unlawful assemblage, preaching anarchist doctrine, and denouncing organized government. On this occasion she was held in custody for several weeks until the $2,000 bail money could be raised, and the resulting month-long trial consequently led to her acquittal.

By 1914 Goldman had become deeply involved in the "right to birth control" movement despite the fact that the dissemination of birth control literature on contraception had been outlawed under the 1873 Comstock Act, which rendered birth control information obscene. For Goldman, the Comstock law was just another example of the government's tendency to encroach upon the freedom of the individual, and her next major arrest occurred in 1916 for disseminating information on birth control. Given the choice of a $100 fine in lieu of 15 days in jail, she opted for detention believing that the sentence would bring greater public attention to the birth control cause.

Shortly thereafter, the United States entered into World War I, instituting the Selective Service Act which required young men between the ages of 21 and 30 to register for the draft. Seeing this as a further infringement on the rights of the individual in the government's attempt to promote capitalism through military aggression, Goldman and fellow anarchist Alexander Berkman organized the No Conscription League of New York. For her activism against the draft, she was arrested on June 15, 1917. Convicted of espionage and conspiracy to prevent persons from registering for the draft, she was ordered to pay a $10,000 fine and was sentenced to two years in prison with the recommendation of deportation once her sentence was completed.

Upon being released from prison in 1919, she immediately resumed her speaking activities but soon discovered that her deportation papers had indeed been signed. After losing a legal appeal in December, she accepted her sentence opting to abandon her legal right to further appeals. Incarcerated at Ellis Island in the immediate days before her departure, she was forced onto a boat that set sail for Europe on December 21, 1919.

Though she had asked to be sent to Soviet Russia because of her intense optimism towards the incipient socialist government, her hopes were soon shattered soon after witnessing the tyranny of the regime, and she eventually began to speak out against its oppressive rule. After a two-year stay in Russia, she spent a brief period in Berlin before moving to England and finally to France, where, with the help of friends, she was able to purchase a small home in Saint Tropez. It was there that she would go on to pen *Living My Life*, her 1934 autobiography. Towards the end of the decade she found time to support the Spanish anarchists by writing articles for European newspapers, even traveling to Spain to assist embattled anarchists in what was to become a lost cause.

From the very beginning of her 20-year exile, Goldman longed to return to the United States, but besides a brief three-month speaking tour in 1934 intended to promote her autobiography, she was never allowed permanent entry into the country. She died on May 14, 1940, from complications from a stroke while living in a small apartment in Toronto, Canada; thus concluded the life of a woman who did all that she could to live by the dictates of her anarchist ideals. Gaining permanent entry into the United States in death, she was buried at Waldheim cemetery in Chicago.

Resources

Bucklin, M. 2004. *Emma Goldman: An Exceedingly Dangerous Woman*. A Nebraska ETV Network Production for the American Experience Series, PBS.

Dalton, D. 1995. The Idea of Anarchism and the Example of Emma Goldman. In *Power Over People: Classical and Modern Political Theory*. Part II Tape 2, Lecture 14. Chantilly, VA: The Teaching Company.

Falk, C. 1984. *Love, Anarchy, and Emma Goldman*. Newark, NJ: Rutgers University Press.

Goldman, E. 1934. *Living My Life*. New York: Garden City Publishing.

Kristyan M. Kouri

Delfina González Valenzuela (ca. 1911–?), María de Jesús González (ca. 1924–?), and Eva González (n.d.)

The González Sisters, or "Las Poquianchis," are on record for being some of the most notorious white slave operators in North America, operating out of the Angel Ranch (El Rancho El Ángel), near San Francisco del Rincon, Guanajuato, Mexico. Young women were lured to the operation with the promise of legitimate employment. These women then were systematically beaten and tortured, sold to brothels for an average of $80, and murdered if they were not compliant, attempted to escape, or lost their attractiveness. Those who were not sold to other brothels were kept at the sisters' own establishments. It is estimated that over 2,000 women were run through the ranch between 1954 and 1963.

In late 1963, three young women had gone missing in and around Guadalajara, one of whom was Maria Hernández. The mothers of these three children made a complaint to the police in León, in Central Mexico. Apparently, they had been approached by a young girl who said that not only had she escaped from a brothel but that their children were being held on a ranch just outside of León. Through investigation, police found the Angel Ranch. One officer commented that as he was looking around the property, he stepped in a soft spot where a woman's hand was uncovered. Storming the house, and then a nearby brothel, they found 19 teenaged girls, aged 14–25. Among these women were the three who had recently gone missing.

Maria Hernández told police a story that was repeated in various forms by many of the women who had been at the ranch. She said she was approached in a park by an older woman with a large mole on her face. This woman was later identified as Josefina Gutierrez, a procurer for the Angel Ranch. She offered Maria a job as a housekeeper in a middle- or upper-class family. Upon her arrival, she was systematically gang-raped and beaten. When she could not work the following day, she was beaten again. She was then sent off to a training brothel in San Francisco del Rincon. It is there that she was found. Josephina eventually told what she knew about her employers and their operation which lead to a formal investigation into this group.

Others recounted how some girls were beaten and starved so badly that they could not work. These women were removed from the brothel and were told that they had "gone to the hospital" and were never seen again. Other stories involved a form of torture called the *cama real*, or "royal bed," which was located at a ranch outside León, where women were sent to die or to receive discipline. The bed consisted of a narrow board where women were forced to lie wrapped in barbed wire, sometimes for days. The bed was designed to cause pain with even the smallest of movements. One woman described being forced to kneel against a wall with a brick in each hand and another on her head and being whipped. Another stated she was left alone to give birth to her baby which later died and was buried on the ranch.

Reports vary as to the results of the search of the grounds of the ranch and brothels. One source states that the bodies of 17 women and 5 babies were found, and another pegs the adult female body count at 80 with a "large number" of infant corpses. Eventually the police established that there were at least 35 murders that took place as part of the slavery ring with some stating there were as many as 100. The ranch undertaker described how she "sprinkled the bodies with kerosene and set them on fire. Then we would call our gravedigger" (Sisters of Shame, 1964).

In October 1964, the courtroom was cleared for the sentencing hearing to protect the sisters against attack. All three sisters were charged with and found guilty of first-degree murder, white slavery, and various other crimes. They received a 40-year prison term; the maximum allowed under Mexican law.

This case is significant as it is one of the few documented cases of a white slavery ring existing post World War II. The fact that this ring was run by three women in the same family was shocking, and several Mexican papers followed this trial with interest. Jorge Ibargüengoitia's 1977 *Las Muertas* (The Dead) is a fictionalized interpretation of the crimes of these women. He used the facts of the case to illustrate the sensationalism of the media. He also utilized actual testimonies and documents to give an accurate representation of what went on at the ranch. Reports of this landmark trial did not, however, make it over the American border; therefore, there are few reports in English on the nature and extent of these sisters' crimes.

Most notably, this case highlights the dangers that face women in poor, developing countries who are looking for work. The sexual exploitation of women into this white slavery ring is representative of similar cases of human trafficking that are more recent. In each case, poor women, desperate to find work to support families, were taken with promises of good work and fair wages and then systematically groomed as fodder for the prostitution industry. The ring operated for almost 10 years without judicial repercussions. It is clear that the sisters had several contacts within the government who were aware of the operations of the ranch and thus allowed it to continue. The sisters received a tip before the police began their initial investigations at the ranch. It was rumored they were preparing to sell their assets and take the money earned from the operation to the United States.

Resources

Ibargüengoitia, Jorge. (1977). *Las Muertas*. México: Joaquín Mortiz. (In Spanish)

"Sisters of Shame." (1964, October 30). *Time*. Retrieved July 17, 2007, from http://www.time.com/time/magazine/article/0,9171,876317,00.html

Hannah Scott

Sandra Good (1944–)

Sandra Good was a member of the notorious Manson family that terrorized California in the 1960s. Good was not involved in the infamous 1969 Tate/La Bianca murders, but she shaved her head and carved an "X" on her forehead during the trial to show her support. The youngest of three girls, Sandra Collins Good was born on February 20, 1944. In her early years she lived in a middle-class home in San Diego, California, but her parents divorced when she was four years old. Her father was a stockbroker, and her mother was a homemaker. Good attended the University of Oregon and Sacramento State College. She has one son, Ivan, who was born on September 16, 1969. The identity of

Sandra Good, one of the members of the notorious Manson "family," talks to reporters in California, 1975. (AP/Wide World Photos)

Ivan's father has not been confirmed; some suspect that the father is her former boyfriend Joel Pugh, son of a Mayo Clinic doctor, and another potential father's name is Charles Manson.

Sandra Good's criminal history spans several years. Good was arrested in 1971 while attempting to help Manson family associate Kenneth Como escape from the Hall of Justice and again in 1972 for trying to hide Aryan brotherhood member Steve Bekins after he robbed a supermarket. Finally, in 1975, Good was arrested for sending threatening letters to corporate executives whom she believed were polluting the earth. After Manson's incarceration, Sandra Good and Lynette Fromme, a second member of the Manson family, moved to Sacramento, California, where the two women became orders in Manson's new religion, the Order of the Rainbow. The two women changed their names to show their devotion to Manson and the order. Sandra took the name "Blue" because of her blue eyes and the ocean, and Lynette took the name "Red" because of her red hair and redwoods. Sandra and Lynette led drug-free lives of abstinence and became more and more concerned with environmentalism. Lynette Fromme went on to attempt to shoot President Gerald R. Ford in 1975, for which she served 34 years in prison and was released on parole in 2009.

The two women created the International People's Court of Retribution (IPCR), a fictitious terrorist group dedicated to ending pollution. In a CBC interview with Barbara Frum in 1975, Good made reference to the IPCR as a "wave of assassins watching those that were killing the wildlife and the earth" (CBC, 1975). Shortly after, Good and several other Family members sent out threatening letters that claimed there were thousands of terrorists in IPCR waiting to assassinate the CEOs of companies that polluted the earth. In a 1990 interview with WGR-radio in Buffalo, New York, Good claimed that 3,000 letters had been sent to the heads of corporations and industries in the United States and Europe (WGR, 1990). She further explained that the letters were not personal threats because "there is no way that I [Good] could give these people the justice that they [the letters] were calling for" (WGR, 1990). In December 1975, Sandra Good was arrested on five counts of conspiracy to send threatening letters through the mail. She was convicted on all charges and served 10 years in prison. Good was incarcerated first in Terminal Island Prison then moved to Pleasanton, California, and finally to Alderson, West Virginia, where she was housed until her release. Good was paroled in 1985 but refused her release terms because authorities would not allow her to move to the town where Manson was incarcerated. She finally agreed to parole conditions that allowed her to relocate to a small town, Bridgeport, Vermont, on Lake Champlain. She has since moved back to California to be closer to Manson. Good, under her nickname "Blue," has been active in developing and maintaining a website dedicated to Manson and his beliefs (All the Way Alive; One World Order). She has continued to be a strong supporter of Manson and is publicly critical of the prosecution of the murders that resulted in Manson's life incarceration.

See also Atkins, Susan; Kasabian, Linda; Krenwinkel, Patricia; Van Houten, Leslie

Resources

"Blue Interview." All the Way Alive, One World Order (website dedicated to Charles Manson). http://www.allthewayalive.com/One_World_Order/blueinterview.html. Retrieved July 15, 2011.

"Blue Thought." All the Way Alive, One World Order (website dedicated to Charles Manson). http://www.allthewayalive.com/One_World_Order/bluethought.html. Retrieved July 15, 2011.

CBC. (1975). Interview with Barbara Frum. Available at: www.archives.cbc.ca/IDC-1–68–368–2086/arts_entertainment/frum/clip4. Retrieved October 25, 2007.

Emerson, Bo. Sandra Collins Good. Available at: www.cielodrive.com. Retrieved October 29, 2007.

Endicott, William. 1975. "Sandra Good Indicted in Death Threat Conspiracy." *Los Angeles Times*. December, 23, B1 and B12.

"Sandra Good, Part of Manson 'Family,' Turns Down Parole. (1985, March 30). *Los Angeles Times*. B1 and B4.

"Two Devotees of Manson Guilty of Death Threats." (1976, March 17) *Los Angeles Times*. 3 and 27.

"Quotes from Blue's Radio Interviews, 1975." All the Way Alive, One World Order (website dedicated to Charles Manson). http://www.allthewayalive.com/One_World_Order/true.blue.html. Retrieved July 15, 2011.

Tara N. Richards

Gessina Gottfried (1798–1828)

Born is Bremen, Germany, Gessina Gottfried was a notorious female serial killer. Little is actually known about her life before she started killing. She confessed to 30 poisonings, 16 of which were fatal. Where possible, she had victims' possessions signed over to her before the victims died, and but she admitted to operating without a conscience. Her crimes stand as some of the earliest recorded cases of serial murder, made even more rare as these murders were committed by a woman.

Although little is known about her upbringing, it is known that at 20 years old Gessina married a drunkard named Miltenberg against her parent's wishes. They had two children. His alcoholism interfered with his ability to sexually satisfy her so she took a lover named Gottfried. When neighbors discovered the affair, she decided to kill her husband by sprinkling a white powder, later found to be mouse poison containing arsenic, in his beer. Wishing to marry Gottfried, she killed her own children by sprinkling poison on their meals. Doctors attributed the deaths to a sudden onset of illness. Her parents were also poisoned over lunch when they objected to the speed of the remarriage. Her parent's deaths were attributed to old age and bowel inflammation. It is suspected that Gottfried was suspicious of these deaths. Gessina began poisoning him slowly, marrying him hours before he died ensuring all his possessions were signed over to her. No suspicions were aroused with his death. Her brother, also an alcoholic, moved in with her after Gottfried's death, succumbing to venereal disease just before signing all his savings over to Gessina. It was reported that she poisoned another unnamed suitor, who willed his estate to her before he died. She also admitted to poisoning an old friend in Hamburg who had asked her to repay a debt.

Gessina Gottfried purchased a large house on the Pelzerstrasse in Bremen. Despite her acquisitions, she ended up being a housekeeper in her own house after the bank foreclosed on her mortgage. The house was bought by a wheelwright named Rumf, his wife, and four children. Rumf had a son during Gessina Gottfried's early tenure as housekeeper, living only one day under Gottfried's care. All remaining family members eventually died shortly thereafter with the exception of Mr. Rumf. He became suspicious after he started feeling ill after each meal, suspecting the white powder that was placed on each dish. Eventually, he took some meat from a meal in to be analyzed. The powder was found to be white arsenic. Gottfried was arrested March 5, 1828, and charged with the murder of six Rumf family members. She boasted of 10 other deaths and another 14 attempts while in custody. At trial she was stripped of her dentures, cosmetics, and the 13 corsets she routinely wore, giving her a skeletal appearance. She confessed to her crimes and testified as to how she liked to watch her victims suffer. She offered nothing by way of defense. She was put to death by decapitation later that year for her crimes. It is recorded that some of her last words were the following: "I was born without a conscience, which allowed me to live without fear."

There is anecdotal evidence that Gottfried was a psychopath or suffering from antisocial personality disorder, given her self-admitted lack of conscience. She liked to control others. She stated that she took all possessions of some of her victims but also admitted to enjoying the suffering of others. It is suggested that she liked the control that others' deaths brought to her life. Although some female serial killers are motivated by financial gain, it is suggested here that she had possessions signed over to her as part of a sadistic practice of dominance and control. She is noteworthy as there are few early documented cases of female serial murderers.

Resource

Newton, Michael. 1993. Gottfried, Gessina Margaretha. In *Bad girls do it!: An Encyclopedia of Female Murderers* (85–86). Port Townsend, WA: Loompanics Unlimited.

Hannah Scott

Rose Greenhow (1814–1864)

Biographers are uncertain of the date of birth of Maria Rosatta O'Neale because she kept her exact age to herself all of her life. It was but one of the many mysteries surrounding a woman destined to be a renowned Confederate spy during the Civil War. She was the middle child in a family of five daughters. Her oldest sister was born in 1810, and her youngest sister was born in 1817. As the middle child, Rose, as she came to be called, was probably born between 1813 and 1814.

The family lived on a small farm in Montgomery County, Maryland. Rose's father, John O'Neale, died at age 34 in April 1817, either by falling from his horse when drunk or being killed by his attending slave who was also inebriated and later hanged even though he protested his innocence. O'Neale's death left his 23-year-old wife, Eliza, in desperate financial straits. After selling first her slaves and then some furnishings to keep her family fed and housed, she was forced to sell nearly everything after 10 years of hardship. In January 1828, she sent Rose and her sister Ellen to live with their aunt and uncle, Maria and Henry Hill, in Washington, D.C., where the couple ran a boarding house for Congressmen. The move remade the sisters' lives from poor farm girls to favorites of the Hill's influential boarders. These important men welcomed the spirited, intelligent, and beautiful young women into their company and confidence. It was here that Rose met and became a close friend of South Carolina senator John C. Calhoun. Their friendship continued until his death at the boarding house in 1850. Rose's oldest sister, Susannah, soon moved to Washington to marry a member of one of the capital's first families, descended from Martha Washington on the paternal side. The marriage provided an introduction for Rose and Ellen into aristocratic Washington society where they mingled with men such as Daniel Webster, Andrew Jackson, Jefferson Davis, and James Buchanan. Their close friends were the nieces and a nephew of Dolley Madison. The latter, James Madison Cutts, courted Ellen and married her in 1833. Rose, still in her late teens, exotic looking with dark hair and brown eyes, had many suitors, and in 1835, she married one of the most eligible bachelors in the city, Robert Greenhow. He was a physician in his early thirties with enviable family connections. At the time, he served with the

Rose Greenhow was a spy for the Confederacy during the American Civil War. She is reported to have continued her intelligence activity even after her capture by the Union in 1861. (Library of Congress)

Department of State as a highly paid librarian and translator of Spanish, French, German, and Italian.

Within seven years, the couple produced three daughters and a son but lost the last two while they were still babies. Another son was born in 1848, but he died the next year, and another daughter was born and soon died the year after that. The Greenhows lost two sons and two daughters in three painful years. Rose's mother died within a few more months, and her close friend and mentor, John C. Calhoun, died in 1850, as she sat by his bedside at the boarding house. Rose had adopted Calhoun's ardent pro-slavery and state's rights positions and believed she must carry on in protests to protect slavery in territories being admitted to statehood.

In her mid-thirties, Rose remained a beautiful and vibrant woman, in spite of the repeated sadness in her life and was ready to join her husband in a new adventure. Greenhow had tired of his work at the State Department and secured a diplomatic assignment in Mexico City from President Zachary Taylor. Leaving their three daughters in Washington with Rose's sister, Ellen, he and Rose set out for Mexico. Upon their arrival, they were welcomed by society leaders, including a French land speculator, Jose Yves Limantour, who held the titles to large parcels of land around a Mexican settlement, Yerba Buena, in the newly admitted state of California. Limantour asked for Greenhow's assistance in proving his land claims in California, and after only six months in Mexico City, the Greenhows left with him for the area that was soon to become San Francisco.

Life in California was not easy since living accommodations were scarce and the gold rush settlers had taken the most desirable accommodations, and the muddy town was a far cry from what Rose had known in Washington. In addition, a devastating fire swept the city in May 1851, and Rose, who missed her children after an absence of over a year, decided to return to Washington without her husband.

After an arduous trip and a few days of rest, once she reached Washington, Rose wasted no time contacting old friends to reestablish her social circle. She began work for James Buchanan in his presidential campaign in 1852. Although Buchanan lost to Franklin Pierce, her loyalty to him would serve her well since Buchanan, in line to become ambassador to the Court of St. James in London, would be elected president four years later. Greenhow paid a visit to his family in the summer of 1852 but returned to San Francisco without Rose and the children. Scarcely nine months later, Rose gave birth to another daughter, named Rose after herself. The child was never to know her father since 10 months later Greenhow fell on a plank walkway in San Francisco suffering injuries that led to a fatal infection six weeks later. Rose filed a lawsuit against the city and was awarded $10,000 (about $250,000 in 2006 dollars according to Measuring Worth statistics). This amount provided her with a substantial nest egg that allowed the two middle daughters to be sent to boarding school and provided an appropriate wedding for the oldest. Her youngest, "Little Rose," was a constant companion.

A small, close-knit group of Southerners in Washington, of which Rose was a central figure, were favored with frequent invitations to the White House during Buchanan's four-year term of office. However in 1860, the election of Abraham Lincoln ended their social domination and brought about a split over slavery that drove wedges between friends and even family members. Rose was outspoken in her defense of Southern states and slavery even though she managed to keep social contacts with those who disagreed with her. She was urged to do so by Confederate General Pierre Beauregard's adjutant in order to gather information from all sources and to use her home as a center to help states that had seceded from the Union. She remained friends with the Confederate president, Jefferson Davis and agreed to help in any way that she could. To prove her loyalty, in July 1861, she passed information concerning Union troops to Beauregard, which Jefferson Davis later credited as key to the Confederate victory at Manassas in the First Battle of Bull Run.

Allan Pinkerton, head of Secret Service, became suspicious and began to monitor her visitors, eventually putting her under arrest after a search of her home uncovered maps and notes about Union military movements. For six months, she was held with Little Rose in her own home, which had been turned into a guarded institution for women prisoners. During those months, she boldly continued to gather information from her guards and visitors, which she transmitted to the Confederacy. Lincoln finally had her moved to the Old Capitol Prison, where she remained with her eight-year-old daughter in squalid conditions for over a year until arrangements were made to exile her to Virginia with a promise not to return until the war was over.

Rose was welcomed as a heroine in Richmond and had scarcely recovered from her voyage when Jefferson Davis sent her a much needed draft for $2,500 as a reward for her services to the Confederate cause (Blackman, 250). Davis, eager to gain recognition and support from the French and English to bolster his troops, soon made an unprecedented decision to send Rose to Europe as his emissary to the heads of those countries. Her cover would be that she was seeking a publisher in England for the diary she kept while in prison. Upon her arrival, she signed a contract for a book, which was published three months after her arrival. Her signature on the contract marked out the letter "e" at the end of O'Neale, and she became known as Rose O'Neal Greenhow, author of *My Imprisonment and the First Year of Abolition Rule at Washington.*

In spite of being entertained by heads of state, being presented in French and English courts, including audiences with Queen Victoria and Napoleon III, and having a romance with Lord Granville, Leader of the British House of Lords, Rose was unsuccessful in her mission to win support for the Confederacy. After a year abroad, she was on her way home after having left Little Rose in a convent in France for safety until the war was over.

She carried the considerable royalties from her book in gold sovereigns which she intended to donate to the Confederate army. As her vessel neared the coast, surrounded by pursuing Union gunboats, a fierce storm ran it aground. Fearing capture by the Union, Rose insisted on escaping by rowboat which was quickly capsized by enormous waves. Weighed down by the gold coins, she drowned and later washed ashore. Her body was wrapped in a Confederate flag at her full military burial in Wilmington, North Carolina, in October 1864. In 1888, the Ladies Memorial Association marked her grave with a marble cross bearing the words: "Mrs. Rose O'Neal Greenhow. A Bearer of Dispatches to the Confederate Government" (*Harper's Monthly*, 124).

Resources

Blackman, Ann. *Wild Rose: The True Story of a Civil War Spy*, Random House Publishers, New York, 2005.

Greenhow, Rose. *My Imprisonment and the First Year of Abolition Rule in Washington.* Richard Bentley, London, 1863.

Harper's Monthly. December 1911–May 1912. Harper & Brothers, New York, 1912.

James, Edward (Ed.). *Notable American Women, Vol. I.* Belknap Press of Harvard University, Cambridge, Massachusetts, 1971.

Marcia Lasswell

Belle Gunness (1859–?)

Belle Gunness was a notorious female serial killer identified as a "black widow" type, killing husbands, lovers, and many of her own children. It is estimated that she murdered anywhere from 13 to 23 people. Although a variety of methods were used, she poisoned most of her victims. Bodies were then chopped up into pieces and buried under various structures on her farm. Belle Gunness often collected insurance monies for their deaths and various arsons she perpetrated.

Belle Gunness was born Brynhild Paulsdatter Storset on November 11, 1859, in Selbu, Norway. Belle emigrated to the United States in 1883, anglicizing her name to Belle Paulson. She lived with her sister Olina (Nellie) Larson and her sister's husband in Chicago until she met Mads Sorrenson in 1884. They adopted Jenny Olson in 1890, and in 1896, Belle bore her first child, Caroline, who died five months after her birth. A second child, Myrtle, was born in 1897. Her first son, Axel, followed in 1898, but he too died in infancy. Lucy was born the following year. Also during this time, a confectionary, in 1896, and a private residence, in 1900, were insured and burned to the ground. Caroline, Axel, and the properties were insured.

Belle Gunness, shown with three of her children. (Library of Congress)

On July 30, 1900, Mads Sorrenson died. Apparently, Belle had given her husband a "powder" for a cold, which sent him into convulsions. The cause of death was determined to be an enlarged heart. He died on the only day that two life insurance policies, filled out in her husband's name, overlapped.

Belle invested the $8,500 insurance claims in a farm near La Porte, Indiana. In 1902, Belle married recently widowed, Peter Gunness. Nine months later he died, in a rather bizarre manner. According to Belle, she stated that Peter must have accidentally tipped a large bowl full of hot brine onto him when reaching for a pair of shoes he had placed on the stove to dry. After being scalded, he had repeated complaints about a cut on his head. The blow was fatal. When asked about it, she stated: "I don't know . . . I picked up the meat grinder from the floor, and I think that must have tumbled on him, one way or another. That is what I think, but I didn't see it" (Shepherd, 246).

Her daughter Jenny confirmed her story, and Belle collected a $2,500 insurance policy. She later gave birth to a child named Phillip. Three men in succession were hired and ended their relationship with Belle rather abruptly. Only Ray Lamphere stayed around the farm even after being fired. She then took out a succession of advertisements in a Norwegian paper. For example: "A rich and good-looking woman, the owner of a pig farm, desires to correspond with a gentleman of wealth and refinement. Object matrimony, Scandinavian preferred" (4 more skeletons in Indiana mystery, 2).

Men began coming to La Porte to marry the rich widow, disappearing suddenly often after making a substantial withdrawal from the bank.

On April 27, 1908, Belle's house burned. The bodies of her children Myrtle, Lucy, and Phillip were found in the basement. Authorities also found the charred, headless body of a woman. Lamphere was charged with the murders. Ten days later, on May 5, while still looking for the head of Belle Gunness. they found the body of Andrew Helgelein. who had been drugged, strangled, cut up. and packaged in old grain sacks. A few feet away were the bodies of Jenny Olson, who had supposedly gone off to school in California, and another unidentified man. In the days to follow, investigators found another body, suspected to be a female, the remains of three more men, two of which were identified as farm hands. The bodies had been sectioned and treated with quicklime, which hampered identification.

Additionally, positive identification of Belle Gunness was difficult. Bottom teeth in the jawbone were used for identification purposes. Belle's body was headless. Further, two doctors' estimated that the woman's body found was probably too small to be Belle's. Upper denture work and lower bridge work, which was attached to a real tooth, was found May 19, 1908. Although she was officially declared dead, the denture work did not prove totally convincing, as it was later offered that it could have been thrown into the fire by Belle. She was sighted several times after her supposed death, and Lamphere was eventually found not guilty of murder but guilty of arson. He died in jail in 1909. He, like others, believed Belle Gunness to be alive and living near La Porte. Her case has inspired many books over the years and a folk song in 1938.

As to motive, it is assumed that she killed all of these people for insurance monies or assets men brought with them. Her own sister remarked: "My sister was crazy for money . . . That was her greatest weakness. As a young woman, she never seemed to care for a man for his own self, only for the money or luxury he was able to give her . . . When living with her first husband in Austin she used to say 'I would never remain with this man if it was not for the nice home he has' " (4 more skeletons in Indiana mystery, 2).

This case is noteworthy for several reasons. As a female serial murderer she clearly used her gender to mask her activities, boldly killing all victims in one location. Belle Gunness also emerged in a time when the rights of women were severely curtailed in the United States. For example, when she first got married, U.S. law stated that women could not hold land if they were married. In her lifetime, newer laws were implemented that stated that widowed and single women could hold and purchase land, but once they married (or remarried), the land would transfer to her husband. Given that Belle was obsessed with money, it is doubtful that she would have separated with her assets easily.

Resources

4 more skeletons in Indiana mystery. (1908, May 7). *New York Times*, 1.

Langlois, J.L. (1985). *Belle Gunness: The Lady Bluebeard*. Bloomington: Indiana University Press.

Shepherd, S.E. (2001). *The mistress of murder hill: The serial killings of Belle Gunness*. Bloomington, IN: 1st Books Library.

Hannah Scott

Clara Harris (1959–)

The Clara Harris case sparked national debate on the mental state and emotional culpability of female offenders. Harris was charged with murdering her adulterous husband and was found guilty of murder with a deadly weapon by "sudden passion."

Clara was a dentist in the state of Texas. David Harris was an orthodontist. They married a decade previous to his murder and had twin sons. Clara and David owned two successful dentist practices in Texas, but Clara owned 51 percent of each practice. While Clara was working at her practice one day, one of her employees had warned her to watch David and to note anything unusual that he was doing. Clara became suspicious. Later, Clara found out that the employees at her dental offices were aware that her husband had been cheating on her with his receptionist.

On July 17, 2002, David Harris admitted his affair, and Clara took advantage of her majority ownership to fire the receptionist, Gail Bridges. David was furious that Clara had released his mistress, and the couple sat down to discuss the situation. David provided Clara with the details of his affair. Shocked and devastated, Clara frantically attempted to become more attractive to her husband. She tried tanning, got new nails, went to the gym, stopped eating, and consulted a plastic surgeon about breast enhancement and liposuction. David and Clara made a list of "comparisons" in which David named all of Bridges's qualities and attributes and compared them to his wife. Clara wrote down all of her "shortcomings" and tried extremely hard to earn her husband back. She also hired a private detective to learn more about Gail Bridges.

On July 24, 2002, David approached Clara and told her that he would be breaking off his relationship with Bridges that night. He was to meet her for dinner and tell her that he loved his wife and was not going to leave her. That night Clara took her stepdaughter out in the car with her to look for David at the place he told her he would be and bring him to be home with his family. She eventually found him with his mistress at the hotel where they had been married a decade earlier. After Clara had a physical altercation with Bridges in the hotel lobby, David Harris screamed, "It's over, it's over," and kicked Clara in the leg.

Clara got into her car, and along with her stepdaughter, she watched David Harris walk Gail Bridges to her car. She then pulled out of her parking spot and ran over David Harris, taking Bridges's car door off. Her stepdaughter screamed and tried to get out of the car. She later testified that Clara intentionally ran over her father, and then she circled around to hit him two more times, killing him. Clara states that her act was an accident and that she only hit him once. The amount of times that Clara Harris ran over her husband was hotly contested in her trial.

Clara's actions have been widely debated. She was a prominent citizen, a dentist, and a business woman. She was a spurned woman who was reportedly trying as hard as she could to salvage her marriage. Her stepdaughter filed a wrongful death suit against her claiming that she intentionally and maliciously killed her father. David's parents continued to stand by Clara through the trial. They forgave her and advocated for her to be released from her sentence so that she could raise her children. David's mother, father, and brother testified during the trial and attested that Clara deeply loved and cared for her family. All involved, including her daughter, stated that Clara tried to do everything possible to make David love her again, that she wouldn't give up on their marriage, and that she had tried to "look pretty" to gain back the attention of her husband.

Murder defendant Clara Harris smiles as her father-in-law testifies in her behalf, 2003. Harris is accused of running down her husband with her car after catching him with another woman. (AP/Wide World Photos)

Clara Harris was interviewed by Oprah Winfrey, and her side of the story was presented to a national audience. Web sites were created, devoted to releasing Clara Harris. Expert testimony was provided arguing that Clara acted in a moment of "sudden passion" and therefore was not rational at the time of the murder. The jury of nine women and three men found her guilty with this stipulation instead of charging her with murder. Over 20 potential jurors were omitted from the jury because they stated that they felt her pain, understood her reaction, and felt that he deserved it.

Clara Harris's case is currently on appeal. She is appealing on the grounds that it would have been impossible to run over David Harris numerous times. Her evidence includes two tapes that demonstrate how the radius of her Mercedes would make such movement impossible. The expert testimony regarding information on these tapes was excluded from the first trial. They are also appealing on the point that the judge disallowed the defense counsel to impeach Lindsey Harris, David's stepdaughter, in spite of repeated inconsistencies in her story. Lastly, the judge would not allow the defense to provide the jury with information on lesser charges.

This case divided the nation into two sides. Clara Harris is currently incarcerated, but some in society feel she should be released because of sympathy for her having "lost it" in the face of her husband's adultery and the thought of losing her family. David's mother, father, and brother, initially supportive of Harris, later became upset that Harris gave custody of the children to a neighbor rather than to them. They filed a successful wrongful death suit against her. Others in society hold the belief that, regardless of what David did and how upset Clara was, she should be held accountable for her actions that fateful day.

Resources

Hollandsworth, Skip. 2002, November. "Suburban Madness." *Texas Monthly*.

Madigan, Nick. 2003, February 14. "Jury Gives 20-Year Term in Murder of Husband." *New York Times*.

Alana Van Gundy-Yoder

Jean Harris (1923–)

Jean Harris was the headmistress of the Madeira School, an exclusive girls' boarding school in McLean, Virginia, but she is best known for being convicted of killing Dr. Herman Tarnower in 1980. Tarnower, a well-known, prominent cardiologist and author of the best-selling book *The Complete Scarsdale Medical Diet*, had been involved with Jean Harris in a long-time romantic relationship.

Jean Harris, born Jean Struven on April 27, 1923, in Cleveland, Ohio, had attended Smith College in Northampton, Massachusetts, where she graduated magna cum laude in 1945 with a major in economics. She was married and had two sons. After her divorce in 1965, she began a relationship with Dr. Herman Tarnower, who gave her many gifts as well as took her on impressive vacations during their approximately 14-year relationship. Tarnower had "a reputation as being a Casanova, regardless of his balding head" and "generally unprepossessing appearance" (Noe 2011). Harris was at the time in her late fifties and considered quite attractive. Tarnower was 69 at the time of his death. While dating Harris, Tarnower had begun a relationship with Lynne Tryforos who was some 20 years younger than Harris. As Tarnower's relationship with Tryforos continued on for more than a few years, it became clear to Harris that she was being replaced by a younger woman.

On March 10, 1980, Jean Harris drove from her school to Tarnower's home in Purchase, New York. She later claimed she had planned to commit suicide with the handgun she had brought with her, after speaking with her former lover one last time. Arriving at Tarnower's home, it was reported that Harris had found the lingerie of Lynne Tryforos on the bedroom floor. There was an argument, and allegedly Herman Tarnower told Jean Harris that she was crazy and ordered her to leave. Harris turned the gun on Tarnower and shot him four times, killing him. She was arrested for second-degree murder. Harris pled not guilty, claiming it was an accident. She was released on $40,000 bail and placed in the United Hospital of Port Chester, New York, for a psychiatric evaluation. She hired a lawyer, Joel Aurnou, and began to start her defense.

Jean Harris, charged with second-degree murder in the shooting of *The Complete Scarsdale Medical Diet* author Dr. Herman Tarnower, is shown leaving the Westchester County Court House in White Plains, New York, 1981. (AP/Wide World Photos)

The case went to trial on November 21, 1980, and lasted 14 weeks. The New York news media focused intensely on the trial, and Harris seemed to make headlines every day. The jury, however, failed to believe her story and found her guilty of second-degree murder.

There was much discussion as to why Harris and her attorney did not use a defense of extreme emotional disturbance, which might have led to a manslaughter conviction and a lighter sentence. Harris insisted that the killing was accidental, and she insisted on going to trial.

During the trial, Jean Harris's reputation as someone with a strong sense of morality was promoted, and it was noted that she had expelled four girls from school for marijuana use. She was also, on the other hand, described as being depressed and confused, and many wondered why her defense did not stress her questionable mental state.

During the trial, it was shown that Harris had written a letter to Tarnower, chronicling the "many wrongs she felt she had suffered on his behalf and pled for better treatment by the doctor. This letter was notable for its rage and pain as well as its extreme hatred for Lynne Tryforos . . . In [this letter] Harris derided Tryforos as a 'vicious, adulterous, psychotic' . . . She repeatedly called Lynne a 'slut' and a 'whore'" (Noe 2011).

Jean Harris was sentenced to 15 years to life and sent to the Bedford Hills Correctional Facility, in Westchester County, New York. There were appeals, but all the appellate courts decided that her trial was fair and that there was no reason to overturn the decision of the lower courts or send it back for a retrial.

In 1993, approximately 12 years after serving time in the correctional facility where she helped found the Fisk House (a part of the prison where model prisoners had their own "room") and where she also tutored and mentored young female prisoners, she was given a pardon by the governor of New York, Mario Cuomo. Today, Harris, in her eighties, has worked for the Children of Bedford Foundation, "which raises funds to help the educational needs of children of the inmates of Bedford Hills" (Kagan 2005). Two made-for-television movies, *The People vs. Jean Harris*, starring Ellen Burstyn and Martin Balsam, and HBO's *Mrs. Harris*, starring Annette Bening and Ben Kingsley, have been produced, and several books have been published about Jean Harris and the killing of Herman Tarnower.

Resources

Alexander, Shana. (1983). *Very Much a Lady: The Untold Story of Jean Harris and Dr. Herman Tarnower*. New York: Little Brown.

Alexander, Shana. (1993). *Marking Time: Letters from Jean Harris to Shana Alexander*. New York: Zebra.

Kagan, Richard. (2005). "A Glimpse into the Imprisonment of Jean Harris." http://www.educationupdate.com/archives/2005/May/html/FEAT-Harris.html

Noe, Denise. (2011). "The Jean Harris Case." Crime Library. www.crimelibrary.com/notorious_murders/women/harris/1.html

Trilling, Diana. (1982). *Mrs. Harris: The Death of the Scarsdale Diet Doctor*. New York: Viking.

Roslyn Muraskin

Masumi Hayashi (1961–)

The whole nation of Japan was shocked in 1998 when 4 people were murdered and 63 people became sick from eating poisoned curry at a neighborhood summer festival. As the police investigated the case, the cunning personality and extended criminal career of the accused, Masumi Hayashi, were slowly revealed. In addition to the murder of these 4, she poisoned her husband and their acquaintances on different occasions in order to make fraudulent life and medical insurance claims. Furthermore, according to the prosecutor, Masumi and her husband paid in total approximately ¥200 million (equivalent to roughly US$1.7 million) for insurance premiums and received about ¥700 million (equivalent to almost US$6 million) through fraudulent insurance claims between 1983 and 1998 (Asahi Weekly, November 3, 2000). Osaka's high court found her guilty of seven crimes, although the police and prosecutor suspected more incidents of insurance fraud (see Table 12).

After Masumi Hayashi's conviction for murder and attempted murder, both Wakayama's district and Osaka's high courts sentenced her to death (Asahi

TABLE 12 Seven Crimes of which Masumi Hayashi Was Convicted by High Court

Charges	Year	Narrative	Damages
Murder/attempted murder	1998	Put arsenic in curry at a summer festival in her neighborhood	Killed 4 people and made 63 others sick
Attempted murder	1998	Put arsenic in their acquaintance's food in an attempt to kill him and to fraudulently obtain insurance money	
Attempted murder	1997	Put arsenic in her husband's food in an attempt to kill him and to fraudulently obtain insurance money	
Attempted tmurder/fraud	1997	Put arsenic in their acquaintance's food in an attempt to kill him and fraudulently obtain life insurance money	Received ¥5.39 million
Fraud[a]	1997	Fraudulently filed an insurance claim that her husband's legs and arms had become paralyzed	Received ¥138 million
Fraud[a]	1996	Fraudulently filed an insurance claim that she had accidentally burned her legs	Received ¥4.59 million
Fraud[a]	1993	Fraudulently filed an insurance claim that her husband had a motorcycle accident (although his injury was actually caused by falling)	Received ¥20.52 million

Note: From 1995 to 1998, the average exchange rate was about ¥120 = US$1 (Bank of Japan 1999).

[a] Kenji was convicted of three counts of frauds in 2000 and released from prison in 2005 after having served a six-year sentence.

Source: Asahi Newspaper, June 28, 2005.

Newspaper, December 12, 2002; June 28, 2005). Although she appealed her sentence to the Japanese Supreme Court, she was denied in 2009. In addition to the notorious nature of the curry incident, the insurance fraud scheme masterminded by Masumi Hayashi raised the public's awareness of the problems in the Japanese insurance system.

Masumi Hayashi was born in Wakayama Prefecture in 1961. Her father was a fisherman, and her mother worked as an insurance agent. After graduating from a public high school, Hayashi went to a nursing school in Osaka Prefecture. Although she completed the course work and graduated from the nursing school, she did not take the national exam to become a registered nurse.

While she was in the nursing school, she started dating Kenji Hayashi, who had a termite control business with a few employees. After Masumi's graduation from the nursing school, they married in 1983 and subsequently had four children.

Masumi Hayashi started working as an insurance agent in 1990. Her insurance business record was relatively good, and she was rewarded a few times for high sales.

However, she frequently obtained new insurance contracts through her husband's gambling friends, many of whom signed multiple contracts themselves (AERA, October 19, 1998). As many people who obtained insurance policies through Masumi Hayashi often later cancelled their policies or made insurance claims, her company started casting doubts on her. The suspicion cast by the insurance company may be the main reason why Hayashi quit her job in 1995.

After Kenji closed his termite control business in 1992, and Masumi quit her job in 1995, both became unemployed. But, using her knowledge of the insurance industry, Masumi masterminded insurance frauds. Masumi and Kenji paid extremely high life insurance premiums by borrowing money from consumer finance loans. They repeatedly utilized their fraudulent insurance scheme and obtained money illicitly. Then they used some of the money to further extend their illegal scheme by returning their loans and purchasing additional policies. Their house expenditures exceeded ¥1 million to ¥200 million (equivalent to roughly US$850,000 to US$1.7 million) per year, and Masumi and Kenji had an extravagant lifestyle until they were arrested in 1998 (Asahi Newspaper, December 12, 2002).

In 1998, 4 people (2 children and 2 adults) died and 63 people got sick by eating curry poisoned with arsenic at a neighborhood summer festival in Wakayama City, which is located in the southwest region of Japan (Chiezo, 2006). As the police investigated the case, they discovered that there were more suspicious incidents of arsenic poisoning surrounding Masumi and Kenji Hayashi. Furthermore, the investigation discovered that large sums of money had been obtained by these two on multiple occasions through fraudulent insurance claims. Based upon such evidence, the police initially arrested Masumi and Kenji Hayashi for insurance fraud. Then two months later, Masumi Hayashi was charged with murder for the curry incident, to which she pleaded not guilty.

Although Masumi Hayashi invoked her right of silence, the police and prosecutor built their case on the basis of circumstantial evidence such as reenactment of people's behaviors at the summer festival. Wakayama's district court determined in 2002 that only Masumi Hayashi had the opportunity to put arsenic into curry. The court suspected that her alienation from other housewives at the summer festival as a primary motive for poisoning the curry. However, the court could not determine the true motive since Masumi Hayashi did not want to talk about her relationship with people in the community (Asahi Newspaper, December 11, 2002; December 12, 2002; June 28, 2005).

Based on circumstantial evidence, Wakayama's district court found Masumi Hayashi guilty of murder and attempted murder and sentenced her to death. Osaka's high court supported Wakayama's district court's decision and rejected her appeal in 2005. She subsequently appealed to the Japanese Supreme Court. Although Masumi Hayashi broke her silence during her appeal to Osaka's high court and claimed her innocence, this high court dismissed her appeal.

The fraudulent insurance scheme masterminded by Masumi Hayashi shocked the insurance industry, and people started to develop skepticism about the Japanese insurance system. The system of insurance companies that allows people to make a contract and pay off claims easily without much investigation came into question, and the public demanded the companies to restructure their systems.

An additional key point of the Masumi Hayashi's case was that she was convicted of murder and attempted murder based on circumstantial evidence, and the appropriateness of such a criminal trial without physical evidence was debated for the first time in the Japanese justice system. There was also a debate as to whether the court could order the television company to submit its interview tapes with Masumi Hayashi as evidence and whether this order constituted an intrusion of freedom of the press (Asahi Newspaper, December 13, 2002). At the end, Osaka's high court decided not to introduce these interview tapes as evidence (Asahi Newspaper, December 17, 2004).

Concerning the freedom of the press, two lawsuits were filed by Masumi Hayashi against a publishing company (Asahi Newspaper, November 19, 2005). First, a tabloid cameraman secretly took a photo of Masumi Hayashi during her trial in the courtroom and published her photo in the magazine, despite the fact that photographing of offenders was prohibited in the courtroom. Second, the same tabloid published a sketch of Masumi Hayashi wearing handcuffs and a rope around her waist during her trial. Although the media was allowed to draw sketches of criminal trials, the artists typically did not draw handcuffs or a rope. The publisher subsequently lost lawsuits in both cases.

Finally, several issues regarding crime victims were raised. The media's insensitive treatment of Masumi Hayashi's neighborhood residents raised a question about their rights of privacy. The negative effects of the media on these residents (i.e., secondary victimization) became the focus of its attention. Furthermore, the families of the murdered victims and those who survived the curry incident were awarded monetary compensation as a result of a civil lawsuit in 2003 (Asahi Newspaper, December 25, 2003). However, even if Masumi Hayashi's assets had been sold through governmental auction, the likelihood that the victims would receive any monetary compensation is slim because the majority of the money collected would be diverted to national taxes. Masumi Hayashi did not pay taxes on her earned insurance money, which is subject to taxation, and the taxation office is expected to receive the money before any other parties get monetary compensation. The Masami Hayashi curry incident reminded people of the weakness of the victim relief measure in Japan.

Resources

AERA. 1998. Wakayama sagi jiken de huhu taiho. [Couple arrested for insurance frauds in Wakayama]. October 19, 10–15.

Asahi Newspaper. May 14, 1999. Wakayama no dokubutsu konyu hokenkin sagi jiken. [The poisoned curry incident and insurance frauds], 30.

Asahi Newspaper. December 11, 2002. Karei dokubutsu jiken, Masumi hikoku ni genkei. [The poisoned curry incident: A severe penalty for Masumi Hayashi], 1.

Asahi Newspaper. December 12, 2002. Hayashi Masumi hikoku ni shikei. [The death penalty for Masumi Hayashi], 1.

Asahi Newspaper. December 12, 2002. Karei jiken hanketsu kosshi. [The poisoned curry incident: A summary of the trial court's verdict], 32.

Asahi Newspaper. December 13, 2002. Karei jiken Wakayama chisai hanketsu: Minpo bideo saiyou ni hamon. [The verdict for the curry incident in Wakayama: Effects of allowing videos as evidence], 37.

Asahi Newspaper. December 25, 2003. Karei jiken: Hayashi Masumi hikoku ni baishou meirei [The curry incident: Monetary compensation for the victims and their families], 18.

Asahi Newspaper. December 17, 2004. Rokuga tepu shoko husaiyou. [The court did not allow videos as evidence], 19.

Asahi Newspaper. June 28, 2005. Hayashi Masumi hikoku nishin mo shikei. [The high court sentences Masumi Hayashi to death], 1.

Asahi Newspaper. November 19, 2005. Mudan satsuei irasuto shouzouken shingai ka [Photographing without permission and violation of privacy rights], 37.

Asahi Weekly. 2000. Hanketsu Hayashi Kenji hikoku ni choeki rokunen hokengaisha no itadeto kyoukun. [The verdict: A six-year sentence for Kenji Hayashi: damages and lessons for insurance companies]. November 3, 150.

Bank of Japan. 1999. *Economic and Financial Developments in the Second Half of Fiscal 1998*. http://www.boj.or.jp/en/type/release/teiki/ar/data/ar9902.pdf. (Accessed February 26, 2007).

Chiezo. 2006. Chiezo. [The encyclopedia of contemporary words]. 439. Tokyo, Japan: Asahi Newspaper.

Yumiko Watanuki, George Kikuchi, and Yoko Baba

Patty Hearst (1954–)

Patty Hearst was one of the most notorious women in the United States in 1974. Having first been kidnapped and then later videotaped robbing a bank with the same militant group that abducted her, Hearst's status as victim quickly changed to that of criminal. The controversy to this case and the focus of the trial was whether Hearst was a victim or a criminal. How does a young, wealthy, yet allegedly defiant, woman move from being a kidnapped victim to an armed robber? The case also called into question her status as a good girl in light of her cohabitation with her fiancé. Finally, the Hearst case signifies the strong impact of psychological trauma on victims and the condition of the Stockholm syndrome.

Patricia Campbell Hearst was born on February 20, 1954, in San Francisco, California, to Randolph A. Hearst and Catherine C. Hearst. Patty's grandfather was William Randolph Hearst, the prominent newspaper publisher who was well-known in his use of tabloid journalism. She grew up in a very wealthy family of five girls. Some claim that Patty received everything that she wanted. In the aftermath of her return to her family, many journalists reported that Patty was spoiled and defiant. However, the 1970s was a decade of distrust of large corporations and the wealthy. Yet, there was also an attempt to hold on to traditions. It is highly probable that Patty was being condemned for stepping

Patty Hearst holds up an executive grant of clemency as she leaves the Federal Correctional Institution in Pleasanton, California, 1979. (AP/Wide World Photos)

out of gender role expectations. For example, as a teenager, Patty had a crush on Steven Weed, a teacher and her math tutor. Patty and Steven had an affair and later moved in together. When Patty was 19 years old, she and Steven became engaged. While Patty did well in school and even earned an award for best student in her freshman year at Menlo College, her affair and cohabitation, especially at such a young age, was highly frowned upon.

On the evening of February 4, 1974, Patty Hearst was kidnapped from her Berkeley apartment. Members of the Symbionese Liberation Army (SLA) knocked on the door, assaulted her fiancé, and kidnapped Hearst at gunpoint. Hearst was kept locked for two months in a closet, and she was continuously physically and sexually assaulted. Patty Hearst's kidnapping was claimed to be a revolutionary political kidnapping in an attempt to free two SLA soldiers who had been recently arrested and were in police custody. The SLA's leader Donald DeFreeze had declared war on the wealthy and powerful. Initially, the SLA's ransom demand called for the Hearst family to distribute several millions of dollars worth of food to the poor. They also demanded that the Hearst family publish SLA propaganda that claimed that the SLA had arrested Patty Hearst and that she was in protective custody.

Patty's father had complied with all demands; however, upon a second demand to distribute food to the poor, Randolph A. Hearst agreed on the condition that Patty be returned. It was at this time that the SLA ceased negotiations. Soon following, the Hearst family received a tape, allegedly from Patty, claiming that she had joined the SLA. The tape showed Patty dressed as a revolutionary holding a gun and standing in front of the SLA emblem. She also claimed that she was given the choice to be released or to join the SLA and fight for the freedom of oppressed people. She chose to stay and fight. Patty was given a new name—Tania. Later, Patty claimed that she was threatened to either join the SLA or be killed.

At 9:40 AM on April 15, 1975, Patty Hearst and four members of the SLA walked guns in hand into the Hibernia Bank in San Francisco, California, and stole over $10,000. Bank surveillance cameras showed Patty holding a carbine rifle. In the robbery, two bystanders were shot. Many have asked why Patty did not flee when she was holding the loaded rifle. Furthermore, the FBI reported that on May 15, 1974, Patty fired 30 shots in an attempt to help SLA soldiers Bill and Emily Harris escape a robbery. Patty Hearst was arrested on September 18, 1975, and convicted of armed bank robbery. She claimed that she was under duress.

During her trial, F. Lee Bailey hired psychiatrists who testified that Patty Hearst had experienced mental deterioration and brainwashing that resulted from the endless violence she experienced while in captivity. Patty was kept locked and blindfolded in a closet, beaten, sexually assaulted, and raped for several weeks. She was also subjected to SLA revolutionary ideologies. After 12 hours of deliberation, the jury found Hearst guilty, and she was sentenced to 25 years in prison. She criticized F. Lee Bailey for exploiting her case for personal gain and even being drunk during her closing statement. While Patty was convicted of the robbery, her case opened the door to the consideration that she could be a victim of the Stockholm syndrome, a condition named for a phenomenon that occurred in 1973 after people taken hostage for six days by bank robbers in Stockholm, Sweden, became emotionally attached to their captors. Characteristic of this syndrome, Patty Hearst was kept isolated, told that no one would rescue her, assaulted, and told she might die. Many believe that she developed positive feelings for her captors whom she relied on to keep her alive and interpreted their later behaviors as regard for her.

Patty Hearst was given a partial pardon from President Carter on February 1, 1979, after serving two years of her sentence. In 1987, she failed to obtain a full pardon from President Reagan but was given a full pardon by President Clinton on his last day in office in January 2001. Patty Hearst married Bernard Shaw, her former bodyguard, and had two children. She has done some acting and has had roles in movies and television shows. Patty Hearst's traumatic experience had tremendous significance for female victims of violence, including domestic violence.

Resources

Boulton, David. 1975. *The Making of Tania: The Patty Hearst Story*. New York: New English Library.

Castiglia, Christopher. 1996. *Bound and Determined: Captivity, Culture-Crossing, and White Womanhood from Mary Rowlandson to Patty Hearst*. Chicago: University Of Chicago Press.

Freedman, Suzanne. 2002. *The Bank Robbery Trial of Heiress Patty Hearst: A Headline Court Case.* Berkeley Heights, NJ: Enslow.

Hearst, Patricia Campbell, and Alvin Moscow. 1981. *Every Secret Thing.* New York: Doubleday.

Venessa Garcia

Leona Helmsley (1920–2007)

Leona Helmsley, better known as the "Queen of Mean," was notorious for her fits of temper and schemes to avoid paying taxes. Her infamous reputation was based on the treatment of her employees, and her belief that she was beyond paying taxes added to her notoriety. It had been reported by many that her fits of temper for very minor infractions by employees usually resulted in personal attacks on the individual, followed by dismissal from the company. She was not always an extremely wealthy person, having started from humble beginnings. Leona was also a generous philanthropist and gave large donations to many charities.

She was born Lena Rosenthal on July 4, 1920, in Ulster County, New York. She was the third in a family of four children. When the economy took a downturn, the family moved several times and eventually settled in Manhattan. Lena was close to her brother and father, but her relationship with her sisters and mother was strained. Lena became bored halfway through high school and dropped out to seek a more interesting life path. A name change was part of this new life, and she finally settled on Leona Mindy Roberts.

Her claims of being employed as a cigarette model for Chesterfield Cigarette Company have not been verified. Leona married Leo Panzirer, and their son Jay was born after four years. Shortly thereafter, they were separated and divorced. Her second husband was her boss, Joseph Lubin, whom she married and divorced twice. With three failed marriages and a son, Leona was on her own again. She did some secretarial jobs and then was hired as a secretary by a real estate firm. There was a shift in ownership of the firm two years later which proved to be a life-changing development for Leona. She found she had a skill for selling real estate. She was confident and diligent, which created a client base for her, and generated profits for the company.

Leona Helmsley, 1991. (AP/Wide World Photos)

By the late 1960s Leona had become very prosperous in the real estate business, though it did not satisfy her ambition and desire for success. While working in the real estate industry, she heard of Harry Helmsley and arranged a meeting through mutual acquaintances. The rumors of romance between Harry and Leona started shortly after she became employed at a Helmsley subsidiary, which was a problem because Harry was married. Harry and his wife Eve were divorced in 1971, however, and Harry married Leona in 1972.

In 1971 Leona had her first encounter with the legal system when she tried to force the residents of a property she managed to purchase their homes. She allegedly verbally abused and threatened tenants until they gave in, but some residents became tired of this treatment and sued her. When she married Harry in 1972, she was reported to be in serious financial trouble.

Harry Helmsley had a dream of building and running a world-class luxury hotel. Once the property for the hotel was secured, the building of the Helmsley Palace Hotel began in 1978. The hotel was completed in 1980, and Harry gave it to Leona to oversee operations. Some hotel employees reported that Leona acted irrationally, bestowing praise in one sentence, then berating the person in the next. She was in charge of operations for all the hotels in the Helmsley corporation. Her mistreatment of employees was believed to have led to an attempt on her and her husband's lives in the 1980s.

In 1989 Leona and Harry Helmsley were indicted for tax fraud, mail fraud, and extortion. They purchased an estate in Greenwich, Connecticut, for $11 million. They did an enormous amount of renovations to the estate, totaling $8 million. They were reluctant to pay for the work because they felt they were grossly overcharged. They charged the majority of the work done on this estate to Helmsley subsidiaries. The contractors and decorators who performed the work became frustrated and filed suit against the Helmsleys. This resulted in 188 counts of tax fraud, and an amount of $1 million in personal income taxes was owed to the government. Leona individually faced federal charges of extortion and mail fraud. The investigation also implicated two ex-employees as accomplices.

When it was time for the trial to begin, Harry Helmsley was deemed incapable of being prosecuted due to failing health. Leona would face the trial alone. The prosecution presented extensive evidence illustrating the extreme lengths to which Leona Helmsley had gone to hide income and fraudulently bill expenses through Helmsley subsidiary companies. She was convicted of 33 felony counts of trying to defraud the government, including tax evasion, mail fraud, and filing false tax returns. The sentence was 16 years in federal prison and a fine of a little more than $7 million to be paid to the federal government. After an appeal in New York Superior Court, all but eight charges were dropped, and she subsequently served 18 months in federal prison.

Harry died in 1997, leaving his entire estate to Leona. Another court trial stemmed from charges filed by ex-employee, Charles Bell, who claimed she fired him for being homosexual. He was awarded $11 million, but an appeal reduced the settlement to $500,000.

Leona died of heart failure on August 20, 2007. Though she was notorious for being tyrannical in her business practices and treatment of her employees, she was also a shrewd business woman. She was generous to many charities and relief funds. The distribution of her estate was a controversial issue. She left $12 million to her dog Trouble and excluded two of her grandchildren. When the matter of the estate came before a judge in 2009, it was ruled that the amount left to Trouble would be reduced to $2 million, and each of the excluded grandchildren received $6 million. The trustee of the estate designated $1 million of the estate to be evenly divided between 10 animal rights and welfare charities, including A.S.P.C.A and Guide Dogs for the Blind.

The majority of the estate was designated for medical research and medical care centers. New York Presbyterian/Weill Cornell Medical Center and Mount Sinai Medical Center were the two largest of the estate donations. The Helmsley Trust is a foundation that also supports different nonprofit agencies to promote research in the areas of health and medicine, conservation, education, and human services.

Resources

A&E Television Networks. 2009. *Bio True Story. Leona Helmsley Biography.* http://www.biography.com/articles/Leona-Helmsley-9334418

CNN.Com. 2007, August. Leona Helmsley, "Queen of Mean," Dies at 87. http://www.cnn.com/2007/US/08/20/helmsley.obit/index.html

Helmsleytrust.org. 2009. http://helmsleytrust.org/

Moss, Michael. 1989. *Palace Coup: The Inside Story of Harry and Leona Helmsley.* New York: Doubleday Publishing.

NYTimes.com. 2009, April. Trustees Begin to Parcel Leona Helmsley's Estate. http://www.nytimes.com/2009/04/22/nyregion/22helmsley.html

Dena Webster

Myra Hindley (1942–2002)

Myra Hindley may have been the most well-known and notorious female criminal of 20th-century Britain. Her case remained prominent in the media from her conviction for murder in 1966 to her death in prison in 2002. She was an almost iconic figure who inspired books, plays, songs, and art exhibits. A police mug shot, taken at the time of her arrest in 1965, depicted 23-year-old Myra with a bleached blonde bouffant hairdo and impassive, unsmiling face. This photo became the defining image of her and the one that usually accompanied news stories, even when she had grown older and changed her appearance completely.

In April 1966, Myra Hindley was convicted jointly with her boyfriend Ian Brady for the murders of two children, Edward Evans and Lesley Ann Downey, and as an accessory after the fact in the murder of John Kilbride. They were both sentenced to life imprisonment, the mandatory penalty for murder in England and Wales. While Hindley and Brady were awaiting trial, the death penalty had been abolished. Because the murders of three children were considered to be particularly horrific crimes, the fact that they could no longer be executed for their crimes increased public interest in the case.

Hindley and Brady lived together in Hindley's grandmother's house in Manchester, an industrial city in northern England. They abducted the children from Manchester and took them to their home, where Brady killed them. They buried the bodies of Lesley and John on the moors. On the evening that they had abducted Edward Evans, they invited Hindley's brother-in-law, David Smith, to visit them. He witnessed Brady attack the boy with a hatchet before strangling him, and then helped Brady and Hindley clean up. When he left their house, he informed the police of what he had seen, and Edward's body was discovered in the house. During the investigation, the police discovered a safe kept by Brady that contained photographs of Lesley Ann without her clothes and a tape recording of her crying and pleading as she was stripped naked. These formed part of the evidence in the case.

Two other children from Manchester were thought to have been murdered by Hindley and Brady, although their bodies had not been found. In 1987, Hindley broke her 21-year refusal to discuss the murders and her role in them during a session with a prison chaplain. She admitted that she and Brady had also killed Pauline Reade and Keith Bennett and attempted to help the police find where their bodies were buried on the moors. The search was successful in finding the remains of Pauline.

The judge in Hindley's trial stated that he believed she could be rehabilitated. While in prison she obtained a university degree and reverted to the Catholicism and religiosity of her girlhood. Her supporters argued that she did not pose a threat to the public and should one day be released. Hindley expressed remorse for her part in the crimes. She stated that she had been infatuated with Brady and willing to do whatever he asked of her. She also said that he was physically violent towards her and that during their relationship, she was afraid of him.

In 1994, Hindley discovered that a "whole life" tariff had been imposed on her in 1990, more than 21 after her original conviction. This meant that a decision had been taken that she should never be released from prison. It was not a penalty that existed at the time she had been sentenced. Supporters helped her to mount a legal challenge against what appeared to be a retrospective punishment, but it was upheld by the House of Lords in 1997. Myra Hindley died in prison in November 2002 and was a rare example of a murderer who was never released.

Hindley's case remained in the public eye throughout her life, and granting her parole or overturning her whole life sentence would likely have proved deeply unpopular with the public. Critics of her punishment have argued that she was kept in prison due to political expediency, rather than an objective assessment of her case. As a woman involved in the abduction and murder of children, Hindley was particularly susceptible to being stereotyped as a witch and a monster. She never managed to replace the image of herself as an expressionless 23-year-old in the public's imagination, and she remained a high example of an evil woman.

Resources

Birch, H. (1993). "If looks could kill: Myra Hindley and the iconography of evil." In H. Birch (ed.), *Moving Targets: Women, Murder and Representation*, London: Virago, 32–61.

Gurnham D. (2003). "The Moral Narrative of Criminal Responsibility and the Principled Justification of Tariffs for Murder: Myra Hindley and Thompson and Venables." *Legal Studies* 23: 605–623.

Murphy, T., and Whitty, N. (2006). "The Question of Evil and Feminist Legal Scholarship." *Feminist Legal Studies* 14(1): 1–26.

Schone, J. M. (2000). "The Hardest Case of All: Myra Hindley, Life Sentences and the Rule of Law." *International Journal of the Sociology of Law* 28(4): 273–289.

Winter, J. (2002). "The Truth Will Out? The Role of Judicial Advocacy and Gender in Verdict Construction." *Social and Legal Studies*, 11(3): 343–367

Lizzie Seal

Xaviera Hollander (1943–)

Known as the "Happy Hooker" for her love of sex work and her best-selling biography of the same name, Xaviera Hollander was arrested and incarcerated for crimes associated with prostitution. But Hollander was no ordinary prostitute. Through the success of her book *The Happy Hooker* and her lengthy career writing about sex for *Penthouse*, Hollander contributed to an era of more open sexual discussion and sexual freedoms for women.

Born on June 15, 1943, in a place now known as Indonesia, Xaviera De Vries spent the first months in relative luxury as her father, Dr. Mick De Vries, was a successful physician who owned a hospital and two expansive villas. But all was lost when the Japanese invaded the Dutch-controlled island and her father was placed in a concentration camp for the crime of being of Dutch/Jewish extraction. Though Hollander and her French/German mother, Germaine De Vries, were detained along with him, Dr. De Vries was soon transferred to a separate camp to tend to the medical needs

British writer Xaviera Hollander, author of *The Happy Hooker*, sits in a swivel chair while promoting her book in London, England, 1972. (AP/Wide World Photos)

of other prisoners. Reunited at the end of the war three-and-a-half years later, the family eventually returned to Holland.

Regrouping in Amsterdam, Hollander's parents reared her in what she describes as a loving home in which she was afforded privileges such as piano lessons and European vacations which helped her achieve fluency in five different languages. Upon graduation from high school, she continued her studies in music and later attained a secretarial position at an advertising agency. Her crowning achievement during this time period was a Best Secretary in Holland award which was bestowed upon her by the Manpower Employment Agency in Amsterdam.

While Hollander's first love affair was with a female high school classmate, she eventually came to enjoy sex with both women and men, developing an almost insatiable need for sexual contact. Her quest for variety did not, however, stop her from falling head over heels in love. After moving to South Africa in the mid 1960s, she began a whirlwind courtship with Carl Gordon, a Jewish American economist, which quickly led to their engagement. Following Gordon to America six months later, Hollander arrived in New York City in December 1967.

Though Hollander soon discovered that her fiancé had a dark side to his personality, she was determined to salvage the relationship—even if it meant enduring both insults and infidelities. But their betrothal ended 14 months later when Gordon left her for a job in South America. Emotionally crushed by his betrayals, she embarked upon what she referred to as a "sex binge."

By this time Hollander was fairly well established in New York City. She had secured a secretarial job at the Dutch Consulate which afforded her a temporary green card, and she had moved into an apartment shared with a female roommate 10 years her senior. Her sexual exploits, however, became a source of tension between the women, and the roommate took to calling her a nymphomaniac in times of anger. And it does indeed seem that Hollander had developed what many modern health care professionals might refer to as a sex addiction. She herself, in fact, came to a very similar conclusion. When comparing herself to her roommate in her memoir, *The Happy Hooker*, she writes that "[her] retreat from reality was the bottle in the same way that mine was sex. At night she would quietly drink herself into a happier world while I would screw myself into mine" (Hollander, Moore, and Dunleavy, 1972: 74).

During this same time period, a series of encounters with people who admonished her for "giving herself away for free" led her to the following conclusion: why not supplement her meager secretarial income with cash she could earn her for doing something she loved? With this realization, she began her career as a prostitute.

Hollander first worked in a brothel run by a small-time New York City madam, but because the working environment in the madam's "house" was so poor, she took to bringing clients to her own apartment. She soon learned, however, that unsavory characters practiced in the art of extortion were watching her every move, and she was forced to navigate a situation common to many prostitutes. On one afternoon, a man posing as a police officer forced his way into Hollander's home, and after attempting to assault her, demanded that she pay him a weekly protection fee. Though Hollander refused, she soon discovered that he had stolen her entire day's pay and some nude photos her former fiancé had taken of her.

In another instance of extortion against Hollander, a moving man, who sensed she was a call girl, offered her his "protective services." When a stranger pressured her to pay him $5,000 for the return of the stolen pictures, Hollander turned to the moving man for help. Murdering the blackmailer in the process, the moving man was indeed able to retrieve the photos. And after charging her for an exorbitant fee several weeks later, he would periodically return to her apartment to extort additional sums of money from her.

Weary of working under the direction of other madams, Hollander eventually made the decision to open her own brothel. In the summer of 1970, she secured an apartment, installed telephones, and hired young, attractive, well-mannered female employees. The vast majority of these women worked as actors, models, flight attendants, and even as a university professor but moonlighted as call girls to make ends meet. But whatever their primary occupation, the women were allotted a percentage of the total cost for their services, and in return for the portion of the fee that went to the brothel, they were provided with clients, a place to work, and an attorney, should they be arrested.

Hollander likened her role as a madam to that of a hostess who helped her customers to relax with a few drinks while waiting for their sexual services and depicted her "house" as "boutique where exclusivity and good-taste prevail" (Hollander, Moore, and Dunleavy, 1972: 174). And her business sense was right on target. For the next two years, she became the most successful madam in New York City.

Working in the sex industry was not, however, always easy for Hollander, and throughout her tenure as both call girl and madam, she was taken into police custody on four different occasions. Her first arrest occurred in February 1970. While Hollander was working in a brothel run by a local madam, eight police officers broke through the door and arrested the call girls on duty. Once in jail, Hollander was photographed and forced to undergo a physical exam before a judge dismissed the entire case.

In another instance, three undercover police officers posing as johns gained entrance into Hollander's private brothel. After spending an hour of laughing, joking, and drinking, they identified themselves as police officers, arrested Hollander and everyone on the premises, and hauled them off to jail. Initially charged with prostitution, the unlicensed storage of alcoholic beverages, and the possession of untaxed cigarettes, Hollander's crimes were later reduced to misdemeanors.

According to Hollander, many of the police she encountered engaged in police misconduct. When she was driven to the police station after her very first bust, the cop sitting beside her grabbed her hand and placed it on his penis. Other police indiscretions involved money. When Hollander was busted in her own brothel, the arresting officers would keep any cash they found lying around her house. And because these raids proved so costly, she found herself paying off corrupt police officials in an attempt to prevent further arrests.

As city leaders developed an increasing awareness of the rampant corruption that existed within the ranks of the New York Police Department, New York City mayor John Lindsay formed the Knapp commission—an undercover operation designed to weed out crooked cops. Hollander ultimately became a central figure in this inquiry because of her involvement with an undercover Knapp commission informant and her pay-offs to the police.

At this same time, Hollander's book *The Happy Hooker* was released, and the publicity generated by the highly publicized Knapp Commission hearings helped to make the book a huge success. But Hollander had been living in the United States without a green card for some time, and her notoriety brought her to the attention of immigration and naturalization services. As a result, she was deported back to Holland in April 1972. With this, her career as a prostitute/madam was essentially over.

Her legal woes, however, were not yet behind her. Resettling in Canada after marrying a Canadian antique dealer Frank Applebaum, Hollander was accused of stealing several nightgowns from an upscale department store and was eventually deported from that country as well.

Hollander managed to remain in the lime light despite her legal setbacks. With her new-found reputation as a person who could write openly and intelligently about sex, she was hired to pen a monthly sex advice column for *Penthouse* magazine—a job that lasted 35 years. Hollander's book, *The Happy Hooker*, and her other writings have been instrumental in increasing the amount and quality of sex discussion in general social discourse. Additionally, Hollander, among others in the 1970s, helped open the door to women's sexuality by demonstrating that women could and should seek sexual pleasure just like men.

As of the publication of this biography, she continues to write, produce plays, and collect modern art. She and her second husband, Philip de Haan, divide their time between their bed-and-breakfast hotel in Amsterdam and a vacation home in Spain.

Resources

Burnham, D. (1970). 7 Police Officers Face Knapp Unit. *New York Times.* November 6.

Dunlap, R., and Hollander, X. (2008). *Xaviera Hollander, The Happy Hooker: Portrait of a Sexual Revolutionary.* Directed by Robert Dunlap. Red Productions. Los Angeles.

Gage, N. (1971). Vice Arrests Follow Knapp Bribe Inquiry. *New York Times.* July 24.

Hollander, X. (2009). *Xaviera Hollander The Happy Hooker.* www.xavierahollander.com.

Hollander, X., Moore, R., and Dunleavy Y. (1972). *The Happy Hooker: My Own Story.* New York: Harper Collins.

Kouri, K. (2009). Personal interview conducted with Xaviera Hollander. January 22.

Parrot, J. (1972). She's Happier in her New Profession. *Los Angeles Times.* April 18.

Kristyan M. Kouri

Karla Homolka (1970–)

Karla Leanne Homolka (aka Karla Bernardo, Karla Teale; currently Leanne Teale) is Canada's most notorious female serial killer. Although she plead guilty to two manslaughters in an agreement for her testimony against her husband, Paul Bernardo (aka the Scarborough Rapist), with whom she committed her crimes, she assisted in the assaults of other teenage girls, including her youngest sister.

She was born on May 4, 1970, in Port Credit, Ontario. She was the first of three of Karel and Dorothy Homolka's girls. She met her husband at a hotel restaurant on October 17, 1987, while attending a convention in Toronto. The couple immediately became intimate and later married on June 29, 1991. In February 1993, the couple legally changed their names to Teale, after the serial killer Martin Thiel in their favorite movie *Criminal Law.* In January, prior to their official name change, Homolka left Bernardo after he beat her in what an attending physician at the St. Catharines General Hospital described as "the worst case of abuse he had ever seen" (Williams, 1998: 285). Homolka sought the legal counsel of George Walker, prior to notifying police that she was implicated in two murders committed by her husband, against whom she was willing to testify. In February 1994, she obtained a divorce on the grounds of cruelty.

Karla Homolka in 1993. (AP/Wide World Photos)

During their time together, the couple drugged, raped, and murdered several girls, videotaping the sexual assaults for later viewing. Their first victim was Tammy Lyn Homolka, Karla's 15-year-old sister, who was raped and killed on December 23, 1994, in the basement of the family home. Tammy was Homolka's Christmas present to Bernardo—a virginal offering to her future husband, who was disappointed that she was not a virgin. To facilitate the assault, Homolka stole Halcion and halothane from work, the Martindale Animal Clinic. Homolka and Bernardo ground the Halcion and mixed it into Tammy's drink. When Tammy passed out, Homolka held a halothane-soaked cloth over her face while she and Bernardo took turns raping her. The combination of food, alcohol, and drugs caused Tammy to vomit, asphyxiating her. The police were called but ruled the death an accident. Because Homolka "ruined" Bernardo's Christmas gift, she tried to make up for it six months later with a similar wedding present. Homolka invited a young friend over whom she had met at her previous employment. Again, Homolka administered alcohol, Halcion, and halothane, and again she and Bernardo took turns raping the 15-year-old, while videotaping the assault. The girl survived this and a later assault.

The couple's next homicide victim was 14-year-old Leslie Erin Mahaffy, whom Bernardo abducted on June 15, 1991. Mahaffy was held captive, tortured, and raped. Because her body was dismembered, the circumstances surrounding her death are unclear. Homolka said she was beaten and strangled by Bernardo, but the only evidence of physical assault were "two unexplained equidistant, asymmetrical, subcutaneous bruises, chest high on either side of her back" (Williams, 1998: 486) suggesting, as Bernardo did, that Homolka tried to suffocate her (CBC, 2006). Mahaffy's body was cut into pieces that were encased in cement and dumped in nearby Lake Gibson. Mahaffy's body was found on Homolka and Bernardo's wedding day by a couple canoeing.

Fifteen-year-old Kristen Dawn French was the couple's last victim. On April 16, 1992, she was abducted from a church parking lot after being lured by Homolka who requested directions with map in hand. French was raped and tortured for several days before Bernardo beat and strangled her prior to attending Easter dinner at the Homolkas. Kristen's naked and beaten body was found April 30, 1992, in a ditch along Number 1 Sideroad, Burlington (Burnside and Cairns, 1995).

On May 14, 1993, Homolka accepted a plea deal, whereby in exchange for testifying against Bernardo, she would received two 12-year terms to be served concurrently for the manslaughters of Mahaffy and French and "blanket immunity" for all related crimes. This agreement was negotiated prior to the discovery of six 8 mm videotapes of the rapes. The Crown entered the agreement out of desperation, as they had little evidence linking Bernardo to the girls' murders. Although the police searched Bernardo's home for 71 days, the tapes were not found until Bernardo told his lawyer, Ken Murray, of their location. However, Murray did not turn the tapes over to the police but kept them for 16 months before handing them over to his replacement, John Rosen, upon his resignation (Chidley, 1995). Because Homolka's July 1993 trial predated Bernardo's May 1995 trial, a media ban was implemented by Judge Francis Kovacs to ensure that information from her trial would not prejudice his. Upon the disclosure of the tapes and evidence of her extensive involvement in the rapes, the public was furious that Homolka received such a light sentence. A petition, signed by 320,000 people, asked the Ministry to revoke her plea agreement (Williams, 2003). Similarly, there were attempts to put conditions on her upon her release from prison. Both efforts were in vain. On April 12, 2005, Ontario Attorney General Michael Bryant affirmed Homolka would not be indicted on additional crimes, and on November 30, 2005, a Québec Superior Court judge, James Brunton, lifted restrictions imposed on Homolka by Judge Jean Beaulieu (CBC, 2005).

Homolka was evaluated numerous times throughout her involvement with the criminal justice system. Early evaluations found she suffered from depression and post-traumatic stress disorder, consistent with spousal abuse syndrome. However, a later evaluation by Dr. Angus McDonald indicated that "Karla Homolka remains something of a diagnostic mystery. Despite her ability to present herself very well, there is a moral vacuity in her which is difficult if not impossible to explain" (Cairns, 2005: 39). Homolka was released from prison on July 4, 2005, and is currently living in Montréal with her son, born on February 2, 2007, and Thierry Bordelais, the baby's father (Gatehouse, 2007).

Resources

Burnside, Scott, and Alan Cairns. 1996. *Deadly Innocence*. New York: Times Warner Books.

Cairns, Alan. 2005. Karla's life behind bars. *Toronto Sun*, June 5.

CBC News Online. 2005. Homolka now free without conditions. November 30. http://www.cbc.ca/canada/story/2005/11/30/homolka051130.html.

CBC News Online. 2006. Indepth: Bernardo. February 21. http://www.cbc.ca/news/background/bernardo/.

Chidley, Joe. 1995. Bernardo: The untold story. *Maclean's*, September 11.

Gatehouse, Jonathon. 2007. Is Karla fit to be a mother? *Maclean's*, June 4.

Williams, Stephen. 1998. *Invisible Darkness*. New York: Bantam Books.

Williams, Stephen. 2003. *Karla: A Pact with the Devil*. Toronto: Cantos International.

Kim S. Ménard

Katherine Howard (1521?–1542)

Katherine Howard was the fifth wife of King Henry VIII and the second to be beheaded. She is a historical example of criminalization related to women's sexuality and childbearing. Howard's alleged sexual improprieties violated expectations of women at the time, and her failure to contribute a child to her royal husband's legacy further underscored her lack of proper contribution as a woman. Allegations resulted in her being found guilty of treason, as handed down by the Council. The act of treason was defined as misrepresenting herself to the King as chaste and sexually innocent and for allegedly committing adultery. This crime was punished in the most severe fashion: capital punishment by beheading.

Howard was 1 of 10 children born to Lord Edmund and Jocasta Culpeper. She is not believed to have been a great beauty even though she did catch the eye of Henry probably within the first month of her being in his court. She had a sweet, childlike quality about her with a propensity to please the men in her life. Howard was raised in the house of her step-grandmother, Agnes Duchess of Norfolk. Given the vast size of the household, over one hundred persons, the living situation was more like a dormitory than a quiet grandmother's house. Howard, being an adolescent girl with minimal supervision, found many opportunities to test her sexuality. It was common for many of the young girls to have boys come into the shared bedroom at night. Howard's first experience was with Henry Mannox, a music teacher, which proved to be inconsequential and was never fully consummated. The second liaison was much more serious and would eventually cost both lovers their lives. Francis Dereham spent many nights in Howard's bedchamber; they consummated their love and even referred to each other as "husband and wife," indicating a pre-contract. By law, a pre-contract existed if a couple engaged in sexual intercourse with a promise of marriage at a later date. In 1539, Howard was invited to court to be a maid of honor to Anne of Cleves, at which point Dereham left for Ireland. Howard apparently forgot her pre-contract with Dereham, probably as her adolescent feelings for Dereham disappeared and in her excitement to be at court.

One way for families to move up in society was to align themselves with other powerful families through marriage. Thus, marriage was largely a political activity which was engaged in to increase wealth, status, and power. Though few could hope for a union with the King specifically, the Howard family was successful. Over time, the family was able to arrange for the marriage of two relations to the King. Katherine Howard's cousin, Anne Boleyn, became Henry's third wife. Her marriage, like Howard's, was arranged by her uncle Thomas Howard, Duke of Norfolk. After two miscarriages, Anne was accused of sexually deviant behavior (incest and adultery) and was beheaded.

Court was where one came to gain favor with the King, a requirement for success, and could be a dangerous place. The definition for treasonous behavior was very broad, and punishment was death. Treasonous behavior involved any intention to do harm to King Henry through either action or thought. Almost any behavior could be viewed as treason. Court was very politically centered as families jockeyed with each other to gain favor with the King. Though the Howard family had already lost one woman to King Henry's suspicious nature, they did not hesitate to sacrifice another. Women were used as pawns by the men in their family, in order to gain the most advantageous position possible within the social hierarchy. Women were not viewed as free agents with desires and a will of their own; they did what they were told. Thus, nobody ever asked Katherine Howard if she wanted to marry King Henry, not that she would have refused. The King was viewed as being just under God, of having a direct line to his wishes and desires. To refuse the King would be an absolutely unthinkable action. Upon being proposed to, Howard, understandably, did not reveal her previous sexual experiences to Henry. She was probably following the example of her step-grandmother and uncle, Duke of Norfolk, who both knew about Dereham and Mannox. King Henry and Katherine Howard were married on July 28, 1540. The King was 30 years Howard's senior, sick and in extremely bad health. He would refuse to see Howard for days at a time, sometimes as many as 10 or 12.

Howard's sexual affairs before marriage and her pre-contract to Francis Dereham were exposed by a family who had something to gain by unseating the Howards from the throne. During the investigation of a pre-contract with Dereham, the possibility was raised that Howard may have engaged in sexual relations with Thomas Culpeper, a member of the King's chambers. Both Howard and Culpeper denied the accusations. Neither of them ever confessed to adultery even when Culpeper was under extreme torture. Katherine Howard was beheaded on February 13, 1542.

Howard had four known or alleged lovers during the course of her life: Henry Mannox, Francis Dereham, Thomas Culpeper, and King Henry VIII. If Howard had been a man, these few sexual experiences would not even be worth noting. She was beheaded on the assumption that she might have committed adultery though this was never proven. Her secret meetings with Culpeper may have been nothing more than an attempt to bribe him into keeping her previous sexual encounters with Dereham quiet. There is a widely held assumption that had Howard borne a child, she would never have been accused of adultery. She failed to become impregnated by a man who was very sick from a wound in his leg and who was quite possibly impotent. In not divulging information about her past she mislead the King, though it should be noted that King Henry divorced Anne of Cleves for this very reason—her failure to divulge a pre-contract. It would seem that because King Henry adored Katherine Howard but was not as fond of Anne of Cleve's, that Howard's indiscretions probably hurt King Henry much more. Her death may have been nothing more than a lover's revenge, which would probably have been overlooked had she had a child. Howard, Dereham, and Culpeper were all executed.

Resources

Fraser, Antonia. 1992. *The Wives of Henry VIII*. New York: Alfred A Knopf.

Harris, Barbara J. Women and Politics in Early Tudor England. *Historical Journal*, 33, No. 2. (1990), 259–281.

Lindsey, Karen. 1995. *Divorced, Beheaded, Survived*. Reading, MA: Addison-Wesley.

Smith, Lacey Baldwin. 1954. English Treason Trials and Confessions in the Sixteenth Century. *Journal of the History of Ideas*, 15, No. 4, 471–498.

Smith, Lacey Baldwin. 1961. *A Tudor Tragedy: The Life and Times of Catherine Howard*. London: The Reprint Society.

Smith, Lacey Baldwin. 1971. *Henry VIII, The Mask of Royalty*. London: Jonathan Cape.

Warnicke, Retha M. Kathryn Howard. *Oxford Dictionary of National Biography*. Accessed April 21, 2007.

Wilson, Derek. 2001. *In the Lion's Court: Power, Ambition and Sudden Death in the Reign of Henry VIII*. New York: St. Martin's Press.

James David Ballard and Shelley Azzarito

Melissa Huckaby (1981–)

The case of Melissa Huckaby, who was convicted of kidnapping, sexually assaulting, and killing eight-year-old Sandra Cantu, demonstrates that women can and do partake in crimes largely committed by men. In fact, the National Center for Post Traumatic Stress Disorders estimates that as many as 14 percent of childhood sexual assault cases are perpetrated by women (Whealin, 2010). But that said, Huckaby's crimes are still quite unusual. When women do engage in the act of molestation, the crime is often committed in association with a male and the age of the victim tends to be somewhat older than that of Sandra Cantu (Finkelhor, 2008). It is also rare for a woman to kill a child other than her own offspring.

Melissa Lawless Huckaby was born on February 23, 1981, to Brian and Judy Lawless in Orange County, California. The information currently available suggests that she had a normal childhood without a history of psychological problems. People who knew her from Brea Olinda High School, which she attended from 1995 to 1999, remembered her as a likable person who was especially interested in dance. She had a number of friends, they recalled, and did not exhibit any kind of deviant behavior (Tully and Ponsi, 2009).

Melissa Huckaby listens to public defender Ellen Schwarzenberg during Huckaby's arraignment in a Stockton, California, courtroom in 2009. (AP/Wide World Photos)

Her parents, who report being baffled by their daughter's violent deeds, contend that her emotional troubles began after being raped by a police officer at the age of 19. Although she was admitted to a series of psychiatric facilities for a number of short-term stays, her father asserts that she never received any long-term therapeutic care. "Whenever she was admitted into a facility," he told NBC's *Today Show* host Matt Lauer, "she would tell the doctor it was 'just a bad moment' [and] the doctor would write it off and release her" (Lauer, 2010). Despite the lack of comprehensive treatment, she was prescribed number of psychiatric medications which she continued to take up until the time of Cantu's murder.

Melissa Huckaby's young adult life was also marked by a host of additional challenges. Her marriage to John Huckaby in May 2003 ended shortly after giving birth to their daughter Madison. Melissa cited alcoholism, domestic violence, and child abduction as the primary reasons for the dissolution of the marriage.[1] And despite brief stints as a medical biller and event planner, she was never able to hold down a job for any period of time. Mired in debt, she subsequently filed for bankruptcy in 2003. She later found it difficult to secure child support payments from John Huckaby and was consequently granted $237 per month in public aid (Tully and Ponsi, 2009).

A lack of financial resources may have led her to engage in the practice of shoplifting. She was convicted of petty theft for stealing items from a Target store in Los Angeles County in 2006, and at the time of her arrest for the murder of Sandra Cantu, she was in the midst of serving a three-year probation sentence for a petty theft conviction in San Joaquin County (Adams, 2009).

In June 2008, Huckaby's paternal grandparents, Connie and Clifford Lane Lawless, asked her to travel to their mobile home at the Orchard Estates mobile home park in Tracy, California, a rural town east of San Francisco, to help them pack for an impending move. The move never took place, and Huckaby and her daughter Madison ended up staying in Tracy. Although Connie Lawless described her unemployed granddaughter as a loner who would intentionally cut herself on her ankles, Huckaby did have, at least, some contact with the people around her at that point. She taught Sunday school in the Clover Road Baptist Church, where her grandfather served as minister, and she formed an on-and-off again relationship with Daniel Plowman, a man she would eventually stand accused of drugging (Simerman and Kazmi, 2010).

The tendency to drug people appears to have been part of an emerging pattern for Huckaby, for in January 2009, Huckaby was also alleged to have drugged a seven-year-old neighbor girl with one of the many psychiatric drugs she was currently taking (Simerman and Kazmi, 2010).

On March 27, 2009, Huckaby lured Sandra Cantu, her neighbor and her daughter Madison's frequent playmate, to the Clover Road Baptist Church located just down the road from her home. And there, within the confines of the church walls, she drugged the child, sexually assaulted her with a rolling pin taken from the church kitchen, and strangled her (Goldman, 2010; Kazmi, 2010a). She then stuffed the child's body into a suitcase and dumped it in a nearby farming trench filled with manure and other liquid waste products (Simerman and Kazmi, 2010).

Though Huckaby engaged in odd behavior immediately following Cantu's disappearance, such as reporting that the suitcase that was ultimately used to dispose of the child's body had been stolen and checking into a hospital after allegedly swallowing an X-Acto knife blade, law enforcement officials did not initially view her as a suspect. FBI experts were instead looking for a "white male, 25–40, with a criminal history of sexual assault or child pornography" (Simerman and Kazmi, 2010), but upon careful examination of the facts, investigators began to compile a case against her.

After being presented with a plethora of evidence linking her to the murder, during a series of interviews with detectives, Huckaby finally admitted to killing the child. She was arrested on April 10, 2009, and ultimately charged with murder with special circumstances including kidnapping, rape with a foreign object, and lewd conduct with a minor.

Huckaby surprised everyone when, on May 10, 2010, she pled guilty to the crime of murder with the special circumstance of kidnapping. According to the *Contra Costa Times*, "prosecutor James Willett decided to make the plea agreement because of the expense of a capital case that would likely be moved to Southern California, followed by perhaps decades of appeal" (Kazmi, June 16, 2010). In agreeing to this plea, Huckaby escaped the death penalty and the charges of rape with a foreign object, and lewd conduct with a minor. The unrelated charges of drugging her ex-boyfriend and a neighbor girl were also dropped (Dillon, 2010; Kazmi, 2010). The plea also allowed Huckaby to avoid a lengthy trial and to retain some contact with her daughter. She was subsequently sentenced to life in prison without parole on June 10, 2010.

On the day of her sentencing, Huckaby told the court that she had no idea why she committed the crime, and at the time of this writing, Huckaby's motive for killing young Sandra Cantu remains uncertain. It is, however, evident that she has been plagued with some sort of psychological ailment. Although theories about just what this ailment might be abound, the Tracy Police Department reported that Huckaby had been diagnosed with bipolar disorder and schizophrenia. Yet, it is unclear just who made this diagnosis and whether she had experienced any of the delusions and hallucinations associated with schizophrenia.

Note

1. John Huckaby told Chris Cuomo of ABC's *Good Morning America* that the charges his former wife lodged against him were false (2009).

Resources

Adams, C. (2009). Sunday school teacher arrested in murder of Sandra Cantu. *Crime Examiner*. www. examiner.com/x-1168-Crime Examiner. April 11.

Breuer, H. (2010). Inside story: Clues to why Melissa Huckaby murdered an eight-year old girl. *People Magazine.* June 27.

Cuomo, Chris. (2009). Television interview with John Huckaby. *Good Morning America.* April 17.

Dillon, Nancy. (2010). Melissa Huckaby, who killed eight-year-old Sandra Cantu, pleads guilty to avoid death penalty. *New York Daily News.* May 10.

Finkelhor, David. (2008). *Childhood Victimization: Violence, Crime, and Abuse in the Lives of Young People.* New York: Oxford University Press.

Goldman, Russell. (2010). Melissa Huckaby used noose to kill eight-year-old Sandra Cantu. http://abcnews.go.com/US/Media/melissa-huckaby-confessed-murderer-year-girl-sent enced-life/story?id=10910285.

Kazmi, S. (2010a). Court records show Huckaby drugged, sexually assaulted Sandra Cantu with rolling pin. *Contra Costa Times.* June 14.

Kazmi, S. (2010b). Melissa Huckaby's parents speak out for first time on NBC's *Today. Contra Costa Times.* July 2.

Lauer, M. (2010). Television interview with Brian Lawless, Judy Lawless, and Joni Hughes. *Today Show.* July 2.

Simerman, J., & Kazmi, S. (2010). A calculated killing: The case against Melissa Huckaby. *Contra Costa Times.* June 21.

Tully, S., & Ponsi, L. (2009). Woman suspected in 8-year-old's slaying grew up in O.C. *Orange County Register.* April 19.

Whealin J. (2010). *Men and Sexual Trauma.* National Center for Post Traumatic Stress Disorders www.ptsd.va.gov.

Kristyan M. Kouri

Dolores Huerta (1930–)

Dolores Huerta is an example of a woman who was apprehended for actions taken during attempts to bring about social change; most of her arrests were grounded in laws that prohibit acts of civil disobedience. A founding member of the United Farm Workers Union, Huerta was arrested on at least 22 different occasions while participating in strikes and demonstrations intended to bring about fair and equitable working conditions to hosts of downtrodden workers.

Born on April 10, 1930, to Alicia and Juan Fernandez, the young Dolores spent the first three years of her life in New Mexico. Upon her parents' divorce, her mother moved her and her four siblings to the San Joaquin Valley, located in Central California. After several years of hard work and careful planning, Alicia Fernandez was able to purchase a restaurant and hotel—an investment that allowed her to provide her children with what Dolores later described as a working-class

United Farm Workers cofounder Dolores Huerta attends a dedication of the César Chávez Monument on the San Jose State University campus in California, 2008. (AP/Wide World Photos)

yet comfortable lifestyle. Dolores's mother often provided needy farm workers with rooms in her hotel for little or no money, and Huerta therefore credits her mother for imbuing her compassion for the plight of farm workers.

Though she did not see much of her father during her formative years, Alicia kept his image alive by speaking of his political work and recounting stories of his attempts to organize New Mexican mine workers. These stories also served to inspire the future labor activist.

Dolores Huerta entered into what is now known as San Joaquin Delta College immediately after high school graduation, completing her degree and teaching credential. It was while teaching elementary school in 1955, a job she obtained soon after graduating from college, that she became acquainted with social activist Fred Ross. Founder of the Community Service Organization (CSO) in Los Angeles, a group dedicated to securing rights for Mexican Americans, Ross was determined to form a chapter in Stockton, California, and he enlisted Huerta and her mother to help him with this cause. "When I saw all the things they were able to do," Huerta told *Ms.* magazine in 1997, "bring in health clinics, fight the police—it was like a revelation." Huerta became acquainted with Cesar Chavez through her work with CSO.

Because both Huerta and Chavez had become frustrated with the CSO's inability to secure basic rights for farm workers, they formed the National Farm Workers Association in 1962, and after merging with the Filipino-based Agricultural Workers Organizing Committee in 1967, the United Farm Workers Union of America (UFW) was born. Throughout these transformations, Huerta served not only as labor organizer, but also as a political lobbyist, contract negotiator, and job action strategist, or, as declassified FBI documents pertaining to the Delano grape strike assert, "the driving force behind the picket lines" (FBI, 1992).

In the beginning, it seemed as though the UFW had won a significant victory in negotiating union contracts with growers, but the growers soon found ways to circumvent union mandates. Typically grapes would be purchased from nonunion farms, and growers would apply their own labels to the fruit to appear as though the grapes had been picked by union farm workers. To combat these practices, Huerta convinced the UFW to launch a nationwide boycott of grapes, a job action that she would ultimately go on to direct. The boycott caught on with Americans throughout the nation, and in 1970, after a sweeping decline in the sale of grapes, the entire California table grape industry bent to the will of the UFW.

All of Huerta's more than 20 arrests took place while engaging in strike activities. Although picketing is considered a guaranteed form of free speech, it must be conducted within the confines of carefully constructed parameters. Strikers who step outside of these boundaries are usually arrested for actions that fall under the rubric of public order crimes which include misdemeanor offenses such trespassing, disturbing the peace, disorderly conduct, or failure to disperse. Though the vast majority of Huerta's arrests for such crimes did not result in convictions, she was sometimes forced to spend as much as a week in jail after being taken into custody. One fairly recent arrest, however, did lead to two subsequent guilty verdicts. While working alongside the Hotel Workers Union in Palm Springs, California, she was arrested, and in 2005, she was convicted of trespassing and disorderly conduct and was sentenced to six months probation.

In their attempts to force the strikers to disperse, the police would sometimes make use of physical force, and Huerta was not immune to these violent tactics—this in spite of her steadfast commitment to nonviolent protest. During a 1988 San Francisco protest rally, she was clubbed so forcefully and hurt so badly that she had to be rushed to a nearby hospital. As a result of these injuries, which ultimately consisted of a ruptured spleen and broken ribs, she sued the city and used the money awarded in damages to launch the Dolores Huerta Foundation, a nonprofit organization "whose mission is to build active communities working for fair and equal access to healthcare, housing, education, jobs, civic participation and economic resources for disadvantaged communities with an emphasis on women and youth" (Dolores Huerta Foundation).

Dolores Huerta found time to form a very large family right in the midst of all her political activism. Celeste and Lori, the first 2 of her 11 children, were born during an early marriage to Ralph Head; Fidel, Emilio, Vincent, Alicia, and Angela arrived while she was married to her second husband, Ventura Huerta; and Juanita, Maria Elena, Ricky, and Camilla were the result of her long-time partnership with Richard Chavez, brother to Cesar.

Over the years, Huerta has become involved in so many social causes that she has been likened to turn-of-the-20th-century social activist Emma Goldman. In addition to her work with the Dolores Huerta Foundation and her ubiquitous union activities, she also spends her time promoting women's causes. She became formally involved in the feminist movement in the 1980s, partly because of the rampant sexism she experienced while working with the male UFW rank-and-file, and perhaps because she has received so little credit for the instrumental role she played in securing rights for farm workers. She became an active member of the National Organization for Women in 1987, and she currently holds a seat on the Feminist Majority executive board. In the fall of 2007 and spring of 2008, she campaigned for Democratic presidential hopeful Hillary Rodham Clinton.

Resources

Dolores Huerta Foundation. http://www.doloreshuerta.org/

Drake, S. S. Dolores Huerta. *Progressive*. September 2000. 34–38

FBI. *The FBI Mission: The Delano Grape Strike*. Washington, DC: Government Printing Office, 1992.

Felner, J. Women of the Year. *Ms*. January/February 1978.

Kouri, Kristyan. Personal interview with Dolores Huerta. January 30, 2008.

Murcia, Rebecca. C. *Dolores Huerta*. Bear, DE: Mitchell Lane Publishers, 2003.

Kristyan M. Kouri

Francine Hughes (1947–)

On the evening of March 9, 1977, Francine Hughes set fire to the bed where her ex-husband lay sleeping, then fled the house with three of her children, arriving at the police station shortly thereafter. In a landmark court decision in November of that year, Francine was declared not guilty by reason of temporary insanity, becoming one of the first women to be acquitted of murder for killing an abusive partner in a way that clearly fell outside traditional notions of self-defense. Her case represents one of the first successful uses of a battered woman's defense, although it was not called that at the time.

Hughes was born in August, 1947, to Hazel and Walter Moran. Her family lived in the country outside of Lansing, Michigan. In her early life, Hughes's father worked the onion fields, and her mother took waitressing jobs on and off as needed. Francine Hughes had two older and three younger siblings.

Although she grew up poor, Francine recalls her childhood as happy—filled with playing outside and enjoying nature. She was very eager to please as a child, getting good grades in school and trying to make a good impression. She suffered only from the occasional reminders of her family's relative poverty—lack of food, secondhand clothing, lack of certainty about the future.

In 1962, when Francine was 15, she met James ("Mickey") Hughes. She married him on November 4 of the following year, after a short courtship. Throughout the 14 years between when Francine married Mickey and when she killed him, Mickey was abusive. He was both physically abusive—hitting and kicking, later threatening her with weapons—and emotionally abusive—putting her down, pointing out any and every flaw. He was possessive of Francine, becoming upset if she visited neighbors or talked to anyone when he wasn't around. Early on, Mickey would apologize after the incidents and promise they would not happen again. Sooner or later, the beatings would resume, and eventually, the apologies stopped. By then, however, the couple had three children and Francine felt trapped. They were often short on money because Mickey was often out of work and did not want Francine to work outside the home. They would settle somewhere, and then get evicted because they couldn't pay the rent, either because Mickey lost a job or used the money for other things. Francine filed for divorce during her fourth pregnancy, prompted mainly by the need to get government benefits so she could feed the children.

Late in 1968, Mickey was in a terrible car accident and nearly lost his life. He remained hospitalized for 40 days and was sent home to recuperate at his parents' home. They depended on Francine to help so she rented the house next door to be close by. Eventually, Mickey moved in with Francine and the kids, despite the divorce—so Francine could take care of him. As Mickey regained his strength, the beatings and constant verbal degradation began again and escalated to a new level of cruelty. He refused to leave and would lash out at the smallest provocation. His abuse began to involve upsetting the children. Although he is never reported as hitting the children as he did Francine, on two occasions, he killed or refused to help animals the kids were attached to, and he had no qualms about beating Francine with them around. He would simply send them outside or upstairs as the beating escalated.

By 1976, Francine was able to earn her GED. After completing it, she received a government grant and began classes at Lansing Business College. Unfortunately, her attending school was a constant sore spot with Mickey, but he didn't force her to quit early on. He would still beat her, threaten to kill her, degrade her, and lash out for seemingly no reason. Francine came to see school as her salvation but still could not seem to get away from Mickey.

On the afternoon of March 9, 1977, Mickey became furious because Francine was late (she had given a fellow student a ride home), because she bought TV dinners for supper, and because he was drunk. He began to beat her and declared that she would not go to school anymore. Francine, in a rare show of defiance, said she wouldn't quit. Mickey was enraged, beating Francine all afternoon, not letting her feed the children, and insisting that she quit. The police came, and left as usual, and the beatings continued. Eventually, Francine gave in and burned her books in the barrel in the backyard as Mickey had ordered. She fixed Mickey something for dinner and then conceded to sex with him. When he fell asleep, Francine brought the children downstairs and thought about her life—how it was ruined and how the kids' lives were just as bad. After a while, she decided that they would all leave and never come back. She had tried to leave many times before, but Mickey always followed and brought her back. She decided the only way to avoid coming back again was to have nothing to come back to. She got the children in the car, doused Mickey's bed in gasoline, lit a match, and left.

Once driving, Hughes was overcome by stress and emotion and drove directly to the county jail where her oldest daughter told the police that their house was on fire (Francine was too hysterical to speak). She was soon taken into custody and confessed to setting the fire that killed her ex-husband. Francine was charged with first-degree murder and felony murder (committing murder while committing the felony of arson). Her trial lasted for eight days, much of which consisted of Francine testifying as to her life with Mickey—his beatings, his cruelty to her and the children, her attempts to leave, her inability to escape the situation. The jury returned with a verdict of not guilty by reason of temporary insanity. Francine was set free.

Her crime and her trial had a tremendous impact on the popular understanding and legal reaction to domestic violence. It received a tremendous amount of press and brought needed attention to the issue of domestic violence and battered women. It came at a time when the public was newly willing and able to see the complexities in a case like hers. It represented a tremendous victory in the feminist cause of shedding light on domestic violence. As a result, there was some inevitable backlash—editorials claiming that to apply the law in such a way opened the floodgates to allow women to kill their husbands. One such article claimed that if the feminists get their way, the numbers of homicides would go up. They quoted a sheriff as saying "I wonder if these people [the feminists] know what they're doing. If they get their way, there are going to be a lot of killings" ("The Law," 1977). Overall, however, the Hughes case paved the way for the public and those in the legal profession to see battered women differently. Rather than having to prove "temporary insanity" during a trial, women in Hughes's position thereafter could present evidence regarding battered women's syndrome as a way of understanding self-defense from the perspective of an abuse victim.

Francine Hughes's story became the subject of a true-crime book (McNulty, 1980) and, later, a made-for-television movie (1984) based on the book, both called *The Burning Bed*. The movie starred Farrah Fawcett. Hughes's case remains one of the most well-known true stories of a woman killing her abusive partner (and being acquitted) to date, and Hughes's story and its impact on the battered women's movement cannot be underestimated.

Resources

Browne, Angela. (1989). *When Battered Women Kill*. New York: The Free Press.

Campbell, J.C., L. Rose, J. Kub, & D. Nedd. (1998). Voices of strength and resistance: A contextual and longitudinal analysis of women's responses to battering. *Journal of Interpersonal Violence*, 13(6), 743–762.

Dutton, M. (1995). Understanding women's responses to domestic violence: A redefinition of Battered Woman Syndrome. *Hofstra Law Review*, 21, 1191–1242.

"The Law: A Killing Excuse." (1977, November 28). *Time*. Retrieved from www.time.com/magazine/article/0,9171,919176-1,00.html

McNulty, Faith. (1980). *The Burning Bed: The True Story of Francine Hughes—A Beaten Wife who Rebelled.* New York: Harcourt Brace Jovanovich.

Sipe, Beth, & Evelyn Hall. (1996). *I Am Not Your Victim: Anatomy of Domestic Violence.* Thousand Oaks, CA: Sage Publications.

Maureen Outlaw

Anne Hutchinson (1591–1643)

Anne Hutchinson was a Puritan woman who would come to be seen as one of the greatest threats to the Massachusetts Bay Colony's heavily structured religious society. Hutchinson was labeled a heretic by the colony's authorities, based on her challenges to the colony's religious order. Yet her willingness to violate societal rules about acceptable female conduct in order to explore and question Puritan doctrines has established Anne Hutchinson over the past few centuries as an early pioneer in the women's right movement and in the fight for religious freedom and tolerance.

Anne Hutchinson was born Anne Marbury in England in 1591 to Francis Marbury and Bridget Dryden. Francis Marbury was a preacher in the Church of England who was arrested several times for denouncing the political assignment of religious leadership, who he viewed as incompetent for their posts. Yet by the time of Anne's birth, Francis Marbury had renounced his former criticisms of the Church and went on to serve as minister of a London parish until his death. Anne's family educated her extensively, and they regularly engaged in energetic theological debates. These intense discussions gave her the opportunity to perfect the assertive, charismatic, and intellectual nature she would display as an adult. She was thus prepared early in life with the skills and knowledge she would need to embark on her challenge of the Puritan doctrines in Massachusetts.

Anne Hutchinson left home when she married William Hutchinson at the age of 21. They established a home in England with William managing a textile business and farming while Anne worked as a midwife. Anne was principally a housewife, taking care of the home and the 15 children that they would eventually come to have. Anne also

Anne Hutchinson led the first organized attack on the male-dominated Puritan religious establishment. Banished from the Massachusetts Bay Colony for her independent views, she has been hailed as one of America's earliest feminists. Illustration from *Harper's Monthly*, v. 102, 1901. (Library of Congress)

found time while living in England to conduct religious meetings for local women examining the Bible and church sermons.

Religion served as the central point of Anne's family's life. Her family had come to favor a Protestant minister named John Cotton who was teaching a growing Puritan theology. Cotton emigrated to Massachusetts in 1632 based on a growing scrutiny of Puritanism by the Church of England. Anne and her family would follow Cotton and the Puritans in 1634 to Massachusetts, looking forward to a more tolerant religious environment based on Puritanism.

In Massachusetts, Anne Hutchinson began conducting religious classes in her home. Initially, these meetings were seen as in compliance with Puritan expectations, as Anne invited women in the community to discuss the religious lessons received through local sermons and through their reading of the Bible. Yet Anne's troubles in the community began as her gatherings grew so popular that they came to include not only significant numbers of women, but men also. While it was problematic according to the Puritan moral code for her to host men in her home, the biggest problems for Anne Hutchinson arose from her challenging Puritan theology.

The Puritan way of life was based on the Covenant of Works doctrine which taught that it was only through good deeds that an individual could gain God's approval and eternal life. Puritan leaders, such as John Withrop, the governor of the Massachusetts Bay Colony, preached the Covenant of Works and designated religious leaders to oversee each individual's adherence to this covenant. Anne Hutchinson began preaching a Covenant of Grace which went in opposition to the Covenant of Works. Specifically, Hutchinson taught that " 'it is not by conduct, not by obeying the commandments, by giving alms, praying, fasting or wearing a long face' " that one gains salvation. Instead, " 'A serene spirit, coming from the consciousness of God's spirit within, proves to the true believer that he is among the elect' " (Rugg, 1930: 119). Anne was thus teaching that one needed only to establish a personal connection with God to gain salvation and that to gain God's grace, it was not necessary to perform all of the duties expected by Puritan leaders. Anne further taught that even a person who was performing all of the duties associated with a virtuous Puritan individual might not gain salvation eternally if that individual did not possess this personal connection with God.

The leaders of the Massachusetts Bay Colony immediately realized the impact that such teachings by Anne Hutchinson could have on the order that they had established in the colony. Overall, she was questioning the legitimacy and competency of the authorities in Massachusetts Bay Colony to enact moral and legal measures deemed to be essential for salvation of the individuals in that society. She was professing to know the way to God's salvation, and that way did not require adherence to the laws and expectations established by Puritan authorities. The leaders of the Massachusetts Bay Colony, led by John Winthrop, thus brought Anne Hutchinson to trial in 1637 to suppress the uprising that was expected to result from her teachings.

Anne Hutchinson was charged with the crime of "'traducing the ministers and their ministry in this country'" and for being "'the breeder and nourisher of all these distempers'" (Curtis, 1930: 62). She was charged with heresy and accused of unacceptably criticizing the teachings of religious authorities, based on her lack of authority on this matter and based on her status as a woman. These charges resulted in her banishment from the colony by the General Court of Massachusetts, and she and her family moved to what is now Rhode Island. Anne Hutchinson and her family would then move to New York following the death of her husband, and she and five of her children would die there as victims of an Indian attack on the colony in which they were residing.

Anne Hutchinson's crimes of challenging religious authorities and going in opposition to norms about appropriate female conduct have been presented as revolutionary contributions to the establishment of rights for women and religious freedom and tolerance in the United States. Anne Hutchinson's legacy today is thus one of a pioneering feminist and intellectual.

Resources

Curtis, Edith. 1930. *Anne Hutchinson: A Biography.* Cambridge: Washburn and Thomas.

LaPlante, Eve. 2004. *American Jezebel: The Uncommon Life of Anne Hutchinson, the Woman Who Defied the Puritans.* New York: HarperSanFrancisco.

Rugg, Winnifred King. 1930. *Unafraid: A Life of Anne Hutchinson.* Boston: Houghton Mifflin Company.

Winship, Michael P. 2005. *The Times and Trials of Anne Hutchinson, Puritans Divided.* Lawrence: University Press of Kansas.

Juanita Ortiz

J

Hélène Jegado (ca. 1803–1851)

Hélène Jegado was a notorious French female serial killer, considered an Angel of Death who primarily targeted people she worked for as a housekeeper and cook. It is estimated she killed 28 people between 1830 and 1850 in northern France. Although she was accused of using arsenic to poison her victims, no one actually ever saw her with the deadly substance. She remains one of France's more notorious criminals.

Born in the summer in Brittany at Plouhinec, department of Morbihan, in 1803, Hélène Jegado was orphaned at the age of 7 and resided with a M. Bubry with whom her two aunts worked as servants. At age 16, one aunt took her into service for M. Conan. In 1833 she went to work for a priest named Le Drogo. Between June 28 and October 3, seven died in his household, including Hélène's visiting sister, Anna; the priest; and both his parents. Although the deaths raised suspicion, Jegado's devout mourning of each death masked her actions. She returned back to the Bubry household to replace her sister where one of Jegado's aunts, the employer's niece and sister, all died within three months. Again Jegado cared and mourned for each one and managed to deflect suspicion.

Jegado then moved on to Locmine to work as a seamstress's apprentice under the widow Marie-Jeanne Leboucher. Both the widow and her daughter died. The widow's son, Pierre Leboucher, did not like Jegado, refused her care, and subsequently improved. Fearing that people would suspect her in these deaths, she left. She was reported to have said to a relative of the deceased, "I'm afraid that people will accuse me of all those deaths. Death follows me wherever I go" (Macclure, 1935: 16). She left the home shortly after taking an offer of a room in the house of the widow Lorey in the same town. Lorey also died. When the widow Cadic, Lorey's niece, arrived, Jegado threw herself at her in great sadness, eliciting much sympathy, lamenting how people die everywhere she goes. By 1835 Jegado was working for Dame Toussant, also of Lacmine, killing four: Anne Eveno (a maid), Toussant's father and daughter, and, eventually, M. Toussant. She was fired by Toussant's son. She now had a reputation of having a "white liver" and had "death in her breath"

(Macclure, 1935: 158). White liver, in this context, was used in conjunction to death in her breath to refer to her presence as somehow being deadly.

Jegado then moved to Auray, where she was accepted as a pensionnaire in the Convent of the Eternal Father. Soon after members of the convent began getting ill, and student's clothes and linens were slashed, Jegado was asked to leave. She resumed her apprenticeship as a seamstress inside Auray with 77-year-old Ann Lecouvrec. Lecouvrec died within two days after eating soup prepared by Jegado. Jegado then attempted to fatally poison Anne Lefur, another employer in Auray. She immediately began work for Mdm. Hetel, but her son-in-law learned of her activities at the convent and dismissed her. Jegado had already poisoned his mother-in-law who died the day after she left. She left and became a cook in Pontivy in the home of Sieur Jouanno, killing their 14-year-old son. Autopsy revealed an inflamed stomach and corroded intestines, but his death was attributed to the fact that he was known to eat a lot of vinegar. In 1836 she murdered M. Kerallic of Hennebont by serving him an herbal tea to nurse a fever. In 1839 she murdered Dame Venon, although the details on this death are not available. In 1841 she killed the granddaughter of M. Dupuy-de-Lome of Lorient, as well as sickening the remainder of his family.

From 1841 to 1849, Jegado appears to have taken a hiatus from killing, turning instead to thievery and alcoholism. By November 6, 1849, she was working for a couple named Rabot. Their son Albert died in December after eating porridge prepared by Jegado. In March 1850, Jegado was given 10 days notice by M. Rabot for stealing wine. All family members became sick the following day. All survived. She then moved onto the Ozaane family, killing their youngest son. He was diagnosed with croup fever. Jegado left immediately to work for M. Roussell whose mother openly chastised Jegado and subsequently became ill, suffering 18 months, but recovering. A fellow housekeeper, Perotte Mace fell ill in August and died in September. Two doctors, Vincent and Guyot, became suspicious of these deaths but autopsy was refused. Jegado was dismissed for stealing wine.

Two weeks later, she began work for a professor of law, M. Bidard. Two servants, Rosalie Sarrazin and Rose Tessier, died despite all administrations by the Bidards to these women. Doctors Pinault and Boudin, friends of the Bidards, became suspicious. Although autopsy on Rosalie did not reveal traces of poison, the doctors persisted, presenting evidence to the procureur-general in the City of Rennes. The three visited M. Bidard and told him of the suspected poisoning, to which Jegado blurted out, "I am innocent!"

The law officer was then said to ask, "Innocent of what? You have not been accused of anything" (Macclure, 1935: 143). Her claim of innocence eventually lead to her arrest and an inquiry into her long past.

There appeared to be no clear motive for these deaths. In some cases it appears she killed to cover up thefts, while in others jealousy resulted in the death of the person she perceived as a rival. She was able to hide behind her gendered, nurturing, and caring identity, despite the fact that she had openly told people, "Wherever I go people die." She was charged with and tried on 3 counts of murder, 3 charges of attempted poisoning, and 11 charges of theft. At her trial, it was commented that she "took snuff and was dirty" (Macclure, 1935: 162). She was found guilty and executed by guillotine at Rennes in December 1851. She remains one of the most prolific serial murderers on record, and her story is made more distinctive by her gender.

Resources

Jones, Richard Glyn. 2004. *Women Who Kill*, 2nd ed. Edison, NJ: Castle Books.

LaSala, Francine. 2002. *Mistresses of Mayhem: The Book of Women Criminals.* Indianapolis, IN: Alpha.

Macclure, Victor. 1935. "Arsenic à la Bretonne," in *She stands accused.* Full text available at the University of Virginia e-text site: http://etext.virginia.edu/toc/modeng/public/MacStan.html

Macclure, Victor. 2005. *She Stands Accused.* New York: Cosino.

Hannah Scott

Genene Jones (1950–)

Genene Jones (aka Genene Anne Jones Turk) is a female serial murderer considered a classic Angel of Death. She was a nurse's assistant prosecuted for killing 2 children under her care and suspected of killing at least 15 others using either heart medications or anesthetic drugs injected into the bloodstream. Her case is also a good illustration of Munchhausen syndrome by proxy directed towards non-familial members, and it became one of the significant forces driving policies and investigations around child and infant deaths.

Genene Jones, one of four adopted children of Dick and Gladys Jones, grew up in San Antonio, Texas. She was born July 13, 1950. From the very beginning of her life she had felt unwanted and unloved. By age 17, she had lost her father to cancer and her disabled brother to injuries sustained from an explosion of her father's sign shop. She married Jimmy DeLany, a high school drop-out, only six weeks after she buried her father. Together, they had two children: a son and a daughter.

After the deaths of her brother and her father, Jones began to show signs of Munchhausen Syndrome. Munchausen syndrome is psychological disorder characterized by the need for great amounts of attention, often medical. Patients lie about symptoms in order to garner medical and other attention. She had begun to lie about events that had happened to her before her senior year of high school. She also began appearing at hospitals in the area with symptoms that were vague such as chest and/or head pain, but which were also indications that something more serious could be indicated. Doctors would issue a series of tests, all of which would turn up with no indication of serious illness. Eventually she became known to the emergency room community in local hospitals, and soon she was not getting the attention she desired and temporarily curtailed her emergency room visits.

She divorced her husband and became a nurse's aide in 1977. She eventually was hired at Bexar County Hospital, a hospital for San Antonio's poor. It is here, in the pediatric intensive care unit, that an alarming number of children began to die under Jones's care. The children in the pediatrics ICU were going into unexpected cardiac arrests on Jones's shift. Eventually, children in her care were found to have died from overdoses of heparin, an anti-coagulant that effectively caused these children to bleed to death.

Jones had moved her locus of her need for medical attention to her young patients' need for medical assistance. In diagnostic terms, she had moved from someone suffering from Munchhausen syndrome to Munchhausen syndrome by proxy. Instead of faking her own symptoms, she began to create symptoms with various drugs and medication in her patients. After the children were in distress, she would heroically try to save them, often receiving praise and/or sympathy for her devotion to trying to save the young life even if she was not successful.

Jones was asked to leave the hospital, rather than prosecuted. She was hired into private practice in Kerrville, Texas, by Dr. Kathy Holland, an intern in the Bexar County Hospital, who believed in Jones's innocence. Within days, a small 14-month-old child, Chelsea McClellan, had mysteriously stopped breathing and had to be resuscitated and taken to emergency at a hospital a few miles away. After dismissing this case as rare, Dr. Holland eventually noticed that, in a single month period, seven children had gone into seizures while being treated by Jones. She also found empty bottles of succinylcholine, a strong drug used by anesthesiologists to relax the body before surgical intubation. Chelsea McClellan was brought back to the office on September 17, 1982, for a check-up, but this time she did not survive. Her mother remembers Genene Jones injecting a clear liquid into her daughters arm and watching her go limp. She tried to stop her but by then it was too late. Jones was dismissed September 28.

Genene Jones was eventually charged with this death and the death of one-month-old Rolando Santos who died of an overdose of heparin, a blood thinner, while being treated by Jones at Bexar County Hospital. While under investigation Jones married a 19-year-old nurse's aid, Garron Ray Turk, in April 1983. She received a 99-year sentence in February 1984 and a 60-year prison sentence in October of that year, respectively, to be served concurrently. She was suspected of killing at least 15 children in the pediatric ICU at Bexar County Hospital for which she was never charged. After her conviction, the hospital where she worked immediately came under scrutiny for its investigation of the sudden increase of child deaths during Jones's tenure. Because of the notoriety of this case, it became instrumental in setting investigation policy around sudden child and infant deaths in hospital settings. In hindsight, the hospital, by not acknowledging the potential for harm that was clearly suspect, allowed for Jones to continue to "save" children, albeit in another location.

This case is also interesting from a diagnostic standpoint, in that it demonstrates behaviorally how a person moved from an illness from Munchhausen syndrome to Munchhausen syndrome by proxy. It also suggests that those who are diagnosed with Munchhausen syndrome may progress to Munchhausen syndrome by proxy if symptoms are not adequately addressed.

Finally, this case ideally demonstrates the power of the master statuses of both gender and caregiver. The protections offered by these very powerful social constructs offered Jones to operate, often in plain sight, as it was assumed that someone of her gender and profession could not hurt a child. She would often inject drugs into children while others were present; in the last case, in front of the child's mother.

Resource

Elkind, Peter. 1983. *The Death Shift: The True Story of Nurse Genene Jones and the Texas Baby Murders*. New York: New American Library.

Hannah Scott

K

Linda Kasabian (1949–)

Linda Kasabian was the star witness in the Tate-LaBianca murder trials that resulted in the convictions of Charles Manson, Charles "Tex" Watson, Susan Atkins, Leslie Van Houten, and Patricia Krenwinkel. Of the six who were arrested, Kasabian emerged as the one to receive the most favor from the court. She provided key testimony for the state at the trial of the other five, and her murder charge was subsequently dropped.

Born Linda Louise Droin on June 21, 1949, in Biddeford, Maine, Linda grew up in a home that was characterized by a lot of parental fighting and childhood sadness. After her father permanently left the house, Linda and her mother grew close. She had a difficult time living with her stepfather whom she disliked because he was abusive to her and her mom. During arguments, Linda would spend time at her grandparents' country home, a place which she enjoyed. She had a special love for animals who she felt were more accepting of her than people were.

At age 16, she left her mother's home in New Hampshire, dropped out of high school, got married, and soon after, got divorced. Linda married again, this time to hippie Robert Kasabian. The two soon headed west "looking," she said, "for God." They both enjoyed the hippies lifestyle, traveling from commune to commune. In March 1968, Linda and Bob had their first child, Tanya. However, problems ensued between them, and Linda and Tanya returned to New Hampshire. In an effort to save the marriage, Bob coaxed Linda out to California where Bob was living with a man, Charles Melton. It was through Melton that Linda first met Manson family member Catherine Share (Gypsy). She also found lots of drugs, lots of sex, and on July 4, 1969, Charles Manson. Married, mother of a two-year-old girl, and pregnant at the time, Kasabian learned about "this beautiful man named Charlie" and the idyllic life his followers led at Spahn Ranch. To Kasabian, it was the "answer to an unspoken prayer." When things failed with Bob, Linda stole $5,000 from Melton, returned to Spahn Ranch with her belongings, and joined the family. Linda later claimed that she thought Manson "could see inside her."

Kasabian had only been a member of the family for six weeks when Manson announced, on August 8, 1969, "Now is the time for Helter Skelter." Selected as the driver, Kasabian joined Tex Watson, Susan Atkins, and Patricia Krenwinkel in traveling to the Tate home. Kasabian maintained that she did not know that there were to be any killings that evening; she thought they were only going there to burglarize the home. Shortly after they arrived, she wit-

Linda Kasabian holds a press conference in Los Angeles after her testimony in the infamous Sharon Tate murders, 1970. (AP/Wide World Photos)

nessed the shooting of Steven Parent while he was trying to exit the property. At this point, she was instructed to go back to the front gate and stand guard while the others went into the residence. As she heard people screaming for their lives, Kasabian ran to the front door, where she found a severely beaten and stabbed Wojciech Frykowski. At the trial, Kasabian recounted that after she saw Frykowski, they looked into each other's eyes and she said, " 'Oh, God, I am so sorry. Please make it stop.' And then he just fell to the ground into the bushes. And then Sadie [Susan Atkins] came running out of the house, and I said, 'Sadie, please make it stop.' And then I said, 'I hear people coming.' And she said, 'It is too late.' " At that point, Atkins asked Kasabian for her knife, saying that she couldn't find it. During this time, Kasabian observed Watson hitting someone over the head and stabbing him; Krenwinkel was in the background, chasing down Abigail Folger with a knife in hand. Kasabian did not directly participate in the murders, later telling Manson, "I'm not you, Charlie—I can't kill anybody."

The next night, Kasabian rode with Manson and other family members to the LaBianca home, but she did not enter the home or see either of the murders. After the murders, Manson gave Kasabian a wallet he had retrieved from the LaBianca home. During her trial, Kasabian claimed that while they were leaving the crime scene, he told her to take the change out of the wallet and wipe off the fingerprints. After they drove for a few blocks, Manson instructed her to throw the wallet out onto the sidewalk. Kasabian said that Manson "wanted a black person to pick it up and use the credit cards so that the people, the establishment would think it was some sort of an organized group that killed these people."

After killing the LaBiancas, Manson and the others drove around, searching for more victims. Manson wanted Kasabian, Atkins, and Clem Grogan to kill a foreign actor, Saladin Nader, whom Kasabian had met once while hitchhiking. Kasabian purposely brought Atkins and Grogan to the wrong door at the Venice Beach apartment complex, thereby aborting the mission.

The next day, August 11, 1969, Manson wanted Kasabian to deliver a message to three family members who were in jail. Seeing this as her only chance to escape, Kasabian drove to New Mexico, leaving Tanya behind at Spahn Ranch. She rejoined her husband, Bob, who wanted to return to the ranch to get Tanya. They later learned that she had been placed in foster care following a raid on August 16. After speaking with a social worker, Linda returned to Los Angeles to retrieve Tanya, and from there, they flew back to New Mexico. Linda later hitchhiked first to her father's home in Florida and then to her mother's home in New Hampshire. California authorities issued a warrant for Linda Kasabian's arrest on December 1, 1969. She voluntarily surrendered to police in Concord, New Hampshire, and was flown back to California. She wanted to tell her version of the story.

Linda Kasabian's attorney, Gary Fleishman, immediately proposed to prosecutors a deal whereby she would testify against other family members in return for complete immunity. Having previously made a deal with Susan Atkins, Prosecutor Vince Bugliosi initially rejected the proposal. When Atkins changed her mind and announced she would not testify at the trial, Bugliosi quickly negotiated a deal with Linda's attorney: the prosecution would petition for immunity after she testified. Kasabian took the witness stand again in a series of trials and retrials, and despite efforts on behalf of the defense attorneys, her testimony remained solid.

After 18 days of testimony, she left the stand. In his closing argument, Bugliosi said Charles Manson "sent out from the fires of hell at Spahn Ranch three heartless, bloodthirsty robots and—unfortunately for him—one human being, the hippie girl Linda Kasabian."

After the trials, Linda Kasabian rejoined her husband and children, moving into a small farm in New Hampshire. She moved to the Pacific Northwest for a while, living under an assumed name. Later, she left her husband and returned to New Hampshire. A car accident left her mildly disabled and unable to work. In a police raid in 1996, Kasabian and one of her daughters who went by the nickname "Lady Dangerous" were arrested for possession of methamphetamine. Her daughter, who was also found in possession of a gun and rock and powder cocaine, was convicted and sentenced to a year in prison. Kasabian once again avoided jail by agreeing to attend drug abuse classes. Her current whereabouts are unknown.

Like many heinous crimes, the Tate-LaBianca murders in 1969 dismantled society's sense of social order. The victims did not know the murderers who delivered a bloody platter of Helter Skelter mayhem and chaos. Charles Manson has been thought by many to be the devil in human form; the women, his faithful servants. But it is still unclear whether Kasabian, or all of the women, were victims of Manson, who preyed on the women's vulnerabilities, or whether the female disciples were themselves evil, as many people believed, and unsuitable for society at large.

See also Atkins, Susan; Good, Sandra; Krenwinkel, Patricia; Van Houten, Leslie

Resources

Bugliosi, Vincent, and Curt Gentry. (1974). *Helter Skelter: The True Story of the Manson Murders*. New York: W.W. Norton & Company.

Didion, Joan. (1993). *The White Album*. New York: Flamingo.

Gilmore, John. (2000). *Manson: The Unholy Trail of Charlie and the Family*. Los Angeles: Amok Books.

King, Greg. (2000). *Sharon Tate and the Manson Murders*. Fort Lee, NJ: Barricade Books.

The Manson Family Today: News and Information. (2007). http://www.mansonfamilyto day.info/manson.htm

Sanders, Ed. (1989). *The Family: The Manson Group and Its Aftermath*. New York: New American Library/Signet.

Sue Cote Escobar

Gladys Cannon Kelly (1942–1987)

The case of Gladys Kelly is one of the most influential cases of women's homicide in U.S. history. It began with a conviction in 1982 of an impoverished African American woman from East Orange, New Jersey, for reckless manslaughter in the death of her husband Ernest and ended as a nationally precedent-setting case for allowing expert testimony about battering in cases of battered women who kill. This 1984 ruling in the New Jersey Supreme Court opened the doors for other state courts to accept battered women's syndrome and other testimony about the psychological effects of battering as a defense for women who killed men who had been abusing them.

Little is known about Kelly's early life. Kelly was born in 1942. According to the defense attorney for the first trial, Charles Lorber (2007), it is most likely that Kelly came to New Jersey from the South as a child with her family or that her family had other roots in the South. Lorber remembers that she had several siblings and that some of them had troubles with the law.

Kelly was married prior to meeting and marrying Ernest Kelly. Little can be found with regard to her marriage to a man named Cannon except that she had at least one child with him. Their child Edith was born around 1963.

Kelly had one reported prior conviction, revealed in the later murder trial. In 1971, prior to marrying Ernest Kelly, Gladys Kelly (then Cannon) was convicted of conspiracy to commit robbery. In her testimony at her murder trial, Kelly stated that she committed the conspiracy with two other people and was given three years of probation. Presumably, she successfully completed probation as no further mention was made of it.

Gladys Cannon met Ernest Kelly, and they were married in 1973. According to available sources, they had a daughter around 1973 named either Janice (Walker, 1989) or Annette (*New Jersey v. Kelly*, 1984). There is no mention of other children in the household other than Ernest's stepdaughter, Edith Cannon, and the couple's daughter in common, Janice or Annette.

The marriage between Gladys and Ernest Kelly was troubled from the beginning. In court records, it is referred to as "stormy" (*New Jersey v. Kelly*, 1984). Kelly testified that Ernest Kelly had knocked her down in public only one day after being married. Most of her husband's beatings occurred in the context of drinking and were frequent (as often as once per week). Other than the first incident of violence right after they were married and the violence on May 24, 1980, which preceded his death, Ernest's attacks were done in private. In fact, Walker (1989) comments that it was due, in large part, to the public nature of the last attack that Kelly felt the need to defend herself.

During these attacks, Ernest would physically assault her as well as threaten her. He beat her up severely on several occasions. He would threaten to "cut off parts of her body" (*New Jersey v. Kelly*, 1984, §II) or kill her if she tried to leave him. He also threatened to abduct their seven-year-old daughter. Gladys was aware that Ernest often carried a dagger with him. After the abuse, Ernest would be contrite and lure Gladys back to convince her to stay in the relationship. In fact, they had separated on several occasions only to have Ernest make promises to change, which persuaded his wife to take him back. This is consistent with the cycle of violence described by Lenore Walker (1989) who describes abusive relationships in terms of alternating battering, "honeymoon" or calm periods, and tension-building periods. In addition to the violence against Gladys Kelly, Kelly's daughter Edith had disclosed that her stepfather had been sexually assaulting her since she was 13. Edith's testimony, however, was excluded from the original court case even though it was relevant for establishing a general pattern of familial violence.

On May 24, 1980, Gladys Kelly killed Ernest Kelly. She stabbed him with scissors in self-defense, according to her version of the story, a version the prosecution disputed. It began the night before when Ernest demanded that Gladys give him money, even though it was needed for groceries for the rest of the week. He promised to give her the money back after he was paid the next day. The next day, Gladys demanded the money back even after he began to hit her. Ernest stormed out of the house to eat with friends. She took their seven-year-old daughter with her to the house, waited for him to finish dinner, and resumed asking for the money he promised to buy food. Ernest had been drinking and told her that she would get it when they got home. The family left together. After walking for some time, Ernest angrily confronted her about going to his friend's house. According to court records (*New Jersey v. Kelly*, 1984, §II), Ernest angrily asked "What the hell did you come around here for?" He then assaulted her, grabbing her dress, and pulled the two of them to the ground. Once he had her on the ground, Ernest reportedly punched or hit Gladys's face, bit her leg, and choked her by pushing his fingers against her throat.

The physical fight drew a crowd of people on the street. According to Kelly, two men were able to pull them apart just as she was feeling like she was going to pass out from being choked. Kelly got up to look for her daughter in the crowd, afraid that Ernest would take her as he had threatened to do many times before. When she found Annette (or Janice), Kelly had discovered that her daughter had picked up her pocketbook after Kelly dropped it during Ernest's attack. Kelly took her pocketbook back. She then observed Ernest coming at her with arms raised, and she feared that he was going to attack her again or kill her. She didn't know if he had gotten a weapon of any sort, and out of fear grabbed a pair of scissors from her pocketbook. She claimed that she was going to scare him away but, instead, ended up stabbing him.

According to Lenore Walker (1989), a consultant on the case, Ernest was taken to the emergency room after he fell down "apparently having a heart attack" (208). Staff in the emergency room assessed him for the possible heart attack and did not tend to the small wound in his chest. They put him in a room and monitored his condition. What they didn't realize was that the myocardium surrounding the heart had been cut, and he was bleeding internally. That is ultimately what killed him. Walker raises the question of whether it would have been a homicide at all if he had gotten appropriate treatment for his injury. Regardless of this information, Kelly was indicted for murder and put on trial in 1982.

During the trial, Kelly's defense team attempted to use testimony regarding Ernest's history of abuse including both his stepdaughter Edith's testimony about his sexual abuse and expert testimony regarding battered women's syndrome from Dr. Lois Veronen, a clinical psychologist who was highly experienced with domestic violence victims. This testimony would establish the imminence and reasonableness of the fear that Ernest would, in fact, kill Kelly and that she acted in self-defense.

The prosecution argued that Gladys Kelly had provoked the attack and that she had ample time to retreat from the scene, a fact that would preclude the use of a self-defense argument. It was also argued by the prosecution that she was angry that Ernest was allegedly going to leave her. Gladys was allowed to provide her side of the story, including the history of experiencing Ernest's violence. However, the trial judge barred the testimony of Dr. Veronen arguing that expert testimony was not allowable to establish defendant's state of mind in self-defense cases. The judge also refused to allow Edith, Ernest's stepdaughter, to testify claiming that it was irrelevant. The trial lasted two weeks and resulted in her conviction of reckless manslaughter and given a five-year prison term at the Clinton Correctional Institution for Women.

Kelly appealed the case, and the conviction was upheld in appellate court where it was stated that expert testimony was not needed because she was testifying about events and fears that the common person could understand. An appeal was filed with the Supreme Court of New Jersey which granted certification in 1983 to hear the case. There were several grounds for the appeal, but the most important was the need for expert testimony to explain the effects of battered women's syndrome and how that led Kelly to believe she needed to defend herself. Amicus curiae briefs (friend of the court briefs) were filed on behalf of Kelly from both the American Psychological Association (APA) and the New Jersey American Civil Liberties Union (ACLU) with the New Jersey Coalition for Battered Women. The APA brief was directed toward establishing the scientific reliability of battered women's syndrome, and the other was directed toward the admissibility of the evidence of battered women's syndrome. Elizabeth M. Schneider, in an unusual move, was allowed to make in-person arguments on behalf of Kelly for the New Jersey ACLU/Coalition for Battered Women, in which she directly addressed the justices on the need for someone to help explain Kelly's story.

Ultimately, the New Jersey Supreme Court decided, in 1984, to reverse the conviction agreeing that Kelly did not receive a fair trial because of the denial of the expert testimony into battered women's syndrome. The jury, they argued, did need someone to explain the reasons why a battered woman wouldn't be able to leave such a home. It was a bittersweet victory for advocates for fair treatment of battered women, however, as the focus was on the woman's failure to leave as opposed to the reasonableness of her actions. The court reversed the conviction and sent the case back for retrial.

The retrial of Gladys Kelly included the testimony of nationally recognized expert, Dr. Lenore Walker (1989), whose account provides most of the additional detail of what happened. While Walker testified to the effects of battered women's syndrome on Kelly, the prosecution called an expert who refuted this. Walker describes the trial as biased in that the trial court judge did not permit continuous testimony and cross-examination, as is customary, in the accommodation of the prosecution's request to cross-examine at several intervals to help clarify details for her. According to Walker, Kelly by this time appeared angry after suffering both at the hands of her husband and now at the hands of the criminal justice system. Her anger played into the stereotypes of the angry black woman and provided an uphill battle with the jury. Ultimately, Kelly was convicted a second time of manslaughter. According to her original defense attorney, Charles Lorber, Kelly died of natural causes while waiting for sentencing.

Gladys Kelly's case stands as the precedent for cases of battered women who kill. It was the first time a key state appellate court had held battered women's syndrome admissible, and it was one of the most thorough considerations of this defense at that point. This opened the door for other states to consider testimony about battering. The syndrome of battered women's syndrome has largely been replaced with broader considerations of the effects of battering, but this discussion could not have happened without the appeal of Gladys Kelly.

Resources

American Civil Liberties Union of New Jersey and the New Jersey Coalition for Battered Women. 1986. Brief and Appendix of Amici Curiae in the Supreme Court of New Jersey, September Term, 1982. State of New Jersey, Plaintiff-Respondent vs. Gladys Kelly, Defendant-Petitioner. Reprinted in *Women Rights Law Reporter*, 9 (3 and 4): 245–252.

Kinsports, Kit, Donald Bersoff, Bruce Ennis, and Nadine Taub (for American Psychological Association). 1983. Brief of Amicus Curiae, American Psychological Association, in support of Defendant-Petitioner, in the Supreme Court of New Jersey, September Term, 1982. State of New Jersey, Plaintiff-Respondent vs. Gladys Kelly, Defendant-Petitioner. On Petition for Certification from the Appellate Division of the Superior Court (Judges Bother and Forman).

Lorber, Charles. Telephone interview. June 20, 2007.

Margolick, David. 1984. "Court Allows Defense to Call Experts on Battered Women" *New York Times* July 25, 1984: A1.

New Jersey v. Kelly. 1984. 97 N.J. 178; 478 A.2d 364; 1984 N.J. Lexis 2698.

Schneider, Elizabeth M. 2000. *Battered Women and Feminist Lawmaking*. New Haven: Yale University Press.

Schneider, Elizabeth M. 1986. "Describing and Changing: Women's Self Defense Work and the Problem of Expert Testimony on Battering." *Women's Rights Law Reporter* 9 (3 and 4): 195–222.

Schneider, Elizabeth M., Mary Dunlap, Michael Lavery, and John DeWitt Gregory. 1988 "Workshop: Lesbians, Gays, and Feminists at the Bar—Translating Personal Experiences into Effective Legal Argument." *Women's Rights Law Reporter* 10 (1 and 2): 107–142.

Walker, Lenore. 1989. *Terrifying Love: Why Battered Women Kill and How Society Responds*. New York: Harper Perennial.

Vickie Jensen

Leila Khaled (1948–)

Leila Khaled, while not the first woman hijacker (according to MacDonald [1991], an Argentine woman was the first woman hijacker), is arguably the most famous. She was involved in the hijacking of two airliners on behalf of Palestinian nationalist freedom fighters, though some consider her and her partners to be terrorists. She was born on April 9, 1944, to a middle-class family in Palestine, in

Leila Khaled, who successfully hijacked a TWA airliner to Damascus, Syria, in 1969, totes a submachine gun at a Palestinian refugee camp in Lebanon, 1970. (AP/Wide World Photos)

the city of Haifa, now a part of Israel. She was a small child when, in 1948, war broke out as a result of the creation of the state of Israel. Her father became involved in Palestinian resistance groups, while her mother escaped with Leila and her siblings (8 siblings at that time) to relatives in Lebanon.

This displacement and subsequent experiences as a refugee motivated Khaled to political action, starting at an early age. Inspired by her father's example, Khaled and her siblings became involved in Palestinian nationalist activities, undertaken with the goal of reclaiming their land from Israel. At 15, she joined the Arab National Movement, an organization promoting the unification of Arab peoples under a left-wing, secular vision of governance. A bright girl, she obtained scholarships to secondary school and then the American University in Beirut. Her education was cut short for lack of funds, and she wound up teaching English to small children in Kuwait.

In 1967, Khaled joined the Popular Front for the Liberation of Palestine (PFLP), founded by George Habash. The PFLP is a left-wing faction of the Palestinian Liberation Organization (PLO) which advocates armed struggle as the most effective means for Palestinians to reclaim their homeland. Khaled enthusiastically took part in guerilla training activities, based in Jordan, where she learned how to fight and use weapons.

On August 29, 1969, Khaled, along with a fellow Palestinian, hijacked a Trans World Airlines (TWA) flight traveling from Los Angeles to Tel Aviv, Israel, with stopovers in Rome and Athens. Handguns and grenades hidden on their person, the two boarded the plane during the Rome stopover. They took over the cockpit mid-flight and, with Khaled taking the lead, they forced the airline personnel to divert the plane to Damascus, Syria. Upon arrival, the hostages were released and the plane blown up. She and her partner escaped without injury. After a brief detention in Syria, she went on to Jordan.

Although the hijackers demanded the release of prisoners held in Israel, the more prominent objective was to thrust the Palestinian cause onto the world stage. In an interview, Khaled relates her reaction to a question posed by one of the hostages, "Who are the Palestinians?": "It said everything—she did not know of our fight— no one did; she did not even know we existed. But after the hijack, everyone knew. That is why we did it" (MacDonald 1991, 110).

This incident made Khaled an idol in Arab countries and propelled her to international fame, the latter helped in no small measure by a classic set of pictures taken of her at the time. As noted in a 2001 *Guardian* piece, she resembled a "delicate Audrey Hepburn," albeit more heavily armed (Viner 2001). In revolutionary circles, she embodied leftist ideals of women as equal partners in armed struggle. More mainstream accounts depicted her as an attractive "girl guerilla." She became so well-known that she felt it endangered her ability to adopt disguises for future PFLP undertakings. As a result, she had plastic surgery on her chin and nose to alter her appearance.

Khaled's second hijacking incident in September 1970 was an even more notable affair. The PFLP's initial plan was to overtake several airplanes, all United States–bound, using them and their passengers to bargain for the release of Palestinian political prisoners, then held in European and Israeli facilities. Khaled and fellow hijacker Patrick Arguello (an American citizen raised in Nicaragua) were assigned to an El Al flight headed to New York (two additional hijackers were kept from boarding in Amsterdam). When she and Arguello attempted to overtake the plane, they were met with resistance by air marshals. Arguello was fatally shot, while Khaled was beaten and captured. The plane was landed in London, and Khaled was taken to a local police station.

Efforts by the PFLP to commandeer three other planes were more successful. The airliners were brought to Jordan, where, as in the 1969 incident, passengers were taken from the planes which were later blown up. A British plane was hijacked a few days later. Throughout that September, the International Red Cross played intermediary in a complex series of machinations between the PFLP and Britain, Jordan, and the United States, among others, to exchange the hostages for Palestinian prisoners is this latter group now including Leila Khaled herself. She was held by Britain during the negotiations for her release. She describes humane treatment by police personnel, and says she received both hate mail and marriage proposals. On September 30, 1970, she, along with a small number of Palestinian prisoners, was released in exchange for the remaining airline hostages.

The 1970 hijacking was her last; PFLP soon discarded this particular method of helping the Palestinians. In subsequent years, Khaled maintained a low-key presence in Lebanon, becoming involved in other PFLP activities. She became a member of the Palestinian National Council, a parliament-like body for the exiled Palestinian community. As of 2000, she was involved in the General Union of Palestinian Women, which works on various issues specific to women and Palestinians in general.

A brief marriage in 1970 ended in divorce. In 1982, she married a physician and fellow PFLP member. She, her husband, and their two sons now live in Jordan.

Khaled has faced steady condemnation for her hijacking activities. Some have pointed to the September 1970 incident in particular as setting the stage for the escalation of air-based terrorism, drawing a direct line between this incident and the attacks of September 11, 2001. In contrast, she views herself as having been a freedom fighter, rather than a terrorist, citing her main concern at the time as drawing international attention to the Palestinian plight. She rejects the idea of harming hostages as an end in itself and has criticized actions that have targeted civilians, for instance, referring to the 9/11 attacks as "criminal." When asked in a 2003 interview about any misgivings concerning her youthful exploits, Khaled replied, "I have no regrets. Every action at the time and within that situation—not at this time, but at that time—was necessary. Part of the objectives was achieved. We succeeded in presenting the Palestinian cause with a force to the world. But freeing all the prisoners was not achieved" (Abdallah 2003).

Resources

Abdallah, Sana. July 21, 2003. Interview: Palestinian Leila Khaled. *United Press International Online.* http://www.upi.com/InternationalIntelligence/Interview_Palestinian_Leila_Khaled/20030721–082110–7107r/ (Accessed March 14, 2007).

Baum, Philip. 2000. "Leila Khaled: In her own words." *Aviation Security International.* http://www.asi-mag.com/editorials/leila_khaled.htm (Accessed on March 8, 2007).

Khaled, Leila, with George Hajjar. 1973. *My people shall live: The autobiography of a revolutionary.* London: Hodder and Stoughton.

MacDonald, Eileen. 1991. *Shoot the women first.* New York: Random House.

Makboul, Lina. 2006. *Leila Khaled: Hijacker.* First Hand Films Website: http://www.leilakhaled.com/ (Accessed on March 13, 2007).

Public Broadcasting Service Online. 2006. Hijacked. *American Experience.* http://www.pbs.org/wgbh/amex/hijacked/index.html (Accessed on March 8, 2007).

Viner, Katherine. 2001. "'I made the ring from a bullet and the pin of a hand grenade.'" *Guardian Unlimited Online.* http://www.guardian.co.uk/g2/story/0,,428510,00.html (Accessed on March 15, 2007).

Angela Taylor

Patricia Krenwinkel (1947–)

Known as a member of the Manson family, Patricia Krenwinkel was involved in two of the nation's most heinous murders of the 20th century. Fully committed to Manson and his vision, Krenwinkel willingly participated in the infamous murders of August 9, 1969, at the home of actress Sharon Tate and director Roman Polanski and again on August 10, 1969, at the home of Rosemary and Leno LaBianca. While Krenwinkel was with the Manson family, she went by numerous aliases, including "Big Patty," "Yellow," "Mary Ann Scott," and "Marnie Reeves." However, to the family, she was best known as Katie.

Patricia Diane Krenwinkel was born in Los Angeles, California. Her father was an insurance salesman, and her mother remained at home; her parents separated when she was about 14 or 15 years old. She had one older sister, Charlene, who became addicted to drugs and died around the age of 29. Krenwinkel attended Los Angeles–area high schools and experienced a difficult adolescence. Krenwinkel had low self-esteem and was often teased for being overweight and having excessive body hair, which was caused by an endocrine system condition. Feeling unattractive and shunned by her peers, she maintained a reclusive persona.

Her parents divorced when she was 17, and Krenwinkel stayed in Los Angeles with her father until she graduated from high school. Her mother moved to Alabama, and Krenwinkel later joined her there where she attended a Catholic college. Krenwinkel had dabbled in teaching Catholic Sunday school and had even considered being a nun at one point in her childhood. Krenwinkel completed only one semester of college before she left and moved back to California. She eventually got her own apartment in Manhattan Beach and got a job in an office as a processing clerk. However, this was not a fulfilling life for her.

In 1967 on Manhattan Beach, Krenwinkel met Charles Manson for the first time. She also met two of "Charlie's Girls," Lynette "Squeaky" Fromme and Mary Brunner. Krenwinkel stated that she slept with Manson that night. For the first time in her entire life, someone had thought she was beautiful. Attention-starved and mesmerized, Krenwinkel decided to go to San Francisco with Manson and the other girls, leaving behind her life on Manhattan Beach. The early years with the Manson family were similar to a long acid trip. As the family grew, Manson, Krenwinkel, and the others drove around the American West in an old school bus, enjoying a life of sex and drugs. During the summer of 1968, Krenwinkel and some other family members spent time with one of the Beach Boys, Dennis Wilson, but they had overstayed their welcome in his home when he found them partying inside, eating his food, and draining him dry financially. Later that same year, Krenwinkel was arrested for possession of marijuana in Mendocino, California, after she and other family girls gave some young people some LSD. By 1969, Manson and his family decided that isolation was the way to go, and to this end, they conned George Spahn, a blind, elderly man, into allowing them to live on his property in the hills above the San Fernando Valley. At Spahn's Movie Ranch, Krenwinkel's devotion to Manson became very intense as she devoted herself to him and to caring for several of the family members' children. At the trial, she described her life with the family at Spahn Ranch: "We were just like wood nymphs and wood creatures. We would run through the woods with flowers in our hair, and Charlie would have a small flute" (Bugliosi and Gentry, 1974: 430).

Krenwinkel's world changed permanently during and following the nights of August 9–10, 1969. On the night of August 9, in the company of Charles "Tex" Watson, Linda Kasabian, and Susan Atkins, Krenwinkel drove to 10050 Cielo Drive, the home of actress Sharon Tate, who was eight months pregnant at the time, and director Roman Polanski, which was located just outside of Los Angeles. Prior to entering the residence, Watson cut the telephone wires leading to the residence; Krenwinkel and the other family girls climbed over a wall at the rear of San Vincente Drive. Krenwinkel maintained that Manson told her to do whatever Watson told her to do, though she has claimed that Manson never mentioned anything about killing anyone that first night. After climbing over the wall, she and the other girls stayed in the bushes where they heard gunshots. Watson had shot and killed one of the victims, Steve Parent, as he was leaving the house to go to his car. Krenwinkel maintained that Watson had told them that they were all there at the house to not only rob but kill everyone. She said that she realized what they were there to do only after they had arrived, not before.

Once inside the home, chaos erupted. Krenwinkel found Abigail Folger in her bedroom and dragged her into the living room. She stabbed her as she fought with her. Folger then tried to escape out the back door, but Krenwinkel pushed her and pinned her to the ground, stabbing her continuously while Folger pleaded for her life. Folger ran out the back door where she was pushed and later stabbed numerous times in the back by Krenwinkel. In total, Folger had been stabbed 28 times. During her trial, Krenwinkel was quoted as saying, "And I had a knife in my hands, and she took off running, and she ran—she ran out through the back door, one I never even touched, I mean, nobody ever got fingerprints because I never touched that door . . . and I stabbed her and I kept stabbing her" (Bugliosi and Gentry, 1974: 430.) She was also asked how it felt, to which she replied, "Nothing, I mean, what is there to describe? It was just there, and it was right" (431).

The next night, August 10, Manson made the orders to kill very clear. So, along with Manson and Krenwinkel, Charles "Tex" Watson, Susan Atkins, Steve Grogan, Leslie Van Houten, and Linda Kasabian drove to the home of grocer Leno LaBianca and his wife Rosemary, in the Los Feliz section of Los Angeles. Manson and Watson entered the house first, and they tied the couple up. Manson then left the house and sent Krenwinkel and Van Houten inside to kill the LaBiancas, leaving Grogan, Atkins, and Kasabian in the car. According to Krenwinkel, she and Van Houten brought Mrs. LaBianca into the master bedroom and proceeded to look through her dresses. When she heard her husband, Leno, scream, Mrs. LaBianca grabbed a lamp and swung at Krenwinkel and Van Houten. She and Van Houten then restrained Mrs. LaBianca, and then Krenwinkel began stabbing her with a kitchen knife. However, the knife blade was too dull and actually broke against Mrs. LaBianca's collar bone. Krenwinkel and Van Houten called for Tex Watson who brought in a sword-like weapon and who Krenwinkel claims ultimately stabbed Mrs. LaBianca, though she and Van Houten also continued to stab her as well.

Krenwinkel left the master bedroom to find Mr. LaBianca lying on the floor in the living room. At the trial, Krenwinkel recalled saying, "You won't be sending your son off to war . . . I guess I put WAR on the man's chest. And then I guess I had a fork in my hands, and I put it in his stomach . . . and I went and wrote on the walls . . . Death to Pigs and Helter Skelter on the refrigerator]" (Bugliosi and Gentry, 1974: 431). Krenwinkel later denied writing the word *war* on his stomach; That act has been attributed to Tex Watson. Before returning to Spahn Ranch, Krenwinkel, Watson, and Van Houten remained at the LaBianca residence eating their food, taking showers, and playing with their two dogs.

Following the murders, a series of raids on Manson's family at Spahn Ranch and then later at Barker Ranch lead to dissolution of the family. A couple of months after the murders, Krenwinkel moved to Alabama to live with her mother until it was "safe" for her to return to Barker Ranch. The orders from Manson never came because he was arrested. During this time, Susan Atkins, who had been jailed on auto theft charges, began telling exploits of the Tate-LaBianca murders to her cellmate. Because of Atkins's confessions and her cellmate's disclosures, Krenwinkel was arrested in Mobile, Alabama, on December 1, 1969. On December 2, Patricia Krenwinkel was indicted for seven counts of first-degree murder and one count of conspiracy to commit murder. Following her Alabama arrest, Krenwinkel asserted that she had left for Alabama because she feared Manson would find her and kill her, thus supporting her attempts to fight extradition to California. In February 1970, she waived extradition proceedings and voluntarily returned to California to stand trial with defendants Manson, Van Houten, and Atkins.

During the trial, Krenwinkel remained loyal to Manson and stood united with the other defendants. They showed loyalty and unity by walking hand-in-hand with each other, singing Manson's songs, shaving their heads, and carving an *X* in their foreheads, just like Manson had done. At the end of the nine-month trial, Krenwinkel was convicted of all counts and was then sentenced to death on March 29, 1971. She, Atkins, and Van Houten were transferred to a new death-row facility built especially for women at the California Institute for Women (CIW). However, this death sentence was automatically commuted to life in prison after the California Supreme Court's decision in *People v. Anderson* invalidated all death sentences given in California before 1972.

At the start of her prison term, Krenwinkel remained loyal to Manson and the family, but over time, she distanced herself from them and the hold it had over her. In doing so, she has kept up a perfect prison record for her nearly 40 years of incarceration at CIW in Chino, California; she has graduated from high school and received a bachelor's degree in human services from the University of La Verne. Krenwinkel remains active with prison 12-step programs such as Alcoholics Anonymous and Narcotics Anonymous and the Long Termers Organization. In addition to these programs, she also works with fellow inmates, teaching them how to read. Additionally, Krenwinkel writes both poetry and music, plays the guitar, plays on a prison volleyball team, and she has even give other inmates dance lessons. Currently, she works with a canine support team where she trains service dogs.

It has been reported that of all of the killers, Krenwinkel has expressed the most remorse for her participation in the Tate-LaBianca murders. In an interview conducted by Diane Sawyer in 1994, Krenwinkel stated that "I wake up every day knowing that I am a destroyer of the most precious thing, which is life; and I do that because that's what I deserve, is to wake up every morning and know that." Despite having been denied parole each of the 13 times she has sought it, Krenwinkel remains positive, works the 12-step programs, and places her faith in a higher power. She was most recently denied parole on January 20, 2011, but she will be eligible again in seven years.

See also Atkins, Susan; Good, Sandra; Kasabian, Linda; Van Houten, Leslie

Resources

ABC News, Channel 7, Chino, California. (November 5, 2007). "Former Manson member trains 'Prison Pups' for disabled," http://www.liveleak.com/view?i=b6e_1194330036, accessed July 3, 2010.

Bugliosi, Vincent, and Curt Gentry. (1974). *Helter Skelter: The True Story of the Manson Murders.* New York: W.W. Norton & Company.

King, Gary C. (2010). "Patricia Krenwinkel: From Manson Groupie to Model Prisoner." Investigation Discovery/Discovery ID. http://investigation.discovery.com/investigation/where-now/krenwinkel/patricia-krenwinkel-02.html, accessed July 3, 2010.

Sanders, Ed. (1989). *The Family: The Manson Group and Its Aftermath.* New York: New American Library/Signet.

Sue Cote Escobar

L

Catherine La Voisin (1640–1680)

Known as "La Voisin" (1640–1680), Catherine Deshayes was a French woman, considered a witch and a serial poisoner, who became a central figure in one of the worst scandals of the 17th century, the "Affair of the Poisons," which involved prominent individuals at the royal court of Louis XIV in France. Born on 1640 in France to a poor woman who was thought to be a sorceress herself, Catherine Deshayes was initiated into what were considered magic powers at an early age. She married Antoine Montvoisin whose businesses in the silk trade and jewelry both led him into bankruptcy. As a result, her husband lapsed into heavy drinking, violently venting his frustrations on her. Having to support him and all her numerous children, she probably turned into the criminal, but lucrative, business of abortion and the preparation of poisons. Her marriage was so unhappy that she never made a secret of her intention to get rid of her husband; indeed, she made several unsuccessful attempts on his life. In any event, Madame Montvoisin engaged in many love affairs with other wizards and alchemists, among whom was Le Sage, who was later also dragged into the Affair of the Poisons.

La Voisin belonged to several Christian congregations in Paris and was a pious worshipper who conceived her occult powers as a gift from God. Her clients, who primarily belonged to French high society, were likely reassured by such a religious devotion to her magical practices. During the late 1660s to the early 1670s, several mysterious deaths of influential members of the nobility followed one after the other. When, in 1676, the Marquise de Brinvilliers, who was accused of having heartlessly poisoned her father and her two brothers, was finally arrested and then prosecuted, she revealed that most of the individuals she knew, "people of quality" (Mossiker 1969, 145), were equally implicated in similar misdeeds. The king, concerned that the spread use of the practice of poisoning could endanger his own safety and that of the royal family, appointed Nicolas de La Reynie, the lieutenant general of the Paris police, to oversee the investigation. In 1679, he also established a special tribunal, known as the *Chambre Ardente,* to prosecute the cases. The court ruled for over three years, issuing 319 subpoenas, arresting 194 people, and sentencing 36 of them to death.

Catherine La Voisin was arrested on March 12, 1679, as she was coming out from mass at her parish church, Notre-Dame de Bonne Nouvelle, in Paris. The search of her premises revealed all sorts of magic powders, venomous potions, sacrilegious objects, as well as a long list of her clients. She was accused of having attempted to poison her husband several times at the instigation of her paramour, Le Sage, and of having performed abortions for a fee, burying the premature infants in her garden. When in March 17, 1679, Le Sage was arrested as well, he provided Nicolas de La Reynie with detailed accounts of the La Voisin's business and customers. He revealed that a small oven was hidden in her house, "where the bones were burned if the infant body seemed too large to lay away in a garden grave" (Mossiker 1969, 185). He also claimed that most of the La Voisin's visitors belonged to the king's entourage, and even a maid of the Marquise de Montespan, one of the favorite mistresses of Louis XIV, had purchased love powders from her.

Catherine La Voisin admitted that some of her customers were indeed prominent figures of the nobility, but she firmly denied having ever served the Marquise de Montespan or even met with her. During her last interrogation, when she was subjected to torture, La Voisin only confessed that "a larger number of persons of all sorts and conditions had come to ask her help in killing off a large number of other persons" (Mossiker 1969, 216), but she refused to utter further names. Catherine La Voisin was burned at the stake in 1680. Spectators at her execution reported that "five or six times, she pushed aside the straw, but finally the flames leaped up, enveloped her, and she was lost to sight . . . So, there you have the death of Mme Voisin, notorious for her crimes and impiety" (219).

See also Brinvilliers, Marquise de; Montespan, Marquise de

Resources

Mossiker, Frances. 1969. *The Affair of the Poisons: Louis XIV, Madame de Montespan, and One of the History's Great Unsolved Mysteries.* New York: Alfred A. Knopf.

Somerset, Anne. 2003. *The Affair of the Poisons: Murder, Infanticide and Satanism at the Court of Louis XIV.* London: Weidenfeld & Nicolson.

Benedetta Faedi Duramy

Debra Lafave (1980–)

In June 2004, Debra Lafave was arrested for molesting a male student who attended the middle school where she taught. In the two years that followed, her case

Former middle school teacher Debra Lafave leaves the Hillsborough County Courthouse after pleading guilty to two counts of lewd and lascivious battery, 2005. Lafave, whose sexual liaisons with a 14-year-old middle school student made tabloid headlines, avoided prison as part of a plea agreement. (AP/Wide World Photos)

garnered a great deal of news media scrutiny. This crime was one of several similar incidents reported between female teachers and male students. However, the media latched on to one unique element in this case—Debra Lafave was incredibly attractive. The crime itself, the legal sanction to the crime, and the social response to both, revealed underlying gender dynamics in attitudes towards child molestation.

Born in 1980, Debra Jean Beasley grew up in Tampa, Florida. Raised in a working-class family, Lafave's mother was a cosmetologist, and her father worked for a local power company; she had one sibling, an older sister named Angie. According to Lafave, her life took at tragic turn at the age of 13. She was raped by her boyfriend in the bathroom of the middle school she attended. The act was interrupted and ended by a school official who mistook the rape as consensual sex. Both Lafave and her boyfriend were punished, and she never clarified what had actually happened because she felt ashamed. According to Lafave, she began drinking heavily at 15 and tried to commit suicide twice during her childhood. In addition, her mother would later assert that Lafave's childhood was fraught with emotional disorders. It was these emotional disorders, later diagnosed as a bipolar condition, which Lafave cited as the reason for her distorted view of sexual relations and the subsequent motivation for her crime (Lauer 2006).

At the age of 18, Lafave enrolled at the University of South Florida, majoring in English. Her sister was killed by a drunk driver in 2001. This incident exacerbated her emotional troubles leading to bouts of depression. These bouts would haunt her throughout the forthcoming years. While at college she met her future husband, Owen Lafave, whom she married in 2003. (They were divorced in 2005.) Following her graduation, she started teaching at Greco Middle School in 2003.

In the spring of 2004, she met the 14-year-old student with whom she had the sexual liaison. Over the course of a couple months, she chaperoned a field trip and gave him rides to basketball games. During these incidents, they flirted with each other, and she admitted to having a crush on him. On June 3, as summer vacation was starting, they had their first sexual liaison at Lafave's townhouse while his cousin was watching television. Ten days later, this was followed by another sexual incident in Lafave's classroom. Over the next three days, the two had sex twice in the backseat of Lafave's car while his 15-year-old cousin was driving. Following the last incident, the cousin told his mother about the relationship who, in turn, told the boy's mother. The boy's mother called the police and reported the crime. Police affidavits later revealed they had sex six times in total.

The police secured the boy's cooperation and convinced him to call Lafave. During these phone calls, Lafave incriminated herself, and she was arrested on June 21. She was brought up on charges of lewd and lascivious battery in two Tampa counties: Hillsborough and Marion. During preliminary negotiations between her defense attorney, John Fitzgibbons, and the prosecution, Fitzgibbons stated that her client was too attractive to be sent to prison. Anticipating a trial, Fitzgibbons planned to use an insanity defense, citing Lafave's diagnosed bipolar disorder. During November 2005, in Hillsborough County, a plea agreement was reached in which Lafave received house arrest for three years, probation for seven years, and life-time registration as a sex offender. When the same plea agreement was rejected by a judge in Marion County, in December 2005, the prosecutors dropped the charges upon urging from the boy's parents who feared the trauma the boy would experience from a trial.

The social reaction to the crime and sentence was layered. There was a great deal of public outrage over the light sentence. This outrage was buoyed by similarly light sentences handed down to an increasing number of female teachers who had molested students. In addition, there was a perception that Lafave's sentence had been positively mitigated by her attractiveness. Her attractiveness received a lot of media coverage, including the claim of her picture being the most sought image on the Internet. What the sentence and social reaction revealed was a gender-based dynamic to child molestation with respect to the perpetrator and victim.

In a 2006 *Time* article that examined the phenomenon of female teachers molesting children, the lighter sentences for Lafave and other female offenders were attributed to the perception that female molesters don't exhibit the stereotypical traits of sexual predators. In addition, unlike female victims, it was noted that male students are likely to be envied and held in higher esteem for having sex with female teachers. Consequentially, it was argued that a double standard has emerged in the legal system, one in which female teachers were generally given light sentences—including probation—whereas, male teachers usually received sentences in excess of 15 years imprisonment. It was this double standard, made so readily apparent by the media coverage, which resulted in the public outcry.

Since the end of her case, Lafave has maintained a low profile working as a waitress and serving out her sentence. However, the media spotlight that her crime and punishment garnered ensure that she is a figure who will not be soon forgotten.

Resources

Denov, Myriam S. 2004. *Perspectives on Female Sex Offending: A Culture of Denial (Society & Welfare).* Burlington, VT: Ashgate Publishing Limited.

Hillsborough County Sheriff's Office. Individual's Charge Report. 2004. Tampa, Florida. http://www.hcso.tampa.fl.us/pub/default.asp?/Online/qdisp/bn=04038892.

Kowal, Jessica. 2005. Women who seduce teens: a series of headlines have been about women bedding boys. We look at what drives these females to commit statutory rape. *Cosmopolitan*, October, 168–169.

Lauer, Matt. 2006. "Debra Lafave: Crossing the Line." *Dateline*, September 13.

Newsome, Melba. 2006. Dangerous Liaisons (seduction of male students by female teachers). *Time*, April, p. B7.

Tampa Bay Online. 2006. "Lafave Case Timeline" Tampa, Florida. http://reports.tbo.com/reports/lafave/.

Matthew Grindal

Lolita Lebron (1919–2010)

Lolita Lebron, a Puerto Rican political activist, made headline news for resorting to violence in her effort to achieve independence for Puerto Rico. While in the United States, she gained fame as a "lead terrorist"; in Puerto Rico and elsewhere, for those who were advocating independence, Lebron became known as a freedom fighter.

Lebron was born in Lares, Puerto Rico, a tiny town famous for its uprising against Spanish colonialism. Lolita and her family lived in poverty. Her father worked as a foreman in a coffee plantation while her mother stayed home taking care of their five children. Lebron was known for her exotic look. In her teenage years, she won the first place in an annual beauty contest, Queen of the Flowers of May. After Lolita became an unwed mother, she sailed for the United States in search of a better life, leaving her daughter, Gladys, in the care of her family. In early 1940, Lebron worked as a seamster for a clothing factory in New York City while attending school at night. Lebron had a brief marriage which resulted in the birth of her son, whom she sent to Puerto Rico to live with her family.

In the New York City of 1940s, Lebron observed explicitly racist signs banning people of color entry to establishments. Contrary to the many stories Lebron had heard of New York being paradise, she described where she lived in New York as a ghetto. Lebron became involved in Puerto Rico's Nationalist party led by Harvard-educated Dr. Pedro Albizu Campos. The goal of the Nationalist party was to attack the expansion of U.S. imperialism on the island by whatever means necessary. Lebron, who was a victim of poverty, worker oppression, and second-class citizenship, was attracted to the ideology of the Nationalist party. In 1951, Campos was arrested and sentenced to 80 years in prison for plotting an attempt to assassinate Harry Truman. Lebron and other Campos's ardent followers continued to hold covert meetings.

On March 1, 1954, Lolita Lebron, together with Andres Figueroa Cordero, Rafael Cancel Miranda, and Irvin Flores attacked the U.S. House of Representatives while more than 240 members of congress were debating an immigration bill. Standing in the visitors' balcony, they fired 30 shots from their automatic pistols, injuring five House members. Alvin Bentley, a 35-year-old member of Congress was shot in the chest, receiving the worst injuries among the five. Witnesses said that while the disturbing noise of gun shooting was going on, they could hear Lolita Lebron yelling, "Long live Puerto Rico." A doorkeeper witnessed that when someone tried to take the Puerto Rican flag out of Lebron's hand, she demanded that they give her

Lolita Lebron, Puerto Rican nationalist, shown at the federal courthouse after her arraignment in the House of Representatives shooting that wounded five members of Congress in 1954. (AP/ Wide World Photos)

back the flag of her country. Lebron and her comrades did not resist their arrest at the scene. Written evidence found at the scene indicated that Lebron saw her place as a freedom fighter for Puerto Rico and accused the United States of betraying basic human principles in their continuous subjugation of it.

At her trial, Lebron testified that she did not wish to hurt anyone, and during the attack, she aimed her gun at the ceiling. The jury believed her. Lolita Lebron was acquitted of the most serious charges she was facing: assault with intent to kill. Along with the other three, she was given a minimum sentence of 70 years in prison. Lolita Lebron was sent to the Federal Correctional Institution for Women in Alderson, West Virginia, where she stayed for the next 26 years.

In 1979, President Jimmy Carter granted clemency to the three assailants: Lebron, Miranda, and Flores. Cordero's sentence was commuted two year earlier because of his deteriorating health. After the release, Lebron and the freed men went through a kind of victory tour before the cheering crowds in New York and Chicago, the epicenters of Puerto Rican communities in the United States. In Puerto Rico, a surging crowd greeted Lebron with signs that read "Welcome, Lolita." Lebron had not softened in her perspective of the righteousness of her role, stating to Puerto Rican supporters upon her return: "We have done nothing to cause us to repent. Everyone has the right to defend his God-given right to liberty" ("Nation," 1979). However, Carlos Romero Barcelo, the governor of Puerto Rico, publicly opposed

Carter's decision in granting the pardon to the attackers, stating that Carter had encouraged terrorism.

On June 26, 2001, in Vieques Island, a municipality of Puerto Rico, Lebron, among others, protested against the use of bombing target practices in the island of Vieques. She and the rest of protesters were arrested with charges of trespassing on U.S. Navy property, resulting in Lebron's imprisonment for 60 days. On May 2003, the Navy gave their facilities to the local Puerto Rican government and moved out of Vieques Island.

Eight years after Lolita returned to Puerto Rico, she married Dr. Sergio Irizarry, a physician who shared the same dream with her—sovereignty for Puerto Rico. Even up into her late eighties, the struggle was not over for the political activist but became expressed in a different manner. Lebron became concerned with preserving the culture of Puerto Rico as well as the undoing the environmental destruction caused by industries and U.S. military bombing practices. Lebron's activities also extended to philanthropic causes like visiting and serving hospital patients. Lebron died in 2010.

To this day bullet holes from the incident still mark the desk of the Republican speaker and the ceiling of the United States House of Representative. Lolita Lebron did not regard herself a terrorist, instead considering herself a proud servant of her country and of her God.

Resources

James, Lesley. 2000. *Women Whom Made a Scene.* Oxford: Raintree Steck-Vaugh Publication.

"Nation: We Have Nothing to Repent." 1979. *Time.* September 24. http://www.time.com/time/magazine/article/0,9171,947395-1,00.htm.

Ojito, Mirta. 1998. Shots that haunted 3 generations. *New York Times.* May 26, p. E1.

Roig-Franzia, Manuel. 2004. "A Terrorist in the House." *Washington Post Magazine,* February 23, w12.

Thompkins, C. M., & D. W. Foster, eds. 1998. *Notable Twentieth-Century Latin American Women.* Westport, CT: Greenwood Press.

Vilar, Irene. 1998. *The Ladies' Gallery.* Translated by Gregory Rabassa. New York: Vintage Books.

Ladan Dejam

Mary Kay Letourneau (1962–)

Mary Kay Letourneau (currently known as Mary Kay Fualaau) was a school teacher infamous for having sex with her student, Vili Fualaau, whom she married after serving seven-and-a-half years for statutory rape.

She was born Mary Katherine Schmitz on January 30, 1962, in Orange County, California, to John and Mary Schmitz. Letourneau was the fourth of Schmitz's seven children; however, John Schmitz had two additional children with his long-time mistress and former student (he had been a professor at Santa Ana College). Letourneau attended Arizona State University until she became pregnant by Steve Letourneau, whom she later married in June 30, 1984. The couple had four children—two boys and two girls. After Letourneau got her degree from Seattle University in 1989, she began teaching at Shorewood Elementary School in Burien, Washington.

Letourneau first met Vili Fualaau when she was the boy's second-grade teacher. It was not until June 1996, after the boy completed grade six and was once again a student in her class, that she began to have sex with him. Fualaau was only 13 years old. However, her criminal activity was not discovered until February 1997, when her husband found love letters. Steve Letourneau's relatives, in whom he confided, reported the affair to local child protection services. Letourneau was pregnant with Fualaau's daughter, Audrey Lokelani, at the time. On February 26, 1997, Letourneau was arrested for child rape. On August 7, 1997, she plead guilty to two counts of second-degree rape of a child, and on November 14, she was sentenced to 89 months in prison by Judge Linda Lau. The court ordered her to confinement in county jail for 180 days with credit for the 100 days she had already spent there but suspended the remaining confinement conditional upon her compliance with the terms of a Special Sexual Offender Sentencing Alternative. Among other restrictions, the terms of her sentence required that she have no contact with her victim, undergo specialized treatment for sexual deviance, have no unsupervised contact with minors including her own biological children, not profit directly or indirectly from any commercialization related to her crime, and take medications and undergo therapy for bipolar disorder. Letourneau received the suspended sentence as part of a plea deal negotiated by her lawyer, David Gehrke, who argued that her actions were in part due to her diagnosis of bipolar disorder. Gehrke brought in psychiatrist Dr. Julia Tybor Moore who said it was Letourneau's condition that caused her to enter into a relationship with Fualaau. Letourneau was released from jail on January 1, 1998. However, she was soon arrested by Seattle Police Officer, Tod Harris, for violating the conditions of her parole on February 3. Letourneau was discovered in a car with Fualaau. In the vehicle she had clothes, her passport, and more than $6,000 in cash, suggesting she was about to abscond. Her original seven-and-a-half year sentence was reimposed, and she was ordered to serve the remainder of her time in prison. On October 16, 1998, Letourneau gave birth to Fualaau's second daughter, Alexis Georgia, conceived while out on parole. However, her obsession with Fualaau did not end with her incarceration. She sent coded messages to him from prison on the labels of the frozen breast milk she sent for their daughter who was being cared for by Fualaau's mother. She also got caught smuggling letters to him in November 1999, garnering her six months in solitary confinement. In May of that year, she divorced her estranged husband Steve, who obtained custody of their four children. In 2000, Letourneau appealed two of her conditions: no unsupervised contact with her biological children and no profiting from her crime. She was successful in June 2000 when these conditions were struck down. After serving her full sentence, Letourneau was released on August 4, 2004. Two days after her release, the then 21-year-old Fualaau applied to have the no contact order on Letourneau lifted, and the request was granted. On May 20, 2005, Letourneau and Fualaau were married in a lavish wedding at Columbia Winery in Woodinville, near Seattle. Sources indicate that the Fualaaus received $750,000 for the exclusive rights to their wedding from *Entertainment Tonight* which recorded the affair. Currently, the couple and their two daughters, whom they gained full custody of in early 2006, are living in Normandy Park, Washington. They are living off of the proceeds from their wedding, their media appearances, and the books they have penned about their story including *Un seul crime, l'amour* (Astudillo, 2007).

Resources

Astudillo, Teresa. 2007. The forbidden love that refused to die. *Daily Telegraph (Australia)*, April 7.

Bartley, Nancy, Cheryl Harris, and Christine Clarridge. 1998. Letourneau's freedom restricted. *Seattle Times*, January 7.

Cloud, John. 1998. A matter of hearts. *Time Magazine*, May 4. http://www.time.com/time/magazine/article/0,9171,988276–1,00.html.

Dress, Christina, Tama-Lisa Johnson, and Mary Kay Letourneau. 2004. *Mass with Mary: The Prison Years*. Trafford, BC, Canada: Trafford Publishing.

Fitten, Ronald K. 1997. Teacher won't go to prison for rape. *Seattle Times*, May 14.

Kiyomura, Cathy. 2005. DSHS may want slice of Letourneau wedding payoff pie. KING 5 News, May 2. www.king5.com/localnews/stories/NW_091304WABletourneausonKC.11421dd7d.html.

Letourneau, Mary Kay, and Vili Fualaau. 1999. *Un seul crime, l'amour* (Only one crime, love). Paris, France: Robert Laffont.

MSNBC. 2006. Letourneau and Fualaau, one year later. *Dateline*, June 2. http://www.msnbc.msn.com/id/13064459/

Olsen, Gregg. 1999. *If Loving You is Wrong*. New York: St. Martin's Press.

Washington v. Letourneau, 100 Wn. App. 424; 997 P.2d 436, 2000.

Kim S. Ménard

Teresa Lewis (1969–2010)

Teresa Lewis is one of the more controversial figures within the women and death penalty debate. Her case brings together several issues including mental capacity and appropriateness of capital punishment as well as how gender plays into considerations in giving women capital sentences. Two images of Lewis exist: (a) a cruel, greedy woman who used sex to mastermind the murder for hire of her husband and stepson for the insurance money; and (b) a mentally challenged woman, extremely vulnerable to the manipulation of a man who wooed her and convinced her to participate in killing her family for his own financial benefit. This case brought many perspectives to renew the argument about effects of gender on death penalty decisions and the inhumanity of the death penalty.

Teresa Lewis smiles at the camera in 2007. Lewis was found guilty of conspiring to have her husband and stepson murdered for insurance money. She was sentenced to death by lethal injection. (AP/Wide World Photos)

Not much is known about Teresa Lewis's early years. She was born Teresa Wilson on April 26, 1969, around Danville, Virginia. Both parents worked in a local textile factory. Lewis's early life was characterized as difficult both from a home life described as "repressive" and from mental challenges related to borderline intellectual functioning IQ.

Growing up and as an adult, Lewis regularly participated in Christian church services and activities. There is some question about how much she practiced her faith, at least in earlier years. Lewis publicly stated that while she went to church twice a week or more, she did not even read her Bible outside of church. Lewis also stated that she did drugs, stole, lied, and had several sexual affairs while she was putting on the face of a "good" church girl.

There are conflicting accounts with regard to Lewis's education with some stating that she dropped out of high school, and the court stating that she had finished high school and attended a year of college. The timing of events is not clear, and it is possible that she dropped out only to finish at a later time. According to Lewis's father, his daughter dropped out of school in 1985 at the age of 16 and ran off to get married to a man named Bean she met from church. Lewis's father described his daughter's life as immoral and self-serving, and he accused her of abandoning her child and having affairs with multiple men including her sister's husband. Lewis publicly admitted having affairs during her marriages. Lewis and her first husband ultimately divorced after having two children including daughter, Christie, who later played a role in Lewis's plan to kill her husband and stepson.

Around the time of Lewis's divorce, she began drinking heavily and is reported to have become addicted to painkillers, taking as many as 600 pills per month to escape physical abdominal pain and the emotional pain of her mother's death. The only prior offense found for Lewis was a charge of forging prescriptions.

Between the time when Lewis married her first husband and her second, victim Julian Clifton Lewis, Lewis is reported to have worked at nearly 50 low-income jobs, jumping from job to job. In March or April 2000, Teresa Lewis was hired at the Dan River textile factory, where she met recently widowed Julian Clifton Lewis, Jr., who was her supervisor. The two fell for each other, and by June, Julian and Teresa began to live together at Julian's home in Danville, Virginia. They were married the following year.

Some, including Lewis's mother-in-law, noticed Lewis's difficulties with some basic daily tasks. For example, she could not manage a checkbook or other household finances. She was unable to buy more than a day's groceries at one time. She was described as being like a child. Her mother-in-law described her as not being quite right. Lewis's questionable mental capacities would later become the cornerstone of her argument in the appeal of her death sentence.

Lewis was portrayed by the prosecution and seen by some others as highly greedy. When her stepson, Jason, died in a car accident in December 2001, Lewis's husband inherited more than $200,000 from his life insurance policy. Lewis allegedly began to think of how to get more money from Julian and his family. Some claim she only wanted Julian Lewis for his money. In early 2002, the couple purchased an acreage and mobile home in Pittsylvania County. At this time, the prosecution claimed that Lewis began to plot ways to get more money. Her greed was intensified when Julian Lewis's other son, Charles, executed a will and took out life insurance listing his father as primary beneficiary and Lewis a secondary beneficiary. Charles, an Army reservist, was about to be deployed to the war in the Middle East and wanted his affairs to be in order.

In the fall of 2002, Lewis met two young men at the local Wal-Mart store: Rodney Fuller and Matthew Shallenberger. After some conversation, Lewis exchanged telephone numbers with Shallenberger. This was the beginning of a sexual affair between them. Lewis allegedly showered Shallenberger with gifts and sex. This relationship quickly led to a conspiracy between Shallenberger, Lewis, and Fuller to kill Lewis's husband for insurance money, which Lewis and Shallenberger would split. The sexual affair and questionable morals of Lewis became important to both defense and prosecution. The defense wished to avoid a jury trial for fear that moral issues would overshadow the facts in the case. The prosecution used the sexually immoral behavior of Lewis as a highly visible and inflammatory part of their case. Particularly damning was Lewis's offering her 16-year-old daughter Christie to Fuller for sex while she and Shallenberger had sex in another car. Prosecution also claimed Lewis had sex with both men.

Lewis provided Shallenberger and Fuller $1,200 to purchase two shotguns, ammunition, and another weapon to kill Lewis's husband. There was one aborted attempt to kill Julian prior to the murders on October 30, 2002. Lewis received news that Julian's son Charles would be staying with them, and the three then planned to kill both of them. On the night of the murders, Lewis left the rear door of her trailer home unlocked for the two men to come in. At some point after midnight, while Lewis was in bed with her husband, the two came into the house. Shallenberger told Teresa to get up, and she went into the kitchen to wait. Shallenberger shot repeated blasts into Julian Lewis while Fuller shot Charles Lewis multiple times. Charles Lewis died instantly, but Julian Lewis did not die until later.

After the murders, Lewis retrieved her husband's wallet, took out $300, and gave half to Shallenberger. Shallenberger and Fuller left, and Lewis waited between 30 and 45 minutes to call 911, after calling her former mother-in-law and a friend. Prosecutors described Lewis as a callous, cruel woman who took careful steps to avoid suspicion. She made a lunch for Julian and placed it into a paper bag with words like "I love you" written on the bag in ink, which was done as she undoubtedly heard her husband's anguish and pain after being shot. Testimony later indicated that Julian never took lunches to work in paper bags. When deputies arrived, Julian Lewis was found curled up in the bedroom moaning "baby, baby, baby." When asked who had shot him, he replied, "my wife knows who done this to me." He died after that.

Lewis initially claimed that two strangers broke into the home and killed her husband and stepson while she hid in the bathroom. Her demeanor was described as strange. When she was informed that her husband and stepson were dead, she did not appear upset. Lewis's story was not consistent with other crime scene evidence. Several days later, Lewis confessed and lead police to Shallenberger who then pointed out Fuller. Lewis had tried to claim assets and insurance money, even before her husband and stepson were buried. These actions were also used to indicate her greed as well as ability to plan the murders.

Teresa Lewis was indicted on November 20, 2002, on two counts of murder for hire and five other charges. Lewis's defense counsel wanted to avoid a trial. They never raised the issue of Lewis's mental capacities or her psychological weaknesses, and the case never went to trial. Lewis waived her right to trial and pleaded guilty in May 2003 to seven offenses, including the two crimes of murder for hire, without any guarantee she would avoid a death sentence. Fuller had already received a life sentence, and the defense did not believe that the judge would give Lewis death. Teresa Lewis was sentenced to death and identified as an evil mastermind of the murders who lured her coconspirators with sex. Judge Strauss of the Pittsylvania Circuit Court stated that she clearly met the legal standard of "depravity of mind."

With Fuller sentenced to life for his role in the murders, Shallenberger was also given a sentence of life as a measure of "fairness" of sentencing between the two. Lewis was remanded to the custody of the Virginia Department of Corrections, where she awaited her execution in complete segregation as the state of Virginia did not have an actual "death row" for women.

In 2004, James E. Rocap, III, took on Lewis's case to pursue an appeal of the death sentence and began additional investigation which revealed three crucial areas not known to or pursued by defense counsel. These were Lewis's low intellectual functioning; symptoms of dependent personality disorder, which hindered her independence; and evidence that Shallenberger was the actual mastermind of the scheme and that Lewis was manipulated by him. When Lewis was administered an IQ test, she scored a full scale IQ of 72, a verbal IQ of 70, and a performance IQ of 79. She was determined to be in the borderline range of mental retardation (borderline intellectual function) but was not diagnosable as retarded nor did she fall below the 70 IQ score established as the minimum cognitive competency allowable for capital punishment. Critics question whether differences in two or three IQ points are meaningful. She was also assessed by three different psychological professionals to have dependent personality disorder which impaired her ability to accomplish daily tasks without help, rendered her vulnerable to stronger individuals—particularly men, and made her eager and even desperate to please. The defense argued that Lewis could not have cognitively or psychologically been the leader of this murder conspiracy but, rather, a follower of the stronger and more intelligent Shallenberger. Investigation in 2004 discovered that Shallenberger had told a former girlfriend in a letter that he manipulated and used Lewis in order to get money to become a drug dealer. He said that Lewis was not very smart and eager to do what he wanted, and this was exactly what he wanted: someone who wanted money and who would fall for his affections. This was repeated to an investigator along with his claim that the money was the only reason he ever had sex with Lewis. Others claimed that Shallenberger fancied himself as a gigolo, a sharp shooter, and that he had sights on becoming a Mafia hit man in New York. Shallenberger killed himself in prison in 2006, but after he made those statements, the defense claimed that Fuller and two others had also substantiated Shallenberger's claim.

The argument that Lewis was too impaired to have planned and led the plot to kill her husband and stepson was soundly rejected by the circuit court. Additional arguments about gender disproportionality were made based on the severity of her sentence compared to similar cases as well as the sentencing of the actual triggermen in this crime. The court explicitly stated that they could not and would not accept an argument based on gender and denied the appeal in March 2004. A subsequent plea for clemency from the governor, Bob McDonnell, was also denied. When Lewis's quest to have the U.S. Supreme Court hear her appeal was denied 7–2 (Justices Sotomayor and Ginsberg dissenting) on September 21, 2010, Lewis's hope for a stay of execution dwindled. The governor denied clemency a second time that same day, and preparations were made for Lewis's execution at Greensville Correctional Center in Jarratt, Virginia. She was executed September 23, 2010, with death proclaimed at 9:13 PM. Her last words were directed toward Kathy Clifton, her stepdaughter and the only remaining immediate relative of Julian Lewis. Lewis apologized to Kathy and expressed her love for her before she died by lethal injection.

The Lewis case gained worldwide attention as countries around Europe and other parts of the world questioned why the United States would execute a retarded woman. The European Union's human rights representative, celebrities, the pope, Amnesty International, and many woman's groups called for clemency. Even Iranian president Mahmoud Ahmadinejad made reference to the case, publicly questioning why the United States would execute such a woman but also criticize Iran's handling of criminals. While the support for Lewis reached a level rarely seen in a death penalty case, the outcome further demonstrates the deep entrenchment of capital punishment in the U.S. criminal justice system and harsher treatment of nonsympathetic, nontraditionally feminine women who kill. Teresa Lewis violated fundamental gender expectations for women: love for family, faithfulness, controlled sexuality. Ultimately, this case raises questions about current definitions of mental capacity and culpability as well as possible gender biases in with regard to capital punishment. Lewis was the 12th woman put to death in the United States since the reinstatement of the death penalty in 1976.

Resources

"Amnesty International Urges Government to Commute Teresa Lewis Execution." www.commondreams.org/newswire/2010/09/14_22. (Retrieved October 10, 2010).

Eckholm, Erik. 2010. "Woman on Death Row Runs Out of Appeals." *New York Times*. September 22. p. A14.

Glod, Maria. 2010. "On Death Row, Killer Pleads for Her Life." *Washington Post*. September 14. p. A08.

Hammack, Laurence. 2010. "Teresa Lewis to be Executed by Lethal Injection." *Roanoke Times* [Roanoke, VA] September 12.

Jones, Ashby. 2010. "High Court Takes a Pass, End is Near for Virginia Woman." WSJ Blog, Law Blog. www.blogs.wsj.com/law/2010/09/22/high_court_takes_a_pass_end_is_near_for_virginia_woman/. (Retrieved October 14, 2010).

Leonard, Tom. 2010. "Is it Because She's a Woman that Double Killer is to be Executed by Lethal Injection?" *Daily Mail*. www.dailymail.co.uk/news/worldnews/article_1313614/Is_Teresa_Lewis_woman_shes_executed_lethal_injection.html#. (Retrieved October 14, 2010).

Lewis v. Commonwealth of Virginia. 2004. Opinion by Chief Justice Leroy R. Hassel., Sr., Circuit Court of Pittsylvania County. Record No. 032153. March 5, 2004.

O'Connor, Anahad. 2010. "Woman, 41, is Executed in Virginia." *New York Times*. September 24. p. A20(L).

Reber, Pat. 2010. "Roundup: Virginia Executes low-IQ Woman Through Injection." *America's Intelligence Wire*. September 24.

Szkotak, Steve. 2010. "Virginia Puts Woman to Death; Rare Female Execution." www.washingtontimes.com/news/2010/sep/24/va_inmate_first_woman_5_years_executed_US. (Retrieved October 15. 2010).

Williams, Carol. 2010. "Woman's Execution Could Signal Shift in U.S. Thinking; Her Death Breaks with Traditional Queasiness Over Such Punishment for Female Criminals." *LATEXTRA;* Metro Desk. Part AA. September 24.

Vickie Jensen

Joan Little (1954–)

Joan (pronounced Jo-Ann) Little was a petty criminal offender in the mid-1970s who went from alleged victim, to alleged murderer, to jail escapee—and became a cause célèbre for the women's movement, the civil rights and black power movements, and the anti-death penalty movement. Her trial in the summer of 1975 for first-degree murder galvanized national focus on the emerging issues of a woman's right to defend herself against male sexual aggression (especially when incarcerated), on sexual and racial inequities in criminal processing, and on the legitimacy of the death penalty.

Joan Little was born May 8, 1954, in Washington, North Carolina, the oldest of eight or nine children in a poor black family. Since her alcoholic stepfather did not contribute to the family income, her mother worked long hours at factory or domestic jobs to keep the family going, and Joan was drafted to look after her younger siblings. But she was bright and rebellious, and by the time she was a teenager, she was misbehaving so badly that her mother sent her to a nearby minimum-security youth training school. When Little ran away from that the school, her mother sent her to live with relatives in Philadelphia and Newark, New Jersey, where she apparently did somewhat better. After returning to North Carolina several years later for a medical procedure, Little rebelled against being placed in a grade below where she believed she belonged and abruptly quit school. A series of menial jobs followed, along with Little becoming increasingly involved with "the wrong crowd" and having run-ins with the law (McNeil, 2001; Reston, 1977).

Though none of Little's first arrests resulted in convictions, she eventually was arrested on a more serious breaking-and-entering charge in 1974 in Greenville, North Carolina. She jumped bail and ran but was soon recaptured. She asked to be detained pending trial at the Beaufort County Jail, rather than at the Correctional Center for Women at Raleigh, which would have been the norm. Depending on which story is believed, this was because she wanted to be closer to her home during her pretrial detention, or she wanted the more relaxed detention available in the small county jail compared to the more rigid custodial arrangements in Raleigh (Reston, 1977). Whatever the reason, her stay at the Beaufort County Jail would prove fateful since it brought Joan into prolonged contact with Clarence Alligood, the white Beaufort County Jail night jailer.

Little's life became news after a deputy entered the Beaufort County jail at about 4:00 AM on the morning of August 27, 1974, to admit a prisoner and found Clarence Alligood lying half-naked and dead from multiple stab wounds. The only woman detainee, Joan Little, was gone. She was immediately suspected of the murder and declared a fugitive, and a massive hunt ensued. For a week Little eluded police, while newspapers gave vivid accounts of "an intentional 'brutal murder' of a night jailer who was acting in the 'line of duty'" (McNeil, 2001: 260). Details about Alligood's pants being off and dried semen trailing down his leg were omitted from press coverage at the time. The search for Little became so fevered that authorities contemplated whether to invoke the "outlaw" clause from a Reconstruction Era law that would have permitted Little to be shot on sight as a dangerous renegade (McNeil, 2001; Reston, 1977). Hearing about this helped impel Little to seek legal assistance and a way to turn herself in safely. She eventually submitted to the North Carolina State Bureau of Investigation accompanied by her attorneys on September 3, 1974.

When finally given an opportunity to tell her side of the story, Little asserted that she had been sexually assaulted by the night jailer and had merely defended herself against him, turning the ice pick he had brought to her cell to intimidate her into her own weapon of defense. She claimed she did not even realize Alligood was dead when she ran away. Nonetheless, the grand jury immediately indicted her for first-degree murder, which at that time carried an automatic death sentence. Activist Angela Davis later claimed that, in a Southern county filled with many people named Alligood, at least one had served on the grand jury that indicted Little, raising questions about how impartial the justice was in this case (Davis, 1975).

Southern justice in the mid-1970s was not known for being kind to blacks who killed whites. Joan Little claimed she fled the jail in fear for her life and stayed on the run once she learned of Alligood's death for the same reason. Given the extent of the police search for her, it is clear that she was able to evade them only with the help of other local blacks—some of whom aided her precisely because the police were so aggressive toward them (Reston, 1977). Once jailed again, this time in Raleigh, Little's case quickly gained national attention, due in part to a story in the *New York Times* in December 1974 and an article by Angela Davis in *Ms.* magazine in June 1975. Supporters quickly began to gather around Little. Support came from a Free Joan Little Committee and a Joann Little Defense Fund which tried to raise money for her $100,000 bail, to support from existing organizations such as the Commission for Racial Justice of the United Church for Christ, the Southern Christian Leadership Conference, the Southern Poverty Law Center, the National

Alliance Against Racial and Political Repression, the National Organization for Women, the Alliance of Lesbian Feminists of Atlanta, and the Black Panther Party (McNeil, 2001).

This unusual combination of supporters exemplifies the way in which Little's case tapped into the concerns of the time. The women's movement had been trying to raise the issue of rape for some time, and here was a case of a woman being prosecuted for defending herself against sexual assault. The black power and civil rights movements had long raged against the inequities of the criminal justice system, and this case of a black woman being sexually coerced by a white male guard was virtual replay of the racial and sexual inequalities of plantation politics. The case also raised uncomfortable issues about the death penalty at a time just after the U.S. Supreme Court had temporarily halted its use in *Furman v. Georgia*. Even before that landmark decision, executions had dropped off to nothing in the United States, and the *Furman* decision acknowledged that executions may have been racially biased in their application in the past. The prospect of giving a death sentence to a young black woman who said she had killed only in self-defense was discomforting.

All of these combined to form national interest in—and support for—Joan Little, both while she was on the run and as she awaited trial. Her lawyers shrewdly encouraged public sympathy for her. And though she was a high school dropout, Little was smart and quickly picked up on the issues that swirled around her. She wrote an essay that appeared in the January 1975 issue of the radical women's newspaper *Off our Backs* in which she articulated her "growing self-awareness" and "her right to defend herself and to have a voice in discussions about her life" (McNeil, 2001: 266). She began to model her behavior after that of her female attorney who was about her same size but more refined (Reston, 1977). Most important, however, she never wavered from her contention that she had acted only to defend herself, even in the highly charged trial, which took place in Raleigh, North Carolina, in the summer of 1975. Despite prosecutorial efforts to make her actions seem like those of a deliberate premeditated killer, Little was so well prepped by her attorneys that she handled the difficult cross-examination exceedingly well. The jury took only 78 minutes to acquit her (Reston, 1977).

Forever a symbol of all individuals caught at the intersection of race, sex, and the criminal justice system, Joan Little's case marked a new sensitivity in American politics to a woman's right to defend her body against male aggression, and the right of blacks to expect fair treatment from the justice system. As Angela Davis noted in her famous *Ms.* magazine essay on Little, it had been presumed up to that time that women who really resisted could not be raped so that women who *were* raped were doubly victimized—-by the rapist and by the system that did not believe them. Black women were victimized once more, since it was historically "acceptable" for white men to take advantage of the black women who were their property as slaves, or who were believed to have provoked their victimization by being sexually seductive (Davis, 1975). Joan Little's case touched on elements of all of these highly sensitive issues, and yet she was quickly acquitted.

Resources

Davis, A. (June, 1975). JoAnne Little: The dialectics of rape. First printed in *Ms.* magazine. Reprinted in James, J. (ed.). (1998). *The Angela Y. Davis Reader*, (149–159). Malden, MA: Blackwell Publishers.

King, W. (December 1, 1974). Killing of Carolina jailer, charged to woman, raises question of abuse of inmates. *New York Times*. p. 41.

Little, J. (December 29, 1974). Self-aware. *Off our backs.* As cited in McNeil (2001).

McNeil, G. R. (2001). "Joanne is you, Joanne is me:" A consideration of African American women and the "Free Joan Little" movement, 1974–1975 (259–279). In B. Collier-Thomas & V. P. Franklin (eds.) *Sisters in the struggle: African American women in the civil rights-black power movement.* New York: New York University Press.

Reston, J. (1977). *The innocence of Joan Little: A Southern mystery.* New York: New York Times Books.

Christine E. Rasche

M

Winnie Mandela (1936–)

Nomzamo Winifred Zanyiwe Madikizela, known to the outside world as Winnie Mandela, was a pivotal political figure in opposition to white supremacy of South Africa. Her political activities were marked with continuous prosecution, arrests, detention in solitary confinement, and life in exile by the South African apartheid government. Winnie was largely accountable for the international attention given to the plight of South Africans and the imprisonment of anti-apartheid leader, Nelson Mandela. After his release, however, she was implicated in and convicted of helping to conceal a murder.

Winnie Mandela was born in Bizana, a poverty-stricken rural area of Southeast Africa. Her father, Columbus Madikizela, was a primary school principal, and her mother, Gertrude, was a teacher. Winnie proved to be an excellent student. At age 16, she received the scholarship to attend the Jan Hofmeyer School of Social Work.

In 1955, Winnie Mandela became the first South African black to receive a degree in medical social work. She was offered a full scholarship to study sociology in the United States, but she decided to turn down the offer and work at Baragwanath Hospital, the only hospital that served the over million blacks who lived in Soweto. While Winnie was researching infant mortality rates, she was confronted with the depth and the scope of dehumanizing poverty that blacks in South Africa experienced. The existing connection between blacks' deprivation from resources and the apartheid system raised Winnie's political consciousness. She began to participate with the African National Council (ANC) which had originally formed to organize a nationwide nonviolent resistance to white supremacy. In 1957, Winnie was introduced to Nelson Mandela, a 39-year-old political activist and one of the ANC's leaders. A year later, Winnie and Nelson were married. In 1960, Nelson was forced to go underground for his political activism. Nelson was arrested in 1962, and the court found him guilty on conspiracy charges, plotting to overthrow the apartheid government. He was sentenced to life imprisonment.

Winnie at age 26 was left alone to keep Mandela's name and work alive as well as to raise their two daughters, Zindi and Zeni. In her 1986 interview, Winnie explained that she was young and politically immature when she married Mandela. As such, it made her path a very difficult one in which she had to fumble her way alone. As Winnie's role in the struggle against apartheid grew, she became the de facto spokesperson for the ANC. Consequently, she became the subject of investigation by the state and local police. In 1962, she was restricted to Soweto and lost her traveling privileges. Five years later, Winnie was sent to prison for a month for her political activity.

Winnie Mandela ponders a question during a speaking engagement in Washington at American University, 1996. Mandela said the struggle to overcome apartheid was a prelude to the challenges of establishing a stable democracy in South Africa. (AP/Wide World Photos)

In May 1969, when Winnie and her daughters were home sleeping, security police began to pound at her door. Under the new Terrorism Act, Winnie was incarcerated in a solitary confinement at the Pretoria Central Prison. Two weeks later, security police began to interrogate her. They wanted to know about the ANC and its communist contacts and whether Nelson Mandela was sending her instruction from Robben Island. Five months later, Winnie was charged for reviving the ANC by recruiting for them; finding targets for sabotage; distributing banned literature; using funerals to further the aims of the ANC; and encouraging hostility between whites and blacks.

On the day of her trial, the state announced that they had 80 witnesses against Winnie, including her youngest sister, Nonyanison, but when the first 20 witnesses stated that they had all been threatened and tortured into testifying, the judge ordered a recess in the trial. In February 1970, the attorney general told the court that the state was dropping the case against Winnie and others who were arrested under the Terrorism Act. But soon after, Winnie was rearrested and returned to solitary confinement for the following seven months. Through the prison grapevine, Winnie learned that her detention had caused international outrage. In September 1970, Winnie among few other political activists were freed. However, she continued to be harassed and was subjected to searches at all hours.

In 1977, Winnie was banished to Brandfort, a small town where the locals did not speak her language. At this point, Winnie Mandela was constantly in the news. The security forces recognized the possible significance of her role and placed her under constant observation. Years later, reflecting back on her life, Winnie described having lived a day-to-day kind of existence. She and her two young daughters were harassed from the moment Nelson Mandela was arrested. It was extremely difficult for her to explain to them why they were constantly under strict surveillance, why security forces were present in their home, why they were constantly being raided, followed, and searched if their mother wasn't a criminal.

In the following decade, in 1991, Winnie's reputation was tarnished when she was charged and convicted of close involvement in a murder case. Winnie appealed her conviction. In February 11, 1991, due to the international pressure and other factors, the ban on the ANC was lifted and Nelson Mandela was released from prison. In 1992, new evidence related to Winnie's involvement in the same murder case surfaced that resulted in her resignation as the head of the ANC's social welfare department. However, the court waived her six-year prison term, and instead, she was ordered to pay a fine. In April 1992, Nelson announced his separation from Winnie. In the following year, despite Winnie's criminal conviction, she was elected president of the ANC's Women League. In 1994, when Nelson Mandela was elected president of South Africa, he appointed Winnie to deputy minister of arts, culture, science, and technology. But Winnie was fired in April 1995 for her ongoing conflict with Nelson. At last, in 1996, the Mandelas were divorced. In years to come, her dented reputation did not destroy Winnie's political career. Many South Africans, especially women, have continued to support her. The 74-year-old political activist has been recently helping women in the areas of education, income generation, and health.

Resources

Gilbey, Emma. 1993. *The Lady. The Life and Times of Winnie Mandela*. London: Cape.

Harrison, Nancy. 1986. *Winnie Mandela*. New York: George Braziller.

Haskins, Jim. 1988. *Winnie Mandela. Life of Struggle*. New York: Putnam & Son.

Hoobler, Dorothy, and Thomas Hoobler. 1987. *Nelson and Winnie Mandela*. New York: Franklin Watts.

Mandela, Nelson. 1994. *Long Walk to Freedom. The Autobiography of Nelson Mandela*. Boston: Little Brown.

Mandela, Winnie. 1985. *Part of My Soul Went with Him*. New York: Norton.

Shreir, Sally, & F. John Harper. 1989. *Women's Movements of the World. An International Directory and Reference Guide*. Letchworth, England: Keesing Publications.

Ladan Dejam

Mother Mandelbaum (1818?–1894)

Mother Mandelbaum (or "Marm" as she was better known) was the most successful fence in New York's criminal history. Between the years of 1864 and 1884, she handled between $5 to $10 million in stolen goods, equivalent to between $120 million and $200 million today. Not much is known about her early life. She was named Fredericka, born to Jewish parents in the German principality of Hesse-Kassel (Bryk, 2003: 1). She arrived in this country with her husband sometime in 1849 (Van Every, 1972: 240).

Police records show her name first appearing in 1862. At that time she was peddling stolen goods door to door. She began managing teams of pickpockets, fencing their takes, and at the same time providing bail and legal defense for them (Bryk, 2003: 1). Mandelbaum and her husband opened a dry-goods and haberdashery store at 79 Clinton Street in the German neighborhood known as Kleine Deutschland in New York City. Later, they were able to purchase the three-story building and a two-story wing in the rear (Van Every, 1972: 240). It was here that she and her husband raised four children, living with them on the second and third floors which were furnished with more elegance than any other place in the city, while they were fronting the biggest fencing operation in New York's history. Mandelbaum had dances and dinners, entertaining lavishly both criminals and police officials and politicians whom were indebted to her (Asbury, 1927: 215).

A one-time warden of Sing Sing described the squat and corpulent Mother Mandelbaum who weighed over 250 pounds, by saying, "The energy of her character seemed to be all drawn down into the capacious thick blubbered reservoir of her body, quiescent in reserve for things more vital than a handshake: and some of it welled up and shone forth in the rich geniality of her smile" (Fried, 1993: 26). It is said that she dealt honestly with the people who brought her stolen property, adhering to a strict code of criminal ethics that made them trust her with absolute confidence. She paid in cash and at times extended advance money for jobs not yet completed. She also paid a $5,000 yearly retainer to the law firm of Howe & Hummel for those of her suppliers who ran afoul of the law. Mandelbaum provided bail money and expenses for their trials, taxing them afterward to recoup her losses (Van Every, 1972: 242). Mandelbaum even declared that her business associates called her Ma "because I give them what a mother cannot sometimes give—money and horses and diamonds" (Fried, 1993: 26).

Mandelbaum used a network of warehouses across the city to house the stolen goods, reselling them all over the East Coast to middlemen in New York and elsewhere (Bryk, 2003: 1). Once the goods were brought into the warehouses, all labels, trademarks, and forms of identification were removed or erased. She accepted everything including stolen bonds, but she loved silks the most. It is said that for years almost everything silk that was stolen went through her (Van Every, 1972: 242).

Mother Mandelbaum ran a school on Grand Street not far from police headquarters. Small boys and girls learned how to be pickpockets and sneak thieves. Advance courses were also offered in burglary, safe-blowing, blackmailing, and confidence schemes. She got scared and shut the school down when the son of a prominent police official applied to the school (Asbury, 1927: 217).

The Great Manhattan Savings Institution Bank Robbery of 1878, which was planned by George Leslie, was financed with Mandelbaum's money. Leslie began planning the heist in 1875 but was murdered by part of the gang a few months shy of the robbery (Lardner and Reppetto, 2000: 76–78). Mandelbaum had an agent working for her identify the body as Leslie's. She is said to have given Leslie a decent burial (Asbury, 1927: 210).

What proved to be Mandelbaum's downfall in the end was her love of silks. District Attorney Peter B. Olney realized that the municipal police would not help him apprehend Mother Mandelbaum. He hired Pinkerton Detectives, who came to her in the guise of thieves, and eventually caught her with some silks in her possession known to be stolen (Van Every, 1972: 243). She was arrested along with her son on July 22, 1884, then released under $21,000 bail. A strong case was made against her, and on December 4, 1884, when she was to face trial, she fled with $1 million in cash to Toronto, where the United States had no extradition treaty. The police could not seize the property put up for bail because Mandelbaum's lawyer Hummell had fraudulently backdated the title documents, transferring the property to Mandelbaum's daughters. Mother Mandelbaum lived in Hamilton, Ontario, Canada, until her death on February 26, 1894 (Bryk, 2003: 3–4).

There is not much societal response to Mandelbaum in general. Because New York had been famous for police corruption for years and because Mother Mandelbaum had held prominent police officials in her power for so long, when Thomas Byrnes became New York's "great detective," the rich and famous began to put their trust in him. When something was stolen, he would promise to get it back for the person. Over the course of many years the idea of the detective agency was born and started to flourish with detectives under his leadership known as "men of prestige" (Lardner and Reppetto, 2000: 83). With Mother Mandelbaum no longer in business, those in society whom she had preyed on must have breathed a huge sigh of relief.

Resources

Asbury, Herbert. 1927. *The Gangs of New York: An Informal History of the Underworld.* Garden City, NY: Garden City Publishing.

Bryk, William. 2003. Fences of New York: Mother Mandelbaum, the Jewish mother of the criminal class. *New York Press*, July 15.

Fried, Albert. 1993. *The rise and fall of the Jewish gangster in America.* New York: Columbia University of Press.

Lardner, James, and Thomas Reppetto. 2000. *NYPD: A City and Its Police*. New York: Henry Holt.

Van Every, Edward. 1972. *Sins of New York: As "Exposed" by the Police Gazette*. New York: Benjamin Blom.

Cora Marie Bradley

Dollree Mapp (1937–)

Dollree (Dolly) Mapp was born in 1937 and lives in St. Albans, New York. She is probably most known for her case establishing stronger requirements for law enforcement to adhere to search and seizure standards.

In 1957 Dollree Mapp was under suspicion of harboring a fugitive wanted in a bombing case. When the police officers in Ohio arrived at the home of Mapp, she refused to allow them to enter her home to search for the fugitive believed to be her home. In due course, the police entered her home by force. In looking for this fugitive she was alleged to be harboring, the police found pornographic material in her home. Dollree Mapp was arrested and ultimately convicted under a state law in Ohio that made possession of pornographic materials illegal (Schmalleger, 2007, 246–247).

Dollree Mapp argued that the materials seized should have been suppressed as the police officers never produced a search warrant for such materials and therefore were the fruits of an illegal search and seizure. She appealed her conviction on the grounds of the basis of freedom of expression. The case of *Mapp v. Ohio* (1961) resulted in the exclusionary rule which led to a change in police training and attitudes. The Fourth Amendment to the U.S. Constitution essentially restrains the police. It tells the police that they must have probable cause to arrest, that they must have a warrant to search, and that the warrant must specify where and what is to be seized. As a result of the Mapp decision, the Fourth Amendment was made applicable to criminal prosecutions at the state level (Muraskin and Roberts, 2009).

Prior decisions of the U.S. Supreme Court, including the case of *Wolf v. Colorado* (1949) had held that the exclusionary rule did not apply to agents acting on behalf of both local and state law enforcement agencies. According to Mr. Justice Clark who delivered the opinion of the Supreme Court, "Appellant stands convicted of knowingly having had in her possession and under her control certain lewd and lascivious books, pictures, and photographs . . . As officially stated in the syllabus to its opinion, the Supreme Court of Ohio found that her conviction was valid though 'based primarily upon the introduction in evidence of lewd and lascivious books and pictures unlawfully seized during an unlawful search of defendant's (Mapp) home'" (170 Ohio St. 427, 428, 166 N.E. 2d 387, 388).

On May 23, 1957 three Cleveland police officers arrived at appellant's (Dollree Mapp) residence in that city pursuant to information that "a person [was] hiding out in the home, who was wanted for questioning in connection with a recent bombing, and that there was a large amount of policy paraphernalia being hidden in the home." Miss Mapp and her daughter by a former marriage lived on the top floor of the two-family dwelling. Upon their arrival at that house, the officers knocked on the door and demanded entrance but appellant, after telephoning her attorney, refused to admit them without a search warrant. They advised their headquarters of the situation and undertook a surveillance of the house. (367 U.S. 643, 644 1961)

The officers again sought entrance some three hours later when four more additional officers arrived on the scene. When Miss Mapp did not come to the door immediately, at least one of the several doors to the house was forcibly opened and the policemen gained admittance. Meanwhile Miss Mapp's attorney arrived, but the officers, having secured their own entry, and continuing in their defiance of the law, would permit him neither to see Miss Mapp nor to enter the house. It appears that Miss Mapp was halfway down the stairs from the upper floor to the front door when the officers, in this highhanded manner, broke into the hall. She demanded to see a search warrant. A paper, claimed to be a warrant, was held up by one of the officers. She grabbed the "warrant" and placed it in her bosom. A struggle ensued in which the officers removed the piece of paper and as a result of which they handcuffed appellant because she had been "belligerent." (367 U.S. 643, 644)

Running roughshod over appellant, a policeman "grabbed" her "twisted [her] hand" and she "yelled [and] pleaded with him" because "it was hurting." Appellant, in handcuffs was then forcibly taken upstairs to her bedroom where the officers searched a draw, a chest of drawers, a closet and some suitcases. They also looked into a photo album and through personal papers belonging to the appellant. The search spread to the rest of the second floor including the child's bedroom, the living room, the kitchen and a dinette. The basement of the building and a trunk found therein was also searched. The obscene materials for possession of which was ultimately convicted were discovered in the course of that widespread search. (367 U.S. 643, 645)

At the trial there was no search warrant produced nor was there any reason produced by the district attorney as to why there was no warrant. It was noted by the Supreme Court that "the rummaging of . . . drawers . . . constitutes the essence of the offence: but it is the invasion of . . . indefensible right of personal security, personal liberty and private property."

It was in the case of *Weeks v. Unites States* (232 U.S. 383 1914) that the court had stated that "the Fourth Amendment . . . put the courts of the United States and

Federal officials, in the exercise of their power and authority, under limitations and restraints [and] . . . forever secure[d] the people, their persons, houses, papers and effects against all unreasonable searches and seizures under the guise of law" (232 U.S. 383, 391–392).

Implicit in their discussion of privacy the court in reviewing their prior decisions stated that "we have no hesitation in saying that were a State affirmatively to sanction such police incursion into privacy it would run counter to the guaranty of the Fourteenth Amendment" (367 U.S. 643, 651).

Accordingly, the court pointed out in their reasoning of *Mapp v. Ohio* that "there are those who say, as did Justice . . . Cardozo, that under our constitutional exclusionary doctrine, '[t]he criminal is to go free because the constable has blundered.' '[t] here is another consideration, the imperative of judicial integrity. The criminal goes free, if he must, but it is the law that sets him free. Nothing can destroy a government more quickly than its failure to observe its own laws or worse, the disregard of the charter of its own existence' "(367 U.S. 643, 659).

The day that Dollree Mapp refused police authorities to enter her home without a proper warrant, impacted the way that the criminal justice system does business:

> [T]he right to privacy embodied in the Fourth Amendment is enforceable against the States and the right to be secure against rude invasions of privacy by state officers is, therefore, constitutional in origin, we can no longer permit that right to remain an empty promise. Because it is enforceable in the same manner to like effect as other basic rights secured by the Due Process Clause we can no longer permit it to be revocable at the whim of any police officer who, in the name of law enforcement itself, chooses to suspend its enjoyment. Our decision, founded on reason and truth, gives to the individual no less that that which honest law enforcement is entitled, and, to the courts, that judicial integrity so necessary in the true administration of justice. (367 U.S. 643, 660).

After the 1957 case in which she was arrested for possession of pornographic material, and the U.S. Supreme Court made a landmark decision regarding search and seizures based on the case, Mapp later made her way back into the news in 1973, when she was arrested for receiving stolen property and drugs. She had sold her home in Cleveland, Ohio, where she was first arrested in 1957, and she moved to New York a few years after her successful Supreme Court case. After the Supreme Court decision of *Mapp v. Ohio*, she subsequently tried her hand at some real estate and had a furniture business. It was in 1973 that "Dolly," as she is known, heard a knock on her door. This time she found a group of Queens County, New York, police detectives at her door. She heard the words, "[W]e have a search warrant, this time" (Krajicek, 2007).

She proceeded to let the officers in, as required by law. "The cops had had Mapp under surveillance for six weeks as a suspected fence for stolen property. In her home police found stolen television sets, furs, silver and antiques. They also found 50,000 $3.00 hits of heroin. She was convicted at trial and sentenced to 20 years in prison under New York's tough [then] new drug laws championed by Governor Nelson Rockefeller. Mapp served more than 9 years, from 1973–1981, before Governor Hugh Carey, who opposed the Rockefeller laws, commuted her sentence" (Krajicek, 2007). This was the second time that Mapp made headlines: first in *Mapp v. Ohio* and then when she was once again arrested in 1973.

To this day Mapp has yet to have forgotten a single detail regarding her arrest back in 1957. "They said they had a warrant, I said: What is your warrant for? When he wouldn't say, I stood firm. I guess I was a little belligerent at times. But I know right from wrong, and I knew I was right in this case. I think I might have died for my rights at that point" (Krajicek, 2007).

Mapp had indicated that the police at that time were probably surprised to find a woman as determined as she was. Women, but particularly black women, "tended to cow to cops in 1957," and she was not the one to give into the officers.

"I was always a determined woman, and I suppose I grew even more determined as a single mother trying to raise a child. I knew I being railroaded, and I said I'm not going to take this lying down. I was determined to take it as far as I needed to take it, and it turned out that meant going to the Supreme Court" (Krajicek, 2007).

Dollree Mapp has said that she had no regrets over her decision. "I stand firm on my convictions. Always have. I believe you don't run away from nothing. You have to be man enough or woman enough to stand and fight if it's something worth fighting for" (Krajicek, 2007). And for Dollree Mapp, *Mapp v. Ohio* was worth fighting for.

Resources

Krajicek, D. (2007). "Dollree Mapp, A Determined Woman." www.crimelibrary.com/about/authors.

Long, Carolyn N. (2006). *Mapp v. Ohio: Guarding Against Unreasonable Searches and Seizures.* Lawrence: University Press of Kansas.

Mapp v. Ohio. (1961). 347 U.S. 643.

Muraskin, R., and A. Roberts. (2009). *Visions for change: Crime and justice in the twenty-first century* (Fifth Edition). Upper Saddle River, NJ: Prentice Hall.

Schmalleger, F. (2007). *Criminal justice today: An introductory text to the 21st century.* Upper Saddle River, NJ: Pearson, Prentice Hall.

Weeks v. United States. (1914). 232 U.S. 383.

Roslyn Muraskin

Marie Antoinette (1755–1793)

Marie Antoinette's life is known for its extravagance and glamorous style, although in the end, she died as a shameful peasant and lowly prisoner. Her aristocratic lifestyle and actions, along with a scandal involving a diamond necklace, resulted in the common people's hatred and rebellion, which in turn led to the French Revolution. She was born Archduchess Marie Antoinette Josephe Jeanne into Europe's most powerful royal family on November 2, 1755. Her parents were very influential figures in Europe: her mother, Maria Theresa, was the empress of the Austrian Empire, and her father, Francis I, was the Duke of Lorraine with the title of Holy Roman emperor. Together they ruled most of Central Europe and had authority over many European kingdoms.

Marie Antoinette grew up in Vienna, the capital of Austria. During her childhood she was trained to be the wife of a noble man and learned to be a charming public figure. Maria Theresa was trying to create an alliance with France and arranged for her daughter to marry the son of King Louis XV, the crown prince of France. The two were wed in 1770, when Marie Antoinette was only 15 years old. Although the young prince was not interested in politics or economics, he was crowned King Louis XVI in 1774, and at the age of 19, Marie Antoinette became queen of France.

The queen was bored of her husband, and of the life in court, and began to make new friends in order to entertain herself. She surrounded herself with men and women of the aristocratic class that she herself belonged to, and rumors of orgies and her infidelities soon began to spread. Many people among the nobility were envious of the queen's lifestyle and insulted by the neglect of her duties to the court. There were many stories circulating among the nobility and common people accusing her of committing sexual acts with men and women of the court and sending funds to Austria. The paternity of her children was also called into question.

Jealousy and envy spread among some of the people surrounding the queen, which soon led to the Diamond Necklace Affair. Three separate people contributed to the unfolding of the affair: Madame Lamotte, a descendant of past Valois nobility who has been trying to gain a position in the court; Prince de Rohan, a high official of the Roman Catholic Church who was unhappy with his exclusion from Marie Antoinette's inner circle; and Boehmer, a jeweler who has been unable to convince the queen to buy an expensive diamond necklace.

Marie Antoinette. (Library of Congress)

Lamotte convinced the two men that she was a lesbian lover of the queen's and that Marie Antoinette indeed wanted the necklace. Rohan obtained the jewel from Boehmer and gave it to Lamotte to give to the queen in attempt to gain her admiration and friendship. When the king and queen found out about the affair, they were enraged, and Marie Antoinette demanded justice, which resulted in a trial in front of the Parliament of Paris. During the trial, details of the private lives of the royal family were revealed in front of the whole nation. In the end, Rohan was acquitted of the charges of insulting the queen, due to the common belief that her lifestyle welcomed such insults. Lamotte was branded on her breasts with a burning iron and imprisoned.

Following the trial, King Louis XVI and Marie Antoinette settled into family life, with the queen spending less time involved with the Paris night life and more time at home with her children. Although the royal family's life seemed to settle, the state of France did not, and in the late 1780s, France had a bad harvest and the poor suffered. The queen tried to aid the poor, but her small acts of kindness went unnoticed. During his time at the throne, Louis XV accumulated debts, and the current king, Louis XVI, was unable to repay them. The country's debt became a crisis, and the crisis worsened between 1778 and 1783 with France's costly aid to the American colonies, at which point the position of the monarchy became fragile.

The common people began to rebel against the monarchy and demanded that unless France created a constitution that gave more power to the people, the rebellion would continue. However, the queen insisted on preserving absolute monarchy and opposed giving more power to the common people. In retaliation, a mob attacked the Bastille prison, which they believed was a symbol of absolute monarchy. Louis XVI was not a forceful king, and although he went to Paris to restore calm, he failed to take prompt action. The mob succeeded in their attack, and no actions were taken against them.

Many leading members of the court fled the country, and although the queen wanted to leave with them, the king refused to leave Versailles. The queen's pride and arrogance made her vulnerable to verbal abuse by the people, and her importance was lowered significantly. On October 4, the people decided they had had enough and formed a mob that would go to Versailles and demand bread from the king. They went in with knives and threatened to harm the queen, but again, ignoring the requests of his wife, the king refused to flee the country or open fire on the mob.

Following the attack and request for bread, the mob insisted that the king and queen follow them to Paris. From that point on, the royal family was vulnerable to attack from the mob who kept a close watch on them. In 1797, after many nobles had already fled the country, and many more were killed, Marie Antoinette finally convinced her husband to leave Paris. The king and queen, with their children, disguised themselves as common travelers and began their escape. However, a citizen recognized them and alerted the people who confronted the royal couple on arrival in Varennes. No one rescued the king, queen, and their children, and they were forced to return to Paris. When they arrived, they were met with complete silence as opposed to the customary cheers of respect and admiration.

The royal family was detained and forced to listen to debates voting to end the monarchy. In September 1792, the Reign of Terror had begun with the murder of hundreds of aristocrats in the prisons. In September 1793, Marie Antoinette was transferred to solitary confinement in the Conciergerie Prison, which served as a holding cell, while she awaited execution. On October 14, the queen faced a trial in which she was attacked more for her acts as a person than a queen. She was found guilty. On October 16, 1793, she rode the garbage cart and was brought to the guillotine. Following her execution, her head was paraded for all to see, and her body was left on the grass before finding its final resting place in an unmarked grave. Even though she faced hatred and close scrutiny by the citizens of France, Marie Antoinette carried herself as a queen until the end, displaying courage in the face of adversity.

Resources

Fraser, Antonia. *Marie Antoinette: The Journey.* New York: Doubleday, 2001.

Lever, Evelyne. Catherine Temerson, translator. *Marie Antoinette: The Last Queen of France.* New York: Farrar Straus Giroux, 2000.

Adi Levy

Marquise de Montespan. *See* Montespan, Marquise de

Regina McKnight (1977–)

Regina McKnight was brought into the national spotlight in the fall of 2003, as the first woman in America to be tried and convicted for using crack cocaine during pregnancy and causing the death of her baby, stillborn at delivery. Many believed it was an act indeterminable in regard to the fetus's ultimate fate as a stillborn, and the trial was heavily saturated with controversy involving moral, racial, and political overtones and factors involved. Advocates on both sides were further divided by the potential ramifications of the 12-year sentence and ruling by the presiding judge and jury of this unique legal battle. The trial brought to light the extent to which the law may regulate the actions of pregnant women in terms of the behavior they engage in weighed against the safety and well-being of their unborn children.

Regina McKnight, convicted in 2001 of homicide by child abuse after her still-born child tested positive for cocaine. On May 12, 2008, the South Carolina Supreme Court issued a ruling overturning McKnight's conviction because she didn't receive adequate counsel. (AP/ Wide World Photos)

Regina McKnight is an African American who was born in 1977 in Horry County, South Carolina, and who remained in the region until the time of her arrest. Throughout the course of her life, she maintained a strong connection and relationship with her mother, on whom she relied for both financial as well as emotional support. This relationship was shattered abruptly in 1998 when McKnight's mother was suddenly killed by a hit-and-run driver, an event that has largely been speculated as a turning point in her life. It may have led to an escalation in her involvement in drug use, arguably as a form of self medication.

Despite this tumultuous and bleak background, McKnight found herself pregnant following the year of her mother's demise, and though expecting a normal and routine birth, she instead delivered a stillborn. During the autopsy of the fetus, trace amounts of substances indicating cocaine use were found. A few months later, she was arrested for homicide, a flexing of preexisting law unknown beforehand but which would evolve over time to include charges in later cases involving child abuse and distribution of a controlled substance to a minor. From the beginning, the legal attempts to regulate motherhood were fraught with instability, as was well illustrated when Regina McKnight's first hearing ended in a mistrial, due largely to the inexperience of the legal system in terms of this recently discovered judicial frontier. A subsequent second trial, however, resulted in a guilty verdict that carried a suspended sentence of a required 12 years in prison.

Debate on both sides intensified over the course of the trial on several key issues, many of which were admittedly plagued by arbitrary and ambiguous factors and circumstances. The prosecution's charge of homicide, for example, denotes the acceptance of the belief that crack cocaine use was the primary reason for the demise of the fetus, when large amounts of medical research have shown evidence to the contrary. The stigma of crack cocaine use made popular in the late 1980s and early 1990s continues to permeate society despite the now well-accepted acknowledgement and understanding of the media's previous exaggeration and distortion of the drug's effects after its initial introduction. Therefore, it's difficult to determine whether the stillborn would have occurred regardless of drug use, making grounds for homicide charges difficult to justify. What's more is that even the prosecution admitted that Regina McKnight most likely did not intend to harm her unborn child, a revelation that would normally exonerate an individual from receiving full-fledged homicide charges and instead usually result in less serious charges along the lines of manslaughter or negligent homicide. Furthermore the success of the conviction raised legal questions as to the breadth to which such actions may lead to judicial hearings. The chief prosecutor for Horry County, South Carolina, expressed these views when he commented that the fact that the cocaine was an illegal substance was not a deciding factor in the case, and he further defined the court's intent by stating that charges would be filed even if a legal substance was used and the mother was determined to be medically responsible for the child's death. This indicated the court's willingness to use such tactics for mothers who put themselves in situations of potential danger for the fetus, theoretically covering everything from frequenting smoky barrooms to unhealthy dieting patterns, a broad spectrum from which to impose regulations and restrictions on indeed. This proposal of intense legal scrutiny on the activities of pregnant women and the plight of McKnight following her ordeal led to public outcry and rallying support from organizations with a vested interest in such matters. Defendants of McKnight counter arguments of these laws being enforced for the well-being of the fetus with evidence to indicate that such legal action may ultimately prove detrimental to the unborn child, as it would act as a deterrent for addicts to seek proper prenatal care or disclose information about drug use to their doctors.

Organizations such as the American Public Health Association, the National Stillbirth Society, and the South Carolina Medical Association collaborated together in order to voice support for Regina McKnight, an effort that eventually led to a review of the case by the Supreme Court. An amicus curiae brief was submitted on behalf of no less than 27 such organizations in support of McKnight, outlining the medical community's oppositional stance to the portrait painted by the prosecution in the original case. In 2002, McKnight's defense attorneys attempted to challenge the constitutionality of a homicide charge given for a stillbirth, yet they were unsuccessful, though the margin by which the decision was reached was noticeably slim.

Regina McKnight's struggle through the legal system was arguably the end result of several collaborating factors that came to a head during her trial. At the time, South Carolina ranked last in the United States in terms of state spending on alcohol and drug treatment facilities, programs, and centers. It was also the only state to have extended its laws regarding child endangerment to include the unborn, meaning that had McKnight been in a hospital in any other state when she delivered her stillborn, legal action would not be sought despite the detection of cocaine in the fetus. Race was also a suspected motivation for moving through with the prosecution, as laws heavily targeting the users of cocaine in crack form have been notoriously harsher than those of the substance in powdered form, and there has been a firm racial dichotomy between users of these separate forms despite the fact that it is essentially the same narcotic. The fact that this case took place in South Carolina, a state with a history heavily impregnated with racial tensions, indirectly supports indicators toward this suspicion. McKnight's stillborn was also classified by law as a "viable fetus" giving ammunition to both the pro life and pro choice movements, causing political waves to ripple across the surface of this landscape while reaching the deepest depths of potential debate. McKnight also validly expressed discontent in terms of her representing counsel who, among other things, failed to attempt to reduce the charges to involuntary manslaughter, failed to undermine the interpretation of preexisting law to form the case against McKnight by the prosecution, and failed to introduce the autopsy report of the fetus into evidence. Factors such as these surmounted into a damaging scenario for the defense and contributed greatly towards the success of the prosecution.

The negligence and ineptness of Regina McKnight's counsel was ironically the primary factor for her case to be submitted for review by the Supreme Court again in 2008, resulting in a reverse of her conviction. The victory was small due to the fact that her projected release date was but a mere two years away; yet, it was important as an illustration of the growing concern of the government's encroachment into the private lives of citizens. Opinions on the actions the courts should be allowed to mandate vary across the diverse population of our nation, and an acceptable solution to approaching such issues will be delicately carved only as time and awareness progress. In this sense, McKnight's case stands as a cornerstone on which the foundation for judicial balance is currently being laid, and the erroneous avenues of action that have been highlighted stand as a beacon for others to both observe and learn from in future legal proceedings.

Resources

Newman, Tony. Supreme Court Will Not Review Murder Conviction of Woman Who Suffered a Stillbirth. *Drug Policy News.* October 6, 2003. http://www.drugpolicy.org/news/pressroom/pressrelease/pr100603.cfm

Petition Filed Today Seeking U.S. Supreme Court Review of Unprecedented South Carolina Decision Treating a Woman Who Suffered a Stillbirth as a Murderer. *National Advocates for Pregnant Women.* May 27, 2003. http://advocatesforpregnantwomen.org/issues/prmcknight.htm

Regina Denise McKnight, Petitioner v. State of South Carolina. 2008. Supreme Court of South Carolina. 378 S.C.

Talvi, Silja. Criminalizing Motherhood. *Nation*. December 3, 2003. http://www.thenation.com/doc/20031215/talvi

Jason Thompson

Sarah Metyard (?–1762) and Sarah Morgan Metyard (?–1762)

Sarah Metyard and daughter Sarah Morgan Metyard were milliners who tortured their apprentices, killing two, in London, England, sometime around 1758. This case is of interest as it reflects a particularly gruesome case, receiving much publicity in media of the time. The British government required that pauper children be protected by making available apprentice positions within various trades. This case also highlights the conditions and dangers facing working pauper children in England before various child labor laws were enacted during the 19th century.

Sarah Metyard, a widower, worked in London taking in five "apprentices" from various parish workhouses to learn the milliner trade. Apprentices were young children, orphaned or sold into the labor pool by family members. Children were often preferred as a source of labor as they did not have to be paid as much as adults—if at all—and their small hands were good at the fine work of making hats, cleaning machinery, and so on.

One of the Metyard apprentices, Ann (Nanny) Nailer, age 13, was systematically beaten and starved until she died sometime after September 29 (Michaelmas), 1758. Before this date, she was fed little and beaten often as she was more sickly than the others and unable to do as much work. Witnesses recounted how Ann Nailer tried to escape just before her death. She was able to leave the Metyard home but was stopped by the milkman at the request of the Metyards just outside the door. Although Ann pleaded with the milkman to let her go as she would be starved to death and was "ill treated," the milkman did not believe the story and returned her to the Metyards.

Witness to the milkman incident, milliner apprentice Philadelphia Dowley testified that the daughter grabbed Ann by the neck, dragged her upstairs, and threw her on a bed where the mother held her head while the daughter beat her with a broken broomstick. Ann Nailer was then placed in the garret, denied food for three days, tied to a door around the waist, and her hands were bound behind her so that she could neither sit nor lie down. She was untied at nights by the daughter so she could rest. The other apprentices were forced to work in a nearby room so that they would experience the consequences of misbehavior vicariously. The day before she died, Dowley stated she was "senseless."

When Ann had been seen hanging from the door, doubled over, on October 4, 1758, by the other apprentices they called for the Metyards. The women released the girl from her bindings and laid her across mother Metyard's lap. Although Ann appeared dead, mother Metyard requested Sarah (Sally) Hinchman go for drops downstairs. Further, the young apprentices were dismissed to the floor below while Ann was administered to. Dowley did not recall the drops being used. Two days later, during a meal, Hinchman was told to go upstairs and fetch Ann, stating that if she promised to behave she could rejoin the group. Knowing Ann was dead, mother and daughter had conspired and left the garret door open and the front door slightly ajar.

When Hinchman said she was not there, the mother stated that she must have run away. Ann's sister would not accept that explanation and she believed that Ann had been killed for she knew that her sister would not leave without her belongings. Eventually Ann's sister was also killed by the Metyards, although sources do not elaborate on how.

Ann's body was kept in a box in the garret for two months until the odor began to cause concern. Although they thought of burning the entire body in the fireplace, concerns about the smell of burning flesh quashed the idea. The body was then hacked into small pieces and placed in a burlap sack and thrown into a gully near Chick Lane by the mother. The hand of Ann, which had a digit removed because of a whitloe (a form of abscess), was retained and burned in the fireplace most probably to hinder positive identification. The body was found shortly after by a night watchman who took it to the coroner. Decomposition and inability to identify the child lead to the assumption by the coroner and police that the body was one of those used for medical purposes and discarded into the gully. No investigation was launched.

The deeds of both came to light four years later, in 1762, when daughter Sarah eventually moved out of the house to take a housekeeping position with a former lodger, Richard Rooker. The mother then took to harassing her daughter and Rooker on a daily basis. This continued even after Rooker took Sarah out to the country as his mistress. Eventually Rooker threatened the elder Metyard with not seeing her daughter. At this point the elder Metyard provoked her and began to mention some odd things occurring at the house on Cock Lane. Younger Sarah responded: "Mother you are the Chick Lane Ghost; remember the gully hole." Later, Rooker asked for clarification on this statement, and the younger Metyard told her story. Rooker encouraged the girl to confess her story, convinced that the judge would show mercy given the daughter's ill treatment by the mother.

At trial, both the mother and the daughter claimed that the other was the instigator of the majority of the violence; the daughter claimed that she was afraid of her mother because of the beatings and "ill treatment" by her. The mother claimed that her daughter committed the majority of the violence of her own accord. In the end, both were found guilty and sentenced to death. The younger Metyard "pleaded her belly," but the women in the courtroom who were called to verify this statement were not convinced she was with child. Mother and daughter were sentenced to hang on the following Monday, July 19, 1762.

Resource

Old Bailey Proceedings Online. (1762, April). Sarah Metyard, Sarah Morgan Metyard, killing: Murder, 14th July, 1762. *Proceedings of the Old Bailey, Ref: t17620714–30.* Retrieved July 16, 2007, from www.oldbaileyonline.org.

Hannah Scott

Montespan, Marquise de (1640–1707)

Françoise Athénaïs (Françoise Athénaïs de Rochechouart de Mortemart, or Marquise de Montespan) was one of the favorite mistresses of Louis XIV, King of France, who became personally involved in the scandal of "the Affair of the Poisons," which brought many poisoning cases to justice. Born on October 5, 1640, in the Château de Lussac, she belonged to one of the oldest and most illustrious families in France. Her father was the Marquis de Lussac, who held several prestigious appointments at the royal court of Louis XIII, and her mother was a lady-in-waiting to the Queen Anne of Austria. Françoise Athénaïs studied at the Covent of Sainte Marie de Saintes and, in 1661, joined the royal court as a maid of honor to the king's sister-in-law, Princess Henrietta Anne of England. Blessed with sovereign beauty and high aspirations, she soon set her eyes on Louis XIV, as another courtesan commented: "She had designs on the King's hearth, and started laying her plans from the day she came to court" (Mossiker 1969, 45).

However, in 1663, Françoise Athénaïs agreed to marry Louis Henri de Pardaillan de Gondrin, Marquis de Montespan, who was the younger brother of her previous fiancée who had tragically died in a duel the year before. The newlywed couple were soon burdened by the Marquis's debts, and the marriage eventually fell apart after the birth of their second child. Discouraged by the lack of ambition and the churlishness of her husband, Françoise Athénaïs de Montespan longed to return to the royal house and attain her previous goals. When in 1665, she was finally summoned to court again as the maid of honor to the queen, Marie Thérèse, she left her family behind without much regret. Once she arrived at court, her strong ambition was soon appeased. Indeed, within only one year, Françoise Athénaïs de Montespan managed to gain Louis XIV's affections, availing herself of the concurrent pregnancies of both the queen and his favorite paramour, Louise de La Vallière. During her long liaison with the king, she bore him eight children who were legitimized and hence integrated into the royal lineage. Acting as an enlightened patroness of the arts and surrounding herself with her protégés, among them Racine, Moliére, and

La Fontaine, Françoise Athénaïs de Montespan gained so much influence and respect at the royal house that she was often referred to as "the King's second wife," or even "the real Queen of France."

In 1669, Louise de La Vallière, who was still, at least nominally, the "favorite" mistress of the king, fell inexplicably ill. She was believed to have been mysteriously poisoned. Two sorcerers, who were on trial at that time before the court of Chatelet, indicated that Françoise Athénaïs de Montespan was responsible for the crime. The case was never made public, and any suspicion of the Marquise de Montespan was rapidly dismissed and forgotten. However, after the successful prosecution of the Marquise de Brinvilliers in 1676 who was held accountable for having ruthlessly poisoned her father and her two brothers, the practice of poisoning was finally acknowledged to be a deadly tool widely employed by the high-ranking society, and, thus, a clear threat to the security of the royal family. Indeed, during her trial, the Marquise de Brinvilliers revealed "[h]alf of the people I know—people of quality— are involved in this same kind of thing . . . and I could drag them all down along with me, should I decide to talk" (Mossiker 1969, 145).

After the decapitation of the Marquise de Brinvilliers, many arrests for the same crime followed one after the other, leading to an infamous scandal better known as "the Affair of the Poisons." A special tribunal, called the Chambre Ardente, was deliberately established to adjudicate those cases in 1679. Over the course of three years, the court issued 319 writs of arrest, sentenced 104 people out of the 194 arrested, and condemned 36 of them to death. Among those doomed to capital punishment was the sorceress Catherine Deshayes, Madame Montvoisin, better known as La Voisin. During her trial, she revealed that many of her clients belonged to the upper echelons of the French nobility. Upon her death, other witches who were imprisoned at Vincennes, and particularly, her daughter, Marie Montvoisin, claimed that Françoise Athénaïs de Montespan had regularly visited La Voisin to purchase her "magic powders." Marie Montvoisin explicitly accused the Marquise de Montespan of having used such potions to retain the King's love, recalling that: "Every time . . . she feared the good graces of the King were diminishing, she advised my mother of it so she could bring a remedy. My mother therefore said Masses over these powders destined for the King. They were powders of love" (Hilton 2002, 199).

Marie Montvoisin further accused Françoise Athénaïs de Montespan of having participated in the black Masses held in 1667–1668 intended to invoke Satan's help to obtain the king's favor and affection. She reported that three to four newborn infants had been sacrificed on behalf of the Marquise de Montespan's demands. The priest who had performed the Masses, who was also imprisoned, confirmed such accusations, recounting that, during the black ceremonies, the Marquise de Montespan recited the following: "I ask for the friendship of the King . . . [and] that the Queen should be sterile and that the King should leave her table and her bed for me; that I should obtain of him all that I ask for myself . . . ; that the King should leave La Vallière and look at her no more, and that, the Queen being repudiated, I can marry the King" (Hilton 2002, 201).

Further allegations that the Marquise de Montespan had conspired to poison Louis XIV were also made. However, the Chambre Ardente never conclusively ruled on the direct involvement of Françoise Athénaïs de Montespan in the Affair of the Poisons. In 1691, no longer a favorite of the King, she retired to the convent of the Filles de Saint Joseph in Paris, where she lived out her final years in solitude and pain. The Marquise de Montespan died in 1707 taking the details of the unsolved mysteries with her.

See also Brinvilliers, Marquise de; La Voisin, Catherine

Resources

Hilton, Lisa. 2002. *Athénais: The Real Queen of France.* London: Little, Brown.

Mossiker, Frances. 1969. *The Affair of the Poisons: Louis XIV, Madame de Montespan, and One of the History's Great Unsolved Mysteries.* New York: Alfred A. Knopf.

Somerset, Anne. 2003. *The Affair of the Poisons: Murder, Infanticide and Satanism at the Court of Louis XIV.* London: Weidenfeld & Nicolson.

Benedetta Faedi Duramy

N

Frances Newton (1965–2005)

Frances Elaine Newton was the 11th woman to be executed in the United States since the reinstatement of the death penalty in 1976. She was lethally injected by the state of Texas on September 14, 2005, for the murder conviction of her husband and two minor children. Newton was the first black woman to be executed in Texas since 1853 and the third woman put to death in Texas since 1976. She is the second black woman to be put to death in the United States since 1976, following Wanda Jean Allen's execution in Oklahoma in 2001.

Newton was born to Iva Jewel Nelms and Bee Henry Nelms, Jr., in 1965. Newton's only recorded previous activity in the criminal justice system included a three-year probation sentence she received in December 1985 for a forgery conviction. She began dating her future husband, Adrian Newton, when they were teenagers, and they had been together for seven years at the time of the murders. Leading up to the deaths, Newton and her husband had been experiencing difficulties with their relationship, and both were engaged in intimate relationships outside the marriage.

On April 7, 1987, Newton's estranged husband (age 23), her son Alton (age 7), and her daughter Farrah (age 20 months) were murdered execution style in their home. Each victim was shot once (Adrian in the head and the two children in the chest), and there was no forced entry into or destruction of the apartment. From the beginning of the investigation until her execution, Newton continually professed her innocence of committing the murders. She theorized that a drug dealer committed the murders. According to police records, Newton's husband used and sold drugs, and Newton believed the killings occurred because of a debt her husband had to another drug dealer.

Newton asserts that the last time she saw her family alive was earlier on the day of their deaths before she left the home to run errands. Newton stated that she found a gun in the apartment earlier in the day and took it with her when she left the home to run errands because she feared the trouble it would cause. After picking up a cousin and on her way to return to the apartment, Newton realized she still had the gun in her car. She took the gun, which she had stored in a bag, into the abandoned house next to her cousin's residence that belonged to Newton's parents. Upon returning to her husband's apartment, Newton and her cousin discovered the bodies. Police officers later retrieved the firearm based on statements provided by Newton and her cousin. The firearm was examined and determined to be the murder weapon. Newton was arrested based on the motive that she killed her family in order to receive life insurance benefits. Newton took out three $50,000 policies on herself, her husband, and her daughter less than a month before the murders. She filed claims on these insurance policies three weeks after the deaths.

Frances Newton, 1998. (AP/Wide World Photos)

Though the victims were found to have been shot at a close range, no blood or tissue was found on Newton and no gunpowder residue was found on her hands or shirt sleeves. The only evidence found on Newton's person was nitrites, which an expert for the prosecution asserted is consistent with gunpowder residue. However, this same expert could not rule out the possibility that the nitrites could have come from gardening fertilizer. Newton's daughter had contact with fertilizer earlier the day of the murders.

During her capital punishment trial, Newton was represented by a court-appointed attorney who did not conduct any interviews or investigation in preparation for the hearing. The attorney, Ronald Mock, has since received several misconduct charges brought against him by the Texas State Bar in other cases and most recently received a suspension of two years lasting through the end of 2007. Although the trial judge allowed Newton to retain a new attorney based on Mock's established incompetence, the judge did not grant a continuance to allow new counsel time to prepare for the defense. This left Newton with the obligation to maintain Mock as her defense attorney. Newton was ultimately convicted and sentenced to death by a jury in October 1988.

Newton's first date of execution was scheduled for December 1, 2004. However, only two hours before the procedure, Texas Governor Rick Perry granted her 120 days to allow for additional testing of the evidence in the case. In spite of this, further testing could not be conducted on the skirt Newton was wearing the evening of the murders because the earlier tests ruined the nitrites on the garment and it was stored in the same container as the clothing the victims wore the night they were killed.

There was never any investigation into a drug-related connection with the murders. In addition, Newton's supporters proclaim there was a mishandling of evidence in the case by the crime analysis laboratory at the Houston Police Department. Questions were raised by Professor David Dow and his Texas Innocence Network at the University of Houston Law Center, which took over as Newton's defense team in the final years of her case. Dow and his students raised the possibility of the existence of another firearm of the same caliber and brand according to information gathered by the police during the initial investigation. Lastly, based on several witness accounts, the timeframe built for the homicides would have left Newton with no more than 20 minutes to shoot her family, clean her clothes and herself, and leave the home.

In addition to Newton's recent legal team, the parents of Newton's husband requested of Texas authorities that Newton not be executed, since they had already lost three members of their family years before. Nevertheless, none of the numerous appeals for reprieve were able to spare Newton from the death penalty. She was given a second execution date of September 14, 2005. Newton did not make a final statement immediately prior to her death warrant being carried out. She was 40 years old when she was executed.

Resources

Carson, David. "Frances Newton." Texas Execution Information Center. http://www.txex ecutions.org/reports/349.asp.

"Media Advisory: Frances Newton Scheduled For Execution." Attorney General of Texas Greg Abbot. https://www.oag.state.tx.us/oagNews/release.php?id=697.

Smith, Jordan. 2005."Without Evidence: Executing Frances Newton." *Austin Chronicle.* Sept. 9. http://www.austinchronicle.com/gyrobase/Issue/story?oid=oid%3A288994.

Hillary Potter

Sarah Osborn (ca. 1640–1692)

Sarah Osborn (aka Osborne, Osburn) was one of first three women accused of witchcraft in Salem, Massachusetts, in late February 1692. The others were Sarah Good and Tituba, a Barbadian slave in the house of the Reverend Samuel Parris, whose daughter and niece were among the young women whose accusations led to the Salem Witch Trials, resulting in the execution of 20 people. As many as 13 died in prison, including Osborn. Sarah Osborn died in chains on May 10, 1692, after having been incarcerated for over two months awaiting trial.

Born Sarah Warren in Watertown, Massachusetts, she married Robert Prince on April 5, 1662, and gave birth to two sons. Prince owned a prosperous farm. When he died in 1674, he left his land in trust to Sarah with the stipulation that she give it to their sons when they reached legal age. Prince's executors were his relatives John and Thomas Putnam, members of a politically and economically influential family in Salem. It was customary for widows to receive one-third of their husband's property, with the remaining two-thirds going to the children.

Soon after Prince's death, Sarah hired Alexander Osborn, an indentured servant from Ireland, to run the farm. Evidence indicates that their economic relationship soon turned romantic. They cohabitated for some time before finally marrying, shocking the Puritan sensibilities of the community. After their marriage, they further shocked the community by filing suit to gain full control of the land that Robert Prince had intended for his sons, in effect denying them their inheritance. The suit would drag on for nearly 25 years.

Scholars contend that these two reasons—cohabitation out of wedlock and challenging the inheritance of her sons—led to her accusation as a witch. Osborn showed disregard of Puritan society's views of sexual behavior by cohabitating, exhibiting what Cotton Mather called the type of "lewd and naughty kind of life" (1862: 33) lived by witches. Perhaps more damning was the challenge to Prince's will. Both of these were particularly taboo for women of the time.

Prince and the Putnams were Salem natives, while the Osborns—Sarah, from another town and Alexander, from another country—were deemed outsiders. Women who "stood in the way of the orderly transmission of property from one generation to another" (Karlsen, 1987: 116), especially from a man to his sons, tended to be considered the disorderly and aberrant women who were accused of witchcraft.

In addition, Osborn had a reputation for being argumentative and challenging authority. During her legal examination, and despite her frail health, she argued with Judge Hathorne. Such defiance was a characteristic shared by many of the women accused of witchcraft. Scholars suggest that her notorious reputation, likely to be a subject of village gossip, was another reason for her accusation. Osborn had not attended church for over a year, further indication to many in Salem that she disregarded both the authority of man *and* God. The Puritan mind was likely to conclude that if she were not worshipping God, she must be worshipping the Devil. The fact that she was over 50 and in poor physical and emotional health was given little consideration.

Osborn's alleged crime consisted of physically tormenting her accusers and tempting them to become witches. It has been suggested that the accusers—the majority of whom were young, orphaned, and single servants with bleak futures— were not only accusing the "witches" of activities that they themselves were guilty of, but were also giving voice to what the community thought and said about the accused. The accusations gave male community leaders their chance to punish women who challenged their authority, thereby establishing what they believed to be the God-given order and hierarchy of the community. The accused served as examples to other disorderly women. Osborn's husband, although guilty of the same activities as she, was never accused of wrongdoing.

Like many accused of witchcraft, Osborn denied both practicing witchcraft and tormenting her accusers. She was bewildered to find herself, a woman of advanced years with a solid social standing, having to answer to such a crime. It is perhaps indicative of her confused state of mind during this examination that she claimed to have heard a voice telling her not to attend worship. She also suggested that the Devil might have taken her shape in order to torment her accusers. According to scholars, Osborn had been sick for most of the winter and was probably exhausted. She may have just been anxious to get the examination over with. Hoffer also comments on the cruelty shown to Osborn and the other witches. The remand into custody of the aged and sickly Osborn, and her confinement in chains, was essentially a death sentence. Osborn never went to trial. The Court of Oyer and Terminer (i.e., to hear and determine), at which the fate of the accused would be decided, did not begin until June 2, 1692, nearly a month after her death.

The crime of witchcraft had a telling impact on the Puritans, whose power had been on the wane for some time. The hysteria wrought by the witchcraft trials, including the accusations of prominent community members, was the final blow. Despite a brief revival during the "Great Awakening" (ca. 1730–1760), Puritan influence would never recover. The trials also predicted how women, especially those who challenged the status quo, would be treated in U.S. society. They would discover that the male establishment was unwilling to cede power to them, witnessed by the fact that it would be nearly 230 years after the witch trials that women would be given the vote, and over 280 years before legislation would be passed to protect women from domestic violence.

Resources

Boyer, P., & S. Nissenbaum. 1974. *Salem Possessed: The Social Origins of Witchcraft.* Cambridge, MA: Harvard University Press.

Breslaw, E. G. 1997. Tituba's Confession: The Multicultural Dimensions of the 1692 Salem Witch-Hunt. *Ethnohistory* 44(3): 535–556.

Burr, G. L. 1914. *Narratives of the Witchcraft Cases: 1648–1706.* New York: Charles Scribner's Sons.

Hoffer, P. C. 1996. *The Devil's Disciples: Makers of the Salem Witchcraft Trials.* Baltimore: Johns Hopkins University Press.

Karlsen, C. F. 1987. *The Devil in the Shape of a Woman: Witchcraft in Colonial New England.* New York: W. W. Norton & Company.

Mather, C. 1862. *Wonders of the Invisible World: Being an account of the tryals of several witches lately executed in New England. To which is added, A farther account of the tryals of the New-England witches. By Increase Mather.* London: J. R. Smith.

Upham, C. W. 2000. *Salem Witchcraft: With an Account of Salem Village and a History of Opinions on Witchcraft and Kindred Subjects.* Mineola, NY: Dover Publications.

James Geistman

P

Dylcia Pagan (1946–)

Dylcia Pagan was arrested on April 4, 1980, for conspiring against the U.S. government. She had been a former member of the Armed Forces of National Liberation of Puerto Rico (FALN), which was a secret and armed organization operating in the United States. Pagan was 1 of 11 Puerto Ricans imprisoned for seditious conspiracy. Pagan was born on October 15, 1946, in "El Barrio" in New York City to Puerto Rican migrant parents. She majored in cinematography and sociology at Brooklyn College, where she also founded the Puerto Rican Student Union. After graduation, she taught social studies in New York City schools and worked for ABC, NEC, and CBS, as well as for the newspaper *El Tiempo.*

Dylcia Pagan, center, speaking to the media after being released from Federal Corrections Institution in Dublin, California, 1999. Four Puerto Rican Nationalist prisoners were released in accordance with a clemency offer by President Clinton. (AP/Wide World Photos)

The objective of the FALN, which was responsible for more than 100 bombings in the United States between 1974 and 1983, was to gain the independence for Puerto Rico and make it into an independent island nation. Former FBI official Oliver Revell stated, "Their purpose was to make it so difficult for the United States to retain sovereignty of Puerto Rico that we would essentially reject and release Puerto Rico" (Black & Feverick, 1999). Pagan was included in a group of 11 FALN members arrested but never convicted of any actual bombings. Pagan and her comrades were sentenced to terms from 35 to 90 years in prison. In an interview with Nuno Andrade, Pagan attributed the length of their prison sentences to the group's refusal to recognize the U.S. judicial system's legitimacy. "We were basically put inside [prison] for such long sentences because of our [political] position," she said. "Eleven Puerto Ricans [stood] before the Federal courts and [said], 'We do not recognize the jurisdiction of the United States courts, we refuse to participate in this trial.' . . . The government, [in order] to [save] face, had to give us these long sentences" (Andrade, 2001).

Pagan was sentenced to 55 years in prison on charges of seditious conspiracy but spent only 20 years in federal prison. Throughout her incarceration Dylcia Pagan remained active in the work of the FALN and maintained her position as "an anti-colonial prisoner of war resisting the illegal U.S. occupation of her homeland." While in prison she helped direct a documentary about the Puerto Rican women prisoners of war (Prison Activist Resource Center, 1999). President Clinton granted Pagan clemency in September 1999. The conditions of her clemency included refraining from the use or advocacy of violence for any purpose and obeying all the statutory conditions of her parole (Black & Feverick, 1999). Dylcia Pagan now lives in Puerto Rico, and the terms of her parole allow her to travel outside of Puerto Rico only twice a year.

Resources

Andrade, N. 2001. www.oneism.com/articles/pagan.html.

Black, C., & Feverick, D. 1999. *Puerto Rican FALN prisoners face clemency decision.* www.CNN.com/US/9909/06/puerto.rico.faln/.

Prison Activist Resource Center. 1999. www.prisonactivist.org/pps+pows/dylcia-pagan. html.

Tara N. Richards

Bonnie Parker (1910–1934)

A handful of influential women over the last one hundred plus years have transformed the way in which women in general are perceived in contemporary America. Historically, women were seen as delicate, vulnerable, and innocent—creatures in need of a man's guidance and help. One of the influential women who helped change this stereotype was Bonnie Parker. She was one of the first female criminals glorified by American popular culture, and while not a typical role model, she influenced how women became to be seen today. Her criminal career helped destroy the delicate, venerable, and passive images that society had assigned to women. After Parker's life, women could hardly be considered weak and helpless. One lesson society learned is that women are as capable of committing terrible and violent crimes as are men.

Bonnie Elizabeth Parker was born on October 1, 1910, in Rowena, Texas. She was one of three children. Her family was poor and struggled to make ends meet. Her father was a bricklayer and died when she was only four years old. Soon after her father's death, her mother moved all the children to Dallas, Texas.

No extensive detail is known about her early life with her family or what she was like as a teenager. Some facts are clear—during her schooling, Parker did well

Depression-era outlaws Clyde Barrow and Bonnie Parker strike a romantic pose. After one of the most sensational manhunts in U.S. history, Barrow and Parker were shot to death by a posse of police officers in an ambush in Bienville Parish, Louisiana, on May 23, 1934. (Library of Congress)

in creative writing classes, where she excelled in writing poetry. She was also known to give introductory speeches for the nearby politicians during election rallies. In her teenage years, she made money by waitressing at local restaurants. She has been described as being an intelligent, personable person who was also social and outgoing. Parker was also known as a strong independent woman despite her petite size of 4 feet 11 inches, 90 pounds. These facts seem like incongruities considering the very aggressive behavior she participated in during her criminal years.

When Parker was 15 years old, she married a man named Roy Thornton in September 1926. Thornton had a long criminal history and spent his life in and out of jail. The two remained together for a little over two years, and in January 1929, they separated but never divorced. At the time of Parker's death, she was still legally married to Thornton.

In 1930 Bonnie meet her future partner in crime, Clyde Barrow. Barrow, like Thornton, had an extensive criminal background. Shortly after their meeting, Barrow was sentenced to prison for a stolen car. Parker stayed loyal to Barrow during his 20-month stay in prison. In 1932, Barrow was released from prison, and the two began a 21-month crime spree.

Their crime spree occurred during the height of the Great Depression, a significant era for the poor in America. The couple's popular image was as the flight of an in-love, romantic but criminal couple. They became Robin Hood–like in the public's eyes. This was despite the fact that their crimes ranged from robbing grocery stores, dry cleaners, gas stations, restaurants, stores, and banks; to kidnappings, casual killings, and assaults. From 1932 to 1934, they traveled the countryside in numerous stolen Fords passing through Texas, New Mexico, Iowa, Kansas, Missouri, Oklahoma, Arkansas, and Louisiana.

They were not successful by at least one measure—during so many robberies, the most money they ever stole at one place was $1,500. Throughout the crime spree, they evaded the police by stealing different automobiles and driving across multiple jurisdictions in 10 states. In December 1932, police discovered two stolen cars in two different states that were linked to them because of a prescription bottle left in the car with Barrows aunt's name on it. This link to the cars resulted in the FBI issuing a warrant for their arrest for interstate transportation of a stolen automobile.

Parker and Barrow were at that point officially on the run from the police and the FBI. During the next year and a half, they engaged in various shoot-outs with the police and escaped time and time again. One instance was during November 1933 in Dallas, Texas, where the police tried to capture them. In January 1934, they helped five prisoners escape a jail, and two prison guards were killed during the breakout that took place in Waldo, Texas. In April 1934, they murdered two police officers in Grapevine, Texas. Soon after, they killed a police constable and kidnapped a police chief in Miami, Oklahoma.

There is no detail of exactly how much involvement Parker had in the murders and robberies. No definitive proof was found that she shot anyone. People close to Parker said that she had never shot a gun in any of the crimes or even during the shoot-outs with the police. Though Parker was assumed by the authorities to have some involvement in the crimes of murder, kidnapping, and robbery, a warrant for far less crimes was issued on May 20, 1933, in Dallas, Texas. This indictment charged her with only interstate transportation of an automobile that was stolen in Illinois and driven across state lines.

During their violent spree, the two managed to kill 12 people, injure dozens more, and hold an estimated 5 people captive. The two created a following of people who were purchasing tabloids to get the latest details on the duo's adventures. Their reputation and relationship was unlike anything that had ever happened before, and to this day there have been few who captured the public's imagination to their degree of notoriety.

Parker and Barrow were both from poor backgrounds. Parker was working a menial job, and Barrows was using crime as a livelihood. Parker's motive for being a criminal was seen as being partly financial and partly for the excitement and thrill. No one is really sure for certain what her exact motives were, but they do know that they both had little money and no real chance for a prosperous future given the Depression era economy.

On May 23, 1934, Bonnie Parker and Clyde Barrow were killed by a group of six police officers along a highway in Gibsland, Louisiana. The police were hiding in nearby bushes to ambush the couple if they should try avoiding a road block. A friend of the couple had tipped the police off regarding their whereabouts, which led to the roadblock. During the shoot-out, 130 rounds were shot into their car. Parker and Barrow were never asked to surrender by the police. When the Texas ranger, Frank Hamer, who headed the ambush, was asked why he killed a woman who was not wanted for any capital offenses, he replied: "I hate to bust the cap on a woman, especially when she was sitting down, however if it wouldn't have been her, it would have been us" (Williams, 2007).

Parker's funeral was a public spectacle with twenty thousand people in attendance. She was buried at Crown Hill Memorial Park in Dallas, Texas. She was only 23 years old when she died. Parker had an impact on U.S. society in that she provided an alternative image of womanhood. She was a murderer and a criminal. Still, she did not care what society thought about her. Her crime spree enabled society to come to terms with the "idea" of a female criminal, and in the process, she probably singlehandedly invented the female gangster image. Her image and story were revived again in 1967 in the critically acclaimed, hugely popular film *Bonnie and Clyde,* starring Faye Dunaway as Bonnie Parker and Warren Beatty as Clyde Barrow. The film did not back away from portraying realistically and graphically the violence of their crimes or the ambush and shoot-out that killed Parker and Barrow.

Resources

Browder, Laura. 2004. "Bonnie and Clyde." *Encyclopedia of the Great Depression*, edited by Robert S. McElvaine. New York: Macmillan Reference.

Federal Bureau of Investigation. "FBI History. Famous Cases. Bonnie and Clyde." http://www.fbi.gov/libref/historic/famcases/clyde/clyde.htm#top.

Phillips-Fein, Kim. 2004. "Crime." *Encyclopedia of the Great Depression,* edited by Robert S. McElvaine. New York: Macmillan Reference.

Robertson, Thomas. 2000. *St. James Encyclopedia of Popular Culture: Bonnie and Clyde.* Detroit: St. James Press.

Williams, Sally. January 21, 2007. Bonnie and Clyde. *Western Mail.*

James David Ballard and Natasha Cooper

Rosa Parks (1913–2005)

Rosa Louise Parks was an African American civil rights activist who was nationally recognized as the "mother of modern day civil rights movement" in America. On December 1, 1955, Parks was arrested for refusing to surrender her seat to a white male passenger on a Montgomery, Alabama, bus. This incident prompted a wave of protest that echoed throughout the United States. It was her very courageous act that changed the view of American people toward African Americans and was influential in redirecting the course of American history.

Rosa Parks was educated in a rural school in Alabama, and she was home-schooled by her mother. When she completed her early education, she enrolled in the Montgomery Industrial School for Girls (Miss White's School for Girls), a private institution. She went on to Alabama State Teachers College High School, where she failed to complete her studies due to the death of her grandmother. As she prepared to go back to Alabama State Teacher's College, her mother fell ill, and she was forced to stay at home to care for her mother, while her brother worked outside the home.

Rosa Parks was an early advocate in the effort to free the Scottsboro Boys, a case that took place in the 1930s. Together she and her husband, Raymond, worked with the National Association of the Advancement of Colored People (NAACP).

After her arrest, black people of Montgomery and sympathizers of other races began to organize, and they promoted a boycott of the city buses, which lasted for over 380 days. Parks had had her first official confrontation on a bus during a rainy day in 1943 when the bus driver demanded that she get off the bus and re-enter through the back door. While exiting the front door, she dropped her purse, and others on the bus ran to pick it up. The bus driver evidently became enraged, and although he allowed her to barely step off the bus, he left, and she was forced to walk five miles home. It was in re-

Rosa Parks is fingerprinted in Montgomery, Alabama. Parks's arrest for refusing to give up her seat on a bus to a white man on December 1, 1955, inspired the Montgomery Bus Boycott, a prolonged action against the segregated Montgomery, Alabama, bus system by African American riders and their white supporters. (Library of Congress)

membering this day when this white bus driver demanded that she move that she felt such determination that she was persuaded to continue her revolt. By Parks's account, the bus driver had said that: "Y'll better make it light on yourselves and let me have those seats." Three of the individuals complied, but Parks would not get up to move to the colored section. She yelled out: "I don't think I should have to stand up" (www.bio.com/articles/Rosa-Parks). The police were called to arrest Rosa Parks. And arrest her they did. She declared in interviews that she was a human being and had rights.

In her biography written by Brinkley (2000), Parks stated that: "People always say that I didn't give up my seat because I was tired, but that isn't true. I was not tired physically, or no more tired than I usually was at the end of the working day. I was not old, although some people have an image of me as being old then. I was forty-two. No, the only tired I was, was tired of giving in."

Like many people of color, Parks was deeply moved by the brutal murder of Emmet Till in August 1955. People who knew Parks described her as a person who, although sweet and soft-spoken, was capable of making statements that screamed loudly. She was a person who understood and believed in the words and writings of Dr. Martin Luther King, the most well-known spokesperson for the boycott who stood for nonviolence. King helped spur the nonviolent movement, which began to take hold throughout the South and the country as whole. Thousands of daring people joined the protest to demand equal rights for all people.

Parks was employed from 1965 to 1988 by Congressman John Conyers from the First Congressional District of Michigan, where she co-founded the Rosa and Raymond Parks Institute for Self Development with Elaine Easton Steele in honor of husband Raymond (1903–1977). The institute's purpose was to motivate and direct youth to achieve their full potential. The institute traced the development of the underground railroad into the civil rights movement and beyond. Journeying primarily by bus as freedom riders did during the 1960s, her theme was "Where have we been? Where are we going?"

Rosa Parks through her life was a modest person who encouraged young people to study those who contributed to world peace. During her life, she was the recipient of more than 43 honorary degrees, including one from Soka University in Japan. In September 1996, Ms. Parks was the recipient of the Medal of Freedom from President Bill Clinton. It is the highest award given to a civilian citizen.

In addition to all her awards, the first Monday following February 4 has been designated as Mrs. Rosa Parks' Day in the state of Michigan. She was the first living person to have a holiday named after her. *Time* magazine voted her as one of the top 100 influential people of the 20th century. Both houses of Congress passed a bill unanimously naming Mrs. Parks as one of 250 individuals to receive the Congressional Gold Medal of Honor.

Rosa Parks is credited with bringing about an awareness of the plight of African Americans and the civil rights struggle. Martin Luther King in his work *Stride Toward Freedom* described Parks's arrest as a precipitating factor with respect to the protest. It was the tip of a history of similar injustices that were taxing and, ultimately, intolerable. Understanding the actions of Mrs. Parks, he explained, could not come without the realization that, eventually, there is a point when humans cannot suffer injustice interminably.

Rosa Parks wrote four books—*Rosa Parks: My Story* (written with Jim Haskins); *Quiet Strength* (written with Gregory J. Reed); *Dear Mrs. Parks: A Dialogue with Today's Youth* (written with Gregory J. Reed); and, *I Am Rosa Parks* (written with Jim Haskins).

Rosa Parks remains an example of a person who had quiet courage, dignity, and tremendous determination which ultimately changed society.

Resources

Brinkley, Douglas. (2000). *Rosa Parks*. New York: Penguin.

Francis, Samuel, Peter Gemma, Patrick Buchanan, and Joseph Sobran. (2006). *Shots Fired: Sam Francis on America's Culture War*. Vienna, VA: Fitzgerald Griffin Foundation.

Hare, Kenneth and Jim Earnhardt. (2005). *They Walked to Freedom: 1955–1956. The Story of the Montgomery Bus Boycott*. Champaign, IL: Spotlight Press.

"Two Decades Later." (1974, May 17). *New York Times*.

Roslyn Muraskin

R

Terri Rachals (1962–)

Terri Rachals is a female serial murder who worked as a nurse and preyed on victims in the intensive care unit (ICU) at Phoebe Putney Hospital in Albany, Georgia. There was no victim preference, other than ICU patients, and all victims were injected with potassium chloride, causing the heart to go into arrest. Although she was charged and indicted with 6 murders and 19 aggravated assaults, she was found guilty of a single aggravated assault. She is suspected of killing six people during the latter part of 1985: Milton Luca (age 68) on October 19; Minnie Houck (age 58) on November 7; Joe Erwin (age 36) on November 10; Robert Parker (age 36) on November 15; Andrew Daniels (age 73) on November 24; and Norris Morgan (age 3) on November 27.

Born in Hopeful, Georgia, Terri Rachals was adopted by the Maples family at the age of two after her mother had a nervous breakdown. At age 11, her adoptive mother died of a stroke, and her adoptive father became a heavy drinker and abusive towards Terri. Rachals states her father was sexually abusive, molesting her until she left home at age 16, although her father denied this accusation. Throughout school she was described as a good student, self-conscious, and hard working. She met Roger Rachals, a printer suffering from cerebral palsy, at a church meeting while attending college in Albany. They were married in 1980, and she started working for Phoebe Putney Hospital a year later after earning her associate's degree in nursing. She had one son, Chad, born around 1984.

In early 1985, Phoebe Putney Hospital administration noticed an increase in their ICU deaths. The ward was put into high security mode for three months, and the deaths stopped. After the release of security measures, the deaths resumed, forcing staff to look at its own ward as a source of the problem. Eventually, upper administration figured out that all deaths had occurred on nurse Rachals's shift. When confronted by FBI agents, she confessed to the killings. She corrected an FBI official who asked about injecting the potassium chloride into the intravenous bags by responding that, for Samuel Bently, it was injected into the plasma bag instead. After the injection, she stated she watched the electrocardiograph (EEG) strip, knowing something was going to happen. She called for a doctor once the EEG started to show signs of poisoning. Further questioning revealed that Terri Rachals was actually unsure if she committed these crimes, given that she often suffered from long periods of loss of memory, or fugue states. She was charged with 6 counts of murder and 20 counts of aggravated assault. She was handcuffed and taken to a psychiatric facility, where, after one month's time, she was deemed fit to stand trial in September 1986.

At trial, Rachals recanted her confession, and defense attorney George Pete Donaldson argued that Rachals was abused as a child, and this abuse caused severe depression which lead her to forget long periods of time. He also brought in psychiatric testimony stating that she was very suggestible. He argued that she confessed because of what was said at the interview by officers and her intense desire to please. The prosecution stated she was a "tigress stalking her prey" and that she sought control and domination because of her feelings of being a "second-class citizen" and low self-esteem emerging from the abuse she experienced as a child. After nine-and-a-half hours of deliberations, five women and seven men returned a verdict of guilty on a single count of aggravated assault, acquitting her of all other charges. She was sentenced to 17 years in prison.

Despite the fact that Rachals was suspected of serial murder, the jury stated that the prosecution "failed to make its case" even with a recanted confession and the admission of fugue states experienced by the offender. The jurors were polled in the newspaper, and many believed the defense's argument that she was mentally ill and highly suggestible but also believed she was guilty and carried out the crimes in "poor mental health."

Throughout the trial, various people commented on what a good nurse she was, how she was a "natural" caregiver and was a very kind person. When asked about the verdict, district attorney Hobart Hind was outraged. He said that the verdict indicated that both the judicial system and the jurors present at that time were faulty. He considered her the most serious murderess of the century. During her trial and incarceration she had several supporters, including her long-time attorney, numerous friends, and family members. Attorney Donaldson stated that her case had changed his life, showing him compassion and giving him a desire to learn why women commit crimes.

While in prison, letters written by Rachals to author Jennifer Furio before 2001 indicate that she had used her time in prison to begin the healing process caused by the childhood sexual abuse. In one letter she wrote while in prison she states: "I am not evil. I love God. I am living normally. I am a victim of abuse. It was extreme and so was my response. I can grieve, but I can no longer ignore the roots of my disorders" (Furio, 2001: p. 37).

In this same letter she acknowledges that she was still not sure what it was that she actually did. She asserted that she was still working through memories of her time in the hospital. Like her memories in her childhood, there are only piecemeal images rather than actual remembrances of that time.

She was released from the Savannah Women's Transitional Center after serving her 17-year sentence in April 2003, and then she completed three years of parole in April 2006. She remains one of the few identified serial murderers to complete a full prison sentence and be released from prison and into public life. As of this writing, her whereabouts is unknown.

Resources

Furio, J. (2001). Terri Rachals. *Letters from prison: Voices of women murderers.* New York: Algora Publishing, 21–44.

Manners, T. (1995). " Terri Rachals" *Deadlier than a male: Stories of female serial killers.* London: Pan Books, 170–209.

Hannah Scott

Leni Riefenstahl (1902–2003)

Leni Riefenstahl is infamous for her film work on behalf of Nazi Germany. Between 1933 and 1936, Riefenstahl was commissioned by the National Socialist Party to create and direct four films highlighting Hitler, Germany, and the Nazi Party. Her most notable work, *Triumph of the Will*, has been held as the greatest propaganda film ever

Leni Riefenstahl (right) directs the filming of *Triumph of the Will*, a Nazi propaganda film, in 1934. Riefenstahl is alternately celebrated as a pioneering filmmaker and excoriated for her role in promoting the Nazi movement. (Library of Congress)

produced. Although she was never a member of the Nazi Party, history has deemed her as "Hitler's filmmaker" and an ardent supporter of Hitler and the Third Reich.

Leni Riefenstahl was born in 1902 as Helene Bertha Amalie in a time when women were not considered to have ambitions beyond their assigned roles as wife and mother. Although her father had intended her to obtain an education, Leni chose the life of an artist. Beginning her career as a dancer, she became immersed in the artistic world, but her life took a new direction when she obtained a role in Arnold Fanck's film, *The Sacred Mountain*, which was a box office success and the Riefenstahl-Fanck team went on to make several films together: *The Great Leap*, *The White Hell of Piz Palu*, *Storm over Mont Blanc*, *White Frenzy*, and *SOS Iceberg*. It was just prior to the filming of *SOS Iceberg* that Riefenstahl first met Adolph Hitler. There was an instantaneous admiration between the two, and Riefenstahl remained enamored with Hitler for the rest of her life. Hitler had seen Riefenstahl's directorial debut, *The Blue Light*, and became interested in her filming the 1933 Nationalist Socialist Party Congress in Nuremberg. Riefenstahl agreed, and she proceeded to film the first of four documentaries, *Victory of Faith*. Although the film was said to be outstanding, Leni was unimpressed with the final product; however, Hitler was able to persuade her to film the conference the following year. Learning from her mistakes from the first attempt, Riefenstahl was able to create what would be considered her masterpiece, *Triumph of the Will*. The film was able to portray a unified Germany under the rule of a godlike Hitler. The documentary helped to guarantee Nazi control over Germany and shape the face of the Third Reich.

With the success of the film's release in 1935, the party leaders commissioned Riefenstahl to direct the third installment of her documentary work on the National Socialist Party, *Day of Freedom*. This third installment illustrated the might of the German military and Hitler's control over it. In contrast to the previous documentaries on Germany and the Third Reich, her fourth and final film funded by the National Socialist party, *Olympia*, chronicled the 1936 Olympics. This final documentary was the encore to her previous masterpiece, *Triumph of the Will*. Using filming techniques that were unheard of in the filming community, Riefenstahl was able to capture the sporting event and its participants in a realistic manner. *Olympia* (1938) was an instantaneous success upon release; the film won numerous awards including the German Film Prize, the state's greatest honor.

In 1939, she began to film *Penthesilea*; however, with the German invasion of Poland that same year, she was forced to shelve the project. Hence, Riefenstahl began filming on the Polish front. It was here that the most damaging material to classify her as more than a mere "sympathizer" occurred. While filming, she was witness to the killing of 31 Polish prisoners in the town of Konskie. Although there has been some disagreement about her role in the incident, evidence suggests that she was not a direct participant in the massacre. Many sources report that she did protest the occurrence; however, her objections fell on deaf ears, even those of her friend and confidant Adolph Hitler. Tired of war, Leni Riefenstahl returned to making movies rather than documentaries/propaganda films. Riefenstahl began filming a shelved project, *Tiefland*. The film took years to finish with Leni Riefenstahl acting as producer, director, writer, and leading lady. When the allied forces entered Germany, filming halted. Upon release after the war, it was a terrible flop.

With the news of Hitler's death, Riefenstahl fled Berlin. She had not foreseen what was to come. Her once-beloved status was gone, and she became viewed as a pariah. Riefenstahl was taken into custody by American troops and held in a detention camp. With her arrival in Salzburg Prison, she was questioned about her relationship with Nazi leaders. She maintained that she was an artist who had occasionally attended official celebrations at the request of the Nazi hierarchy. She failed to admit she had been a longtime friend and patron of Hitler and the Nazi party. She was cleared by the American occupiers and released. With the French occupation of the territory, Riefenstahl had to go through denazification hearings to ascertain her level of complicity with Hitler's regime. The first denazification hearing occurred in 1948 and found her free of "political incrimination." Upon appeal by the French military government in 1949, she was again cleared of the charges against her. The third trial conducted by the Baden Commission found her innocent of specific crimes, but classified her as a "fellow traveler" who had willingly served the Third Reich. The ruling was extremely controversial since witnesses had testified that she had used gypsy prisoners to work on her film *Tiefland*. Moreover, two days prior to the ruling, *Revue* released the photos at Koskie, which placed Riefenstahl at the murders, which conflicted with her admission of ignorance. Nevertheless, her status was upheld, and Riefenstahl was free to work again since the classification of "fellow traveler" carried no prohibitions or penalties.

Although Riefenstahl was able to avoid any reprisals for her relationship with the Reich, her career suffered and her reputation was ruined. No film company would associate with her; she was, in essence, ostracized from the movie picture industry. It was not until 1962 that Riefenstahl made a comeback with her "discovery" of the Nubas in the Sudan. Rather than film the tribe, Riefenstahl turned to photographs. Her work with "her" Nubas led to the publishing of two books. In 2002, she again reinvented herself with her work on underwater photography releasing her documentary on life in the oceans, *Underwater Impressions*. A year later, Leni Riefenstahl died of cancer and ended a brilliant yet controversial career.

Until her death, Leni Riefenstahl maintained that she was guilty of nothing but being an artist. Many argued that her love of art led her to an obsession to create perfection at any cost. Her unwillingness to see "the real Hitler" and her own ambition allowed her to become a successful director at a time when women were relegated to domesticity, but eventually at a cost. Like many others in Nazi Germany, Riefenstahl chose to ignore the atrocities surrounding her.

Resources

Bach, Steven. 2007. *Leni: The life and work of Leni Riefenstahl.* New York: Alfred A. Knopf.

Berg-Pan, Renata. 1980. *Leni Riefenstahl.* Boston: Twayne Publishers.

Knopp, Guido. 2001. *Hitler's women.* New York: Routledge.

Müeller, Ray. 1993. *The wonderful horrible life of Leni Riefenstahl.* 188 min. Kino Video, Videocassette.

Trimborn, Jurgen. 2007. *Leni Riefenstahl: A life.* New York: Faber and Faber.

Tammy S. Garland

Christina Riggs (1971–2000)

Christina Marie Riggs was a licensed nurse and the fifth woman in the United States to be executed after the reinstatement of the death penalty in 1976. When she was put to death for the murder of her two preschool-aged children, she became the first woman to be executed in Arkansas in almost 150 years. During the sentencing, she pleaded for the jury to give her the death penalty in anticipation of being reunited with her deceased children. As Riggs stated: "There is no way no words can express how sorry I am for taking the lives of my babies . . . now I can be with my babies, as I always intended" (CNN Special Report, 2007: 1). As she requested for her death penalty, she was put to death by a lethal injection of potassium chloride, which is also the drug Riggs had initially planned to use to kill her children.

Riggs was executed by lethal injection on Thursday May 2, 2000, in Arkansas. Society has been unwilling to believe that women are capable of committing murder, and therefore, there is a tendency to justify women criminal's actions by associating them with mental illness or disability. Even Riggs's mother and lawyer explained Riggs's actions by claiming that post-traumatic stress disorder was the leading cause of her mental instability. What makes Riggs's case unique is the fact that she was not viewed by the prosecutor and the jurors as mentally ill or deficient but rather as and individual who was completely and willingly capable of murder.

Christina Riggs was born in 1971 in Lawton, Oklahoma. Between the ages of 7 and 13, she had been sexually abused by her stepbrother and also by a neighbor. In adolescence, she experienced low self-esteem as a result of being abused and overweight, and she began drinking alcohol and smoking marijuana. Once she graduated from high school, she went on to receive her license as a practical nurse and began working at the Veterans Administration hospital in Oklahoma City. In October 1991, she was pregnant with her son Justin, but his father chose to play no role in Justin's life. In July 1993, Christina married John Riggs and shortly after their wedding, she became pregnant again; however, she had a miscarriage. After the miscarriage, Christina was placed on Prozac after reporting feelings of depression and thoughts of suicide. In December 1994, Christina gave birth to her daughter

Shelby, but soon after the birth of their daughter, Christina went through a painful divorce. As a single mom with little financial support from the children's fathers, she began to feel frustrated with long work hours and high living expenses.

On November 4, 1997, during her shift at the hospital, Christina Riggs stole some antidepressants (Elavil), morphine, and potassium chloride. Around 10:15 PM, she made her two children drink half of an Elavil each in order to make them drowsy. While Justin was asleep, she injected him with potassium chloride, but she was unaware of the fact that the drug had to be diluted in order for it to work accordingly. Unfortunately, instead of feeling drowsy, Justin woke up screaming in pain, and Riggs ended up giving her son morphine as a pain reliever and suffocated him with a pillow. After her son's reaction to the potassium chloride injection, she decided not inject her daughter, and, instead, she suffocated her with a pillow as well. Christina wrote a suicide note to her mother and to her ex-husband explaining how her life had been full of disappointments, and she felt that by killing her children they would not have to suffer as she had.

The prosecutors and jurors held the view that Riggs killed her children because they had become an inconvenience to her lifestyle. According to the prosecution, she was a woman who frequented local bars and karaoke nights. She informed the detectives that she had been planning to kill herself and her children for about two to three weeks prior. However, the jurors viewed Riggs's motive as relating to her late night lifestyle. According to Riggs, 20 minutes after killing her children, she took numerous antidepressant pills and injected herself with potassium chloride causing her to become unconscious. The prosecution explained how Riggs would leave her children unattended in order to go out to bars. The recorded confession to the murder proved that she had been plotting to kill her children for several weeks. The following morning, Riggs's mother Carol Thomas arrived at her daughter's home and found the two dead children on the bed along with her daughter laying unconscious on the floor. She quickly called 911 for help, and once they got there they took Christina to the hospital and stabilized her.

Christina Riggs was charged and arrested on two counts of capital murder on November 6, 1997. Her trial began June 23, 1998, and she pleaded not guilty by reason of mental disease or defect, The defense claimed that Christina had suffered from depression along with low self-esteem and that she had experienced extreme forms of depression and had a family history of depression and suicide. The defense also brought up the claim that as a victim of sexually abuse, Riggs's mental state was unstable. In regard to the recorded confession, the defense believed that it was irrelevant because she was still drowsy from the drug overdose, which caused her to hallucinate. However, the court denied the notion that she was still drowsy during the recording because there were no signs of hallucination. According to *Riggs vs. State* (1999), Riggs claimed that she had been isolated from her family during her statement, and she retained counsel that resulted in an infringement of her Fifth and Sixth Amendment rights.

On June 30, 1998, the jury had reached a verdict of guilty on two counts of capital murder after only 55 minutes. The prosecutor explained that the jury was able to see her as a selfish woman who believed that her children were an inconvenience. During sentencing, Christina Riggs pleaded to the jury for the death penalty, and the jury granted her request. Society tends to be reluctant to charge women with capital murder and sentence them to death. What lead to her conviction was that the idea that a mother could murder her own children violated society's gender norms.

The Riggs case was an example of how society reacts and severely punishes women who they believe intentionally killed their own children. There were many mixed feelings about her execution, and many explained that her being put to death was assisted suicide because she wanted to die. Others believed that Christina Riggs was not a criminal but rather as a woman who made a mistake because she was incapable of dealing with the overwhelming frustrations of life. For instance, William F. Shultz, executive director of Amnesty International USA, stated that the state of Arkansas should show compassion toward Riggs (Yellin, 2000). On May 2, 2000, Christina Marie Riggs was put to death by lethal injection; the execution went smoothly and ended in about nine minutes. Even though some viewed Riggs as a self-centered and selfish killer, her last words were "now I can be with my babies, as I always intended" (Chen, 2000).

Resources

Chen, Julie. 2000. Woman executed in Arkansas. *CBS News Transcript,* May 3, Newscast.

Christina Marie Riggs v. State of Arkansas. 1999. No. CR 98-1281, 1-19. Retrieved from http://caselaw.findlaw.com/ar-supreme-court/1007799.html.

CNN Special Report. 2007. "Last Words on Death Row." CNN, December 10, 1-6. Retrieved from http://articles.cnn.com/2007-12-10/us/court.last.words_1_death-row-ricky-lee-sanderson-texas?_s=PM:US.

Frye, Cathy. 2000. Special Report: 'I'm sorry, Momma' One week before her death by lethal injection, Christina Riggs sat for an interview. She said she wanted people to understand what she was thinking when she smothered her children. *Arkansas Democrat-Gazette*, May 7, A1.

Yellin, Emily. 2000. "Arkansas Executes a Woman Who Killed Both Her Children." *New York Times*, May 3. Retrieved from http://www.nytimes.com/2000/05/03/us/arkansas-executes-a-woman-who-killed-both-her-children.html.

Karunya Jayasena and Janet Jimenez

Ethel Rosenberg (1915–1953)

In June 1953, Ethel Rosenberg was executed, along with her husband Julius Rosenberg, for supplying atomic secrets to the Soviet Union. Arrested in 1950,

Ethel Rosenberg holds the arm of her husband Julius Rosenberg, who is in handcuffs. (Library of Congress)

the controversial circumstances surrounding their trial, conviction, and execution provide a stunning reflection of the anticommunist hysteria of that time period.

On September 28, 1915, Ethel Greenglass, the daughter of Jewish European immigrants, was born in a predominantly Jewish working-class region of Manhattan. It was here that she would spend all of her youth and formidable years. Ethel's father ran a sewing machine repair shop, and her mother worked as a housewife. She was the second oldest of four children and the only daughter. One of her younger brothers, David, would figure prominently during the travails that surrounded Ethel's final years.

Although Ethel was regarded as a recluse during her early adolescent years, she developed a love for acting and singing during high school. At the age of 16 she started working at National New York Packing and Shipping as a stenographer, and it was here where her political activism was spawned. As a direct witness and eventual victim of National's unfair labor practices, she became one of the first people to file and successfully win an appeal to the National Labor Relations Board.

This activism was nurtured and grew due to the immediate influence of communist and other progressive groups actively present within the area she lived. Ethel would often sing at progressive gatherings and rallies, combining the two passions that meant the most to her. It was at one of these rallies where she met Julius Rosenberg, whom she married in 1939.

Ethel and Julius Rosenberg continued their activism throughout the 1940s, and during this time they had two children. Julius found employment with the Signal Corps, only to lose it in 1945 when his political affiliations came under scrutiny. He then established his own business, partnering with two of Ethel's brothers. This business floundered, creating tensions between Ethel's family and Julius. During this period, the Rosenbergs experienced their worst financial times while Ethel focused primarily on raising her two children.

In June 1950, Ethel's younger brother, David Greenglass, was implicated in an elaborate espionage ring that provided the Soviets with atomic secrets during the World War II. David had been stationed at Los Alamos from 1944 to 1945, and with assurances from the FBI to not indict his wife (Ruth), he implicated Julius and later Ethel as part of the espionage ring. Julius was arrested on July 17, and Ethel was arrested on August 11.

The Rosenbergs' arrest came at a time when American society was highly suspicious of foreign and American communists alike. In 1949, the Soviet Union had detonated its first atomic bomb. Although many of the Los Alamos scientists and President Truman had stated that it would only a matter of years before the Soviet Union developed the technology to create an atomic bomb, an anticommunist hysteria that had seized America led to the belief that the Soviet Union had secured the technology primarily through domestic espionage by American communists. These fears were exacerbated when Alger Hiss, a prominent State Department official, was accused of espionage in 1948 and convicted of perjury in 1950.

David Greenglass asserted that he provided Julius with names of Los Alamos scientists and a roughly drawn sketch for a high explosive lens mold which were passed on to Soviet agents. The sketch would later, after the executions, be called amateurish and useless by several of the Los Alamos scientists—a sentiment corroborated by decrypted documents from KGB agents (the Venona Files) that were declassified by the National Security Administration in 1995. Under further FBI questioning, David would go on to remember incidents that implicated Julius as being a greater participant. In addition, David and Ruth would go on to remember that in February 1951, a full eight months after they had been initially questioned and six months after Ethel's arrest, that Ethel also participated in the ring by typing up notes secured by Julius. Later in his life, David recanted this latter statement.

The allegations against Ethel are now regarded as having been an unfortunate consequence of the anticommunist zeal and hysteria present in America at the time. These allegations and the subsequent capital charges were used by the FBI to try and secure leverage against Ethel and Julius to name other American communists who were active in the espionage ring. Their refusal to name other communist members resulted in the increased likelihood that, once convicted, they would be sentenced to death; this was an oddity given the significantly lighter sentences handed down to other convicted spies who had much more prominent roles in the spy ring, yet were willing to implicate others.

The trial for Ethel and Julius commenced on March 6, 1951. In addition to the overall political climate making it difficult for Ethel and Julius to receive a fair trial, the trial itself was littered with both poor advice by defense attorney Emmanuel Bloch and questionable conduct by the presiding judge, Irving Kaufman, and the U.S. attorney, Irving Saypol. Ethel and Julius were advised to take the Fifth Amendment right against self-incrimination whenever they were asked about their communist ties. This led to a sense among the jurors that they were hiding incriminating acts. Also, they were tried under the General Espionage Act of 1917 instead of the Atomic Energy Act of 1946 which superseded it. This decision allowed the court to impose a death sentence if the alleged espionage had occurred during wartime, the assumption being that the espionage was done to benefit an enemy nation. However, in this case, the alleged espionage had occurred during the World War II, when the

Soviet Union was an American ally. Finally, after the conviction, Kaufman sought advice for the appropriate sentence from several individuals including Irving Saypol. On March 29, 1951, Julius and Ethel were found guilty. On April 5, 1951, they were sentenced to death.

Despite numerous worldwide appeals to have their sentences commuted, President Eisenhower refused to grant clemency. In addition, the conviction was affirmed twice by the Circuit Court of Appeals; the Supreme Court refused to grant certiorari at least six times, in the end vacating a stay by Justice Douglas on a 6–3 vote. Ethel and Julius Rosenberg were executed on July 19, 1953.

The events surrounding the final three years of Ethel Rosenberg's life provides a historical reflection of the McCarthy era and the real-life consequences that ensued from ideological hysteria. The telling image her story provides of this historical time ensures that she is a figure who will not be soon forgotten. Due to a confession in 2008 by Morton Sobell, a classmate of Julius Rosenberg, it now appears that Julius Rosenberg was in fact a spy, but Ethel Rosenberg, also executed, was most probably not (Roberts 2008).

Further Reading

Meeropol, Robert. 2004. *An Execution in the Family: One Son's Journey* [Paperback]. New York: St. Martin's Griffin.

Philipson, Ilene.1992. *Ethel Rosenberg: Beyond the Myths.* Newark, NJ: Rutgers University Press.

Roberts, Sam. 2008. "Father Was a Spy, Sons Conclude with Regret." *New York Times.* September 17. p. B1.

Matthew Grindal

S

Margaret Sanger (1879–1966)

Margaret Sanger was an advocate for birth control who developed awareness for the need of contraceptives in the United States during the early 1900s, a period during which such devices as well as information on birth control were considered obscene and indecent. In 1912, she began her life-long crusade for providing women with the ability to plan their pregnancies even before the phrase "birth control" had been established. Although Sanger supported the development of modern medical methods of birth control, her greatest achievement was promoting the idea that every woman had the right of control over her body and reproductive capabilities and that these were basic and universal concepts that applied to every woman. Many of her writings were considered illegal under the Comstock Law of 1873 because they contained information about sex education that was considered to be obscene. Sanger was considered a criminal for promoting birth control and was the target of raids and other harassment; she was placed on trial, and on some occasions even sent to jail. Sanger opened the first U.S. birth control clinic and founded the American Control League in 1921, now known as the Planned Parenthood Federation of America. While for some, Margaret Sanger was a sort of heroine, to others she was perceived as immoral, deserving to be labeled as an outcast from society for threatening its moral integrity.

Margaret Sanger was born in Corning, New York, on September 14, 1879. She was the daughter of Anne Purcell Higgins, who out of 18 pregnancies had only 11 live births. Anne Higgins died of cervical cancer and tuberculosis in 1896. With the financial support of her sisters, Sanger attended Claverack College in Hudson. She then enrolled in a hospital's nursing program in White Plains, New York, to become an obstetrical nurse. In 1902, she married architect William Sanger and had three children—two sons and a daughter. Sanger left the nursing profession in 1912 to educate women about birth control, a topic she believed would help improve their lives. In 1913, Margaret and William Sanger separated and later divorced. She was remarried in 1922 to James Noah Slee.

In 1912, she began writing two columns for the daily newspaper the *New York Call* entitled, "What Every Mother Should Know" and "What Every Girl Should Know." These columns included modest accounts and information regarding sex, puberty, and descriptions of the reproductive organs using medical terms. These articles indirectly challenged the Comstock Law of 1873, a law that was lobbied through Congress and the state legislature by antipornography advocates. Under this law, distributing contraceptive devices and birth control information through the U.S. postal service was prohibited. In 1914, Sanger caught the attention of Anthony Comstock himself when she began writing *The Woman Rebel,*

Margaret Sanger, U.S. birth control reform leader. (Library of Congress)

a monthly magazine that advocated for contraception. Comstock proceeded to impede upon attempts at circulating the magazine, making it undeliverable by mail. Margaret was summoned to court. Due to the risk of imprisonment, she fled to England, but only after writing and creating a plan of mass distribution of her pamphlet, *Family Limitations*, which explained all the details she knew about birth control and how to use it. Once in England, 10 million copies of the pamphlet were distributed in the United States. One copy was sent to the judge in charge of Sanger's case. *Family Limitations* received huge publicity. In 1916, Sanger returned to the United States and faced her first trial, *The People v. Margaret Sanger.* After refusing the assistance of a lawyer, she appeared on her own behalf in front of the judge. A large crowd of sympathizers gathered at her trial to publicly express their support. Because of the commotion caused by people cheering for Sanger inside and outside the court, the government decided to dismiss the case because they did not want Sanger becoming a political "martyr" (Wardell, 1980: 740).

Margaret Sanger opened the first birth control clinic in the United States in 1916 in Brownsville, a section of Brooklyn. The clinic was illegal, but it provided women with some contraceptive methods and gave simple instructions on how to use them. Ten days after being opened, the clinic was raided by the New York City police and Sanger was arrested. The next day, she was bailed out and immediately reopened the clinic. She was subsequently sent to jail a second time. Charges against Sanger included selling indecent pamphlets, running a public nuisance, and distributing birth control information. In 1917, Sanger faced her second trial. She refused to promise to abide by the law in the future, and as punishment, was returned to jail for 30 days. In 1918, Judge Frederick Crane made it legal for women to obtain information about birth control and contraceptives from doctors if they claimed a reason involving personal health, a victory for Sanger and her cause.

Margaret Sanger's motivation for defying the Comstock Law was that, as a nurse, she encountered many women dying from constant childbirth or blood poisoning after having illegal abortions done. Other women committed suicide in order to prevent themselves from having more children. During this time period, the maternal mortality rate was over 50 times what it is today (Hoyert, 2007: 1–2), and in light of such circumstances, Sanger saw a need for birth control. She perceived her actions as necessary to promote the enhancement of life for all women.

Sanger's impact on society was significant and left a lasting impression contributing to understanding and reform in women's lives. She helped reduce maternal death rates by providing women with contraceptive devices and information on how to use them to prevent pregnancies. Her struggle made possible the first FDA approved oral contraceptive pill in 1960, and her petitions in court led the way for the private use of contraceptives to become a constitutional right in 1965. Above all, the purpose of Margaret Sanger's birth control crusade was to allow women to take control of their fertility and thus gain a degree of autonomy they had previously been denied. Freeing women from the risk of unwanted or life-threatening pregnancies, they reached a position from which to better promote their advancement. Sanger died in 1966.

Resources

Coigney, Virginia. 1969. *Margaret Sanger: Rebel with a Cause*. New York: Doubleday & Company.

Douglas, Emily T. 1975. *Margaret Sanger: Pioneer of the Future*. Garrett Park, MD: Garrett Park Press.

Hoyert, D. L. 2007. Maternal Mortality and Related Concepts. National Center for Health Statistics. *Vital Health Statistics* 3(33).

Lader, Lawrence. 1955. *The Margaret Sanger Story and the Fight for Birth Control*. New York: Country Life Press.

"Margaret Sanger (1879–1966)." *Harvard University Open Collections Program: Women Working, 1800–1930*. http://ocp.hul.harvard.edu/ww/sanger.html

Sanger, Margaret. 1959. *My Fight for Birth Control*. New York: Division of Maxwell Scientific International.

Wardell, Dorothy. 1980. Margaret Sanger: Birth Control's Successful Revolutionary. *American Journal of Public Health* 70(7): 736–742.

Prana Yenkosky and Jason Thompson

Sophie Scholl (1921–1943)

Sophie Scholl was a player in one of the few instances of German organized resistance to Nazi dictatorship. Although condemned as a criminal by the government of Nazi Germany, she acted for freedom. She was born on May 9, 1921, to a middle-class family, the fourth of five children. Her father was a businessman who had a brief stint as mayor of Forchtenberg, Germany, when she was a baby. Her parents encouraged all their children to be open-minded and to question authority. Sophie and her siblings they were given a wide berth for making their own decisions about politics, and they were even allowed to participate in Hitler Youth organizations.

A serious, studious child, her early years were unremarkable, although they included a stint in the Nazi youth organization Der Bund Deutscher Mädel (The League of German Girls). In late adolescence, she participated in a reading group consisting of her siblings and other members of her family's social network. As she grew older, she became gradually disillusioned with the message and activities of National Socialism. Scholl's rising skepticism was likely solidified by her father's brief detention for antigovernment remarks and her older brother Hans's arrest for involvement in an unauthorized youth organization.

Her attitudes and actions went against the grain of the stereotypical ideas about women that were a key aspect of Nazism. In an excerpt from a letter to her boyfriend, reproduced in a biography by Dumbach and Newborn (2006), she says, "I'm sure you'll find what I'm writing very unfeminine. It's ridiculous for a girl to involve herself in politics. She should let her feminine feelings dominate her thoughts. Especially compassion. But I believe that first comes thinking, and that feelings, especially about little things that affect you directly, maybe about your own body, deflect you so that you can hardly see the big things anymore" (45).

In 1940, Scholl graduated secondary school and enrolled in vocational school, partially as a failed effort to avoid compulsory work in the National Labor service—a prerequisite for going on to university. In May 1942, after her work stint was completed, she took up the study of biology and philosophy at the University of Munich where Hans was enrolled as a medical student.

While living with her brother, she became aware of his involvement with a group called the White Rose. Motivated by varying ideologies, this small group of friends, mostly medical students, had become disenchanted with Hitler's Germany and wished to exhort their fellow citizens to challenge the regime. Their method lay chiefly in distributing a series of leaflets mailed from Munich and other cities to selected individuals across Germany. First targeted toward intellectuals and then addressed to the population at large, they pushed Germans to resist the Nazi system, reject the ideology, and become aware of the larger atrocities that were occurring as part of the war effort and beyond.

Sophie joined the organization, becoming treasurer and helping to copy and distribute the leaflets. On February 18, 1943, she and her brother placed leaflets outside of classrooms at their university. At one point, they threw a bunch of them onto a wide plaza. Discovered by a school custodian, they were detained and questioned by the Gestapo. The police found a draft leaflet in Hans's pocket—this linked the siblings to a third White Rose member, Christoph Probst, who was arrested shortly afterwards.

In the late morning of Monday, February 22, 1943, Sophie, her brother, and Probst were put on trial, accused of treason and of helping the opponents of the Reich. They were tried before the People's Court, the Nazi institution for countering political opponents. During the proceedings, at one point Sophie interjected: "Somebody had to make a start. What we said and wrote are what many people are thinking. They just don't dare say it out loud." (Dumbach and Newborn, 2006, 157). Having confessed to their activities, all three were found guilty and sentenced to death by guillotine. The executions were rapidly carried out; by shortly after 5:00 PM that same day, all three were dead. Sophie Scholl was 21 years old.

Soon afterwards, other core members of the group, along with associates and family members, were taken into custody. Three other White Rose members were executed later that year. Others, punished for assisting the group, were sentenced to varying terms of imprisonment.

It is not clear how much the German public knew of Sophie or the group at the time of the executions, although a few months later one leaflet, obtained by the Allies, was airdropped over Germany. After the end of the war, a book by Inge Scholl relating her siblings' story gave wider notice to the White Rose. Currently, the Scholls, along with other members of the group, are viewed as icons of resistance. Sophie in particular has attained supreme heroine status, especially among the young in Germany. Schools have been named after her, and several movies have been made of her life, including the Academy Award–nominated *Sophie Scholl: The Final Five Days* (http://www.sophiescholl-derfilm.de/).

Resources

Dumbach, Annette, and Jud Newborn. 2006. *Sophie Scholl & The White Rose.* Oxford: Oneworld Publications.

Henderson, Simon. 2005. The White Rose and the definition of resistance. *History Review* 53: 45–47.

Robertson, Jenna. 2004. Leaflets of The White Rose. *The White Rose Website.* http://www.jlrweb.com/whiterose/leaflets.html (Accessed March 6, 2007).

Rothemund, Marc. 2005. *Sophie Scholl: The Final Days.* Zeitgeist Films DVD.

Scholl, Inge, and Arthur R. Schultz, trans. 1970. *Students against Tyranny; The Resistance of the White Rose, Munich, 1942–1943.* Middletown, CT: Wesleyan University Press.

Wittenstein, George J. 1997. Memories of the White Rose. *The History Place: Points of View.* http://www.historyplace.com/pointsofview/white-rose1.htm (Retrieved on March 6, 2007).

Angela Taylor

Assata Shakur (1947–)

Assata Shakur's background as a female African American militant, who achieved a high ranking role in the Black Liberation Army (BLA), establishes her as a relevant figure in contemporary American history. Through her involvement in this organization, she struggled against the oppression encountered by African Americans to gain liberation in the United States. Many believe that Shakur's case draws attention to institutional flaws within the American judicial system while highlighting the conflict between government ideology and individual principle.

Shakur was born Joanne Deborah Chesimard on July 16, 1947, in New York City, though most of her childhood was spent in Wilmington, North Carolina. She was a student at Borough of Manhattan Community College and City College of New York in the 1960s. After completing her degree, Shakur became an active member of the BLA, an auxiliary of the Black Panther Party (BPP).

The BPP was an African American paramilitary organization active in the late 1960s founded to promote civil rights and self-defense. Its radical approach to social reform made the group a target for law enforcement, contributing to the development of the Counter Intelligence Program (COINTELPRO), a covert program orchestrated by the FBI. The BLA was an underground, black nationalist, Marxist organization comprised largely of former Black Panthers to rise above racial oppression and injustice by any means necessary. These organizations were subsequently under intense surveillance by the COINTELPRO which aimed to examine and subdue dissident political organizations whose outlined design included politically radical elements, including those that desired the overthrow of

A member of the Black Liberation Army, Assata Shakur was convicted in 1973 of killing New Jersey State Trooper Werner Foerster as he lay on the ground. She escaped from prison in 1979 and fled to Cuba. (AP/Wide World Photos)

the U.S government. Its purpose was to "expose, disrupt, misdirect, discredit, or otherwise neutralize" the activities of these movements (http://www.albionmonitor. com/9905a/jbcointelpro.html). Because Shakur was a member of the BLA, her advocates argue this was the reason she became a target for government harassment. She had previously been arrested several times before for a variety of different offenses ranging from bank robberies to attempted murder. Subsequent trials for these crimes resulted in acquittals and dismissals.

On May 2, 1973, on a highway in New Jersey, Assata Shakur and two companions, Zayd Malik Shakur (no relation) and Sundiata Acoli (legal name Clark Squire), were stopped by state troopers Werner Foerster and James Harper. There is considerable debate over what happened next, though there was a shoot-out that left two people dead: Shakur's close friend Zayd Shakur and officer Werner Foerster. Officer James Harper and Assata Shakur were both wounded as a result of the fray.

There are two accounts for what happened on the New Jersey turnpike. According to police reports, state trooper Foerster pulled over a white Pontiac containing three suspects because of a broken taillight. Officer Harper became suspicious when the driver, Zayd Shakur, would not say who owned the vehicle. During the search that followed, Foerster uncovered a loaded ammunition clip. Soon after, the suspects opened fire with automatic pistols striking Foerster's chest and Harper in the left shoulder. Evidence presented in court suggests that Acoli shot Foerster with his own weapon two additional times in the head. During the trial that followed, Harper maintained that he received his wound from Assata, though he later retracted this accusation.

Assata Shakur's representatives, however, claim that she and her colleagues were political targets and victims of racial profiling. After stopping the Shakur and her friends for "DWB" or "Driving While Black," the state troopers physically and verbally assaulted Acoli and Zayd Shakur—a confrontation that led to the shoot-out. Afterwards Zayd Shakur lay dead, and though Acoli escaped, he was taken into custody two days later. Assata Shakur was arrested and alleges that she was physically abused and questioned by police while injured. Her autobiography includes accounts of an interrogation during which she was repeatedly punched by the interviewing officers.

Despite evidence that indicated that Shakur was not the shooter, she was jailed without bail for four years pending trial as an accomplice to murder. She was found guilty on March 25, 1977. Forensic evidence to support Shakur's defense argument was used to prove that she was shot with her hands raised. A pathologist testified that there was "no conceivable way" the first bullet could have hit Shakur's clavicle if her arm was down. Additionally, forensic examination did not find gun residue on her hands which supports the claim that she did not kill officer Foerster.

Following sentencing, Shakur was transferred to the Federal Women's Prison Camp in Alderson, West Virginia; it was there she met Puerto Rican Nationalists

Lolita Lebron and Mary Alice who introduced her to the concept of Liberation Theology (which interprets the teachings of Jesus Christ to address political and social struggles). After the maximum security unit was closed in 1978, Shakur was transferred to the Clinton Correctional Facility for Women in New Jersey.

On November 2, 1979, she escaped the Clinton Correctional Facility. Though very little is known about the events leading up to her escape, journalist Asha Bandele who interviewed Shakur, reported that on Black Solidarity Day, several armed people came into the prison's visiting room, and after holding a few guards as hostages, Shakur was able to escape (http://www.assatashakur.org/hands-off1.htm). In 1984, she resurfaced in Cuba, where she received political asylum from President Fidel Castro after asserting that she never received a fair trial.

There have been many extradition attempts to return Shakur to the United States from Cuba. These attempts have included a letter to Pope John Paul II from New Jersey superintendent Carl Williams in 1997 asking the Pope to raise the issue of Shakur's extradition during his talks with Fidel Castro. Shakur countered this by writing her own letter to the Pope, in which she stated, "I am not writing to ask you to intercede on my behalf. I ask nothing for myself. I only ask you to examine the social reality of the United States and to speak out against the human rights violations that are taking place." (http://www.assatashakur.org/pope.htm).

In 2005, the FBI classified Shakur as a "domestic terrorist" and increased the reward for assistance in her capture to $1 million. Despite the label of terrorist, Shakur remains supported by a number of U.S. politicians including Maxine Waters and Charles Barron, as well as the "Hands off Assata" campaign, which depicts her as a contemporary freedom fighter. She has also formerly had a scholarship from Manhattan Community College named after her and a documentary about her life released in 1997 entitled *Eyes of the Rainbow*. Shakur's case continues to receive national attention and remains a heavily debated topic within the realms of academia. She is still considered an enemy of the state and currently resides in Cuba where she continues to maintain that she is innocent.

Resources

Assata Shakur website (current communication and general resource information) http://www.AssataShakur.org

Bandele, Asha. 2003. "The Life of an Outlaw" [interview]. *Vibe*. May, 2003.

James, Joy. 2003. *Imprisoned Intellectuals: America's Political Prisoners Write on Life, Liberation and Rebellion*. Lanham, MD: Rowman & Littlefield.

Scheffler, Judith A. 2002. *Wall Tappings: An International Anthology of Women's Prison Writings, 200 A.D. to the Present*. New York: Feminist Press.

Shakur, Assata. 1987. *Assata: An Autobiography*. Chicago: Westport, CT: Lawrence Hill Books.

Williams, Evelyn. 1993. *Inadmissible Evidence: The Story of the African American Trail Lawyers who Defended the Black Liberations Army.* New York: Lawrence Hill Books.

Jason Thompson and Michelle Hartzog

Fusako Shigenobu (1945–)

As a cofounder and leader of the Japanese Red Army, a radical leftist group, Fusako Shigenobu organized numerous terrorist attacks worldwide in the 1970s and 1980s. While the group's primary goal was to instigate a world revolution and to overthrow the Japanese government, its terrorist attacks often involved hijackings and hostage takings to negotiate the release of political prisoners held in various countries (Table 13). In particular, the Japanese Red Army gained international notoriety in 1972 for their machine gun and grenade attack at Lod Airport in Tel Aviv, Israel, in which they killed 26 people (10 of whom were Puerto Ricans on a pilgrimage) and wounded more than 70 (*Japan Times*, 1972).

After having been on the International Criminal Police Organization's (Interpol's) wanted list for nearly 30 years, Shigenobu's arrest in Japan in 2000 came as a surprise because she had been believed to be living in Lebanon where she was regarded as a hero who had successfully orchestrated many terrorist attacks for the Palestinian cause. Although she pleaded not guilty, she was sentenced to 20 years in prison for attempted murder and kidnapping charges for taking part in an attack on the French embassy in the Hague, Netherlands, in 1974 (*Japan Times*, 2006a).

TABLE 13 Major Terrorist Attacks by the Japanese Red Army

Year	Incident	Place
1972	Lod Airport attack by machineguns and grenades	Tel Aviv, Israel
1973	Hijacking of a Japan Airlines airplane	The Netherlands
1974	Blowing up storage tanks at an oil refinery for the Vietnam War	Singapore
1974	Hostage taking at the Japanese embassy	Kuwait
1974	Hostage taking at the French embassy	The Hague, the Netherlands
1975	Hostage taking at the American and Swedish embassies	Kuala Lumpur, Malaysia
1977	Hijacking of a Japan Airlines airplane	Dhaka, Bangladesh
1986	Gun shooting at the Japanese, Canadian, and American embassies	Jakarta, Indonesia
1987	Firing rockets at the British and American embassies	Rome, Italy
1988	Bombing a U.S. military recreational facility	Naples, Italy

Sources: Shigenobu (2001); *Japan Times* (2000).

After the lower court's ruling, Shigenobu filed an appeal against the 20-year prison sentence (*Japan Times*, 2006b). During her trial at the lower court, Shigenobu announced a disbanding of the Japanese Red Army (*Japan Times*, 2001).

Fusako Shigenobu was born in 1945 in Tokyo; her father was a member of a pre–World War II right-wing organization. After graduation from high school, Shigenobu got a clerical job at a major soy sauce manufacturer. Shigenobu was often frustrated, however, with the way her supervisors devalued female workers' abilities. Her suggestions during meetings were often ignored as they were not in accord with the company's traditional managerial system.

In order to pursue her dream of becoming a school teacher, Shigenobu entered the night division of a private university. On the very first day that she went to the university, however, there was a sit-in protest against a tuition increase. Such student protests were common across Japan in the 1960s. When one of the protesters explained the reason for the protest and asked her to join them, she spontaneously joined simply because "there was not any reason to say no" (Shigenobu, 2001: 37–38). That was the beginning of Shigenobu's involvement in the new left movement.

Typical to female members involved at the time, Shigenobu's initial responsibility in the movement was acting in support functions. During violent protests and clashes with police, Shigenobu along with her female peers would follow the male protesters, providing medical aid to the injured. But Shigenobu also proved her ability to manage meetings as well as to solicit money for the movement.

As the Japanese police strengthened their pressure against the new left movement by arresting its members, Shigenobu, a strong advocate of world revolution, sought to develop ties with guerrilla groups overseas in order to establish an international military base for the movement. At the time, Lebanese militias were inviting foreigners to undertake guerrilla training in order to liberate Palestinians. As Shigenobu perceived this liberation fight was also a fight against imperialism, she moved to Lebanon with some other members in 1971 to prove her theory of world revolution; during this time, she cofounded the Japanese Red Army.

While male members underwent physical and guerrilla training to become revolutionary fighters, Shigenobu produced a book and a film depicting the Japanese Red Army's role in fighting for the Palestinian cause. Despite such efforts for world revolution and armed action by members of the Japanese Red Army, the radical movement in Japan started to self-destruct and lose its power. In 1972, the United Army, another faction of the radical left from which the Japanese Red Army was descended, had a violent purge killing its own members, including Shigenobu's best friend Mieko Toyama (Steinhoff, 1996).

Compelled to show for Japanese radicals "what the true fight is, what the true death is" (Shigenobu, 2001: 80), the Japanese Red Army undertook the terrorist attack at Lod Airport. This random shooting by three members in a baggage claim area was regarded as a major achievement towards the Palestinian cause. While more than two dozen tourists were killed and many more were injured, the Japanese attackers (two died during the attack, while Kozo Okamoto was arrested) were hailed as heroes. As Shigenobu gained celebrity status, her responsibilities as the leader of the Japanese Red Army broadened. Subsequently, the group undertook numerous terrorist attacks involving hijackings and hostage takings throughout the 1970s and 1980s.

Despite the heinous terrorist attacks that Shigenobu orchestrated, a close look at her life reveals her feminine character (Steinhoff, 1996). As male members went through violent clashes with the police, Shigenobu's role to follow the protesters to attend to the injured was a typical responsibility for female members. As she proved her abilities in organizing support functions, she also supervised other female peers. These background support activities by Shigenobu and other women were critical to keeping the new left movement going. Even after she cofounded the Japanese Red Army, her primary responsibilities were public relations, political analysis, recruitment of new members, and solicitation of funding, while male members primarily conducted terrorist attacks. Shigenobu also proved her intellectual abilities by publishing several books on topics including political analyses of Middle Eastern events and theoretical treatises of the Japanese Red Army's position in world revolution.

Furthermore, Shigenobu's feminine character is evident in her decision to return to Japan after more than two decades away during which she was on Interpol's wanted list. As the membership of the Japanese Red Army decreased, she needed to find other people who could take care of Okamoto, whose health condition was deteriorating. Okamoto, arrested in the Lod Airport attack, had been subsequently released through hostage negotiations and was living in Lebanon. Moreover, although Shigenobu's role as a mother had been less known because of her secretive life for safety reasons, her recent biography exhibited her love for her daughter, Mei (Shigenobu, 2001).

Undoubtedly, the Japanese Red Army was a predominantly male organization that implemented numerous terrorist attacks. Nonetheless, Shigenobu achieved her leadership position in the organization by performing distinctively feminine roles. Unlike key males in the new left movement who were often authoritative and assertive, Shigenobu was always cooperative and feminine in the male world of the radical left movement.

Resources

Japan Times. 1972. 3 Japanese kill 26 at Tel Aviv. June 1, p. 1.

Japan Times. 2000. Chronology of the Japanese Red Army. November 9, p. 2.

Japan Times. 2001. Shigenobu declares end of Japanese Red Army. April 16, p. 4.

Japan Times. 2006a. Red Army founder gets 20 years. February 24, p. 1–2.

Japan Times. 2006b. Red Army founder appeals ruling. March 7, p. 2.

Shigenobu, Fusako. 2001. *Ringo no kinoshita de anatawo umouto kimeta* [I decided to give birth to you under the apple tree]. Tokyo, Japan: Gentousha.

Steinhoff, Patricia G. 1996. Three women who loved the Left: Radical woman leaders in the Japanese Red Army movement. In *Re-imaging Japanese women*, ed. Anne E. Imamura, 301–324. Los Angeles: University of California Press.

George Kikuchi, Yoko Baba, and Yumiko Watanuki

Susan Smith (1971–)

Susan Smith, a working-class secretary, lived a dysfunctional life wrought with physical and sexual abuse, psychological illness, and interpersonal relationship problems that culminated in the murder of her own children. Susan Smith (then Susan Vaughan) was born in Union, South Carolina, in 1971 to parents who married young and fought often. Her father created a violent environment at home in which he physically assaulted Susan's mother and threatened to kill her mother and himself. Both Susan and her half brother attempted suicide as children on separate and unrelated occasions. Susan and her brothers lived in fear at home until Susan's parents divorced and her father committed suicide. Weeks later, her mother remarried to a man named Bev Russell who fondled, molested, and sexually assaulted Susan for years. Susan became sexually active early in life with several male coworkers at the local grocery store where she worked. She became pregnant by one married coworker, aborted the baby, and subsequently attempted suicide by ingesting a large dosage of over-the-counter medications. Shortly after her recovery Susan began dating another coworker, David Smith, became pregnant again with his child, and immediately married David in 1991 at the early age of 19. Susan's life continued on a chaotic and traumatic path due to a second pregnancy and a rocky relationship, plagued with many infidelities, which ultimately ended with Susan filing for divorce.

Because David and Susan worked together at the local grocery store, Susan decided to find other employment and secured a job as a secretary for Conso Products, the largest employer in Union, South Carolina. Susan began dating Tom Findlay, the son of the owner of Conso Products; however, he was unprepared to continue the relationship due to the relationship complications posed by her two young boys. Tom Findlay wrote Susan a letter on October 17, 1994, emphasizing that the presence of her children were preventing him from being able to continue a romantic relationship with her. Susan was distraught, depressed, and mentally and emotionally traumatized. A week after receiving the rejection letter, on October 25, Susan Smith put her two children, three-year-old Michael and one-year-old Alex, in the

Susan Smith, center, is escorted out of the Union County Courthouse after a jury delivered a guilty verdict in her murder trial, 1995. (AP/Wide World Photos)

backseat of her car and drove for miles trying to calm herself down. She ended at John D. Long Lake and contemplated suicide. Instead, she positioned the car on the boat docking ramp, exited the vehicle leaving her two sleeping boys in the backseat, closed the car door, and let the car slowly roll into the lake. Susan then ran a quarter mile to a nearby home and hysterically told the residents that a black man hijacked her car with her two children inside.

Susan Smith's story was instantly exposed to the national media. For nine days police investigators were searching for the "missing" boys, and television media and newspaper agencies widely distributed the frenzied and sensationalized story about a black man kidnapping two white children. During this time, many young black men were questioned and targeted by police, and the racial aspect of the crime upset many of Union's residents. David Smith, accompanied by Susan Smith, made a televised plea for the kidnapper to safely return their children. Police investigators immediately became suspicious of Susan Smith's alibi and repeatedly interviewed her about the facts of the case. Both David and Susan were asked to take polygraph tests. David consistently passed polygraph tests whereas the results of Susan's polygraphs were inconclusive. After nine days of investigating, the sheriff again confronted Susan Smith about her involvement in the death of her children, and she confessed to the murder of her children. Susan Smith signed a confession, was arrested, and charged with two counts of murder. She was held without bail at York County Jail. She was then held for eight months before trial at a women's correctional facility in Columbia. During this time, the public expressed outrage over the fabricated racial element and subsequent police targeting of young black males. Susan's brother made a public apology to the black community as well as the larger society for Susan's actions and assured the public that she never intended for her alibi to negatively impact the black community. The black community of Union quickly joined forces toward healing and repairing the social damage and held a town meeting designed to eliminate feelings of pain and racial discrimination and promote reconciliation within all communities.

While awaiting trial, Susan Smith was diagnosed with having dependent personality disorder but was deemed mentally competent to stand trial. On July 10, 1995, her trial began in Union, South Carolina. A jury of seven whites and five blacks were selected, of which nine were male and three were female. Many argued that the trial should have received a change in venue due to the close-knit nature of the city and residents of Union. In fact, many of the jurors knew some of the witnesses who testified in court. Furthermore, others argued that a jury comprised of mostly men would not produce a fair and objective jury given that Susan Smith was a mother who was diagnosed with a mental disorder and who had been sexually victimized during her youth. After the trial, the jury found Susan Smith guilty of murdering her two young sons. Although the prosecution sought the death penalty, the jury declared she would spend her life incarcerated and sentenced her to 30 years to life in prison. Prior to sentencing, Susan's stepfather, Bev Russell, wrote her a letter of apology for sexually abusing her during her childhood. He expressed feelings of guilt for victimizing her and said that he, too, was partly to blame for her actions due to years of abuse.

Susan Smith's chaotic life was riddled with instability, abuse, and terror beginning in early childhood and extending throughout her life. Susan developed a dependent personality disorder and was repeatedly victimized by the men in her life beginning with her father, continuing with her stepfather, and ending with her unhealthy romantic relationships with men outside her family.

Resources

Eftimiades, Maria. (1995). *Sins of the Mother.* New York: St. Martin's Paperbacks.

Rekers, George. (1996). *Susan Smith: Victim or Murderer.* Lakewood, CO: Glenbridge Publishing.

Smith, David, with Carol Calef. (1995). *Beyond All Reason: My Life with Susan Smith.* New York: Kensington Books.

Kathleen A. Fox

Ruth Snyder (1895–1928)

Ruth Snyder murdered her husband in 1927. Her case was publicized widely and she was heavily stigmatized. No one could believe that a woman could commit such a heinous act. Her case was affected by the predominant gender norms on the time and used to justify and reinforce them. Snyder's image was used as an example of what a woman should not be. By vilifying her actions, womanhood was reinstated as something soft, delicate, and never violent.

Growing up, Ruth Snyder had always been an ambitious child. She began working as a telephone operator as the age of 13. She took various classes on business and bookkeeping. She met her husband, Albert Snyder, when she was hired to work for him. Ruth was 20 years old when she married Albert Snyder. Ruth and Albert Snyder lived a suburban life in Queens Village, New York. In 1925 the Long Island

RUTH BROWN SNYDER   HENRY JUDD GRAY

The front page of the *New York Daily News*, 1928, headline read "Dead!" with pictures of Ruth Brown Snyder and Henry Judd Gray, who were executed via the electric chair at Sing Sing Prison for the murder of Albert Snyder. (Library of Congress)

housewife met a corset salesman named Judd Gray. Snyder, who was 32 years old at the time, was a tall, attractive blonde. The two soon realized their sexual attraction and began an affair. Snyder's husband, Albert, worked as the art editor of the magazine *Motorboat* and usually was not home during the day. They had a 9-year-old daughter, Lorraine. Because Lorraine attended school during the day and Albert was not home, Snyder and Gray could meet often. Lorraine was sometimes left at a hotel lobby while they went to a room.

Snyder became bored with her husband, who was 14 years older than she. She suggested that she had been a victim of neglect. Furthermore, Snyder attempted to convince Gray that her husband abused her and must therefore be killed. Gray refused her initial demands. However, in March 1927, Gray accepted Snyder's proposition. They worked out a plan to commit the murder. Gray traveled from Syracuse to New York by train, then took a bus to Long Island. When he got to the Snyder home, he walked around for about an hour drinking from his flask. Finally he entered through the back door as planned. The Snyder family was away at a party and would be gone for a while. Gray hid in a spare room in which Snyder had left a dumbbell, chloroform, and rubber gloves for the murder.

The Snyder family returned from the party at 2:00 AM on March 20, 1927, and Albert Snyder immediately fell asleep. Ruth Snyder, however, found Gray, and the two had sex that night. Afterwards, Gray got the dumbbell weight and went with Snyder to where her husband was sleeping with the blankets over his head. Gray brought down the weight onto Albert Snyder's head. The blow, however, was not strong enough to kill him. He woke up and screamed. Snyder then took the weight and killed her husband herself. The couple also strangled him with picture wire and put a chloroform-soaked cloth in his nose. They then knocked over some things around the house to make it seem as though a robbery had occurred. Snyder's hands and feet were also loosely tied to make it seem as though she was also an innocent victim. Minutes after Gray left, Snyder began banging on nine-year-old Lorraine's door. Lorraine removed the gag from her mother's mouth and was told to go get help: she ran to her neighbor's house and the police were called.

Police began to question Snyder, and she confessed almost at once. However, she claimed that the murder was all Gray's fault. Judd Gray was found hiding in his hotel room and immediately said he had not been to New York. However, his train ticket was found in his trashcan, and he was left with no choice but to confess. Like Snyder, he said it was not his fault and blamed the whole thing on her. The two lovers turned on each other after that, each blaming the other for the murder.

The trial attracted media frenzy. Ruth Snyder and Judd Gray became the center of media attention, as their case monopolized the headlines. Both defendants had different defense attorneys arguing their innocence. Snyder's attorneys, Edgar Hazelton and Dana Wallace, stated that Albert Snyder was not loving or affectionate enough to keep a marriage functioning. They also argued that Judd manipulated Ruth into the crime by setting up a $50,000 double indemnity insurance on Albert Snyder. Hazelton and Wallace attempted to present the image of Snyder as a loving wife and mother. When she took the stand, Snyder presented her own account: she claimed to be a suffering wife. She said that her husband usually ignored her and that it was she who read to Lorraine from the Bible and took her to Sunday School. She stated that it was Gray who tricked her into setting up an insurance policy for her husband. Gray's lawyers, William Millard and Samuel Miller, on the other hand, presented him as a law-abiding citizen who was manipulated by the so-called domineering Snyder. These lawyers suggested that Gray's mind was impaired by passion and lust. Gray, like Snyder, presented an account of himself as an innocent victim. He claimed that Snyder had already attempted to kill Albert Snyder several times before and that it was she who took the insurance policy out. Additionally, he said she had been the one to give the death blow.

The jury was out for an hour and forty minutes and returned with a verdict of "guilty" for both Ruth Snyder and Judd Gray and recommended a punishment of death on May 19, 1927. Ruth Snyder was led to the electric chair at about 11:00 PM on January 12, 1928. She was the first woman since 1899 to die at the Sing Sing Prison's electric chair in New York. At the moment in which the electric current was running through Snyder's body, a photographer named Thomas Howard with a camera strapped to his leg snapped a picture of her death. The image ran in a New York tabloid, *Daily News*, the very next day.

Ruth Snyder's case had a lot to do with gender in the 1920s. There were two images that emerged for Ruth during the trial. One was that of "the Bloody Blonde" who must be put to death because of her crime; the other image was that of the "Marble Woman" who lacked proper feminine emotions and had transgressed gender boundaries (Ramey 2004: 627). Snyder was presented as a cold and unemotional killer. She did not portray culturally defined characteristics of a lady, wife, and mother. Therefore, she was often referred to as a "non-woman" (Ramey 2004: 642). Many reporters used the Snyder case as an example of women threatening the patriarchal order and power in the family as well as the state. A popular novel *Double Indemnity* (1935), written by James M. Cain (which in 1994 was made into a popular and critically acclaimed movie of the same name, starring

Barbara Stanwyck and Fred MacMurray), was based on the story of Ruth Snyder and Judd Gray.

Resources

Noe, Denise. 2011. "The Murder of Albert Snyder." TruTV Crime Library: Notorious Murders; Death in the Family. http://www.crimelibrary.com/notorious_murders/family/al bert_snyder/8.html

Ramey, Jessie. 2004. "The Bloody Blonde and the Marble Woman: Gender and Power in the Case of Ruth Snyder." *Journal of Social History* 37(3): 625–650.

Taylor, Troy. 2004. "The Dumb-bell Murder: The Crime of Ruth Snyder & Judd Gray" http://www.prairieghosts.com/ruth_judd.html

Daniella Reynoso

Kathleen Soliah (1947–)

Kathleen (Ann) Soliah, alias Sara Jane Olson, was finally captured in June 1999 by the FBI for a crime she had committed 23 years earlier. In August 1975, Kathleen Soliah, a member of Symbionese Liberation Army (SLA), had allegedly planted pipe bombs beneath two Los Angeles Police Department (LAPD) marked vehicles. Her arrest made headline news, and "soccer mom" became the media's shorthand for Kathleen Soliah. Those who knew her well were outraged for they believed Soliah was much more complicated than being described as a soccer mom. They said that although Olson shed her real name and background, she never had abandoned her radical ideology.

Soliah was born in 1947 in Fargo, North Dakota. In her middle-class family, she was the eldest child of Marin and Elsie Soliah. Marin was a high school English teacher and Elsie was a homemaker. In the early 1950s Soliah's family moved to Palmdale, California. Growing up, Soliah wanted to be an inspiring actress, so she began to make her childhood dream a reality by taking acting classes at Antelope Valley College. She became interested in political literature and started to develop her views on politics. She then enrolled as a theater major in the University of California, Santa Barbara (UCSB). During this time the vastly published news related to Vietnam War was an important factor in strengthening Soliah's political views.

Soliah's image about law officials changed when a series of demonstrators who were against the war were confronted by law enforcement. When she graduated, Soliah and her boyfriend, Jim Kilgore, who had studied economics at UCSB, moved to Monterey, California, where Soliah was an actress and a part-time waitress. Soliah and Kilgore were introduced into the SLA which was known for its extremist urban guerillas in the 1970s. Soon after becoming a member of SLA, Soliah's sister and brother joined the organization.

In August 1975, Soliah sneaked into the LAPD's parking lot and planted pipe bombs beneath two of the marked police vehicles. However, the pipe bombs that Soliah had planted did not explode. They were discovered after one of the bombs had fallen down, leading to the examination of all the vehicles parked in the department. For Soliah, planting the pipe bombs was a retaliation in response to the Compton shooting, in which six of the SLA members were killed by the LAPD. Two weeks prior to Soliah planting bombs, in a rally held in the Ho Chi Minh Park, Soliah had given a speech in front of a crowd of Berkeley radicals, undercover police, and people who were simply there looking for a familiar face from anti–Vietnam War days. Soliah in her fiery speech said, "I am a soldier of SLA."

Soon after Soliah had planted the pipe bombs under the police cars, she disappeared from California and left to Minnesota, where she legally changed her name to Sarah Jane Olson. Soon, she married her husband Dr. Fred Peterson. The couple lived in Zimbabwe for two years. In Zimbabwe, she worked as an English teacher while her husband practiced medicine. Later, they returned to Minnesota where Olson gave birth to their three daughters. Olson was a stay-at-home mom who was highly engaged in her community. Olson was politically conscious and active; she protested apartheid; rallied against American policy in Central America; helped organized a progressive bookstore; and campaigned for women's rights. According to Olson's parents, their daughter Kathleen never was hiding from the officials. She even visited them in Palmdale and indirectly requested a negotiation with the FBI, but it was denied. However, in May 1999, a viewer recognized Mary Jane Olson's pictures in the *America's Most Wanted* TV show and immediately called the show's hotline from which the federal officials were given tips about Soliah's whereabouts. On June 16, 1999, Soliah's white minivan was surrounded by law enforcement officials and federal agents who were there to capture and book Olson for attempted murder.

During her bail hearing in downtown Los Angeles, 1999, former Symbionese Liberation Army fugitive Kathleen Soliah, accused of planting bombs under police cars 24 years earlier, looks up at her attorney in Federal Court. (AP/Wide World Photos)

Initially, Olson denied the charge. Within days after Olson's arrest, her upper-class neighbors raised a million dollars and bailed Olson out. However, eventually, she acknowledged her crime. The prosecution team was interested in charging Olson with other SLA crimes. Olson retained Stuart Hanlon to defend her. Hanlon had been the defense attorney for Bill and Emily Harris, two of the SLA members who were charged with kidnapping. There were many difficulties and delays during the Olson trial. A number of key witnesses were either dead or close to dying. Olson's case (which in 1975 had 28 witnesses) suddenly became shaky and circumstantial. Olson's defense attorney Hanlon resigned to meet family obligations. At this point, Olson, out of funds, was provided with a public defender, Henry Hall.

During her testimony, Olson expressed remorse for the bombing attempt. "I'm incredibly sorry," Olson said at the hearing. She added "I can't take it back, so I have to take responsibility, and that's what I'm doing now." But she maintained that she was never a member of the leftist 1970s revolutionary group. In February 2003, Olson was sentenced to two consecutive terms of 10 years in prison. Olson served her time at the Central California Women's Correctional Facility in Chowchilla. Her story has continued to receive media attention. She was released from prison on March 17, 2009, and allowed to serve her parole in Minnesota.

Resources

Mackey, Robert. "Former Symbionese Liberation Army Member Released From Prison." *New York Times.* March 17, 2009. http://thelede.blogs.nytimes.com/2009/03/17/former-symbionese-liberation-army-member-to-released/?scp=2&sq=kathleen%20soliah&st=cse

Taylor, Michael. "Ex-Fugitive Soliah Is Released After Posting $1 Million Bail." *San Francisco Chronicle.* July 21, 1999. http://articles.sfgate.com/1999–07–21/news/17693982_1_los-angeles-county-bank-robbery-kathleen-soliah

Ladan Dejam

Bathsheba Spooner (1746–1778)

Bathsheba Spooner was hanged in Worcester, Massachusetts, on July 2, 1778, for murdering her husband. Spooner's execution was remarkable for a few reasons. First, she was the first woman to be executed in the American colonies by colonial citizens rather than the British. Second, she was five months pregnant upon her execution.

Bathsheba Spooner (born Bathsheba Ruggles) was the daughter of two prominent citizens: her father was a descendent of royalty and a general in the army, and her mother was a wealthy land and store owner. She was the favored child out of six, and she grew up in an affluent environment that provided her great wealth and privilege. She married Joseph Spooner at a young age and gave birth to four children, one of which passed away.

Bathsheba reportedly had a great dislike for her husband, found him unmanly, and was utterly repulsed by him. It has also been suggested that he had a severe drinking problem and an affair with their servant. She eventually began an affair with a young revolutionary soldier named Ezra Ross whom she had nursed back to health after a war injury. Bathsheba became pregnant with his child and began to hatch plans to murder her husband. After unsuccessfully trying to convince Ross to kill her husband numerous times, she enlisted the help of two other soldiers to carry out her plans. All three soldiers waited for Joshua Spooner to come home from an evening out, and then they beat him to death. Under Bathsheba's instruction, they later placed him in the family well.

The three men maintain that Bathsheba was the mastermind of the murder plot. She was reportedly sitting behind the curtains of the front door and heard her husband yell out for help but did not help him. After their job was done, the three soldiers reported to Bathsheba that her plan had been executed. Each reported that Bathsheba appeared to be in a high state of confusion. She paid each of them money from a money box that her husband kept upstairs and gave them his clothing. She then asked them to go to the well and fetch some water, seemingly not comprehending why they could not get water from the well. When they explained to her again that her husband was dead and placed in the well, she reiterated that it could not be true. The three men were arrested the next day wearing her dead husband's clothing and shoes and riding her husband's horse. Bathsheba was then arrested and placed in jail for murder.

The three men were indicted on charges ranging from abetting to murder, and Bathsheba was charged with inciting, moving, abetting, counseling, and procuring the murder of her husband. All pled not guilty even though the three men had signed a written confession. They came before the Massachusetts Superior Court, 5 judges, and 12 jurors, and after a one day trial, they were sentenced to hang within two months. Bathsheba requested numerous stays of execution nearly a month later, in the hopes that the court would allow her deliver her child (she was four months pregnant at the time). Her stay of execution was denied, and one month later she was executed. Upon her death an autopsy showed that she was carrying an otherwise healthy baby boy. Reporting of the autopsy was not widely made public until nearly 60 years after her execution.

The Bathsheba Spooner trial has been romanticized and presented in numerous ways over the last 200 years. Her trial took place prior to the constitutional right against self-incrimination, the fundamental right to due process, the right to counsel, the right to appeal, and the ability for a woman to divorce her husband. Each of the individuals had a different role in Spooner's murder, yet they were given the same punishment. Although the confessions of the three men were supposed to be omitted from trial, notes were made by the prosecutor and the judge that referred to their confessions.

As a wealthy, upper-class woman of society who was the daughter of an army general, Bathsheba was expected to live by the gender and class norms of her time period. She was to serve her husband, not be allowed to think independently, and stay in a marriage that was unfulfilling to her. Throughout the trial and execution, Bathsheba refused to admit her guilt and make a public confession. This only added to the impression that she had a "rebellious" nature, for which she had already been known. The midwives and women who examined her for pregnancy had such aversion to her norm violations that they all maliciously agreed that she was not pregnant in order for the execution to take place. Her pregnancy was debated by the judge, viewed by others as an excuse for amoral behavior, became irrelevant for her pleas to extend her life, and was ultimately denied by those within the legal system.

Bathsheba was viewed as, tried as, and hanged as a man. It has been suggested she felt trapped, in despair, and angry at her inability to leave a marriage to a husband she did not love. Bathsheba was the first American woman to be executed by someone other than the British, and she was the first women on record to be executed while pregnant. In the minister's final address to Bathsheba, he commented that it was grievous that society found her in that position as a woman. He then bid her a solemn and final farewell. Her execution became entertainment, was a historical moment, and continues to be debated to this day.

Resources

Bullock, Chandler. (1939). *The Bathsheba Spooner Murder Case*. Worcester, MA. American Antiquarian Society.

Navas, Deborah. (1999). *Murdered By His Wife*. Amherst: University of Massachusetts Press.

Peleg, Chandler. (1844). "The Trial of Mrs. Spooner and Others." *American Criminal Trials*, 2.

Alana Van Gundy-Yoder

Gloria Steinem (1934–)

Gloria Steinem is one of the most widely recognized and influential women of the feminist movement. She is a political activist, an outspoken journalist, and an advocate for the rights of women all over the world. Steinem has spent her life trying to break down gender barriers, and she views crime as being directly impacted by inequality.

Steinem was born in Toledo, Ohio, on March 25, 1934. Born to Ruth Nuneviller and Leo Steinem, she had a tumultuous upbringing that she managed to handle with grace. Her mother suffered from depression and anxiety, and her father traveled as an antique salesman. Leo Steinem eventually divorced Ruth, leaving Gloria to take care of her mother, run and organize the house, pay the bills, and work numerous jobs to provide for her family.

Despite these difficulties, Steinem was elected vice president of her senior class, placed second in a beauty pageant, was an accomplished tap dancer, was chosen as a princess-in-waiting at her high school ball, and was accepted into Smith College, a prestigious women's only college. Her acceptance and graduation from Smith College would prove a pivotal time in her life.

Unlike other women of her time, Steinem did not go to college to be married; she was an accomplished and independent woman who was interested in gaining her education. She majored in government, became active in a democratic political campaign, and spent a year touring Europe. In her senior year of college, she was inducted into

Gloria Steinem is an American feminist, journalist, and a spokeswoman for women's rights. She founded *Ms.* magazine in 1972, the same year this photo was taken. (Library of Congress)

an International National Honor Society and was elected class historian. When Steinem graduated she won a scholarship to study in India and went to study abroad. On her way to India, she stayed with one of her friends who lived in England. During her stay in England, Steinem found out that she was pregnant. After choosing to end her pregnancy, she became empathetic to women's circumstances all throughout the world. It was here that her political crusade began.

Steinem was a leader in the women's movement in many ways. Her most recognized advancement was that of allowing women to control their own bodies. She fought for the poor, the oppressed, and the struggling. In India, she protested government policy regarding the unequal distribution of land and wrote a guidebook for the Indian government. In the United States, she worked for the Independent Service for Information, a group that encouraged youth to discuss democratic ideals. She began publishing articles regarding the treatment of women in the workforce, the way that a woman must choose between a career and a marriage, and the political process. Steinem's broad impact, writing talent, and her utter devotion to her beliefs helped to shatter the world of American women as it was then known.

Steinem cofounded the National Women's Political Caucus, the Women's Action Alliance, and the Coalition of Labor Union Women. She started the magazine

Ms., founded Choice USA and the Ms. Foundation for Women, and actively supported the Equal Rights Amendment. She served on the Democratic National Committee and demonstrated against the impact pornography has on women. Steinem has been an invited guest on many national television shows and has been included in many film documentaries that focus on feminist issues. She has published numerous books and countless articles with a focus ranging from Marilyn Monroe to rebellion and revolution. In 1972 she was named the Woman of the Year by *McCall's* magazine, and in 1993, she was inducted into the National Women's Hall of Fame.

Steinem's advocacy for democracy and equality spilled over to the family and to the educational system. She was a champion for women's and children's rights. Her own abortion allowed her to share the "shame" of women all over the world. She was a leader for the right for women to choose to govern and make decisions for their own body, and as a result of her and many other women's efforts, abortion was decriminalized in the United States. She participated and organized rallies supporting the women's movement. She toured the world lecturing women on their rights (one of those being reproductive freedom), gaining information on their needs, calling for the equal representation of women in all aspects of life, and comforting the oppressed.

Steinem's work for those who had suffered from childhood sexual abuse and domestic violence stemmed from her views on inequality. Steinem viewed crime against women as a way for men to dominate women. She believed that the core of violence against women is when one individual is deemed inferior to another, and the only way for the superior individual to maintain power is through violence. In Western society, males are often encouraged to be violent and their violence may be condoned. Steinem's work within the family structure, political sphere, and educational system has called for society to stop socializing males to think they need to prove masculinity through violence, control, and a lack of emotion. She has called for new laws and legislation that would recognize the seriousness of crimes against women. She has been an advocate against pornography and its exploitation of women. Steinem's epic battle for women's rights has contributed to the decriminalization of abortion, a new viewpoint on the relationship between gender and crime, and work toward a full realization of the Equal Rights Amendment.

Steinem's political activism, while most notably in the area of women's rights, has also included activities protesting other forms of inequality and supporting civil rights. Steinem's only documented arrest came in December, 1984, when she was arrested with 100 other people, including 19 members of Congress, for protesting the United States' export of munitions to the government of South Africa. To this day, Steinem continues to speak out and write about women's and other civil rights issues.

Resources

"Arrested at Embassy." *Gadsden Times*, p. A10. December 20, 1984.

Gilbert, L., and G. Moore. (1981). *Particular Passions*. New York: Clarkson N. Potter.

Heilbrun, Carolyn. (1995). *The Education of A Woman*. New York: Dial Press.

Ladensohn Stern, Sydney. (1997). *Gloria Steinem: Her Passions, Politics, and Mystique*. Secaucus, NJ: Birch Lane Press.

Marcello, P.C. (2004). *Gloria Steinem: A Biography*. Westport, CT: Greenwood Press.

The official Web site of Gloria Steinem. (2010). www.gloriasteinem.com.

Alana Van Gundy-Yoder

Martha Stewart (1941–)

Martha Stewart is a prominent business mogul who rapidly achieved success, fame, and wealth as a result of her efforts as an author, model, stock broker, magazine editor, and television icon. Born to a middle-class family, Martha Stewart (Martha née Kostyra) was taught and perfected homemaking skills including gardening, cooking, sewing, and housecleaning, among a variety of other household abilities.

Martha Stewart is best known as the president, chief executive officer, and host of her own television show *Martha Stewart Living Omnimedia* as well as the editor in chief of her magazine *Martha Stewart Living*. In short, Martha Stewart is a common household name within the United States. Stewart's reputation became even more pronounced after the national media exposed allegations of her involvement with insider trading. Insider trading refers to using material, nonpublic information about a security in order to get an advantage in buying or selling a security when that would be a breach of a fiduciary duty or other relationship of trust and confidence. Insider trading violations can also include providing tips about securities and using such misappropriated tips to

Martha Stewart and her lawyer John Tigue enter U.S. District Court in New York, 2003. Stewart faced trial on charges that she obstructed justice and lied to investigators after the sale of ImClone Systems stock in 2001. (AP/Wide World Photos)

buy or sell securities. The criminalization of Martha Stewart is a celebrated case of white collar crime that has clear implications for discussing gender and crime.

As a former stock broker, Martha Stewart remained avidly engaged as an investor in the stock market. The SEC believed that on December 27, 2001, Martha Stewart engaged in insider trading by allegedly obtaining confidential information from her stockbroker, Peter Bacanovic, regarding the biopharmaceutical company ImClone, in which she held stock. According to the SEC, Bacanovic informed Stewart that the Food and Drug Administration (FDA) had decided to deny ImClone's request to market a new drug called Erbitux. Although this confidential information had not yet been made public, Bacanovic allegedly informed Stewart of this undisclosed fact and Stewart, in turn, instructed Bacanovic to sell all 3,928 of her ImClone shares. Martha Stewart avoided a loss of $45,673 by selling all 3,928 shares of ImClone stock (SEC 2003).

Interestingly, the federal government did not indict or charge Martha Stewart with insider trading. Instead, the SEC filed securities and fraud charges against Martha Stewart on June 4, 2003. According to the SEC, Martha Stewart and Peter Bacanovic fabricated false information (i.e., committed fraud), which was provided to the federal government in an attempt to conceal their engagement in insider trading. Whereas the SEC considered Stewart's and Bacanovic's statements as fraudulent, the two insisted that their original agreement was for Bacanovic to sell all of Stewart's ImClone stocks if the price per stock dropped below $60 per share. On December 28, 2001, ImClone announced the FDA's denial to market the new pharmaceutical drug, and their stock subsequently dropped to $46 per share.

Martha Stewart was obligated to stand trial along with Peter Bacanovic in a federal court for three securities and fraud charges: making false statements, obstruction of justice, and conspiracy. It has been argued that joint trials place defendants at significant disadvantages before and during the trial (Moohr 2006). For example, rules regarding the exclusion of hearsay do not apply in cases where coconspirators are on trial together. Furthermore, juries often have difficulty separating the evidence, testimony, and demeanor of one defendant from the other, which becomes problematic when one defendant has behaved criminally and the other has not. This legal disadvantage significantly affected Martha Stewart as she was found guilty of the perjury Peter Bacanovic committed.

Martha Stewart and Peter Bacanovic were found guilty in federal court, and Stewart was sentenced to 5 months in federal prison followed by 5 months of house arrest and 2 years of probation. Peter Bacanovic received the same incarceration sentence of 10 months (split between prison and house arrest) in addition to a civil penalty of $75,000. As part of a civil settlement, Martha Stewart was also obligated to repay the $45,673 she saved by selling her ImClone stocks along with $12,389 for interest, totaling $58,062. A maximum civil financial penalty of $137,019 was also charged to Stewart which represented three times the amount Stewart initially avoided by selling the stocks. Furthermore, Stewart lost the right to act as director of a public company for 5 years, and limitations on serving or being employed by a public company were imposed on her (SEC 2006). The financial cost endured by Martha Stewart and her company for legal fees, time spent incarcerated, and negative publicity is unknown, although estimates place the number as *exponentially* higher than the financial gain would have been for selling the ImClone stock shares (valued at $45,673).

In light of the fact that 95 percent of all persons charged with crimes plead guilty to (mostly lesser) charges in exchange for lighter punishments, it is remarkable to note that Martha Stewart was one of the few who did not plead, but rather decided to go to trial. The fact that Stewart was not charged for the original crime in which the government believed her to have engaged in (insider trading) is equally peculiar. Explanations for this oddity are unknown, yet speculations have been made regarding insufficient evidence and—even more perplexing—that Stewart did not commit insider trading. For example, Stewart allegedly acted on the nonpublic information that others (namely, Bacanovic) illegally provided. In this respect, Martha Stewart was privy to information that was beyond her own control, whereas her associates proactively broke the law by knowingly informing Stewart of illegal information. Some could argue, then, that other actors are guilty of insider trading and should have received the brunt of the scrutiny and punishment. In spite of this, Martha Stewart received the greater sentence (which tacked on two years of probation) and a fine significantly greater than Bacanovic's fine.

Martha Stewart's gender likely had a substantial influence in this case—from the investigation and the prosecution to the sentencing. It is important to note that engagement in insider trading is certainly not uncommon in business; however, the federal government chose Martha Stewart—a woman—to prosecute. Given that men still outnumber women in business careers, it can be argued that men are more likely to engage in insider trading than women (perhaps due, in part, to opportunity). Prior to the criminal investigation, Martha Stewart was well-known for conducting her business in an authoritative and aggressive fashion which reminded many of the way in which one might see that a *man* would conduct a business. It is certainly possible, many believe, that Stewart's style and behavior was considered threatening to both men and women who may have been uncomfortable with her stereotypically "unfeminine" or less feminine demeanor. Therefore, it is not unreasonable to consider the possibility that Stewart's gender strongly affected decisions made by investigators and other criminal justice actors.

Other scholars have observed that the three charges against Stewart (making false statements, obstruction of justice, and conspiracy) were duplicative in nature, overly aggressive, and excessive (Moohr 2006). It is possible the government (through the SEC) believed her to be an attractive target—a famous female billionaire—whose demise might generally deter potential insider traders. Unfortunately, it is virtually impossible to determine the number of deterred insider traders due to the media exposure of the high-profile Martha Stewart case. Martha Stewart's true criminality is also unknown in terms of her involvement with insider trading as well as fraud. It is, however, obvious that Stewart's ordeal has not deterred her from continuing to pursue her career as magazine editor, television icon, and entrepreneur. After the years of negative media publicity, the charges, the trial, and the five months in federal prison, Stewart continues today to embody a successful professional who is relatively unscathed by the chain of events known to some as the "criminalization of Martha Stewart."

Resources

Moohr, Geraldine Szott. (2006). What the Martha Stewart Case Tells Us About White Collar Crime. *Houston Law Review 43*(3): 591–619.

U.S. Securities and Exchange Commission. (2003, June 4). SEC Charges Martha Stewart, Broker Peter Bacanovic with Illegal Insider Trading. http://www.sec.gov/news/press/2003–69.htm

U.S. Securities and Exchange Commission. (2006, August 7). Martha Stewart and Peter Bacanovic Settle SEC's Insider Trading Charges. http://www.sec.gov/news/press/2006/2006–134.htm

Kathleen A. Fox

Lucy Stone (1818–1893)

Lucy Stone was a well-known suffragist during the 19th century. Although she was known for her work on women's rights, she is perhaps most notorious for being the first woman in the United States to retain her maiden name after marriage. Her very controversial and public stances on slavery and women's rights (particularly in marriage) made her vulnerable to criticism, ostracism, and public scrutiny which led her into conflict with the law.

Lucy Stone was born in the farming community of West Brookfield, Massachusetts, in 1818. Lucy was the eighth of nine children born in the Stone household; however, two siblings had died prior to her birth. Of the Stone siblings, she was closest in age to her older brother by two years, Luther. It was with him who she would begin a rivalry until she left home. Literary accounts maintain that Lucy was smarter and more outgoing than her older brother; however, it seemed that no matter how hard she tried, her brother was always favored by her parents and praised for his scholarly achievements. Lucy had not realized that it was expected for boys to receive an education, but girls were to remain at home and tend to domestic matters until it was time to marry. This was definitely not the life that Lucy had dreamed.

From an early age, she had witnessed the power that men held over their wives and resolved never to marry.

An education was deemed unnecessary in a girl's life, and they often quit school at an early age. At age 12, Lucy had to persuade her father to allow her to continue her education. Since there was no money for her education, and her father refused any support in her education, Lucy began teaching in the district schools to save money for her education. She was able to attend school by alternating working and attending seminary. Lucy Stone entered Mount Holyoke Female Seminary in 1839. At Mount Holyoke, she realized that she wanted a formal education rather than one that encouraged women to stay in their place as an unequal partner to man. It took her several years to

Lucy Stone in a photo taken sometime between 1840 and 1860. (Library of Congress)

save enough money to pay for her first year at Oberlin College, the first college to admit both women and blacks. Oberlin was more conservative than Stone's liberal ideology. Stone was an ardent reader of the works of Garrison and the Grimkés; however, the college did not support confronting slavery and women's rights head on, ideas that were considered outlandish at the time. It was at Oberlin that Stone decided she would become a women's rights reformer and began speaking on the subject. On August 25, 1847, Lucy Stone received her diploma from Oberlin College and became the first woman from Massachusetts to receive a college degree. She had to boycott the writing of her graduation essay since women were not allowed to read in public at a "gentlemen's meeting." It is ironic that 36 years later she would return to Oberlin as a guest speaker.

Upon her graduation, Stone returned home and began teaching. However, she did not take long to return to public speaking. Stone's first public speaking engagement on women's rights paradoxically occurred in her brother Bowman's Evangelical Congregational Church. Her speeches would lead to great controversy in the small Massachusetts towns. Although the women's rights movement was Stone's passion, she began working as a lecturer for the Massachusetts Anti-Slavery Society. Stone was able to argue that antislavery and women's rights were twin causes. However, when this approach created controversy with the Anti-Slavery Society, she began speaking about each issue separately until she eventually dedicated all her time to lecturing on women's rights. Stone became a very popular orator, and her name was used to draw audiences across the country to women's rights conferences. She soon became the face of the National Woman Suffrage Association (NWSA).

In 1851, Stone spoke before the Massachusetts legislature in an attempt to convince the state body to pass a constitutional amendment to grant women full civil rights. She failed in her objective for a state constitutional amendment. However, it was here that she met Henry Blackwell. Although she had vehemently objected to the institution of marriage, Henry Blackwell convinced Lucy Stone to marry him after a two-year courtship. On their wedding day, they read a protest recognizing that women remained an independent being rather than a possession upon marriage. Lucy Stone became the first woman in the United States to not take her husband's name. This caused a great amount of controversy in the media; however, the greatest controversy over the marriage was within Stone's own circle. Many in the NWSA felt she had betrayed their cause by getting married and feared she would abandon the plight of women altogether. Although Stone remained committed to obtaining equality and continued to lecture, she continued to be questioned about her commitment especially with the birth of her first and only child, Alice Stone Blackwell. With the birth along with illnesses that plagued the family, Stone had to cut back on her lectures. This created such turmoil that she finally turned over the NWSA helm to Elizabeth Cady Stanton.

The cutback in the frequency of Stone's public speaking did not keep her from engaging in protest against a system that favored men. After the birth of their child, Stone's husband left frequently on business, leaving her to largely raise the child alone. During this time in 1858, Stone protested a property tax assessment claiming that it represented taxation without representation as women were not allowed to vote. Law enforcement was sent to her home, and some of her furniture was confiscated for auction. The revenue from this auction met the tax bill, and Stone was not pursued any further by tax officials. The publicity from her refusal to pay tax provided a visible focus for the cause of women's rights and became the material of continued legend.

Stone's antislavery opinions were well known publicly. In 1856, she was accused in court of supplying a knife to a former slave, Margaret Garner, who had killed her own child to prevent its being enslaved. While Stone escaped formal charges, she stated that she agreed with the passion of this woman to free her child through death when there would be no freedom in a life in slavery. Stone engaged in a great deal of public speaking and, by the Civil War, devoted all her time to the antislavery movement. When the war ended, she campaigned for an amendment to grant all people equality; however, to her dismay, when the Fourteenth Amendment was passed by Congress, it introduced the word "male" into the Constitution. Deeply hurt by this setback, Stone still supported the ratification of both the Fourteenth and Fifteenth Amendments. It was this act that created a bitter division between her and her allies, Susan B. Anthony and Elizabeth Cady Stanton. This division led to the creation of the American Woman Suffrage Association (AWSA). It approached the women's rights movement more conservatively than the NWSA which was led by Anthony and Stanton. In 1870, she, along with her husband, founded the *Woman's*

Journal, considered by many to be the voice of the women's movement. It took over 20 years for the AWSA and NWSA to reconcile their differences and begin, once again, to fight for the same goal: women's rights. Lucy Stone died three years later in 1893 never seeing her dream come to fruition; it would take almost three decades after her death for women to receive the right to vote. This great feat would have never been achieved without the work and dedication of Lucy Stone, and thus, she will always be remembered for her commitment to the women's rights movement.

Resources

Blackwell, Alice Stone. 1971. *Lucy Stone, pioneer of woman's rights.* New York: Kraus Reprint.

Hays, Elinor Rice. 1961. *Morning Star: A Biography of Lucy Stone 1818–1893.* New York: Harcourt, Brace, and World.

Kerr, Andrea Moore. 1992. *Lucy Stone: Speaking out for equality.* New Brunswick, NJ: Rutgers University Press.

Million, Joelle. 2003. *Woman's voice, woman's place: Lucy Stone and the birth of the woman's rights movement.* Westport, CT: Praeger.

Tammy S. Garland

Mary Surratt (1823–1865)

Mary Elizabeth Jenkins Surratt was the first woman ever to be executed in the United States. She was charged and convicted as a conspirator in the plot to assassinate President Lincoln and was hanged on July 7, 1865. Her relationship with John Wilkes Booth and her familiarity with the other conspirators established her guilt. A public that was war weary and outraged by Lincoln's assassination observed the newspaper accounts of her closely. These daily reports portrayed her with the features of a criminal and exaggerated her physical stature to create an image that fit what, at the time, was the face of a murderer (Larson 2008). These distortions reflect the social perceptions of Mary Surratt's crime: a woman who was involved in politics and conspiracy was monstrous.

Mary Surratt was born in 1823 in Waterloo, Maryland. Her mother, widowed when Mary was two, remained independent, raising her children and managing a plantation and slaves on her own. She provided her daughter with an example of a woman who succeeded on her own. Mary was educated in a Catholic girls' school and became a devout Catholic, a fact that might have contributed to prejudices against her by the Protestant tribunal.

She married John Surratt in 1840. It was Mary who managed their affairs, and perhaps, his death was a relief to her as his alcoholism led to financial sacrifices and to abuse (Larson 2008). By this time, most of the land John Surratt had acquired was leased or in second mortgages, and the tavern they owned was operated by John Lloyd, who became a key witness against Mary. To maintain financial stability was a struggle, and Mary Surratt opened a boarding house in Washington DC. One of her frequent visitors was her son John's friend, John Wilkes Booth. This relationship with Booth determined her guilt. Mary Surratt, as President Andrew Johnson stated, "kept the nest that hatched the egg" (cited in Larson 2008).

Mrs. Surratt was seen as guilty long before her trial. She disregarded the boundaries of her woman's role of dependence upon the protection and support of a man. Mary Surratt's life choices contradicted the basic myths of the Southern woman as docile, delicate, and confined to the home. Contemporary historians of Southern women's history, as well as current research into the Civil War era, have documented that the notions of separate spheres and women's domesticity were powerful ideologies of the time, though they were often undermined by women's participation in the war as blockade runners and spies (Rable 1989). The belief that women were vulnerable and that their interests were confined to the home gave these Confederate agents and spies protection from suspicion. Mary Surratt, dedicated to the Southern cause, was in the position to aid and abet those agents and spies, including her son and his friend John Wilkes Booth.

Mary's son John took over the responsibilities his father had been given as a postmaster in the town named for him, Surrattsville. This appointment gave John the opportunity to serve the Confederacy as a courier. His activities for the Confederacy led to his meeting with Booth and confirmed suspicions of Mary's contributions to the conspiracy.

Mary Surratt was frequently visited by Booth in the absence of her son. It was well-known that John assisted Booth with the original plan to kidnap Lincoln. That Booth met with Mary during this time was considered proof that she knew of the proposed attack against Lincoln. On the day of the assassination, April 14, 1865, Booth handed her a wrapped package that she was to give to John Lloyd who had possession of the weapons that would be used. This package contained field glasses, but Mary's errand included informing Lloyd to have the guns ready. This was given as evidence that Mary conspired in the assassination. It has been this fact that continues to be contested.

Mary Surratt's visibility as a woman who violated the codes of domesticity may have contributed to her conviction. Women's historians, however, have argued for Mary Surratt's guilt without much discussion of her vulnerability as a woman who disregarded her place. Among these historians, Kate Larson, in *The Assassin's Accomplice* (2008), has noted that Mary Surratt was motivated as a conspirator by her allegiance to the Confederacy. However, the evidence of the case against Mary Surratt depended upon the testimonies of several men without any letters, papers, or physical and material evidence to prove her guilt. It was only years later, during the trial of John Surratt Junior, that evidence seemed to determine Mary's guilt (Larson 2008).

Yet, in 1865, gender was a factor in Mary Surratt's conviction. David DeWitt, who recorded the proceedings in *The Judicial Murder of Mary E. Surratt* (1895), referred again and again to Mary Surratt's unimpeachable faith, a faith characteristic of true femininity. According to DeWitt, it was incontrovertible evidence that a woman, who in her final confession to her priest declared her innocence, must be innocent. Surratt's lawyers based their defense on her femininity. A devout woman, they claimed, was incapable of a crime leading to murder. The attorneys called character witnesses and priests to prevail upon the judges.

In the highly controversial request for pardon issued to President Andrew Johnson, it has been demonstrated that whether or not he reviewed the proposal in time, there was the fear that a pardon based upon her womanhood would set a precedent for exonerating all women in cases of serious crime (Busch 1957).

The claim of her attorney Reverdy Johnson at the opening of the trial still had the potential, however, to exonerate her. A military tribunal was, according to Reverdy Johnson, inappropriate. A panel of military men, still reeling from the slaughter of war and the public horror at the assassination of Lincoln, was biased. If indeed, Lincoln's death was a war crime, the provisions of such a tribunal were responsible for Mary's conviction. According to Francis X. Busch in *Enemies of the State* (1957), both John Lloyd and Louis Weichmann, the key witnesses whose testimonies condemned Mary, were excluded from criminal charges by testifying in the trial. These men knew Booth and John Surratt, as well as George Azerodt and Lewis Powell, two other conspirators.

Lloyd in fact waited for Booth to pick up the package from Mary. He had hidden the "shooting irons" Booth used (DeWitt 1895). Weichmann, living in the house and friends with John, may have known more than he admitted. In DeWitt's primary account and according to other historians, Lloyd's credibility was undermined by his drunkenness. The record has demonstrated inconsistency about whether Lloyd was too drunk to understand Mary's instructions concerning the guns. During the trial, however, Weichmann was characterized as a serious student of theology and allied with the Union's cause; Lloyd was sober enough to repair Mary's wagon and right minded enough to identify her role in the conspiracy.

Whether or not Mary Surratt actively participated in the conspiracy to assassinate President Lincoln now seems more uncertain. But outrage and fear about her crime were inseparable from the outrage, fear, and instability that reigned at the conclusion of the Civil War, which assured her conviction. As a woman and with the reputation of a political activist who acted with criminal intent, the trial of Mary Surratt further destabilized a society that depended on women staying in their place. The sentiment after her execution, therefore, was one of horror and remorse: a woman should not have suffered the same indignity as a man, and a woman should not be guilty of murder.

Resources

Busch, Francis X. (1957). *Enemies of the State*. London and Melbourne: Arco Publications.

DeWitt, David Miller. (1895). *The Judicial Murder of Mary E. Surratt*. Baltimore: John Murphy.

Larson, Kate. (2008). *The Assassin's Accomplice*. New York: Basic Books.

Moore, Guy W. (1954). *The Case of Mrs. Surratt*. Norman: Oklahoma University Press.

Rable, George C. (1989). *Civil Wars: Women and the Crisis of Southern Nationalism*. Urbana: University of Illinois Press.

"Surratt House Museum." www.surratt.org

Mrs. Surratt's Story. http://www.surratt.org/su_hist.html

Susan Bohrer

Aung San Suu Kyi (1945–)

Dr. Aung San Suu Kyi is an internationally renowned opposition leader in Burma and, until late 2010, an imprisoned Nobel laureate. Her formal name combines those of her father Aung San, founder of the Burmese army; her mother Khin Kyi, an early voice for Burmese democracy; and her grandmother Suu, mother to three anticolonial activists. Her country's name entails contention, having been changed to the Union of Myanmar in 1989 through a military-run process of expunging labels given during its colonial history. But she is listed in several places—including a list of proposed United Nations secretaries-general, compiled by human rights group Equality Now—as Prime Minister-Elect of Burma Daw Suu Kyi. Though elected by a landslide popular vote in 1990, she has been unable to serve and is usually under house arrest. In that she violated Myanmar law, she is technically a criminal, but she is also a victim of Myanmar sanctions, which are illegal.

The leader of the National League for Democracy, Aung San Suu Kyi was placed under house arrest by the military government of Myanmar in 1989; she was released from house arrest in May 2002 and then rearrested in May 2003. (AFP/Getty Images)

Suu Kyi's father was born into a resistance movement and widely involved in efforts against British rule throughout the 1930s. He led an "independence" army from Japanese-occupied Thailand in March 1942 to end British rule, only to see Japanese rule begin. Though Japan declared Burma nominally independent in August

1943, he led a new revolt two years later that made that separation final—only to see British rule return again. While recovering from leading the march into Burma in 1942, Aung San met senior nurse Ma Khin Kyi at the Rangoon General Hospital. They married within months and had four children in rapid succession. On June 19, 1945, British Commonwealth forces invaded Thailand from Burma. That same day, Aung San's third child and only daughter was born. Of the two brothers, Lin drowned at age eight and Oo moved to San Diego, California. Aung San was assassinated July 19, 1947, only months before Burma's independence was complete, leaving two-year-old Suu Kyi as the political heir to a decades-long struggle for Burmese self-determination.

Following the assassination, Khin Kyi became involved in social planning and policy before being appointed ambassador to India. Suu Kyi accompanied her there and attended high school and college in New Delhi before going to Oxford University. She received a degree in philosophy, politics, and economics from St. Hugh's College. There, she met Michael Aris who was studying Tibetan civilization, and they married in 1972. (In the interim, she had gone to New York for graduate study. However, she was living with Ma Than E, a family friend and staff member at the United Nations, whose secretary-general at the time was U Thant of Burma. Suu Kyi had quickly become involved in UN activities, both formally and as a volunteer.) She spent most of the next 18 years in England where Aris took a position at Oxford University. She bore two sons, Michael in 1974 and Kim in 1977. Suu Kyi then completed her PhD from the University of London and began writing, first three travel books aimed at juveniles and then a journal article on "Socio-Political Currents in Burmese Literature." She has since authored or co-authored a dozen books, all regarding the life she has led *since* her family years in London.

Both Suu Kyi and Burma changed course in 1988: She returned home to Rangoon in March when her mother had a stroke, only months before the resignation of General U NeWin, who had been the military dictator since 1962. Public demonstrations grew throughout the summer and came to a head in a violent revolt on August 8 (the so-called 8888 Uprising), which was met with military opposition that killed an estimated thousands of protesters. Suu Kyi entered the political arena within a week; in an August 15 open letter to the government, she called for multiparty elections. On August 26, she gave a speech to hundreds of thousands of demonstrators, calling for a democratic government. On September 18, the military performed a bloody coup, rebranded the Burmese Socialist Programme Party as the State Law and Order Restoration Council (SLORC), and imposed martial law, including arresting and sentencing without trial as well as prohibiting political assemblies of more than four people. Within one week, and in direct defiance, Suu Kyi formed the National League for Democracy (NLD), named herself general-secretary, and began a national speaking tour.

The next year began with her mother's funeral. Throughout spring and summer, Suu Kyi continued to endure harassment and violence from state troops, and on July 20, 1989, she was given her first house arrest. She had grown bold during 10 months of appearances, including once walking directly toward guns pointed at her, and her violation of new martial restrictions finally attracted sanctions. However, though martial law permitted three years of detention without a charge or trial, she would be held for six, monitored for five, then re-detained on September 23, 2000. As the result of covert UN negotiations, she was released May 20, 2002. She attracted supportive crowds wherever she appeared. She was re-arrested May 30, 2003, following a military attack in which many of her supporters were wounded or killed.

Her most recent detention has been extended three times: first, despite direct opposition from UN Secretary-General Kofi Annan; second, in violation of both Burmese and international law; and third, for permitting an American man who had sneaked into her house to remain for several days. (The latter extension came only weeks before her most recent statutory detention would have ended, raising suspicion about its motives. Originally, a three-year sentence to hard labor, it was commuted by the junta under international pressure. The intruder received a seven-year prison sentence, which was not commuted.) She was thus under house arrest until her release on November 13, 2010, by the generals who held her captive. Since 1989, she had been confined for all but six-and-a-half years.

Despite her initial detention, the NLD won 59 percent of the vote and over 80 percent of the parliamentary seats (394 out of 492) in a May 27, 1990, election, compared to only 10 seats (less than 3%) for the military's National Unity Party. However, SLORC refused to acknowledge those results and prohibited the NLD from forming a new government, helping attract a steady stream of formal international opposition. Suu Kyi has received several dozen commendations for her persistence, including the Sakharov Prize (1990), the Nobel Peace Prize (1991), the Simon Bolivar International Prize (1992), the Honorary Companion of the Order of Australia (1996), the Presidential Medal of Freedom (2000), the UNESCO Madanjeet Singh Prize for the Promotion of Tolerance & Non-Violence (2002), the Gwangju Prize for Human Rights (2004), the Congressional Gold Medal (2008), and the Mahatma Gandhi International Award for Peace and Reconciliation (2009). Throughout this period, she has continued writing and pushing for democracy.

In awarding its prize in 1991, the Nobel Committee referred to Suu Kyi's struggle as "one of the most extraordinary examples of civil courage in Asia in recent decades" (Norwegian Nobel Committee, 1991). (She used the prize money to create a health and education trust in Burma.) A delegation of Nobel laureates, denied entry into Burma in 1993, began a long series of high-profile pleas for her release, including UN delegations in 2004, 2006, and 2008. (A 2009 visit was cancelled by the junta.) She has received international support from dozens of nations and organizations, including Freedom Forum, the Human Rights Action Center, International

IDEA, and Amnesty International, which has deemed her case a priority. Her forced seclusion has been represented by an empty chair at meetings of the Elders, created and led by Nelson Mandela, and by an empty car in a Chrysler advertisement featuring Nobel laureates. She has even been celebrated in popular media, including the 1995 movie *Beyond Rangoon* about the 8888 Uprising, as well as popular songs by U2, Damian Rice, and State Radio.

However, international reactions have not been universally critical of the Myanmar government. Leaders in both Thailand and Vietnam have opposed both support for Suu Kyi and a focus on her in relations with Burma. Several UN resolutions have been opposed by China, which continues a close political and economic relationship with the military junta. The junta itself fears support for her and has said she is a danger to the stability and community peace in Burma. It has, however, paid costs for her continued isolation. For example, in the fall of 2007, it brutally ended protests by Buddhist monks when one group reached her gate, leading to international critique. The junta has also tried leveraging access to her for its own benefit. Suu Kyi has encouraged international sanctions against Burma and discourages tourism to and investment in the country. A one-hour meeting with foreign diplomats on October 9, 2009, was thus permitted by government leaders, who themselves are restricted by current financial and travel restrictions. However, the only political aftermath was a resolution by ASEAN (Association of Southeast Asian Nations) against Suu Kyi's imprisonment.

Multiparty elections were held November 7, 2010—the first since those Suu Kyi won 20 years earlier; however, the elections attracted both domestic and international criticism. Suu Kyi's own party, the NLD, had been formally disbanded when it chose to boycott the elections, refused to register by the May 6 deadline, and was disqualified. NLD members who opposed the boycott created and registered the national Democratic Force on July 11, using NLD's bamboo hat icon. (Suu Kyi had opposed splintering the opposition any further, in a field that already has 40 parties, 6 government related.) Ultimately, the election was cancelled in many areas; turnout was under 20 percent in remaining areas; and charges of fraud, bribery, and intimidation were rampant.

Suu Kyi's most recent detention, six days later, occurred after seven years of confinement to a dilapidated lake house that lost its roof and electricity during a spring 2008 storm and had since gone unrepaired. While detained, she released some video statements and wrote for her own website, but she was permitted only limited contact with others and was subject to ongoing condemnation through state-run media. At a rally less than a week after her release, she called for unity—welcomed by the NLD, which has referred to her not only as their leader but as an inspiration for democracy. She remains without her children, who live in London, and her husband, who died of prostate cancer in 1999 after being permitted only five visits with her in 10 years.

Resources

Ling, Bettina. 1998. *Aung San Suu Kyi: Standing Up for Democracy in Burma (Women Changing the World Series)*. New York: Feminist Press of CUNY.

Norwegian Nobel Committee. 1991. "The Nobel Peace Prize." www.nobelprize.org/nobel_prizes/peace/laureates/1991/press.html.

Suu Kyi, Aung San. 1998. *Letters from Burma*. New York and London: Penguin.

Victor, Barbara. 2002. *The Lady: Aung San Suu Kyi: Nobel Laureate and Burma's Prisoner.*, Boston and London: Faber & Faber.

Wintle, Justin. 2007. *The Perfect Hostage: A Life of Aung San Suu Kyi*. London: Hitchinson.

Ellis Godard

T

Gwen Taketa (1947–)

Gwen (Fumiko) Taketa was found guilty of five felony counts relating to illicit drugs by a Hawaii jury in March 1986. Her conviction made her a rare inmate in the state's female prison because she was unlike the other inmates in that she was a successful college-educated Japanese businesswoman with no prior criminal history (des Marets, 2006). Prosecutors, however, painted her as a drug kingpin (nicknamed the Ice Queen), who had to be dealt with harshly despite her gender, race, and noncriminal background to stem drug trafficking in the state.

Born in 1947, Taketa was the first of six children. Her father was a Maui plantation supervisor in their single paycheck family. Parent-child ties were close; even her lesbianism was quietly accepted. Scholastically she excelled, having had since grade school, college as a goal. Her parents had only high school education.

Taketa's peers were from similar middle-class backgrounds whose delinquencies involved underage cigarette smoking, beer drinking, and drag racing—all just for fun for which the police gave only warnings. They never identified themselves as a female gang defying the system.

Taketa thus lived a normal life, upholding cultural expectations of a Japanese family with its stress on filial piety, achievement, and community. Her strong involvement with family, school, and relatively law-abiding peers and her positive self-concept and realistic educational goals insulated her from any serious delinquency during this period.

Leaving college life after earning a bachelor's in communication, however, exposed her to a more deviant world—the local drug scene in Waikiki's gay bars. Partying with drugs became an almost weekly fun activity, but eventually it grew costly. Taketa decided to develop her own contacts to buy wholesale rather than pay $5 per pill, $20 per bag of marijuana, and $50 per half gram of cocaine. Eventually, she set up buys for her friends, taking a cut for this freelancing service. Taketa doesn't recall who most influenced her transformation as a drug dealer. No other family member used drugs or was a criminal. She admits being the only black sheep.

Recalling the events leading up to her arrest, Taketa claimed she was entrapped by an acquaintance that had promised to deliver a kilo of cocaine. The shipment, however, was intercepted by the DEA, and her acquaintance was co-opted to set up a sting, but Taketa didn't buy the poor quality cocaine. The next day she was nevertheless arrested, with the DEA confiscating about 200 Quaalude pills, some marijuana bags, and a couple of grams of cocaine. Out on $10,000 bail, Taketa was indicted a year later on two Class A felonies relating to the promotion of controlled substances (20 years imprisonment for each count); one Class B felony relating to conspiracy to promote drugs (10 years); and two Class C felonies relating to the possession of drug paraphernalia (5 years each). Between her arrest and trial, her life was in limbo; she wasn't working as a sales rep for tourist items any longer, and partying definitely wasn't enjoyable anymore. Under possible surveillance, she had to stay out of further trouble. Nevertheless, in March 1986, she was convicted and received the unexpected consecutive sentence of 60 years, not the usual 20 years or even probation that such offenses usually elicited for first-timers. Taketa felt that she was dealt a harsher sentence because she was not the stereotypical Asian female and especially because a lesson had to be taught about drug trafficking in the state.

Her assessment of her prison experience, however, was that it was a good adventure, made more memorable by lesbian friendships, though banned, and easier by inmates showing her how to survive inside the walls. In exchange, given her higher education, Taketa became their legal advocate, filing so many inmate complaints and requests that the system was overwhelmed. Understanding the inmate subculture with its expectations of sisterhood and family, Taketa risked negative stigmatization as a troublemaker and harassment by the guards. By manipulating the system's need for order, she was able to set up dances and fundraisers for playground and library needs, and she even sold contraband to inmates becoming known, as a result, as their godmother.

To further avoid the boredom of prison routines, Taketa continued her formal education, earning a Phi Beta Kappa key and an associate's degree in the process. By doing so, she effectively bridged her pre-arrest and post-arrest life by maintaining some role continuity through her educational and entrepreneur endeavors and by participating in the close-knit inmate community with its system of exchanges and lesbian relationships. Prison deprivations were consequently minimized by her new lesbian friendships, power and status enhancement as an inmate, and by downplaying her loss of freedom and her stigmatic status as a convicted felon.

Serving only 5 years, Taketa received an early parole (Lee, 2006); while on parole, she earned a master's in social work and became an employment specialist for a private social service agency. After 13 years there, she left to become a counselor with the state despite her criminal past. She realizes today that such stigmatization will remain an indelible part of her life. She was finally discharged from her parole in February 1995 (Lee, 2006).

Resources

Becker, Gay. 1997. *Disrupted Lives.* Los Angeles: University of California Press.

Des Marets, Jo. 2006. Face-to-face Interview. Hawaii Paroling Authority. Honolulu, Hawaii.

Lee, Donna. 2006. Telephone Interview. Hawaii Paroling Authority. Honolulu, Hawaii.

Taketa, Gwen. 1990. "How I Spent My Summer Vacation, Or Da Secret Sex Lives of Da Little Green Things." Unpublished essay.

Taketa, Gwen. 2006. Interviews, emails, phone calls between July 2006 and January 2007. Honolulu, Hawaii.

Deanna Chang

Marybeth Tinning (1942–)

Marybeth Tinning, a female serial murderer, killed eight of her children, from 1972 to 1985, all by suffocation. Tinning exhibited many of the characteristic traits of Munchhausen syndrome by proxy, as she, the killer, not only received attention from being pregnant but also from the eventual sudden deaths of her children. Her case is significant as all murder victims were either diagnosed with SIDS (sudden infant death syndrome) or Reye's syndrome. In essence, any investigation into murder was curtailed once the diagnoses was offered, thus allowing Marybeth to continue to bear and adopt children whom she would eventually kill.

Not much is known about Tinning's childhood. Marybeth Tinning lived in the small town of Schenectady, New York, in a modest apartment with her husband and two children. Tragedy befell Tinning when her father died suddenly of a heart attack, in November 1971, when she was seven months pregnant with her third child. This child, Jennifer, was born December 26, 1971, but survived only one week succumbing to hemorrhagic meningitis on January 3, 1972. It has been suggested that the attention she received at this time as the result of these two very sudden and unexpected deaths gave Tinning attention she craved. Although there is no real evidence of Munchhausen syndrome in Tinning prior to this time, it was very shortly after the death of this infant that the outward behaviors of Munchhausen syndrome by proxy began to emerge.

Seventeen days after the death of Jennifer, her youngest boy, Joey, suddenly died. Tinning reported that he went into convulsions and then suddenly stopped breathing. He had been brought in days earlier with similar symptoms. The hospital staff diagnosed Joey's death as Reye's syndrome, a relatively newly discovered disease in 1972. Six weeks later, Barbara Tinning was brought into the hospital and died under identical circumstances as Joey, with an identical diagnosis.

Four months later, in July 1972, the Tinnings were approved to foster a 10-year-old girl. Tinning started to exhibit bizarre behavior. In the restaurant where she worked, fellow waitresses reported that she was constantly looking for approval and lied about being pregnant. She came to work with her hair dyed drastically different colors, with no or partial eyebrows, often penciled in with great, big, black lines.

The foster child was sent back after Timothy was born in December 1973. Timothy was found lifeless in his crib three weeks later. Timothy was labeled a victim of SIDS, another disease newly discovered in the early 1970s. Suspicion around these deaths began to grow between medical staff in both local hospitals. Shortly after Timothy's funeral, Marybeth Tinning's husband was taken to hospital from an overdose of phenobarbital, which his wife had also had access to. Hospital staff assumed it was an attempted suicide. Earlier that night he had mentioned to his brother that his food had tasted bitter.

Nathan was born healthy on March 30, 1975. Doctors tested Nathan for genetic defects, but test results were negative. Tinning declined an offer for an apnea monitor, which could warn Tinning when the child had stopped breathing. Nathan stopped breathing five months later while Tinning was driving. In early spring of 1978, Joe and Marybeth Tinning were approved for the adoption of a child, Michael. However, while waiting for the adoption to go through, she became pregnant. Michael came to the house during Tinning's pregnancy. Mary Francis was born October 29, 1978, and died January 20, 1979. Again, the doctors suggested the apnea monitor, but she refused.

After supposedly being surgically sterilized, she became pregnant again. Jonathan was born November 19, 1979. He was brought into the emergency twice within 11 weeks for similar symptoms. Doctors looking over this case did not feel that SIDS was a reasonable diagnosis for several reasons and began to suspect foul play. This was followed by the sudden death of adopted Michael in February 1981. An autopsy revealed pneumonia, thus hampering any further investigation around this death.

Marybeth Tinning's last child, Tami Lynne, was born August 22, 1985. She too died like the others. However, enough evidence was collected to charge Tinning. She was found guilty of depraved indifference to human life and was sentenced to 20 years to life in prison. Over the course of the trial, she admitted to the smothering of Tami Lynne, Timothy, and Nathan only. She was never tried for the other deaths. In 2009, she was denied parole, with the parole board noting that she continued to be a danger to society ("Marybeth Tinning Loses Parole Bid," 2009). She was once again denied in 2011.

Marybeth Tinning is led from Schenectady County Court by Sheriff Bernard Waldron, 1986. Although nine of Tinning's young children died over the course of 14 years, she was formally charged with only one death. (AP/Wide World Photos)

This case is significant in that the notoriety of the case sparked investigation and research into SIDS and Reye's syndrome. These diagnoses had hampered investigation in what eventually became obvious: Marybeth was killing her children. She was also exhibiting classic symptoms of Munchhausen syndrome by proxy, whereby an individual craves attention, usually medical, but acquires it through the harm of others. Child death cases in which diagnoses of SIDS or Reye's syndrome were made were re-examined, as a result of this case and others like it, for potential homicidal behavior in many Western nations. Policies around the treatment of children in hospitals, presenting with similar symptoms as all eight of Marybeth's victims, were also re-examined in many hospitals.

This case also highlights the power of gender roles, and specifically the role of motherhood, in the case of homicides such as these. In retrospect, it was obvious that Marybeth was killing her children. Hospital personnel in this case became blinded by the fact that the woman who was bringing in these lifeless little bodies was the mother of these children. Under any other circumstances, foul play would have been suspected. The possibility that she may be harming her own children was not even considered until it was proven that seven of her children, including her adopted child, were murdered instead of dying from diseases thought to be genetically linked.

Resources

Egginton, J. (1989). *From the Cradle to the Grave: The Short Lives and Strange Deaths of Marybeth Tinning's Nine Children*. New York: Jove Books.

Marybeth Tinning Loses Parole Bid. 2009. *North Country Gazette*. http://www.northcoun trygazette.org/2009/04/04/tinning_loses/.

Hannah Scott

Tokyo Rose. *See* d'Aquino, Iva

Harriet Tubman (1820–1913)

Harriet Tubman is known by the legend that surrounds her and by the name Moses, given to her to reflect her defiance of the laws of slavery and her fight for freeing African American slaves. In Tubman's biography by the white abolitionist Sarah Bradford and in other accounts during her lifetime, as well as in current juvenile biographies, it is noted that Harriet Tubman earned that title through her efforts as a rescuer, spy, and nurse.

In 1820 Harriet Tubman was born in Cambridge, Maryland, to the slaves Harriet Greene and Ben Ross. The baby girl was named Araminta, a reminder of her

African ancestry. As a teenager, she took the name of Harriet as a sign of her adulthood. By the age of six, she was hired out by her family's master, Brodess (Brodas in some versions), as an assistant to a weaver. However, she returned to the plantation of her master, very ill with the measles and with bronchitis caused by the dust and fibers. Tubman demonstrated her lack of interest and skill in domestic tasks when she was returned home once again from a position as a house servant. She was still a little girl, a factor that as a matter of course was ignored by her mistress. She was beaten until she was scarred, and she was bedridden for weeks. Tubman's inability to perform the expected duties within the realm of women's work foreshadows her continued resistance to the role assigned to her by her gender and her race. For in 19th-cen-

Portrait of Harriet Tubman, leader of the Underground Railroad. (Library of Congress)

tury America, the idea of separate spheres, women in the home and men at work in the world, was almost as powerful a belief as the belief that African Americans were of an inferior race.

Tubman's failure at women's work was fortunate. Instead of being confined to the kitchen or the nursery, she toiled in the fields along with the male slaves, including her father. The exceptional physical strength attributed to Harriet Tubman was less her mythical power than a consequence of years of hard physical labor. In addition, side by side with her father, she learned about healing plants and the lore of survival in the woods. These skills were essential to her success as a guide for runaway slaves and to her military career.

Harriet Tubman was 11 when the stories of Nat Turner's rebellion circulated. While news of his uprising was circulated, so were the tales of the Underground Railroad and slaves who escaped into the North, where freedom awaited them. These stories had a significant influence throughout the South. The Southern economy suffered from the loss of valuable labor and property with each slave that left. Moreover, slaves, like Harriet Tubman, learned that there were abolitionists and free African Americans ready and able to assist in the journey to freedom.

Harriet Tubman's recognition of the power each slave represented by his/her disobedience, and by running away, was demonstrated when she was in her early teens when she either barred the way of an overseer pursuing a runaway slave, or she refused to tie the runaway slave when he was captured so that the escapee could be whipped. In his anger, the captor threw a two-pound lead weight. It was intended for the slave who defied him but hit Tubman instead. As a result of this blow to her head, Tubman experienced episodes in which she lost consciousness, which were most likely a form of epilepsy, for the rest of her life. It is, however, Tubman's interference that was important. She resisted bondage through her act, and in retrospect, it was this resistance that culminated in her leadership as she dared to fight for her own freedom and the freedom of other slaves.

Tubman's own Underground Railroad escape occurred in 1849. Already married to John Tubman for six years, Tubman hoped he would go with her. However, as a free man, he had more to risk and little to gain. This 1849 excursion was the first of many trips North. Each trip she took was in defiance of the law. By 1850, her illegal activity was underscored by the Fugitive Slave Law. This law obligated the North to return slaves to their owners. The rewards in place as a result of the law encouraged the return of slaves; emphasized that slaves were the valuable property of their masters; and increased the risks that runaways took by defying the laws of slavery.

Harriet Tubman ran enormous risks to lead approximately 300 African Americans out of slavery. The price for her return continued to rise. From $12,000, the reward grew to between $40,000 and $60,000; the demand for her capture was a measure of the impact of her rebellion against the legal and political system that perpetuated the holding of humans as property.

Harriet Tubman's resistance is often described as that of a rescuer. This characterization reinforces how her first biographer, Sarah Bradford, characterized her—a "simple" woman of great courage—and how contemporary children's books depict her—a beloved hero (Bradford, 1901; Petry, 1983). In these versions of her story, Harriet Tubman depends upon the good will of others. This version has been emphasized by her relationship with prominent abolitionists: William Still, Thomas Garrett, William Garrison, and William Seward. As Tubman faced danger, she outwitted her enemies as a trickster. The scheme of baffling her former master by disguising herself as an old woman flustered by her chickens, for example, portrayed Tubman as clever and wily (Bradford, 1901). Harriet Tubman's militant, revolutionary, and political power was diminished within the prevailing idealization of a woman who gained by guise and who was dependent on men.

Tubman broke the law, and she conspired with the radical John Brown who was hanged for his own abolitionist plot. In addition, in 1863, Tubman led Colonel Montgomery's troops in battle. This effort resulted in the release and relocation of 800 slaves to Sea Island, South Carolina. As a military leader, she fought for the equal pay and recognition of African American troops who served in the Civil War. Even her work as a war nurse required physical and mental strength beyond what was considered womanly. At the end of the war, she fought for the right to a military pension and was denied this right until her second husband, who had served in the Navy died (Humez, 2003). This too was a political battle waged against discrimination.

Harriet Tubman's postwar efforts indicate that, even after the war, she persisted in a struggle against oppression. She was an active advocate for suffrage, and her voice was joined with that of Susan B. Anthony. Tubman addressed the National Association of Colored Women and frequently spoke on women's right to vote (Humez, 2003).

Harriet Tubman's later years were dedicated to providing for the poor and infirm, as well as to public speaking. She proposed a shelter for elderly and ill African Americans that would be named the John Brown Home and located in Auburn, New York, where she resided. Her career as a public speaker was to finance this project and was an opportunity to assert her place in history by repeating her own stories. Her goal for the John Brown Home was never fulfilled, though, she maintained a home for the elderly and the ill. The stories of her life, however, have a critical place in history.

Resources

Bradford, Sarah H. (1901). *Harriet Tubman: The Moses of Her People* (Rev. ed.) New York: J.J. Little.

Humez, Jean. (2003). *Harriet Tubman: The Life and the Life Stories.* Madison: University of Wisconsin Press.

Lee, Butch. (2000). *Jailbreak Out of History.* New York: Stoopsale Books.

Petry, Ann. (1983). *Harriet Tubman* (Rev. ed). New York: Amistad and Collins.

Susan Bohrer

Karla Faye Tucker (1959–1998)

Karla Faye Tucker was executed on February 3, 1998, having served 14 years on death row and been denied a reprieve of execution by then-governor of Texas, George W. Bush, for her role in the deaths of Jerry Lynn Dean and Deborah Thornton. She became the first woman to be executed in Texas since 1863 and the second woman to be executed in the United States since the death penalty was reinstated in 1976. Tucker attracted global attention as her execution neared, largely due to her gender and her religious conversion during incarceration.

Tucker was born November 18, 1959, to Carolyn Moore and Lawrence Tucker. She grew up in Houston, Texas, the youngest of three girls. Tucker's parents separated when she was 10 years old, and the girls resided with their father for three years before being sent to live with their mother in the hopes that she would be better able to manage their increasingly troublesome behavior. Tucker attended school until the seventh grade after which she traveled with the Allman Brothers Band. Still a teenager, she married Steven Griffith, and the couple cared for the child of a friend for approximately five years until their relationship dissolved. Following her separation from Griffith, Tucker continued to use drugs, which had been a regular part of her life since age 8, and worked as a prostitute, taking after her mother who had introduced her to the sex trade at the age of 14.

Tucker later became involved in a relationship with Daniel Ryan Garrett while her long-time friend Shawn, who had also traveled with the Allman Brothers Band, had married Jerry Lynn Dean. Approximately one month before the night of the offence, Tucker had assaulted Dean for having defaced photographs of her mother, who had died from drug abuse on December 24, 1979. Shortly thereafter, Jerry Lynn Dean assaulted Shawn, prompting her to move in with Tucker and her room-mates. On the night leading up to the offense, Tucker was heavily intoxicated, having ingested alcohol, speed, and a host of other drugs over a two-week period. She had not slept for three nights due to her significant intake of speed.

In the early morning hours of June 13, 1983, 23-year-old Tucker, her then boy-friend, 37-year-old Garrett, and a mutual friend, James Liebrant, went to Dean's apartment to steal his motorcycle. Upon discovering Dean in the apartment with Deborah Thornton, whom Dean had met at a party earlier that evening, Garrett proceeded to hit Dean on the head with a hammer until Tucker entered with a pickax and struck him to death. Tucker and Garrett then turned to Thornton, who was hiding in the bedroom, and struck her to death with the pickax. The victims were found dead with more than 20 stab wounds each, the pickax left embedded in Thornton's chest. Dubbed the "Pickax Murderer," Tucker boasted about her role in the murders and claimed that she had experienced sexual gratification with each strike of the ax. She later denied this claim, explaining that she had simply been trying to impress her friends.

Tucker was arrested July 21, 1983, and indicted for capital murder; she pleaded not guilty before the court though she never denied her role in the murders. A jury found her guilty of capital murder on April 19, 1984, and sentenced her to death on April 25, 1984. She was detained in Harris County Jail until December of that year, before being transferred to the female death row in the Mountain View Unit of the Texas Department of Criminal Justice. Tucker testified against former boyfriend and co-defendant in the murders, Garrett, who was sentenced to death January 10, 1985, but died of liver disease on June 15, 1993, while serving his sentence. Not long after her incarceration, Tucker attended a religious service at the prison where she was detained. She soon converted to Christianity and, on June 24, 1995, married prison chaplain Dana Brown by proxy. (Although Tucker took Dana Brown's last name to become Karla Faye Tucker Brown, she is still best known as Karla Faye Tucker.)

For nearly a decade, Tucker and her attorneys attempted to appeal her case and ultimately sought executive clemency to commute her sentence to life imprison-ment. A number of supporters emerged during this time, including Pat Robertson of the conservative Christian Coalition of America, Pope John Paul II, and Deborah Thornton's brother. With the exception of one stay of execution in 1992, all of Tucker's applications and appeals were denied—the Texas Court of Criminal Appeals upheld Tucker's conviction and sentence in 1998, and the Supreme Court of the United States refused to hear her case.

In a letter to the governor and Texas Board of Pardons and Paroles, published in the *Houston Chronicle*, and in an interview for CNN talk show *Larry King Live*, Tucker claimed that her request for clemency should not be granted on the basis of gender, despite the media's focus on gender in coverage of her execution. Rather, Tucker argued that she no longer posed a threat to the public and could make an important contribution to society through prison ministry. Tucker's attorneys made a formal submission to the 18-member Texas Board of Pardons and Paroles, requesting it recommend to the governor of Texas a commutation of her sentence to life imprisonment. Because the board denied this request, the governor of Texas could only invoke his independent authority to grant a one-time 30-day reprieve of execution. George W. Bush denied this request, claiming there was no doubt about Tucker's guilt and the courts had had the opportunity to review the legal issues of her case.

Having exhausted all possibilities for appeal and commutation, Karla Faye Tucker was executed by lethal injection in Huntsville, Texas, on February 3, 1998, and pronounced dead at 6:45 PM. In her final statement prior to execution, she apologized to the families of the victims and thanked her supporters. Tucker had attracted significant media attention and public sympathy, and several academic scholars have since examined the role of race, gender, sexuality, femininity, and faith in her execution and the public's response (Beckman, 2004; Cooey, 2002; Farr, 2000; Howarth, 2002; Sigler, 2007).

Resources

Beckman, Karen. 2004. Dead woman glowing: Karla Faye Tucker and the aesthetics of death row photography. *Camera Obscura 19*(1): 1–41.

Cooey, Paula M. 2002. Women's religious conversions on death row: Theorizing religion and state. *Journal of the American Academy of Religion 70*(4): 699–717.

Farr, Kathryn A. 2000. Defeminizing and dehumanizing female murderers: Depictions of lesbians on death row. *Women & Criminal Justice 11*(1): 49–66.

Howarth, Joan W. 2002. Executing white masculinities: Learning from Karla Faye Tucker. *Oregon Law Review 81*: 183–230.

King, Larry. 1998. Karla Faye Tucker: Live from death row. *CNN Larry King Live Transcript* (#98011400V22), January 14.

Long, Walter C. 1999. Karla Faye Tucker: A case for restorative justice. *American Journal of Criminal Law 27*: 117.

Lowry, Beverly. 1992. *Crossed over: A murder, a memoir.* New York: Knopf.

Sigler, Mary. 2007. Mercy, clemency, and the case of Karla Faye Tucker. *Ohio State Journal of Criminal Law 4*: 455–486.

Strom, Linda. 2000. *Karla Faye Tucker set free: Life and faith on death row.* New York: Random House.

Tucker, Karla Faye. 1998. Excerpts from Karla Faye Tucker's letter. *Houston Chronicle,* 21 January, A25.

Katherine R. Rossiter

V

Leslie Van Houten (1949–)

In a 1977 interview with Barbara Walters, Leslie Van Houten expressed her regret for the Tate-LaBianca murders, though she did not expect much forgiveness in return. For much of her time since the Tate-LaBianca murders, Van Houten has openly expressed remorse for her participation in the crimes. She has spent much of her imprisoned life at California Institution for Women (CIW), where she is serving a life sentence for the murders of wealthy Los Angeles grocers Rosemary and Leno LaBianca on the night of August 10, 1969, and for conspiring in the murders on the night previous, August 9, of Abigail Folger, coffee heiress; Voytek Frykowski, Folger's lover; teenager Stephen Parent; Hollywood hair stylist Jay Sebring; and actress Sharon Tate, who was eight months pregnant.

Born Leslie Louise Van Houten in Altadena, California, Van Houten lived much of her early life in Monrovia. The young Leslie Van Houten is remembered for her kindness and joy. She expressed this joy through cheerleading and being twice elected homecoming princess. During her adolescence, Van Houten's happiness took a dark turn. Her parents divorced when she was 14 years old. Around this time, Van Houten began to experiment with LSD. Becoming pregnant just before she turned 17, she had an abortion she claims she did not want. Feeling a need for love and a sense of purpose in her life, Van Houten broke away from her family and plunged into the Haight-Ashbury drug scene in San Francisco. In 1968, while in Berkeley, she connected with drifters Bobby Beausoleil, an aspiring actor; his wife Gail; and Catherine Share, who went by the name "Gypsy." Gypsy often told stories of "the family" and a wild, fabulous man she knew: Charlie Manson, who was their leader.

Van Houten met Manson within a month of meeting and hanging with the Beausoleils and Gypsy, and she soon fell under Mason's charismatic influence. When she joined the family, Van Houten maintained that it was only so that she could remain close to Beausoleil. However, in 1969, when Beausoleil was found guilty of the murder of Gary Hinman, a music teacher, and then jailed, Van Houten chose to stay with Manson.

Van Houten recalled in a 1994 interview with the *Washington Post* that Manson's teachings were simple and that everyone fed into what he had to say. Manson taught them to distrust their conscience and to be ashamed. They were taught to see what they had learned as children as being part of a deliberate attempt by parents and society to control them. Manson then presented himself as the freedom to this societal control. Manson also encouraged everyone to let go of their sexual inhibitions; in fact, one of Van Houten's responsibilities was to entertain the local bikers. She claims she later realized Manson used family women as payment for his drug deals.

Shortly before the murders of August 9–10, 1969, Van Houten recalls that it was a dangerous time for Manson and the family. Their acid trips became more frequent and violent, and his message more urgent. During this time, Manson talked about the inevitability of a race war, which he described as an apocalyptic battle in which blacks would rise up against their white oppressors and kill them. Manson was influenced by the Beatles'

Former Charles Manson follower Leslie Van Houten is taken to the courtroom during 1978 proceedings in Los Angeles where a jury found her guilty of first-degree murder in the 1969 killings of Leno and Rosemary LaBianca. (AP/Wide World Photos)

White Album, which he played endlessly. He claimed that during the war, the family would be safe. At the end of this war, family members would be made into gods and eventually rule the Earth when blacks realized that they were unable to do it by themselves.

Though the plans were undoubtedly delusional, Van Houten and the others believed every word that came out of Manson's mouth. For Van Houten, "Helter Skelter" came to fruition on the night of August 10, when Manson drove her, Charles "Tex" Watson, Patricia Krenwinkel, Susan Atkins, Steve Grogan, and Linda Kasabian to the LaBianca residence in the Los Feliz section of Los Angeles. Alone, Manson went into the house first. A few minutes later, he came out to let the others know that the couple was tied up, and then he ordered Watson, Krenwinkel, and Van Houten to go inside and kill them. Manson told them to do whatever Watson said.

Van Houten and Krenwinkel entered the house and found Rosemary LaBianca in a bedroom, where they paused for a moment to sit with her. Then, Van Houten covered Mrs. LaBianca's head with a pillowcase and, together with Krenwinkel, tied an electrical cord from a nearby lamp around Mrs. LaBianca's neck. Suddenly, she panicked at hearing LaBianca's husband's screams from another room where Watson stabbed him to death. Van Houten held Mrs. LaBianca down while Krenwinkel stabbed her repeatedly and very hard in the chest, bending the knife against her collarbone. Despite her painful injuries, Mrs. LaBianca continued to struggle, causing Van Houten to knock a lamp away from her. At that moment, Van Houten called assistance from Watson and reportedly told him that she wasn't able to kill Mrs. LaBianca. Van Houten then left the room. She stood in the hallway and stared blankly into a nearby room to somewhat remove herself from what was happening. Watson finished stabbing Mrs. LaBianca with a sword-like knife; he then handed Van Houten a knife and told her to join him. Van Houten stabbed Mrs. LaBianca over a dozen times, even though she was certain she was already dead. The autopsy revealed several postmortem wounds on Mrs. LaBianca's body, though no one could determine their cause. Following the murders, Van Houten cleaned everything for fingerprints and put on some of Mrs. LaBianca's clothing, since hers were likely covered with blood. Then, she, Krenwinkel, and Watson began to eat cheese and drink milk from the refrigerator, which bore blood-laden messages such as "Death to Pigs" and "Helter Skelter."

In the months following the murders, Van Houten, Manson, Krenwinkel, and Atkins were tried in Los Angeles. Watson had a separate trial, due to the fact that he was in Texas fighting extradition at that time. Of the defendants, Van Houten, the youngest, was considered the least devoted to Manson. Therefore, of all the defendants, Van Houten was considered the most likely to be given mercy for her role in the killings. However, during the trial, she behaved uncooperatively and inappropriately, often disrupting the proceedings with giggling, mainly when the murders of Sharon Tate and the LaBiancas were being discussed. During the sentencing phase of the trial, Van Houten stated with little emotion or remorse that "[s]orry is only a five-letter word. How do I feel? I feel like it happened." As a result, any sympathy she may have had with the jury quickly vanished. All defendants were convicted, found guilty of murder, and subsequently sentenced to death on March 29, 1971. However, after the California Supreme Court invalidated death sentences imposed in California prior to 1972 with *People v. Anderson*, the defendants' sentences were automatically commuted to life in prison.

Van Houten went through several lawyers and trials before her final conviction. Donald Barnett, her first attorney, was dismissed following his cross-examination of Manson. Marvin Part, her second lawyer, wanted to demonstrate Van Houten's mindset during the crime, which he viewed as being influenced by LSD and Manson. Van Houten differed, stating that she "was influenced by the war in Vietnam and TV" (Linder, 2010). Dismayed, Manson urged Van Houten to fire Part. Her third attorney, Ronald Hughes, also suggested that Manson influenced Van Houten. During the trial, Hughes disappeared and eventually turned up dead.

Though Manson family members were suspected of the killing, no one was ever charged.

In 1976, a California State Appellate Court overturned Van Houten's first-degree murder conviction on grounds that Van Houten was not granted her motion for a mistrial following attorney Hughes's disappearance. The jury could not reach a verdict during the first re-trial. Consequently, Van Houten was released on bond. During this time, she stayed with Los Angeles High School teacher Linda Grippi, re-learned how to drive, and went with Grippi to ballet classes. The impact that Van Houten had on those students, who were flirting with drugs, was profound. Grippi reported that Van Houten's influence was so profound that many of the students just straightened themselves out.

In 1978, the court tried her for a third time and convicted her of first-degree murder, felony robbery murder, and conspiracy to commit murder. She mounted a defense of diminished capacity, resulting from her extensive use of hallucinogenic drugs, but the jury did not accept it. By her sentencing in 1978, many people had recognized that Leslie Van Houten had changed tremendously. Even the sentencing judge at this third and final trial appeared distraught as he sentenced Van Houten back to prison for the rest of her life.

With only one mark on her prison record—her relationship to ex-convict Bill Cywin—Van Houten's time behind bars has been uneventful. Van Houten's transformation throughout her years in prison has been remarkable. Clinical and staff psychiatrists have noted significant progress and change in her mental health and fitness and her productivity behind bars. California Superior Court Judge Bob Krug confirmed this progress by stating in 2002 that Van Houten had been a model prisoner for 30 years, completing all available prison programs and helping other inmates. Judge Krug further noted that Van Houten was actually already eligible for parole in 1978 since she had already served eight years in prison and her sentence allowed for the possibility of parole. Since that time, Van Houten has gone before the board of parole hearings and has applied for parole 18 times, but she has not yet been successful.

Over the years, Van Houten has often challenged her parole denials. In 2004, Van Houten was denied parole. She challenged this denial in federal court, but the attorney general has opposed her petition. The parole board last denied Van Houten parole on August 30, 2007. Like many heinous crimes, the Tate-LaBianca murders dismantled society's sense of social order. The victims did not know the murderers who delivered them to society on a bloody platter of "Helter Skelter" mayhem and chaos. Charles Manson has been thought to be the Devil in human form—the women, his faithful servants. Even with the exchange of evidence for immunity or remorseful statements at parole hearings, it is difficult to know Leslie Van Houten's fate. Her hearing for the 2004 parole denial, originally scheduled for 2009, was held on July 6, 2010. Leslie Van Houten's 19th bid for parole was

president. Van Lew did not go without a fight. She tried, to no avail, to regain her position under Hayes and Garfield. While in Richmond, the city's elite ostracized Van Lew for her Union sympathies, and she lived the rest of her life in her family mansion in poverty. She was supported only by an annuity from the family of a Union soldier whom she had assisted. Her grave was unmarked until a Union soldier she assisted commissioned a tombstone that reads:

Elizabeth L. Van Lew 1818–1900

She risked everything that is dear to man—friends-fortune-comfort-health-life itself—all for the one absorbing desire of her heart—that slavery might be abolished and the union preserved. This boulder from the Capitol Hill in Boston is a tribute from Massachusetts friends. (Ryan 2001: 54–55)

Van Lew is a member of the Military Intelligence Hall of Fame, one of the minority of women who have been members.

Resources

Ryan, David. 2001. *A Yankee Spy in Richmond: The Civil War Diary of "Crazy Bet" Van Lew.* Mechanicsburg, PA: Stockpole Books.

Varon, Elizabeth. 2003. *Southern Lady, Yankee Spy: The True Story of Elizabeth Van Lew, A Union Agent in the Heart of the Confederacy.* New York: Oxford University Press.

Melencia Johnson

Rachel Wall (1760–1789)

Rachel Wall was a pirate and the last woman to be hanged in the state of Massachusetts. Aside from her prominence as one of only a few female pirates, her story also provides an illustration of post–Revolutionary War small-scale piracy. Although Rachel was hanged for a crime unrelated to her exploits as a pirate, she made her piracy well-known in her dying confession which was printed in the October 7, 1789, edition of the *Boston Goal.*

Rachel Wall was born in Carlisle, Pennsylvania, in 1760. She grew up in a conventional, religious farm family and was 16 years old when the Declaration of Independence was signed. Rachel left home at a young age but returned for two years before running off with a sailor named George Wall. Rachel married George, and they traveled together to New York and to Boston. In Boston, George left Rachel in order to work aboard a fishing schooner. Rachel remained in Boston, working as a servant to a wealthy family. After two months, George returned to Boston to collect Rachel. They left to meet George's fishing schooner but missed their ship because they had fallen into "bad company" (Weatherby, 1998) and had been out drinking. Because they had no money and no form of employment, George Wall decided that he and Rachel, along with their friends, should become pirates.

Rachel had no previous experience with piracy, but George and his friends had plundered ships when they had served aboard privateers during the Revolutionary War. Rachel's role in George's piracy scheme was to act as bait. Following a storm, George and the crew made the ship look ragged and sea-battered, while Rachel screamed for help to alert a nearby ship. When the captain and crew of the ship boarded Wall's vessel, George and his crew killed them and plundered their ship. While some accounts state that both George and Rachel had a hand in killing the crews of the ships that they plundered, others state that Rachel did not kill (Weatherby, 1998). Rachel herself stated that she had never murdered anyone. Once the pirates had relieved the vessel of all valuables, they sank the ship and disposed of the bodies of its crew. The crew used the storm to explain the destruction of the victim ship and the death of its crew.

Variations of this ruse of false distress were played out into the following summer, until the crew mistook the eye of a hurricane for the end of the storm, leading to the destruction of their ship. All crew members but Rachel were killed, including Rachel's husband George. Rachel was rescued by a passing ship and was dropped off in Boston, where she returned to her old job as a servant in Beacon Hill. An opposing account of the end of Rachel's piracy states that George was killed during a fight with another ship, and Rachel took command of the ship, sailing to safety. According to this account, Rachel actively chose to quit piracy following the death of her husband rather than being forced into that position.

Undated woodcut of the famous New England pirate, Rachel Wall. Stockton, Frank Richard. (*Buccaneers and Pirates of our Coasts*, 1919)

After Rachel Wall's "retirement" from piracy, she continued to steal valuables from ships docked in Boston Harbor. According to some sources, Wall crept onto ships at night and stole from the sailors as they slept (Weatherby, 1998). The only crime for which Wall was caught, however, was the alleged theft of another women's fancy bonnet. Wall stole the bonnet off of the woman's head, placed it on her own, and ran off down the street. She was overtaken by an officer of the law and was taken to jail. It was for this crime that Wall was convicted and hanged on Boston Common on October 7, 1789. Her trial was September 10, 1789, and the charge was that she committed a felony when she assaulted Margaret Bender and took from her a bonnet valued at seven shillings (Weatherby, 1998). She also confessed to another act of robbery for which someone else had been charged. However, Rachel Wall maintained until her death that she was innocent of the theft of the bonnet.

Although Rachel Wall was a pirate, her piracy had little to do with the crime for which she was executed. However, Rachel Wall was vocal about her former acts of piracy in her final confession. She may have been hanged as a common thief but clearly she wished to be remembered as a pirate. The extent of her involvement in the acts of George Wall's pirate crew is debatable, but her participation in piracy is not.

Resources

Rogozinsky, Jan. 1995. *Pirates!: Brigands, Buccaneers, and Privateers in Fact, Fiction, and Legend*. New York: Facts on File.

Wall, Rachel. 1789. "Life, Last Words and Dying Confessions of Rachel Wall." *Boston Goal*. October 7. Evans Early American Imprint microcard series, No. 22235. Columbia, SC: University of South Carolina.

Weatherby, Myra. 1998. *Women Pirates: Eight Stories of Adventure*. Greensboro: Morgan Reynolds.

Weatherby, Myra. 2006. *Women of the Sea: Ten Pirate Stories*. Greensboro: Morgan Reynolds Publishing.

Ariel E. Allison

Yvonne Wanrow (1943–)

Yvonne Wanrow was an American Indian woman who was sentenced to two 20-year terms and one 5-year sentence for murder and attempted murder. Her criminal prosecution brought to light the lack of women's equal protection under the law.

In 1972, Yvonne Wanrow's son was assaulted by William Wesler, a neighbor. Wesler had previously molested another child in the neighborhood and had given her a sexually transmitted disease (the daughter of Shirley Hooper). Wanrow's son fled his assailant and came home to report the occurrence to his mother. Wanrow contacted the police and was subsequently told that they were unable to arrest him at that time. Wanrow and Hooper spoke to their landlords and consequently found out that Wesler had molested another child in the area and had spent time in a mental institution. The landlord suggested that Wanrow and Hooper stay together in their home and keep his gun for protection.

The two women later called family members over to Hooper's home and stayed up all night to protect their children. After an invitation to reconcile differences from one of their family members, Wesler and a friend of his came to the house. As he entered the residence, Wesler made a comment to Wanrow about her nephew and moved towards the three-year-old child. Wanrow shot and killed Wesler and shot his friend. Wanrow and Hooper called the police, and Wanrow calmly confessed to the police.

As an American Indian female, Wanrow initially lacked access to legal counsel within the criminal justice system. She originally pled guilty until a new attorney, provided for by the Center for Constitutional Rights, advised her to plea not guilty by reason of temporary insanity and self-defense. While she was initially convicted of second-degree murder and first-degree assault, Wanrow's trial was reversed on appeal, and a retrial was mandated. Her retrial resulted in a plea to reduced charges, and her sentence was decreased to five years probation and 2,000 hours of community service. Wanrow spent her time speaking for the women's movement and the American Indian Movement, counseling alcoholics and volunteer teaching to students on her reservation.

Wanrow's trial brought numerous issues to light. Her attorneys argued that her confession was gained by illegal means and that and expert testimony focusing on her American Indian background and culture was banned from delivery. Of the most importance to feminists and proponents of women's rights was the manner in which the jury was instructed. At her original trial, the jury was instructed to base their decision on the standards of a "reasonable man." Upon appeal, Wanrow's attorney pointed out that, due to this standard of masculinity, Wanrow was denied equal protection of the law. Instructing the jury in masculine terminology presented a precedent that was unequal to Wanrow's gender status. This did not allow the jury to consider her perceptions, her status as a mother, or an acceptable level of defense when a female felt threatened by a male.

Wanrow's appeals process resulted in what is known as the "Wanrow jury instruction," which stipulates that juries must be instructed to consider the facts in gender-neutral terminology. This advance in court instruction also allows the jury to consider what a female will find "reasonable" and "justifiable" instead of judging them by male standards. Utilizing gender-neutral terminology within the court system helps afford females equal protection under the law.

Wanrow's case also demonstrated how cultural narrative is used in the legal process. Wanrow was on welfare, was divorced with children, had problems with alcohol, and was an American Indian. Calling attention to her cultural narrative and background as an American Indian female, her attorneys argued that she must be convicted or sentenced according to her distinct background, both as a woman and as an American Indian. Wanrow's trial brought attention to the plight and oppression of women and minorities in a time of political and social turmoil, and the trial highlighted the complex social positioning of females within the criminal justice system.

Citing the Civil Rights Act of 1964, which prohibits discrimination based on gender, race, color, religion, and national origin, Wanrow's case provided the framework and guidelines for new jury instruction, equal consideration of defendants, and equal protection for females. It served to focus society on women's rights, cultural background, and the victimization of women and children by males.

Resources

Jones, Ann. 1980. *Women Who Kill*. New York: Holt, Rinehart, and Winston.

Schuetz, Janice. 1994. *The Logic of Women on Trial: Case Studies of Popular American Trials*. Carbondale: Southern Illinois University Press.

Alana Van Gundy-Yoder

Rosemary West (1953–)

Rosemary West was one of the few female serial killers who, in the 1980s and 1990s, terrorized a society with a rash of kidnappings, rapes, and murders of young women. Most female serial killers commit their crimes alone; however, one-third of the female serial killers in the United States act in partnership with another person, usually an intimate other. Rose West and her husband, Fred West, terrorized Gloucester, England, raping and killing young women. The rarity of the sexually aggressive female serial killer who steps so far out of her gender roles by raping other females makes this case a significant break from societal definitions of womanhood. Furthermore, Rose West's first victim was her stepdaughter; this crime represented to many the ultimate betrayal of womanhood.

Rosemary Letts was born on November 29, 1953, to Bill and Daisy Letts. One of seven children, Rose's siblings and mother endured constant violence at the hands of her schizophrenic father. Even prior to her birth, Bill Letts was very abusive to her mother. The beatings lead Daisy Letts into a state of depression. Finally, in 1953, Daisy Letts was hospitalized and treated with electroshock therapy. Shortly after this hospitalization, Daisy became pregnant with Rose. It is uncertain if the electroshock therapy did any damage to the fetus; however, it is known that as a young child, Rose would rock her body so hard in her cot that she would slide it across the room. As she grew older, Rose would rock only her head for hours. She was believed to be slow and was called "Dozy Rosey."

While receiving affection from Bill Letts was extremely hard, Rose appeared to be his pet gaining affection that none of the other children received. It is claimed that as her father's favorite, Rose was able to escape his beatings. However, others claim that Bill Letts beat and raped his daughter. Furthermore, as

Undated photo of British serial killer Rosemary West and her husband Fred, who was found hanged in his prison cell awaiting trial on 12 murder charges in 1997. (AP/Wide World Photos)

a young teenager, Rose started having sexual relations with older men. Fred West, a man 12 years her senior, would turn out to be the love of her life. Rose met Fred in 1969 at the bakery where she worked. As an impressionable 15 year old, Rose took to Fred's gifts and soon moved in with him in order to raise his children, Ann Marie and Charmaine.

In 1970, when Fred West was arrested and incarcerated, Rose began beating their children. After his nine-month stint in prison, Fred joined in on the beating of his children, especially Charmaine, who had been fathered by another man. In 1971, Fred and Rose West killed and buried Charmaine and Fred's former wife Rena when she came to claim her children. From this point on, Rose and Fred's crimes became more violent and extended beyond the victimization of their own children.

On February 24, 1994, a warrant was served to search the house of Fredrick West for the remains of Heather West, the daughter of Rosemary and Fredrick West. Heather disappeared at the age of 16 in 1987. Police believed that Fred West killed her and buried her under the patio. The next day, Fred confessed to the police that he killed his daughter, cut her body in three pieces, and buried her. He also claimed that Rose had nothing to do with the murder. Twenty minutes later he denied the entire story. However, after learning that the police found three human bones, though they were not Heather's, he once again confessed, giving all of the gory details. In 1994, upon further investigation and confessions, Fred and Rose West were charged with murder. Fred West was charged with 12 murders. Rose West was charged with 10 murders, including the murder of Fred's first child Charmaine (in 1971), Fred and Rose West's first child Heather (in 1987), a lodger in the West house Shirley Robinson (in 1977), and seven other victims. In their crimes, Fred and Rose West often befriended or kidnapped young women, held them captive in their house on 25 Cromwell Street in London, sexually assaulted them, and then murdered them.

Rose West's trial started on October 3, 1995. During her 31-day trial, Rose West was depicted as an unfeminine, aggressive, manipulative, violent, sexual predator. Furthermore, it was revealed that Rose had prostituted herself in their home and had even became pregnant from a client. In all, Rose had three children from other men while married to Fred West. These actions are not believed to belong to the ideal woman who may claim victim status. While Rose West was convicted of 10 murders, the evidence against her was only circumstantial. The prosecution used Rose's sexual deviance as well as her inability to behave as a good woman and a good mother as the basis for the murder charges. The defense counsel, on the other hand, tried to show that one can not assume that murder is linked to sexual deviance.

Officials had the initial confessions of Fred West, who continuously professed Rose's innocence. However, after Rose's rejection of Fred West, he hanged himself in his cell on January 1, 1995. Since Fred West was not able to stand trial, some claim that Rose West was inadvertently standing trial for both of their crimes.

On November 22, 1995, Rose was convicted of 10 murders and sentenced to life imprisonment.

Resources

Gordon, Burn. 1999. *Happy Like Murderers: The True Story of Fred and Rosemary West.* London: Farber and Farber.

Klein, Shelley. 2003. *The Most Evil Women in History.* New York: Barnes & Noble Books.

Sounes, Howard. 1995. *Fred and Rose: The Full Story of Fred and Rose West and the Gloucester House of Horrors.* London: Little Brown & Company.

Vronsky, Peter. 2007. *Female Serial Killers: How and Why Women Become Monsters.* New York: Berkley Books.

Winter, Jo. 2002. "The Trial of Rose West: Contesting Notions of Victimhood." In H. Carolyn and Y. Richard (eds.), *New Visions of Crime Victims*, 173–196. Portland, OR: Hart Publishing.

Venessa Garcia

Charlotte Anita Whitney (1867–1955)

Charlotte Anita Whitney was a political radical whose legacy has been primarily legal. An appellate case bearing her name serves as a hallmark in free speech case law. She can also be regarded as important sociologically, as the story of her life illustrates the costs and benefits that social affiliation pose in criminal as well as cultural processes. Though a later observer described her as a "frail, quiet-mannered, soft-voiced woman [who] maintained a stoic poise which was conceded to be remarkable" (Reed, 1922: 93), her relentless dedication to the downtrodden has been lost in the legalistic intricacies of case law and the historical stigmatization of communism.

Whitney, the daughter of a San Francisco lawyer, was born into privilege. Both finance magnate Cyrus W. Field and Supreme Court Justice Stephen Johnson Field were her uncles. Her family's wealth and prestige permitted voyages to the East Coast with both educational and personal import. She graduated from Wellesley College in 1889, and in 1893, she famously visited the College Settlement House in New York City's slums. The latter experience ignited her passion for social work and led her back to California, not to retire in San Francisco comfort but across the Bay to the social and economic slums of Oakland.

After serving six years in a county-wide nonprofit position, her attentions turned statewide and political, as her contributions to serving marginalized persons began to coalesce and intensify. Whitney began by leading a women's suffrage campaign in California, and then she assisted similar efforts in other states, more than a decade before the Nineteenth Amendment allowed women to vote. During that time, she became involved in efforts to exercise and protect speech by the socialist organization Industrial Workers of the World (IWW). She formally joined the Socialist Party in 1914 but found it insufficiently ambitious. When Whitney and other members of the party's "radical" wing were ejected from the party's 1919 national convention in Chicago, she founded the Communist Labor Party (CLP). She helped draft the party's constitution which explicitly noted intent to unify American workers into a working-class movement, and pledged to take the principles of Communism and revolutionary industrial unionism and help put them into practice.

Her increasing radicalism, however, contrasted sharply with national trends. Only two years earlier, the Bolshevik revolution in Russia had sparked a "red scare" of antiradical, revolution-fearing hysteria in the United States. The same year she formed what would become simply the Communist Party, California passed the 1919 Criminal Syndicalism Act, which expressly prohibited "advocating, teaching or aiding and abetting . . . unlawful acts of force and violence . . . as a means of accomplishing a change in industrial ownership or control, or effecting any political change" (California statute of 1919 as cited in H.R.M., 1922: 512.

After giving a speech on "the negro question" to the California Civic League on November 18, 1919, Whitney was arrested on five counts of violating the act and, specifically, of having attended the Chicago convention. Her first lawyer was recused for a 104-degree fever and died one week later; a second had insisted he was "not competent" to take charge and that Whitney did not desire his representation, but he was nevertheless compelled by the judge to represent her. Thus subject both to national hysteria and judicial obstinacy, Whitney was convicted on the first count of having organized and joined the party for the purposes of advocating, teaching, and aiding and abetting criminal syndicalism. Although she barely contested that charge, she was ultimately victorious by several measures. While she received a prison sentence of 1 to 14 years at San Quentin Penitentiary, she only served 11 days, due to poor health. And though 8 years of legal appeals went unsuccessful, she was ultimately pardoned by Governor Friend Richardson on June 21, 1927, based on a concurring opinion *against* her in her final appeal effort, as well as an effort organized on her behalf.

The years of legal wrangling concerned whether the state has the power, such as through the 1919 Act, to restrict First Amendment rights to free speech and freedom of assembly when that speech and assembly threaten the state itself.

In its original case against Whitney (*People v. Whitney*, 57 Cal. App. 449, 207), the state of California charged that the Community Labor Party was an instrument of syndicalism, which the act clearly defined as teaching and encouraging violent overthrow of state authority. Asserted linkages to violence were tenuous at best: The California CLP had endorsed the national CLP, which had endorsed the national

IWW, which had endorsed the California IWW, members of which had been found guilty of acts of violence in Bakersfield, California. Whitney *did* testify in the original trial that neither she nor the other organizers had intended the CLP to be violent or to violate any known law. And in the later appellate process, her lawyers contended that she had not known the convention would turn violent, that she had tried to object to resolutions calling for aggressive means, and that she had offered resolutions toward peaceful means. However, nowhere in the seminal legal history that followed did Whitney's attorneys ever contest that the Communist Party posed a threat nor that Whitney had joined them. (Worse, she continued her involvement, first at the Chicago convention and later as an alternate delegate to state meetings.) Indeed, Justice Louis Brandeis practically *complained* that no such argument had been made, writing that Whitney "did not claim that . . . there was no clear and present danger of serious evil, nor did she request that the existence of these conditions of a valid measure thus restricting the rights of free speech and assembly be passed upon by the court of a jury" (*People v. Whitney*, 57 Cal. App. 449, 207). Moreover, as he noted, the party had been created for the purpose of teaching criminal syndicalism, violent or not. Indeed, the threat of violence was arguably an important primary difference between the Socialist Party Whitney had left and the Communist Party she had started. As such, the 1919 Act was clearly violated. The question remained, whether the act was constitutional.

Whitney appealed on 16 counts, including asserting Fourteenth Amendment violations of due process and equal protection. (Her lawyers had oddly argued that the act prohibited syndicalism by those seeking a shift from capitalism but not by those who would defend it. Justice Earnest T. Stanford ruled that it was within the discretionary power of the state and was not, in fact, arbitrary. The District Court of Appeals (in *Whitney v. California*, 269 U.S. 530 [1925]), the California Supreme Court, and the United States Supreme Court (in *Whitney v. People of State of California*, 274 U.S. 357 [1927]) all denied Whitney's claims, the latter in dual opinions issued on May 16, 1927. (An initial appeal to the U.S. Supreme Court had been denied on technical grounds in 1925.)

The majority opinion, written by Justice Sanford, ruled that the state has the power to identify and define evils, and invoked the Court's recent opinion in *Gitlow v. New York* (1925), that free speech can be restricted. (Notably, Whitney was represented by New York lawyers Walter Pollak and Walter Nelles, who also represented Benjamin Gitlow.) But Sanford, and the seven justices who joined his opinion, went beyond the previous Holmes test of clear and present danger, arguing that the state has the power to punish words that merely have a potential to threaten even if they don't rise to a direct threat.

The opinion written by Justice Brandeis (joined by Oliver Wendell Holmes), while formally a concurring opinion, entailed stark differences and subtle dissent and had the most lasting legal impact. Both opinions agreed on the Fourteenth

Amendment questions before the court, and that, as Brandeis wrote, "although the rights of free speech and assembly are fundamental, they are not in their nature absolute." However, whereas Stanford wrote that "every presumption is to be indulged in favor of the validity of the statute" and that only restrictions that were considered arbitrary or unreasonable could be found unconstitutional, Brandeis suggested that there must be limits to the state's power to prohibit First Amendment exercises. Further, he argued that citizens in a democracy have a responsibility to criticize government policy, "the function of speech [being] to free men from the bondage of irrational fears." In place of "clear and present danger," he argued that the danger must be both serious and imminent: "The fact that speech is likely to result in some violence or in destruction of property is not enough to justify its suppression. There must be the probability of serious injury to the State" (*Whitney v. People of State of California*).

Further, he suggested what has been called a "time to answer" test, the danger of words not being clear and present if they can be contested, as should be part of the democratic process. "Even advocacy of violation [of the law], however reprehensible morally, is not a justification for denying free speech where the advocacy falls short of incitement" (*Whitney v. People of State of California*). That position would later be taken up by Justices William O. Douglas and Hugo L. Black in the second half of the century, and ultimately adopted in *Brandenburg v. Ohio* (395 US 444, 1969), which explicitly overturned the *Whitney* decision.

Whitney continued her efforts—political, sociological, and criminal—for the rest of her life. She was a Communist candidate for California state treasurer in 1924, receiving over 100,000 votes. In 1935, she faced convictions for election fraud, distribution of communist literature, and lecturing without a permit. She became national chairman of the Community Party in 1936, was twice nominated for the U.S. Senate, and got nearly 99,000 votes in 1950, despite anticommunist attacks by Ronald Reagan and Joe McCarthy. Just five years later, on February 3, 1955, she passed away in San Francisco. By the time her legacy ruling was overturned 14 years later, in *Brandenburg v. Ohio*, a second "red scare" had struck America as communism became a threat not just of worker revolt but of international annihilation. Twenty years beyond that, iconic events worldwide would be heralded as the death of communism. Whitney's legacy has thus been dually lost—Sanford's opinion was overturned years after she died, and communism has been stigmatized to the point of its reported death.

Resources

Bhagwat, Ashutosh. 2004. "The Story of *Whitney v. California*: The Power of Ideas." In *Constitutional Law Stories*, ed. Michael C. Dorf, 383–408. New York: Foundation Press.

Blasi, Vincent. 1988. "The First Amendment and the Ideal of Civic Courage: The Brandeis Opinion in *Whitney v. California.*" *William & Mary Law Review* 653.

Collins, Ronald, and David Skover. 2005. "Curious Concurrence: Brandeis' Vote in *Whitney v. California.*" *Supreme Court Review* 333.

Dee, Juliet. 2003. "Whitney v. California." In *Free Speech on Trial: Communication Perspectives on Landmark Supreme Court Decisions*, ed. Richard A. Parker. Tuscaloosa: University of Alabama Press.

H.R.M., 1922. "Criminal Law: Criminal Syndicalist Act: Constitutional Law: Validity Under the Act Under the Free Speech Clause. *California Law Review*, 10: 512–518.

People v. Whitney, 57 Cal. App. 449, 207.

Reed, Alma. 1922. "Woman Tests Free Speech: Case Against Anita Whitney for Syndalicism Up to Supreme Court." *New York Times* (September 17), 93.

Rubens, Lisa. 1986. "The Patrician Radical: Charlotte Anita Whitney." *California History* 158.

Whitney v. People of State of California, 274 U.S. 357 [1927].

Ellis Godard

Aileen Wuornos (1956–2002)

Aileen Wuornos was a female serial killer who was deemed "too aggressive" in her killings. Aileen Wuornos was considered to be a predatory killer. As a highway prostitute who sought out her victims, shot, and then robbed them, Wuornos defied societal ideas of female normalcy and deviance. Adding to the defiance of her gender role expectations, Wuornos was also lesbian. During her trial, her deviant behaviors and lesbianism were used by both the prosecution and the defense.

Aileen Wuornos was born on February 29, 1956, to Diane Wuornos and Leo Pittman. Abandoned by their parents, Aileen and her brother Keith were raised by their maternal grandparents, Britta and Lauri Wuornos. Until she was 11, Aileen and Keith were led to believe that, Britta and Lauri were their parents and that their aunts and uncles were their siblings. Diane had married Leo at the young age of 14; however, they divorced when Diane was pregnant with Aileen. Leo was known to beat Diane and engage in criminal behaviors. Eventually, Leo was given a life sentence for kidnapping and raping a 7-year-old girl. While in prison, he committed suicide.

It has been reported that Aileen and Keith were physically abused and neglected by their grandparents. Britta Wuornos, Aileen's grandmother, was an alcoholic who turned her head from the abuse her husband Lauri gave to their children and grandchildren. Aileen also claimed to being sexually abused by her grandfather. Although this accusation was not substantiated, researchers speculate that Aileen's extreme hate for Lauri Wuornos coupled with her early sexual experiences as well as Lauri's advances on Aileen's mother Diane would not preclude this possibility.

As a child, Aileen was known to have uncontrollable and unprovoked outbursts. She was also sexually active by the age of 11, selling sexual favors for cigarettes and loose change or a couple of dollars. Aileen Wuornos was frequently in trouble and running away. She would spend nights sleeping in the woods, in abandoned cars, or at the house of her only childhood friend, Dawn Nieman. In 1971, Britta became very ill and although she needed hospitalization, Lauri never called an ambulance. Britta died of cirrhosis of the liver when Aileen was 15 years old. It was at this time that Lauri blamed Aileen and her brother Keith for Britta's death. Lauri threatened to kill the children if their mother did not take them away. Although Aileen never got along with her grandparents, Britta's death, Aileen's hostile behavior at her funeral, and Lauri's threats resulted in Aileen's final departure from her home. Lauri's children believe that he let Britta die when he neglected to call an ambulance.

Aileen Wuornos admitted that she was a prostitute by the age of 15 when she hitchhiked across the country to settle in Florida following her grandmother's funeral. In addition to prostitution, she engaged in other crimes such as check forgery, shoplifting, identity and car theft, and ultimately armed robbery. She spent most of her time on her own and initially expressed disgust for lesbians; however, after serving three years in prison for robbing a convenience store with a .22 caliber gun, she claimed to be a lesbian. Wuornos did not have any significant relationships until she met Tyria (Ty) Moore in a gay bar in 1986. Prior to her four-and-a-half year relationship with Ty, the longest relationship Wuornos ever had had lasted two months. Wuornos was the one in control within her relationship with Ty, and although Ty maintained her job as a hotel maid, they often had trouble making ends meet. They often moved from hotel to hotel, sometimes sleeping in the woods or staying with Ty's sister and her husband. Throughout their relationship, Wuornos prostituted herself on the highways of Florida trying making a living to support both herself and Ty.

In early December 1989, Wuornos got into the car of Richard Mallory on Florida's Interstate 4. Mallory was a well-known patron of prostitutes with a distant past of attempted rape for which he spent nine years in a Maryland

Convicted serial killer Aileen Wuornos waits to testify in the Volusia County courthouse in Daytona Beach, Florida, 2001. Wuornos was sentenced to death six times for killing middle-aged men along the highways of central Florida in 1989 and 1990. (AP/ Wide World Photos)

prison. Wuornos's goal that night was to make some money by prostituting herself, but she ended the encounter by pumping four bullets into the body of Richard Mallory, stealing his car, his wallet, and other personal possessions. Wuornos returned home with Mallory's car in order to move her and Ty's possessions from their hotel room to an apartment. According to Ty, Wuornos was calm and collected that night and gave no indication of her murderous act. The next day she returned to the scene of the crime in order to bury the body and clean and abandon Mallory's car. That night Wuornos told Ty, "I killed a guy today." Ty claimed that she wanted to leave Wuornos at that point, but she was too afraid.

In the next 12 months, Wuornos proceeded to shoot and kill six other clients and rob them of their possessions. After being seen fleeing the scene of a car accident, Wuornos was arrested for the highway murders. With the help of Ty, the police were able to gain a confession from Wuornos on January 16, 1991. In her confession, however, Wuornos gave several accounts as to why she killed Richard Mallory. In the end, Wuornos claimed that Mallory tried to rape her and that she had to kill him in self-defense. Wuornos claimed that each of her seven victims (Richard Mallory, Dick Humphreys, Troy Burress, David Spears, Charles Carskaddon, and Walter Gino Antonio) assaulted, threatened, or raped her. She was not charged with the murder of Peter Sims because his body was never found; however, Wuornos was suspected of his murder as well.

On January 14, 1992, Aileen Wuornos was tried for Mallory's murder. By this time, Wuornos claimed that Mallory had raped and tortured her. Mallory's sexual criminal history was not brought into the trial. However, due to Florida's Williams Rule, evidence of Wuornos's other murders was presented. Florida's Williams Rule allows the presentation of evidence related to other cases if it helps to demonstrate a pattern. With evidence of the other murders presented in the Mallory case, establishing a viable self-defense was extremely difficult. Wuornos became very hostile and argumentative during her testimony, which was extremely damaging to her case. On January 27, after two hours of deliberation, the jury returned a guilty verdict. In her angered response, Wuornos yelled to the jury, "I'm innocent! I was raped! I hope you get raped! Scumbags of America!" Wuornos pleaded no contest to three other murders and guilty to the murders of Carskaddon and Antonio. In all she was given five death sentences. Aileen Wuornos was executed on October 9, 2002, by lethal injection.

While Aileen Wuornos's crimes were unacceptable and tragic, this case exemplified society's willingness to demonize female offenders. These murders and the circumstances do not compare to those of male serial killers who often incorporate sexual fantasies through control and/or torture. While Wuornos claimed to be a victim, evidence also points to a financial motivation. Furthermore, while most women kill family members or intimate others, Wuornos focused on strangers in a predatory fashion. Another component of Aileen Wuornos's case that worked to demonize her was her claim to be a victim of multiple rapes. Society often denies that prostitutes can be raped. That is, it is assumed that prostitutes enjoy the risks of their chosen profession, or, they are thought to deserve being raped. Furthermore, the claim of multiple rapes is often dismissed as implausible by society although research shows that this is quite common, especially among sex workers.

Resources

Gehring, Krista. 2006. "A Star is Formed: Media Construction of the Female Criminal." In R. Muraskin and S. F. Domash (eds.), *Crime and the Media: Headlines vs. Reality*, 117–132. Upper Saddle River, NJ: Pearson Prentice Hall.

Keitner, Chimene I. 2002. Victim or Vamp? Images of violent Women in the Criminal Justice. *Columbia Journal of Gender and the Law* 11: 38–72.

MacLeod, Marlee. 2011. "Aileen Wurnos: Killer Who Preyed on Truck Drivers." TruTV Crime Library. http://www.trutv.com/library/crime/nororious_murders/wmen/wuor nos/10.html.

Shipley, Stacey L., and Bruce A. Arrigo. 2004. *The Female Homicide Offender: Serial Murder and the Case of Wuornos*. Upper Saddle River, NJ: Pearson Education.

Vronsky, Peter. 2007. *Female Serial Killers: How and Why Women Become Monsters*. New York: Berkley Books.

Venessa Garcia

Donna Yaklich (1955–)

Donna Yaklich was in her early thirties in 1988 when she began serving a 40-year sentence for conspiring to kill her husband, Dennis, a 6-foot 5-inch man of muscular build and member of the Pueblo, Colorado, police department. Donna Yaklich admitted to hiring the two young brothers who were the triggermen. She was too terrified to kill him herself. His body was found in her driveway on December 12, 1985. Yaklich's case exposed the depths of desperation of an abused wife, one who turned to hired killers to do the job for her.

Donna and Dennis began dating in 1977, two months after Dennis's first wife, Barbara, had died, according to published reports. Donna and Dennis had a child together, a son, and cared for Dennis's children from his previous marriage. Donna described in court how her marriage had been rocky from the start, how Dennis had beaten her many times, choked her, put the barrel of the gun he carried into her face, and played psychological games that included showing her photographs of homicide cases. Her defense also told the jury that Dennis used steroids and that the drugs made him violent.

Because he was a police officer, Donna felt she could not go to authorities for help. She believed they would protect Dennis and not believe her. She told jurors she tried to get away, but she felt that there was no place she could go without being found. Once, she fled to a battered women's shelter in Denver. Though Dennis did not find her, she said she returned home on her own after she spoke to her husband on the telephone, and he asked her to forgive him. But psychological abuse continued, according to Donna, so she turned to Ed and Charles Greenwell, two brothers she had met who agreed to kill Dennis. Both eventually pleaded guilty for the slaying. Donna's defense had maintained that she suffered from battered wife's syndrome and that her actions were justified.

A debate emerged, however, because her case illustrated a different angle from similar cases in which battered wife's syndrome had been used as a defense. In such cases, it is more common for an abused wife to act aggressively, going after her husband with a gun or a knife. But in Donna's case, she had spent months discussing her husband's slaying and the terms of payment with the Greenwill brothers. And prosecutors asserted that Donna's motive was to gain more than $250,000 in life insurance that Dennis had bought.

Lenore Walker, a psychologist and expert on battered wife's syndrome who testified on Donna's behalf, said women in Donna's situation feel so terrorized they turn to others they perceive as having power and plead for their help. It is often an unfortunate circumstance because, later, these women may face conspiracy to commit murder charges. Juries have been notably less lenient in deciding conspiracy cases, according to Lenore Walker, author of *Terrifying Love: Why Battered Women Kill and How Society Responds*. The Yaklich case is included among the case histories presented in the Walker book.

On May 23, 1988, a Pueblo jury acquitted Donna of first-degree murder but convicted her of conspiracy. Her attorneys, Stanley Marks and Richard Hostetler, believed Donna's sentence would be light. Contrary to what her attorneys had predicted, District Court Judge Jack Seavy handed Donna a 40-year sentence.

Decades later, after she had served 20 years of her sentence, Donna's story inspired an investigation into the death of Dennis's first wife, Barbara, who had died at the age of 35. Her death was attributed to a diet drug overdose. A special task force was assembled, but investigators found that while Barbara died under suspicious circumstances, there was no proof that she had been killed by Dennis.

Meanwhile, Donna's case brought national headlines along with a documentary on the Oxygen Network series, *Snapped*, and a 1994 made-for-TV movie, *Cries Unheard: The Donna Yaklich Story*, starring *Charlie's Angels* star Jaclyn Smith. In 2006, she was transferred to a community-based, residential treatment center after serving less than 20 years in prison. She was released from custody in December, 2010.

Resources

Delaney, Ted. May 13, 1988. Yaklich relates stories of abuse at husband's hand. *Gazette*, Colorado Springs.

Delaney, Ted. May 14, 1988. Yaklich: Husband's death was "mistake"—No other way out, she says. *Gazette*, Colorado Springs.

Delaney, Ted. July 30, 1988. Sentence squelches qualified victory. *Gazette*, Colorado Springs.

Walker, Lenore. 1989. *Terrifying Love: Why Battered Women Kill and How Society Responds*. New York: Harper Collins.

Susan Abram

Andrea Yates (1964–)

The Andrea (Kennedy) Yates murder trial, appeal, and subsequent second trial stirred controversy and drew renewed attention to the behaviors of people who

In 2006, Andrea Yates, left, who has admitted drowning her five children in a bathtub at the family home, arrives at the Harris County Criminal Justice Center with Mary Parnham, wife of her defense attorney George Parnham. Yates's defense attorney asked for a delay in the start of the capital murder retrial for the 2001 bathtub drowning deaths of her children. (AP/Wide World Photos)

are mentally ill, particularly women who develop postpartum depression, or in the Yates case, postpartum psychosis. Both are mental disorders that may occur in some women after giving birth.

Andrea was born on July 2, 1964, in Houston, Texas. In high school, she was captain of the swim team, an officer in the National Honor Society, and valedictorian of her 1982 graduating class. After high school, Andrea attended the University of Houston, where she completed a two-year nursing program. She went on to obtain her registered nursing license from the University of Texas, School of Nursing in Houston. Upon graduation, Andrea worked as a registered nurse at the University of Texas M. D. Anderson Cancer Center from 1986 until 1994. Andrea met her future husband, Rusty, in 1989 when they were both 25. They married in 1993 and "planned on having as many children as nature provided" (Montaldo, n.d., Andrea Meets Rusty Yates).

Their first child, Noah, was born in February 1994. John, their second child, was born in December 1995. After John's birth, Andrea Yates began to withdraw from people. She became reclusive. She stopped jogging and swimming. In 1996, Rusty accepted a job in Florida. The family moved to Seminole, Florida and lived in a 38-foot travel trailer. Andrea got pregnant while in Florida, but miscarried. In 1997, they returned to Houston, Texas, living in their trailer until Rusty's parents and in-laws persuaded him to move to a bigger home. Rusty purchased a 350 square foot, renovated bus from a traveling minister who preached "the role of women is derived from the sin of Eve and that bad mothers who are going to hell create bad children who will go to hell" (Montaldo, n.d., Michael Woroniecki). Andrea embraced the minister's sermons. Paul, their third child, was born in September 1997, and Luke, their fourth, was born in February 1999.

On June 16, 1999, Rusty was at work when he received a phone call from Andrea who begged him to come home. When he arrived, Andrea was shaking and chewing on her fingers. The next day, after Andrea had taken an overdose of pills, Rusty took her to the hospital where she was diagnosed with major depression and admitted. Her doctor halted her antipsychotic drugs and sent her home after only marginal improvement on June 24, 1999. At the insistence of Andrea's parents, Rusty purchased a house. Andrea had viewed her life on the bus as failing herself and her children. In the new home, Andrea began to return to the activities she enjoyed—swimming, cooking, and socializing. Rusty wanted another child; he ignored warnings from Andrea's last doctor that additional pregnancies might trigger the psychotic behavior again. Andrea stopped taking birth control medication, and on November 30, 2000, Mary, their fifth child was born. On March 12, 2001, Andrea's father died and her mental state began to collapse. She frantically read the Bible, stopped talking, and began mutilating herself. She would not feed their newborn.

On June 20, 2001, Andrea Yates drowned her five children in the bathtub. She called 911 first and then Rusty, who was at work at the time. " 'It's time. I finally did it,' she said before telling him to come home and then hanging up. Rusty called back to ask what happened. 'It's the kids,' she said. He asked which of the five and she responded, 'All of them' " (Berryman et. al., 2006, para. 4).

Andrea's 2002 trial lasted three weeks. The jury found her guilty of capital murder and sentenced her to life in prison. After an appeal, a second trial convened in 2006. Andrea's attorneys argued that severe postpartum psychosis and a delusional state, in which Andrea believed that Satan was inside her, caused her to believe that killing the children would save them. They also noted that Andrea's family has a history of mental illness. The jury in this second trial found Yates "not guilty by reason of insanity." She was committed to a state mental hospital in Texas.

Yates's crime, trial, and verdict, though not the first of its kind, "underlies . . . the dramatic chasm that divides public perceptions and myths about mental illness from what psychiatrists and other experts know to be its reality" (Colb 2002, 1). Societal reaction to the Yates verdict of "not guilty by reason of insanity" remains split. Those who feel that Yates is morally responsible for her crime of infanticide believe that she should have received life in prison at the least. Those who understand the scientific and medical implications of severe major depression believe that someone who is clinically diagnosed with a mental disorder should not be subject to the same punishment as someone who is not. Still, they recognize that proving mental illness, especially postpartum psychosis, can be a challenge. Voicing another belief, biblical feminists view Yates as a desperate woman, caught up in a strict, conservative Christian culture in which women carry the sin of Eve (Eggenbroten 2001–2002, 5).

The National Institute of Mental Health estimates that "10 to 15 percent of all mothers become depressed during the first six months after the birth of a child" (*New York Times* 2004). Postpartum psychosis is rare—1 in 500 births—and usually ends, if detected, a few days after giving birth. Yates was at greater risk for prolonged postpartum psychosis because she had prior bouts of depression, had a succession of children, and her family has a history of mental illness. Under Texas law, a "not guilty by reason of insanity" verdict requires that a judge review the case annually with jail time no longer than a conviction verdict. Andrea Yates, however, committed a capital murder, and she might spend the rest of her life in confinement.

Public and private mental health organizations have made mental illness a major priority, specifically as it relates to women, but many in our society continue to view persons with mental disorders who commit a crime not as sick people but as criminals.

Resources

Berryman, A., Fowler, D., Hylton, H., and Fulton, G. (2006, July). The Yates odyssey. *Time Magazine.* http://www.time.com/time/magazine/article/0,9171,1001706,00.html.

CBS News.com (2009). *Andrea Yates found not guilty.* http://www.cbsnews.com/sto ries/2006/07/26/national/main1837248.shtml?tag=currentVideoInfo; videoMetaInfo

Colb, Sherry F. (2002, March 27). The Andrea Yates verdict: A nation in denial about mental illness. *FindLaw.* http://writ.news.findlaw.com/colb/20020327.html

Eggenbroten, A. (2001–2002). A biblical feminist looks at the Andrea Yates tragedy (electronic version). *Newsletter of the Evangelical Ecumenical Women's Caucus,* 25, 4.

Montaldo, C. (n.d.). Profile of Andrea Yates (Supplemental Material]. *About.com Guide.* Retrieved from http://crime.about.com/od/current/p/andreayates.htm

U.S. Department of Health and Human Services. (1999). *Mental health: A report of the surgeon general.* Rockville, MD: U.S. Department of Health and Human Services, Substance Abuse and Mental Health Services Administration, Center for Mental Health Services, National Institutes of Health, National Institute of Mental Health.

Why women are more vulnerable to depression than men [Special advertising supplement]. (2004, October 24). *New York Times.* 2, 5.

Dorothy F. Striplin

Lila Young (ca. 1902–1967)

Lila Gladys Young (aka "The Butterbox Baby Killer") ran an orphanage with her husband from 1928 until 1945 near Halifax, Nova Scotia, on the east coast of Canada. Although it is not clear exactly how many infant and child deaths she is responsible for, one handyman testified that he remembered burying anywhere from 100 to 125 infants placed in butterboxes on land owned by Young's parents. All children reportedly died from neglect and malnutrition. Although this case is relatively recent, witnesses are difficult to find as many feel that they would incriminate themselves if they were to talk about working conditions at this orphanage. She remains, to this day, Canada's most prolific serial murderer.

Lila and William Young opened the Life and Health Sanitarium in their four-room cottage in East Chester, Nova Scotia, Canada, in 1928. At first, most people agreed that the sanitarium was opened with good intentions. Both Lila and her husband had strong ties to the Seventh-Day Adventist faith, and Lila was said to have a very caring nature. She had a degree from the National School of Obstetrics and Midwifery, and he was a graduate of the National School of Chiropractic, both awarded in 1928 during their stay in Chicago. By 1929, the majority of her clients were pregnant women and eventually the name of the sanitarium changed to the Ideal Maternity Home and Sanatorium.

Soon Lila began to realize that she could make considerable monies if she sold the children, rather than just giving the children away to a loving home. Children were often sold to couples who wanted children, with some sales to couples in the United States. Laws at the time forbid adoption to families where the child and the adoptive family did not have the same religious background. The Youngs were unconcerned about this stipulation, and many Jewish families were allowed to adopt non-Jewish children, and their lives were spared. Problem children were sold to farmers, often at a discounted rate, to ensure a source of free indebted labor.

Those who were not adopted, often because they had slight imperfections, were starved to death on a diet of sugar water and/or molasses, often lasting no more than two weeks. In some cases, women who wanted to keep their children were told their children had taken ill and died if there was a prospective buyer for a child. Those infants who were killed were buried on the property and in the surrounding area in small pine butterboxes provided by the local dairy.

By 1933, the business was geared for expansion, with additions made to the original building, and a new home for the Youngs. By 1938, the mortgage had been paid off completely. Women who could not afford birthing services at the home could work off their debt by working at the home until their debt was paid. This ensured a constant source of cheap labor. Although official suspicion began in 1933 with the appointment of Dr. Frank Roy Davis to the Health Portfolio in the local government, the orphanage continued to operate. Interestingly, Lila had developed quite a groundswell of local and political support. It is suspected she was supported by the elite of the community, as well as the poor, as many people had discretely used her services. By 1940, changes in the Maternity Boarding House Act required that maternity homes be licensed. The Ideal Maternity Home applied and was denied.

This case holds significance for many reasons. Lila Young ran one of the few examples of a black market adoption agency that existed at this time. Women were charged anywhere from $300 to $500 for birthing services, while adoptive parents made generous "contributions" to the Ideal Maternity Home, ranging from $1,000 to $10,000. It is estimated that birthing services for the women generated as much as $60,000 per year. Significantly more money came from the selling of babies to couples who could not have children of their own. It has been estimated that approximately 700 babies were sold at an average price of $5,000 during the operation of the orphanage (an estimated $3.5 million in revenue). This case clearly exhibits the profitability to be found in selling children at that time.

Finally, this case highlights the lack of protections for small children and infants prior to World War II. Because of the restrictions on reproductive rights, and the strong taboos on women having children out of wedlock, the environment for abuses of these stigmatized women and unwanted children was ripe. Women used the Youngs' services because Lila Young promised to be discrete. The birth mothers seldom came back to check on the services they had paid or worked for. Further, Lila handled most inquiries about children by stating that they had been adopted or, in some cases, that they had died of illness. These agencies were not regulated, and therefore, finding verification for her claims was difficult. Many of the survivors of this orphanage have banded together to search for other survivors and adoptees. A movie, *The Butterbox Babies*, was made in 1996, documenting the story of Lila Young's activities, bringing national and international attention to her crimes.

Resource

Cahill, B.L. (2006). *Butterbox babies: Baby sales, baby deaths. New revelations 15 year later.* Halifax, NS, Canada: Fernwood Publishing.

Hannah Scott

Z

Anna Zwanziger (1760–1811)

Anna Marie Schonleben in Nuremberg, Germany, in 1760. The death of both parents by the time she was 5 years old left her an orphan. She was moved among relatives after her parents' deaths, but at the age of 10, an affluent male relative became Anna's guardian and made certain that she became educated. When she was 15 however, he introduced Anna to Mr. Zwanziger, a man more than 30-years-old. Anna's guardian forced her to marry this man, against her wishes.

Anna Zwanziger gave birth to two children during this marriage, but the marriage was doomed from the start. Her husband spent the majority of his time, and the family's money, on alcohol. Anna Zwanziger attempted suicide twice but failed both times. Because her husband continued to spend the family's money on alcohol, Anna Zwanziger had to find a way to support her family, and prostitution was her solution. Upon her husband's death, when she was 33 years old, Anna Zwanziger began taking on housekeeping and cleaning jobs to meet expenses and maintain a livelihood. It has been asserted that she moved from prostitution to housekeeping because she felt the latter employers might be more suitable as future partners.

In her mid-forties, Anna Zwanziger became determined to find a second husband. She secured a job with a Bavarian judge named Glaser who was separated from his wife. Though her role was that of housekeeper and cook for the judge, she considered him a potential spouse. Viewing the estranged wife as a threat, Zwanziger lured the wife back to the house and began poisoning her tea with large doses of arsenic, an easily accessible substance at that time. When the judge did not propose to Zwanziger, even after his wife's death, Zwanziger began poisoning guests who came to his home. Judge Glaser eventually began questioning Zwanziger's meals and continued to lack interest in her sexually. Anna Zwanziger consequently decided to leave his residence to for a job with another legal professional.

Still seeking a second husband, Anna Zwanziger discovered that her new employer, Judge Grohmann, already had a fiancée. Believing herself once again to have been rejected by her male employer, Anna Zwanziger decided to ensure that he would marry no one else. This time, however, rather than looking at potential recipients of his affection, she targeted him. Using arsenic again, she began poisoning Grohmann's food and drink. He ultimately died, but because he had frequently suffered from gout, the authorities decreed his death to be from "natural causes." Zwanziger was, consequently, free to continue killing.

In a third household, she worked as a nurse for Judge Gebhard, a man seeking a caretaker for his sickly wife who had just given birth. Anna Zwanziger began poisoning Gebhard's wife, assuming he would desire Anna once his wife was gone. Again, arsenic was her weapon of choice. Although Gebhard's wife accused Anna of poisoning her, no one believed her and she died a horrible death, as had her other victims.

When Gebhard then failed to show Anna Zwanziger attention, she began poisoning others in the household. Soon anyone who visited the home was poisoned, as well as several of Gebhard's other servants. Ultimately, Judge Gebhard noticed an odd white substance in the bottom of his drink and became suspicious of Zwanziger. He immediately asked Zwanziger to leave his employ.

Zwanziger was furious at how she was being treated. Before leaving the Gebhard home, she went to the kitchen and put large amounts of arsenic into the coffee, salt, and sugar jars. Then, she gave Gebhard's baby an arsenic-infused biscuit to chew on; the child also became ill and died.

Because of his continuing suspicions, Judge Gebhard had his kitchen foods and staples tested. The test revealed arsenic. However, Anna Zwanziger had disappeared. On October 18, 1809, she was located and arrested with a packet of arsenic in her pocket. During her trial, which lasted for months, she steadfastly maintained her innocence in the deaths of her past employers and/or their family members.

However, when the police exhumed the bodies of Mrs. Glaser and Judge Grohmann, arsenic was found, and Anna Zwanziger finally admitted to murder. Her motive: "She couldn't bear to look at their healthy, happy faces and wanted to see them writhe in pain" (Davis, 2001). Though not all of her poisoning victims died, she was successful in killing four people, including an infant. She also stated that if she had not been caught, she would have continued killing. The courts, however, denied her any future opportunities; she was beheaded in July 1811.

Prior to her execution, Anna Zwanziger confessed that she enjoyed poisoning people. For her, using arsenic to kill was not for vengeance but had, instead, become a source of pleasure. She even admitted that, like a drug, she was unable to resist the urge to poison, and she agreed that her own death was the only way to stop her addiction.

Resource

Davis, Carol Anne. 2001. *Women Who Kill*. London: Allison & Busby Limited.

Devon Thacker Thomas

APPENDICES: STATISTICS AND REPORTS ON WOMEN AND CRIME

In the following appendices, statistics from the FBI and the Bureau of Justice provide information on these topics: (a) arrests of women and girls, including trends by sex (gender) from the most recent figures through 2009; (b) gender of offenders according to victims for personal crimes of violence; and (c) numbers of prisoners by gender and incarceration rates, and death penalty imposed on women who have been sentenced for execution. Following these tables is a report, "Death Penalty for Female Offenders. January 1, 1973, Through October 31, 2010," by Victor Streib, which provides additional material that summarizes the most current information on the execution and case status of women who have been sentenced to death.

The statistics presented here represent summary data that provide the best available summary of the picture of women's offending. It is crucial to understand the origins of many of these data in order to assess what one is seeing and to make appropriate conclusions. Each picture of gender and offending is slightly different and has its strengths and weaknesses. The reader is cautioned to make conclusions that are appropriate to what the data show and do not show.

A. ARRESTS

TABLE A.1 Ten-Year Arrest Trends, by Sex, 2000–2009

[8,649 agencies; 2009 estimated population 186,864,905; 2000 estimated population 172,176,040]

Offense charged	Male Total			Male Under 18			Female Total			Female Under 18		
	2000	2009	Percent change	2000	2009	Percent change	2000	2009	Percent change	2000	2009	Percent change
TOTAL[a]	6,491,372	6,174,287	−4.9	1,047,690	807,818	−22.9	1,874,217	2,087,303	+11.4	407,526	354,012	−13.1
Murder and nonnegligent manslaughter	6,755	6,437	−4.7	576	599	+4.0	844	756	−10.4	80	53	−33.8
Forcible rape	16,139	12,469	−22.7	2,652	1,792	−32.4	169	148	−12.4	22	28	+27.3
Robbery	58,443	67,906	+16.2	14,861	17,342	+16.7	6,663	9,384	+40.8	1,532	1,994	+30.2
Aggravated assault	240,528	209,078	−13.1	31,550	22,685	−28.1	60,787	58,236	−4.2	9,583	7,247	−24.4
Burglary	151,244	159,017	+5.1	51,950	40,897	−21.3	23,497	29,764	+26.7	7,013	5,740	−18.2
Larceny-theft	454,947	451,750	−0.7	146,160	106,852	−26.9	258,379	354,854	+37.3	85,599	90,011	+5.2
Motor vehicle theft	67,551	38,987	−42.3	23,314	9,412	−59.6	12,558	8,486	−32.4	4,802	1,942	−59.6
Arson	8,820	6,432	−27.1	4,922	3,138	−36.2	1,556	1,300	−16.5	662	477	−27.9
Violent crime[b]	321,865	295,890	−8.1	49,639	42,418	−14.5	68,463	68,524	+0.1	11,217	9,322	−16.9
Property crime[b]	682,562	656,186	−3.9	226,346	160,299	−29.2	295,990	394,404	+33.2	98,076	98,170	+0.1
Other assaults	590,790	592,155	+0.2	98,731	88,631	−10.2	179,874	211,334	+17.5	43,968	46,494	+5.7
Forgery and counterfeiting	40,765	31,152	−23.6	2,746	889	−67.6	26,468	18,840	−28.8	1,398	388	−72.2
Fraud	116,447	78,550	−32.5	3,871	2,637	−31.9	100,219	61,385	−38.7	2,003	1,454	−27.4
Embezzlement	6,207	5,743	−7.5	686	224	−67.3	6,249	6,013	−3.8	638	169	−73.5
Stolen property; buying, receiving, possessing	62,320	52,247	−16.2	15,179	9,570	−36.3	13,151	14,057	+6.9	2,812	2,320	−17.5

Vandalism	143,680	133,421	−7.1	62,404	48,203	−22.8	26,230	29,090	+10.9	8,863	7,554	−14.8
Weapons; carrying, possessing, etc.	86,024	90,182	+4.8	20,096	18,553	−7.7	7,614	8,040	+5.6	2,287	2,143	−6.3
Prostitution and commercialized vice	18,886	11,639	−38.4	332	167	−49.7	25,779	25,757	−0.1	397	624	+57.2
Sex offenses (except forcible rape and prostitution)	50,319	42,609	−15.3	10,103	7,061	−30.1	3,831	4,019	+4.9	745	738	−0.9
Drug abuse violations	771,170	806,669	+4.6	102,909	86,857	−15.6	167,968	189,039	+12.5	18,757	16,800	−10.4
Gambling	3,984	2,877	−27.8	431	304	−29.5	584	482	−17.5	27	8	−70.4
Offenses against the family and children	67,421	53,001	−21.4	3,029	1,701	−43.8	18,828	17,574	−6.7	1,738	988	−43.2
Driving under the influence	734,872	651,424	−11.4	10,500	6,033	−42.5	144,794	190,445	+31.5	2,183	2,052	−6.0
Liquor laws	311,989	244,047	−21.8	66,585	41,879	−37.1	94,783	96,795	+2.1	30,753	25,980	−15.5
Drunkenness	363,705	331,804	−8.8	11,406	7,381	−35.3	56,312	66,608	+18.3	2,846	2,456	−13.7
Disorderly conduct	280,158	257,713	−8.0	69,814	61,616	−11.7	89,049	96,319	+8.2	29,020	31,138	+7.3
Vagrancy	13,151	13,189	+0.3	1,287	824	−36.0	3,721	3,628	−2.5	360	223	−38.1
All other offenses (except traffic)	1,720,089	1,746,701	+1.5	186,628	145,383	−22.1	460,661	530,612	+15.2	65,789	50,653	−23.0
Suspicion	2,757	958	−65.3	575	119	−79.3	696	335	−51.9	174	33	−81.0
Curfew and loitering law violations	67,275	50,288	−25.3	67,275	50,288	−25.3	21,915	21,915	−27.1	30,078	21,915	−27.1
Runaways	37,693	26,800	−28.9	37,693	26,800	−28.9	32,423	32,423	−39.5	53,571	32,423	−39.5

[a]Does not include suspicion.

[b]Violent crimes are offenses of murder and nonnegligent manslaughter, forcible rape, robbery, and aggravated assault. Property crimes are offenses of burglary, larceny-theft, motor vehicle theft, and arson.

Source: Federal Bureau of Investigation. Crime in the United States. Table 33. http://www2.fbi.gov/ucr/cius2009/data/table_33.html.

TABLE A.2 Five-Year Arrest Trends, by Sex, 2005–2009

[9,651 agencies; 2009 estimated population 192,575,487; 2005 estimated population 186,517,601]

| | Male | | | | | | Female | | | | | |
| | Total | | | Under 18 | | | Total | | | Under 18 | | |
Offense charged	2005	2009	Percent change	2005	2009	Percent change	2005	2009	Percent change	2005	2009	Percent change
TOTAL[a]	7,387,112	6,999,896	−5.2	1,072,951	933,186	−13.0	2,328,402	2,360,522	+1.4	448,722	404,317	−9.9
Murder and nonnegligent manslaughter	8,179	7,471	−8.7	756	747	−1.2	1,005	869	−13.5	88	56	−36.4
Forcible rape	17,066	14,289	−16.3	2,684	2,134	−20.5	212	172	−18.9	56	38	−32.1
Robbery	70,325	76,306	+8.5	18,661	20,105	+7.7	8,865	10,233	+15.4	1,951	2,216	+13.6
Aggravated assault	245,046	225,292	−8.1	32,669	25,695	−21.3	64,094	62,273	−2.8	10,041	8,071	−19.6
Burglary	174,890	176,704	+1.0	48,636	46,194	−5.0	29,738	31,558	+6.1	6,366	6,105	−4.1
Larceny-theft	489,368	517,082	+5.7	121,909	122,850	+0.8	311,727	405,250	+30.0	89,047	103,184	+15.9
Motor vehicle theft	82,705	46,703	−43.5	22,048	11,775	−46.6	17,515	9,959	−43.1	4,527	2,382	−47.4
Arson	9,770	7,142	−26.9	5,035	3,406	−32.4	1,940	1,457	−24.9	802	516	−35.7
Violent crime[b]	340,616	323,358	−5.1	54,770	48,681	−11.1	74,176	73,547	−0.8	12,136	10,381	−14.5
Property crime[b]	756,733	747,631	−1.2	197,628	184,225	−6.8	360,920	448,224	+24.2	100,742	112,187	+11.4
Other assaults	677,259	665,940	−1.7	116,749	99,969	−14.4	222,433	234,696	+5.5	57,700	51,608	−10.6
Forgery and counterfeiting	48,539	35,015	−27.9	2,002	1,012	−49.5	32,429	21,226	−34.5	949	419	−55.8
Fraud	120,597	84,764	−29.7	3,619	2,934	−18.9	101,738	65,647	−35.5	1,933	1,579	−18.3
Embezzlement	6,560	6,159	−6.1	461	239	−48.2	6,631	6,459	−2.6	365	192	−47.4
Stolen property; buying, receiving, possessing	70,996	55,717	−21.5	12,626	10,406	−17.6	16,629	13,148	−20.9	2,307	2,013	−12.7

Vandalism	163,956	156,806	-4.4	64,250	55,650	-13.4	33,741	34,394	+1.9	10,253	8,834	-13.8
Weapons; carrying, possessing, etc.	121,704	104,946	-13.8	28,398	21,500	-24.3	10,739	9,119	-15.1	3,405	2,457	-27.8
Prostitution and commercialized vice	17,924	13,105	-26.9	275	197	-28.4	32,953	27,709	-15.9	741	675	-8.9
Sex offenses (except forcible rape and prostitution)	56,144	47,954	-14.6	10,627	8,307	-21.8	5,109	4,368	-14.5	1,092	953	-12.7
Drug abuse violations	1,022,878	930,152	-9.1	111,771	102,338	-8.4	242,534	212,255	-12.5	22,852	19,086	-16.5
Gambling	6,524	6,231	-4.5	1,358	1,223	-9.9	567	586	+3.4	31	18	-41.9
Offenses against the family and children	68,478	60,511	-11.6	2,415	1,976	-18.2	22,007	20,091	-8.7	1,547	1,117	-27.8
Driving under the influence	744,389	733,761	-1.4	9,497	6,976	-26.5	178,347	214,911	+20.5	2,704	2,330	-13.8
Liquor laws	301,462	280,477	-7.0	57,358	48,804	-14.9	109,796	114,805	+4.6	32,370	30,884	-4.6
Drunkenness	323,717	347,376	+7.3	8,218	7,492	-8.8	58,915	70,203	+19.2	2,591	2,573	-0.7
Disorderly conduct	346,952	327,950	-5.5	96,322	77,679	-19.4	122,695	119,782	-2.4	46,095	38,263	-17.0
Vagrancy	18,620	16,445	-11.7	1,160	817	-29.6	5,310	4,131	-22.2	322	206	-36.0
All other offenses (except traffic)	2,070,416	1,972,015	-4.8	190,799	169,178	-11.3	613,711	605,969	-1.3	71,565	59,290	-17.2
Suspicion	2,114	971	-54.1	226	119	-47.3	362	381	+5.2	102	35	-65.7
Curfew and loitering law violations	67,831	54,080	-20.3	54,080		-20.3	23,599	23,599	-18.9	29,101	23,599	-18.9
Runaways	34,817	29,503	-15.3	29,503		-15.3	35,653	35,653	-25.6	47,921	35,653	-25.6

aDoes not include suspicion.

bViolent crimes are offenses of murder and nonnegligent manslaughter, forcible rape, robbery, and aggravated assault. Property crimes are offenses of burglary, larceny-theft, motor vehicle theft, and arson.

Source: Federal Bureau of Investigation. *Crime in the United States*. Table 35. http://www2.fbi.gov/ucr/cius2009/data/table_35.html.

TABLE A.3 Current Year Over Previous Year Arrest Trends, by Sex, 2008–2009

[11,310 agencies; 2009 estimated population 224,035,573; 2008 estimated population 222,163,484]

	Male						Female					
	Total			Under 18			Total			Under 18		
Offense charged	2008	2009	Percent change	2008	2009	Percent change	2008	2009	Percent change	2008	2009	Percent change
TOTAL[a]	7,640,534	7,394,270	-3.2	1,079,484	976,538	-9.5	2,510,670	2,514,440	+0.2	467,876	432,979	-7.5
Murder and nonnegligent manslaughter	8,113	7,723	-4.8	815	737	-9.6	974	931	-4.4	61	60	-1.6
Forcible rape	15,808	14,906	-5.7	2,359	2,189	-7.2	189	187	-1.1	38	40	+5.3
Robbery	82,549	79,722	-3.4	22,491	19,908	-11.5	11,026	10,898	-1.2	2,349	2,267	-3.5
Aggravated assault	249,642	244,031	-2.2	30,759	27,123	-11.8	68,590	68,412	-0.3	9,575	8,918	-6.9
Burglary	194,315	186,328	-4.1	54,136	48,423	-10.6	33,571	32,995	-1.7	7,652	6,341	-17.1
Larceny-theft	548,430	550,408	+0.4	135,022	129,359	-4.2	390,535	430,794	+10.3	107,706	109,283	+1.5
Motor vehicle theft	57,144	47,126	-17.5	14,220	11,264	-20.8	11,913	10,239	-14.1	2,705	2,334	-13.7
Arson	8,891	7,464	-16.0	4,321	3,527	-18.4	1,670	1,505	-9.9	605	529	-12.6
Violent crime[b]	356,112	346,382	-2.7	56,424	49,957	-11.5	80,779	80,428	-0.4	12,023	11,285	-6.1
Property crime[b]	808,780	791,326	-2.2	207,699	192,573	-7.3	437,689	475,533	+8.6	118,668	118,487	-0.2
Other assaults	696,537	699,135	+0.4	110,518	103,892	-6.0	241,577	247,510	+2.5	57,566	54,546	-5.2
Forgery and counterfeiting	41,312	38,200	-7.5	1,305	1,101	-15.6	25,702	23,125	-10.0	659	467	-29.1
Fraud	98,149	90,429	-7.9	3,634	3,101	-14.7	78,205	69,760	-10.8	1,950	1,682	-13.7
Embezzlement	7,616	6,487	-14.8	549	259	-52.8	8,240	6,728	-18.3	403	201	-50.1
Stolen property; buying, receiving, possessing	66,123	61,491	-7.0	12,799	11,488	-10.2	17,005	16,129	-5.2	2,960	2,677	-9.6
Vandalism	173,154	162,543	-6.1	68,134	57,864	-15.1	35,798	35,661	-0.4	10,606	9,186	-13.4
Weapons; carrying, possessing, etc.	117,737	109,084	-7.3	25,944	22,091	-14.9	9,682	9,577	-1.1	2,772	2,580	-6.9

Prostitution and commercialized vice	15,234	14,507	-4.8	263	203	-22.8	31,431	29,832	-5.1	756	690	-8.7
Sex offenses (except forcible rape and prostitution)	52,437	50,862	-3.0	9,570	8,913	-6.9	4,852	4,772	-1.6	1,021	1,042	+2.1
Drug abuse violations	961,288	941,094	-2.1	104,916	101,001	-3.7	223,523	219,109	-2.0	20,322	19,624	-3.4
Gambling	3,091	3,548	+14.8	375	436	+16.3	477	592	+24.1	21	13	-38.1
Offenses against the family and children	64,462	60,878	-5.6	2,759	2,194	-20.5	21,812	20,787	-4.7	1,573	1,238	-21.3
Driving under the influence	835,121	812,236	-2.7	8,724	7,736	-11.3	228,819	236,698	+3.4	2,824	2,540	-10.1
Liquor laws	332,096	305,560	-8.0	61,187	52,654	-13.9	130,202	125,468	-3.6	37,254	33,338	-10.5
Drunkenness	387,855	368,958	-4.9	8,945	7,866	-12.1	75,640	73,872	-2.3	2,906	2,668	-8.2
Disorderly conduct	360,391	345,338	-4.2	91,385	81,531	-10.8	132,544	129,193	-2.5	45,204	40,959	-9.4
Vagrancy	18,151	18,552	+2.2	2,179	1,479	-32.1	5,380	5,087	-5.4	874	578	-33.9
All other offenses (except traffic)	2,140,820	2,076,130	-3.0	198,107	178,669	-9.8	645,273	639,443	-0.9	71,474	64,042	-10.4
Suspicion	930	1,051	+13.0	139	131	-5.8	262	393	+50.0	45	36	-20.0
Curfew and loitering law violations	69,138	59,650	-13.7	69,138	59,650	-13.7	31,688	26,487	-16.4	31,688	26,487	-16.4
Runaways	34,930	31,880	-8.7	34,930	31,880	-8.7	44,352	38,649	-12.9	44,352	38,649	-12.9

[a]Does not include suspicion.

[b]Violent crimes are offenses of murder and nonnegligent manslaughter, forcible rape, robbery, and aggravated assault. Property crimes are offenses of burglary, larceny-theft, motor vehicle theft, and arson.

Source: Federal Bureau of Investigation. *Crime in the United States*. Table 37. http://www2.fbi.gov/ucr/cius2009/data/table_37.html.

TABLE A.4 Arrests. Females, by Age, 2009

[12,371 agencies; 2009 estimated population 239,839,971]

Offense charged	Total all ages	Ages under 15	Ages under 18	Ages 18 and over	Under 10	10–12	13–14	15	16	17	18
TOTAL	2,714,361	128,883	460,927	2,253,434	1,795	23,046	104,042	96,462	115,385	120,197	130,097
Total percent distribution[a]	100.0	4.7	17.0	83.0	0.1	0.8	3.8	3.6	4.3	4.4	4.8
Murder and nonnegligent manslaughter	1,020	8	69	951	1	1	6	9	29	23	35
Forcible rape	208	23	45	163	1	7	15	9	7	6	7
Robbery	11,919	547	2,523	9,396	0	64	483	544	669	763	885
Aggravated assault	72,905	3,056	9,747	63,158	45	634	2,377	2,074	2,346	2,271	2,556
Burglary	35,109	1,945	6,863	28,246	58	395	1,492	1,456	1,591	1,871	2,243
Larceny-theft	463,508	30,641	116,330	347,178	379	6,068	24,194	22,811	29,867	33,011	33,258
Motor vehicle theft	11,408	683	2,646	8,762	3	60	620	664	687	612	602
Arson	1,617	308	552	1,065	15	87	206	108	81	55	45
Violent crime[b]	86,052	3,634	12,384	73,668	47	706	2,881	2,636	3,051	3,063	3,483
Violent crime percent distribution[a]	100.0	4.2	14.4	85.6	0.1	0.8	3.3	3.1	3.5	3.6	4.0
Property crime[b]	511,642	33,577	126,391	385,251	455	6,610	26,512	25,039	32,226	35,549	36,148
Property crime percent distribution[a]	100.0	6.6	24.7	75.3	0.1	1.3	5.2	4.9	6.3	6.9	7.1
Other assaults	269,736	21,327	59,135	210,601	284	4,478	16,565	12,320	13,396	12,092	10,316
Forgery and counterfeiting	25,425	57	504	24,921	3	11	43	75	105	267	746
Fraud	69,393	293	1,762	67,631	14	36	243	267	455	747	1,437
Embezzlement	7,177	9	203	6,974	0	1	8	12	54	128	332
Stolen property; buying, receiving, possessing	17,300	711	2,811	14,489	13	120	578	611	696	793	937
Vandalism	38,504	3,814	9,782	28,722	119	1,013	2,682	1,761	2,079	2,128	2,083
Weapons; carrying, possessing, etc.	10,511	1,112	2,767	7,744	54	266	792	492	588	575	501
Prostitution and commercialized vice	39,437	82	844	38,593	2	1	79	175	220	367	1,383
Sex offenses (except forcible rape and prostitution)	5,337	528	1,109	4,228	26	136	366	220	179	182	249
Drug abuse violations	242,414	4,142	21,002	221,412	23	481	3,638	3,874	5,337	7,649	12,181
Gambling	904	1	38	866	0	0	1	5	13	19	42
Offenses against the family and children	22,332	354	1,295	21,037	12	74	268	322	293	326	497
Driving under the influence	251,695	70	2,668	249,027	10	6	54	134	604	1,860	5,169
Liquor laws	128,132	3,952	34,049	94,083	26	326	3,600	5,696	9,595	14,806	24,297

19	20	21	22	23	24	25–29	30–34	35–39	40–44	45–49	50–54	55–59	60–64	65 and over
134,691	124,382	108,434	99,536	95,009	89,849	381,314	275,486	240,329	215,857	179,511	99,500	42,964	18,592	17,883
5.0	4.6	4.0	3.7	3.5	3.3	14.0	10.1	8.9	8.0	6.6	3.7	1.6	0.7	0.7
46	44	61	44	36	42	173	128	82	108	70	46	18	10	8
9	13	13	3	8	7	31	16	21	17	8	5	5	0	0
785	679	581	543	501	429	1,709	1,028	811	685	461	200	66	21	12
2,765	2,911	2,931	2,749	2,725	2,630	11,314	8,395	7,161	6,526	5,362	3,014	1,206	508	405
2,059	1,764	1,629	1,312	1,259	1,131	5,062	3,511	2,843	2,289	1,712	840	360	138	94
27,879	22,513	18,630	15,949	14,607	13,638	54,579	37,902	31,140	27,010	22,653	14,036	7,029	3,525	2,830
534	513	426	428	403	375	1,796	1,210	938	733	488	212	66	22	16
48	35	32	43	30	35	174	124	108	124	135	62	36	15	19
3,605	3,647	3,586	3,339	3,270	3,108	13,227	9,567	8,075	7,336	5,901	3,265	1,295	539	425
4.2	4.2	4.2	3.9	3.8	3.6	15.4	11.1	9.4	8.5	6.9	3.8	1.5	0.6	0.5
30,520	24,825	20,717	17,732	16,299	15,179	61,611	42,747	35,029	30,156	24,988	15,150	7,491	3,700	2,959
6.0	4.9	4.0	3.5	3.2	3.0	12.0	8.4	6.8	5.9	4.9	3.0	1.5	0.7	0.6
10,355	10,458	10,526	9,927	9,335	8,824	37,207	27,107	23,860	20,783	16,537	8,694	3,731	1,640	1,301
1,066	1,223	1,102	1,037	1,049	1,099	5,088	4,003	3,102	2,414	1,635	848	319	137	53
1,896	2,290	2,166	2,254	2,236	2,320	12,287	10,779	10,186	8,093	5,438	3,183	1,577	837	652
488	388	378	332	278	296	1,125	873	779	628	489	321	152	72	43
891	820	788	751	686	630	2,844	1,974	1,490	1,232	820	384	152	57	33
1,958	1,728	1,746	1,561	1,362	1,307	5,145	3,351	2,723	2,253	1,866	944	381	176	138
443	445	422	390	378	345	1,409	922	728	657	529	295	158	65	57
1,932	1,946	1,817	1,731	1,617	1,409	6,275	4,779	5,136	4,947	3,579	1,529	393	91	29
266	241	193	185	168	176	670	526	500	422	342	153	84	37	16
13,113	12,225	11,381	10,186	9,867	9,333	39,392	26,802	23,166	21,798	18,243	9,145	3,288	935	357
54	68	13	14	13	16	66	54	75	84	102	98	68	54	45
550	633	730	815	895	963	4,558	3,838	3,051	2,080	1,315	658	265	102	87
7,219	8,342	12,713	12,551	12,143	11,083	44,220	29,811	26,618	26,295	25,143	15,186	7,175	3,235	2,124
25,167	19,285	2,253	1,480	1,208	997	3,810	2,952	2,923	3,207	3,332	1,809	797	322	244

(Continued)

TABLE A.4 Arrests. Females, by Age, 2009 *(Continued)*

[12,371 agencies; 2009 estimated population 239,839,971]

Offense charged	Total all ages	Ages under 15	Ages under 18	Ages 18 and over	Under 10	10–12	13–14	15	16	17	18
Drunkenness	78,141	504	2,814	75,327	13	48	443	545	659	1,106	2,376
Disorderly conduct	139,315	16,744	44,722	94,593	131	3,415	13,198	9,839	9,916	8,223	6,321
Vagrancy	5,655	164	601	5,054	0	22	142	169	161	107	293
All other offenses (except traffic)	696,621	17,595	67,793	628,828	336	2,606	14,653	15,020	17,173	18,005	21,289
Suspicion	424	10	39	385	3	1	6	6	10	13	17
Curfew and loitering law violations	27,504	7,442	27,504	–	73	1,042	6,327	6,658	7,460	5,944	–
Runaways	40,710	12,761	40,710	–	151	1,647	10,963	10,586	11,115	6,248	–

[a]Because of rounding, the percentages may not add to 100.0.

[b]Violent crimes are offenses of murder and nonnegligent manslaughter, forcible rape, robbery, and aggravated assault. Property crimes are offenses of burglary, larceny-theft, motor vehicle theft, and arson.

Source: Federal Bureau of Investigation. *Crime in the United States.* Table 40. http://www2.fbi.gov/ucr/cius2009/data/table_40.html.

19	20	21	22	23	24	25–29	30–34	35–39	40–44	45–49	50–54	55–59	60–64	65 and over
2,729	2,536	3,407	3,056	2,950	2,628	11,147	8,265	8,405	9,734	9,640	5,463	2,000	692	299
5,512	5,135	5,548	4,780	4,372	3,911	15,507	10,573	9,537	8,647	7,568	4,141	1,722	703	616
314	246	179	123	133	112	547	508	689	695	639	370	138	44	24
26,589	27,879	28,740	27,272	26,728	26,093	115,121	86,014	74,208	64,370	51,383	27,843	11,769	5,152	8,378
24	22	29	20	22	20	58	41	49	26	22	21	9	2	3
–	–	–	–	–	–	–	–	–	–	–	–	–	–	–
–	–	–	–	–	–	–	–	–	–	–	–	–	–	–

TABLE A.5 Arrests, by Sex, 2009

[12,371 agencies; 2009 estimated population 239,839,971]

| Offense charged | Number of persons arrested | | | | | | Percent distribution[a] | | |
	Total	Male	Female	Percent male	Percent female		Total	Male	Female
TOTAL[a]	10,741,157	8,026,796	2,714,361	74.7	25.3		100.0	100.0	100.0
Murder and nonnegligent manslaughter	9,775	8,755	1,020	89.6	10.4		0.1	0.1	*
Forcible rape	16,442	16,234	208	98.7	1.3		0.2	0.2	*
Robbery	100,702	88,783	11,919	88.2	11.8		0.9	1.1	0.4
Aggravated assault	331,372	258,467	72,905	78.0	22.0		3.1	3.2	2.7
Burglary	235,226	200,117	35,109	85.1	14.9		2.2	2.5	1.3
Larceny-theft	1,060,754	597,246	463,508	56.3	43.7		9.9	7.4	17.1
Motor vehicle theft	64,169	52,761	11,408	82.2	17.8		0.6	0.7	0.4
Arson	9,509	7,892	1,617	83.0	17.0		0.1	0.1	0.1
Violent crime[b]	458,291	372,239	86,052	81.2	18.8		4.3	4.6	3.2
Property crime[b]	1,369,658	858,016	511,642	62.6	37.4		12.8	10.7	18.8
Other assaults	1,036,754	767,018	269,736	74.0	26.0		9.7	9.6	9.9
Forgery and counterfeiting	67,357	41,932	25,425	62.3	37.7		0.6	0.5	0.9
Fraud	162,243	92,850	69,393	57.2	42.8		1.5	1.2	2.6
Embezzlement	14,097	6,920	7,177	49.1	50.9		0.1	0.1	0.3
Stolen property; buying, receiving, possessing	82,944	65,644	17,300	79.1	20.9		0.8	0.8	0.6
Vandalism	212,981	174,477	38,504	81.9	18.1		2.0	2.2	1.4
Weapons; carrying, possessing, etc.	130,941	120,430	10,511	92.0	8.0		1.2	1.5	0.4
Prostitution and commercialized vice	56,640	17,203	39,437	30.4	69.6		0.5	0.2	1.5
Sex offenses (except forcible rape and prostitution)	60,422	55,085	5,337	91.2	8.8		0.6	0.7	0.2

Offense charged	Total	Male	Female	Percent male	Percent female	Percent distribution total	Percent distribution male	Percent distribution female
Drug abuse violations	1,305,191	1,062,777	242,414	81.4	18.6	12.2	13.2	8.9
Gambling	8,067	7,163	904	88.8	11.2	0.1	0.1	*
Offenses against the family and children	87,889	65,557	22,332	74.6	25.4	0.8	0.8	0.8
Driving under the influence	1,112,384	860,689	251,695	77.4	22.6	10.4	10.7	9.3
Liquor laws	447,496	319,364	128,132	71.4	28.6	4.2	4.0	4.7
Drunkenness	471,727	393,586	78,141	83.4	16.6	4.4	4.9	2.9
Disorderly conduct	518,374	379,059	139,315	73.1	26.9	4.8	4.7	5.1
Vagrancy	26,380	20,725	5,655	78.6	21.4	0.2	0.3	0.2
All other offenses (except traffic)	2,946,277	2,249,656	696,621	76.4	23.6	27.4	28.0	25.7
Suspicion	1,517	1,093	424	72.1	27.9	*	*	*
Curfew and loitering law violations	89,733	62,229	27,504	69.3	30.7	0.8	0.8	1.0
Runaways	73,794	33,084	40,710	44.8	55.2	0.7	0.4	1.5

Note: * = Less than one-tenth of 1 percent.

[a]Because of rounding, the percentages may not add to 100.0.

[b]Violent crimes are offenses of murder and nonnegligent manslaughter, forcible rape, robbery, and aggravated assault. Property crimes are offenses of burglary, larceny theft, motor vehicle theft, and arson.

Source: Federal Bureau of Investigation. *Crime in the United States.* Table 42. http://www2.fbi.gov/ucr/cius2009/data/table_42.html.

TABLE A.6 Trends, Cities, by Sex, 2008–2009

[8,275 agencies; 2009 estimated population 155,344,295; 2008 estimated population 153,870,093]

Offense charged	Male						Female					
	Total			Under 18			Total			Under 18		
	2008	2009	Percent change	2008	2009	Percent change	2008	2009	Percent change	2008	2009	Percent change
TOTAL[a]	5,701,583	5,494,797	−3.6	884,010	799,180	−9.6	1,920,138	1,918,882	−0.1	390,761	361,643	−7.5
Murder and nonnegligent manslaughter	5,966	5,602	−6.1	647	585	−9.6	692	643	−7.1	51	50	−2.0
Forcible rape	11,449	10,759	−6.0	1,754	1,568	−10.6	127	130	+2.4	29	26	−10.3
Robbery	70,428	67,651	−3.9	19,476	17,227	−11.5	9,543	9,463	−0.8	2,072	2,022	−2.4
Aggravated assault	187,580	182,925	−2.5	24,099	20,994	−12.9	53,480	52,952	−1.0	7,624	6,943	−8.9
Burglary	143,181	137,090	−4.3	41,283	37,659	−8.8	25,783	25,256	−2.0	6,192	5,176	−16.4
Larceny-theft	452,441	456,752	+1.0	115,012	110,192	−4.2	337,948	373,269	+10.5	95,953	97,364	+1.5
Motor vehicle theft	42,810	34,687	−19.0	10,992	8,603	−21.7	8,971	7,646	−14.8	2,077	1,791	−13.8
Arson	6,659	5,468	−17.9	3,469	2,800	−19.3	1,209	1,097	−9.3	459	418	−8.9
Violent crime[b]	275,423	266,937	−3.1	45,976	40,374	−12.2	63,842	63,188	−1.0	9,776	9,041	−7.5
Property crime[b]	645,091	633,997	−1.7	170,756	159,254	−6.7	373,911	407,268	+8.9	104,681	104,749	+0.1
Other assaults	528,071	527,055	−0.2	85,150	79,825	−6.3	183,843	187,405	+1.9	45,480	42,753	−6.0
Forgery and counterfeiting	31,655	28,874	−8.8	1,016	864	−15.0	19,376	17,432	−10.0	527	374	−29.0
Fraud	60,122	57,126	−5.0	2,896	2,443	−15.6	43,158	40,072	−7.2	1,519	1,336	−12.0
Embezzlement	5,813	4,923	−15.3	447	208	−53.5	6,489	5,182	−20.1	329	159	−51.7
Stolen property; buying, receiving, possessing	51,202	47,284	−7.7	10,850	9,764	−10.0	13,795	13,152	−4.7	2,644	2,385	−9.8

Vandalism	136,785	127,288	−6.9	55,938	47,005	−16.0	28,410	28,006	−1.4	8,665	7,385	−14.8
Weapons; carrying, possessing, etc.	92,594	85,251	−7.9	21,262	18,225	−14.3	7,584	7,518	−0.9	2,182	2,034	−6.8
Prostitution and commercialized vice	14,126	13,374	−5.3	239	175	−26.8	29,320	27,893	−4.9	692	636	−8.1
Sex offenses (except forcible rape and prostitution)	36,710	35,851	−2.3	6,732	6,359	−5.5	3,959	3,759	−5.1	810	775	−4.3
Drug abuse violations	728,856	703,920	−3.4	83,919	80,579	−4.0	165,599	159,104	−3.9	15,882	15,273	−3.8
Gambling	2,598	2,745	+5.7	337	407	+20.8	354	378	+6.8	17	8	−52.9
Offenses against the family and children	26,378	27,123	+2.8	1,672	1,652	−1.2	13,578	13,673	+0.7	1,111	990	−10.9
Driving under the influence	520,544	495,964	−4.7	5,906	5,221	−11.6	149,511	151,809	+1.5	2,004	1,773	−11.5
Liquor laws	266,182	244,615	−8.1	46,989	40,246	−14.4	103,839	99,472	−4.2	28,540	25,469	−10.8
Drunkenness	334,247	318,915	−4.6	7,789	6,843	−12.1	63,767	62,588	−1.8	2,522	2,315	−8.2
Disorderly conduct	307,347	295,566	−3.8	78,918	70,183	−11.1	113,560	110,385	−2.8	39,255	35,649	−9.2
Vagrancy	16,385	16,361	−0.1	1,955	1,315	−32.7	4,674	4,042	−13.5	784	499	−36.4
All other offenses (except traffic)	1,529,191	1,480,535	−3.2	163,000	147,145	−9.7	467,564	461,498	−1.3	59,336	52,982	−10.7
Suspicion	712	481	−32.4	118	67	−43.2	174	163	−6.3	35	16	−54.3
Curfew and loitering law violations	66,115	56,760	−14.1	66,115	56,760	−14.1	29,954	24,905	−16.9	29,954	24,905	−16.9
Runaways	26,148	24,333	−6.9	26,148	24,333	−6.9	34,051	30,153	−11.4	34,051	30,153	−11.4

[a] Does not include suspicion.

[b] Violent crimes are offenses of murder and nonnegligent manslaughter, forcible rape, robbery, and aggravated assault. Property crimes are offenses of burglary, larceny-theft, motor vehicle theft, and arson.

Source: Federal Bureau of Investigation. Crime in the United States. Table 45. http://www2.fbi.gov/ucr/cius2009/data/table_45.html.

TABLE A.7 Arrest Trends, Metropolitan Counties, by Sex, 2008–2009

[1,195 agencies; 2009 estimated population 47,724,783; 2008 estimated population 47,402,595]

	Male						Female					
	Total			Under 18			Total			Under 18		
Offense charged	2008	2009	Percent change	2008	2009	Percent change	2008	2009	Percent change	2008	2009	Percent change
TOTAL[a]	1,355,319	1,320,026	−2.6	148,865	135,120	−9.2	413,087	413,902	+0.2	58,820	54,722	−7.0
Murder and nonnegligent manslaughter	1,605	1,520	−5.3	130	116	−10.8	209	194	−7.2	9	8	−11.1
Forcible rape	2,946	2,740	−7.0	405	404	−0.2	39	38	−2.6	2	9	+350.0
Robbery	10,584	10,395	−1.8	2,855	2,484	−13.0	1,271	1,222	−3.9	259	231	−10.8
Aggravated assault	46,063	45,200	−1.9	5,380	4,983	−7.4	11,554	11,702	+1.3	1,625	1,637	+0.7
Burglary	35,498	33,831	−4.7	9,483	7,804	−17.7	5,561	5,405	−2.8	1,102	863	−21.7
Larceny-theft	72,528	71,542	−1.4	16,187	15,606	−3.6	42,664	46,532	+9.1	10,220	10,280	+0.6
Motor vehicle theft	10,761	9,362	−13.0	2,473	2,084	−15.7	2,214	1,932	−12.7	471	380	−19.3
Arson	1,566	1,400	−10.6	671	553	−17.6	321	296	−7.8	117	88	−24.8
Violent crime[b]	61,198	59,855	−2.2	8,770	7,987	−8.9	13,073	13,156	+0.6	1,895	1,885	−0.5
Property crime[b]	120,353	116,135	−3.5	28,814	26,047	−9.6	50,760	54,165	+6.7	11,910	11,611	−2.5
Other assaults	116,313	118,572	+1.9	19,397	18,415	−5.1	39,949	41,905	+4.9	9,286	9,184	−1.1
Forgery and counterfeiting	7,166	7,016	−2.1	227	197	−13.2	4,370	4,003	−8.4	93	69	−25.8
Fraud	24,569	21,306	−13.3	521	507	−2.7	21,774	18,031	−17.2	318	235	−26.1
Embezzlement	1,440	1,227	−14.8	94	43	−54.3	1,324	1,167	−11.9	63	39	−38.1
Stolen property; buying, receiving, possessing	11,686	10,944	−6.3	1,561	1,369	−12.3	2,563	2,319	−9.5	251	212	−15.5
Vandalism	25,264	24,495	−3.0	9,132	7,849	−14.0	5,142	5,362	+4.3	1,437	1,337	−7.0

Weapons; carrying, possessing, etc.	19,257	17,722	−8.0	3,976	3,296	−17.1	1,645	1,576	−4.2	513	478	−6.8
Prostitution and commercialized vice	987	1,032	+4.6	20	24	+20.0	2,018	1,865	−7.6	62	53	−14.5
Sex offenses (except forcible rape and prostitution)	10,913	10,575	−3.1	1,952	1,795	−8.0	629	715	+13.7	148	180	+21.6
Drug abuse violations	171,242	172,071	+0.5	16,668	16,193	−2.8	41,447	42,448	+2.4	3,314	3,287	−0.8
Gambling	333	578	+73.6	21	23	+9.5	77	180	+133.8	2	4	+100.0
Offenses against the family and children	28,383	24,699	−13.0	819	378	−53.8	5,860	4,813	−17.9	336	159	−52.7
Driving under the influence	199,271	199,979	+0.4	1,617	1,346	−16.8	51,340	54,515	+6.2	480	423	−11.9
Liquor laws	41,081	38,188	−7.0	9,098	7,950	−12.6	16,505	16,437	−0.4	5,580	5,260	−5.7
Drunkenness	37,416	35,025	−6.4	773	724	−6.3	8,130	7,618	−6.3	248	259	+4.4
Disorderly conduct	36,005	33,814	−6.1	9,304	8,458	−9.1	12,886	12,730	−1.2	4,439	3,975	−10.5
Vagrancy	1,568	1,903	+21.4	209	157	−24.9	665	973	+46.3	86	74	−14.0
All other offenses (except traffic)	431,443	416,451	−3.5	26,461	23,923	−9.6	123,445	122,015	−1.2	8,874	8,089	−8.8
Suspicion	147	501	+240.8	10	56	+460.0	68	220	+223.5	7	19	+171.4
Curfew and loitering law violations	2,705	2,607	−3.6	2,705	2,607	−3.6	1,551	1,373	−11.5	1,551	1,373	−11.5
Runaways	6,726	5,832	−13.3	6,726	5,832	−13.3	7,934	6,536	−17.6	7,934	6,536	−17.6

[a]Does not include suspicion.

[b]Violent crimes are offenses of murder and nonnegligent manslaughter, forcible rape, robbery, and aggravated assault. Property crimes are offenses of burglary, larceny-theft, motor vehicle theft, and arson.

Source: Federal Bureau of Investigation. Crime in the United States. Table 51. http://www2.fbi.gov/ucr/cius2009/data/table_51.html.

TABLE A.8 Arrest Trends, Nonmetropolitan Counties, by Sex, 2008–2009

[1,840 agencies; 2009 estimated population 20,966,495; 2008 estimated population 20,890,796]

	Male						Female					
	Total			Under 18			Total			Under 18		
Offense charged	2008	2009	Percent change	2008	2009	Percent change	2008	2009	Percent change	2008	2009	Percent change
TOTAL[a]	583,632	579,447	-0.7	46,609	42,238	-9.4	177,445	181,656	+2.4	18,295	16,614	-9.2
Murder and nonnegligent manslaughter	542	601	+10.9	38	36	-5.3	73	94	+28.8	1	2	+100.0
Forcible rape	1,413	1,407	-0.4	200	217	+8.5	23	19	-17.4	7	5	-28.6
Robbery	1,537	1,676	+9.0	160	197	+23.1	212	213	+0.5	18	14	-22.2
Aggravated assault	15,999	15,906	-0.6	1,280	1,146	-10.5	3,556	3,758	+5.7	326	338	+3.7
Burglary	15,636	15,407	-1.5	3,370	2,960	-12.2	2,227	2,334	+4.8	358	302	-15.6
Larceny-theft	23,461	22,114	-5.7	3,823	3,561	-6.9	9,923	10,993	+10.8	1,533	1,639	+6.9
Motor vehicle theft	3,573	3,077	-13.9	755	577	-23.6	728	661	-9.2	157	163	+3.8
Arson	666	596	-10.5	181	174	-3.9	140	112	-20.0	29	23	-20.7
Violent crime[b]	19,491	19,590	+0.5	1,678	1,596	-4.9	3,864	4,084	+5.7	352	359	+2.0
Property crime[b]	43,336	41,194	-4.9	8,129	7,272	-10.5	13,018	14,100	+8.3	2,077	2,127	+2.4
Other assaults	52,153	53,508	+2.6	5,971	5,652	-5.3	17,785	18,200	+2.3	2,800	2,609	-6.8
Forgery and counterfeiting	2,491	2,310	-7.3	62	40	-35.5	1,956	1,690	-13.6	39	24	-38.5
Fraud	13,458	11,997	-10.9	217	151	-30.4	13,273	11,657	-12.2	113	111	-1.8
Embezzlement	363	337	-7.2	8	8	0.0	427	379	-11.2	11	3	-72.7
Stolen property; buying, receiving, possessing	3,235	3,263	+0.9	388	355	-8.5	647	658	+1.7	65	80	+23.1
Vandalism	11,105	10,760	-3.1	3,064	3,010	-1.8	2,246	2,293	+2.1	504	464	-7.9

Weapons; carrying, possessing, etc.	5,886	6,111	+3.8	706	570	−19.3	453	483	+6.6	77	68	−11.7
Prostitution and commercialized vice	121	101	−16.5	4	4	0.0	93	74	−20.4	2	1	−50.0
Sex offenses (except forcible rape and prostitution)	4,814	4,436	−7.9	886	759	−14.3	264	298	+12.9	63	87	+38.1
Drug abuse violations	61,190	65,103	+6.4	4,329	4,229	−2.3	16,477	17,557	+6.6	1,126	1,064	−5.5
Gambling	160	225	+40.6	17	6	−64.7	46	34	−26.1	2	1	−50.0
Offenses against the family and children	9,701	9,056	−6.6	268	164	−38.8	2,374	2,301	−3.1	126	89	−29.4
Driving under the influence	115,306	116,293	+0.9	1,201	1,169	−2.7	27,968	30,374	+8.6	340	344	+1.2
Liquor laws	24,833	22,757	−8.4	5,100	4,458	−12.6	9,858	9,559	−3.0	3,134	2,609	−16.8
Drunkenness	16,192	15,018	−7.3	383	299	−21.9	3,743	3,666	−2.1	136	94	−30.9
Disorderly conduct	17,039	15,958	−6.3	3,163	2,890	−8.6	6,098	6,078	−0.3	1,510	1,335	−11.6
Vagrancy	198	288	+45.5	15	7	−53.3	41	72	+75.6	4	5	+25.0
All other offenses (except traffic)	180,186	179,144	−0.6	8,646	7,601	−12.1	54,264	55,930	+3.1	3,264	2,971	−9.0
Suspicion	71	69	−2.8	11	8	−27.3	20	10	−50.0	3	1	−66.7
Curfew and loitering law violations	318	283	−11.0	318	283	−11.0	183	209	+14.2	183	209	+14.2
Runaways	2,056	1,715	−16.6	2,056	1,715	−16.6	1,960	1,960	−17.2	1,960	1,960	−17.2

[a]Does not include suspicion.

[b]Violent crimes are offenses of murder and nonnegligent manslaughter, forcible rape, robbery, and aggravated assault. Property crimes are offenses of burglary, larceny-theft, motor vehicle theft, and arson.

Source: Federal Bureau of Investigation. *Crime in the United States*. Table 57. http://www2.fbi.gov/ucr/cius2009/data/table_57.html.

TABLE A.9 Arrest Trends, Suburban Areas, by Sex, 2008–2009

[6,008 agencies; 2009 estimated population 94,512,203; 2008 estimated population 93,792,021]

	Male						Female					
	Total			Under 18			Total			Under 18		
Offense charged	2008	2009	Percent change	2008	2009	Percent change	2008	2009	Percent change	2008	2009	Percent change
TOTAL[a]	2,855,567	2,764,735	-3.2	397,850	361,410	-9.2	932,258	935,325	+0.3	162,412	152,145	-6.3
Murder and nonnegligent manslaughter	2,355	2,193	-6.9	200	182	-9.0	295	288	-2.4	14	18	+28.6
Forcible rape	5,348	4,984	-6.8	802	797	-0.6	63	67	+6.3	8	15	+87.5
Robbery	21,703	21,796	+0.4	5,896	5,329	-9.6	2,739	2,790	+1.9	537	528	-1.7
Aggravated assault	82,775	81,907	-1.0	10,920	10,246	-6.2	21,627	21,929	+1.4	3,417	3,370	-1.4
Burglary	69,118	66,127	-4.3	19,702	16,871	-14.4	11,018	10,950	-0.6	2,389	1,977	-17.2
Larceny-theft	194,747	194,848	+0.1	48,941	46,307	-5.4	130,924	145,246	+10.9	34,053	34,614	+1.6
Motor vehicle theft	18,428	16,151	-12.4	4,512	3,818	-15.4	3,846	3,510	-8.7	905	779	-13.9
Arson	3,613	3,158	-12.6	1,886	1,578	-16.3	618	570	-7.8	263	214	-18.6
Violent crime[b]	112,181	110,880	-1.2	17,818	16,554	-7.1	24,724	25,074	+1.4	3,976	3,931	-1.1
Property crime[b]	285,906	280,284	-2.0	75,041	68,574	-8.6	146,406	160,276	+9.5	37,610	37,584	-0.1
Other assaults	244,098	246,006	+0.8	44,201	41,948	-5.1	86,277	88,761	+2.9	21,852	20,966	-4.1
Forgery and counterfeiting	14,985	14,553	-2.9	505	466	-7.7	9,543	8,838	-7.4	256	171	-33.2
Fraud	44,356	39,896	-10.1	1,370	1,194	-12.8	36,843	31,592	-14.3	740	610	-17.6
Embezzlement	2,708	2,306	-14.8	191	75	-60.7	2,775	2,408	-13.2	125	80	-36.0
Stolen property; buying, receiving, possessing	24,518	23,283	-5.0	4,524	4,139	-8.5	6,148	5,753	-6.4	1,019	926	-9.1
Vandalism	63,615	59,784	-6.0	26,464	22,147	-16.3	12,371	12,191	-1.5	4,125	3,569	-13.5

Offense												
Weapons; carrying, possessing, etc.	37,696	35,083	-6.9	8,997	7,650	-15.0	3,258	3,368	+3.4	1,024	1,047	+2.2
Prostitution and commercialized vice	1,935	1,857	-4.0	58	63	+8.6	3,496	3,181	-9.0	102	88	-13.7
Sex offenses (except forcible rape and prostitution)	19,448	18,688	-3.9	3,776	3,462	-8.3	1,297	1,357	+4.6	358	389	+8.7
Drug abuse violations	346,821	342,702	-1.2	42,438	41,141	-3.1	83,654	83,694	*	8,804	8,472	-3.8
Gambling	680	976	+43.5	69	104	+50.7	127	259	+103.9	8	5	-37.5
Offenses against the family and children	35,867	32,555	-9.2	1,422	941	-33.8	9,447	8,478	-10.3	720	525	-27.1
Driving under the influence	371,886	362,717	-2.5	3,771	3,277	-13.1	104,185	107,158	+2.9	1,239	1,046	-15.6
Liquor laws	125,109	117,333	-6.2	26,650	23,326	-12.5	51,470	50,741	-1.4	16,194	14,810	-8.5
Drunkenness	115,485	110,265	-4.5	3,399	3,000	-11.7	25,273	24,658	-2.4	1,143	1,110	-2.9
Disorderly conduct	132,422	125,380	-5.3	37,425	33,765	-9.8	47,557	46,945	-1.3	17,142	15,734	-8.2
Vagrancy	3,637	3,933	+8.1	498	364	-26.9	1,100	1,419	+29.0	148	138	-6.8
All other offenses (except traffic)	847,782	813,856	-4.0	74,801	66,832	-10.7	256,486	251,617	-1.9	26,006	23,387	-10.1
Suspicion	405	641	+58.3	68	84	+23.5	133	293	+120.3	21	25	+19.0
Curfew and loitering law violations	13,195	12,158	-7.9	13,195	12,158	-7.9	6,431	6,071	-5.6	6,431	6,071	-5.6
Runaways	11,237	10,230	-9.0	11,237	10,230	-9.0	13,380	11,486	-14.2	13,380	11,486	-14.2

Note. Suburban areas include law enforcement agencies in cities with less than 50,000 inhabitants and county law enforcement agencies that are within a metropolitan statistical area. Suburban areas exclude all metropolitan agencies associated with a principal city. * = Less than one-tenth of 1 percent.

[a]Does not include suspicion.

[b]Violent crimes are offenses of murder and nonnegligent manslaughter, forcible rape, robbery, and aggravated assault. Property crimes are offenses of burglary, larceny-theft, motor vehicle theft, and arson.

Source: Federal Bureau of Investigation. *Crime in the United States.* Table 63. http://www2.fbi.gov/ucr/cius2009/data/table_33.html.

B. OFFENDERS ACCORDING TO VICTIMIZATION DATA

These tables provide data from the National Crime Victimization Survey, conducted by the U.S. Bureau of Justice Statistics (a division of the Department of Justice). The data reflect victims' perceptions of the offenders who victimized them violently. These data include crimes that may not have been known to police, but they are also limited by both victim memory and by victims' willingness to report in the survey that they had been victimized. (For more on victimization see "Victimization and Women's Offending" in part 1.)

TABLE B.1 Personal Crimes of Violence, 2007: Percent Distribution of Single-offender Victimizations, by Type of Crime and Perceived Gender of Offender

Type of crime	Number of single-offender victimizations	Perceived gender of offender		
		Male	Female	Not known and not available
Crimes of violence	4,074,630	75.6	20.1	4.2
Completed violence	1,171,330	78.5	19.4	2.1*
Attempted/threatened violence	2,903,300	74.5	20.4	5.1*
Rape/sexual assaulta	226,590	94.9	5.1*	0*
Robbery	297,500	86.3	11.7	2*
Completed/property taken	208,430	81.6	15.5*	2.9*
With injury	89,950	75.7	21.5*	2.8*
Without injury	118,470	86	11.1*	2.9*
Attempted to take property	89,070	97.4	2.6*	0*
With injury	23,100*	89.9*	10.1*	0*
Without injury	65,970	100	0*	0*
Assault	3,550,540	73.5	21.8	4.7
Aggravated	643,570	83.8	13.3	2.9*
Simple	2,906,960	71.3	23.6	5.1

Note: Detail may not add to total shown because of rounding.

aIncludes verbal threats of rape and threats of sexual assault.

*Estimate is based on 10 or fewer sample cases.

Source: Bureau of Justice Statistics. Filename: cv0738.csv. Table 38. Percent distribution of single-offender victimizations, by type of crime and perceived gender of offender. Data source: *National Criminal Victimization Survey*, 2007 NCJ 227669. Produced by: Cathy Maston. Authors: Patsy Klaus and Cathy Maston. Data of version: 02/03/10.

TABLE B.2 Personal Crimes of Violence, 2007: Percent Distribution of Multiple-offender Victimizations, by Type of Crime and Perceived Gender of Offenders

Type of crime	Number of multiple-offender victimizations	Perceived gender of offenders			
		All male	All female	Male and female	Not known and not available
Crimes of violence	937,200	69.10	10.30	13.10	7.50
Completed violence	365,130	72.3	13.3	9.8	4.6[b]
Attempted/threatened violence	572,070	67.1	8.5	15.1	9.4
Rape/sexual assault[a]	8,310[b]	100b	0[b]	0[b]	0[b]
Robbery	273,640	82.4	8.1[b]	5.7[b]	3.8[b]
Completed/property taken	213,030	78.6	9.2[b]	7.4[b]	4.8[b]
With injury	70,600	79.4	20.6[b]	0[b]	0[b]
Without injury	142,420	78.2	3.6[b]	11[b]	7.2[b]
Attempted to take property	60,610	95.7	4.3[b]	0[b]	0[b]
With injury	20,330[b]	100[b]	0[b]	0[b]	0[b]
Without injury	40,270	93.6	6.4[b]	0[b]	0[b]
Assault	655,240	63.2	11.4[b]	16.3	9.2
Aggravated	183,180	65.3	3.9[b]	23.5	7.4[b]
Simple	472,060	62.3	14.3	13.5	9.9

Note: Detail may not add to total shown because of rounding.

[a] Includes verbal threats of rape and threats of sexual assault.

[b] Estimate is based on 10 or fewer sample cases.

Source: Bureau of Justice Statistics. Filename: cv0744.csv. Table 44. Personal crimes of violence, 2007: Percent distribution of multiple-offender victimizations, by type of crime and perceived gender of offenders. Data source: *National Criminal Victimization Survey*, 2007 NCJ 227669 Produced by: Cathy Maston. Authors: Patsy Klaus and Cathy Maston. Data of version: 02/03/10.

C. GENDER, PRISONERS, AND THE DEATH PENALTY

These tables, adapted from the Bureau of Justice Statistics' report "National Prisoner Statistics," concern both incarceration and the death penalty and provide a specific look at gender and sentencing. Those who are incarcerated are a small proportion of those who commit crimes, and there are demonstrated patterns in the kinds of persons who are more likely to receive correctional sentences than others. (See "Criminal Justice System and Women: Corrections and Correctional Issues" in part 1.) These data provide a census of both rate (adjusted for population) and raw numbers of those who are in correctional facilities and sentenced to death.

TABLE C.1 Females Prisoners under the Jurisdiction of State or Federal Correctional Authorities, by Jurisdiction, December 31, 2000, 2007, and 2008

| Region and jurisdiction | Number of female prisoners | | | | |
	December 31, 2000	December 31, 2007	December 31, 2008	Average annual percent change, 2000–2007	Percent change, 2007–2008
U.S. total	93,234	114,505	114,852	3	0.3
Federal	10,245	13,338	13,273	3.8	−0.5
State	82,989	101,167	101,579	2.9	0.4
Northeast	9,082	9,694	9,844	0.9	
Connecticut[a]	1,406	1,496	1,502	0.9	0.4
Maine	66	139	156	11.2	12.2
Massachusetts	663	790	751	2.5	−4.9
New Hampshire	120	202	234	7.7	15.8
New Jersey	1,650	1,410	1,299	−2.2	−7.9
New York	3,280	2,754	2,587	−2.5	−6.1
Pennsylvania	1,579	2,463	2,954	6.6	19.9
Rhode Island[a]	238	282	243	2.5	−13.8
Vermont[a]	80	158	118	10.2	−25.3
Midwest	14,598	17,929	17,741	3	−1
Illinois	2,849	2,824	2,721	−0.1	−3.6
Indiana	1,452	2,295	2,493	6.8	8.6
Iowa[b]	592	717	749	2.8	4.5
Kansas	504	625	569	3.1	−9
Michigan	2,131	2,080	1,957	−0.3	−5.9
Minnesota	368	602	628	7.3	4.3
Missouri	1,993	2,522	2,449	3.4	−2.9
Nebraska	266	399	390	6	−2.3
North Dakota	68	147	160	11.6	8.8
Ohio	2,808	3,822	3,913	4.5	2.4
South Dakota	200	369	355	9.1	−3.8
Wisconsin	1,367	1,527	1,357	1.6	−11.1
South	39,652	48,503	49,050	2.9	1.1
Alabama	1,826	2,158	2,231	2.4	3.4
Arkansas	772	1,066	1,060	4.7	−0.6
Delaware[a]	597	577	557	−0.5	−3.5
District of Columbia	356	*	*	**	**
Florida	4,105	6,854	7,151	7.6	4.3
Georgia[b]	2,758	3,545	3,692	3.7	4.1

(Continued)

TABLE C.1 Females Prisoners under the Jurisdiction of State or Federal Correctional Authorities, by Jurisdiction, December 31, 2000, 2007, and 2008 *(Continued)*

Region and jurisdiction		Number of female prisoners				
		December 31, 2000	December 31, 2007	December 31, 2008	Average annual percent change, 2000–2007	Percent change, 2007–2008
	Maryland	1,219	1,184	1,060	−0.4	−10.5
	Mississippi	1,669	1,962	1,981	2.3	1
	North Carolina	1,903	2,626	2,778	4.7	5.8
	Oklahoma	2,394	2,607	2,524	1.2	−3.2
	South Carolina	1,420	1,604	1,633	1.8	1.8
	Tennessee	1,369	1,923	2,129	5	10.7
	Texas	13,622	13,931	13,853	0.3	−0.6
	Virginia	2,059	2,933	2,967	5.2	1.2
	West Virginia	303	634	648	11.1	2.2
West		19,657	25,041	24,944	3.5	−0.4
	Alaska[a]	284	564	503	10.3	−10.8
	Arizona[b]	1,964	3,460	3,766	8.4	8.8
	California	11,161	11,628	11,620	0.6	−0.1
	Colorado	1,333	2,335	2,294	8.3	−1.8
	Hawaii[b]	561	746	728	4.2	−2.4
	Idaho	493	800	758	7.2	−5.3
	Montana	306	301	363	−0.2	20.6
	Nevada	846	1,179	982	**	**
	New Mexico	511	576	569	1.7	−1.2
	Oregon	596	1,060	1,109	8.6	4.6
	Utah	381	632	640	7.5	1.3
	Washington	1,065	1,514	1,404	5.2	−7.3
	Wyoming	156	246	208	6.7	−15.4

*Not applicable. After 2001, responsibility for sentenced felons from the District of Columbia was transferred to the Federal Bureau of Prisons.

** Not calculated.

[a] Prisons and jails form one integrated system. Data include total jail and prison populations.

[b] Prison population based on custody counts.

Source: Bureau of Justice Statistics, p08at04.csv. Appendix table 4. Females prisoners under the jurisdiction of state or federal correctional authorities, by jurisdiction, December 31, 2000, 2007, and 2008. Report title: Prisoners in 2008 NCJ 228417. Data source: National Prisoner Statistics, 1b. William J. Sabol, PhD, Heather C. West, PhD, and Matthew Cooper. Date of version: December 8, 2009.

TABLE C.2 Imprisonment Rates of Sentenced Prisoners under Jurisdiction of State and Federal Correctional Authorities, by Gender and Jurisdiction, December 31, 2007, and 2008

		Imprisonment rate					
		2007			2008		
Region and jurisdiction		Total	Male	Female	Total	Male	Female
U.S. total		506	955	69	504	952	68
	Federal	59	112	8	60	113	7
	State	447	844	61	445	840	61
Northeast		306	598	30	306	597	30
	Connecticut[a]	410	794	45	407	787	45
	Maine	148	284	18	151	289	19
	Massachusetts[b]	249	499	13	218	434	13
	New Hampshire	222	420	29	220	410	35
	New Jersey	308	597	32	298	578	29
	New York	322	635	27	307	605	25
	Pennsylvania	365	710	38	393	762	42
	Rhode Island[a]	235	463	21	240	475	19
	Vermont[a]	260	495	32	260	504	24
Midwest		393	743	52	392	741	52
	Illinois	350	668	42	351	669	41
	Indiana	426	791	71	442	818	77
	Iowa[c]	291	542	47	291	538	49
	Kansas	312	584	44	303	570	40
	Michigan	499	971	41	488	951	39
	Minnesota	181	341	23	179	336	24
	Missouri	506	948	83	509	957	81
	Nebraska	243	449	41	247	455	42
	North Dakota	221	394	46	225	400	50
	Ohio	442	838	65	449	851	66
	South Dakota	413	736	92	412	738	87
	Wisconsin	397	748	50	374	709	43
South		556	1,050	79	552	1,043	77
	Alabama	615	1,180	85	634	1,215	88
	Arkansas	502	949	73	511	969	72
	Delaware[a]	482	945	47	463	906	45
	Florida	535	1,013	73	557	1,054	76
	Georgia[c]	563	1,069	72	540	1,021	74

(Continued)

TABLE C.2 Imprisonment Rates of Sentenced Prisoners under Jurisdiction of State and Federal Correctional Authorities, by Gender and Jurisdiction, December 31, 2007, and 2008 *(Continued)*

Region and jurisdiction		Imprisonment rate					
		2007			2008		
		Total	Male	Female	Total	Male	Female
	Maryland	404	793	39	403	796	33
	Mississippi	734	1,385	121	735	1,389	121
	North Carolina	361	696	41	368	707	42
	Oklahoma	665	1,211	131	661	1,203	132
	South Carolina	524	1,009	64	519	1,000	63
	Tennessee	424	804	61	436	824	66
	Texas	669	1,244	97	639	1,191	87
	Virginia	490	921	74	489	918	75
	West Virginia	333	610	68	331	604	69
West		438	807	67	436	803	67
	Alaska[a]	447	785	82	430	752	79
	Arizona[c]	554	1,009	97	567	1,031	101
	California	471	880	62	467	872	62
	Colorado	465	829	96	467	834	93
	Hawaii[a]	338	594	79	332	585	74
	Idaho	483	854	106	474	844	99
	Montana	356	649	62	368	660	74
	Nevada[b]				486	880	76
	New Mexico	313	580	54	316	583	56
	Oregon	369	686	56	371	688	58
	Utah	239	428	46	232	415	45
	Washington	273	500	46	272	501	43
	Wyoming	394	686	95	387	687	79

Note: Imprisonment rate is the number of prisoners sentenced to more than 1 year per 100,000 U.S. residents.

[a]Prisons and jails form one integrated system. Data include total jail and prison populations.

[b]The 2008 imprisonment rate includes 4,012 male prisoners sentenced to more than one year but held in local jails or houses of corrections in the Commonwealth of Massachusetts. The 2007 imprisonment rate includes 6,200 sentenced males held in local jails or houses of corrections in the Commonwealth of Massachusetts and an estimated number of sentenced prisoners in Nevada. See Methodology.

[c]Prison population based on custody counts.

Source: Bureau of Justice Statistics, p08at10.csv. Appendix table 10. Imprisonment rates of sentenced prisoners under jurisdiction of state and federal correctional authorities, by gender and jurisdiction, December 31, 2007 and 2008. Report title: Prisoners in 2008 NCJ 228417. Data source: National Prisoner Statistics, 1b. Authors: William J. Sabol, PhD, Heather C. West, PhD, and Matthew Cooper. Date of version: December 8, 2009.

TABLE C.3 Estimated Number of Sentenced Prisoners under State or Federal Jurisdiction, by Gender, Race, Hispanic Origin, and Age, December 31, 2008

Age	Male				Female			
	Total[a]	White[b]	Black[b]	Hispanic	Total[a]	White[b]	Black[b]	Hispanic
Total[c]	1,434,800	477,500	562,800	295,800	105,300	50,700	29,100	17,300
18–19	23,800	6,500	10,400	4,900	1,000	400	300	200
20–24	208,400	59,400	85,000	48,400	11,500	5,400	3,000	2,300
25–29	246,400	66,000	102,800	60,000	16,000	7,300	4,400	3,100
30–34	238,100	70,700	96,800	54,400	18,500	8,900	5,000	3,200
35–39	226,700	75,200	90,500	45,900	20,800	9,900	5,900	3,200
40–44	202,500	75,500	77,400	35,600	17,900	8,700	5,100	2,600
45–49	136,300	53,100	51,300	22,600	10,700	5,200	3,100	1,500
50–54	75,800	31,600	27,000	12,300	5,000	2,500	1,400	700
55–59	39,100	19,000	11,900	6,200	2,100	1,300	500	300
60–64	19,200	10,700	4,700	3,000	1,000	600	200	200
65 or older	15,800	9,300	3,700	2,200	600	400	100	100

Note: Totals based on prisoners with a sentence of more than one year.

[a]Includes American Indians, Alaska Natives, Asians, Native Hawaiians, other Pacific Islanders, and persons identifying two or more races.

[b]Excludes persons of Hispanic or Latino origin.

[c]Includes persons under age 18.

Source: Bureau of Justice Statistics, p08at13.csv. Appendix table 13. Estimated number of sentenced prisoners under state or federal jurisdiction, by gender, race, Hispanic origin, and age, December 31, 2008. Report title: Prisoners in 2008 NCJ 228417. Data source: National Prisoner Statistics, 1b. Authors: William J. Sabol, PhD, Heather C. West, PhD, and Matthew Cooper. Date of version: December 8, 2009.

TABLE C.4 Estimated Rate of Sentenced Prisoners under State or Federal Jurisdiction per 100,000 U.S. Residents, by Gender, Race, Hispanic Origin, and Age, December 31, 2008

Age	Male Total[a]	White[b]	Black[b]	Hispanic	Female Total[a]	White[b]	Black[b]	Hispanic
Total[c]	952	487	3,161	1,200	68	50	149	75
18-19	528	238	1,532	614	23	16	44	25
20-24	1,916	893	5,553	2,474	112	86	202	131
25-29	2,238	1,017	7,130	2,612	153	115	301	167
30-34	2,366	1,217	8,032	2,411	190	155	380	174
35-39	2,159	1,171	7,392	2,263	201	156	434	183
40-44	1,903	1,090	6,282	2,032	169	127	364	170
45-49	1,202	671	4,056	1,523	93	65	211	106
50-54	713	407	2,385	1,085	45	31	106	61
55-59	429	276	1,325	739	22	18	44	30
60-64	259	184	738	502	12	9	25	23
65 or older	95	69	294	186	3	2	6	4

Note: Totals based on prisoners with a sentence of more than one year. Rates are per 100,000 U.S. residents in each reference population group.

[a]Includes American Indians, Alaska Natives, Asians, Native Hawaiians, other Pacific Islanders, and persons identifying two or more races.

[b]Excludes persons of Hispanic or Latino origin.

[c]Includes persons under age 18.

Source: Bureau of Justice Statistics, p08at14.csv. Appendix table 14. Estimated rate of sentenced prisoners under state or federal jurisdiction per 100,000 U.S. residents, by gender, race, Hispanic origin, and age, December 31, 2008. Report title: Prisoners in 2008 NCJ 228417.Data source: National Prisoner Statistics, 1b. Authors: William J. Sabol, Ph.D., Heather C. West, Ph.D., and Matthew Cooper. Date of version: December 8, 2009.

TABLE C.5 Estimated Number of Sentenced Prisoners under State Jurisdiction, by Offense, Gender, Race, and Hispanic Origin, Year End 2006

Offense		All inmates	Male	Female	White[a]	Black[a]	Hispanic
	Total	1,331,100	1,238,900	92,200	474,200	508,700	248,900
Violent		667,900	638,100	29,800	217,100	256,400	145,300
	Murder[b]	144,500	135,700	8,800	34,700	61,400	36,800
	Manslaughter	16,700	14,900	1,800	6,900	6,100	2,400
	Rape	54,800	54,400	400	26,600	16,900	7,400
	Other sexual assault	105,500	104,100	1,400	56,800	20,600	23,900
	Robbery	179,500	172,400	7,100	37,500	91,500	33,900
	Assault	136,600	128,800	7,900	42,800	49,800	34,700
	Other violent	30,300	27,800	2,400	11,800	10,100	6,100
Property		277,900	251,200	26,700	135,300	96,000	25,000
	Burglary	138,000	132,300	5,700	68,700	53,600	2,800
	Larceny	51,600	43,800	7,800	23,300	17,600	7,200
	Motor vehicle theft	27,100	25,500	1,600	10,900	7,100	7,900
	Fraud	34,400	25,000	9,400	19,200	10,000	2,900
	Other property	26,800	24,700	2,100	13,300	7,600	4,200
Drug offenses		265,800	240,500	25,400	72,100	117,600	55,700
Public-order offenses[c]		112,300	106,100	6,200	48,200	35,400	21,000
Other/unspecified[d]		7,200	2,900	4,300	1,400	3,300	1,900

Note: Totals based on prisoners with a sentence of more than 1 year. Detail may not add to total due to rounding.

[a]Excludes Hispanics and persons identifying two or more races.

[b]Includes negligent manslaughter.

[c]Includes weapons, drunk driving, court offenses, commercialized vice, morals and decency offenses, liquor law violations, and other public-order offenses.

[d]Includes juvenile offenses and other unspecified offense categories.

Source: Bureau of Justice Statistics, p08at15.csv. Appendix table 15. Estimated number of sentenced prisoners under state jurisdiction, by offense, gender, race, and Hispanic origin, yearend 2006. Report title: Prisoners in 2008 NCJ 228417. Data source: National Prisoner Statistics, 1b. Authors: William J. Sabol, PhD, Heather C. West, PhD, and Matthew Cooper. Date of version: December 8, 2009.

TABLE C.6 Estimated Percent of Sentenced Prisoners under State Jurisdiction, by Offense, Gender, Race, and Hispanic Origin, Year End 2006

Offense		All inmates	Male	Female	White[a]	Black[a]	Hispanic
	Total	100	100	100	100	100	100
Violent		50.2	51.5	32.3	45.8	50.4	58.4
	Murder[b]	10.9	11	9.5	7.3	12.1	14.8
	Manslaughter	1.3	1.2	2	1.5	1.2	1
	Rape	4.1	4.4	0.5	5.6	3.3	3
	Other sexual assault	7.9	8.4	1.5	12	4.1	9.6
	Robbery	13.5	13.9	7.7	7.9	18	13.6
	Assault	10.3	10.4	8.5	9	9.8	13.9
	Other violent	2.3	2.2	2.6	2.5	2	2.5
Property		20.9	20.3	28.9	28.5	18.9	10
	Burglary	10.4	10.7	6.2	14.5	10.5	1.1
	Larceny	3.9	3.5	8.5	4.9	3.5	2.9
	Motor vehicle theft	2	2.1	1.8	2.3	1.4	3.2
	Fraud	2.6	2	10.2	4	2	1.2
	Other property	2	2	2.3	2.8	1.5	1.7
Drug offenses		20	19.4	27.5	15.2	23.1	22.4
Public-order offenses[c]		8.4	8.6	6.7	10.2	7	8.4
Other/unspecified[d]		0.5	0.2	4.6	0.3	0.6	0.8

Note: Totals based on prisoners with a sentence of more than 1 year. Detail may not add to total due to rounding.

[a]Excludes Hispanics and persons identifying two or more races.

[b]Includes negligent manslaughter.

[c]Includes weapons, drunk driving, court offenses, commercialized vice, morals and decency offenses, liquor law violations, and other public-order offenses.

[d]Includes juvenile offenses and other unspecified offense categories.

Source: Bureau of Justice Statistics, p08at16.csv. Appendix table 16. Estimated percent of sentenced prisoners under state jurisdiction, by offense, gender, race, and Hispanic origin, yearend 2006. Report title: Prisoners in 2008 NCJ 228417. Data source: National Prisoner Statistics, 1b. Authors: William J. Sabol, PhD, Heather C. West, PhD, and Matthew Cooper. Date of version: December 8, 2009.

TABLE C.7 Elapsed Time since Sentencing for Inmates under Sentence of Death on December 31, 2008, by Gender, Race, and Hispanic Origin

Inmates under sentence of death	Elapsed time since sentencing (months)	
	Mean	Median
Total	147	141
Male	148	142
Female	110	107
White[a]	150	145
Black[a]	149	144
Hispanic	131	122

[a]Excludes persons of Hispanic/Latino origin.

Source: Bureau of Justice Statistics, Capital Punishment, 2008. Table 17. Statistical Tables NCJ 228662. Data source: National Prisoner Statistics (NPS-8). Authors: Tracy L. Snell. Date of version: November 13, 2009.

D. DEATH PENALTY FOR FEMALE OFFENDERS

JANUARY 1, 1973, THROUGH OCTOBER 31, 2010[1]

by Victor Streib

Preface

Beginning with the first legislative enactments of modern death penalty statutes in 1973, we now have over thirty-six years of death sentences being imposed in American jurisdictions. This post-1973 time period is referred to as the current era of the death penalty, operating under quite different laws and procedures than did earlier death penalty eras. This report, now available primarily in electronic format, supersedes the written report, "Capital Punishment of Female Offenders," generated quarterly by this author from 1984 through early 1998. The burdens of constant corrections and updates, coupled with the difficulties of worldwide distribution of regular issues of a printed, hard copy report, led us to this electronic format.

The data herein are updated as often and as quickly as possible, with the last date of entry noted on the cover page. However, given the difficulty of gathering complete information from all jurisdictions and as soon as cases develop, these reports may under-report the number of female offenders under death sentences. The subjects of these reports are female offenders sentenced to death. They are not all referred to as women since some were as young as age fifteen at the time of their crimes. However, no such very young female offenders are currently under death sentences.

One final source of confusion and occasional inaccuracy is the difference between being legally under a sentence of death and being physically on a prison's death row. These reports chronicle the exact dates of imposition and reversal or removal of the death sentence by a court or executive officer. Therefore, the list of female offenders currently under death sentences excludes those for whom the sentence has been legally reversed or removed even if the case is still being reviewed or reconsidered. However, it is not uncommon for such a person to continue to be housed on the prison's death row even though no longer legally under a death sentence. The list also includes those female offenders under death sentences who are housed temporarily in local jails or prisons rather than the jurisdiction's death row prison. Such temporary housing typically occurs (1) when the individual has just been sentenced to death but not yet transported to the death row prison or (2) when she is serving as a witness or defendant in another trial or proceeding and must be located nearby. In either case, they are under sentences of death but are not physically on death row and often are not even known or listed by the prison officials.

It is left to other documents and to other organizations to argue about the pros and cons of this practice, with the hope that these data will inform those arguments and deliberations. Therefore, these reports take no position on the legality, the wisdom, or the morality of the death penalty for female offenders. The author of these reports has been involved with this issue for twenty-five years as a researcher and as an attorney. References to some of those involvements can be found in Appendix C to this report. Please feel free to contact the author if further information is desired.

Recent Developments

(1)   From 1973 through late 2010, the leading states for sentencing women to death are California and Texas with nineteen each, Florida with seventeen, and North Carolina with sixteen.

(2)   As of late 2010, California has sixteen women on death row, and Texas has ten.

(3)   Currently on death row are fourteen women who killed their husbands or boyfriends, and another eleven women who killed their children. One other women killed both her husband and her children, and three other women killed a young niece, nephew, or child in their care. These twenty-nine women account for almost half of the fifty-five women now on death row.

(4)   The most recent execution of a female offender was of Teresa Lewis in Virginia on September 23, 2010.

(5)   The most unusual fairly recent development is the rebirth of federal death penalties for women. No women had received federal death sentences in the entire current era (beginning in 1973) until one such sentence was imposed in late 2005 and another in early 2008.

Screening Female Offenders From the Death Penalty

(1)   Women account for about 10.0% of murder arrests annually;

(2)   Women account for only 2.0% (167/8,292) of death sentences imposed at the trial level;

(3)   Women account for only 1.7 % (55/3,261) of persons presently on death row; and

(4)   Women account for only 1.0 % (12/1,232) of persons actually executed in this modern era.

Death Sentences Imposed Upon Female Offenders In Current Era

(1) A total of 167 death sentences have been imposed upon female offenders from 1973 through late 2010. Table D.1 below provides these data by individual year.

(2) These 167 death sentences for female offenders constitute just 2% of all death sentences during this time period.

(3) The annual death sentencing rate for female offenders during the last decade has averaged four per year.

TABLE D.1   Death Sentences Imposed Upon Female Offenders, January 1, 1973, Through October 31, 2010

Year	Total death sentences	Death sentences for females	Percent of total	Year	Total death sentences	Death sentences for females	Percent of total
1973	42	1	2.4	1994	315	5	1.6
1974	149	1	0.7	1995	326	7	2.1
1975	298	8	2.3	1996	323	2	0.6
1976	233	3	1.3	1997	281	2	0.7
1977	137	1	0.7	1998	306	7	2.3
1978	185	4	2.1	1999	284	4	1.4
1979	151	4	2.6	2000	235	8	3.4
1980	173	2	1.1	2001	167	2	1.2
1981	223	3	1.3	2002	169	5	3.0
1982	267	5	1.8	2003	153	2	1.3
1983	252	4	1.6	2004	140	5	3.6
1984	284	8	2.8	2005	138	5	3.6
1985	262	5	1.9	2006	115	5	4.3
1986	300	3	1.0	2007	115	1	0.9
1987	287	5	1.7	2008	111	3	2.7
1988	291	5	1.7	2009*	55**	0	0
1989	258	11	4.2	2010**	90**	0	0
1990	251	6	2.4	Totals	8,292**	167	2.0
1991	268	7	2.6				
1992	287	10	3.5				
1993	287	6	2.0				

*as of December 31, 2010

**estimates

(4) The wide fluctuations in annual death sentencing rates are unexplained by changes in statutes, court rulings, or public opinion.

(5) These 167 death sentences for female offenders since 1973 have been imposed by twenty-five individual states and by the federal government, comprising about two-thirds of the thirty-nine death penalty jurisdictions during this time period. Table D.2 below provides these data by jurisdiction and race of offender.

TABLE D.2 State-by-State Breakdown of Death Sentences for Female Offenders, January 1, 1973, through June 30, 2009

State	Total death sentences	White offenders	Black offenders	Latina offenders	American Indian offenders
Texas	19	11	7	1	0
California	19	10	3	6	0
Florida	17	13	3	1	0
North Carolina	16	10	4	0	2
Ohio	12	6	6	0	0
Alabama	11	8	3	0	0
Mississippi	9	7	2	0	0
Oklahoma	8	7	1	0	0
Illinois	7	1	4	2	0
Pennsylvania	7	3	4	0	0
Georgia	6	5	1	0	0
Missouri	5	4	0	1	0
Indiana	4	2	2	0	0
Arizona	3	3	0	0	0
Federal	2	2	0	0	0
Kentucky	3	3	0	0	0
Louisiana	3	2	1	0	0
Maryland	3	1	0	0	2
New Jersey	3	3	0	0	0
Arkansas	2	2	0	0	0
Idaho	2	2	0	0	0
Nevada	2	1	1	0	0
Tennessee	2	2	0	0	0
Delaware	1	1	0	0	0
South Carolina	1	1	0	0	0
Virginia	1	1	0	0	0
Total	167	110	42	11	4

(6) The top five states (Texas, California, Florida, North Carolina, and Ohio) account for essentially half (83/167) of all such sentences since 1973.

(7) Virginia, a leading death penalty state for male offenders, has imposed only one death sentence on a female offender since 1973 (and executed her on 9–23–2010)

(8) Appendix A to this report provides a detailed listing of name, race, jurisdiction, dates of crimes and sentences, and current status for each female death sentence.

Executions of Female Offenders

(1) Actual execution of female offenders is quite rare, with only 569 documented instances in the 378 years from 1,632 through late 2010.

(2) Beginning with the earliest American colonial period, executions of female offenders constitute about 2.8% (569/20,000) of all American executions.

(3) From 1900 through late 2010, 0.6% (51/8,557) of all executions have been of female offenders. Table D.3 (pp. 695-96) provides these data by year and by executing jurisdiction.

(4) Comparing these post-1900 data with data from previous American eras reveals that this practice is even rarer now than in previous centuries.

(5) Executions of female offenders in the current era (1973–late 2010) are listed in Table D.4 (p. 696).

(6) Only twelve (1.0%) of the 1,232 total executions since 1973 have been of female offenders. This execution pace has changed recently, with only one (0.2%) of the 434 executions from 1973 to 1997 being a female offender. Since 1998, eleven (1.4%) of the 798 total executions have been of female offenders.

(7) This recent (1998 to late 2010) execution pace matches almost exactly that beginning in 1900 so it appears that the 1973–1997 lull in executions of female offenders was atypical and that we have now returned to our normal rate.

Females Under Death Sentences
As of October 31, 2010

(1) Of the 167 death sentences imposed since 1973, only fifty-five women remained under sentences of death in eighteen states and under federal jurisdiction as of late 2010. Tables D.5 and D.6 (p. 697) provide data describing the offenders and victims in these cases.

(2) These fifty-five women comprise only 1.7% of the approximately 3,261 persons currently on death row.

TABLE D.3 Executions of Female Offenders by State, January 1, 1900, through October 31, 2010

State of execution	Date of execution	Name of offender	Race of offender	Age at crime of offender
Alabama	01-24-1930	Gilmore, Selena	Black	[adult]
	09-04-1953	Dennison, Earle	White	54
	10-11-1957	Martin, Rhonda Belle	White	48
	05-10-2002	Block, Linda Lyon	White	45
Arizona	02-21-1930	Dugan, Eva	White	49
Arkansas	05-02-2000	Riggs, Christina Marie	White	26
California	11-21-1941	Spinelli, Eithel Leta Juanita	White	52
	04-11-1947	Peete, Louise	White	58
	06-03-1955	Graham, Barbara	White	32
	08-08-1962	Duncan, Elizabeth Ann	White	58
Delaware	06-07-1935	Carey, May H.	White	52
Federal (NY)	06-19-1953	Rosenberg, Ethel[1]	White	37
Federal (MO)	12-18-1953	Heady, Bonnie Brown	White	41
Florida	03-30-1998	Buenoano, Judias	White	28
	10-09-2002	Wuornos, Aileen	White	33
Georgia	03-05-1945	Baker, Lena	Black	44
Illinois	1-28-1938	Porter, Marie	White	38
Louisiana	02-01-1929	LeBoeuf, Ada	White	38
	02-08-1935	Moore, Julia (Powers)	???	[adult]
	11-28-1942	Henri, Toni Jo (Annie)	White	26
Mississippi	01-13-1922	Perdue, Pattie	Black	[adult]
	10-13-1922	Knight, Ann	Black	[adult]
	04-29-1937	Holmes, Mary	Black	32
	05-19-1944	Johnson, Mildred Louise	Black	34
New York	03-29-1909	Farmer, Mary	White	29
	01-12-1928	Snyder, Ruth Brown	White	33
	08-09-1934	Antonio, Anna	White	27
	06-27-1935	Coo, Eva	White	40
	07-16-1936	Creighton, Mary Francis	White	36
	11-16-1944	Fowler, Helen	Black	37
	03-08-1951	Beck, Martha	White	29
North Carolina	01-01-1943	Phillips, Rosana Lightner	Black	25
	12-29-1944	Williams, Bessie May	Black	19
	11-02-1984	Barfield, Velma	White	52
Ohio	12-07-1938	Hahn, Anna Marie	White	32
	01-15-1954	Dean, Dovie Smarr	White	55
	06-12-1954	Butler, Betty	Black	25

TABLE D.3 Executions of Female Offenders by State, January 1, 1900, through October 31, 2010 *(Continued)*

State of execution	Date of execution	Name of offender	Race of offender	Age at crime of offender
Oklahoma	07-17-1903	Wright, Dora	Black	[adult]
	01-11-2001	Allen, Wanda Jean	Black	29
	05-01-2001	Plantz, Marilyn Kay	White	27
	12-04-2001	Smith, Lois Nadeen	White	41
Pennsylvania	02-23-1931	Schroeder, Irene	White	22
	10-14-1946	Sykes, Corrine	Black	22
South Carolina	01-15-1943	Logue, Sue Stidman	White	43
	01-17-1947	Stinette, Rose Marie	Black	49
Texas	02-03-1998	Tucker, Karla Faye	White	38
	02-24-2000	Beets, Betty Lou	White	46
	09-14-2005	Newton, Francis Elaine	Black	21
Vermont	12-08-1905	Rogers, Mary Mabel	White	21
Virginia	08-16-1912	Christian, Virginia	Black	17
	09-23-2010	Lewis, Teresa	White	33

Note: Ethel Rosenberg's capital crime was espionage, the only one of these 20th- and 21st-century executions of female offenders that was for a crime other than murder.

TABLE D.4 Executions of Female Offenders by States During Current Era, January 1, 1973, through June 30, 2010

Date of execution	Date of crime	Executing state	Name of offender	Race and age at crime & execution
11-02-1984	02-01-1978	North Carolina	Barfield, Velma	white; ages 52 & 58
02-03-1998	06-13-1983	Texas	Tucker, Karla Faye	white; ages 23 & 38
03-30-1998	09-16-1971	Florida	Buenoano, Judias	white; ages 28 & 54
02-24-2000	08-06-1983	Texas	Beets, Betty Lou	white; ages 46 & 62
05-02-2000	11-04-1997	Arkansas	Riggs, Christina Marie	white; ages 26 & 29
01-11-2001	12-01-1988	Oklahoma	Allen, Wanda Jean	black; ages 29 & 41
05-01-2001	08-26-1988	Oklahoma	Plantz, Marilyn Kay	white; ages 27 & 40
12-04-2001	07-04-1982	Oklahoma	Smith, Lois Nadeen	white; ages 41 & 61
05-10-2002	10-04-1993	Alabama	Block, Linda Lyon	white; ages 45 & 54
10-09-2002	12-01-1989; 05-24-1990; 07-30-1990; 09-11-1990	Florida	Wuornos, Aileen	white; ages 33 & 46
09-14-2005	04-07-1987	Texas	Newton, Francis Elaine	black; ages 21 & 40
09-23-2010	10-30-2002	Virginia	Lewis, Teresa	white, ages 33 & 41

TABLE D.5 Characteristics of Offenders in Female Death Penalty Cases in Force as of June 30, 2009

Age of offender at crime	Current age of offender	Race of offender
ages 18–19 = 4 (7%)	ages 20–29 = 3 (5%)	American Indian = 1 (2%)
ages 20–29 = 22 (40%)	ages 30–39 = 14 (25%)	Black = 12 (22%)
ages 30–39 = 20 (36%)	ages 40–49 = 21 (38%)	Latin = 6 (11%)
ages 40–49 = 7 (13%)	ages 50–59 = 4 (8%)	White = 36 (64%)
ages 50–59 = 2 (4%)	ages 60–69 = 5 (9%)	
	ages 70–79 = 1(2%)	
Totals = 55(100%)	55 (100%)	55 (100%)

TABLE D.6 Characteristics of Victims in Female Death Penalty Cases in Force as of October 31, 2010

Age of victim at crime	Race and sex of victim
ages 0–4 = 8 (10%)	Asian Male = 1 (1%)
ages 5–9 = 16 (21%)	Asian Female = 1 (1%)
ages 10–19 = 11 (14%)	Black Male = 2 (3%)
ages 20–29 = 12 (15%)	Black Female = 3 (4%)
ages 30–39 = 12 (15%)	Latin Male = 8 (12%)
ages 40–49 = 6 (8%)	Latin Female = 10 (13%)
ages 50–59 = 4 (5%)	White Male = 33 (42%)
ages 60–69 = 2 (3%)	White Female = 20 (26%)
ages 70–79 = 4 5%)	
ages 80–89 = 3 (4%)	
Totals = 78 (100%)	78 (100%)

(3) One-quarter (14/55) of these fifty-five death-sentenced women killed their husbands or boyfriends; and another one-fifth (11/55) killed their children. One young woman killed both her husband and her children, and three other women killed a young niece, nephew, or child in their care.

(4) The present ages of these 55 female offenders range from 27 to 77 years old, and they have been on death row from less than one year to almost twenty-five years.

(5) Appendix B to this report provides the names of these offenders and some brief details about their crimes and sentences. Multiple sentencing dates mean that the earlier death sentence was reversed but then a new death sentence was imposed.

Appendix A   Death Sentences Imposed
On Females, January 1, 1973,
Through June 30, 2009

Year, name, and race of offender	Sentencing jurisdiction	Date of crime	Date of sentence	Current status
1973:				
Ward, Mamie Lee (black)	North Carolina	07-19-1973	09-17-1973	reversed in 1976
1974:				
Hunt, Rozell O. (American Indian)	North Carolina	07-01-1973	06-10-1974	reversed in 1976
1975:				
Boykin, Margie (white)	North Carolina	08-14-1975	12-01-1975	reversed in 1976
Dodds, Catherine (white)	Louisiana	01-27-1975	??-??-1975	reversed in 1976
Glenn, Mabel (black)	California	03-??-1975	10-21-1975	reversed in 1979
Kozeak, Marie (white)	California	??-?? 1975	??-??-1975	reversed in 1976
Lockett, Sandra (black)	Ohio	01-15-1975	04-??-1975	reversed in 1978
Osborne, Alberta (white)	Ohio	12-15-1974	06-02-1975	reversed in 1978
Sanders, Janet [aka Miller] (white)	Oklahoma	02-24-1975	08-26-1975	reversed in 1977
Smith, Rebecca (white)	Georgia	08-31-1974	01-30-1975	reversed in 1983
1976:				
Brown, Faye B. (black)	North Carolina	09-02-1975	01-05-1976	reversed in 1977
Jacobs, Sonia (white)	Florida	02-20-1976	08-20-1976	reversed in 1981
Wernert. Patricia white	Ohio	11-18-1975	11-22-1976	reversed in 1978
1977:				
Smith, Benita (black)	Ohio	05-03-1977	11-30-1977	reversed in 1978
1978:				
Anderson, Mary (white)	Texas	01-03-1978	08-29-1978	reversed in 1982
Barfield, Velma (white)	North Carolina	02-01-1978	12-02-1978	Executed on 11-02-1984
Bracewell, Debra (white)	Alabama	08-15-1977	05-17-1978	reversed in 1981
Detter, Rebecca (white)	North Carolina	06-02-1977	09-26-1978	reversed in 1979
1979:				
Binsz, Michelle (white)	Oklahoma	03-18-1979	10-23-1979	reversed in 1984
Burnett, Linda (white)	Texas	06-01-1978	03-20-1979	reversed in 1983
Cunningham, Emma (white)	Georgia	01-01-1979	10-26-1979	reversed in 1983
Tyler, Shirley (black)	Georgia	10-22-1979	12-04-1979	reversed in 1985

(Continued)

Year, name, and race of offender	Sentencing jurisdiction	Date of crime	Date of sentence	Current status
1980:				
O'Bryan, LaVerne (white)	Kentucky	07-05-1979	09-12-1980	reversed in 1982
Perillo, Pamela (white)	Texas	02-24-1980	9-2-1980 & 11-13-1984	reversed in 1998
1981:				
Buttrum, Janice (white)	Georgia	09-03-1980	08-31-1981	reversed in 1989
Stebbing, Annette (white)	Maryland	04-09-1980	04-30-1981	reversed in 1985
Thomas, Patricia (black)	Alabama	02-28-1981	12-28-1981	reversed in 1990
1982:				
Cannaday, Attina (white)	Mississippi	06-03-1982	09-23-1982	reversed in 1984
Ford, Priscilla (black)	Nevada	11-27-1980	04-29-1982	died of natural causes in 2005
Foster, Doris (American Indian)	Maryland	01-29-1981	2-8-1982 & 04-04-1984	commuted in 1987
Smith, Nadean (white)	Oklahoma	07-04-1982	12-29-1982	executed on 12-2-2001
Whittington, Teresa (white)	Georgia	01-02-1982	05-07-1982	reversed in 1984
1983:				
Grant, Rosalie (black)	Ohio	04-01-1983	10-21-1983	commuted in 1991
Neelley, Judith (white)	Alabama	09-23-1982	04-18-1983	commuted in 1999
Summers, Sheila (white)	Nevada	09-14-1982	12-20-1983	reversed in 1986
Young, Sharon (white)	Ohio	06-12-1983	09-30-1983	reversed in 1986
1984:				
Foster, Doris (American Indian)	Maryland	01-29-1981	4-4-1984 & 02-08-1982	commuted in 1987
Hendrickson, Patricia (white)	Arkansas	03-10-1983	04-13-1984	reversed in 1985
Jackson, Andrea (black)	Florida	05-16-1983	2-10-1984 2-21-1992 & 12-13-95	reversed in 1997
Moore, Marie (white)	New Jersey	01-??-1983	11-19-1984	reversed in 1988
Perillo, Pamela (white)	Texas	02-24-1980	11-13-1984 & 9-2-1980	reversed in 1998
Tucker, Karla Faye (white)	Texas	06-13-1983	04-25-1984	executed on 02-03-1998
Williamson, Celia (white)	Mississippi	03-23-1982	03-14-1984	reversed in 1987
Windsor, Karla (white)	Idaho	09-06-1983	02-28-1984	reversed in 1985
1985:				
Beets, Betty (white)	Texas	08-06-1983	10-14-1985	executed on 02-24-2000

(Continued)

Year, name, and race of offender	Sentencing jurisdiction	Date of crime	Date of sentence	Current status
Brown, Debra (black)	Ohio	07-13-1984	06-18-1985 & 06-23-86	commuted in 1991
Buenoano, Judias (white/Latina)	Florida	09-16-1971	11-26-1985	executed on 03-30-1998
Houston, Judy (white)	Mississippi	06-03-1984	11-30-1985	reversed in 1988
Thacker, Lois (white)	Indiana	11-03-1984	06-27-1985	reversed in 1990
1986:				
Brown, Debra (black)	Indiana	06-18-1984	06-23-1986 & 06-18-85	would be on death row but in Ohio prison
Cooper, Paula (black)	Indiana	05-14-1985	07-11-1986	reversed in 1989
Owens, Gaile (white)	Tennessee	02-17-1985	01-15-1986	now on death row
1987:				
Caillier, Carla (white)	Florida	11-20-1986	03-19-1987	reversed in 1988
Casteel, Dee Dyne (white)	Florida	08-20-1983	09-16-1987	reversed in 1990
Cox, Donna Sue (Allen) (white)	North Carolina	07-12-1986	10-30-1987	reversed in 1992
Dudley, Kaysie (white)	Florida	09-30-1985	01-27-1987	reversed in 1989
Foster, Lafonda (white)	Kentucky	03-09-1986	04-24-1987	reversed in 1991
1988:				
Green, Elizabeth (black)	Ohio	01-04-1988	07-11-1988	commuted in 1991
Haney, Judy M. (white)	Alabama	01-01-1984	11-18-1988	reversed in 1997
Newton, Francis (black)	Texas	04-07-1987	11-17-1988	executed on 09-14-2005
Wacaser, Nila (white)	Missouri	08-28-1987	05-31-1988	reversed in 1990
Walker, Altione (white)	Alabama	03-31-1988	12-15-1988	reversed in 1992
1989:				
Allen, Wanda (black)	Oklahoma	12-01-1988	04-26-1989	executed on 01-11-2001
Balfour, Susie (black)	Mississippi	10-07-1988	10-14-1989	reversed in 1992
Coffman, Cynthia (white)	California	11-07-1986	08-30-1989	now on death row
Harris, Louise (black)	Alabama	03-11-1988	08-11-1989	reversed in 2004
Jones, Patricia (white)	Oklahoma	04-??-1988	12-07-1989	reversed in 1995
Lampkin, Beatrice (black)	Ohio	11-04-1988	04-26-1989	commuted in 1991
Landress, Cindy (white)	Indiana	04-23-1988	06-26-1989	reversed in 1992
Plantz, Marilyn (white)	Oklahoma	08-26-1988	03-31-1989	executed on 05-01-2001
Rivers, Delores (black)	Pennsylvania	01-30-1988	03-16-1989	reversed in 2005
Stager, Barbara (white)	North Carolina	02-01-1988	05-19-1989	reversed in 1991

(Continued)

Year, name, and race of offender	Sentencing jurisdiction	Date of crime	Date of sentence	Current status
Twenter, Virginia (white)	Missouri	05-04-1988	01-06-1989	reversed in 1991
1990:				
Butler, Sabrina (black)	Mississippi	04-11-1989	03-14-1990	reversed in 1992
Hunt, Deidre M. (white)	Florida	10-20-1989	09-13-1990	reversed in 1992
Jennings, Patricia (white)	North Carolina	09-19-1989	11-05-1990	now on death row
MaHaley, Marilyn (white)	North Carolina	03-17-1990	12-17-1990	reversed in 1992
McDermott, Maureen (white)	California	04-28-1985	06-15-1990	now on death row
Smith, Rebecca (white)	South Carolina	07-17-1989	12-10-1990	reversed in 1992
1991:				
Copeland, Faye (white)	Missouri	1986-1988	04-27-1991	reversed in 1999
Gay, Yvette (black)	North Carolina	05-30-1990	08-10-1991	reversed in 1993
Isa, Maria (Latina)	Missouri	11-06-1989	12-19-1991	reversed in 1993
Milke, Debra Jean (white)	Arizona	12-02-1989	01-18-1991	now on death row
Moore, Blanche (white)	North Carolina	10-07-1986	1-18-1991	now on death row
Smith, Geraldine (black)	Illinois	06-??-1987	02-20-1991	reversed in 1997
Williams, Dorothy (black)	Illinois	07-31-1989	04-18-1991	commuted in 2003
1992:				
Alfaro, Maria (Latina)	California	06-15-1990	07-14-1992	now on death row
Cardona, Ana (Latina)	Florida	11-02-1990	04-01-1992	reversed in 2002
Garcia, Guinevere (white)	Illinois	07-24-1991	10-09-1992	commuted in 1996
Hill, Doneta (black)	Pennsylvania	06-20-1990	4-9-1992 & 03-24-1991	reversed in 2005?
Jackson, Andrea (black)	Florida	05-16-1983	02-21-1992 02-10-1984 & 12-13-95	reversed in 1997
Phillips, Shirley (white)	Missouri	10-03-1989	04-06-1992	reversed in 1997
Wuornos, Aileen (white)	Florida	12-01-1989 05-24-1990 07-30-1990 & 9-11-90	01-31-1992 05-15-1992 05-15-1992 & 5-15-92	executed on 10-09-2002
1993:				
Ballenger, Vernice (white)	Mississippi	07-10-1983	01-13-1993	reversed in 2000
Larzelier, Virginia (white)	Florida	03-08-1991	05-11-1993	reversed in 2005
Mulero, Marilyn (Latina)	Illinois	05-12-1992	11-12-1993	reversed in 1997
O'Donnell, Kelly (white)	Pennsylvania	11-11-1992	07-01-1993	reversed in 1999
Row, Robin Lee (white)	Idaho	02-10-1992	12-16-1993	now on death row
Thompson, Catherine (black)	California	06-14-1990	06-10-1993	now on death row
1994:				
Carrington, Celeste (black)	California	01-26-1992 & 3-11-92	11-23-1994	now on death row

(Continued)

Year, name, and race of offender	Sentencing jurisdiction	Date of crime	Date of sentence	Current status
King, Carolyn (black)	Pennsylvania	10-??-1993	11-30-1994	now on death row
Lyon, Linda [Block] (white)	Alabama	10-04-1993	12-21-1994	executed on 05-10-2002
Pulliam, Latasha (black)	Illinois	03-21-1991	06-15-1994	commuted in 2003
Samuels, Mary E. (white)	California	12-08-1988 & 6-?-1989	09-16-1994	now on death row
1995:				
Dalton, Kerry Lyn (white)	California	06-26-1988	05-23-1995	now on death row
Frank, Antoinette (black)	Louisiana	03-04-1995	09-13-1995	now on death row
Henderson, Cathy (white)	Texas	01-21-1994	05-25-1995	now on death row
Jackson, Andrea H. (black)	Florida	05-16-1983	12-13-1995 02-10-1984 & 02-21-92	reversed in 1997
Sheppard, Erica (black)	Texas	06-30-1993	03-03-1995	now on death row
Spunaugle, Delpha (white)	Oklahoma	08-15-1993	03-31-1995	reversed in 1997
Young, Caroline (Latina)	California	06-18-1993	10-27-1995	died of natural causes in 2005
1996:				
Anderson, Melanie (white)	North Carolina	08-24-1994	09-26-1996	reversed in 2003
Pike, Christa Gail (white)	Tennessee	01-12-1995	03-29-1996	now on death row
1997:				
Nelson, Leslie (white)	New Jersey	04-20-1995	05-??-1997 & 03-30-01	reversed in 2002
Routier, Darlie (white)	Texas	06-06-1996	02-04-1997	now on death row
1998:				
Brookshire, Kelly (white)	Georgia	02-07-1997	11-20-1998	now on death row
Buenrostro, Dora (Latina)	California	10-25-1994	10-02-1998	now on death row
Gonzalez, Veronica (Latina)	California	07-21-1995	07-20-1998	now on death row
Holberg, Brittany (white)	Texas	11-13-1996	03-27-1998	now on death row
McCarthy, Kimberly (black)	Texas	07-28-1997	12-??-1998 & 11-01-02	now on death row
Riggs, Christina (white)	Arkansas	11-04-1997	06-30-1998	Executed on 05-02-2000
Williams, Jacqueline (black)	Illinois	11-16-1995	05-11-1998	commuted in 2003
1999:				
Basso, Susan (white)	Texas	08-28-1998	09-01-1999	now on death row
Eubanks, Susan (white)	California	10-27-1996	10-13-1999	now on death row
Mata, Bernina (Latina)	Illinois	06-27-1998	10-28-1999	commuted in 2003
Parker, Carlette (black)	North Carolina	05-12-1998	04-01-1999	now on death row

(Continued)

Year, name, and race of offender	Sentencing jurisdiction	Date of crime	Date of sentence	Current status
2000:				
Byrom, Michelle (white)	Mississippi	06-04-1999	11-18-2000	now on death row
Carlson, Doris (white)	Arizona	10-25-1996	03-31-2000	reversed in 2002
Caudill, Virginia (white)	Kentucky	03-15-1998	03-24-2000	now on death row
Johnson, Shonda (white)	Alabama	12-01-1999	01-19-2000	reversed in 2005
Kemmerlin, Chris (white)	North Carolina	03-24-1999	10-18-2000	reversed in 2002
Nieves, Sandi (white)	California	06-30-1998	10-06-2000	now on death row
Tharp, Michelle (white)	Pennsylvania	04-18-1998	11-14-2000	now on death row
Walters, Christina (Amer. Indian)	North Carolina	08-17-1998	07-06-2000	now on death row
2001:				
Markman, Beth Ann (white)	Pennsylvania	10-04-2000	[2001]	reversed in 2007
Nelson, Leslie (white)	New Jersey	04-20-1995	03-30-2001 & 05-??-97	reversed in 2002
2002:				
Blackmon, Patricia (black)	Alabama	05-??-1999	06-07-2002	now on death row
Caro, Socorro (Latina)	California	11-22-1999	04-05-2002	now on death row
Carty, Linda (black)	Texas	05-16-2001	02-21-2002	now on death row
McCarthy, Kimberly (black)	Texas	07-28-1997	11-01-2002 & 12-??-98	now on death row
Michaud, Michelle (white)	California	12-02-1997	09-25-2002	now on death row
2003:				
Lewis, Teresa (white)	Virginia	10-30-2002	06-03-2003	Executed on 09-23-2010
Roberts, Donna (white)	Ohio	12-11-2001	06-21-2003 & 10-29-07	now on death row
2004:				
Andrew, Brenda (white)	Oklahoma	11-20-2001	09-22-2004	now on death row
Adrian, Wendi (white)	Arizona	10-08-2000	12-22-2004	now on death row
Berry, Kenisha (black)	Texas	11-29-1998	02-19-2004	reversed in 2007
Charbonneau, Linda (white)	Delaware	09-23-2001 & 10-17-01	06-04-2004	reversed in 2006
Rodriguez, Angelina (Latina)	California	09-09-2000	01-12-2004	now on death row
2005:				
Diar, Nicole (white)	Ohio	08-27-2003	11-02-2005	reversed in 2008
Gobble, Tierra (white)	Alabama	12-15-2004	10-26-2005	now on death row
Johnson, Angela (white)	Federal (Iowa)	07-25-1993 & 11-05-93	12-20-2005	now on death row
Richardson, Chelsea (white)	Texas	12-11-2003	06-01-2005	now on death row

(Continued)

Year, name, and race of offender	Sentencing jurisdiction	Date of crime	Date of sentence	Current status
Walter, Shonda (black)	Pennsylvania	03-25-2003	04-19-2005	now on death row
2006:				
Chamberlain, Lisa Jo (white)	Mississippi	02-20-2004	08-04-2006	now on death row
Coleman, Lisa Ann (black)	Texas	07-26-2004	07-07-2006	now on death row
Fulgham, Kristi Leigh (white)	Mississippi	05-10-2003	12-09-2006	now on death row
Holmes, Brandy (white)	Louisiana	01-01-2003	02-21-2006	now on death row
Snyder, Janeen Marie (white)	California	04-17-2001	09-07-2006	now on death row
2007:				
Roberts, Donna (white)	Ohio	12-11-2001	06-21-2003 & 10-29-07	now on death row
2008:				
Cole, Tiffany Ann (white)	Florida	07-08-2005	03-06-2008	now on death row
Lucio, Melissa Elizabeth (Latin)	Texas	02-16-2007	08-??-2008	now on death row
Montgomery, Lisa (white)	Federal (MO)	12-16-2004	04-04-2008	now on death row
2009:				
Sarinano, Cathy Lynn	California	12-25-2005	06-29-2009	now on death row
Scott, Christie Michelle	Alabama	09-16-2008	08-??-2009	now on death row
2010				
[apparently none]				

APPENDIX B

CASE SUMMARIES FOR FEMALE OFFENDERS UNDER DEATH SENTENCES AS OF OCTOBER 31, 2010

Alabama

(last execution of female by Alabama on 5–10–2002)

(4 female offenders now on Alabama's death row)

Blackmon, Patricia: Black; age 29 at crime and now age 39 (DOB 11–3–1969); murder of black female age 2 (her adopted daughter) in Dothan in May 1999; sentenced on 6–7–2002.

Gobble, Tierra Capri: White; age 21 at crime and now age 26 (DOB: 4–18–1983); murder of white male age 4 months (her son) in Dothan on 12–15–2004; sentenced on 10–26–2005.

Johnson, Shonda Nicole (aka: Richards): White, age 28 at crime and now age 41 (DOB 9–30–1969); murder of white male age 29 (1 of her 3 husbands)in Jasper (Walker County) on 11–30–1997; sentenced on 10–22–1999.

Scott, Christie Michelle: White; age 30 at crime and now age 30 (DOB: 8–10–1978); arson and murder of white male age 6 (her son) in Russellville (Franklin County) on 9–16–2008; jury recommended life sentence on 7–11–2009, but judge sentenced her to death in early August 2009.

Arizona

(last execution of female by Arizona on 2–21–1930)
(2 female offenders now on Arizona's death row)

Andriano, Wendi: White; age 30 at crime and now age 38 (DOB: 8–6–1970); murder of white (?) male age 33 (her husband) in Mesa on 10–8–2000; sentenced on 12–22–2004.

Milke, Debra Jean: White; age 25 at crime and now age 45 (DOB: 3–10–1964); murder of white male age 4 (her son) in Maricopa County on 12–2–1989; sentenced on 1–18–1991.

California

(last execution of female by California on 8–8–1962)
(16 female offenders now on California's death row)

Alfaro, Maria del Rosio [aka Rosie]: Latin; age 18 at crime and now age 37 (DOB: 10–12–1971); burglary, robbery and murder of white female age 9 in Anaheim on 6–15–1990; sentenced 7–14–1992.

Buenrostro, Dora Luz: Latin; age 34 at crime and now age 49; murder of Latin females ages 4 and 9 and Latin male age 8 (her children) in San Jacinto on 10–25–1994 and 10–27–1994; sentenced on 10–2–1998.

Caro, Socorro: Latin; age 42 at crime and now age 52 (DOB: 3–27–1957); murder of Latin males ages 5, 8, and 11 (her children) in Santa Rosa Valley (Ventura County) on 11–22–1999; sentenced on 4–5–2002.

Carrington, Celeste Simone: Black; age 30 at crimes and now age 47 murders (during burglaries) of Latin male age 34 on 1–26–1992 in San Carlos and of white female age 36 in Palo Alto on 3–11–1992; sentenced on 11–23–1994.

Coffman, Cynthia Lynn: White; age 24 at crime and now age 47 (DOB 1–19–1962); murder of white female age 20 in San Bernardino County on 11–7–1986; sentenced on 8–31–1989.

Dalton, Kerry Lyn: White; age 28 at crime and now age 49; murder of white female age 23 in Live Oak Springs on 6–26–1988; sentenced on 5–23–1995.

Eubanks, Susan: White; age 33 at crime and now age 46; murder of four white males ages 4, 6, 7, and 14 (her children) in San Marcos (San Diego County) on 10–27–1996; sentenced on 10–13–1999.

Gonzalez, Veronica: Latin; age 26 at crime and now age 40; murder of Latin female age 4 (her niece) in San Diego on 7–21–1995; sentenced on 7–20–1998.

McDermott, Maureen: White; age 37 at crime and now age 62 (DOB 5–15–1947); murder of white male age 27 in Van Nuys (Los Angeles County) on 4–28–1985; sentenced on 6–8–1990.

Michaud, Michelle Lyn: White; age 38 at crime and now age 48; kidnapping, sexual assault, and murder of white female age 22 in Pleasanton (Alameda County) on 12–2–1997; sentenced on 9–25–2002.

Nieves, Sandi Dawn: White; age 34 at crime and now age 45; murder of four Latin females ages 5, 7, 11 and 12 (her children) in Saugus (north of Los Angeles) on 6–30–1998; sentenced on 10–6–2000.

Rodriguez, Angelina: Latin; age 32 at crime and now age 41; murder of Latin male age 41 (her husband) in Montebello (Los Angeles County) on 9–9–2000; sentenced on 1–12–2004.

Samuels, Mary Ellen: White; age 40 at crimes and now age 61; murder (she hired killer) of white male age 40 (her husband) on 12–8–1988 in Northridge (Los Angeles County) and of white male age 27 (her husband's killer) in Ventura County on 6–27–1989; sentenced on 9–16–1994.

Sarinano, Cathy Lynn: White, age 30 at crime and now 35; murder of Latin mage age 13 (her nephew) in Riverside on 12–25–2005; sentenced on 6–26–2009.

Snyder, Janeen Marie: White; age 21 at crime and now age 29; murder of white female age 16 in Rubidoux (Riverside County) on April 17, 2001; sentenced on September 7, 2006.

Thompson, Catherine: Black; age 42 at crime and now age 61; murder (she hired killer) of black male (her husband) in Westwood (Los Angeles County) on 6–14–1990; sentenced on 6–10–1993.

Federal

(last execution of a female by the federal government on 12–18–1953)
(2 female offenders now on federal death row)

Johnson, Angela Jane: White; age 29 at crime and now age 45; murder of white male age 34, white female age 31, white female age 10, and white female age 6 in Mason City, Iowa, on 7–25–1993; and murder of white male age 32 in Mason City, Iowa on 11–5–1993; sentenced on 12–20–2005.

Montgomery, Lisa M.: White; age 36 at crime and now age 41; murder of white female age 23 in Skidmore (Nodaway County), Missouri on 7–16–2004; sentenced on 4–4–2008.

Florida

(last execution of female by Florida on 10–9-2002)
(1 female offender now on Florida's death row)

Cole, Tiffany Ann: White, age 23 at crime and now age 27; murder of white female age 61 and white male age 61 in Jacksonville (Duval County), Florida, on 7–8–2005; sentenced on 3–6–2008.

Georgia

(last execution of female by Georgia on 3–5–1945)
(1 female offender now on Georgia's death row)
Brookshire, Kelly Renee [aka Gissendaner]: White, age 28 at crime and now age 41 (YOB: 1968); murder of white male age 30 (her husband) in Gwinnett County on 2–7–1997; sentenced on 11–20–1998.

Idaho

(Idaho has never executed a female offender)
(1 female offender now on Idaho's death row)
Row, Robin Lee: White; age 35 at crime and now age 51 (DOB 9–12–1957); murder/arson of white male age 34 (her husband), white male age 10 (her son), and white female age 8 (her daughter) in Boise on February 10, 1992; sentenced on 12–16–1993.

Indiana

(Indiana has never executed a female offender)
(1 female offender now on Indiana's death row)
Brown, Debra Denise: Black; age 21 at crime and now age 46 (DOB 11–11–1962); murder of black female age 7 in Gary on 6–18–1984; sentenced on 6–23–1986; (serving life sentence in Ohio but sentenced to death in Indiana).

Iowa

(see Federal)

Kentucky

(last execution of female by Kentucky on 2–7–1868)
(1 female offender now on Kentucky's death row)
Caudill, Virginia Susan: White; age 37 at crime and now age 48 (DOB: 9–10–1960); robbery and murder of black female age 73 in Lexington on 3–15–1998; sentenced on 3–24–2000.

Louisiana

(last execution of female by Louisiana on 11–28–1942)
(2 female offenders now on Louisiana's death row)

Frank, Antoinette: Black; age 22 at crime and now age 38 (DOB: 4–30–1971); robbery and murder of white male age 25 (police officer), Asian male age 17, and Asian female age 24 in New Orleans on 3–4–1994; sentenced on 9–13–1995.

Holmes, Brandy: White; age 23 at crime and now age 29; robbery and murder of white male age 70 in Blanchard (Cado Parish) on 1–1–2003; sentenced on 2–21–2006.

Mississippi

(last execution of female by Mississippi on 5–19–1944)

(3 female offenders now on Mississippi's death row)

Byrom, Michelle: White; age 43 at crime and now age 52 (DOB: 11–3-1956); murder (she hired killer) of white male age 56 (her husband) in Tishomingo County on 6–4–1999; sentenced on 11–18–2000.

Chamberlin, Lisa Jo (aka Chamberlain): White; age 31 at crime and now age 36 (DOB: 9–30–1972); murder of white male age 34 and white female age 37 in Hattiesburg (Forrest County) on 3–20(?)–2004; sentenced on 8–4–2006.

Fulgham, Kristi Leigh: White; age 26 at crime and now age 33 (DOB: 8–27–1976); murder (she hired killer) of white male age 28 (her husband) in Longview (Oktibbeha County) on 5–10–2003; sentenced on 12–9–2006.

Missouri

(see Federal)

North Carolina

(last execution of female by North Carolina on 11–2–1984)

(4 female offenders now on North Carolina's death row)

Jennings, Patricia JoAnn [aka Wells]: White; age 47 at crime and now age 66 (DOB: 8–24–1942); murder of white male age 77 (her husband) in Wilson County on 9–19–1989; sentenced on 11–5-1990.

Moore, Blanche Kiser [aka Taylor]: White; age 56 at crime and now age 76 (DOB: 2–17–1933); murder of white male age 50 (her boyfriend) in Alamance County on 10–7–1986; sentenced on 1–18–1991.

Parker, Carlette Elizabeth: Black; age 34 at crime and now age 46 (DOB: 6–12–1963); murder of white female age 86 in North Raleigh (Wake County) on 5–12–1998; sentenced on 4–1–1999.

Walters, Christina S.: American Indian; age 20 at crime and now age 30 (DOB: 7–15–1978); murder of white female age 19 and white female age 25 north of Fayetteville in Cumberland County on 8–17–1998; sentenced on 7–6–2000.

Ohio

(last execution of female by Ohio on 6–12–1954)
(1 female offender now on Ohio's death row)

Roberts, Donna Marie: White; age 58 at crime and now age 65 (DOB: 5–23–1944); murder of white male age 56 (her husband) near Warren (Trumbull County) on 12–11–2001; sentenced on 6–21–2003; reversed on 8–2–2006; resentenced on 10–29–2007.

Oklahoma

(last execution of a female by Oklahoma on 12–4–2001)
(1 female offender now on Oklahoma's death row)

Andrew, Brenda E.: White; age 37 at crime and now age 45 (DOB: 12–16–1963); murder of white male age 39 (her husband) in Oklahoma City on 11–20–2001; sentenced on 9–22–2004.

Pennsylvania

(last execution of female by Pennsylvania on 10–14–1946)
(3 female offenders now on death row)

King, Carolyn Ann [aka Ewell; Goodman; Kline]: Black; age 28 at crime and now age 43 (DOB: 12–9–1965); robbery and murder of white female adult in October 1993 in Lebanon; sentenced on 11–30–1994.

Tharp, Michelle Sue: White; age 29 at crime and now age 40 (DOB: 1–20–1969); murder of white female age 7 (her daughter) in Burgettstown (Washington County) on 4–18–1998; sentenced on 11–14–2000.

Walter, Shonda Dee (aka Walters]: Black; age 23 at crime and now age 29 (DOB: 7–16–1979); murder of white male age 83 in Lock Haven (Clinton County) on 3–25–2003; sentenced on 4–19–2005.

Tennessee

(last execution of female by Tennessee in 1837)
(2 female offenders now on death row)

Owens, Gail Kirksey: White; age 32 at crime and now age 56 (DOB 9–22–1952); murder (she hired killer) of white male adult (her husband) in Shelby County on 2–17–1985; sentenced on 1–15–1986.

Pike, Christa Gail: White; age 18 at crime and now age 33 (DOB: 3–10–1976); murder of Latin female age 19 in Knoxville on 1–12–1995; sentenced on 3–29–1996.

Texas

(last execution of female by Texas on 9–14–2005)

(10 female offenders now on death row)

Basso, Suzanne Margaret: White; age 44 at crime and now age 55 (DOB: 5–15–1954); murder of white male (her boyfriend) age 59 in Houston (Harris County) on 8–25–1998; sentenced on 9–1–1999.

Carty, Linda Anita: Black; age 42 at crime and now age 50 (DOB: 10–5–1958); kidnapping and murder of Latin female age 20 (and victim's infant son) in Houston (Harris County) on 5–16–2001; sentenced on 2–21–2002.

Coleman, Lisa: Black; age 28 at crime and now age 33; murder of black male age 9 in Arlington (Tarrant County) on 7–26–2004; sentenced on 7–7–2006.

Henderson, Cathy Lynn: White; age 37 at crime and now age 52 (DOB: 12–27–1956); murder of white male age 3 months (she was babysitter) near Austin (Travis County) on 1–21–1994; sentenced on 5–25–1995.

Holberg, Brittany Marlowe: White; age 23 at crime and now age 36 (DOB: 1–7–1973); murder of white male age 80 in Amarillo (Randall County) on 11–13–1996; sentenced on 3–27–1998.

Lucio, Melissa Elizabeth: Latin; age 38 at crime and now age 40 (DOB: 7–18–1968); murder of Latin female age 2 1/2 (her daughter) in Harlington (Cameron County) on 2–16–2007; sentenced on 8–??–2008.

McCarthy, Kimberly Lagayle: Black; age 36 at crime and now age 48 (DOB: 5–11–1961); murder of white female age 71 in Lancaster (Dallas County) on 7–21–1997; sentenced on 12-?-1998; reversed in 2001; resentenced to death on 11–1–2002.

Richardson, Chelsea Lea: White; age 19 at crime and now age 25 (DOB: 3–26–1984); murder of white male age 46 and white female age 45 in Mansfield (Tarrant County) on 12–11–2003; sentenced on 6–1–2005.

Routier, Darla Lynn: White; age 26 at crime and now age 39 (DOB: 1–4–1970); murder of white male age 5 (her son) in Rowlett (Dallas County) on 6–6–1996; sentenced on 2–4–1997.

Sheppard, Erica Yvonne: Black; age 19 at crime and now age 35 (DOB: 9–1–1973); murder of white (?) female age 43 in Houston (Harris County) on 6–30–1993; sentenced on 3–3–1995.

APPENDIX C

SELECTED CITATIONS TO AUTHOR'S PUBLICATIONS CONCERNING CAPITAL PUNISHMENT OF FEMALES

Death Penalty for Women and Girls in North Carolina, 1 ELON UNIVERSITY LAW REVIEW 65 (2009) (with Elizabeth Rapaport).

THE FAIRER DEATH: EXECUTING WOMEN IN OHIO (Athens, OH: Ohio University Press) (2006).

Rare and Inconsistent: The Death Penalty for Women, 33 FORDHAM URBAN LAW JOURNAL 609 (2006).

DEATH PENALTY IN A NUTSHELL (St. Paul, MN: West Group) (2003) (2nd ed. 2005) (3rd ed. 2008).

Executing Women, Children, and the Retarded: Second Class Citizenship in Capital Punishment, in AMERICA'S EXPERIMENT WITH CAPITAL PUNISHMENT at 201 (1998) and at 301 (2nd ed. 2003) (James R. Acker, Robert M. Bohm, & Charles S. Lanier, eds.) (Durham, NC: Carolina Press).

Gendering the Death Penalty: Countering Sex Bias in a Masculine Sanctuary, 63 OHIO STATE LAW JOURNAL 433 (2002).

Sentencing Women to Death, 16(1) CRIMINAL JUSTICE (ABA) 24 (Spring 2001).

Women on Death Row, in ENCYCLOPEDIA OF WOMEN AND CRIME 45 (Nicole Rafter, ed.) (Phoenix: The Oryx Press) (2000).

Capital Punishment of Female Offenders, in WOMEN IN PRISON (Shirley Dicks, ed.) (Amherst, NY: Prometheus Books) (1998).

America's Aversion to Executing Women, 1 OHIO NORTHERN UNIVERSITY WOMEN'S LAW JOURNAL 1 (1997).

Death Penalty for Lesbians, 1 NATIONAL JOURNAL OF SEXUAL ORIENTATION LAW 104 (1994) (available at http://sunsite.unc.edu/gaylaw).

Death Penalty for Battered Women, 20 FLORIDA STATE LAW REVIEW 163 (1992).

Death Penalty for Female Offenders, 58 UNIVERSITY OF CINCINNATI LAW REVIEW 845 (1990).

Executing Juvenile Females, 22 CONNECTICUT LAW REVIEW 3 (1989) (with Lynn Sametz).

Note

1. Issue #65. Copyright 2010 by Victor Streib. Used by permission.

SELECTED BIBLIOGRAPHY

Historical and Contemporary Core Sources in Women's Offending

Adler, Freda. 1975. *Sisters in Crime: The Rise of the New Female Criminal*. New York: McGraw Hill.

Atkins, Susan, and Brenda Hoggett. 1984. *Women and the Law*. Oxford: Basil Blackwell.

Bach, Steven. 2007. *Leni: The Life and Work of Leni Reifenstahl*. New York: Alfred A. Knopf.

Barrows, Sydney. 1986. *Mayflower Madam: The Secret Life of Sydney Biddle Barrows*. New York: Arbor House.

Baskin, Deborah, and Ira Sommers. 1998. *Casualties of Community Disorder: Women's Careers in Violent Crime*. Boulder, CO: Westview.

Baunach, Phyllis. 1985. *Women in Prison*. New Brunswick, NJ: Transaction Books.

Bicknell, Anna L. 2009. *The Story of Marie-Antoinette*. New York: Cornell University Press.

Bosworth, Mary, and Jeanne Flavin. 2006. *Race, Gender, and Punishment: From Colonialism to the War on Terror*. New Brunswick, NJ: Rutgers Press.

Brock, Deborah. 1998. *Making Work, Making Trouble: Prostitution as a Social Problem*. Toronto: University of Toronto Press.

Broidy, Lisa, and Robert Agnew. 1997. "Gender and Crime: A General Strain Theory Perspective." *Journal of Research in Crime and Delinquency* 34: 275–306.

Browne, Angela. 1987. *When Battered Women Kill*. New York: The Free Press.

Browne, Angela, Brenda Miller, and Eugene Maguin. 1999. "Prevalence and Severity of Lifetime Physical and Sexual Victimization Among Incarcerated Women." *International Journal of Law and Psychiatry* 22(3–4): 311–322.

Byron, Christopher. 2002. *Martha, Inc.: The Incredible Story of Martha Stewart Living*. New York: Wiley.

Campbell, Anne. 1993. *Men, Women, and Aggression*. New York: Basic Books.

Carlen, Pat. 1983. *Women's Imprisonment: A Study in Social Control*. London: Routledge.

Carr, Nicole T., Kenneth Hudson, Roma S. Hanks, and Andrea N. Hunt. 2008. "Gender Effects along the Juvenile Justice System." *Feminist Criminology* 3: 25–43.

Chesler, Ellen. 1992. *Women of Valor: Margaret Sanger and the Birth Control Movement in America*. New York: Simon and Schuster.

Chesney-Lind, Meda. 1989. "Girls' Crime and Woman's Place: Toward a Feminist Model of Female Delinquency." *Crime and Delinquency* 35: 5–29.

Chesney-Lind, Meda. 2006. "Patriarchy, Crime and Justice." *Feminist Criminology* 1(1): 6–26.

Chesney-Lind, Meda, and J.M. Hagedorn, eds. 1999. *Female Gangs in America: Essays on Girls, Gangs, and Gender.* Chicago: Lakeview Press.

Clinton, Catherine. 2004. *Harriett Tubman: The Road to Freedom.* Boston: Little and Brown.

Collier-Thomas, Bettye, and V.P. Franklin. 2001. *Sisters in the Struggle: African American Women in the Civil Rights-Black Power Movement.* New York: New York University Press.

Cook, Sandy, and Susanne Davies, eds. 1999. *Harsh Punishment: International Experiences of Women's Imprisonment.* Boston: Northeastern University Press.

Daly, Kathleen. 1989. "Gender and Varieties of White Collar Crime." *Criminology* 27(4): 769–794.

Daly, Kathleen. 1994. *Gender, Crime, and Punishment.* New Haven: Yale University Press.

Daly, Kathleen, and Meda Chesney-Lind. 1988. "Feminism and Criminology." *Justice Quarterly* 5: 497–538.

Daly, Kathleen. 1997. "Different Ways of Conceptualizing Sex/Gender in Feminist Theory and Their Implications for Criminology." *Theoretical Criminology* 1(1): 25–51.

De Coster, Stacy, and Karen Heimer. 2006. "Crime at the Intersections: Race, Class, Gender, and Violent Offending." In Ruth Peterson, Lauren Krivo, and John Hagan (eds.), *The Many Colors of Crime: Inequalities of Race, Ethnicity, and Crime in America,* 138–156. New York: New York University Press.

DeHart, Dana. 2008. "Pathways to Prison: The Impact of Victimization in the Lives of Incarcerated Women." *Violence Against Women* 14: 1362–1381.

DeKeseredy, Walter. 2000. *Women, Crime, and the Canadian Criminal Justice System.* Cincinnati: Anderson.

Denov, Myriam. 2004. *Perspectives on Female Sex Offending: A Culture of Denial.* Burlington, VT: Ashgate.

Dodge, Mara. 2002. *Whores and Thieves of the Worst Kind: A Study of Women, Crime, and Prisons: 1835–2000.* DeKalb: Northern Illinois University Press.

Eaton, Mary. 1993. *Women After Prison.* Philadelphia: Open University Press.

Erlanger, Rachel. 1978. *Lucrezia Borgia: A Biography.* New York: Hawthorn Books.

Esbensen, Finn-Aage, Dana Peterson, Terrance J. Taylor, and Adrienne Feng. 2010. *Youth Violence: Sex and Race Differences in Offending, Victimization, and Gang Membership.* Philadelphia: Temple University Press.

Faith, Karlene. 1993. *Unruly Women: The Politics of Confinement and Resistance.* Vancouver: Press Gang Publishers.

Fentinan, Linda. 2009. "Pursuing the Perfect Mother: Why America's Criminalization of Maternal Substance Abuse Is Not the Answer—A Comparative Legal Analysis." *Journal of Gender and the Law* 15: 389–465.

Filetti, Jean S. 2001. "From Lizzie Borden to Lorena Bobbitt: Violent Women and Gendered Justice." *Journal of American Studies* 335: 471-484.

Gado, Mark. 2008. *Death Row Women: Murder, Justice, and the New York Press.* Westport, CT: Praeger.

Gentry, Curt. 1964. *The Madams of San Francisco.* Garden City, NY: Doubleday.

Giallombardo, Rose. 1966. *Society of Women: A Study of a Women's Prison.* New York: John Wiley.

Gilfus, Mary. 1992. "From Victims to Survivors to Offenders: Women's Routes of Entry and Immersion into Street Crime." *Women and Criminal Justice* 4: 63–90.

Gillespie, Cynthia. 1989. *Justifiable Homicide: Battered Women, Self Defense, and the Law.* Columbus: Ohio State University Press.

Girschick, Lori. 1999. *No Safe Haven: Stories of Women in Prison.* Boston: Northeastern University Press.

Goldman, Emma. 2006. *Living My Life.* New York: Penguin Books.

Goldsmith, Margaret L. 1976. *Seven Women Against the World.* Westport, CT: Hyperion Press.

Gooch, Steve. 1978. *The Women Pirates Ann Bonny and Mary Read.* London: Pluto Press.

Hagan, John. 1987. "Class in the Household: A Power-Control Theory of Gender and Delinquency." *American Journal of Sociology* 92: 788–816.

Hammer, Richard. 1990. *The Helmsleys: The Rise and Fall of Harry and Leona.* New York: New American Library.

Haskins, James. 1988. *Winnie Mandela: Life of Struggle.* New York: Putnam.

Hearst, Patricia Campbell, and Alvin Moscow. 1982. *Every Secret Thing.* Garden City, NY: Doubleday.

Heidensohn, Frances. 1985. *Women and Crime.* Basingstoke: Macmillan.

Heidensohn, Frances. 1968. "The Deviance of Women: A Critique and an Enquiry." *British Journal of Sociology* 19(2): 160–175.

Hendley, Nate. 2007. *Bonnie and Clyde: A Biography.* Westport, CT: Greenwood Press.

Hollander, Xaviera. 2002. *Child No More: A Memoir.* New York: Regan Books.

Humphries, Drew. 1999. *Crack Mothers: Pregnancy, Drugs, and the Media.* Columbus: Ohio State University Press.

Jensen, Vickie. 2001. *Why Women Kill: Gender Equality and Homicide.* Boulder, CO: Lynne Rienner.

Kruttschnitt, Candace, and Kristin Carbone-Lopez. 2006. Moving Beyond the Stereotypes: Women's Subjective Accounts of Their Violent Crime. *Criminology* 44(2): 321–352.

Langlois, Janet L. 1985. *Belle Gunness, The Lady Bluebeard.* Bloomington: Indiana University Press.

Leonard, Elizabeth Dermody. 2002. *Convicted Survivors: The Imprisonment of Battered Women Who Kill.* Albany: SUNY Press.

Maher, Lisa. 1997. *Sexed Work: Gender, Race, and Resistance in a Brooklyn Drug Market.* Oxford: Clarenden Press.

Maher, Lisa, and Kathleen Daly. 1996. "Women in the Street Level Drug Economy: Continuity or Change?" *Criminology* 34(4): 465–491.

McNulty, Faith. 1981. *The Burning Bed.* Toronto: Bantam Books.

Messerschmidt, James. 1986. *Capitalism, Patriarchy, and Crime: Toward a Socialist Feminist Criminology.* Totowa, NJ: Rowman and Littlefield.

Meyer, Cheryl, and Michelle Oberman. 2001. *Mothers Who Kill Their Children: Understanding the Acts of Moms from Susan Smith to the "Prom Mom."* New York: New York University Press.

Miller, Jody. 2008. *Getting Played: African-American Girls, Urban Inequality, and Gendered Violence.* New York: New York University Press.

Miller, Jody. 1998. "Up It Up: Gender and the Accomplishment of Street Robbery." *Criminology* 36: 37–66.

Miller, Jody. 2001. *One of the Guys: Girls, Gangs, and Gender.* New York: Oxford University Press.

Miller, Susan. 2005. *Victims as Offenders: The Paradox of Women's Violence in Relationships.* New Brunswick, NJ: Rutgers University Press.

Moore, Lucy. 2007. *Liberty: The Lives and Times of Six Women in Revolutionary France.* New York: HarperCollins.

Nadelson, Reggie. 1972. *Who Is Angela Davis? The Biography of a Revolutionary.* New York: P. H. Wyden.

Naffine, Ngaire. 1988. *Female Crime: Construction of Women in Criminology.* London: University College of London Press.

Naffine, Ngaire. 1996. *Feminism and Criminology.* Philadelphia: Temple University Press.

Naffine, N., and F. Gale. 1989. "Testing the Nexus: Crime, Gender, and Unemployment." *British Journal of Criminology* 29(2): 144–156.

O'Brien, Patricia. 2001. *Making It In the Free World: Women in Transition From Prison.* Albany: SUNY Press.

Oberman, Michelle. 2008. *When Mothers Kill Kids: Interviews from Prison.* New York: New York University Press.

Odem, Mary E. 1995. *Delinquent Daughters: Protecting and Policing Adolescent Female Sexuality in the United States, 1885–1920.* Chapel Hill: University of North Carolina Press.

Ogle, Robbin, and Susan Jacobs. 2002. *Self Defense and Battered Women Who Kill.* Westport, CT: Praeger.

Owen, Barbara. 1998. *"In the Mix": Struggle and Survival in a Women's Prison.* Albany: SUNY Press.

Pence, Irene. 2001. *Buried Memories: The Chilling True Story of Betty Lou Beets, the Texas Black Widow.* New York: Pinnacle Books.

Ptacek, James. 1999. *Battered Women in the Courtroom: The Power of Judicial Responses.* Boston: Northeastern University Press.

Rafter, Nicole Hahn, and Frances Heidensohn, eds. 1995. *International Feminist Perspectives in Crime: Engendering a Discipline.* Buckingham: Open University Press.

Richie, Beth. 1996. *Compelled to Crime: The Gender Entrapment of Battered Black Women.* New York: Routledge.

Ross, Ishbel. 1954. *Rebel Rose: Life of Rose O'Neal Greenhow, Confederate Spy.* New York: Harper.

Salisbury, Emily J., and Patricia Van Voorhis. 2009. "Gendered Pathways: A Quantitative Investigation of Women Probationers." *Criminal Justice and Behavior* 36: 541–566.

Scherr, Marie. 1970. *Charlotte Corday and Certain Men of the Revolutionary Torment.* New York: AMS Press.

Schiller, Lawrence. 1970. *The Killing of Sharon Tate: The Exclusive Story of Susan Atkins.* New York: Signet.

Scholl, Hans, Inge Jens, and Sophie Scholl. 1987. *At the Heart of the White Rose: Letters and Diaries of Hans and Sophie Scholl.* New York: Harper and Row.

Schuetz, Janice. 1994. *The Logic of Women on Trial: Case Studies of Popular American Trials.* Carbondale: Southern Illinois University Press.

Schur, Edwin. 1984. *Labeling Women Deviant: Gender Stigma and Social Control.* New York: McGraw Hill.

Schwartz, Martin, and Dragan Milovanovic. 1999. *Race, Gender, and Class in Criminology: The Intersections.* New York: Garland Publishing.

Seagrave, K. 1992. *Women Serial and Mass Murderers: A Worldwide Reference, 1580–1990.* London: McFarland and Co.

Sharp, Susan. 2003. *The Incarcerated Woman: Rehabilitative Programming in Women's Prisons.* Upper Saddle River, NJ: Prentice Hall.

Shipley, Stacey L., and Bruce A. Arrigo. 2004. *The Female Homicide Offender: Serial Murder and the Case of Wuornos.* Upper Saddle River, NJ: Pearson Education.

Simkins, Sandra, and Sarah Katz. 2002. "Criminalizing Abused Girls." *Violence Against Women* 8: 1474–1499.

Simon, Rita. 1975. *Women and Crime.* Lexington, MA: Lexington Books.

Simpson, Sally. 1991. "Caste, Class, and Violent Crime: Explaining Differences in Women's Offending." *Criminology* 29(1): 115–135.

Simpson, Sally, and Lori Ellis. 1995. "Doing Gender: Sorting our the Caste and Crime Conundrum." *Criminology* 33(1): 47–81.

Skiffer, LaTanya. 2008. *How Black Female Offenders Explain their Crime and Describe Their Hopes: A Case Study of Inmates in a California Prison.* Lewiston, NY: Edwin Mellon Press.

Smart, Carol. 1976. *Women, Crime, and Criminology: A Feminist Critique.* London: Routledge.

Solinger, Rickie, ed. 2010. *Interrupted Life: Experiences of Incarcerated Women in the United States.* Berkeley: University of California Press.

Steffensmeier, Darrell J., and Emilie A. Allan. 1996. "Gender and Crime: Toward a Gendered Theory of Female Offending." *Annual Review of Sociology* 22: 459–487.

Vernon, Virginia. 1964. *Enchanting Little Lady: The Criminal Life of the Marquise de Brinvilliers.* London: Abelard-Schuman.

Victor, Barbara. 1998. *The Lady: Aung San Suu Kyi, Nobel Laureate and Burma's Prisoner.* Boston: Faber and Faber.

Visher, Christy. 1983. "Gender, Police Arrest Decisions, and Notions of Chivalry." *Criminology* 21: 5–28.

Ward, David, and Gene Kassebaum. 1965. *Women's Prison: Sex and Social Structure.* Chicago: Aldine.

Wilczynski, Ania. 1991. "Images of Women Who Kill Their Infants: The Mad and the Bad." *Women and Criminal Justice* 2: 71–88.

Wood, Ean. 2000. *The Josephine Baker Story.* London: Sanctuary.

Young, Vernetta. 1980. "Women, Race, and Crime." *Criminology* 18: 26–34.

Zaitzow, Barbara, and Jim Thomas, eds. 2003. *Women in Prison: Gender and Social Control.* Boulder, CO: Lynne Rienner.

Selected Secondary Textbooks and Textbook Readers

Belknap, Joanne. 2010. *The Invisible Woman: Gender, Crime, and Justice*, 4th edition. Belmont, CA: Thomson Wadsworth.

Chesney-Lind, Meda. 2004. *The Female Offender: Girls, Women, and Crime.* Thousand Oaks, CA: Sage.

Chesney-Lind, Meda, and Lisa Pasko, eds. 2004. *Girls, Women, and Crime: Selected Readings.* Thousand Oaks, CA: Sage.

Chesney-Lind, Meda, and Randall Shelden. 2003. *Girls, Delinquency, and Juvenile Justice.* Belmont, CA: Thomson/Wadsworth.

Heimer, Karen, and Candace Kruttschnitt, eds. 2006. *Gender and Crime: Patterns of Victimization and Offending.* New York: New York University Press.

Muraskin, Rosllyn, ed. 2012. *Women and Justice: It's a Crime.* Upper Saddle River, NJ: Prentice-Hall.

Pollock, Joycelyn. 2001. *Women, Prison, and Crime.* Belmont, CA: Wadsworth.

Price, Barbara, and Natalie Sokoloff. 2003. *The Criminal Justice System and Women: Offenders, Prisoners, Victims, and Workers*, 3rd edition. New York: McGraw Hill.

Renzetti, Claire, and Lynne Goodstein, eds. 2001. *Women, Crime, and Criminal Justice: Original Feminist Readings.* Los Angeles: Roxbury.

Roberts, Dorothy. 1998. *Killing the Black Body: Race, Reproduction, and the Meaning of Liberty.* New York: Vintage.

Schram, Pamela, and Barbara Koons-Witt. 2004. *Gender (in)Justice: Theory and Practice in Feminist Criminology.* Long Grove, IL: Waveland.

Silvestri, M., and C. Crowther-Dowey. 2008. *Gender and Crime.* Thousand Oaks, CA: Sage.

Van Wormer, Katherine Stuart, and Clemens Bartollas, eds. 2007. *Women and the Criminal Justice System.* Boston: Pearson.

INDEX

Boldface page numbers reflect main entries.

Abolition Democracy (Davis), 374
abortion and criminalization, 223–229
    1840–1806 period, 226–227
    1890–1900 antiabortion policy, 227
    Hawaii Court of Appeals ruling, 231
    Model Penal Code, 227–228
    New York Revised Statutes (1829), 225
    19th century policy evolution, 225–226
    Revised "Crimes and Punishments" law, 224
    state laws, 226–227
    Supreme Court cases, 228–229
    therapeutic exceptions (NYS), 225
Abu-Jamal, Mumia, 374
Adams, Anthony, 11
Adams, Elizabeth, 415
adjudication. *See* criminal adjudication
Adler, Freda, 101
Affair of the Poisons (France), 543
African American women. *See also* Allen, Wanda Jean; women of color; Wright, Dora
    anti-court testimony laws, 131, 278
    black feminism, 130
    comparison with Latinas, 131
    comparison with white criminality, 123
    drug-related incarceration odds, 126
    early-vs. late-onset criminality, 103, 127
    femininity construction by, 135
    incarceration overrepresentation, 123–124, 127–129, 192
    interviews regarding police treatment, 190
    IPV in lesbian partnerships, 198–199
    prostitution data, 86
    rape of female slaves, 83
    release rates vs. African American men, 125
    stereotypes of, 130–133, 281
    victimization by male police, 190, 193, 195
African National Council (ANC), 525–527
age and women's offending, 99–114
    age-graded social control, 103
    age invariance theory, 100–101
    changes in data, research methods, 104–107
    crime mix, 108–109
    Criminal Career and Life Course Study, 105
    developmental life course criminology, 102–103
    Dunedin Multidisciplinary Health and Development Study, 102
    duration, 109–111
    frequency, 108
    future research directions, 112–114
    gender in the life course perspective, 103–104
    general information, 99–100
    life course theory, 101–102
    Lola (case study), 99
    participation, 107–108
    Racine Wisconsin adult onset study, 104, 105
    Women's Reformatory Study, 103–106
age-crime curve, 100
age-graded social control, 103

age invariance theory, 100–101

Agricultural Workers Organizing
Committee, 477

Ah Toy, 21, **277–279**, 360

*Akron v. Akron Center for Reproductive
Health* (1983), 228

Alarid, Leanne Fiftal, 90

Albright, Gerald, 309

alcohol and drug offenses, 21–23, 154–156.
See also substance abuse

Alcoholics Anonymous (AA), 504

Alderson Federal Women Penitentiary, 174

Alexander VI (Pope), 328–330

Alice, Mary, 580

Allan, Emilie A., 40, 41, 101, 103, 173

Allen, Wanda Jean, 64–65, 134, **279–281**

Alliance of Lesbian Feminists of Atlanta, 523

Alligood, Clarence, 522

Allitt, Beverly, 14, 71, **282–283**

American Civil Liberties Union, 497

American Control League, 573

American Indian Council of the Reformed
Church of America, 356–357

American Indian Movement (AIM), 167,
169, 289–290, 633–634

American Indian women, 127, 133. *See also*
Aquash, Anna; Wanrow, Yvonne

American Law Institute's Model Penal
Code, 227

American Psychiatric Association, 88, 433

American Psychological Association (APA),
497

American Public Health Association, 538

American Woman Suffrage Association
(AWSA), 601

Amnesty International, 428, 568, 608

Anarchist Exclusion Act, 436

Anderson, George (Arthur Dunlop), 302

Anderson, K. B., 203

Andrew, Phil, 371

Andrews, E. Ray, 310

Angel Ranch, 437

Angels of Death. *See* Allitt, Beverly;
Bombeek, Cecile; Jegado, Hélène;
Jones, Genene

Annan, Kofi, 607

anomie/strain theory, 35–37

Anthony, Casey, **284–288**

Anthony, Cindy, 286

Anthony, Susan B., 407, 601, 618

antisocial personality disorder, 65, 66. *See
also* Atkins, Susan; Hindley, Myra;
Huckaby, Melissa; Krenwinkel, Patricia; Van Houten, Leslie; Wuornos,
Aileen

antisodomy laws, 88

Antoinette, Marie. *See* Marie Antoinette

Antonio, Walter Gino, 643

Aquash, Anna, 167, **289–291**

Aquash, Nogeeshik, 290–291

Arab National Movement, 499

Archbold, C. A., 202, 203

Are Prisons Obsolete? (Davis), 374

Arguello, Patrick, 500

Armed Forces of National Liberation of
Puerto Rico (FALN), 553–554

ASEAN (Association of Southeast Asian
Nations), 608

The Assassin's Accomplice (Larson),
603–604

Association for Support of Children's
Rights, 394

Association of Southeast Asian Nations
(ASEAN), 608

Atkins, Susan, 13, 66, **291–295**, 492–493,
624

Atomic Energy Act (1946), 570

Aurnou, Joel, 452

Austria/Australia, infanticide legal status, 60

Avakame, E. F., 197

Axis Sally. *See* Gillars, Mildred Elizabeth
Sisk

"baby farms" (of Amelia Dyer), 14

Bacanovic, Peter, 597–598

Badlands movie, 425

Baez, Jose, 287

Bailey, F. Lee, 459

Baker, E. D., 361

Baker, Josephine, **297–299**

Balagoon, Kuwasi, 354

Ballard, James David, 166

*The Bandit Queen: The True Story of
Phoolan Devi* (Sen), 376

Bandit Queen of India. *See* Devi, Phoolan

The Bandit Queen of India: An Indian Woman's Amazing Journey from Peasant to International Legend (Devi), 171

Barfield, Velma, 14, 69–70, 145–146, **299–301**

Barker, Arizona "Ma," 17, **302–303**

Barker, Doyle Wayne, 309–310

Barker-Karpis Gang, 302–303

Baro, A. L., 202

Barron, Charles, 580

Barrow, Clyde, 17, 554–557. *See also* Parker, Bonnie

Barrows, Sydney, 21, **303–306**

Bàthory, Elizabeth, 69, **306–308**

battered husband's syndrome, 235

battered spouse syndrome, 235

battered women (battered women's syndrome), 147. *See also* Bobbitt, Lorena; Hughes, Francine; Kelly, Gladys Cannon; Thurman, Tracy

  criminal adjudication and, 232–235

  as defendant vs. victim, 233

  defined, 245

  failures in legal protections for, 4–5, 147

  individual state codification, 235

  New Jersey Coalition for Battered Women, 497

  as pathway to prison, 245

  Violence Against Women Act, 85, 147

  work of Lenore Walker, 150–153

Battered Women's Justice Project (2008), 149

Beauchamp, Jereboam, 358

Beaufort County Jail (North Carolina), 521–522

Beauregard, Pierre, 445

Beausoleil, Bobby, 293, 623

Bedford Hills Children's Center, 353. *See also* Clark, Judith

Bedford Hills Correctional Facility for Women (NYS), 353, 452

Beets, Betty, 14, 145–146, **308–310**

Beets, James Donald, 309–310

Beirne, Piers, 165, 173

Bell, Charles, 461–462

Bell, Mary, 157, **310–312**

Bell, Norma, 311

Belle Boyd in Camp and Prison (Boyd), 333

Bellotti v. Baird (1979), 228

Bembo, Pietro, 330

Bence, Eli, 326–327

Bennett, Keith, 463

Bentley, Alvin, 512

Berk, R. A., 196

Berkman, Alexander, 435–436

Bernardo, Paul (Scarborough Rapist), 468–470

Bevan, Catherine, **312–314**

Bevan, Henry, 312

Bexar County Hospital (Texas), 488

Biggers, J. R., 154

biological perspectives of women's criminality, 57–63

  Lombroso/early perspectives, 57–58

  mothers who kill their children, 60–63

  sexuality and menstruation, 58–59

bipolar disorder, 69, 73. *See also* Dann, Laurie; Huckaby, Melissa; Lafave, Debra; Letourneau, Mary Kay

Bishop, Amy, 14, **314–317**

Black Liberation Army (BLA), 133, 344, 353–354, 578

Black Movement, 169, 373

Black Panther Party (BPP), 164, 373, 523, 578

Black Tigresses, 380

Black Widow killer. *See* Doss, Nannie

Blackjack Hall of Fame, 389

Blackwell, Henry, 601

Blakey, David, 398–399

Blanchard, Susan, 417

Blee, Kathleen, 163

Block, Carolyn Rebecca, 105, 108–110

Blues Legacies and Black Feminism (Davis), 374

Bobbitt, John Wayne, 319–321

Bobbitt, Lorena, **318–321**

Boleyn, Anne, 471

Bombeek, Cecile, 14, 70, **321–322**

Bonnie and Clyde movie, 557. *See also* Parker, Bonnie

Bonny, Anne, 17, **323–324**

Borden, Abby Durfee Gray, 326–328
Borden, Andrew Jackson, 326–328
Borden, Lizzie, **325–328**
borderline personality disorder, 65–66
Borgia, Cesare, 328–330
Borgia, Lucrezia, **328–330**
Boroughs, Deborah, 91
Bottcher, Jean, 82
Boudin, Kathy, 354
Bowers v. Hardwick (Supreme Court decision), 88
Bowser, Mary Elizabeth, 628
Box, S., 39
Boyd, Belle, **330–333**
Boyns, David, 166
Brady, Ian, 463
Brame, Robert, 103
Brandenburg v. Ohio (Supreme Court decision), 640
Branson, Robert Franklin, 308
Bremer, Edward George, 303
Bridges, Gail, 449–450
Brinvilliers, Marquise de, **333–335**
Broderick, Betty, **335–337**
Broidy, Lisa M., 103–104
Brokaw, Frances Seymour, 417
Brown, Debra, 13–14, **337–340**
Brown, Joyce Ann, **341–343**
Brown, Martin, 311–312
Brown, W. O., 291
Brown, Waverly, 353
Bruce, Martha Jean, 342–343
Brundidge, Harry, 368
Brunner, Mary, 293, 502
Brunson, R. K., 192, 195
Buchanan, James, 443, 444
Buck, Marilyn, 167, **343–345**
Bugliosi, Vince, 493
Bureau of Justice Statistics data
    African American overrepresentation, 123
    imprisonment by gender, race, origin, 242
    inmate mental health, 256
    Latina overrepresentation, 126
    male/female victimization surveys, 187, 196
    mental health problems in prison, 256
    pre-incarceration abuse, 254
    rape with aggravating factors, 199
    sentenced prisoners under state jurisdiction, 243
    violent crime victimization, 195
    women under sentence of death, 251
Burlingame, D., 202
The Burning Bed movie, 149, 481. *See also* Hughes, Francine
Burress, Troy, 643
Busch, Francis X., 604
Bush, George W., 90, 168–169, 228, 229, 419, 618
Buttafuoco, Joey, 412–414
Buttafuoco, Mary Jo, 413
The Butterbox Babies movie, 651
"Butterbox Baby Killer." *See* Young, Lila
Byrd, Robert C., 344

Calhoun, Cheshire, 88
California Gold Rush, 277, 360, 387, 444
California Institution for Women (CIW), 295, 504
Campbell, Anne, 11, 68
Campos, Pedro Albizu, 511
Canada, infanticide legal status, 60
Canary, Martha Jane (Calamity Jane), 388
Cantu, Sandra, 473–475
Cao, Liqun, 11
Carey, Hugh, 533
Carrington, Peter J., 108
Carskaddon, Charles, 643
Carter, Jimmy, 459
Casey, James Patrick, 361
Castro, Fidel, 580
Cauffman, Elizabeth E., 103–104
Celebrity Rehab with Dr. Drew tv show, 416
Celeste, Richard, 340
Center for Constitutional Rights, 633
Central California Women's Facility (Chowchilla), 292, 295, 337, 591
Centurion Ministries, 343
César Chávez Monument (San Jose, CA), 477
"Charlie's Girls" (Charles Manson). *See* Atkins, Susan; Brunner, Mary; Fromme, Lynette "Squeaky"; Good, Sandra; Hindley, Myra; Krenwinkel, Patricia; Van Houten, Leslie

Chávez, César, 477
Che-Lumumba Club (Communist Party), 373
Cheng Chui Ping (Zheng Cui Ping), **347–349**
Cheng I Sao, 17, **349–351**
Chesney-Lind, M., 39, 82, 144, 145, 189–190, 248
Chicano Movement, 169
child abuse and neglect, 142–146. *See also* Wuornos, Aileen
   legislative intervention, 142–143
Child Abuse Prevention and Treatment Act (1974), 143
Child Savers Movement (early 1900s), 143
children
   abuse by pedophiles, 91–92
   killing of, by their mothers, 60–63
   prostitution by, 156
   sexual abuse of, 82
Children of Bedford Foundation, 453
Children's Act (1908) (England), 390
Ch'ing Yih Szaou. *See* Cheng I Sao
Chivers, Thomas Holley, 359
Choice USA, 595
Christian Coalition of America, 620
Christian Right organization, 89
Civil Rights Act (1964), 201, 634
Civil Rights Movement (U.S.), 297–298, 343
Civil War (U.S.), 83, 167, 330–331, 333, 395, 445
Clark, Judith, **352–354**
Clark, Justice, 530
Cleghorn, Mildred, **355–357**
Clinton, Bill, 197, 554, 559
Clinton, Hillary Rodham, 479
Clinton Correctional Facility for Women (NJ), 580
Coalition of Labor Union Women, 594
cocaine addiction, 70, 155
cognitive/learning deficits, 63–65
Coleman, Alton, 338–340. *See also* Brown, Debra
Coleman, Travis, 409–410
Collins, Patricia H., 83
Collison, Merle, 424
Colvert, Robert, 423
commercialized vice, 20–21
Commission for Racial Justice of the United Church for Christ, 522

Commission on Accreditation for Law Enforcement Agencies (CALEA), 202
Committee to Free Debra Gindorf, 433
Committees for Correspondence for Democracy and Socialism, 374
Communist Labor Party (CLP), 638
Communist Party youth organization, 373
Community Service Organization (CSO), 477
The Complete Scarsdale Medical Diet (Tarnower), 451–452
Comstock, Anthony, 574
Comstock Act (1873), 436, 573–574
Conciergerie Prison (France), 363, 536
Congressional legislation
   abortion funding, 228
   Child Abuse Prevention and Treatment Act, 143
   Comstock Law (1873), 574
   Fourteenth Amendment, 601
   freeing prisoners of war (1912), 356
   Medal of Honor to Rosa Parks, 559
   public funding assistance, 5
   Sentencing Reform Act (1984), 211
Constitution (U.S.)
   Equal Protection Clause, 231
   Fifth Amendment, 570
   First Amendment, 638, 640
   Fourteenth Amendment, 201, 601, 639–640
   Fourth Amendment, 530, 531–532
   Nineteenth Amendment, 638
   Sixth Amendment, 567
Convention against Torture and Other Cruel, Inhuman or Degrading, Treatment or Punishment and its Optional Protocol, 182
Convention on the Elimination of All Forms of Discrimination against Women, 182
Convention on the Elimination of Racial Discrimination, 182
Convention on the Rights of the Child, 182
Cook, Ann, **357–359**
Cora, Belle, **360–362**
Cora, Charles, 360–362
Corday, Charlotte, 15, **362–364**

Cordero, Andres Figuero, 512

Cornfield, Bernie, 415

corrections and correctional issues, 241–264

abuse and victimization, 254–255

assessment and screening, 253–254

community reentry, 263–264

death penalty, 250–251

drug use, 255–256

education, job skills, training, 261–263

female prisoners, 244–245

gender differences in prison adaptations, 249–250

gender-policies and practices, 246–248

incarceration trends, 241–244

management and supervision, 251–253

mental health, 256–257

parenting issues, 257–260

women and pathways to prison, 245–246

Cotton, Mary, 14, **364–366**

Counter Intelligence Program (COINTEL-PRO), 578

Covenant of Works doctrine (Puritans), 483

Crane, Frederick, 575

Crenshaw, Kimberle, 83

Crime in the United States reports. *See* FBI Uniform Crime Reports statistics

criminal adjudication, 209–235

abortion and criminalization, 223–229

battered women, 232–235

death sentences, 219–220

drug trafficking cases, 215–216

"evil women" perspective, 210

federal sentencing, 211–217

gender disparities in outcomes, 209–210

gender disparity studies, 215

Hispanic/black defendants, 216

interaction effect on sentence outcomes, 212

length of imprisonment period, 214–217

maternal substance abuse, 230–232

outcomes for white collar-offenders, 211–214

path modeling studies, 212

prosecutorial charging decisions, 220–223

sentence disparities, 214–215

social world perspective on sentencing, 210–211

state sentencing, gender disparities, 217–219

suspended sentences, 213

Criminal Career and Life Course Study, 105, 108

Criminal Cases Review Commission (2003), 400

Criminal District Court for the Parish of New Orleans, 421

Criminal Women, the Prostitute, and the Normal Woman (Lambroso & Ferrero), 170

Crittenden, Alexander P., 407

Crow, Matthew S., 126, 133

Cruz-Vera, Luis Rogelio, 317

Culpepper, Thomas, 472

Cuny, Marie-Therese, 376

Cuomo, Mario, 453

Cussen, Desmond, 399, 400

Cutts, James Madison, 443

Czolgosz, Leon, 435

d'Aquino, Iva (Tokyo Rose), 166, **367–369**

Daly, Kathleen, 107

Daniels, Andrew, 561

Dann, Laurie, 69, **370–372**

Dann, Mary and Carrie, 167

Dann, Russell, 370

Davies, K., 198–199

Davis, Angela, 134, 164, **372–374,** 522

Davis, Carla P., 106

Davis, Jefferson, 443–445

Davis, Jeffrey, 409

Davis, Maria Ragland, 317

De Coster, Stacy, 135

De Vries, Mick and Germaine, 464

Dean, Charles, 65

Dean, Jerry Lynn, 618, 619

Dear Mrs. Parks: A Dialogue with Today's Youth (Parks with Reed), 559

Declaration of the Rights of Women (Gouze), 167

Defendants of Regina McKnight, 538

DeFreeze, Donald, 458–459

DeHärt, Dana D., 157

Demuth, Stephen, 125

Department of Homeland Security (U.S.), 169

Department of Justice (U.S.) data
abuse of convicted men, women, 141
drug coping by prostitutes, 86–87
intimate partner violence, 84
males/serious vs. violent crime arrests, 105
race of women under sentence of death, 251
sexual assault reports, 81, 91

dependent personality disorder, 66–67. *See also* Gillars, Mildred Elizabeth Sisk; Lewis, Teresa

Dereham, Francis, 471–472

Dershowitz, Allen, 320

Deshayes, Catherine, 543

"Developing a Sociological Theory for the Empirical Understanding of Terrorism" (Boyns & Ballard), 166

developmental life course criminology, 102–103

Devi, Phoolan, 171, **374–377**

Devi: The Bandit Queen (Giddy & Shears), 376

Deviant Children Grown Up (Robins), 107

Devlin, Bernadette, 167, **377–379**

DeWitt, David, 604

DeWolfe, Thomas, 369

Dhanu (Thenmuli Rajaratnam), 15, **379–381**

Diagnostic and Statistical Manual of mental Disorders, 4th edition (DSM-IV)
absence of postpartum depression, 433
antisocial personality disorder, 66
personality disorders, 65
postpartum depression, 60

Diamond Necklace Affair (France), 534

Dill, Bonnie Thornton, 122

diversity and women's offending, 121–136
African American female perspective, 130–131
definitions, 122
drugs example, 128–129
impacts of stereotypes, 132–135
Latinas/other women of color perspective, 131–132

need for "intersectionality," 135
patterns and trends, 122–128

Doerner, Jill K., 125

Dolores Huerta Foundation, 478

domestic abuse syndrome, 235

Domestic Violence Experiment (Minneapolis) (1984), 197

Domestic Violence Offender Gun Act (1996), 197

Donizetti, Gaetano, 330

Dorothea Dix State Hospital (North Carolina), 300

Doss, Nannie, 15, **382–384**

Double Indemnity (Cain), 588–589

Dow, David, 547

Dowley, Philadelphia, 540–541

Downey, Lesley Ann, 463

Drexler, Melissa, 13, **384–386**

drug abuse. *See* substance abuse

drug-connected women, as pathway to prison, 245–246

drug crimes, 21, 128–129

drug trafficking cases, 18, 180, 215–217, 611–612

Due Process Clause (Constitution), 532

Duluth Domestic Violence Intervention programs, 154

Dumont, Eleanor, **387–389**

Dunedin Multidisciplinary Health and Development Study, 102

Dunlop, Arthur, 302

Durose, M. R., 189

Dwight Correctional Center (Illinois), 428

Dyer, Amelia, 14, **389–391**

Ebadi, Shirin, **393–395**

Ebrahimi, Amir Farshad, 394

Edgar, Jim, 428

Edmonds, Sarah, **395–398**

Eisenhower, Dwight, 571

Eklavya Sena self-defense group, 376

Elder, Glen, 102

Elliott, Delbert S., 108

Ellis, George, 399

Ellis, Ruth, **398–400**

embezzlement, 9, 18–19, 27–28, 156, 187, 191, 215

Enemies of the State (Busch), 604
Engel, R. S., 203
Equal Employment Opportunity Act (1972), 201
Equal Rights Amendment, 595
Erni, T., 68
Erwin, Joe, 561
escort services, 20–21, 85. *See also* Barrows, Sydney
Estes, Richard J., 157
Etiquette for Consenting Adults (Barrows), 305
Evans, Edward, 463
Everleigh, Ada, **400–402**
Everleigh, Minna, **403–405**
"evil women" perspective, 210

facilitators (defined), 91
Fair, Laura, 69, 170, **407–408**
Fair Sentencing Act (2010), 129
Falling, Christine, **408–410**
Fallmer, Clara, **410–412**
FALN (Armed Forces of National Liberation of Puerto Rico), 553–554
Family Limitations pamphlet (Comstock), 574
Farrell, Joanna, 321
Farrington, David P., 109
Fawcett, Farrah, 481
FBI Most Wanted List, 372, 373
FBI Uniform Crime Reports statistics, 9
    age and offending data, 106
    aggravated assault, 188
    alcohol and drug offenses, 21
    battered women, 233
    forcible rape, 84
    male vs. female arrests, 188
    persons arrested by sex, 191
    property crime, 18–19
    rapes/sexual offenses, 15
    reporting by race or gender (not both), 122–123
    robbery, 16
    "runaway" children, 143–144
    victimization surveys, 187–188
    violent arrests, 10–11
Federal Correctional Institution for Women (West Virginia), 512

Federal Corrections Institute (California), 345
Federal Medical Center (FMC) (Texas), 345
Federal Sentencing Guidelines
    drug trafficking cases, 215–216
    implementation (1987), 211
    post-implementation female sentencing, 214–217
federal sentencing of women, 211–217
    drug trafficking cases, 215–216
    federal districts study, 212
    gender disparity studies, 215
    Hispanic/black defendants, 216
    legal-bureaucratic model, 212–213
    length of imprisonment period, 214–217
    outcomes for white collar-offenders, 211–214
    path modeling studies, 212
    post-Federal Sentencing Guidelines, 214–217
    sentence disparities, 214–215
    suspended sentences, 213
Federal Women's Prison Camp (West Virginia), 579–580
Feldman, T. B., 68
Felson, R. B., 199
female police officers
    contemporary issues facing, 202–205
    historical overview, 201–202
"female public enemy." *See* Barker, Arizona "Ma"
feminist criminology, 139–140
feminist (women's) movement, 169. *See also* Davis, Angela; Fonda, Jane; Steinem, Gloria
    African American feminists, 131
    analyses of rape, 83
    assumptions about men and women, 31
    biblical feminists, 648
    critique of criminology, 121, 128
    "double strain" concept, 36–37
    FBI infiltration of, 169
    Francine Hughes case impact, 481
    Huerta's involvement, 478
    lesbians ignored by, 88
    Little as cause célèbre, 521, 523
    Lorena Bobbitt incident reaction, 320
    1970s period, 121, 200

1960s reaction to violence, 196

second generation movement, 38

Stone's *Woman's Journal*, 601–602

support for Joan Little, 523

support for Laura Fair, 407

thoughts on women's offending, 15–16, 41, 177

Wanrow's speaking for, 633–634

feminist pathways and criminal careers, 76–77

Fergusson, David M., 109

Ferraro, K., 154

Ferrero, Guglielmo, 170

Ferrero, William, 57–58

Fifth Amendment (Constitution), 570

filicide (defined), 8, 60

First Amendment (Constitution), 638, 640

Fisher, Amy, **412–414**

Fleishman, Gary, 493

Fleiss, Heidi, 21, **415–416**

Flores, Irvin, 512

Foerster, Werner, 579

Folger, Abigail, 492

Fonda, Henry, 417

Fonda, Jane, **416–419**

Ford, Gerald, 369, 440

forensic psychiatry, 428

Fort Sill Apache Tribe, 355–357. *See also* Cleghorn, Mildred

Fourteenth Amendment (Constitution), 201, 601, 639–640

Fourth Amendment (Constitution), 530–531, 531–532

Frank, Antoinette, **419–421**

Free Joan Little Committee, 522

Freedom Forum organization, 607

French, Kristen Dawn, 469

Friedman, Leon, 354

Fromme, Lynette "Squeaky," 440, 502

Frum, Barbara, 440

Frykowski, Voytek, 291, 294

Frykowski, Wojciech, 492

Fualaau, Vili, 513–515

Fugate, Caril, 13–14, 64, **422–425**

Fuller, Rodney, 517–518

Furman v. Georgia (Supreme Court decision), 523

Fyfe, J. J., 197

Gandhi, Rajiv, 15

Garcia, George, 428

Garcia, Guin, 145, 156, **427–428**

Garrett, Thomas, 617

Garrison, William, 617

gay and lesbian sexual issues, 8, 88–91, 169

Gehrke, David, 514

Gelsthorpe, L., 26

gender norms

creation/impacts of, 7

described, 42–43

female political prisoners and, 173

hegemonic masculinity and, 5–7, 6, 9, 16, 76

influence on Snyder case, 586

liberated gender ideologies vs., 40

limitations to females, 44

male gender-specific roles and, 82

moral development and, 43

outcomes influenced by, 46

Rosenberg's alleged violations of, 568

variability over time, 101, 112

gender-responsive programs and services, 246–248

gender systems, contexts of, 3–7. *See also* men vs. women

defined, 3–4

hegemonic masculinity, 5–7, 9, 16, 76

male-female similarities, differences, 26–29

political representation, 5

structural aspects, 4

women's crime, 4–5, 7–9

workforce opportunities, 4

gendered theories of women's offending. *See* women's offending, gendered theories

General Espionage Act (1917), 570

Germany, infanticide legal status, 60

Giallombardo, Rose, 74

Giddy, Isobelle, 376

Gilbert, David J., 354

Gillars, Mildred Elizabeth Sisk (Axis Sally), 67, 166, **429–431**

Gindorf, Debbie, 145–146, 152, **431–433**

Gindorf, Randy, 432

"girl guerilla." *See* Khaled, Leila

Girondists (French political group), 362–363. *See also* Corday, Charlotte

Girshick, Lori B., 142, 145

Gitlow v. New York (Supreme Court decision), 639

global women's crime issues, 177–183
consequences of offending, 180–181
explanations, 179–180
international policymaking, 181–182
patterns of crime, 179
sources of data, 178–179

Glueck, Sheldon and Eleanor, 104–106

Gold Rush (California), 277

Goldman, Emma, 164, **434–437**

González Valenzuela, Delfina, María de Jesús González, and Eva González, **437–439**

Gonzalez, Zenaida, 286

Good, Sandra, **439–441**

Good, Sarah, 549

Good Friday Agreement, 378

Gordon, Carl, 465

Gordon, M., 154

Gottfredson, Michael, 101, 104

Gottfried, Gessina, **441–442**

Gouze, Marie, 167

Graham, John, 291

Grana, S. J., 189

Gray, Judd, 587–589

Great Manhattan Savings Institution Robbery (1878), 529

Green, John C., 89

Greenberg, David, 101, 103

Greenhow, Rose, **443–446**

Greensville Correctional Center (Virginia), 519

Greer, Kimberly R., 89–90

Grogan, Clem, 492–493

Grogan, Steve, 294, 624

Grognan, Steve, 503

Gunness, Belle, **446–448**

Gurevich, Liena, 133

Habash, George, 499

Hagan, John, 74–75

Hale, C., 39

Handbook for Prison Managers and Policymakers on Women and Imprisonment (UNODC), 182–183

"Hanoi Jane." *See* Fonda, Jane

The Happy Hooker (Hollander), 464–465, 467

Hardinge, Samuel Wylde, Jr., 332–333

harmed and harming women (pathway to prison), 245

Harper, Hames, 579

Harris, Angela, 83

Harris, Bill and Emily, 591

Harris, Clara, **449–451**

Harris, David, 449–451

Harris, Jean, **451–453**

Harris, Lindsey, 451

Harris v. McRae (1980), 228

Hayashi, Kenji, 454

Hayashi, Masumi, **453–456**

Hearst, Patty, 72, 164, **457–459**

Hearst, Randolph and Catherine, 458

Hearst, William Randolph, 458

hegemonic masculinity, 5–6, 5–7, 9, 16, 76

Heimer, Karen, 135

Helmsley, Harry, 461

Helmsley, Leona, 20, **460–462**

Henry VIII (King of England), 470–472

Herman, Didi, 89

Hershberger, Mary, 418–419

Hibernia Bank (San Francisco, CA), 459

Hickey, Eric, 14

hijacking of a TWA jet. *See* Khaled, Leila

Hill-Collins, Patricia, 130

Hinchman, Sarah (Sally), 541

Hindley, Myra, 12, 66, **462–464**

Hinman, Gary, 291, 292, 295

Hirschfeld, Michael L., 354

Hirschi, Travis, 101, 104

Hislop, Julia, 82, 91

histrionic personality disorder, 65, 67

Hitler, Adolph, 563–565, 576

Hollander, Xaviera, 21, **464–467**

Hollywood Madame. *See* Fleiss, Heidi

Home Sweet Home radio program (Gillars), 430

homicide offending
by African Americans, Latinas, 124
by battered women, 233–234
caretaking burden and, 45
by child abuse, 536–539
economic disadvantage and, 32–33
European Sourcebook data, 179

of family, intimate partners, 4–5, 12, 146, 149–154
FBI statistics, 9
female underrepresentation, 27
gender equality and, 39
infanticide, 60–61
juvenile female homicide, 32
maternal substance abuse and, 230–231
men vs. women (NYC data), 123
by minority parents, 133
motives for, 11, 12–13
racial heterogeneity and, 34
serial/mass killings, 13–14
Homolka, Karla, **468–470**
Homolka, Tammy Lyn, 469
Horwood, L. John, 109
Hostetler, Richard, 648
Hotel Workers Union (California), 478
Houck, Minnie, 561
Houston Police Department, 547
Howard, Katherine, **470–472**
Howe, Brian, 311
Huckaby, Melissa, 16, 66, 92, **473–475**
Huerta, Dolores, 134, **476–479**
Hughes, Francine, 149, **479–481**
Hughes, Mickey, 479–481
Human Rights Action Center, 607
Human Rights Watch report (1996), 90
Humphreys, Dick, 643
Hutchinson, Anne, 164, **482–484**

I Am Rosa Parks (Parks with Haskins), 559
I Phoolan Devi, The Autobiography of India's Bandit Queen (Cuny & Rambali), 376
Ibargüengoitia, Jorge, 438–439
incarceration of women
abuse and victimization, 254–255
assessment and screening, 253–254
community reentry, 263–264
death row prisoners, 250–251
drug use, 255–256
education, job skills, training, 261–263
gender differences in adaptations, 249–250
management and supervision, 251–253
mental health issues, 256–257
parenting issues, 257–260
trends, 241–244

Indian Peacekeeping Force (IPKF), 379
Indianapolis Police Department, 204
Industrial Workers of the World (IWW), 638–639
Infant Life Protection Act (1897) (England), 390
infanticide, 8, 60–62, 390, 648
initiating partners (defined), 91
intensive care unit murders. *See* Rachals, Terri
International Covenant on Civil and Political Rights, 182
International Covenant on Economic, Social and Cultural Rights, 182
International Criminal Police Organization, 581
International IDEA, 607–608
International People's Court of Retribution (IPCR), 440
intimate partner violence (IPV), 146–149. *See also* battered women; Bobbitt, Lorena
described, 146
increasing arrests for, 147–148
Latina survivors of, 198
in lesbian relationships, 198
Office of Domestic Violence establishment, 147
police response to, 195–199
rape, 195
statutes by individual states, 149, 154
women of color cases, 198–199
and women's homicide offending, 149–154
IQ (intelligence quotient) and criminal behavior, 63–64. *See also* Allen, Wanda Jean; Brown, Debra; Fugate, Caril; Lewis, Teresa; West, Rosemary
Irish Hunger Strike (1980–1981), 378
Irish Republican Socialist Party (IRSP), 378
Islamic Revolution (1979), 393–394

Jackson, Andrew, 443
Jackson, George, 164, 373
Jagger, Bianca, 428
Jagger, Mick, 415
Japanese Red Army, 581–583
Japanese Supreme Court, 454–455
Jegado, Hélène, **485–487**

Jensen, Robert, 424
Jensen, Vickie, 11
Joann Little Defense Fund, 522
Jobson, Tracey, 283
John Paul II (Pope), 620
Johnson, Adriel D., 317
Johnson, Cassidy Marie, 409
Jones, Genene, 14, **487–489**
Jones, Palmer and Maggie, 339
The Judicial Murder of Mary E. Surratt
    (DeWitt), 604
Just Between Us Girls (Barrows), 305
Justice Denied (Joyce Ann Brown), 343
Juvenile Justice and Delinquency Prevention
    Act (1974), 106–107

Karpis, Alvin, 302
Kasabian, Linda, 13, 293, 294, **491–494,**
    624
Kasabian, Robert (Bob), 491
Keating, Frank, 281
Kellor, Frances, 58
Kelly, Ernest, 494–496
Kelly, Gladys Cannon, 12, 132, 152,
    494–498
Kelly, Liz, 15
Kennedy, Randall, 83
Kentucky Tragedy, 359. *See also* Cook,
    Ann
Kerry, John, 419
Khaled, Leila, 165, **498–501**
Kilgore, Jim, 589–590
Kim Anh Vietnamese Restaurant, 420
King, Carol, 424
King, Martin Luther, Jr., 558–559
Kishwar, Madhu, 376
Knapp Commission, 467
Koischewitz, Max Otto, 430–431
Kovacs, Francis, 470
Kramer, John, 125
Krenwinkel, Patricia, 13, 66, 291, 293, 295,
    492, **501–505,** 624
Ku Klux Klan (KKK), 163–164
Kunselman, Julie C., 126, 133

La Due. Charles, 410–412
La Voisin, Catherine, **507–508**

LaBianca, Rosemary, 294, 491, 493,
    504–505, 623, 624–626
LaCaze, Rogers, 420
Lady Ching. *See* Cheng I Sao
Lafave, Debra, 16, **508–510**
Laisure, Donald Lee, 295
Lambroso, Cesare, 170
Land, Kenneth C., 111
Lane, Billy York, 308–309
larceny-theft, 9, 18–19, 32–33, 106, 191
Larson, Kate, 603
Las Muertas (The Dead) (Ibargüengoitia),
    438–439
Latinas (Latin women)
    African American women comparison,
        126
    death row underrepresentation, 128
    diversity perspective of, 131–132
    drug offenses, 125–126
    homicide commitment rates, 123
    incarceration overrepresentation, 127
    incarceration rates, 123–125
    IPV in lesbian partnerships, 198–199
    stereotypes of, 133
Lau, Linda, 514
Laub, John H., 101, 103, 104
Lautenberg Amendment (Domestic Vio-
    lence Gun Act) (1996), 197
Lawless, Connie and Clifford, 474
Lawrence v. Texas (Supreme Court deci-
    sion), 88
Lazarro, Tony, 285–286
Leahy, Joseph G., 317
Leathers, Gloria, 279–281
Leaving Valentine (Ward), 425
Lebron, Lolita, **511–513,** 579–580
Lederman, Lawrence, 354
Lee, Clark, 368
Lee, John Henry, 300–301
legal-bureaucratic model, of federal sentenc-
    ing, 212–213
lesbian relationships, 8, 89–91, 169. *See also*
    Allen, Wanda Jean; Taketa, Gwen;
    Wuornos, Aileen
Leslie, George, 529
lethal injection deaths
    Aileen Wuornos, 643

Betty Lou Beets, 310
Christina Riggs, 566, 568
Frances Newton, 545
Kara Faye Tucker, 620
Teresa Lewis, 516, 520
usage data, 251
Velma Barfield, 301
Wanda Jean Allen, 280–281
Letourneau, Mary Kay, 16, 92, **513–515**
Lewis, Charles, 518
Lewis, Julian Clifton, 517–520
Lewis, Teresa, 64, 67, **515–520**
"liberated female crook" myth, 39
liberation theory, 38, 40
Liberation Tigers of Tamil Eelam (LTTE)
    (Tamil Tigers), 15, 380–381
life course theory, 101–102
life span patterns. *See* age and women's
    offending
Limantour, Jose Yves, 444
Little, Joan, 15, 158, **521–524**
Living My Life (Goldman), 436
Lokelani, Audrey, 514
Lombroso, Cesare, 57–58, 363–364
Long Island Lolita. *See* Fisher, Amy
Long Termers Organization (prison pro-
    gram), 504
Looking Cloud, Arlo, 291
Lorber, Charles, 494
Los Angeles Police Department (LAPD),
    201, 589
Louis XIV (King of France), 542, 544
Louis XV (King of France), 534–535
Louis XVI (King of France), 534–535
Louis XVIII (King of France), 542
Louisiana Correctional Institute for Women,
    421
Louisiana Supreme Court, 421
Lubin, Joseph, 460
Luca, Milton, 561
Lucrèce Borgia opera (Hugo), 330
Lucrezia Borgia opera (Donizetti), 330
Lutesinger, Kathryn, 294
Lynne, Tami, 614

MacKinnon, Catherine, 88
macro-level criminology, 25

Madame Moustache. *See* Dumont, Eleanor
Madison, Dolley, 443
Madonna/whore duality of womanhood, 82,
    84–85
Mahaffy, Leslie Erin, 469
Maher, L., 9
Mallory, Richard, 642–643
Manatu-Rupert, Norma, 132
Mandela, Nelson, 525, 608
Mandela, Winnie, **525–527**
Mandelbaum, Mother, **528–529**
Mann, John, 369
Mann Act (1910), 170
Mannox, Henry, 472
Manson (Charles Manson) followers. *See* At-
    kins, Susan; Brunner, Mary; Fromme,
    Lynette "Squeaky"; Good, Sandra;
    Grognan, Steve; Hindley, Myra; Kren-
    winkel, Patricia; Van Houten, Leslie;
    Watson, Charles "Tex"
Mapp, Dollree, **530–533**
Mapp v. Ohio (Supreme Court decision),
    530–532
Marat, Jean Paul, 15, 362–364. *See also*
    Corday, Charlotte
marginalization hypothesis, 36
Marie Antoinette, **534–536**
Marks, Stanley, 648
Marolla, Joseph, 84
Marshall, Richard "Dickie," 291
Marx, Karl, 122
masculinity, hegemonic, 5–7, 9, 16, 76
Massachusetts Anti-Slavery Society, 600
maternal substance abuse, 230–232. *See
    also* McKnight, Regina
Maternity Boarding House Act (1940), 650
Matthews, Jane, 91
Mauron, S., 68
May 19 Communist Organization, 352–353.
    See also Clark, Judith
Mayflower Madame. *See* Barrows, Sydney
*Mayflower Madame: The Secret Life of Syd-
    ney Biddle Barrows* (Barrows), 304
Mazerolle, Paul, 109
McCarthy, Joe, 640
McClellan, Chelsea, 488
McClosky, Jim, 343

McDonald, Angus, 470

McDonnell, Bob, 519

McKinley, William, 435

McKnight, Regina, 15, 22, 70, 129, 156, **536–539**

Meadow, Roy, 70

Memoirs from the Women's Prison (Saadawi), 168

men vs. women (boys vs. girls)

  age invariance theory, 100–101

  anger control, 12

  anomie/strain theory, 35–37

  arrest table, 191

  commercialized vice, prostitution, 20–21

  dangerous crime patterns, 10

  gender disparities in outcomes, 209

  government rule, 4–5

  hegemonic masculinity, 5–6, 76

  homicide arrests, 13–14

  juvenile offending data, 108

  less serious offending, 29

  offending gap, 9

  pay, 4

  personality disorders, 65–67

  robbery, 16–18

  running away, 144

  serial killing, 14

  sexual abuse, 144–145

  total offending data, 25, 27

  violence and aggression, 81–82

  weapons charges arrests, 11

menstruation, 58–59, 61, 407

Messerschmidt, James, 76, 165, 173

Metyard, Sarah, and Sarah Morgan Metyard, **540–542**

middle-range theories, of female offending, 41

Miller, Jody, 10, 75

Miller, S. L., 192, 195

Minneapolis Domestic Violence Experiment (1984), 196

Minnesota state sentencing guidelines, 217–219

Miranda, Rafael Cancel, 512

Mock, Ronald, 546

Modestin, J., 68, 73

Moffitt, Terrie, 102, 103, 111

money laundering, 215, 348–349. *See also* Cheng Chui Ping (Zheng Cui Ping)

Monitoring the Future survey, 188

Monster movie, 8

Montespan, Marquise de, **542–544**

Montvoisin, Madame, 543

Moore, Julia Tybor, 514

Moore, Tyria (Ty), 642–643

Morgan, Norris, 561

Morris, A., 26

Morton, Joann Brown, 69

Most, Johann, 435

Mother Earth magazine (Goldman), 435

Mother of all Snakeheads. *See* Cheng Chui Ping (Zheng Cui Ping)

Mothers (Fathers) for the Advancement of Social Systems (MASS), 343. *See also* Brown, Joyce Ann

mothers who kill their children, 60–63

Mount Sinai Medical Center (New York), 462

Mrs. Ching. *See* Cheng I Sao

Mrs. Harris (made-for-tv movie), 453

Ms. Foundation for Women, 595

Munchausen syndrome, 14, 70–71, 282–283, 409. *See also* Allitt, Beverly; Falling, Christine; Jones, Genene; Tinning, Marybeth

Munchausen syndrome by proxy, 488

Murphy, A. K., 193

Murphy, Peter, 313–314

Murray, Ken, 469–470

My Imprisonment and the First Year of Abolition Rule at Washington (Greenhow), 445

Nader, Saladin, 493

Naffine, N., 37

Nagy, Ivan, 415

Naiburg, Eric, 414

Nakamoto, George, 369

Narcotics Anonymous (NA), 504

National Alliance Against Racism and Political Repression, 374, 522–523

National Association for the Advancement of Colored People (NAACP), 298, 557

National Association of Colored Women, 618

National Black Women's Health Project, 374

National Center for Post Traumatic Stress Disorders, 473

National Center for Women and Policing, 201

National Center on Child Abuse and Neglect, 91

National Collaborative Perinatal Project, 105

National Committee of the Communist Party, 374

National Crime Victimization Report (Census Bureau personnel), 26

National Crime Victimization Survey (2006), 84, 188, 197, 198, 199

National Farm Workers Association, 477

National Incident-Based Reporting System (NIBRS), 106, 199

National Institute of Corrections, 247

National Institute of Justice, 196

National Institute of Mental Health, 648

National League for Democracy (NLD) (Burma), 606–608

National Organization for Women, 478–479, 523

National Research Council, 199

National Security Agency (NSA), 419

National Stillbirth Society, 538

National United Committee to Free Angela Davis, 374

National Woman Suffrage Association (NWSA), 600–601

National Women's Political Caucus, 594

National Youth Risk Behavior Survey, 188

National Youth Survey, 108

Nationalist Party of Puerto Rico, 511–512

Nationalist Socialist Party Congress (Germany), 564, 576

Native Americans, 356–357

   American Indian Movement, 167, 169, 289–290, 634

   anti-court testimony laws, 131, 278

Natural Born Killers movie, 425

Nazi propaganda radio programs, 430

Nebraska Board of Parole, 425

Nebraska National Guard, 424

"Nebraska" song (Springsteen), 425

Nebraska State Pardon Board, 425

neonaticide (defined), 61

New Jersey ACLU/Coalition for Battered Women, 497

New Jersey v. Kelly court decision, 495

New Left radical movement, 344

New Orleans Police Department (NOPD), 419–421

New York City Police Department, 467

New York Presbyterian/Weill Cornell Medical Center, 462

New York Revised Statutes (1829), 225

New Zealand, infanticide legal status, 60

Newton, Frances, **545–547**

Nineteenth Amendment (Constitution), 638

No Conscription League, 436

Nobel Peace Prize. *See* Ebadi, Shirin

North Carolina State Bureau of Investigation, 522

North Carolina Supreme Court, 196

Northern Ireland Civil Rights Association, 377

Office of Domestic Violence (1979), 147

O'Grandy, Edward, 353

Olson, Sara Jane. *See* Soliah, Kathleen

Oki, Kenkichi, 369

Oklahoma Indian Welfare Act (1936), 356

Oklahoma State Penitentiary, 279

Olney, Peter B., 529

Omnibus Crime Control Act (1994), 197

Opelousas Junior Police (Louisiana), 419

Opium Wars (China), 277

Orleans Parish Criminal District Court (Louisiana), 421

Osborn, Sarah, **549–551**

Owens, Marie, 201

Oxygen Network tv series, 646

Pagan, Dylcia, 134, 374, **553–554**

Paltrow, Lynn, 22

Pandering (Fleiss), 416

Panzirer, Leo, 460

Paoline, E. A., 204

paranoid schizophrenia, 69
Parent, Steven, 492
Parker, Bonnie, 17, **554–557**
Parker, Robert, 561
Parks, Rosa, **557–559**
Parris, Samuel, 549
Partial-Birth Abortion Ban Act (2003), 229
Peck, Clare, 282
pedophiles, 91
Peltier, Leonard, 290
PEN Prison Writing Program, 345. *See also* Buck, Marilyn
Penal Reform International organization, 182
Pennsylvania Sentencing Guidelines, 217
Penthouse magazine, 464, 467
People v. Anderson (California Supreme Court), 295, 504
The People v. Margaret Sanger (Supreme Court decision), 574
The People vs. Jean Harris (made-for-tv movie), 453
People's Court (Nazi Germany), 577
People's Democracy group, 377
Perry, Rick, 546
Pershing, Linda, 320
personality disorders, 65–69, 73
Pettus, Detra, 280
Phillips, Scott W., 148
Pine Ridge Reservation (South Dakota), 290–291
Pinkerton Detectives, 529
Piquero, Alex R., 103
piracy. *See* Bonny, Anne
Planned Parenthood Federation of America, 573. *See also* Sanger, Margaret
Planned Parenthood of Central Missouri v. Danforth (1976), 228
Planned Parenthood of Southeastern Pennsylvania v. Casey (1992), 229
Plantation Club (New York City), 297
Pleck, E., 196, 232
Plowman, Daniel, 474
Podila, Gopi, 317
Poe, Edgar Allen, 359
Polanski, Roman, 501–503

Police-Public Contact Survey (2005), 189189
policing and women, 187–205
    arrests for prostitution, 191
    current trends in arrests, 190–192
    female police officers, 201–205
    interaction of race and sex, 192–193
    intimate partner violence, response to, 195–199
    offenders vs. victims, 193–194
    rape and sexual assault, response to, 199–200
    sex equality in policing, 201
    traditional policing styles, 188–190
    women victims/survivors of crime, 194–195
Politian (Poe), 359
political assassinations, 15. *See also* Corday, Charlotte; Dhanu; Surratt, Mary
political women and criminalization, 163–175
    class, race, age, religion, sexual orientation, 172–173
    crimes against the state, 165–169
    definitions and types, 163–165
    fate of women within the system, 173–174
    international political crimes by the state, 171
    political crimes by the state, 169–171
Pollak, Otto, 58–59
Pollock, Joycelyn, 21
Popular Front for the Liberation of Palestine (PFLP), 499–500
post-traumatic stress disorder (PTSD), 68, 151, 432, 470, 473, 566
postmenstrual syndrome (PMS), 58–59
postpartum depression, 60–62, 432–433. *See also* Gindorf, Debbie; Yates, Andrea
    causes of, 61–62
    connection to killing of children, 61
    DSM-IV definition, 60
    National Institute of Mental Health data, 648
postpartum psychosis, 8, 60, 62. *See also* Yates, Andrea
power-control theory (Hagan), 74–75

President's Commission on Law Enforcement and Administration of Justice (1967), 201
Pretoria Central Prison (South Africa), 526
Prison Activist Resource Center and Critical Resistance, 374
prison inmates (female), 89–91
    African American overrepresentation, 123–124, 127–129, 192
    Latina incarceration rates, 123–125
    victimization of, 158
Prison Rape Elimination Act (PREA Act), 90–91
Prisons, Democracy, and Empire (Davis), 374
Prom Mom. *See* Drexler, Melissa
property crime, 18–20
prostitution, 82, 85–87. *See also* Ah Toy; Barrows, Sydney; Fleiss, Heidi; Hollander, Xaviera
    aspects of, 20–21
    child prostitution, 156
    drug use by, 86–87
    escort services, 20–21, 85
    "high-end," 87
    historical background, 85–87
    offending patterns, 9, 18, 27
    reasons for, 28, 32, 36–37, 43
    state statutes, 191
    victimization and, 156–158
psychological perspectives
    cognitive/learning deficits, 63–65
    general disorders, 67–70
    Munchausen syndrome, 14, 70–71, 282–283, 409
    personality disorders, 65–67, 65–69, 73
    Stockholm syndrome, 71–73, 457–459
psychotics, 60, 62, 65, 68, 92
Puerto Rican Nationalist Party, 579–580
Puritan statutes (Massachusetts), 196, 549–550

Quiet Strength (Parks with Reed), 559
Quinn, Pat, 433

Rachals, Terri, **561–563**
Racine Birth Cohort, 111

Racine Wisconsin adult onset study, 104, 105
Rackham, Jack (Calico Jack), 323–324
Radio Berlin, 430
Radio Tokyo, 368–369
Rajaratnam, Thenmuli. *See* Dhanu (Thenmuli Rajaratnam)
Rambali, Paul, 376
Rankin, Jeannette, 164
rape and sexual assault, 15–16, 199–200
    anti-rape movement, 85
    crisis centers, 200
    marital rape, 84
    rape "myths," 199
    sexual abuse and, 83–85
Raphael, Jody, 86
Reade, Pauline, 463
Reading Baby Farmer. *See* Dyer, Amelia
Reagan, Ronald, 640
Red Bank Special Unit, 312
Reign of Terror (France), 536
reluctant partners (defined), 91
Rescue the Word (Buck), 345
Resistance Conspiracy Case, 344. *See also* Buck, Marilyn
revictimization rates, 142
Revised "Crimes and Punishments" law (Connecticut), 224
Rice, Condoleezza, 169
Richardson, William H., 360–362
Riefenstahl, Leni, **563–565**
Riggs, Christina, **566–568**
The Rights of the Child (Ebadi), 394
Rios, Thelma, 291
Rocap, James E., III, 519
Roche, Michael, 369
Rodriquez, Lucy, 174
Roe v. Wade (1973), 228–229
Rogers, Woodes, 323–324
Rooker, Richard, 541
Rosa and Raymond Parks Institute for Self-Development, 559
Rosa Parks: My Story (Parks with Haskins), 559
Rosen, John, 470
Rosenberg, Ethel, 167, **568–571**
Rosenberg, Julius, 568–571

Rossiter, Lyle Harold, Jr., 428
Rules for the Protection of Juveniles Deprived of their Liberty, 182

Saadawi, Nawal El, 168
Sampson, Robert J., 101, 103, 104
Sanger, Margaret, **573–575**
Santos, Rolando, 488
Sarrazin, Rosalie, 486
Savannah Women's Transitional Center, 563
Sawyer, Diane, 505
Scarborough Rapist (Paul Bernardo), 468
Schauer, E. J., 191
schizophrenia, 68
Schneider, Elizabeth M., 497
Scholl, Sophie, 167, **576–577**
Schulz, D. M., 202, 203
Scott, Eugene, 340
Scully, Diana, 84
Sein Féin political party, 378
Selective Service Act, 436
Sen, Mala, 376
sentencing decisions, social world perspective, 210–211
Sentencing Reform Act (1984), 211
serial murder/mass killings, 13–14, 306, 321–322. *See also* Bàthory, Elizabeth; Bombeek, Cecile; Cotton, Mary; Doss, Nannie; Falling, Christine; Jegado, Hélène
Seward, William, 617
sex crimes, 81, 92, 100–101. *See also* prostitution
Sex Tips DVD (Fleiss), 416
sexual abuse. *See also* intimate partner violence; rape and sexual assault
adulthood consequences of, 155
of children, 82, 144–145, 157
female inmates, 89–91, 141–142, 244
lesbianism and, 89–91
male inmates and, 89–91, 141
rape laws and, 83–85
by women, 15–16
sexual assault nurse examiners (SANE), 200
sexual harassment, 83

sexual offending, 81–93. *See also* Huckaby, Melissa; prostitution; rape and sexual assault
DOJ sexual assaults reports, 81
facilitators (defined), 91
homosexuality and the law, 88–89
influence of male relationships, 82
initiating partners (defined), 91
inmates, lesbian relationships, 89–91
pedophiles, 91–92
psychotics, 60, 62, 65, 68, 92
rape laws/sexual abuse, 83–85
reluctant partners (defined), 91
seducers/lovers, 91
sexual abuse, 83–85, 89–91
sexual victimization, 37, 65, 82, 155
sexuality. *See also* prostitution
connection to romance with men, 15–16
hegemonic masculinity and, 5–6, 9, 16, 76
male-centered focus on, 19
use for criminal gain, 17, 27, 43–44
sexuality and menstruation, 58–59, 61, 407
Sforza, Giovanni, 329
Shakur, Assata, 133, **578–580**
Shallenberger, Matthew, 517–519
Shapiro, Deborah, 86
Share, Catherine, 491
Sharp, Solomon, 358
Shaw, Bernard, 459
Shears, Richard, 376
Sheridan, Mary, 70–71
Sherman, L. W., 196
Sherwood, Grace, 170
Shigenobu, Fusako, 165, **581–583**
Shultz, William F., 568
sibling incest, 292
SIDS (sudden infant death syndrome), 56, 71, 613–615
Simms, William Gilmore, 359
Simpson, Sally, 11
Sinder, Peter G., 148
Sister Godfrida of the Apostolic Congregation of St. Joseph. *See* Bombeek, Cecile
Sixth Amendment (Constitution), 567
Sizemore, Tom, 416
Skiffer, LaTanya, 127, 134

Sklansky, D. A., 202
Smith, David, 463, 584–585
Smith, E. L., 190, 192
Smith, Susan, 12, **584–586**
Snakehead Queen. *See* Cheng Chui Ping
  (Zheng Cui Ping)
Snyder, Ruth, **586–589**
Sobol, James J., 148
social scientific perspectives
  dynamics of the context, 75–76
    feminist pathways, criminal careers,
      76–77
    socialization, 73–75
social world perspective, on sentencing, 210
socialization (defined), 73–75
Society for the Prevention of Cruelty to
  Children (late 1800s), 142
Soledad Brothers Defense Committee, 373
Soliah, Kathleen, 72, **589–591**
South Carolina Medical Association, 538
Southern Christian Leadership Conference,
  522
Southern Poverty Law Center, 522
Spears, David, 643
Special Sexual Offender Sentencing Alter-
  native, 514
Spooner, Bathsheba, **591–593**
Spousal Assault Replication Program
  (SARP), 197–198
St. Petersburg Police Department, 204
*Standard Minimum Rules for the Adminis-
  tration of Juvenile Justice*, 182
*Standard Minimum Rules for the Treatment
  of Prisoners* (UN), 182, 183
Stanton, Elizabeth Cady, 601
Starkweather, Charles, 422–424
The State of Texas vs. Joyce Ann Brown
  (Dallas County Court), 342
state sentencing, gender disparities, 217–219
statutory rape, 16, 513
Steffensmeier, Darrell J., 40, 41, 100, 101,
  103, 125, 173
Steinem, Gloria, **593–595**
Stenberg v. Carhart (2000), 229
Stephens, B. Joyce, 148
Stern, Howard, 321
Stewart, Martha, 20, **596–599**

Still, William, 617
Stockholm syndrome, 71–73, 457–459. *See
  also* Hearst, Patty; Soliah, Kathleen
Stone, Lucy, **599–602**
Storey, Tonnie, 339–340
Stork Club (New York City), 298
street women, as pathway to prison, 245
Streifel, C., 40, 100
Stride Toward Freedom (King), 559
Struckman-Johnson, Cindy and David, 90
Student Non-Violent Coordinating Committee, 373
Students for a Democratic Society (SDS),
  344
substance abuse
  assault arrests with, 28
  Casey Anthony, 285
  criminalization and, 230–232
  male vs. female rates, 27
  maternal substance abuse, 230–232
  morphine addiction, 70
  relation to crime, 154–156
  schizophrenia and, 73
  Susan Atkins, 292
  Velma Barfield, 300
  victimization and, 154–156
  Wisconsin Court of Appeals ruling,
    231
sudden infant death syndrome (SIDS), 56,
  71, 613–615
Sullivan, Alan, 338
Support of Children's Rights, Association
  for, 394
Supreme Court decisions
  Bowers v. Hardwick, 88
  Brandenburg v. Ohio, 640
  Furman v. Georgia, 523
  Gitlow v. New York, 639
  Lawrence v. Texas, 88
  Maher v. Roe, 228
  Mapp v. Ohio, 530–532
  The People v. Margaret Sanger, 574
  *Planned Parenthood of Central Missouri
    v. Danforth,* 228
  *Planned Parenthood of Southeastern
    Pennsylvania v. Casey,* 229
  Roe v. Wade, 228–229

Thornburgh v. American College of Obstetricians & Gynecologists, 228
Weeks v. United States, 531
Whitney v. People of State of California, 639–640
Wolf v. Colorado, 530
Supreme Court of Ohio, 530
Surratt, Mary, 15, **602–604**
Suthanthirap Paravaikal (The Freedom Birds), 380
Suu Kyi, Aung San, 168, **605–608**
Swindle, William, 409
Symbionese Liberation Army (SLA), 458–459, 589–591

Taketa, Gwen, 23, **611–612**
Tamil Tigers, 15, 380–381
Tarnower, Herman, 451–452
Tate, Sharon, 291, 294, 491, 493, 504–505, 623, 626
Taylor, Rene, 341–342
Temple, Virginia and Rachelle, 339–340
temporary insanity, 407–408, 479, 481, 633
Terrifying Love: Why Battered Women Kill and How Society Responds (Walker), 646
Terrorism Act (South Africa), 526
Tessier, Rose, 486
Texas Board of Pardons and Paroles, 620
Texas Criminal Court of Appeals, 342–343, 620. *See also* Brown, Joyce Ann
Texas State Bar, 546
Thornburgh v. American College of Obstetricians & Gynecologists (1986), 228
Thornton, Deborah, 618
Thornton, Roy, 555
"three-strikes" laws, 243–244
Thurman, Tracy, 147
Tigue, John, 596
Tinning, Marybeth, 71, **613–615**
Title VII of the Civil Rights Act (1964), 201
Tokyo Rose. *See* d'Aquino, Iva (Tokyo Rose)
Torres, Haydee, 174
Tracy (CA) Police Department, 475
treason. *See* d'Aquino, Iva (Tokyo Rose); Gillars, Mildred Elizabeth Sisk

Triumph of the Will (Riefenstahl), 563–564
truth-in-sentencing laws, 243–244
Tryforos, Lynne, 451–452
Tubman, Harriet, **615–618**
Tucker, Karla Faye, **618–620**
Turks, Annie, 338–339
Turner, Nat, 616
Turner, Ted, 418
12-Step programs, 295, 504–505
Tye, Yee Ah, 278

Ulmer, Jeffrey T., 125
UN Commission on Crime Prevention and Criminal Justice (19th session, 2010), 183
UN Congress on the Prevention of Crime and the Treatment of Offenders (1955), 182
UN Economic and Social Council (1957), 182
UN Office on Drugs and Crime (UNODC), 182–183
UN Standard Minimum Rules for the Treatment of Prisoners, 182
Unal, H., 36
Underground Railroad, 616–617
United Farm Workers Union of America (UFW), 476–478. *See also* Huerta, Dolores
United Nations Rules for the Treatment of Women Prisoners and Non-custodial Measures for Women Offenders, 183
Universal Declaration of Human Rights, 182
"up-crime-ing" of young girls, 106
U.S. Secret Service (USSS), 419

Van Houten, Leslie, 13, 66, 291, 294, 295, 491, 503–504, **623–627**
Van Lew, Elizabeth, **627–629**
Venkatesh, S. A., 193
victimization. *See also* battered women; intimate partner violence; rape and sexual assault
African American women and, 132
and alcohol/drug abuse and crime, 154–156
childhood vs. adults, 65

early offending and, 113
homicide victimization, 61
influence on crime, 77
inmate victimization, 41, 158
lessened experiences of call-girls, 87
National Crime Victimization Survey,
    26, 84
physical victimization, 82
and prostitution, 156–158
race survey comparisons, 195
resistance to, 10
revictimization rates, 142
sexual victimization, 37, 65, 82, 155
of slave women, 131
violent victimization histories, 140–154
vulnerabilities to, 42, 76
women in the drug trade and, 22, 69
Vietnam Veterans Against War (VVAW),
    418–419
Vietnam War, 418
Vigilante Committee (1851), 278
Violence Against Women Act (1994), 85,
    147–148, 197, 198
Violent Crime Control and Law Enforce-
    ment Act (1994), 216
Violent Crime Victimization Rate by Gen-
    der survey, 194
violent victimization histories
    child abuse and neglect, 142–146
    general abuse, 141*t*
    intimate partner violence, 146–149
    physical abuse, 141*t*
    sexual abuse, 141*t*, 144–145
Virginia Department of Corrections,
    518–519
Visher, C. A., 190, 192
Visher, Christy, 133
Vision of Invasion drama (Koischewitz),
    430–431
Vu, Cuong, 420
Vu, Ha, 420

Walker, Lenore, 132–133, 150–152,
    495–497, 646
Wall, Rachel, **631–632**
Walters, Marlene and Harry, 339–340
Wanrow, Yvonne, 133, **633–634**

War on Drugs campaign, 244
Ward, Lauer and Clara, 424
Ward, Liza, 425
Warren, Janet, 68, 82, 91
Warren, Robert Penn, 359
Washington Sentencing Reform Act (1981),
    218
Waters, Maxine, 580
Watson, Charles "Tex," 291, 293, 294, 492,
    502–503, 624
Weather Underground radical group, 344,
    354
Weber, Max, 122
Webster, Daniel, 443.
Webster v. Reproductive Health Services
    (1989), 228
Weeks v. United States (Supreme Court de-
    cision), 531
Weiner, Neil Alan, 157
Weisheit, R., 39
Weller, Sheila, 414
Wells, Alice Stebbin, 201
West, Candace, 81
West, Fred, 635–637
West, Rosemary, 65, 156, **635–637**
Wheat, Verita, 340
Wheaton, E. M., 191
White Album (Beatles), 293
white-collar crime. *See also* Helmsley,
    Leona; Stewart, Martha
    Adler's research, 38
    federal sentencing studies, 211–215, 217
    ignoring of, 172–173
    media coverage, 20
White Rose group (Germany), 576–577
Whitehouse, James, 295
Whitney, Charlotte Anita, **637–640**
Whitney v. People of State of California
    (Supreme Court decision), 639–640
Willett, James, 475
Williams, Donna, 339–340
Williams, Ronald, 420
Wilson, Dennis, 502
Wimmer, Carl D., 229
Winchell, Walter, 298
Winfrey, Oprah, 450
Winkler, Mary, 170

Winter Soldier Investigation, 418
Wisconsin Court of Appeals ruling, 231
witchcraft. *See* Osborn, Sarah
Wittrock, S. M., 36
Wolf v. Colorado (Supreme Court decision), 530
Wolves in the Fold (Fair), 408
The Woman Rebel (Comstock), 574
Women, Culture, and Politics (Davis), 374
Women, Race, and Class (Davis), 374
women of color. *See also* African American women; Latinas (Latin women)
   crack addiction pregnancies, 129
   diversity perspectives, 131–132
   IPV cases, 198–199
   prejudicial experiences of, 121–122
   rape/sexual assault and, 200
   severe sentencing responses, 123, 126, 128
Women's Action Alliance, 594
Women's Christian Temperance Union, 326, 327–328
women's criminality
   biological perspectives, 57–63
   defined, 7–9
   diagnosing/defining, 55–57
   individual risk factors, 25–26
   macro-level patterns of offending, 26–29
   offending rates, 26
   psychological perspectives, 63–73
Women's Economic Agenda Project (1994), 172
Women's Ku Klux Klan (WKKK), 163
Women's League (African National Council), 525–527
women's movement. *See* feminist (women's) movement
women's offending
   age and, 99–114
   alcohol and drug offenses, 9, 21–23
   commercialized vice, 20–21
   diversity and, 121–136

homicide, 4, 12–15
   larceny-theft, 9, 18–19, 32–33, 106, 191
   male vs. female rates, 26–29
   non-negligent manslaughter, 9
   nonviolent crime, 18
   property crime, 18–20
   prostitution, 9, 20–21
   rape/sexual offenses, 9, 15–16
   robbery, 16–17
   social scientific perspectives, 73–77
   victimization and, 139–159
   violent crime, 10–12
women's offending, gendered theories, 41–46
   gender norms, 42–43
   gendered paradigm of offending, 41–42
   middle-range theories, 41
   moral development, affiliative concerns, 43
   physical strength, aggression, 42
   sexuality, 43
   social control, 43–46
Women's Reformatory Study (Glueck), 103–106
Worden, R. E., 203
World Festival of Youth and Students (Finland), 373
World League Against Racial Discrimination, 298
Wright, Dora, 279
Wuornos, Aileen, 8, 14, 66, 143–144, **641–644**

Yaklich, Donna, 152, **645–646**
Yates, Andrea, 8, 62, **646–649**
Young, Lila, **649–651**

Zambrano, Ruth Enid, 121, 122
Zero Hour Japanese radio show, 367
Zimmerman, Don, 81
Zwanziger, Anna, **653–654**

ABOUT THE EDITOR
AND CONTRIBUTORS

Editor

VICKIE JENSEN is a professor of sociology at California State University at Northridge. She earned her doctorate in sociology in 1997 from the University of Colorado at Boulder. She has published in the areas of diversity and violence, family violence, gender and corrections, and homicide, most notably the book *Why Women Kill: Gender Equality and Homicide* (2001). Her current research interests include intimate partner violence, PTSD and children, and traumatic childbirth.

Contributors

SUSAN ABRAM is a reporter for the *Los Angeles Daily News*, where she covers crime, education, and public health. She also currently writes for a series for the paper called LA@Night. Susan also has worked at the *Stamford Advocate*, in Connecticut, where she won four Society of Professional Journalism awards and was nominated for a New York Deadline Club Award. Other stories have appeared in the *Los Angeles Times*, *LA Weekly*, *Venice*, *Latin Style*, and *Rapport* magazines. She holds a degree in sociology from California State University, Northridge, and in journalism from California State University, Fullerton.

CELESTA A. ALBONETTI is a professor of sociology at the University of Iowa. She holds a courtesy appointment in the College of Law. Since receiving her PhD in 1984 from the University of Wisconsin–Madison, her research has focused primarily on developing theoretical perspectives of judicial and prosecutorial discretion in state and federal courts. Her research has been published in *Social Forces*, *Journal of Quantitative Criminology*, *Law and Society Review*, *Criminology*, *Social Problems*, *American Sociological Review*, *American Journal of Sociology*, *Iowa Law Review*, and the *Journal of Gender, Race, and Justice*.

ARIEL E. ALLISON is an MA student in sociology, with an emphasis in criminology, at the University of Oklahoma. Her areas of academic interest are women and crime, foreign and domestic terrorism, the sociology of mass movements, and Iranians and Iranian Americans.

SHELLEY AZZARITO earned a BA in general sociology in 2007 from California State University at Northridge. Her interests include pursuing a law degree.

YOKO BABA received her PhD from the University of Oklahoma in 1987. Currently she is professor in the justice studies department at San Jose State University, San Jose, California. Her research interests are in the areas of intimate partner violence, juvenile delinquency, and victimology. Her recent research involves the maintenance of the language and culture in the Japanese Brazilian communities in Brazil and Japanese Brazilian return migrants to Brazil.

KARREN BAIRD-OLSON is an associate professor of sociology at California State University at Northridge. She has published in the areas of victimization, American Indians and crime, and American Indian studies.

JAMES DAVID BALLARD is a professor of sociology at California State University, Northridge. His doctorate comes from the University of Nevada at Las Vegas, and his concentrations include political sociology, criminology, and deviance. He is the author of over 100 articles, book chapters, and various governmental documents primarily focused on transportation-related terrorism attacks, radiological terrorism, and attacks against nuclear waste shipments/storage facilities.

ROSEMARY BARBERET, PhD, is an associate professor in the sociology department at John Jay College of Criminal Justice, City University of New York, and director of the Master of Arts in International Crime and Justice degree program. Dr. Barberet's publications and research interests focus the use of criminal justice data and research in policymaking, crime indicators, victimization, gender and crime, and cross-cultural methodology. She has served two terms as chair of the International Division of the American Society of Criminology and has been awarded the Herbert Bloch Award of the American Society of Criminology for service to the society. She currently represents the International Sociological Association at the United Nations.

LIZETTE BARRIENTOS graduated from California State University, Northridge, in 2009 with an MA in clinical psychology. She is currently attending Alliant University's Forensic PhD program. Her research interests include psychopathy, forensic assessment, competency to stand trial issues, insanity pleas, and mental illness in corrections.

CAROLYN REBECCA BLOCK was senior research analyst at Illinois Criminal Justice Information Authority, Chicago, until her recent retirement, where she maintained (and continues to maintain) the Chicago Homicide Dataset since 1965 and the CWHRS (Chicago Women's Health Risk Study) dataset since 2000. She was a founder (with Richard Block) in 1991 of the Homicide Research Working Group (HRWG). She has worked to establish and support the Working Group on Practitioner /Researcher Collaboration on Research and the Working Group on Criminological Careers Outside of Academia. Her research focuses on homicide, homicide prevention, spatial analysis, time series, and criminal careers.

SUSAN BOHRER is a lecturer in writing and is tutor coordinator at the University of California, Merced. She has written about 19th-century women as well as women and disability.

CORA MARIE BRADLEY is a graduate student at the University of Central Oklahoma. She has written articles for a women's folklore encyclopedia and has been published in the *New Plains Review*. In 2008, she won the Sigma Tau Delta national award for her grant proposal, "Extending Literacy to Those Usually Forgotten."

KATHRYN A. BRANCH is an assistant professor of criminology and criminal justice at the University of Tampa. Her research interests include the secondary effects of sexual assault disclosures; women's use of intimate partner violence; and the role of social support in women's use of aggression against an intimate partner.

NICOLE T. CARR is the director of Student Academic Success and Retention and an associate professor of sociology at the University of South Alabama. Her research interests in criminology include gender and crime, specifically inequality in outcomes for women and girls. She is currently collaborating on a book that examines female reports of criminal activities across the life course. Dr. Carr earned he PhD From Louisiana State University, and her BA and MA from the College of William and Mary.

DEANNA CHANG earned her PhD from University of Hawaii, where she received the American Sociological Association's Minority Fellowship Dissertation Award. She was professor and chair of sociology at Indiana University of Pennsylvania before she retired in 2008. She did research and presented research in the area of domestic violence, victimization, and identity transformation among other topics in crime and deviance.

NATASHA COOPER earned her BA in sociology from California State University at Northridge in 2008. Her specialty was in crime and criminal justice.

REBECCA CSIKOS is an undergraduate honors student at the University of Tampa. She is pursuing a double degree in criminology and psychology. Her research interests include the impact of a death sentence on offender's family members and the psychological aspects associated with serial killers and murderers.

KIM DAVIES is a sociology professor and chair of the department of sociology, criminal justice, and social work at Augusta State University, Augusta, Georgia. She is author of *The Murder Book: Examining Homicide* (2007) and various articles about women as criminals or victims. She teaches classes on sociological methodology, murder, deviance, violence and the South, and women and crime.

LADAN DEJAM earned her MA in sociology from California State University at Northridge, where she specialized in women's issues in Iran. She is currently working on credentials for secondary education teaching.

JO-ANN DELLA GIUSTINA is an assistant professor at Bridgewater State College (Massachusetts), where she teaches courses in gender and crime, homicide, criminal law and procedure, domestic violence, and restorative justice. She also teaches Inside-Out classes at Old Colony Correctional Center (Bridgewater, Massachusetts). She received her PhD in criminal justice from City University of New York (John Jay College) with a specialization in women and crime and her JD degree from Chicago-Kent College of Law. As an attorney, Dr. Della Giustina was an assistant Cook County (Illinois) public defender and a law clerk to Illinois Appellate Court Justice David Cerda. She wrote *Why Women Are Beaten and Killed: Sociological Predictors of Femicide* (2010) as well as several book chapters and journal articles She is a licensed attorney in Massachusetts, New York, and Illinois.

BENEDETTA FAEDI DURAMY is an associate professor at Golden Gate Law School, San Francisco, where she teaches international human rights, and gender and children's issues in international law. She received her JSD from Stanford Law School in 2010. She is the author of "From Violence against Women to Women's Violence in Haiti" was awarded the 2009 Stanford Richard S. Goldsmith Writing Award in Dispute Resolution and the 2008 Marjorie Lozoff Graduate Essay Prize at the Michelle R. Clayman Institute for Gender Research, Stanford University. It was published in 2010 in the *Columbia Journal of Gender and Law*. Her article "The Double Weakness of Girls: Discrimination and Sexual Violence in Haiti," in *Stanford Journal of International Law* (2008) was awarded the 2007 Carl Mason Franklin Prize in International Law at Stanford Law School.

SUE COTE ESCOBAR, JD, PhD, professor in the division of criminal justice at California State University, Sacramento, earned her JD from the State University of New York at Buffalo School of Law and her PhD (sociology) in 2000 from the State University of New York at Buffalo. Recent publications include a report, "Determining the Size of the Methamphetamine Problem in California," prepared for the California Office of Emergency Services, Drug Enforcement Section; and two articles, "Same-Sex Domestic Violence" and the "Cycle of Violence," for Fisher and Lab's 2010 *Encyclopedia of Victimology and Crime Prevention*. Dr. Escobar also published an edited crime theory anthology in 2002 entitled *Criminological Theories: Bridging the Past to the Future*. She is currently working on a comprehensive victimology textbook (estimated to be published 2012).

KATHLEEN A. FOX is an assistant professor in the College of Criminal Justice at Sam Houston State University. Dr. Fox earned her PhD in criminology, law, and society from the University of Florida. Her research interests include crime victimization, gangs, fear of crime, gender, and campus safety and security issues. Her work has recently appeared in *Justice Quarterly, Journal of Criminal Justice, Crime & Delinquency,* and the *Journal of Interpersonal Violence*.

VENESSA GARCIA is an associate professor of criminal justice at Kean University, Union, New Jersey. She received her MA and PhD in sociology at the State University of New York University at Buffalo. Her family court research resulted in a book *Domestic Violence and Child Custody Disputes: A Resource Handbook for Judges and Court Managers*. Her research in policing has been published in the *Journal of Contemporary Criminal Justice, Journal of Criminal Justice, Police Practice and Research: An International Journal, Handbook of Police Administration*, and *Contemporary Issues in Law Enforcement and Policing*. In 2005, she won the New Scholar of the Year from the Division of Women and Crime of American Society of Criminology.

TAMMY S. GARLAND is an assistant professor at the University of Tennessee at Chattanooga, where she teaches courses in victimology, juvenile justice, media and crime, corrections, and methods. She received a BA in history from the University of Kentucky in 1993, an MS in criminal justice from Eastern Kentucky University in 1999, and a PhD in criminal justice from Sam Houston State University in 2004. Her current research emphasis include victimology, victimization of the homeless, women and crime, popular culture, and juvenile justice.

JAMES GEISTMAN is a lecturer of criminal justice at Wayne State University in Detroit. His research interests include policing and stalking. His dissertation explores the effects of patriarchy on criminal justice majors.

ARINA GERTSEVA is a research associate for the Social and Economic Sciences Research Center (SESRC) at Washington State University. Dr. Gertseva received her PhD in sociology in 2009 from Washington State University. Her academic background and training is in research methods, statistics, sociology, and criminology. Her current research interests include the linkage between victimization and offending during the transition from childhood to early adulthood, as well as the geography of crime.

JENNIFER C. GIBBS is an assistant professor in the Department of Criminal Justice at West Chester University. She earned a PhD from the University of Maryland, College Park. Her research interests include violence against women, policing, terrorism, and the scholarship of teaching and learning.

ELLIS GODARD is an assistant professor of sociology at California State University, Northridge. His research interests include legal behavior as a labeling process, and he has written about nonlegal means of handling conflicts in settings ranging from reality shows to virtual reality.

ERIN ELIZABETH GOURLEY is a graduate from Kean University in New Jersey with a bachelor's degree in criminal justice and a second degree in police science. Her area of research is in animal cruelty and criminal behavior.

MATTHEW GRINDAL is currently a doctoral student at University California, Riverside. His research interests include the examination of identity-related processes and their role in intergroup behavior, as well as their ability to explain various criminal outcomes.

MICHELLE HARTZOG is finishing an MSW from the University of Southern California, with an interest in becoming a clinical licensed social worker. She has participated in the University of Chicago's PhD program in sociology, where she was awarded an OMSA Research Initiative grant to study academic achievement of African Americans in postsecondary education. Her research interests include gender, education, and the African American experience.

REBECCA HAYES-SMITH currently is an assistant professor at Central Michigan University in the department of sociology, anthropology, and social work. Her research focuses on racial and gender inequalities in the criminal justice system. Recent work appears in the journals: *Critical Criminology*, *Contemporary Justice Review*, and *Deviant Behavior*.

NAYLA HUQ earned her BA degree in English from UCLA and is currently an MA student in sociology at California State University, Northridge. Her research interests are social movements/revolutions, influence of religion on social movements, green movements, and hegemonic culture in the media.

KARUNYA JAYASENA earned her BA and MA in sociology from California State University at Northridge. Her research interests include women and terrorism.

JANET JIMENEZ earned her BA from California State University at Northridge in sociology.

MELENCIA JOHNSON is a doctoral student at Southern Illinois University–Carbondale. Her interests include criminology, sociology of gender, and female crime.

CRYSTAL KELLY earned her BA in journalism/public relations from California State University, Northridge, in 2008. Currently, she is an MA student in sociology at California State University, Northridge.

GEORGE KIKUCHI is an assistant professor of criminology at California State University, Fresno. He received his Ph.D. in sociology from Purdue University in 2008. He is a certified crime and intelligence analyst from the California Department of Justice and has worked as a crime analyst intern at several law enforcement agencies in the U.S. Additionally, he has worked as a postdoctoral researcher at the National Research Institute of Police Science, Japan, affiliated with the National Police Agency of Japan. His current research interests include spatio-temporal analyses of crime and data mining in crime analysis.

BARBARA A. KOONS-WITT received her doctorate degree from Michigan State University. She is currently an associate professor in the department of criminology and criminal justice at the University of South Carolina. Her research focuses on sentencing, corrections, and women offenders. She also examines situational factors related to violent offending by women. Dr. Koons-Witt currently serves on the editorial boards of *Feminist Criminology* and *Women & Criminal Justice*. In addition to these journals, her work has appeared in *Criminology, Crime & Delinquency, Justice Quarterly*, and *Journal of Criminal Justice*.

KRISTYAN M. KOURI studied sociology and marriage and family therapy at the University of Southern California, where she earned a MA and a PhD. Her research interests include cultural sociology and the interactions between race, class, and gender. Her scholarly publications focus upon black/white interracial couples and service-learning. A public sociologist, Dr. Kouri also uses her knowledge in ways that are designed to bring about positive social change, and in this regard, she has recently written a number of opinion pieces for the *Los Angeles Daily News*.

MARCIA LASSWELL is a professor emeritus from California State Polytechnic University, Pomona, California, and the author of such books as *No-Fault Marriage, Styles of Loving*, and *Equal Time*, and numerous articles in both scholarly journals and in popular magazines and newspapers. She has a clinical practice in Claremont, California.

ADI LEVY earned her BA in general sociology in 2009 from California State University at Northridge. She is currently working toward her MS in counseling leading to a career in marriage and family therapy. Her interests include children, delinquency, family violence, and foster care.

ANISE LONEY is a student at the University of Tampa. She is pursuing a major in liberal studies with a concentration in social science and a minor in women's studies and criminology. Her research interests include women who kill, female soldiers who have been assaulted by other soldiers, and minority women in the military.

SHANA MAIER is an associate professor of criminal justice at Widener University, Chester, Pennsylvania. She earned her PhD from the University of Delaware. Her research interests include violence against women and the perceptions and experiences of rape victim advocates and sexual assault nurse examiners.

KIM S. MÉNARD is an assistant professor of criminal justice at Penn State Altoona. She received her PhD from the Pennsylvania State University, University Park campus in 2003. Her research follows two tracks: (a) gender differences in interpersonal offending and victimization and (b) victims' reporting behavior and criminal justice involvement.

CARLOS MORAN earned his BA from California State University, Northridge, where he was involved in American Indian issues through the American Indian Student Association.

ROSLYN MURASKIN is a professor of criminal justice at the C.W. Post Campus of Long Island University and the director of the Long Island Women's Institute. She earned her PhD at the Graduate Center of the City University of New York in criminal justice. She is the author/editor of *It's a Crime: Women and Justice*, 5th edition (forthcoming) and *Visions for Change: Crime and Justice in the Twenty-First Century*, 5th edition (forthcoming). She is the author of *Key Correctional Issues*, 2nd edition (2010). She is also the editor of a Women's Series for Prentice Hall, having edited books ranging from various issues in women and crime, programming in women's prisons, and women in law enforcement careers. She is the editor of the journal *Criminal Justice Series: A Critical Journal of Crime, Law, and Society*. She has received several awards and has served in several leadership roles in criminal justice professional organizations.

ANNIE NEIMAND is a graduate of California State University, Northridge, in sociology. She is currently pursuing doctoral studies at the University of Florida in social psychology and gender. She is interested in identity development, self-perception, and bonding among young women.

JUANITA ORTIZ received her bachelor's degrees in sociology and political science from the University of Oklahoma. She completed her master's degree in sociology and is currently working on her PhD in sociology. She has recently been named a National Hispanic Scholar; a College of Arts & Sciences Second Century Scholarship Recipient; and the editorial assistant for *Feminist Criminology*, the official journal of the Division on Women and Crime of the American Society of Criminology. As a graduate student, Mrs. Ortiz's research has primarily focused on issues relating to prisoner re-entry and child fatality trends in Oklahoma.

SHARON S. OSELIN is an assistant professor of sociology at California State University, Los Angeles. Her research interests include gender, crime and deviance, social movements, and sex workers, and she has published articles in a variety of journals on these topics. She is currently working on a book project that examines how and why women leave street prostitution.

MAUREEN OUTLAW is an assistant professor of sociology at Providence College. Her research focuses on intimate partner violence, the role of the motive of control, gender, and situational factors affecting violence.

KAY KEI-HO PIH is an associate professor of sociology at California State University, Northridge. His research interests include transnational and organized crimes, gangs, race and inequality, and Asian American communities in the United States.

GILLIAN M. PINCHEVSKY received her master of arts degree from the University of Maryland–College Park. She is currently pursuing her doctorate in the department of criminology and criminal justice at the University of South Carolina. Her research interests focus on policing issues and intimate partner violence.

CAMILA KÜHL PINTARELLI received a law degree from Campinas Pontifical Catholic University, São Paulo, Brazil. She is a member of Brazilian Criminal Science Institute (IBCCRIM—www.ibccrim.org.br).

HILLARY POTTER is assistant professor of sociology at the University of Colorado at Boulder. She holds a BA and a PhD in sociology from the University of Colorado at Boulder and an MA in criminal justice from the John Jay College of Criminal Justice. Dr. Potter's research has focused on the intersections of race, gender, and class as they relate to crime and violence, and she is currently researching race variations in intimate partner homicides; intimate partner abuse among interracial couples; and community intervention in intimate partner abuse. Dr. Potter is the author of *Battle Cries: Black Women and Intimate Partner Abuse* (2008) and the editor of *Racing the Storm: Racial Implications and Lessons Learned from Hurricane Katrina* (2007).

CHRISTINE E. RASCHE, PhD, is a professor emeritus in the department of criminology and criminal justice, University of North Florida, where she continues to teach graduate courses several times a year. Most of her research contributions over the years have been in the area of women and crime, a field which she continues to actively study.

DANIELLA REYNOSO graduated with a MA in sociology from California State University, Northridge.

TARA N. RICHARDS is a graduate of the University of Tennessee in Knoxville, Tennessee, where she earned a BA in political science with a minor in French and received a MS in criminal justice at the University of Tennessee at Chattanooga. She is now a doctoral candidate at the University of South Florida, where she is a research coordinator at the Louis de la Parte Florida Mental Health Institute.

KATHERINE R. ROSSITER is a doctoral student in the School of Criminology at Simon Fraser University in British Columbia, Canada. Her research interests include trauma and recovery for women at the interface of the mental health and criminal justice systems, women's imprisonment, and intimate partner violence and homicide.

PREETA SAXENA earned her MA in sociology, with a focus on gender issues, from California State University at Northridge. She is currently a doctoral student at University of California at Riverside.

CORINA SCHULZE is an assistant professor of political science and criminal justice at University of South Alabama, Mobile. With a particular emphasis on the contributions of feminist criminology in the study of crime and punishment, she teaches a course on gender and the criminal justice system. She is currently working on the first national survey of maternity leave policies in U.S. police departments.

JENNIFER SCHWARTZ is an associate professor of sociology at Washington State University—Pullman. She earned her PhD in sociology and criminology at the Pennsylvania State University. Her research aims to better understanding and explaining offending and social control trends in girls' and women's crime and substance use.

HANNAH SCOTT is an associate professor in the Faculty of Social Sciences and Humanities and a founding faculty member at the University of Ontario Institute of Technology (UOIT). She is the author of several publications including "The Female Serial Murderer: The Well Kept Secret of the 'Gentler Sex'" (Mellen Press) and "Victimology: Canadians in Context" (Oxford University Press). She is also the founder and Director of the Centre for Evaluation and Survey Research at UOIT. Her research interests lie in the areas of victimology, homicide studies, statistics, research methods, and more recently, drug courts in Canada.

LIZZIE SEAL is currently a lecturer in criminology at School of Applied Social Sciences, Durham University, United Kingdom. She earned her PhD from Bristol University in England, focusing on gender representations of women who kill. Her research interests include women who kill, popular culture and crime, public opinions on the death penalty, historical criminology, and cultural criminology.

YASMIN SERRATO earned her MA and BA in sociology from California State University, Northridge, where she was very active in the sociology honorary society, Alpha Kappa Delta.